BUTT-NAKED BABY BLUES

Other Baby Blues® books from Andrews McMeel Publishing

Guess Who Didn't Take a Nap?
I Thought Labor Ended When the Baby Was Born
We Are Experiencing Parental Difficulties. . . Please Stand By
Night of the Living Dad
I Saw Elvis in My Ultrasound
One More and We're Outnumbered!
Check, Please. . .
threats, bribes & videotape
If I'm a Stay-At-Home Mom, Why Am I Always in the Car?
Lift and Separate
I Shouldn't Have to Scream More Than Once!
Motherhood Is Not for Wimps

Treasuries

The Super-Absorbent Biodegradable Family-Size Baby Blues®
Baby Blues®: Ten Years and Still in Diapers

BUTT-NAKED BABY BLUES®

A Baby Blues® Treasury by Rick Kirkman & Jerry Scott

**Andrews McMeel
Publishing**

Kansas City

Baby Blues is syndicated internationally by King Features Syndicate, Inc. For information, write King Features Syndicate, Inc., 888 Seventh Avenue, New York, New York 10019.

02 03 04 05 QUD 10 9 8 7 6 5 4 3

ISBN: 0-7407-1852-5

Library of Congress Catalog Card Number: 2001088684

For Kim, who keeps life full of surprises.

—J.S.

To Debbie Morrone for giving our children a safe and loving start.

—R.K.

WANDA

"Earth mother." That's what Wanda calls herself. Especially on laundry days when it seems like half of the topsoil on the planet is ground into the knees of the kids' jeans.

Mother of two, nurturer of three (men can be so helpless!), Wanda is a stay-at-home mom who does her best to keep the household running smoothly. And with two kids to feed, transport, and clean up after, it's no easy task. She figures that she spends 40 percent of her time driving the kids around, 40 percent doing housework, and 40 percent cooking. This leaves a full negative 20 percent of her day to take care of herself. Which, come to think of it, probably explains her shock at the appearance of the woman she sees looking back at her from the mirror these days.

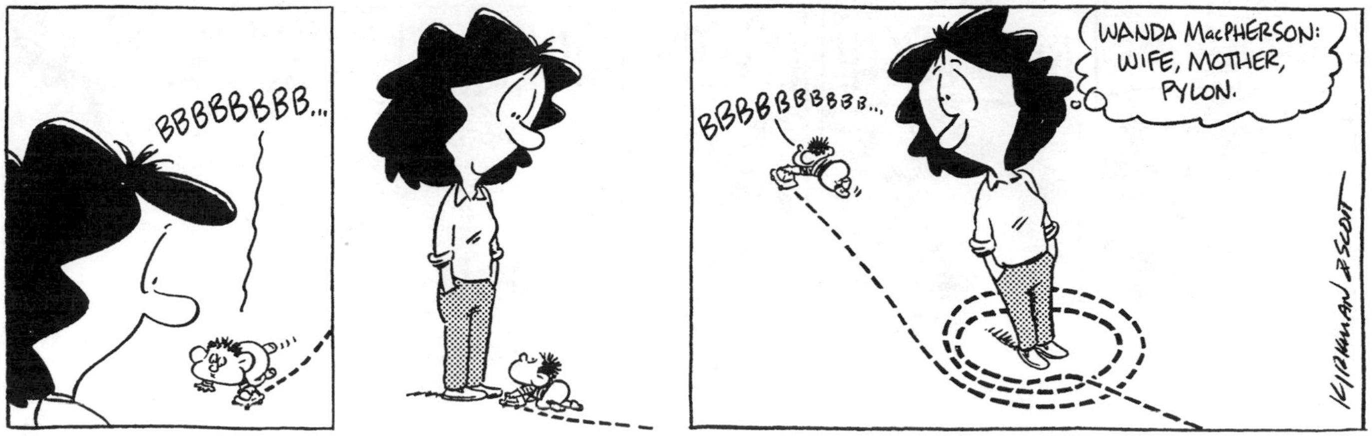
BBBBBBBB...
BBBBBBBBBBB...
WANDA MacPHERSON: WIFE, MOTHER, PYLON.
KIRKMAN & SCOTT

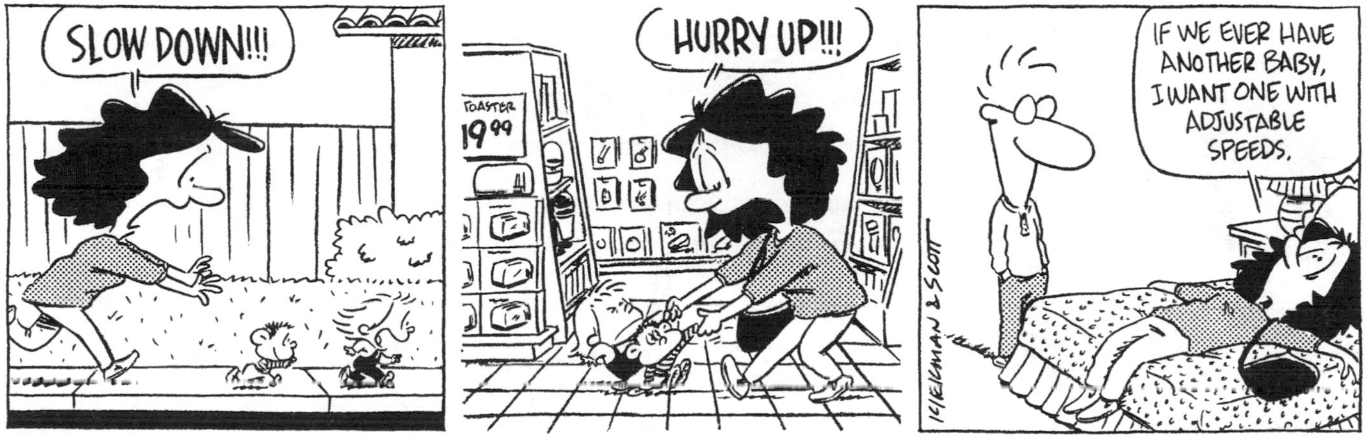
SLOW DOWN!!!
HURRY UP!!!
TOASTER 19.99
IF WE EVER HAVE ANOTHER BABY, I WANT ONE WITH ADJUSTABLE SPEEDS.
KIRKMAN & SCOTT

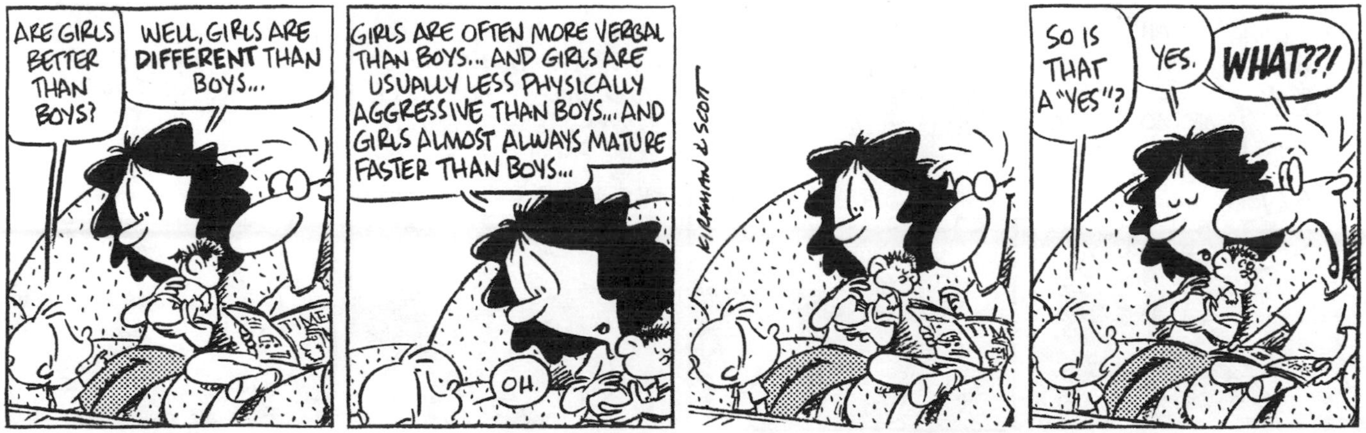
ARE GIRLS BETTER THAN BOYS?
WELL, GIRLS ARE **DIFFERENT** THAN BOYS...
GIRLS ARE OFTEN MORE VERBAL THAN BOYS... AND GIRLS ARE USUALLY LESS PHYSICALLY AGGRESSIVE THAN BOYS... AND GIRLS ALMOST ALWAYS MATURE FASTER THAN BOYS...
OH.
KIRKMAN & SCOTT
SO IS THAT A "YES"?
YES.
WHAT??!

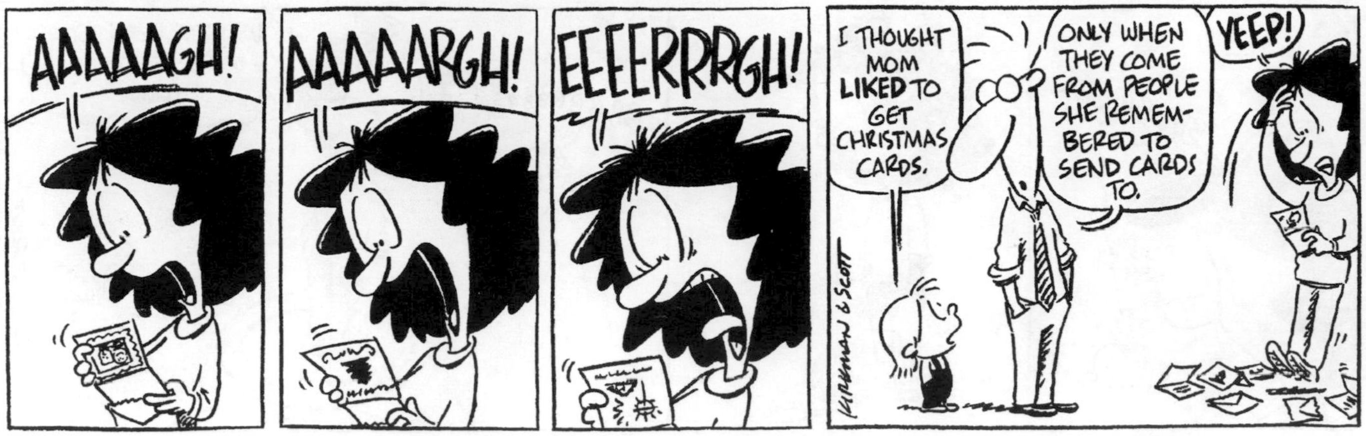
AAAAAGH!
AAAAARGH!
EEEERRRGH!
I THOUGHT MOM LIKED TO GET CHRISTMAS CARDS.
ONLY WHEN THEY COME FROM PEOPLE SHE REMEMBERED TO SEND CARDS TO.
YEEP!
KIRKMAN & SCOTT

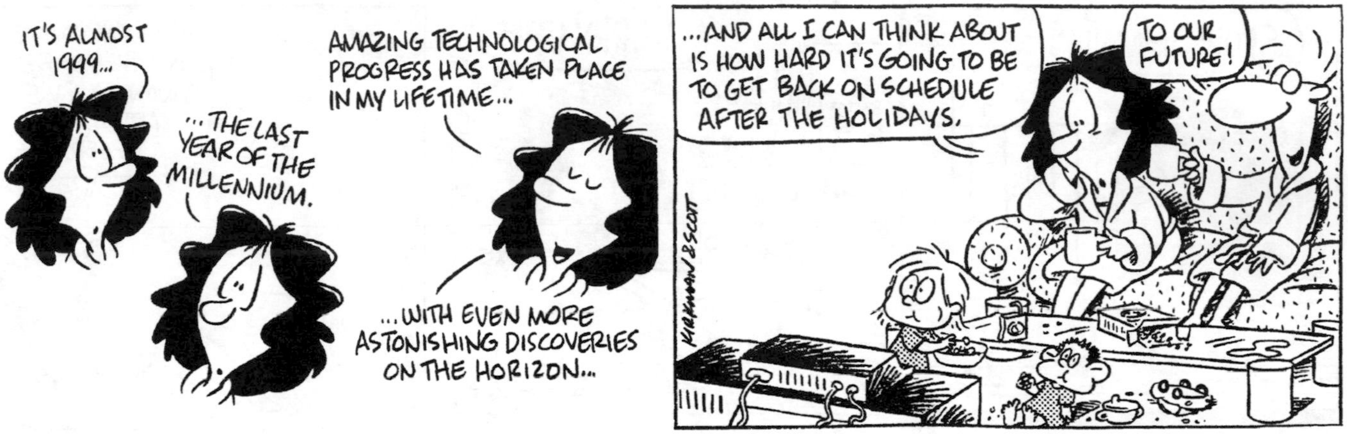
IT'S ALMOST 1999...
...THE LAST YEAR OF THE MILLENNIUM.
AMAZING TECHNOLOGICAL PROGRESS HAS TAKEN PLACE IN MY LIFETIME...
...WITH EVEN MORE ASTONISHING DISCOVERIES ON THE HORIZON...
...AND ALL I CAN THINK ABOUT IS HOW HARD IT'S GOING TO BE TO GET BACK ON SCHEDULE AFTER THE HOLIDAYS.
TO OUR FUTURE!
KIRKMAN & SCOTT

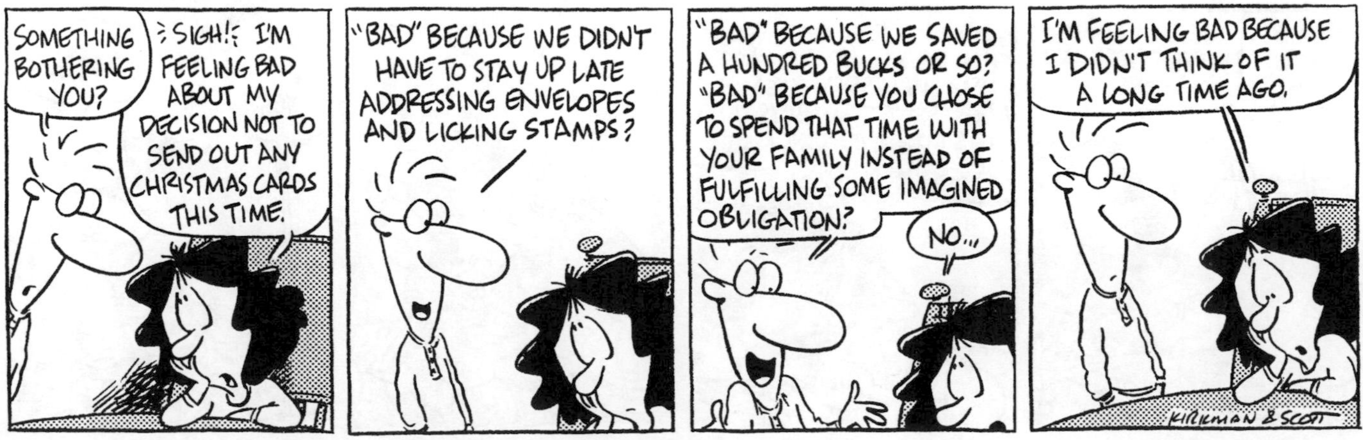
SOMETHING BOTHERING YOU?
SIGH! I'M FEELING BAD ABOUT MY DECISION NOT TO SEND OUT ANY CHRISTMAS CARDS THIS TIME.
"BAD" BECAUSE WE DIDN'T HAVE TO STAY UP LATE ADDRESSING ENVELOPES AND LICKING STAMPS?
"BAD" BECAUSE WE SAVED A HUNDRED BUCKS OR SO? "BAD" BECAUSE YOU CHOSE TO SPEND THAT TIME WITH YOUR FAMILY INSTEAD OF FULFILLING SOME IMAGINED OBLIGATION?
NO...
I'M FEELING BAD BECAUSE I DIDN'T THINK OF IT A LONG TIME AGO.
KIRKMAN & SCOTT

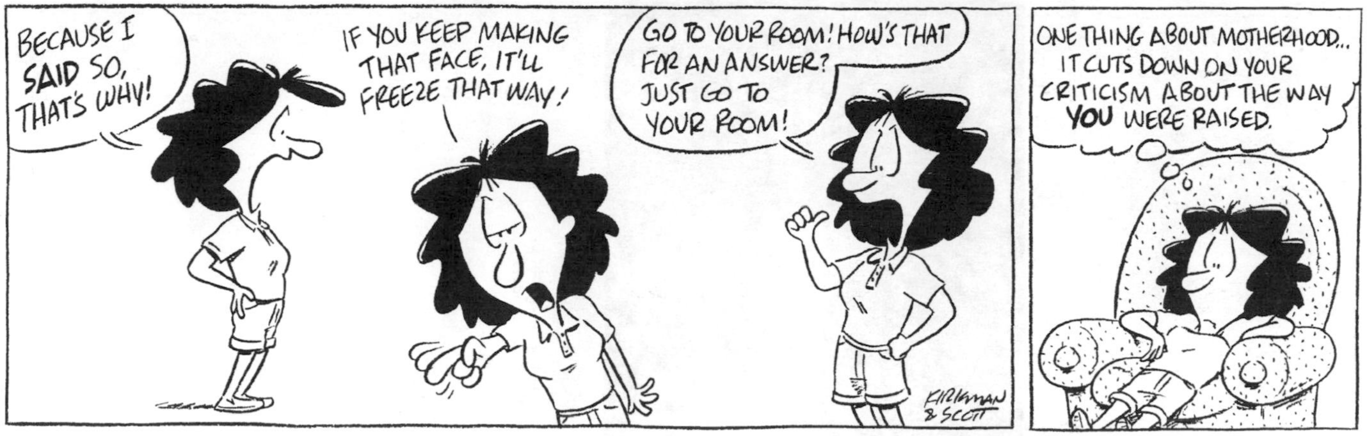
BECAUSE I SAID SO, THAT'S WHY!
IF YOU KEEP MAKING THAT FACE, IT'LL FREEZE THAT WAY!
GO TO YOUR ROOM! HOW'S THAT FOR AN ANSWER? JUST GO TO YOUR ROOM!
KIRKMAN & SCOTT
ONE THING ABOUT MOTHERHOOD... IT CUTS DOWN ON YOUR CRITICISM ABOUT THE WAY YOU WERE RAISED.

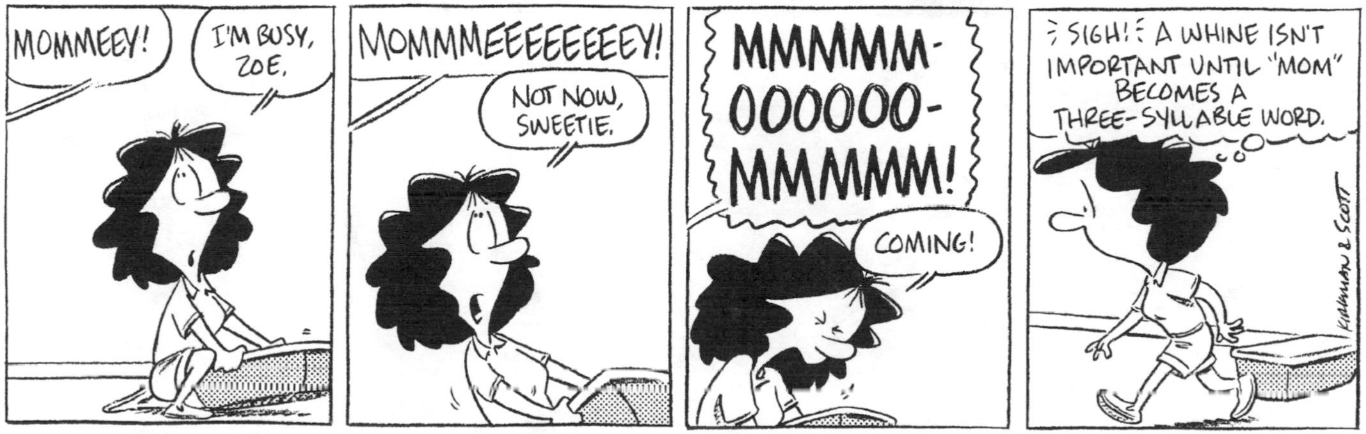
MOMMEEY!
I'M BUSY, ZOE.
MOMMMEEEEEEEEY!
NOT NOW, SWEETIE.
MMMMM-OOOOOO-MMMMM!
COMING!
SIGH! A WHINE ISN'T IMPORTANT UNTIL "MOM" BECOMES A THREE-SYLLABLE WORD.
KIRKMAN & SCOTT

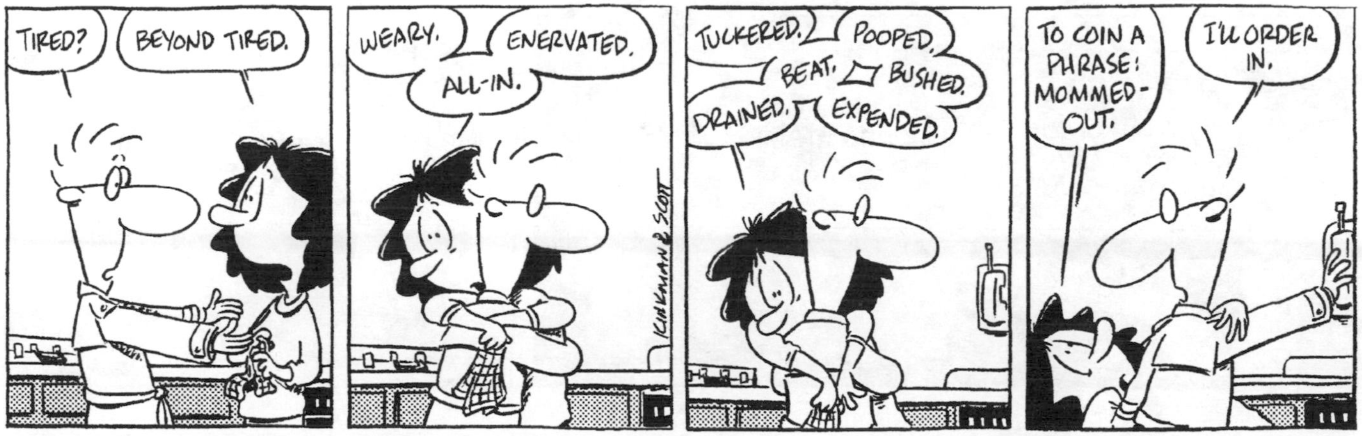
TIRED?
BEYOND TIRED.
WEARY.
ENERVATED.
ALL-IN.
KIRKMAN & SCOTT
TUCKERED.
POOPED.
BEAT.
BUSHED.
DRAINED.
EXPENDED.
TO COIN A PHRASE: MOMMED-OUT.
I'LL ORDER IN.

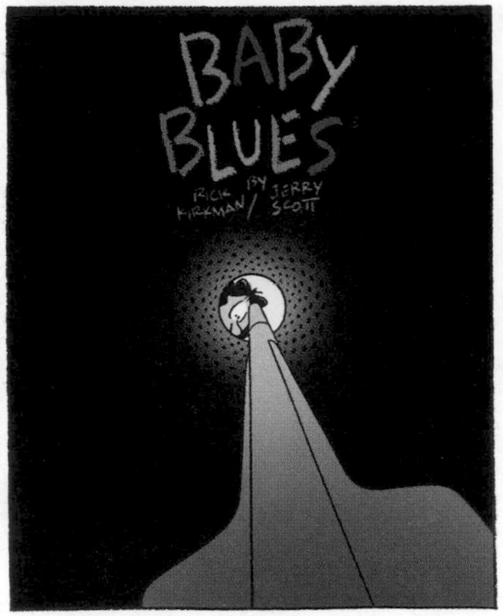
BABY BLUES
RICK KIRKMAN / BY JERRY SCOTT

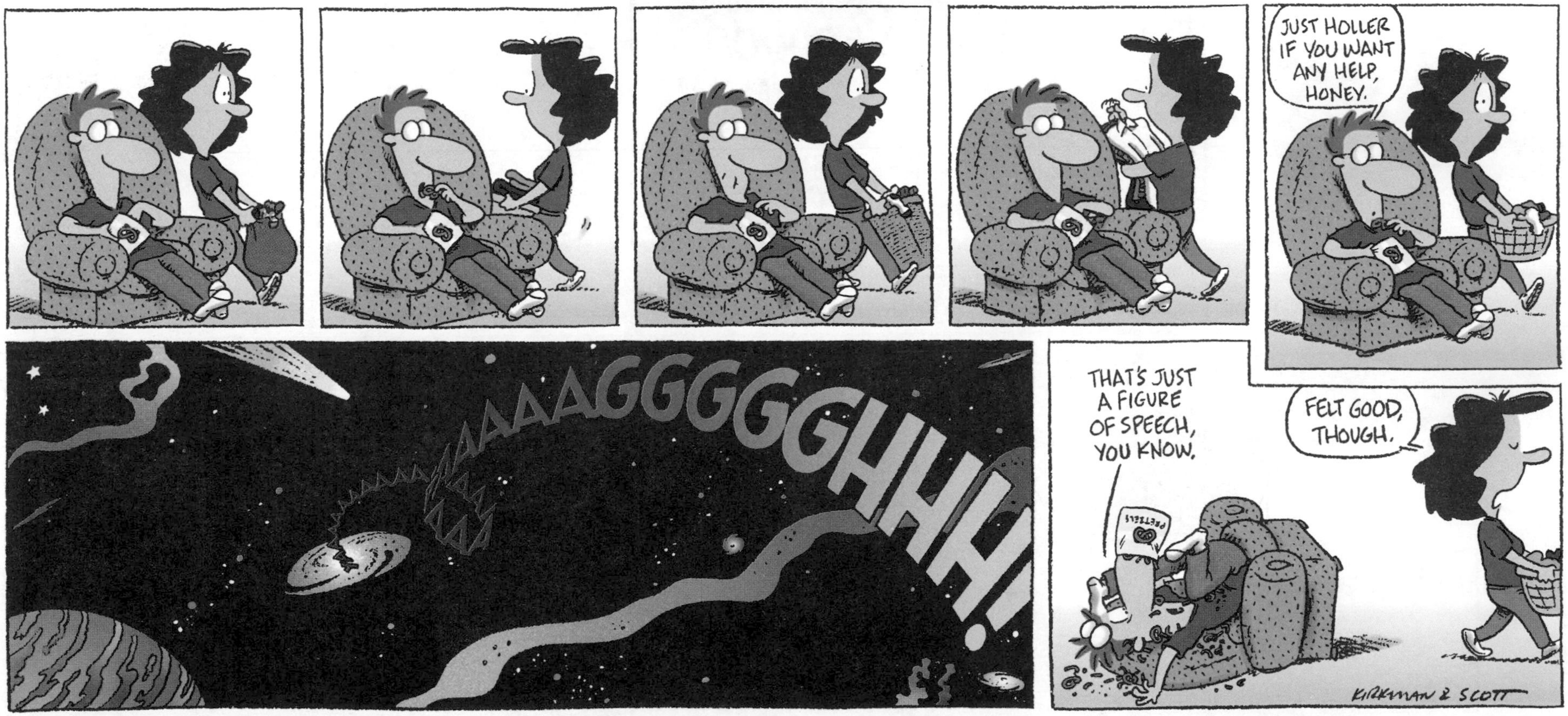
JUST HOLLER IF YOU WANT ANY HELP, HONEY.
AAAAAAAAGGGGGHHHH!
THAT'S JUST A FIGURE OF SPEECH, YOU KNOW.
FELT GOOD, THOUGH.
PRETZELS
KIRKMAN & SCOTT

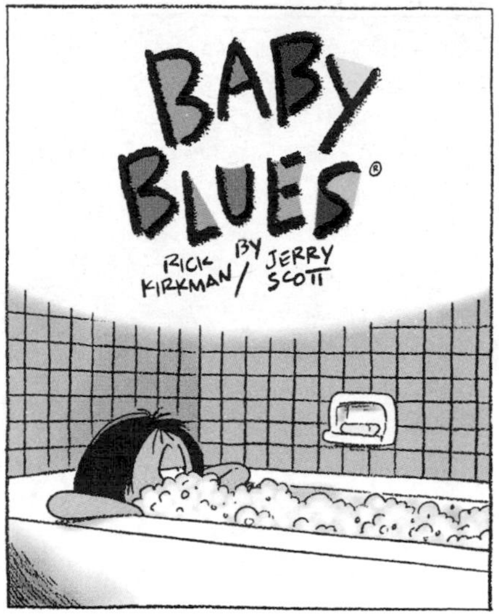
BABY BLUES®
BY RICK KIRKMAN / JERRY SCOTT

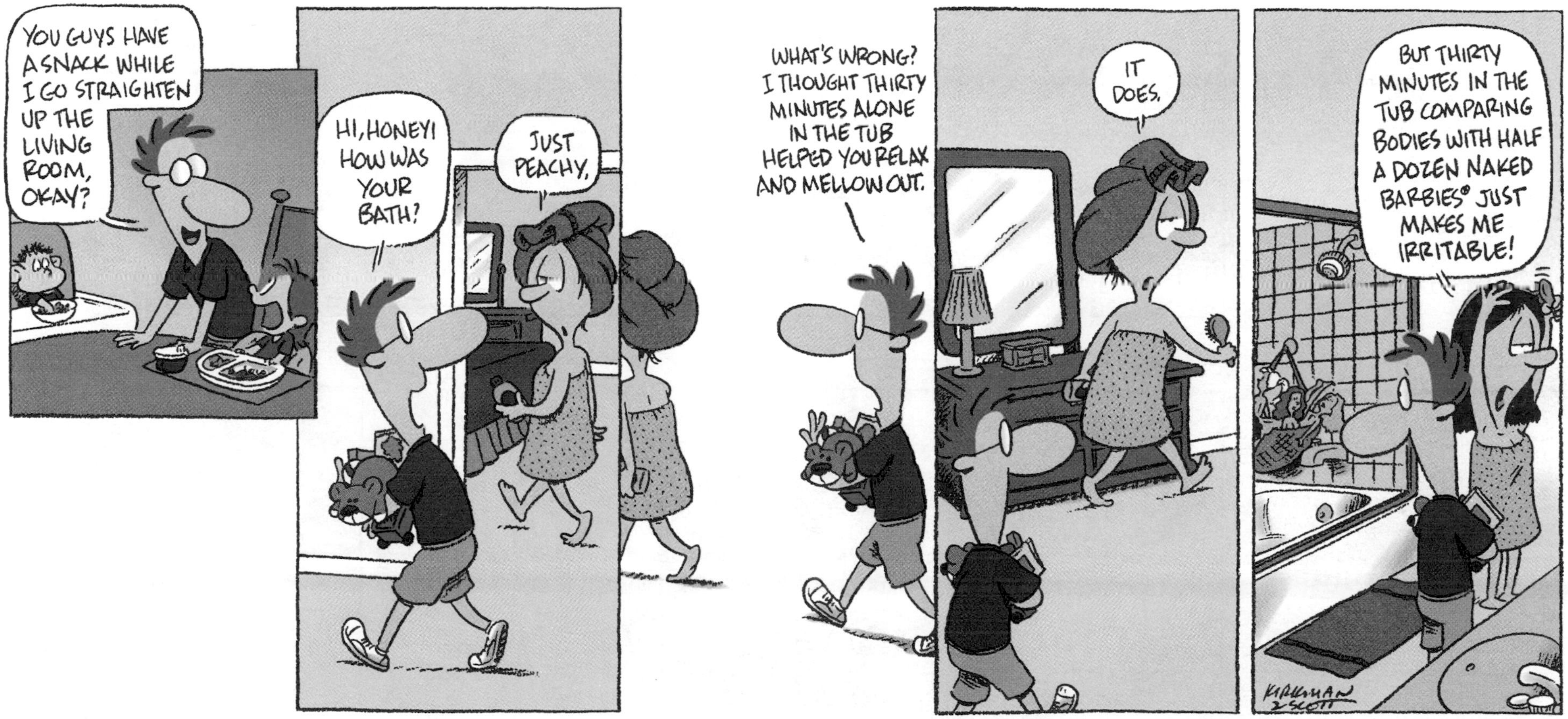
YOU GUYS HAVE A SNACK WHILE I GO STRAIGHTEN UP THE LIVING ROOM, OKAY?
HI, HONEY! HOW WAS YOUR BATH?
JUST PEACHY.
WHAT'S WRONG? I THOUGHT THIRTY MINUTES ALONE IN THE TUB HELPED YOU RELAX AND MELLOW OUT.
IT DOES.
BUT THIRTY MINUTES IN THE TUB COMPARING BODIES WITH HALF A DOZEN NAKED BARBIES® JUST MAKES ME IRRITABLE!
KIRKMAN & SCOTT

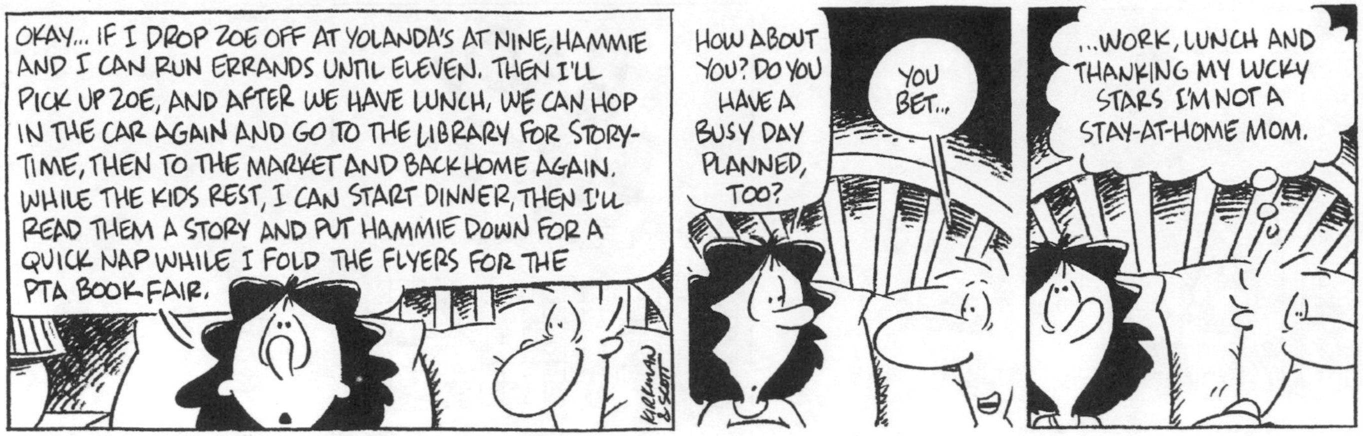
OKAY... IF I DROP ZOE OFF AT YOLANDA'S AT NINE, HAMMIE AND I CAN RUN ERRANDS UNTIL ELEVEN. THEN I'LL PICK UP ZOE, AND AFTER WE HAVE LUNCH, WE CAN HOP IN THE CAR AGAIN AND GO TO THE LIBRARY FOR STORY-TIME, THEN TO THE MARKET AND BACK HOME AGAIN. WHILE THE KIDS REST, I CAN START DINNER, THEN I'LL READ THEM A STORY AND PUT HAMMIE DOWN FOR A QUICK NAP WHILE I FOLD THE FLYERS FOR THE PTA BOOK FAIR.
HOW ABOUT YOU? DO YOU HAVE A BUSY DAY PLANNED, TOO?
YOU BET...
...WORK, LUNCH AND THANKING MY LUCKY STARS I'M NOT A STAY-AT-HOME MOM.

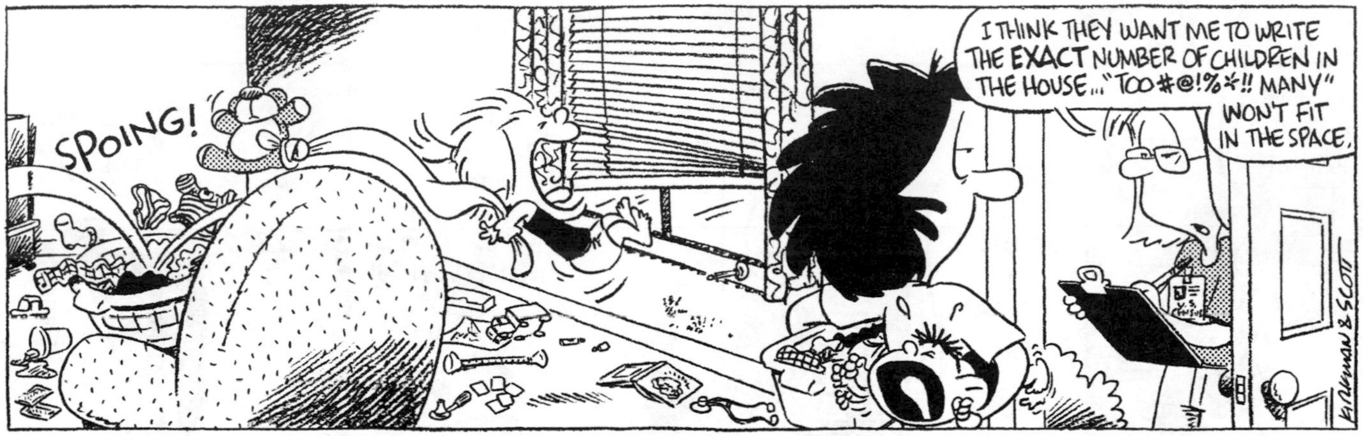
SPOING!
I THINK THEY WANT ME TO WRITE THE **EXACT** NUMBER OF CHILDREN IN THE HOUSE... "TOO #@!%*!! MANY" WON'T FIT IN THE SPACE.

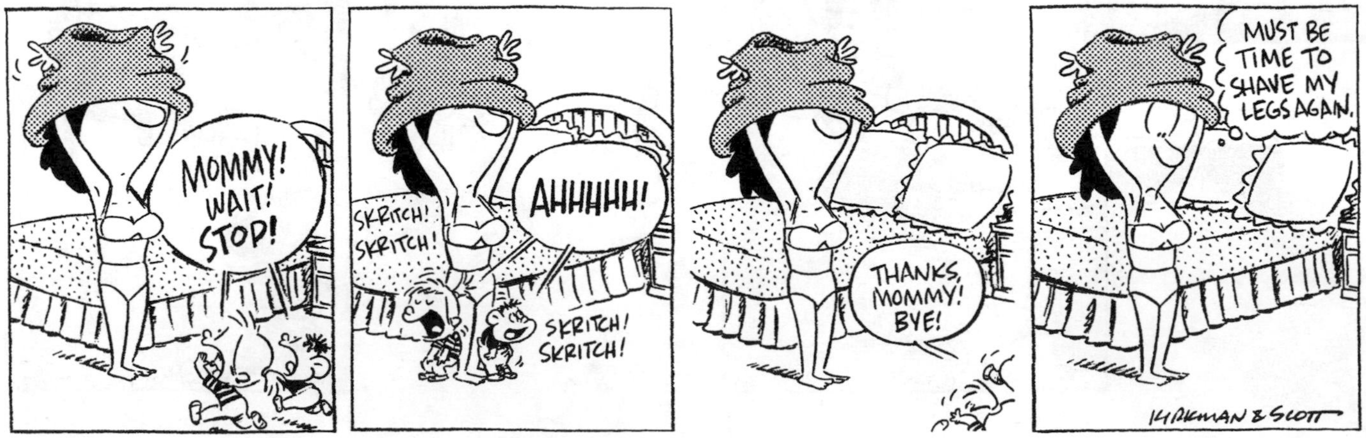
MOMMY! WAIT! STOP!
SKRITCH! SKRITCH!
AHHHHH!
SKRITCH! SKRITCH!
THANKS, MOMMY! BYE!
MUST BE TIME TO SHAVE MY LEGS AGAIN.

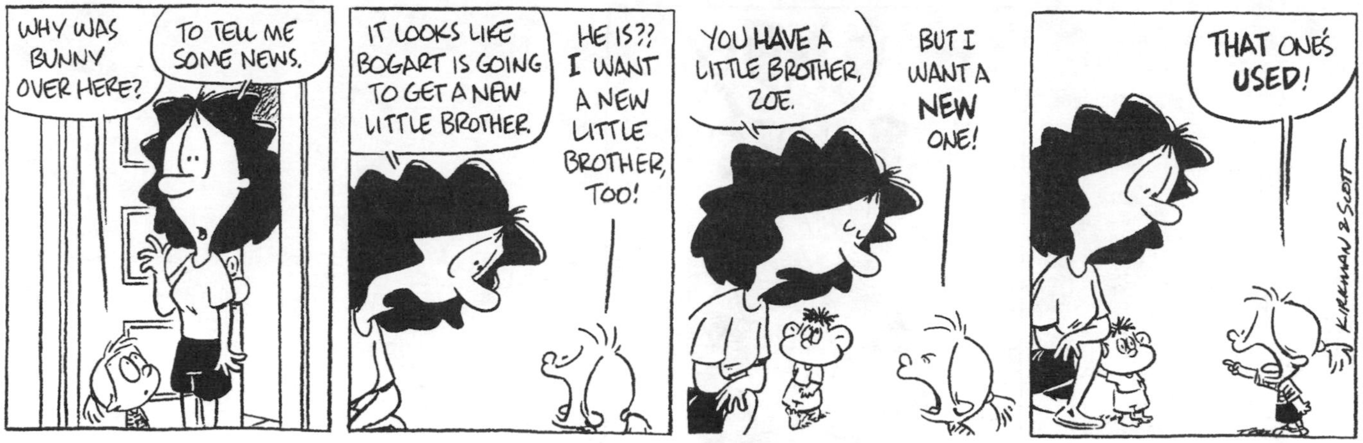
WHY WAS BUNNY OVER HERE?
TO TELL ME SOME NEWS.
IT LOOKS LIKE BOGART IS GOING TO GET A NEW LITTLE BROTHER.
HE IS?? I WANT A NEW LITTLE BROTHER, TOO!
YOU HAVE A LITTLE BROTHER, ZOE.
BUT I WANT A NEW ONE!
THAT ONE'S USED!
KIRKMAN & SCOTT

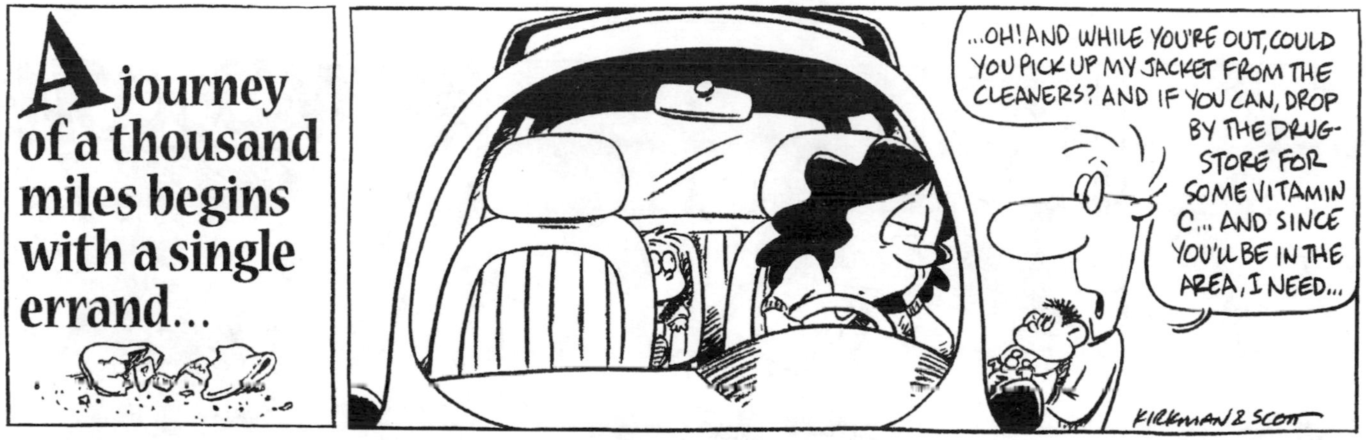
A journey of a thousand miles begins with a single errand…
…OH! AND WHILE YOU'RE OUT, COULD YOU PICK UP MY JACKET FROM THE CLEANERS? AND IF YOU CAN, DROP BY THE DRUG-STORE FOR SOME VITAMIN C… AND SINCE YOU'LL BE IN THE AREA, I NEED…
KIRKMAN & SCOTT

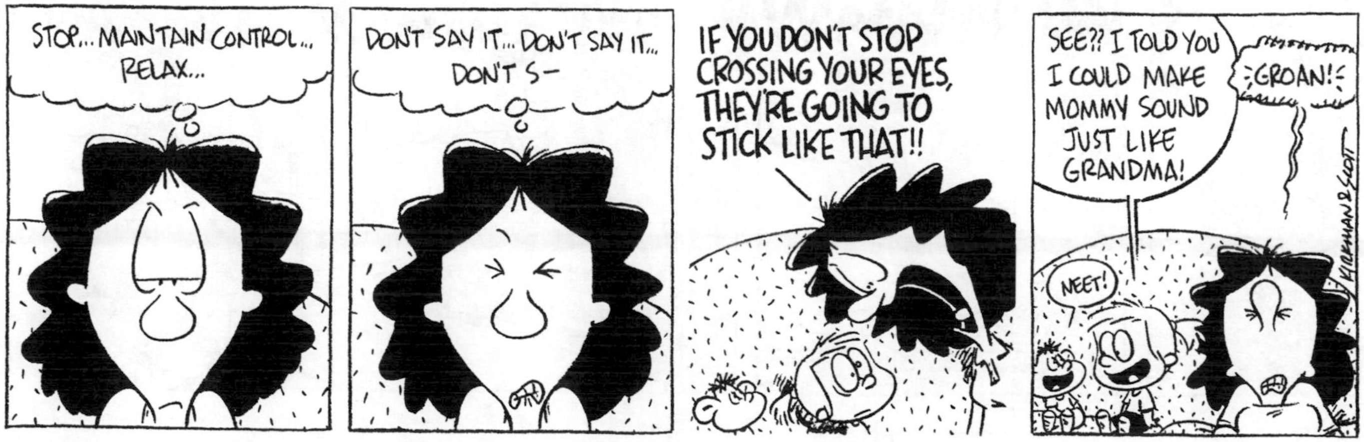
STOP… MAINTAIN CONTROL… RELAX…
DON'T SAY IT… DON'T SAY IT… DON'T S–
IF YOU DON'T STOP CROSSING YOUR EYES, THEY'RE GOING TO STICK LIKE THAT!!
SEE?? I TOLD YOU I COULD MAKE MOMMY SOUND JUST LIKE GRANDMA!
GROAN!
NEET!
KIRKMAN & SCOTT

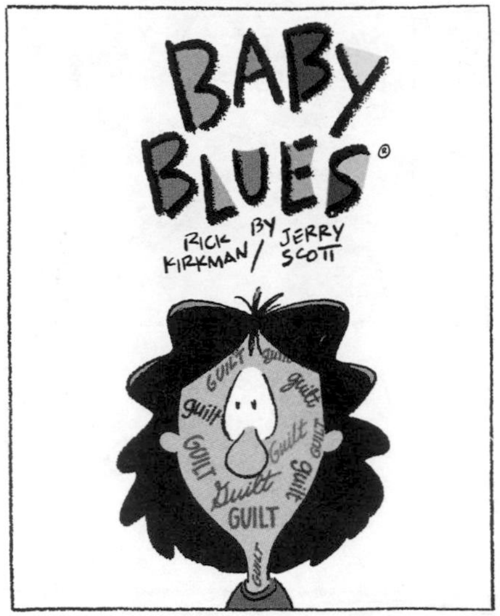
BABY BLUES®
RICK KIRKMAN / BY JERRY SCOTT
GUILT guilt GUILT Guilt guilt GUILT Guilt Guilt GUILT GUILT

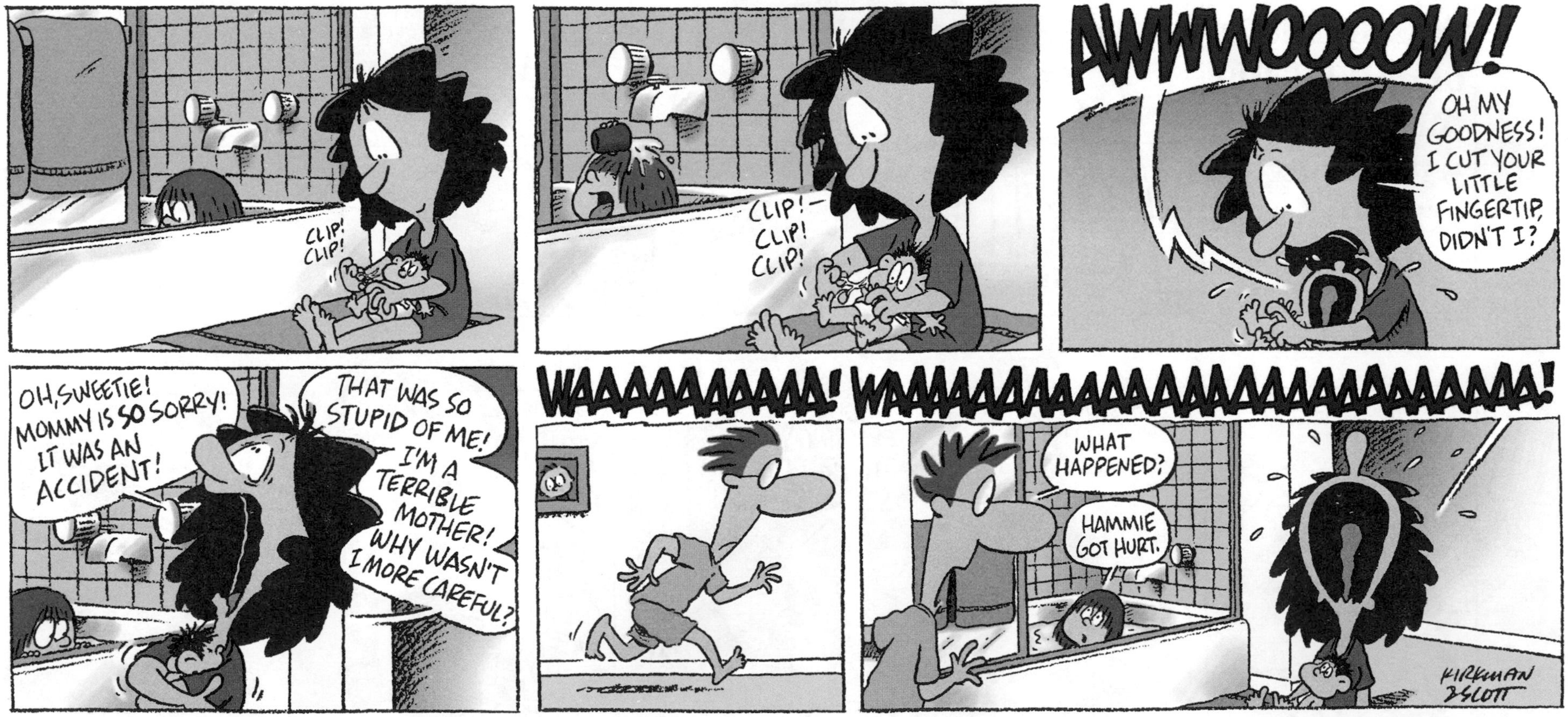
CLIP! CLIP!
CLIP! CLIP! CLIP!
AWWWOOOOOW!
OH MY GOODNESS! I CUT YOUR LITTLE FINGERTIP, DIDN'T I?
OH, SWEETIE! MOMMY IS SO SORRY! IT WAS AN ACCIDENT!
THAT WAS SO STUPID OF ME! I'M A TERRIBLE MOTHER! WHY WASN'T I MORE CAREFUL?
WAAAAAAAAAA! WAAAAAAAAAAAAAAAAAAAAAAAAAAAAA!
WHAT HAPPENED?
HAMMIE GOT HURT.
KIRKMAN & SCOTT

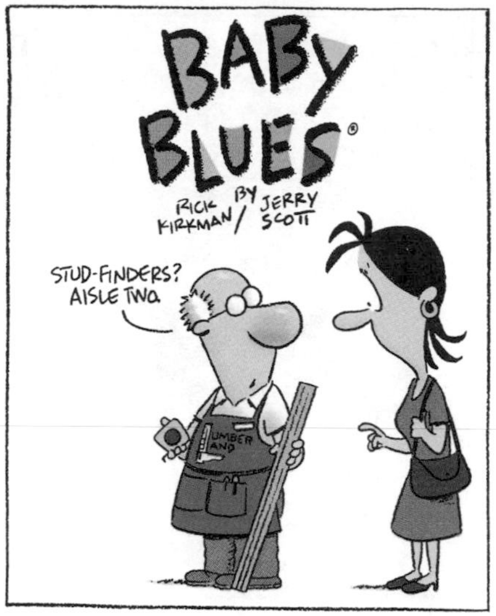
BABY BLUES®
BY RICK KIRKMAN / JERRY SCOTT
STUD-FINDERS? AISLE TWO.

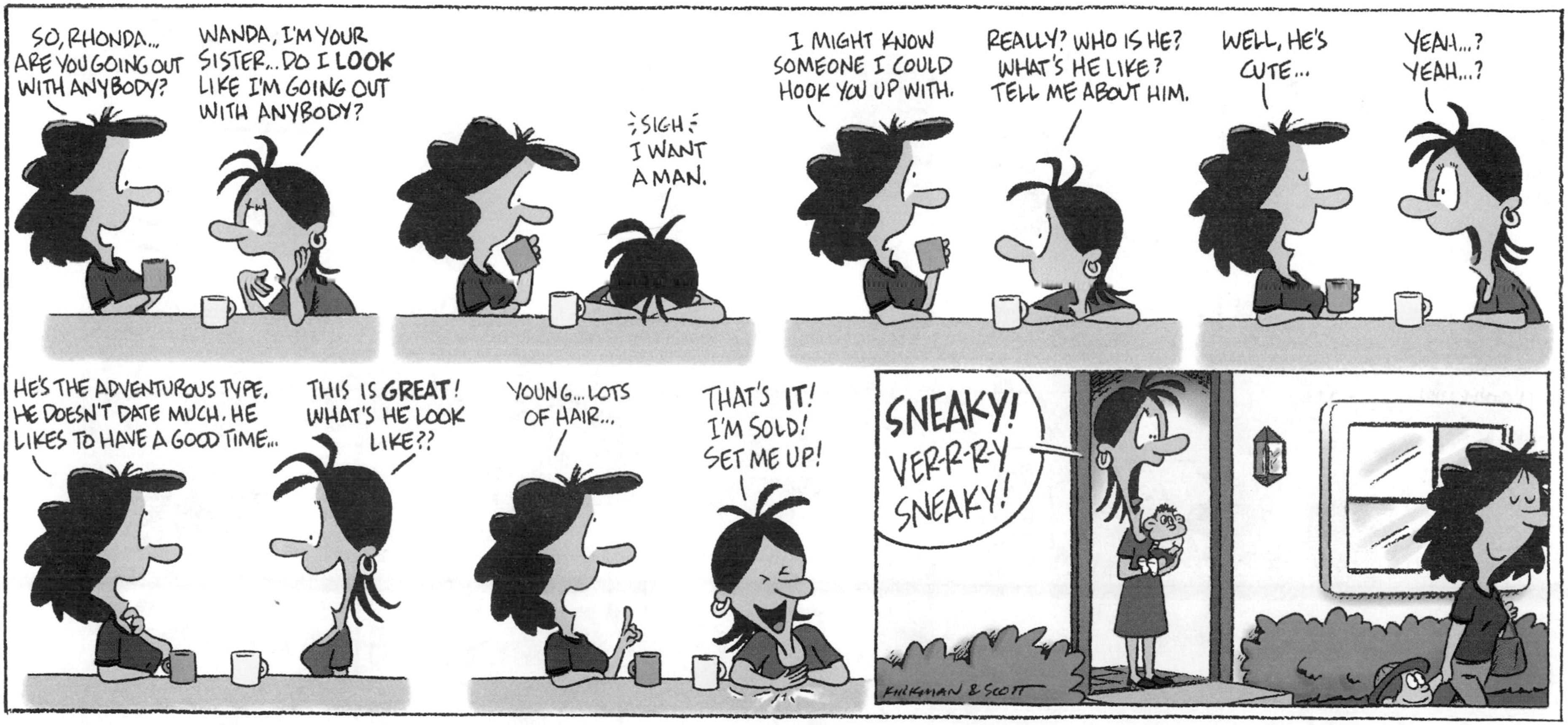
SO, RHONDA... ARE YOU GOING OUT WITH ANYBODY?
WANDA, I'M YOUR SISTER... DO I LOOK LIKE I'M GOING OUT WITH ANYBODY?
SIGH I WANT A MAN.
I MIGHT KNOW SOMEONE I COULD HOOK YOU UP WITH.
REALLY? WHO IS HE? WHAT'S HE LIKE? TELL ME ABOUT HIM.
WELL, HE'S CUTE...
YEAH...? YEAH...?
HE'S THE ADVENTUROUS TYPE. HE DOESN'T DATE MUCH. HE LIKES TO HAVE A GOOD TIME...
THIS IS GREAT! WHAT'S HE LOOK LIKE??
YOUNG... LOTS OF HAIR...
THAT'S IT! I'M SOLD! SET ME UP!
SNEAKY! VER-R-R-Y SNEAKY!
KIRKMAN & SCOTT

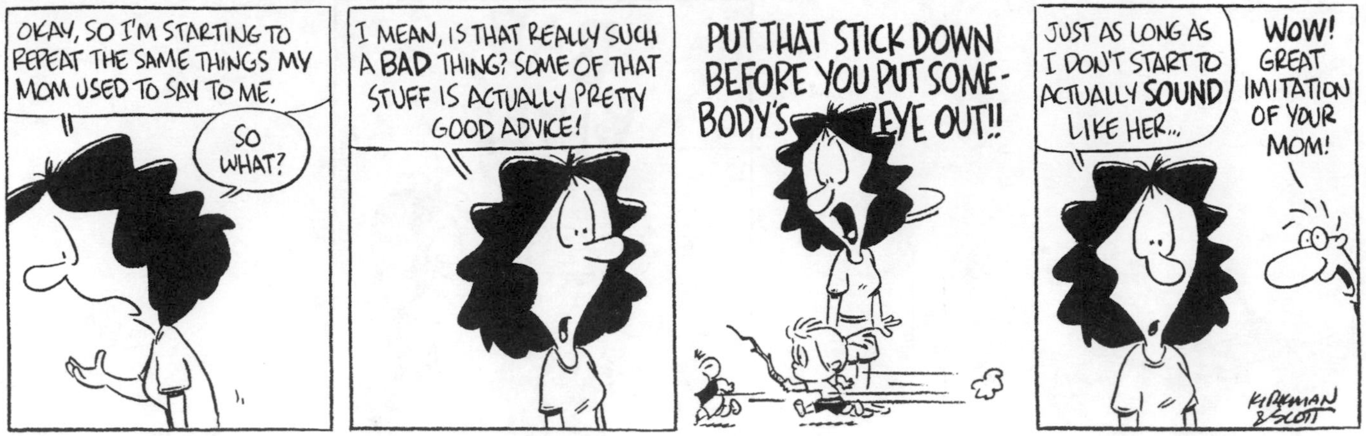
OKAY, SO I'M STARTING TO REPEAT THE SAME THINGS MY MOM USED TO SAY TO ME.
SO WHAT?
I MEAN, IS THAT REALLY SUCH A BAD THING? SOME OF THAT STUFF IS ACTUALLY PRETTY GOOD ADVICE!
PUT THAT STICK DOWN BEFORE YOU PUT SOME-BODY'S EYE OUT!!
JUST AS LONG AS I DON'T START TO ACTUALLY SOUND LIKE HER...
WOW! GREAT IMITATION OF YOUR MOM!
KIRKMAN & SCOTT

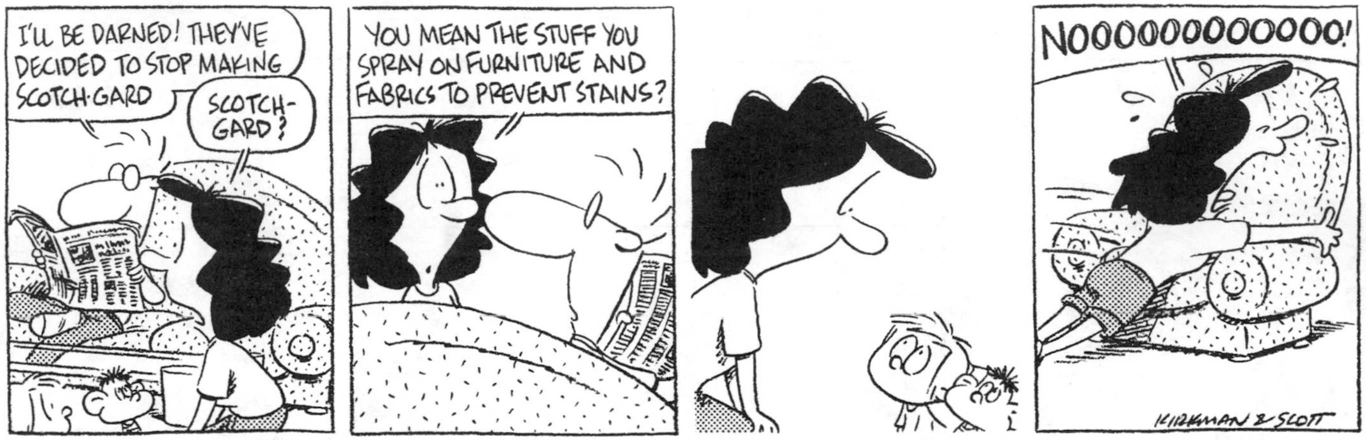
I'LL BE DARNED! THEY'VE DECIDED TO STOP MAKING SCOTCH-GARD
SCOTCH-GARD?
YOU MEAN THE STUFF YOU SPRAY ON FURNITURE AND FABRICS TO PREVENT STAINS?
NOOOOOOOOOOOO!
KIRKMAN & SCOTT

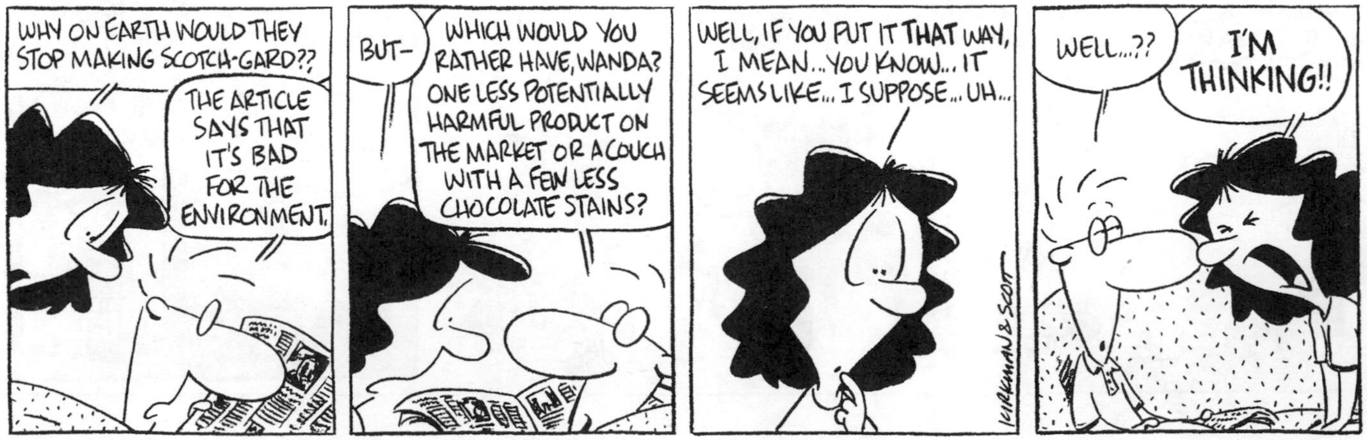
WHY ON EARTH WOULD THEY STOP MAKING SCOTCH-GARD??
THE ARTICLE SAYS THAT IT'S BAD FOR THE ENVIRONMENT.
BUT-
WHICH WOULD YOU RATHER HAVE, WANDA? ONE LESS POTENTIALLY HARMFUL PRODUCT ON THE MARKET OR A COUCH WITH A FEW LESS CHOCOLATE STAINS?
WELL, IF YOU PUT IT THAT WAY, I MEAN... YOU KNOW... IT SEEMS LIKE... I SUPPOSE... UH...
KIRKMAN & SCOTT
WELL...??
I'M THINKING!!

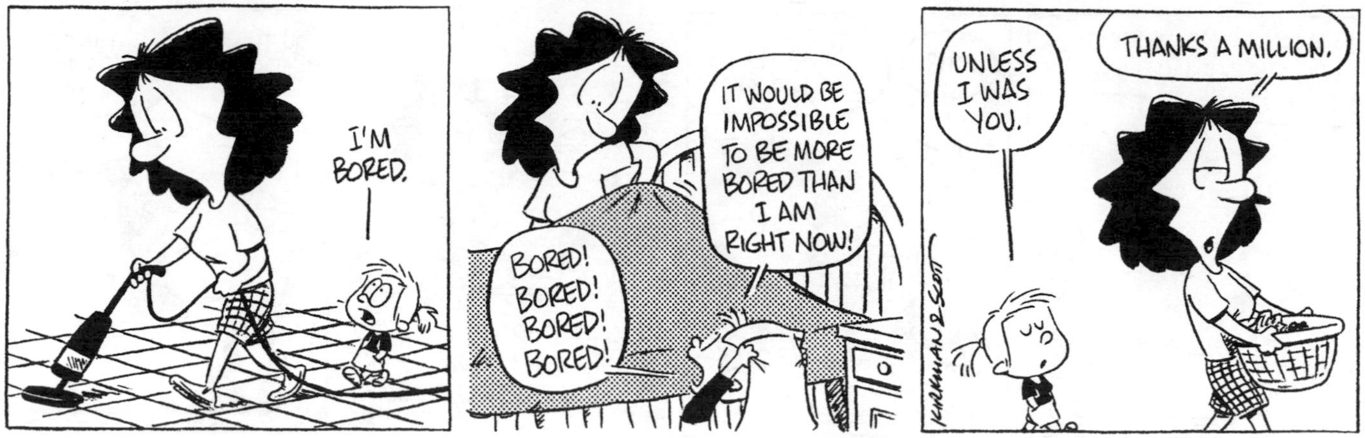
I'M BORED.
IT WOULD BE IMPOSSIBLE TO BE MORE BORED THAN I AM RIGHT NOW!
BORED! BORED! BORED! BORED!
UNLESS I WAS YOU.
THANKS A MILLION.
KIRKMAN & SCOTT

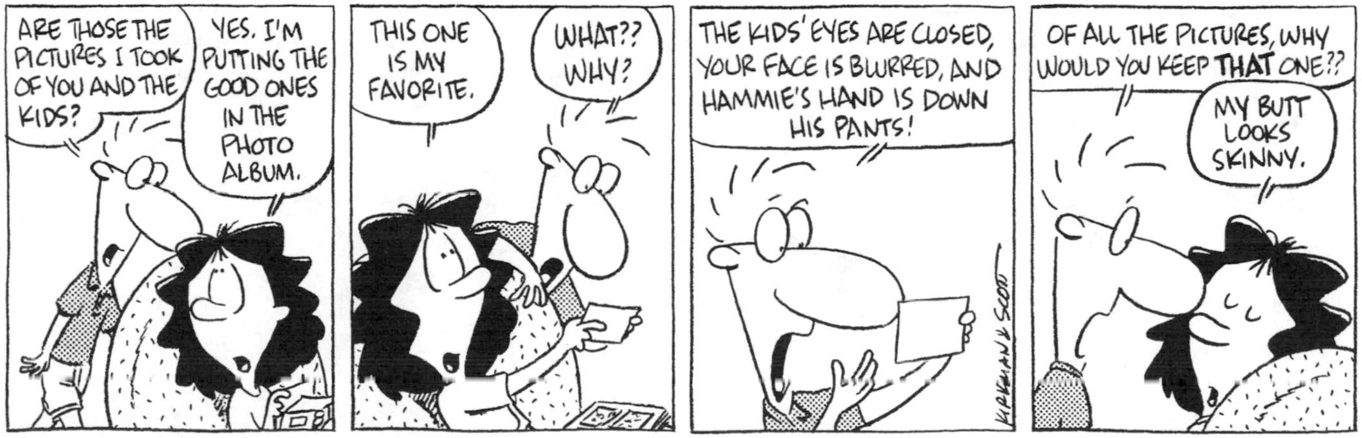
ARE THOSE THE PICTURES I TOOK OF YOU AND THE KIDS?
YES. I'M PUTTING THE GOOD ONES IN THE PHOTO ALBUM.
THIS ONE IS MY FAVORITE.
WHAT?? WHY?
THE KIDS' EYES ARE CLOSED, YOUR FACE IS BLURRED, AND HAMMIE'S HAND IS DOWN HIS PANTS!
KIRKMAN & SCOTT
OF ALL THE PICTURES, WHY WOULD YOU KEEP **THAT** ONE??
MY BUTT LOOKS SKINNY.

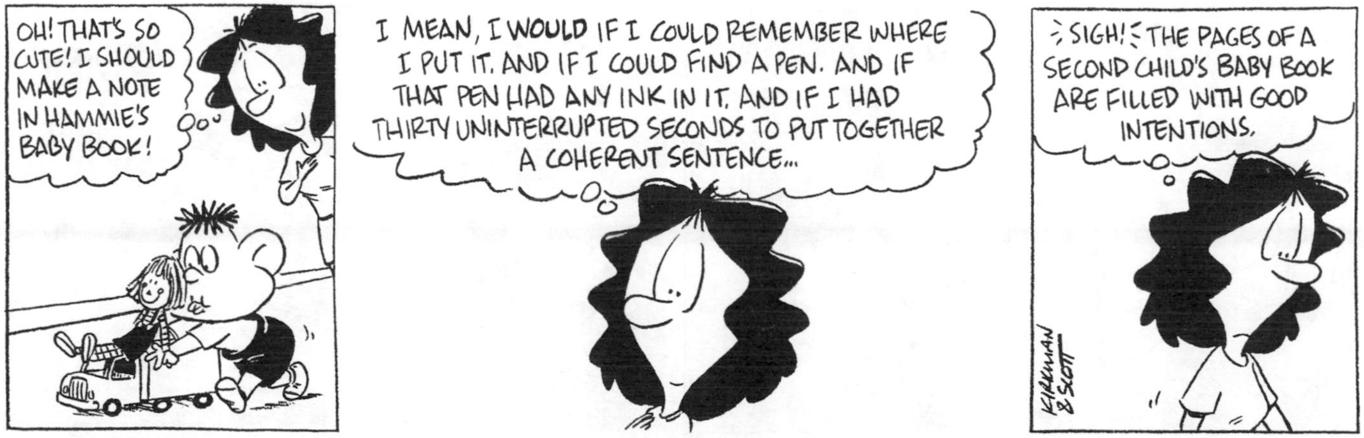
OH! THAT'S SO CUTE! I SHOULD MAKE A NOTE IN HAMMIE'S BABY BOOK!
I MEAN, I **WOULD** IF I COULD REMEMBER WHERE I PUT IT. AND IF I COULD FIND A PEN. AND IF THAT PEN HAD ANY INK IN IT. AND IF I HAD THIRTY UNINTERRUPTED SECONDS TO PUT TOGETHER A COHERENT SENTENCE...
SIGH! THE PAGES OF A SECOND CHILD'S BABY BOOK ARE FILLED WITH GOOD INTENTIONS.
KIRKMAN & SCOTT

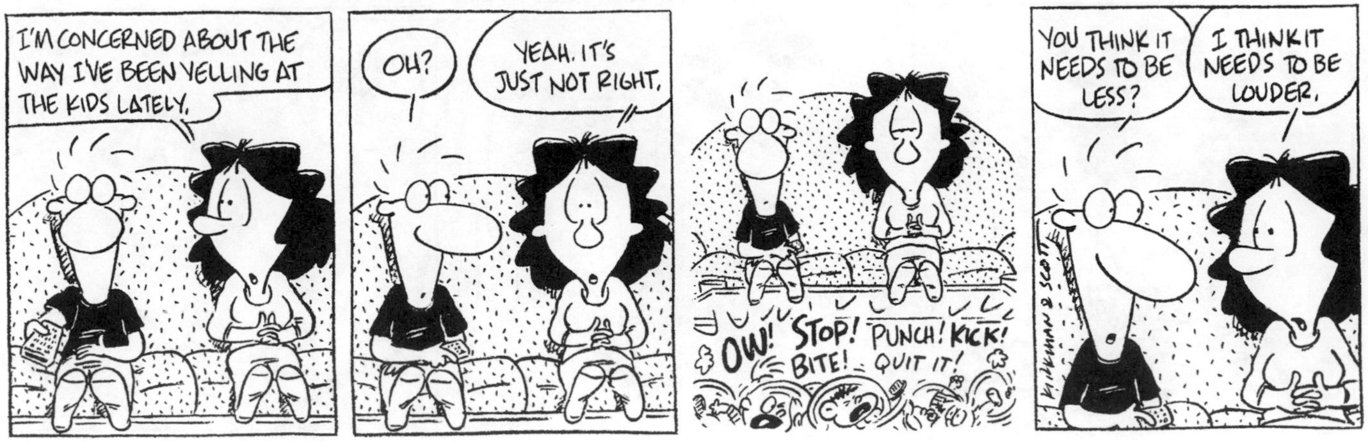
I'M CONCERNED ABOUT THE WAY I'VE BEEN YELLING AT THE KIDS LATELY.
OH?
YEAH. IT'S JUST NOT RIGHT.
OW! STOP! BITE! PUNCH! KICK! QUIT IT!
YOU THINK IT NEEDS TO BE LESS?
I THINK IT NEEDS TO BE LOUDER.
KIRKMAN & SCOTT

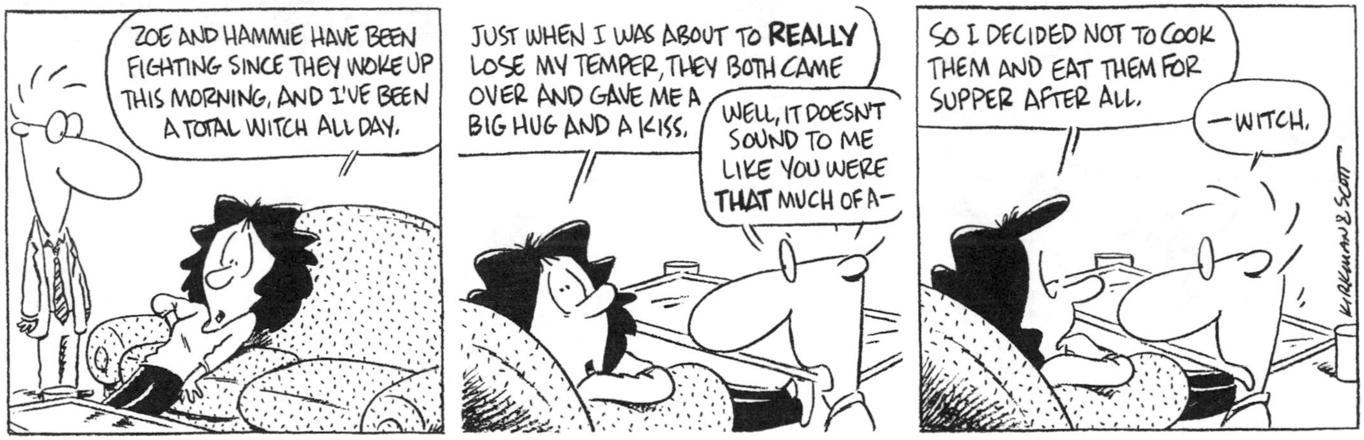
ZOE AND HAMMIE HAVE BEEN FIGHTING SINCE THEY WOKE UP THIS MORNING, AND I'VE BEEN A TOTAL WITCH ALL DAY.
JUST WHEN I WAS ABOUT TO REALLY LOSE MY TEMPER, THEY BOTH CAME OVER AND GAVE ME A BIG HUG AND A KISS.
WELL, IT DOESN'T SOUND TO ME LIKE YOU WERE THAT MUCH OF A—
SO I DECIDED NOT TO COOK THEM AND EAT THEM FOR SUPPER AFTER ALL.
—WITCH.
KIRKMAN & SCOTT

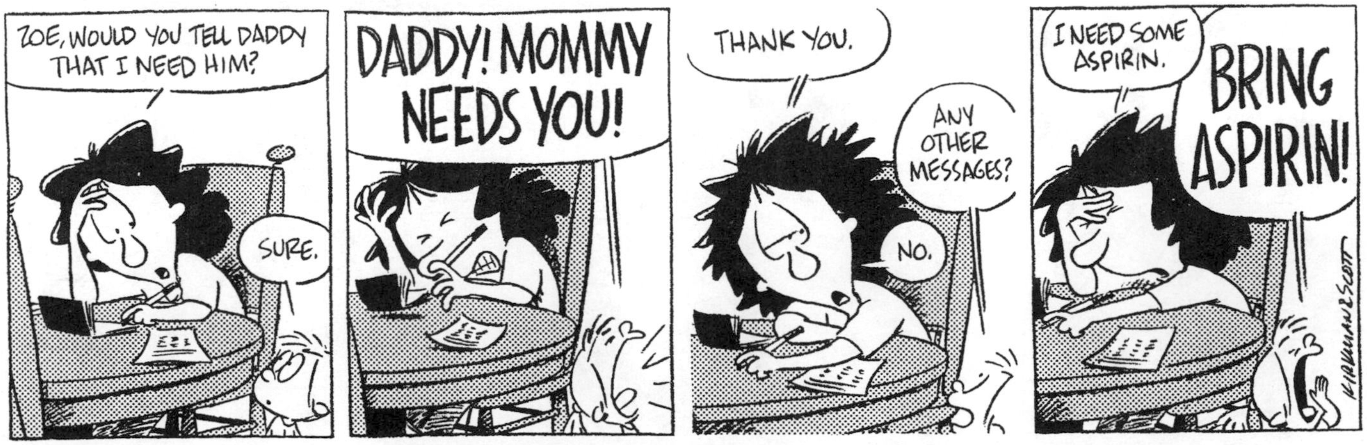
ZOE, WOULD YOU TELL DADDY THAT I NEED HIM?
SURE.
DADDY! MOMMY NEEDS YOU!
THANK YOU.
ANY OTHER MESSAGES?
NO.
I NEED SOME ASPIRIN.
BRING ASPIRIN!
KIRKMAN & SCOTT

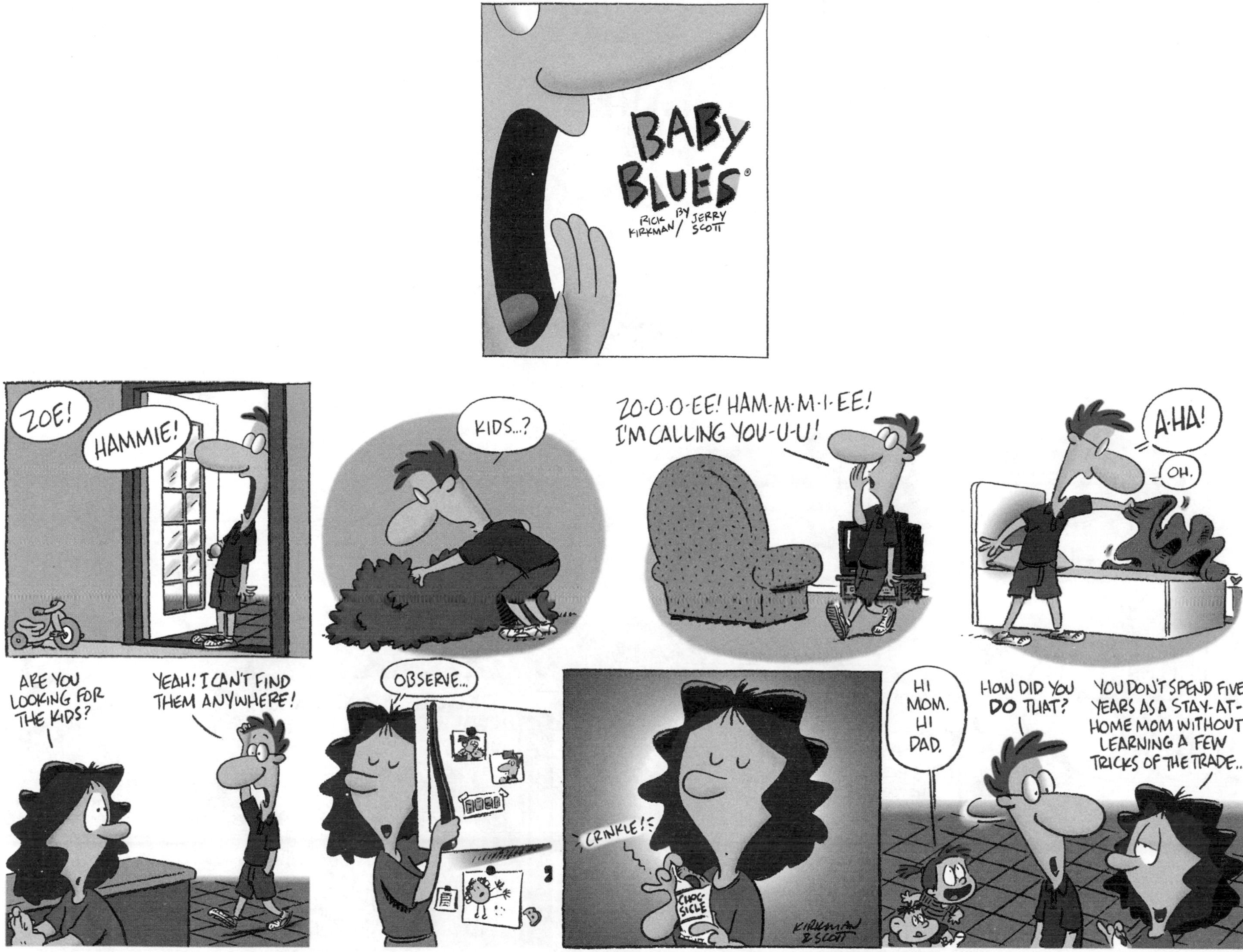
BABY BLUES®
BY RICK KIRKMAN / JERRY SCOTT
ZOE!
HAMMIE!
KIDS...?
ZO-O-O-EE! HAM-M-M-I-EE! I'M CALLING YOU-U-U!
A-HA!
OH.
ARE YOU LOOKING FOR THE KIDS?
YEAH! I CAN'T FIND THEM ANYWHERE!
OBSERVE...
CRINKLE!
CHOC-SICLE
KIRKMAN & SCOTT
HI MOM. HI DAD.
HOW DID YOU DO THAT?
YOU DON'T SPEND FIVE YEARS AS A STAY-AT-HOME MOM WITHOUT LEARNING A FEW TRICKS OF THE TRADE...

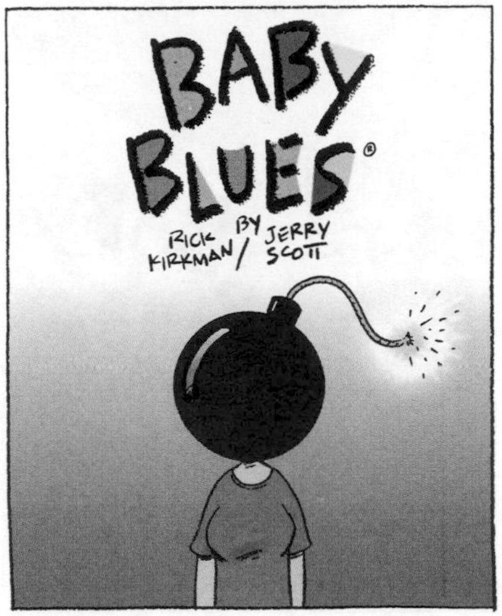

BABY BLUES®
BY RICK KIRKMAN / JERRY SCOTT

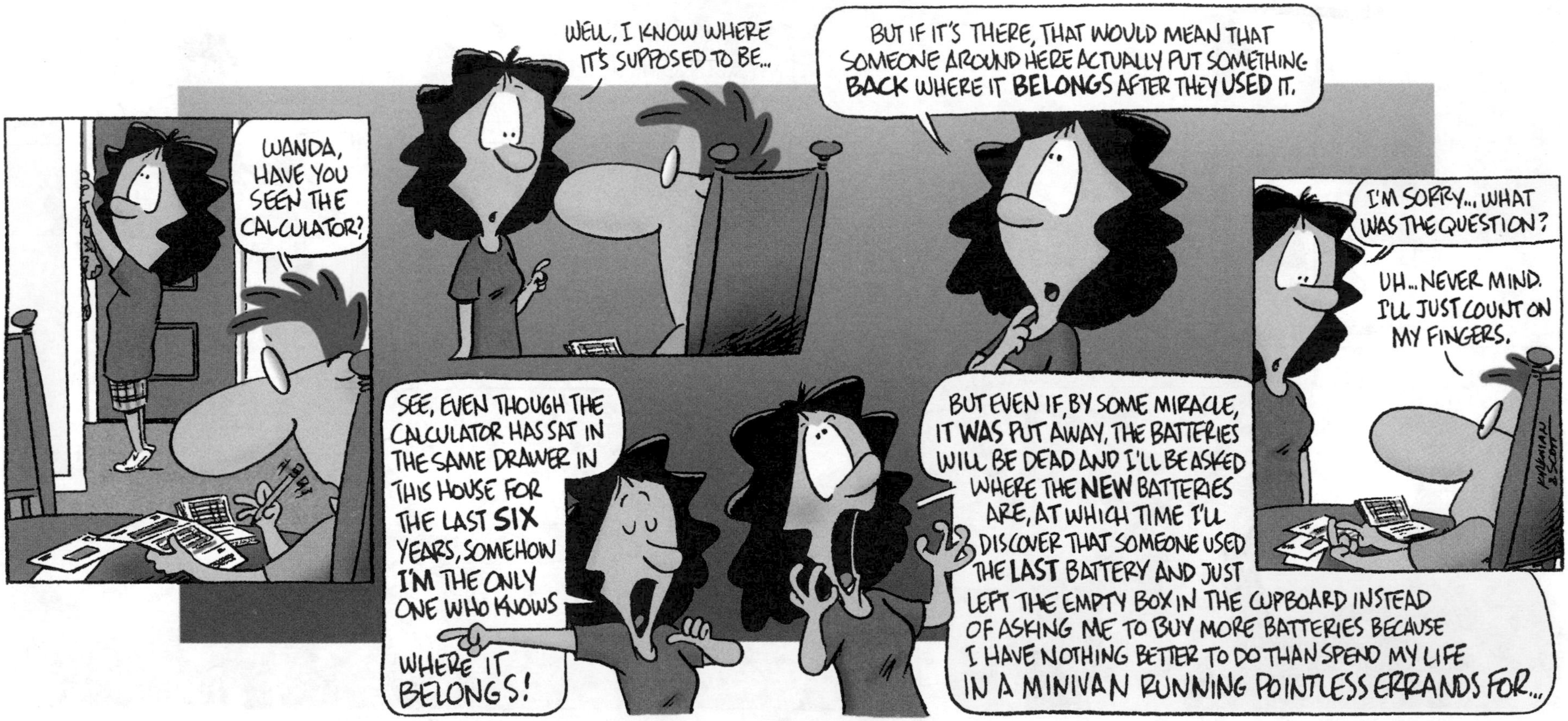

WANDA, HAVE YOU SEEN THE CALCULATOR?
WELL, I KNOW WHERE IT'S SUPPOSED TO BE...
BUT IF IT'S THERE, THAT WOULD MEAN THAT SOMEONE AROUND HERE ACTUALLY PUT SOMETHING BACK WHERE IT BELONGS AFTER THEY USED IT.
SEE, EVEN THOUGH THE CALCULATOR HAS SAT IN THE SAME DRAWER IN THIS HOUSE FOR THE LAST SIX YEARS, SOMEHOW I'M THE ONLY ONE WHO KNOWS WHERE IT BELONGS!
BUT EVEN IF, BY SOME MIRACLE, IT WAS PUT AWAY, THE BATTERIES WILL BE DEAD AND I'LL BE ASKED WHERE THE NEW BATTERIES ARE, AT WHICH TIME I'LL DISCOVER THAT SOMEONE USED THE LAST BATTERY AND JUST LEFT THE EMPTY BOX IN THE CUPBOARD INSTEAD OF ASKING ME TO BUY MORE BATTERIES BECAUSE I HAVE NOTHING BETTER TO DO THAN SPEND MY LIFE IN A MINIVAN RUNNING POINTLESS ERRANDS FOR...
I'M SORRY... WHAT WAS THE QUESTION?
UH... NEVER MIND. I'LL JUST COUNT ON MY FINGERS.

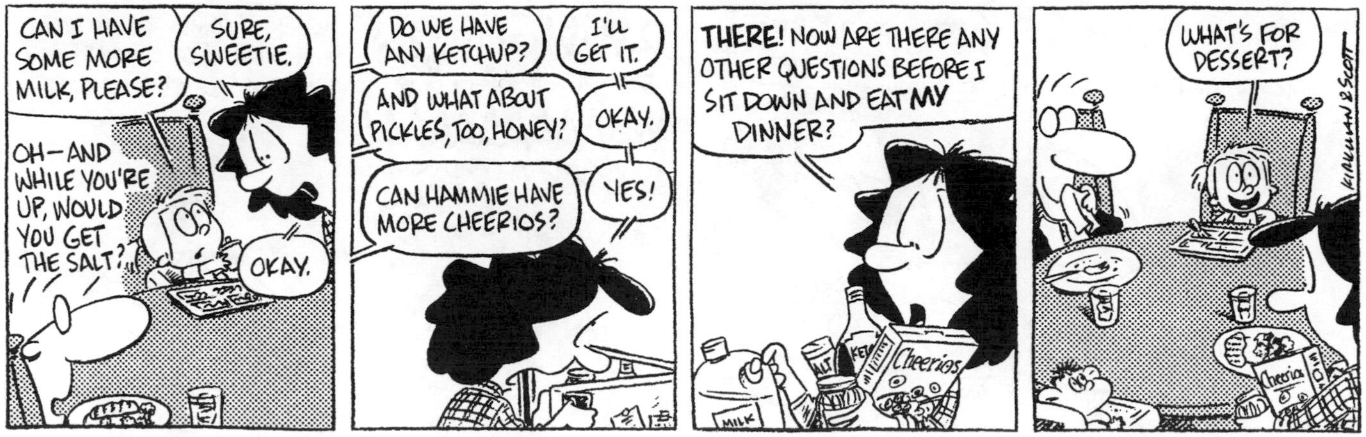
CAN I HAVE SOME MORE MILK, PLEASE?
SURE, SWEETIE.
OH—AND WHILE YOU'RE UP, WOULD YOU GET THE SALT?
OKAY.
DO WE HAVE ANY KETCHUP?
I'LL GET IT.
AND WHAT ABOUT PICKLES, TOO, HONEY?
OKAY.
CAN HAMMIE HAVE MORE CHEERIOS?
YES!
THERE! NOW ARE THERE ANY OTHER QUESTIONS BEFORE I SIT DOWN AND EAT MY DINNER?
MILK
Cheerios
WHAT'S FOR DESSERT?
KIRKMAN & SCOTT

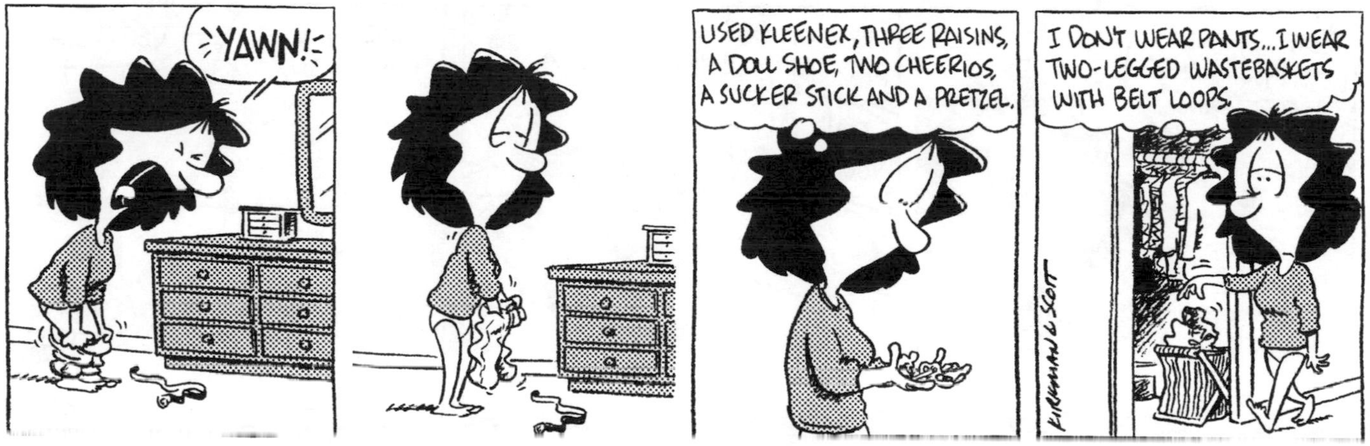
YAWN!
USED KLEENEX, THREE RAISINS, A DOLL SHOE, TWO CHEERIOS, A SUCKER STICK AND A PRETZEL.
KIRKMAN & SCOTT
I DON'T WEAR PANTS...I WEAR TWO-LEGGED WASTEBASKETS WITH BELT LOOPS.

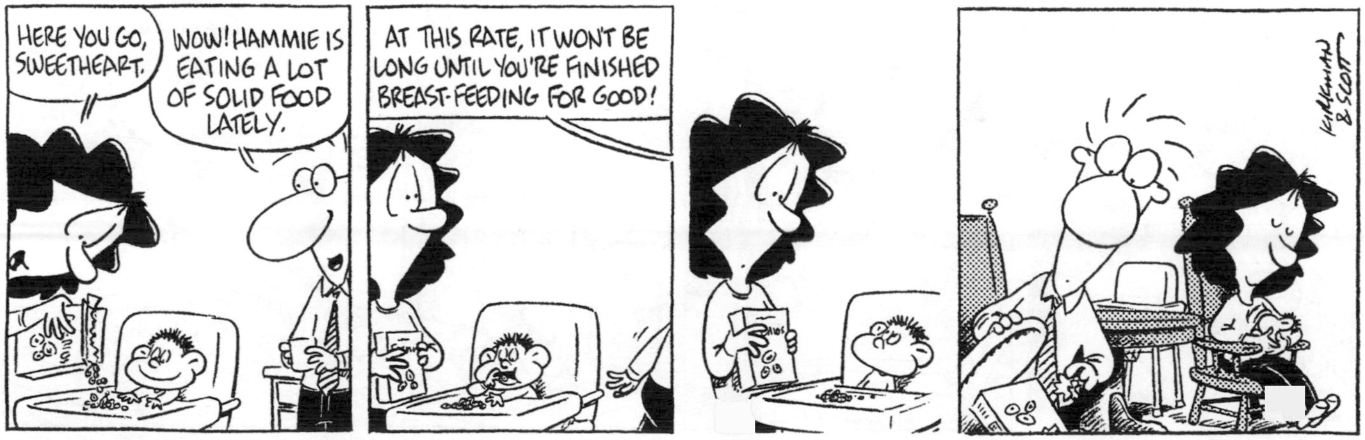
HERE YOU GO, SWEETHEART.
WOW! HAMMIE IS EATING A LOT OF SOLID FOOD LATELY.
AT THIS RATE, IT WON'T BE LONG UNTIL YOU'RE FINISHED BREAST-FEEDING FOR GOOD!
KIRKMAN & SCOTT

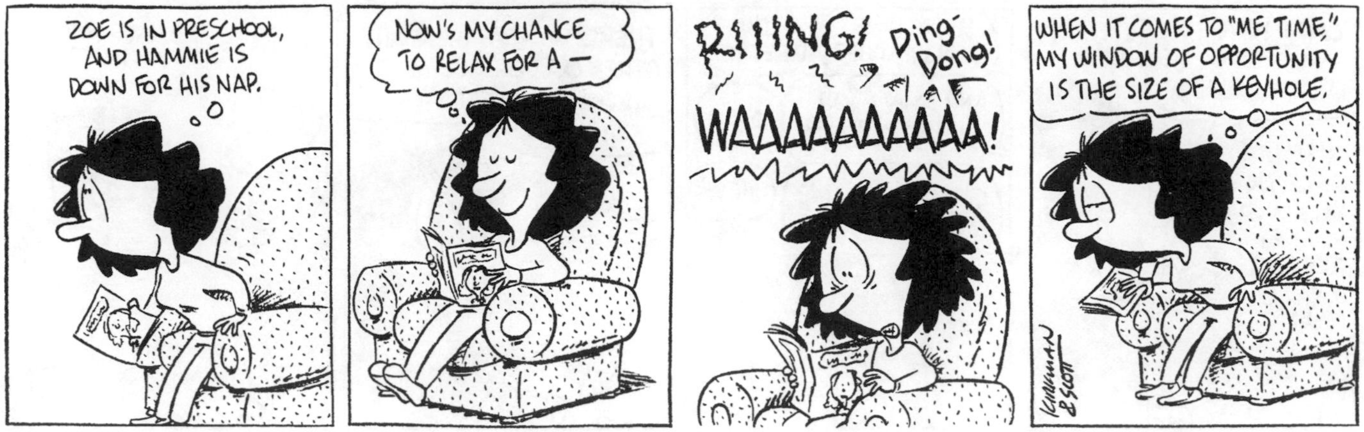
ZOE IS IN PRESCHOOL, AND HAMMIE IS DOWN FOR HIS NAP.
NOW'S MY CHANCE TO RELAX FOR A —
RIIING! Ding-Dong!
WAAAAAAAAAA!
WHEN IT COMES TO "ME TIME," MY WINDOW OF OPPORTUNITY IS THE SIZE OF A KEYHOLE.
KIRKMAN & SCOTT

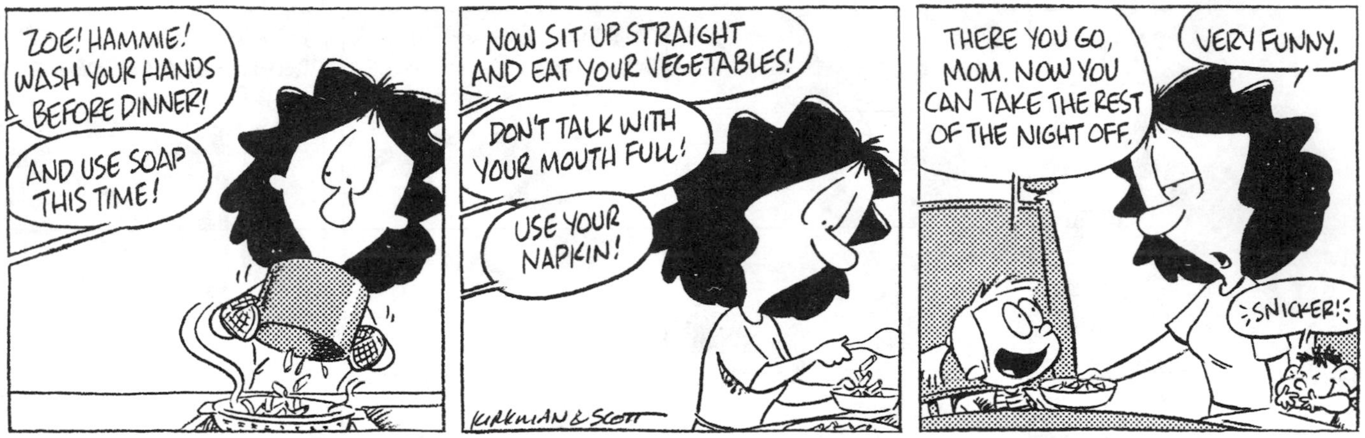
ZOE! HAMMIE! WASH YOUR HANDS BEFORE DINNER!
AND USE SOAP THIS TIME!
NOW SIT UP STRAIGHT AND EAT YOUR VEGETABLES!
DON'T TALK WITH YOUR MOUTH FULL!
USE YOUR NAPKIN!
KIRKMAN & SCOTT
THERE YOU GO, MOM. NOW YOU CAN TAKE THE REST OF THE NIGHT OFF.
VERY FUNNY.
SNICKER!

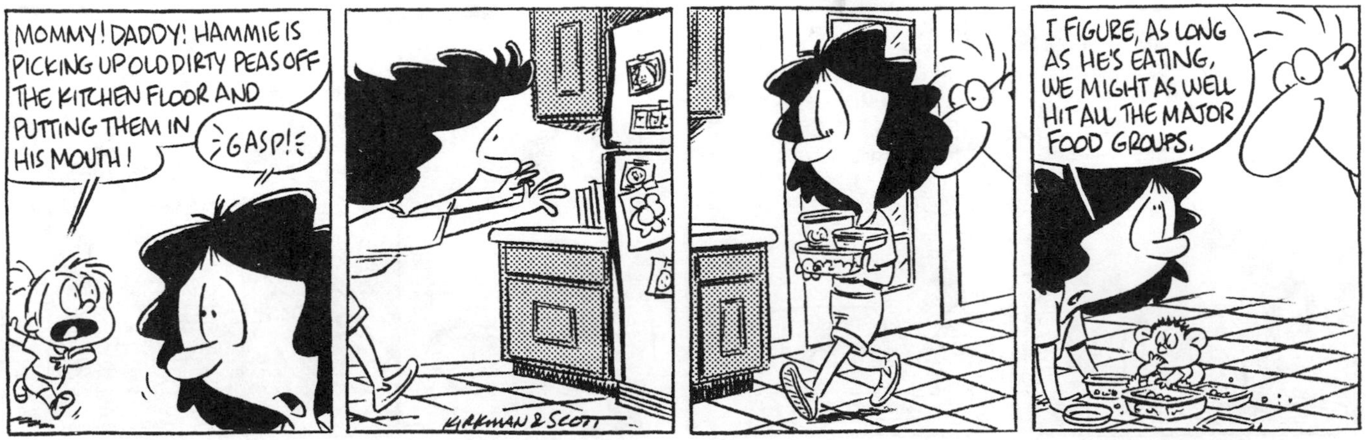
MOMMY! DADDY! HAMMIE IS PICKING UP OLD DIRTY PEAS OFF THE KITCHEN FLOOR AND PUTTING THEM IN HIS MOUTH!
GASP!
KIRKMAN & SCOTT
I FIGURE, AS LONG AS HE'S EATING, WE MIGHT AS WELL HIT ALL THE MAJOR FOOD GROUPS.

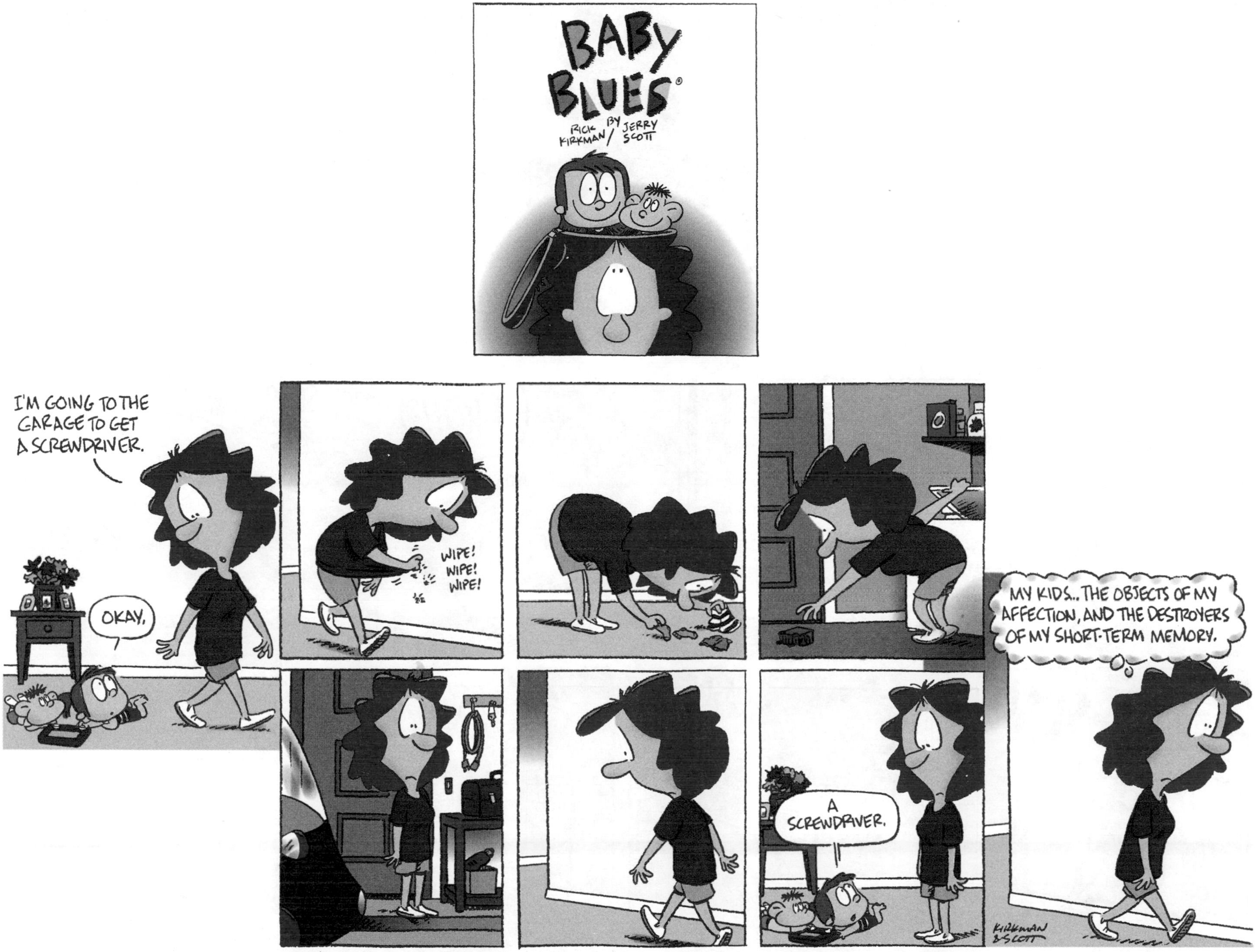
BABY BLUES®
BY RICK KIRKMAN / JERRY SCOTT
I'M GOING TO THE GARAGE TO GET A SCREWDRIVER.
OKAY.
WIPE! WIPE! WIPE!
A SCREWDRIVER.
MY KIDS... THE OBJECTS OF MY AFFECTION, AND THE DESTROYERS OF MY SHORT-TERM MEMORY.
KIRKMAN & SCOTT

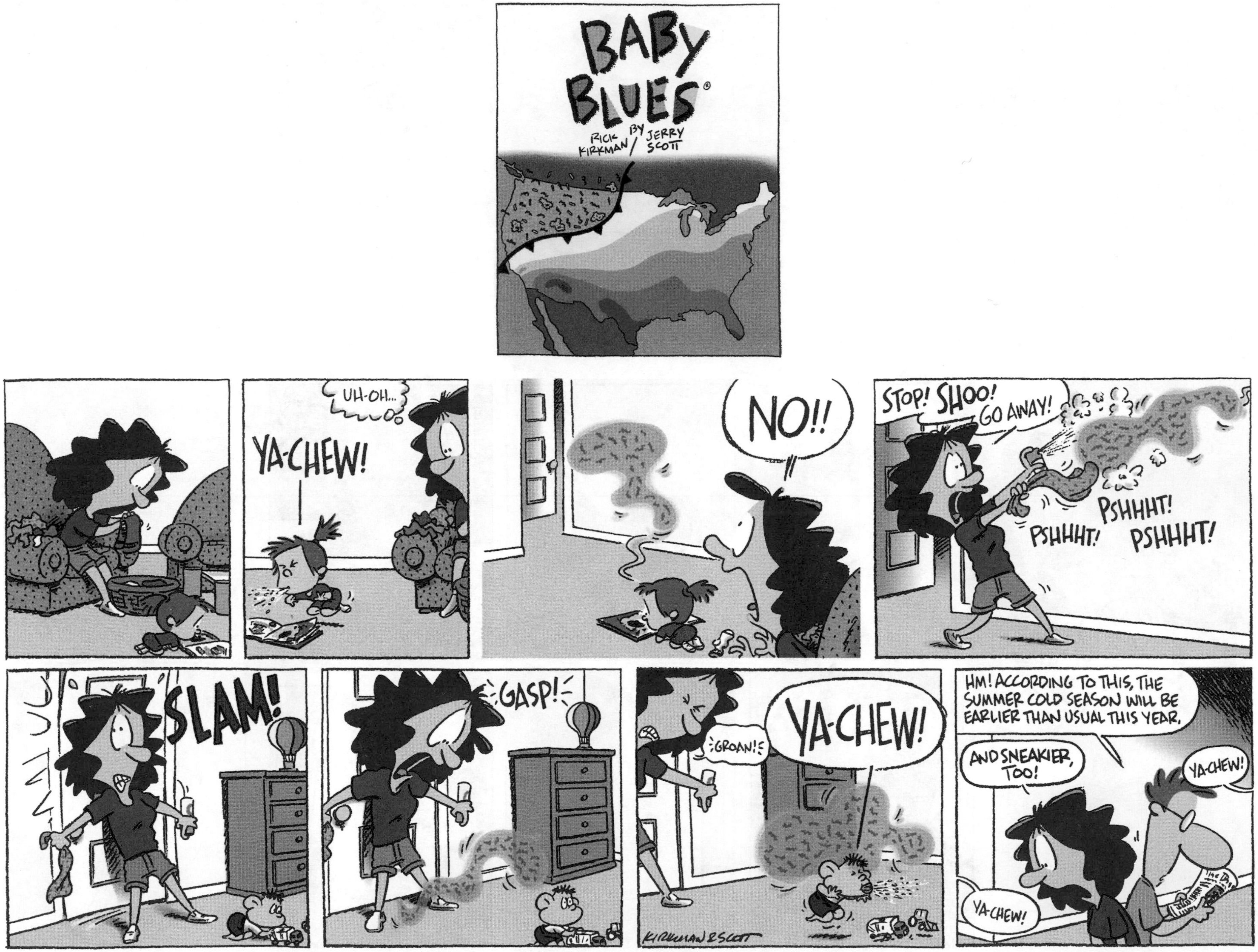
BABY BLUES®
BY RICK KIRKMAN / JERRY SCOTT
UH-OH...
YA-CHEW!
NO!!
STOP! SHOO! GO AWAY!
PSHHHT! PSHHHT! PSHHHT!
SLAM!
GASP!
GROAN!
YA-CHEW!
KIRKMAN & SCOTT
HM! ACCORDING TO THIS, THE SUMMER COLD SEASON WILL BE EARLIER THAN USUAL THIS YEAR.
AND SNEAKIER, TOO!
YA-CHEW!
YA-CHEW!

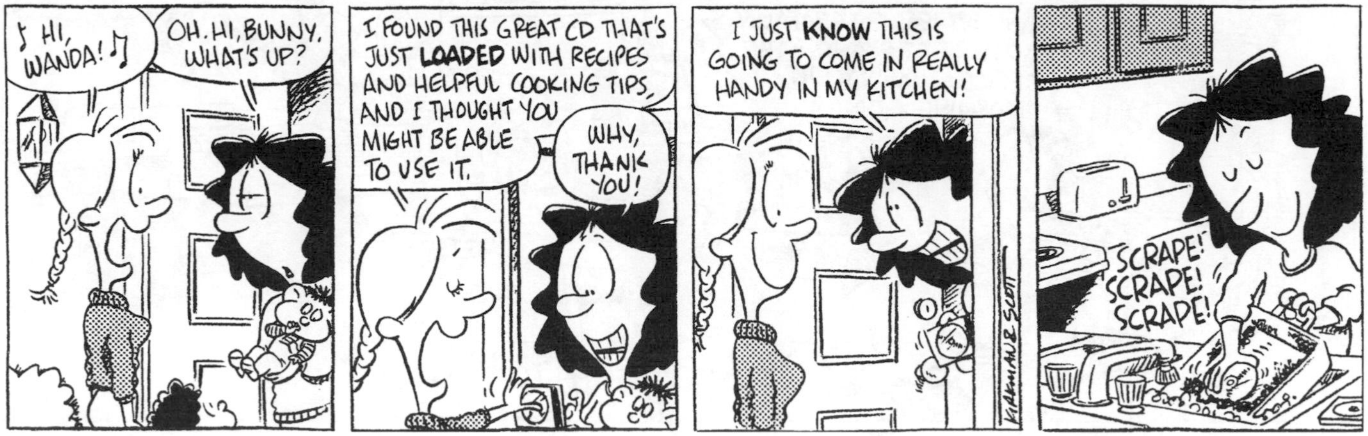
♪ HI, WANDA! ♫
OH. HI, BUNNY. WHAT'S UP?
I FOUND THIS GREAT CD THAT'S JUST **LOADED** WITH RECIPES AND HELPFUL COOKING TIPS, AND I THOUGHT YOU MIGHT BE ABLE TO USE IT.
WHY, THANK YOU!
I JUST **KNOW** THIS IS GOING TO COME IN REALLY HANDY IN MY KITCHEN!
KIRKMAN & SCOTT
SCRAPE! SCRAPE! SCRAPE!

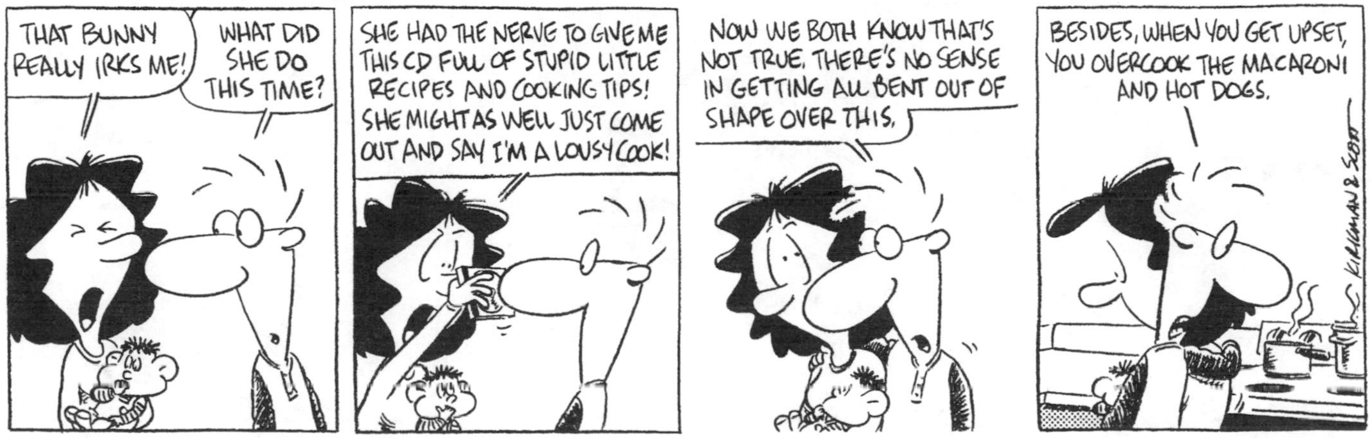
THAT BUNNY REALLY IRKS ME!
WHAT DID SHE DO THIS TIME?
SHE HAD THE NERVE TO GIVE ME THIS CD FULL OF STUPID LITTLE RECIPES AND COOKING TIPS! SHE MIGHT AS WELL JUST COME OUT AND SAY I'M A LOUSY COOK!
NOW WE BOTH KNOW THAT'S NOT TRUE. THERE'S NO SENSE IN GETTING ALL BENT OUT OF SHAPE OVER THIS.
BESIDES, WHEN YOU GET UPSET, YOU OVERCOOK THE MACARONI AND HOT DOGS.
KIRKMAN & SCOTT

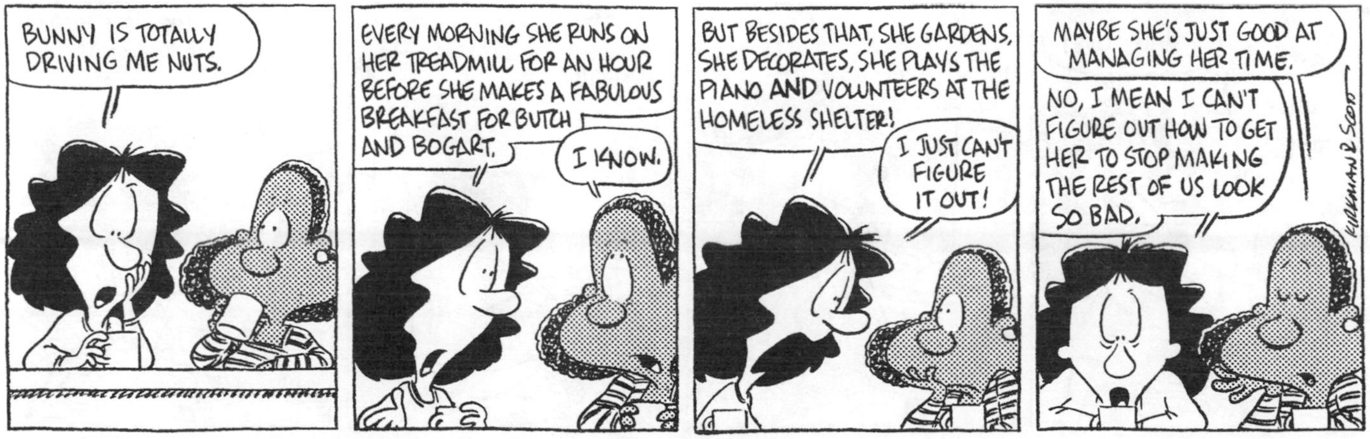
BUNNY IS TOTALLY DRIVING ME NUTS.
EVERY MORNING SHE RUNS ON HER TREADMILL FOR AN HOUR BEFORE SHE MAKES A FABULOUS BREAKFAST FOR BUTCH AND BOGART.
I KNOW.
BUT BESIDES THAT, SHE GARDENS, SHE DECORATES, SHE PLAYS THE PIANO **AND** VOLUNTEERS AT THE HOMELESS SHELTER!
I JUST CAN'T FIGURE IT OUT!
MAYBE SHE'S JUST GOOD AT MANAGING HER TIME.
NO, I MEAN I CAN'T FIGURE OUT HOW TO GET HER TO STOP MAKING THE REST OF US LOOK SO BAD.
KIRKMAN & SCOTT

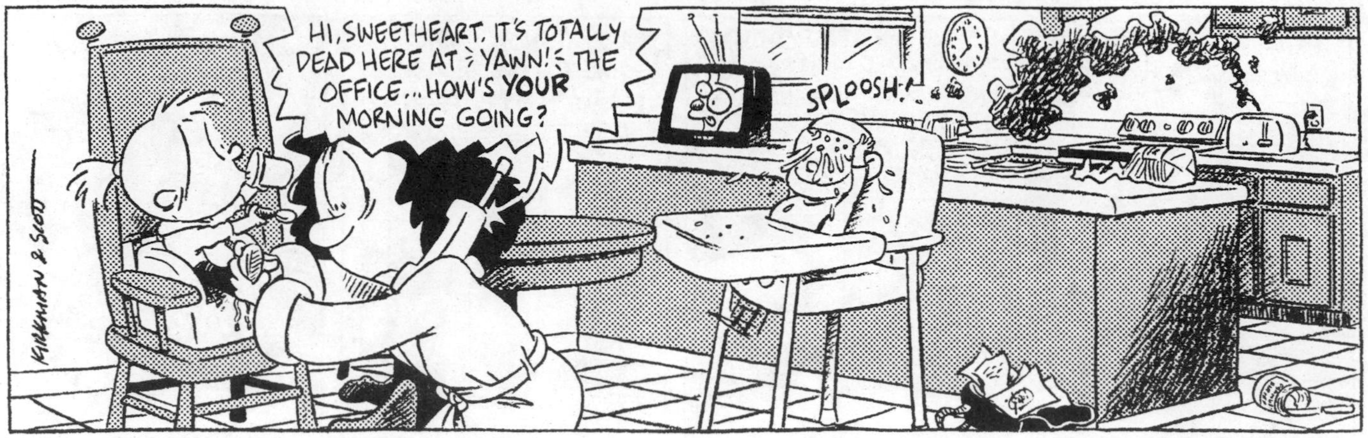
HI, SWEETHEART. IT'S TOTALLY DEAD HERE AT ~YAWN!~ THE OFFICE... HOW'S **YOUR** MORNING GOING?
SPLOOSH!
KIRKMAN & SCOTT

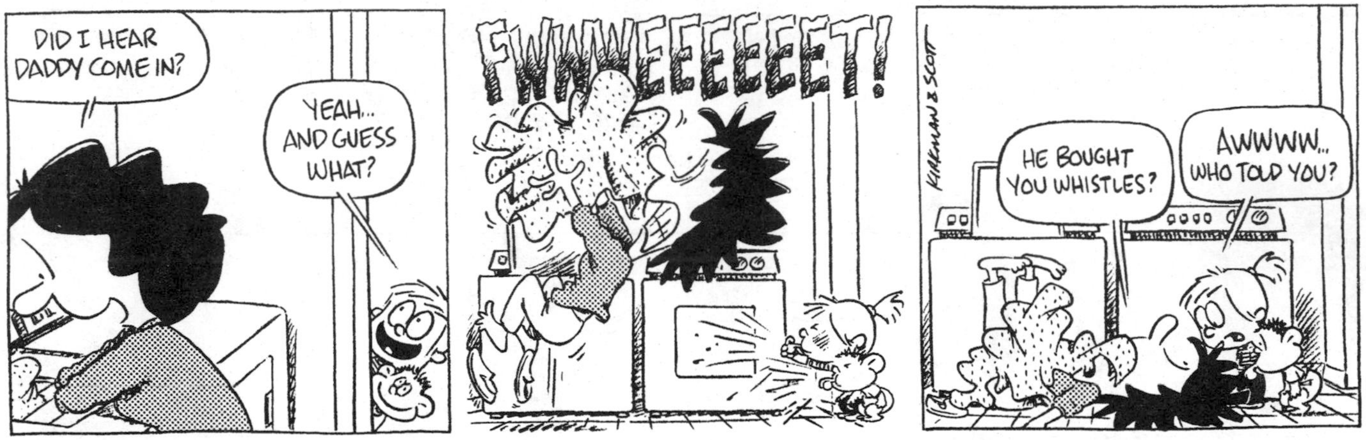
DID I HEAR DADDY COME IN?
YEAH... AND GUESS WHAT?
FWWWEEEEEEET!
KIRKMAN & SCOTT
HE BOUGHT YOU WHISTLES?
AWWWW... WHO TOLD YOU?

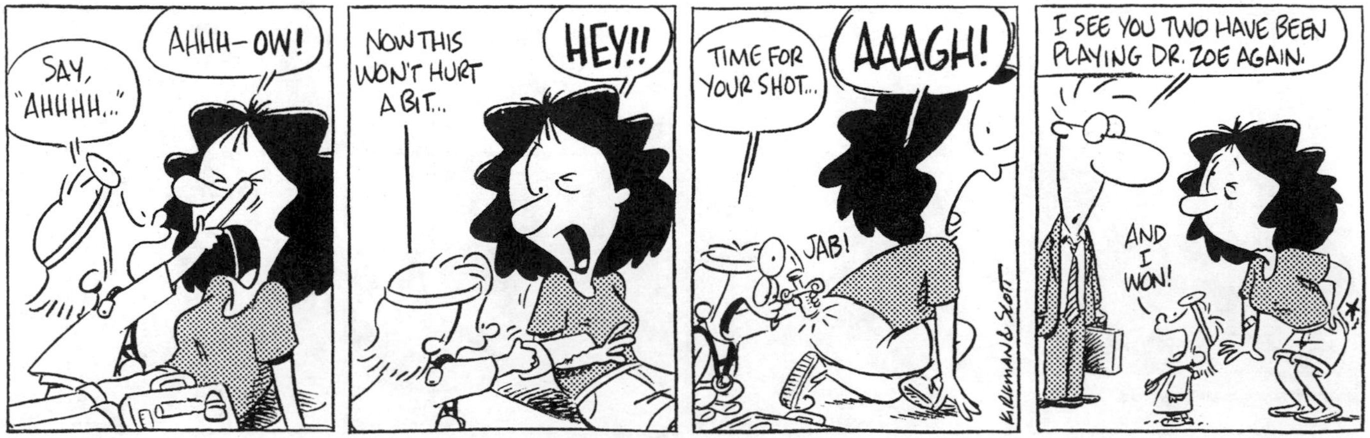
SAY, "AHHHH..."
AHHH-OW!
NOW THIS WON'T HURT A BIT...
HEY!!
TIME FOR YOUR SHOT...
AAAGH!
JAB!
KIRKMAN & SCOTT
I SEE YOU TWO HAVE BEEN PLAYING DR. ZOE AGAIN.
AND I WON!

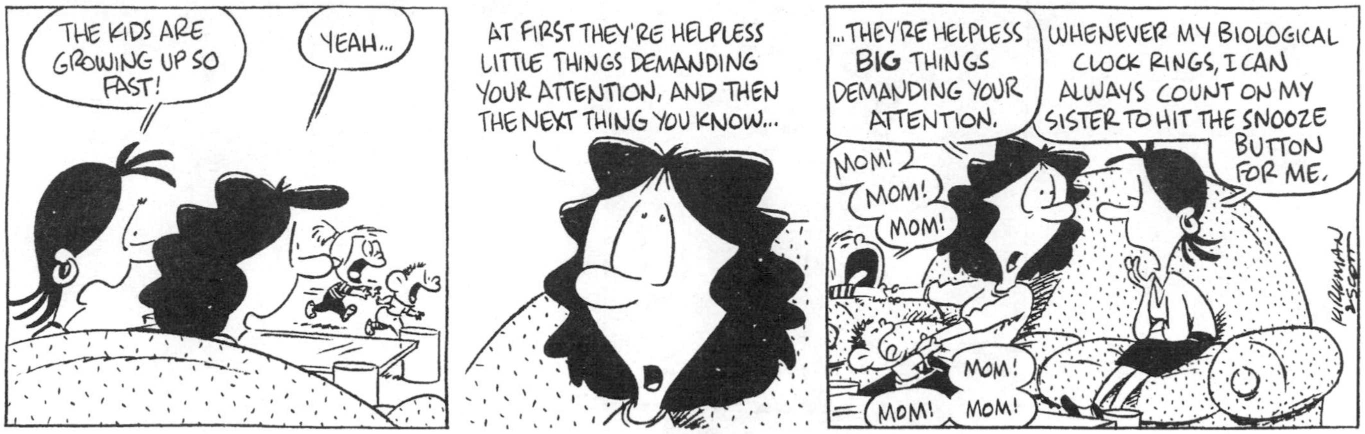
THE KIDS ARE GROWING UP SO FAST!
YEAH...
AT FIRST THEY'RE HELPLESS LITTLE THINGS DEMANDING YOUR ATTENTION, AND THEN THE NEXT THING YOU KNOW...
...THEY'RE HELPLESS BIG THINGS DEMANDING YOUR ATTENTION.
WHENEVER MY BIOLOGICAL CLOCK RINGS, I CAN ALWAYS COUNT ON MY SISTER TO HIT THE SNOOZE BUTTON FOR ME.
MOM!
MOM!
MOM!
MOM!
MOM!
MOM!
KIRKMAN & SCOTT

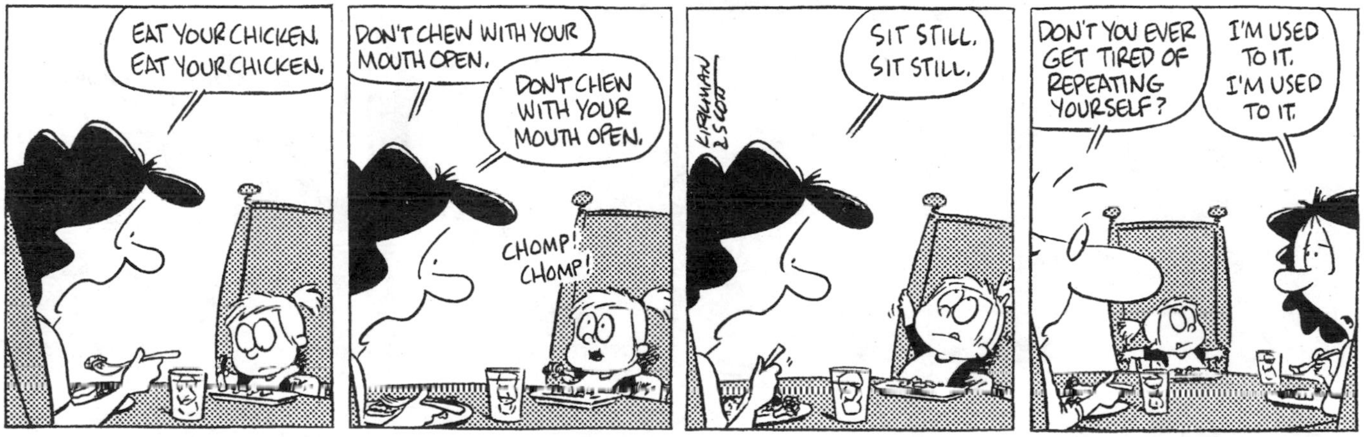
EAT YOUR CHICKEN. EAT YOUR CHICKEN.
DON'T CHEW WITH YOUR MOUTH OPEN.
DON'T CHEW WITH YOUR MOUTH OPEN.
CHOMP! CHOMP!
KIRKMAN & SCOTT
SIT STILL. SIT STILL.
DON'T YOU EVER GET TIRED OF REPEATING YOURSELF?
I'M USED TO IT. I'M USED TO IT.

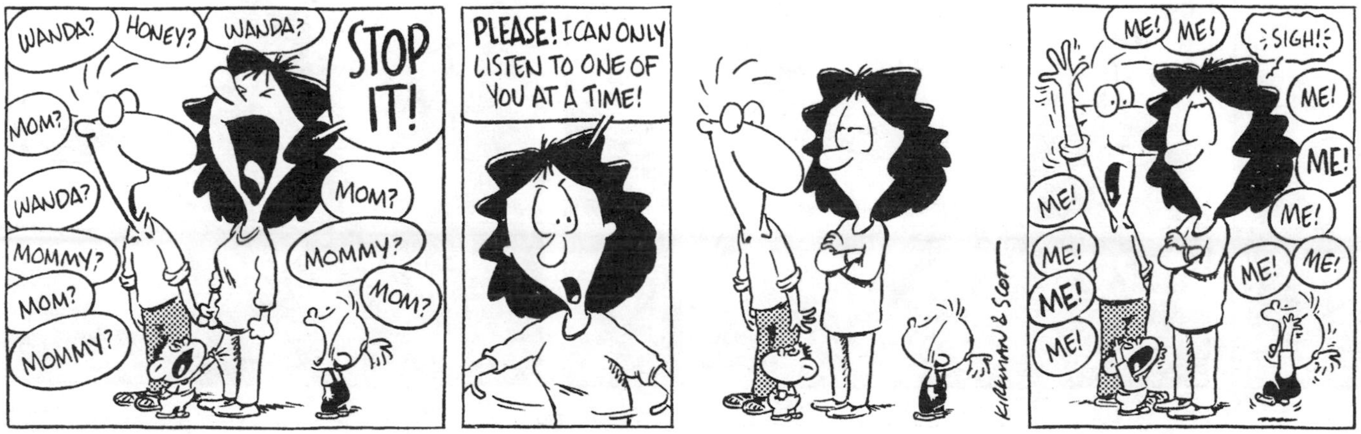
WANDA?
HONEY?
WANDA?
MOM?
WANDA?
MOMMY?
MOM?
MOMMY?
STOP IT!
MOM?
MOMMY?
MOM?
PLEASE! I CAN ONLY LISTEN TO ONE OF YOU AT A TIME!
KIRKMAN & SCOTT
ME!
ME!
SIGH!
ME!
ME!
ME!
ME!
ME!
ME!
ME!
ME!
ME!

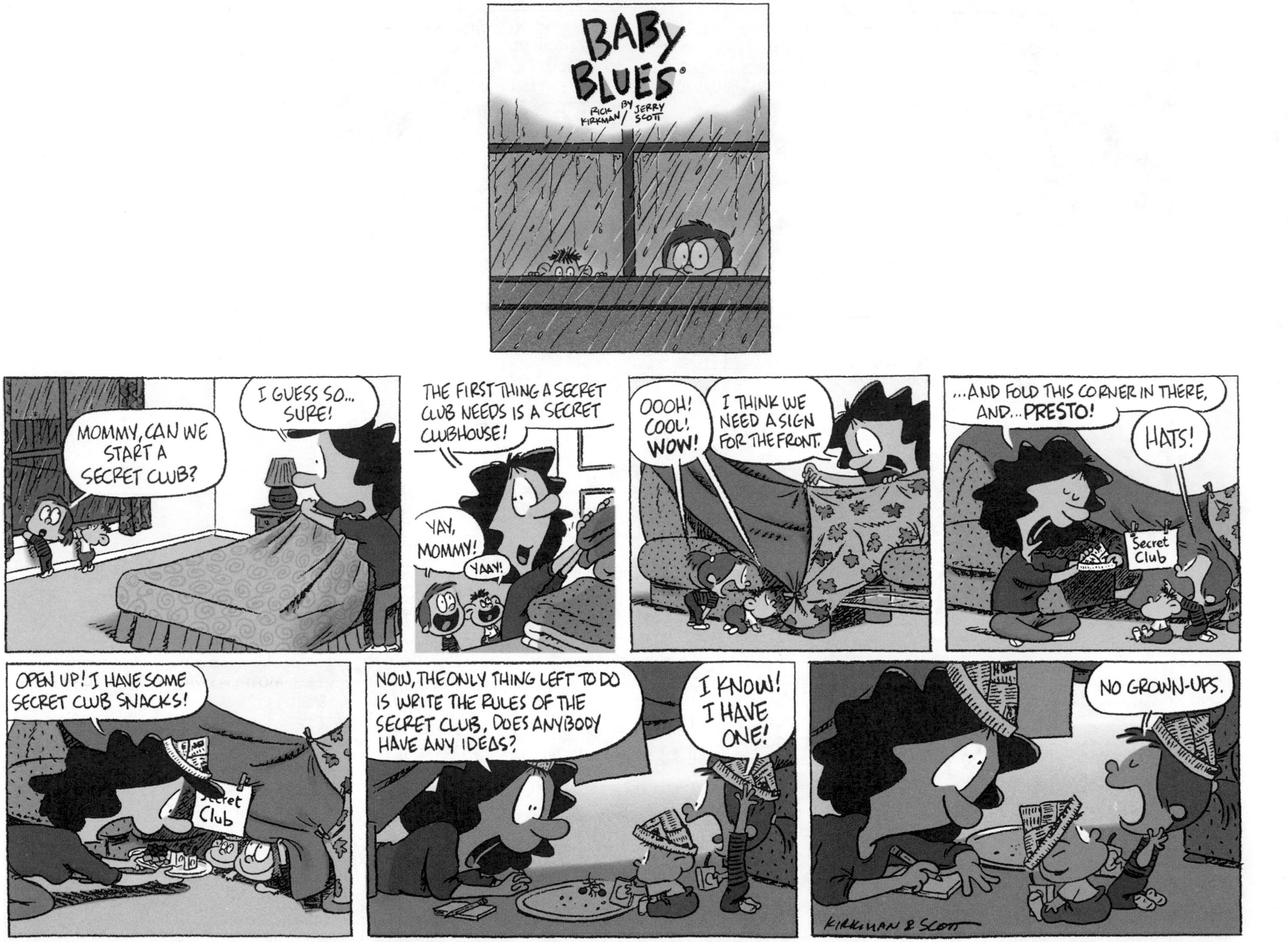
BABY BLUES®
RICK KIRKMAN / BY JERRY SCOTT
MOMMY, CAN WE START A SECRET CLUB?
I GUESS SO... SURE!
THE FIRST THING A SECRET CLUB NEEDS IS A SECRET CLUBHOUSE!
YAY, MOMMY!
YAAY!
OOOH! COOL! WOW!
I THINK WE NEED A SIGN FOR THE FRONT.
...AND FOLD THIS CORNER IN THERE, AND... PRESTO!
HATS!
Secret Club
OPEN UP! I HAVE SOME SECRET CLUB SNACKS!
Secret Club
NOW, THE ONLY THING LEFT TO DO IS WRITE THE RULES OF THE SECRET CLUB. DOES ANYBODY HAVE ANY IDEAS?
I KNOW! I HAVE ONE!
NO GROWN-UPS.
KIRKMAN & SCOTT

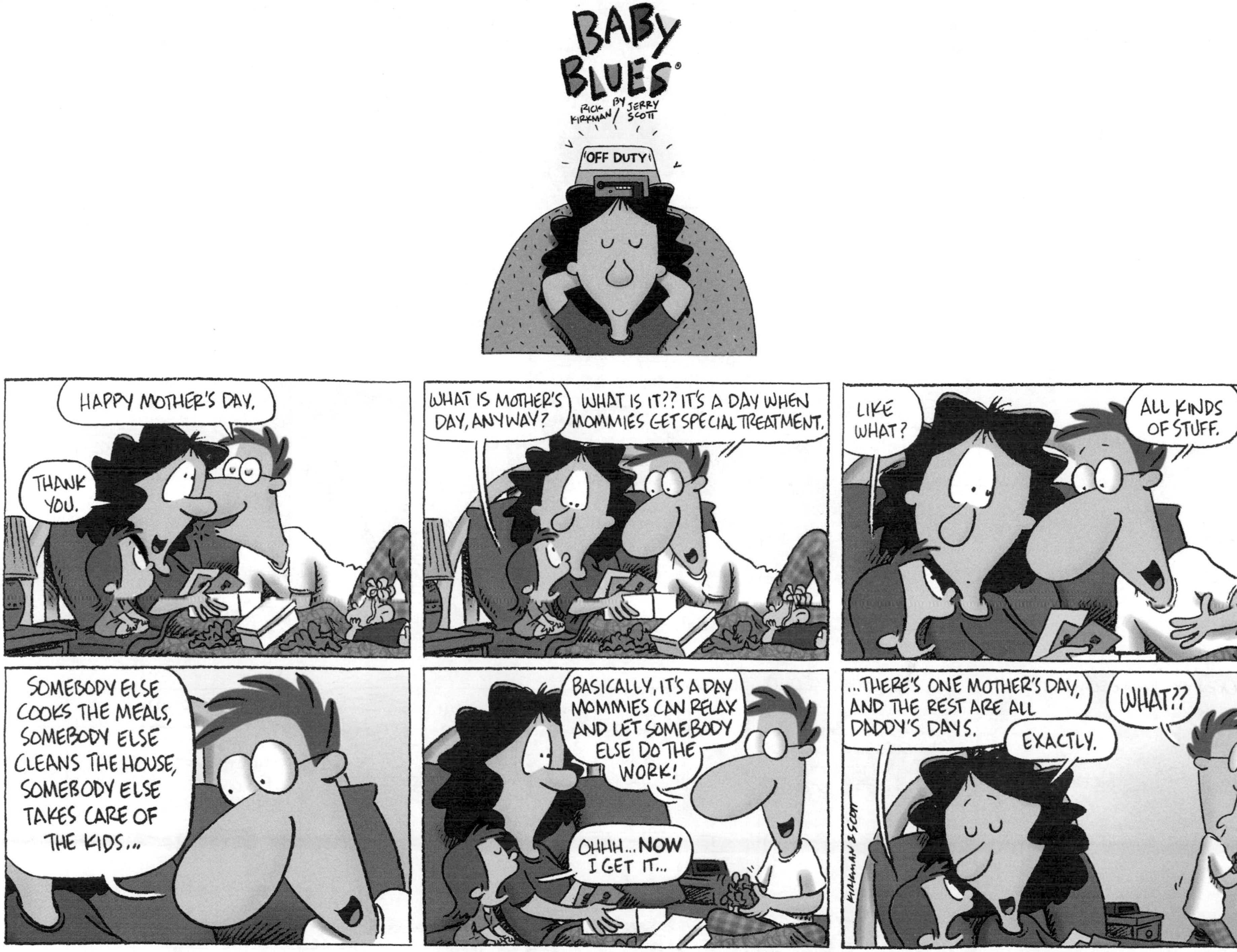
BABY BLUES®
RICK KIRKMAN / JERRY SCOTT
OFF DUTY
HAPPY MOTHER'S DAY.
THANK YOU.
WHAT IS MOTHER'S DAY, ANYWAY?
WHAT IS IT?? IT'S A DAY WHEN MOMMIES GET SPECIAL TREATMENT.
LIKE WHAT?
ALL KINDS OF STUFF.
SOMEBODY ELSE COOKS THE MEALS, SOMEBODY ELSE CLEANS THE HOUSE, SOMEBODY ELSE TAKES CARE OF THE KIDS...
BASICALLY, IT'S A DAY MOMMIES CAN RELAX AND LET SOMEBODY ELSE DO THE WORK!
OHHH... NOW I GET IT...
...THERE'S ONE MOTHER'S DAY, AND THE REST ARE ALL DADDY'S DAYS.
WHAT??
EXACTLY.
KIRKMAN & SCOTT

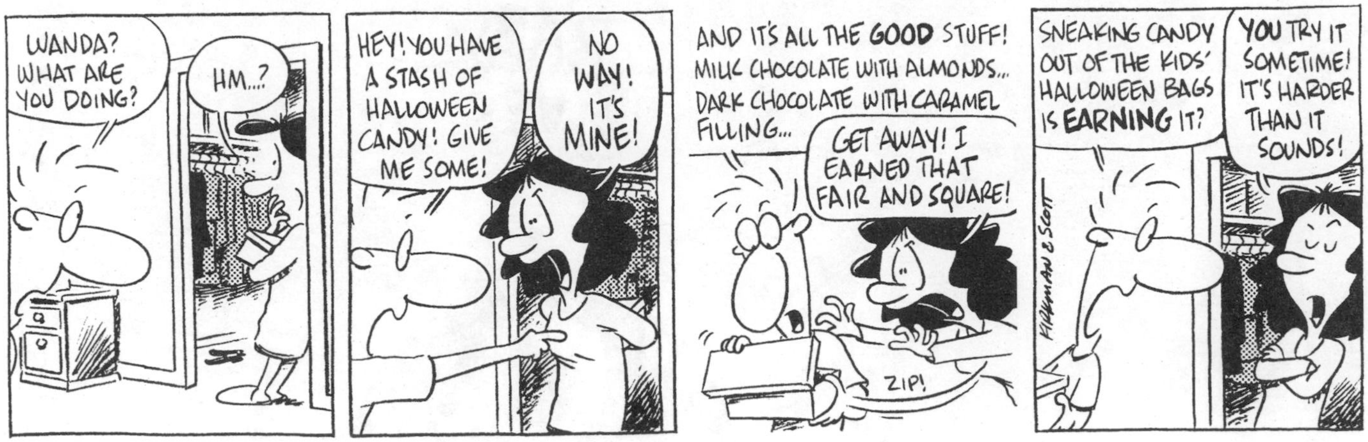
WANDA? WHAT ARE YOU DOING?
HM...?
HEY! YOU HAVE A STASH OF HALLOWEEN CANDY! GIVE ME SOME!
NO WAY! IT'S MINE!
AND IT'S ALL THE GOOD STUFF! MILK CHOCOLATE WITH ALMONDS... DARK CHOCOLATE WITH CARAMEL FILLING...
GET AWAY! I EARNED THAT FAIR AND SQUARE!
ZIP!
KIRKMAN & SCOTT
SNEAKING CANDY OUT OF THE KIDS' HALLOWEEN BAGS IS EARNING IT?
YOU TRY IT SOMETIME! IT'S HARDER THAN IT SOUNDS!

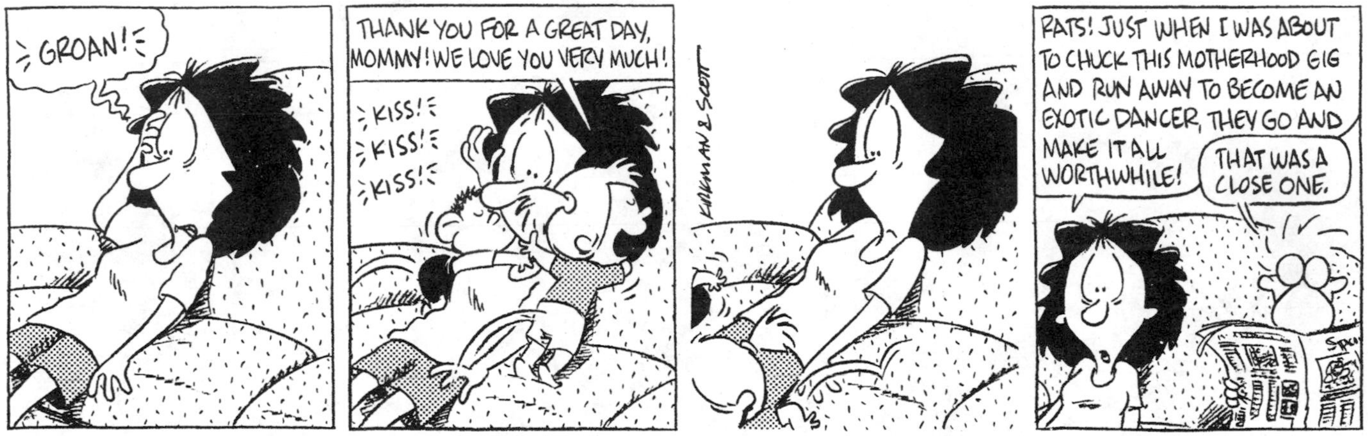
GROAN!
THANK YOU FOR A GREAT DAY, MOMMY! WE LOVE YOU VERY MUCH!
KISS!
KISS!
KISS!
KIRKMAN & SCOTT
RATS! JUST WHEN I WAS ABOUT TO CHUCK THIS MOTHERHOOD GIG AND RUN AWAY TO BECOME AN EXOTIC DANCER, THEY GO AND MAKE IT ALL WORTHWHILE!
THAT WAS A CLOSE ONE.

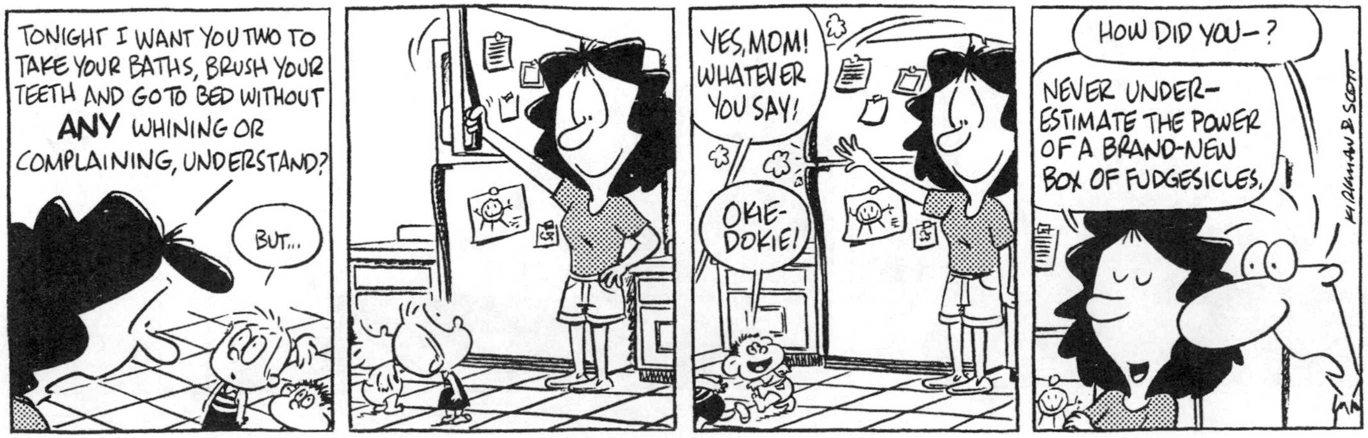
TONIGHT I WANT YOU TWO TO TAKE YOUR BATHS, BRUSH YOUR TEETH AND GO TO BED WITHOUT ANY WHINING OR COMPLAINING, UNDERSTAND?
BUT...
YES, MOM! WHATEVER YOU SAY!
OKIE-DOKIE!
HOW DID YOU—?
NEVER UNDER-ESTIMATE THE POWER OF A BRAND-NEW BOX OF FUDGESICLES.
KIRKMAN & SCOTT

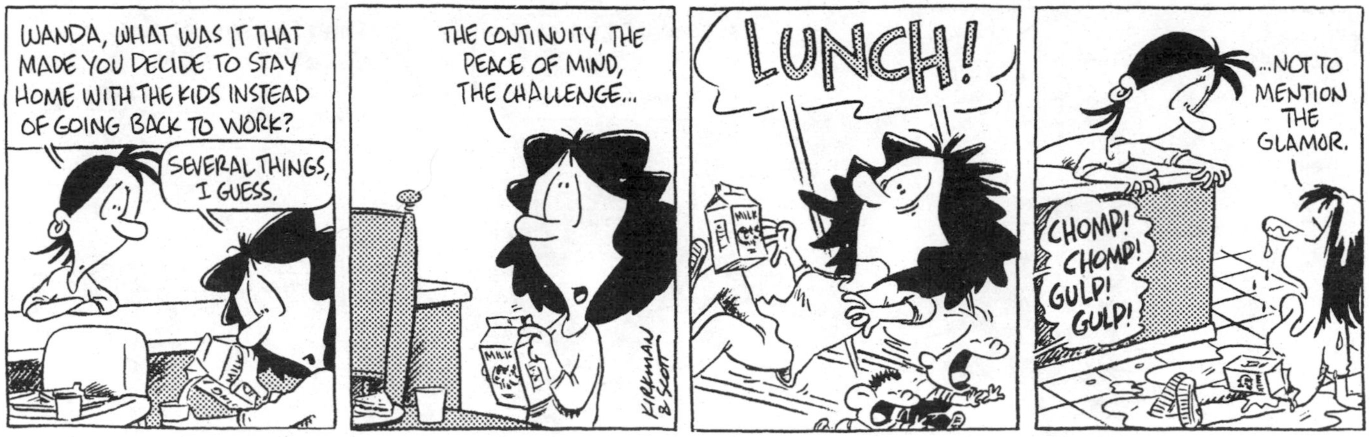
WANDA, WHAT WAS IT THAT MADE YOU DECIDE TO STAY HOME WITH THE KIDS INSTEAD OF GOING BACK TO WORK?
SEVERAL THINGS, I GUESS.
THE CONTINUITY, THE PEACE OF MIND, THE CHALLENGE...
KIRKMAN & SCOTT
LUNCH!
CHOMP! CHOMP! GULP! GULP!
...NOT TO MENTION THE GLAMOR.

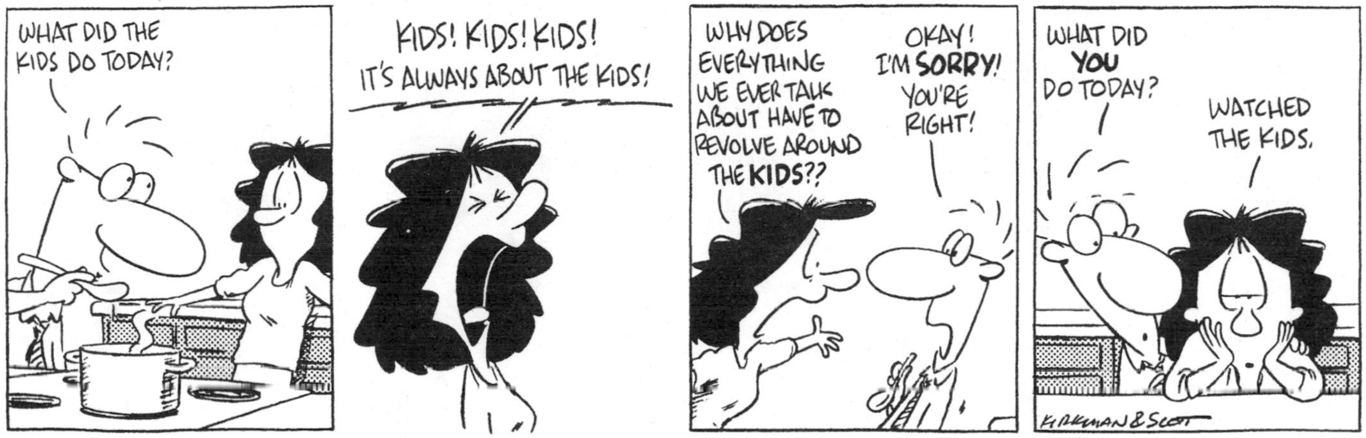
WHAT DID THE KIDS DO TODAY?
KIDS! KIDS! KIDS! IT'S ALWAYS ABOUT THE KIDS!
WHY DOES EVERYTHING WE EVER TALK ABOUT HAVE TO REVOLVE AROUND THE **KIDS**??
OKAY! I'M **SORRY**! YOU'RE RIGHT!
WHAT DID **YOU** DO TODAY?
WATCHED THE KIDS.
KIRKMAN & SCOTT

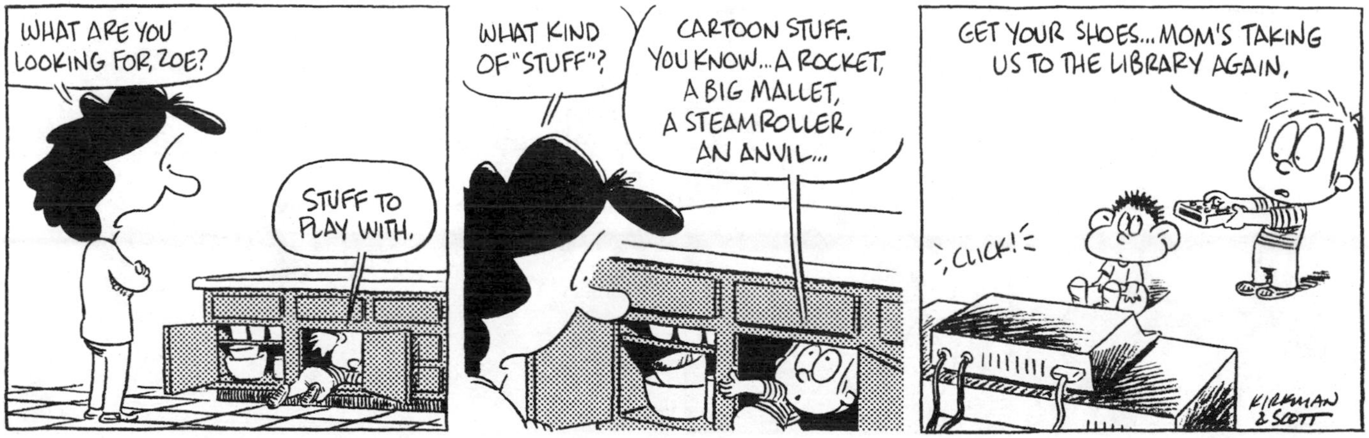
WHAT ARE YOU LOOKING FOR, ZOE?
STUFF TO PLAY WITH.
WHAT KIND OF "STUFF"?
CARTOON STUFF. YOU KNOW... A ROCKET, A BIG MALLET, A STEAMROLLER, AN ANVIL...
GET YOUR SHOES... MOM'S TAKING US TO THE LIBRARY AGAIN.
CLICK!
KIRKMAN & SCOTT

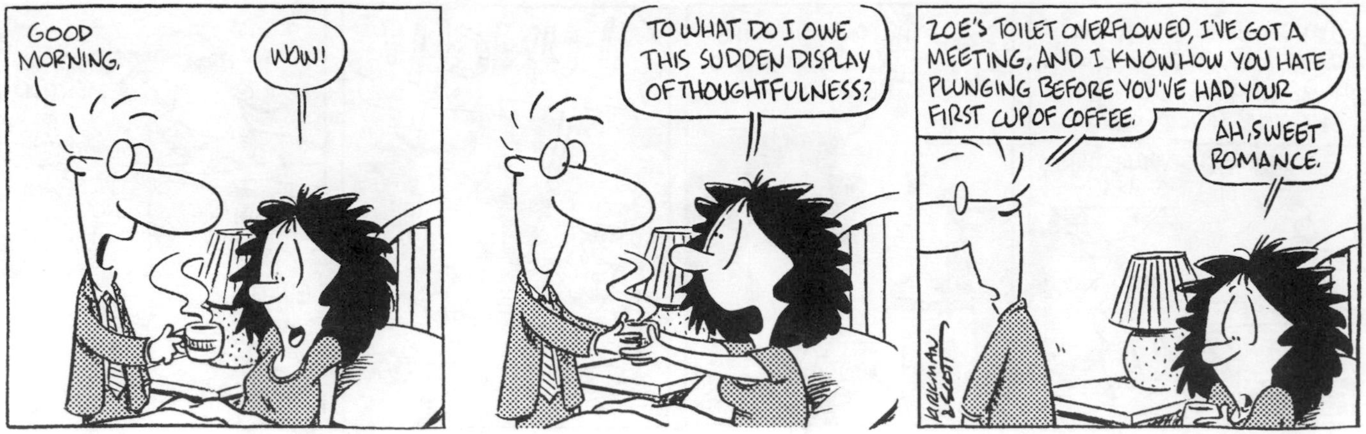
GOOD MORNING.
WOW!
TO WHAT DO I OWE THIS SUDDEN DISPLAY OF THOUGHTFULNESS?
ZOE'S TOILET OVERFLOWED, I'VE GOT A MEETING, AND I KNOW HOW YOU HATE PLUNGING BEFORE YOU'VE HAD YOUR FIRST CUP OF COFFEE.
AH, SWEET ROMANCE.
KIRKMAN & SCOTT

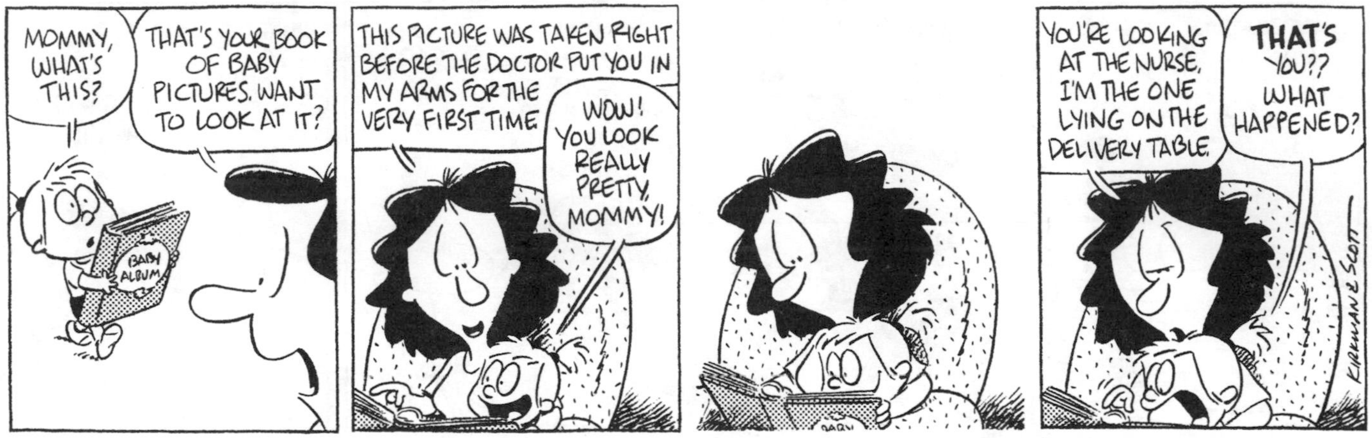
MOMMY, WHAT'S THIS?
THAT'S YOUR BOOK OF BABY PICTURES. WANT TO LOOK AT IT?
BABY ALBUM
THIS PICTURE WAS TAKEN RIGHT BEFORE THE DOCTOR PUT YOU IN MY ARMS FOR THE VERY FIRST TIME.
WOW! YOU LOOK REALLY PRETTY, MOMMY!
YOU'RE LOOKING AT THE NURSE. I'M THE ONE LYING ON THE DELIVERY TABLE.
THAT'S YOU?? WHAT HAPPENED?
KIRKMAN & SCOTT

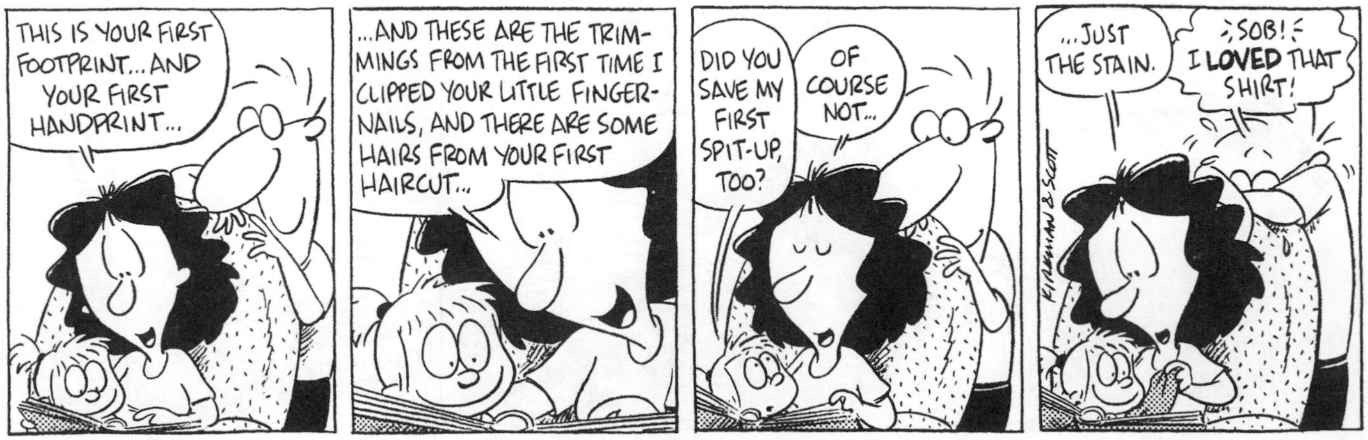
THIS IS YOUR FIRST FOOTPRINT... AND YOUR FIRST HANDPRINT...
...AND THESE ARE THE TRIMMINGS FROM THE FIRST TIME I CLIPPED YOUR LITTLE FINGERNAILS, AND THERE ARE SOME HAIRS FROM YOUR FIRST HAIRCUT...
DID YOU SAVE MY FIRST SPIT-UP, TOO?
OF COURSE NOT...
KIRKMAN & SCOTT
...JUST THE STAIN.
SOB! I **LOVED** THAT SHIRT!

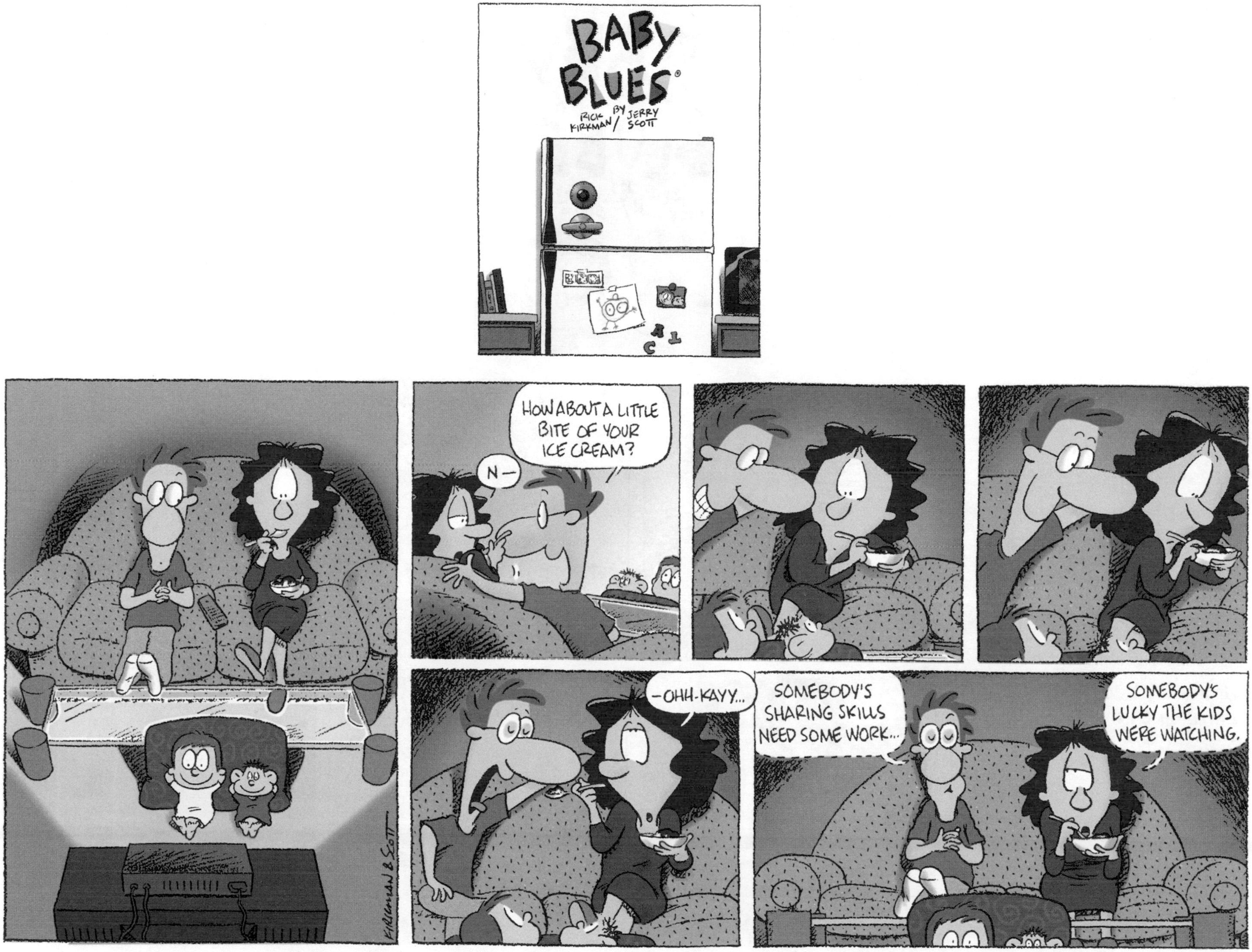
BABY BLUES®
RICK KIRKMAN / BY JERRY SCOTT
KIRKMAN & SCOTT
HOW ABOUT A LITTLE BITE OF YOUR ICE CREAM?
N—
—OHH-KAYY...
SOMEBODY'S SHARING SKILLS NEED SOME WORK...
SOMEBODY'S LUCKY THE KIDS WERE WATCHING.

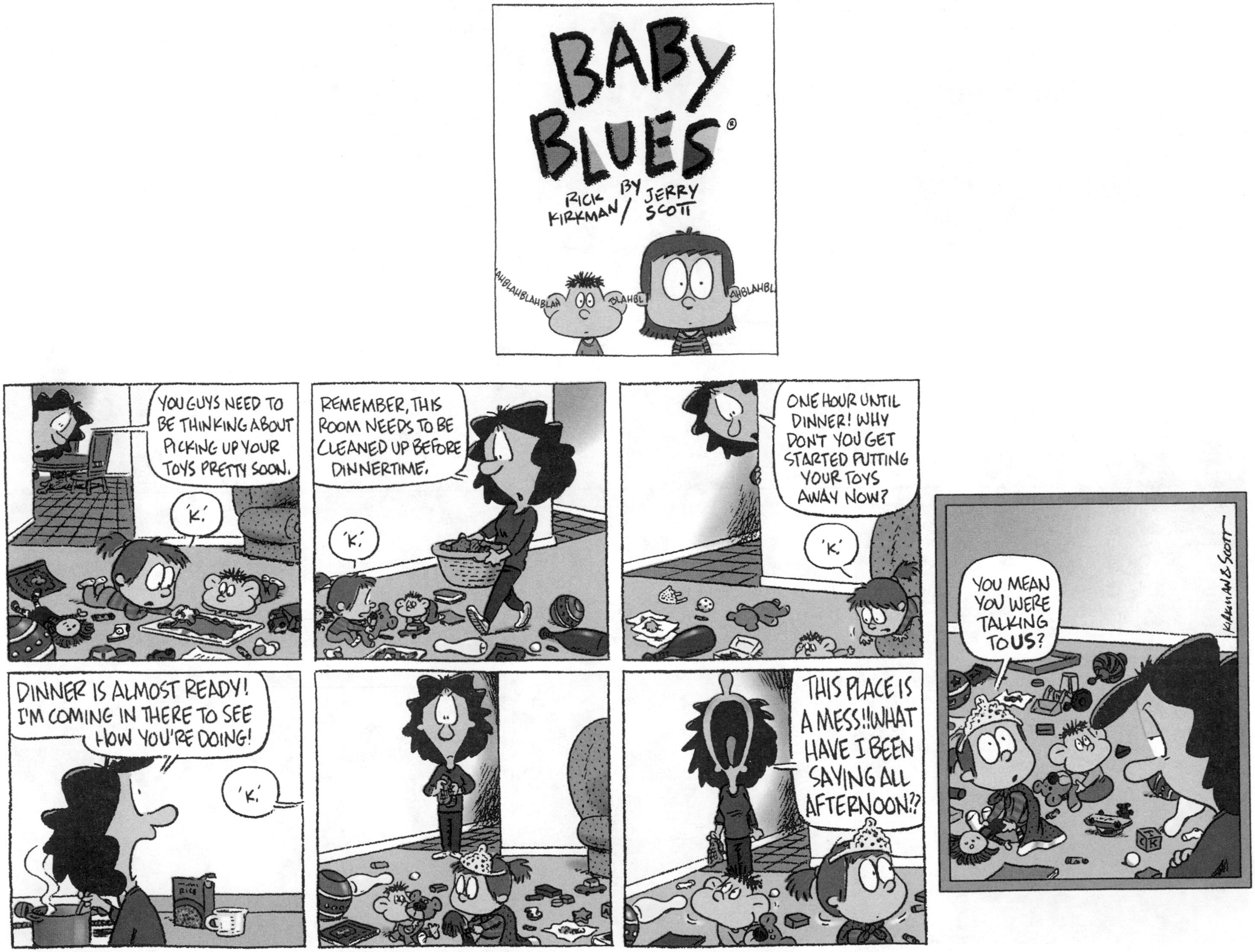
BABY BLUES®
BY RICK KIRKMAN / JERRY SCOTT
YOU GUYS NEED TO BE THINKING ABOUT PICKING UP YOUR TOYS PRETTY SOON.
'K.'
REMEMBER, THIS ROOM NEEDS TO BE CLEANED UP BEFORE DINNERTIME.
'K.'
ONE HOUR UNTIL DINNER! WHY DON'T YOU GET STARTED PUTTING YOUR TOYS AWAY NOW?
'K.'
DINNER IS ALMOST READY! I'M COMING IN THERE TO SEE HOW YOU'RE DOING!
'K.'
THIS PLACE IS A MESS!! WHAT HAVE I BEEN SAYING ALL AFTERNOON!?
YOU MEAN YOU WERE TALKING TO US?
KIRKMAN & SCOTT

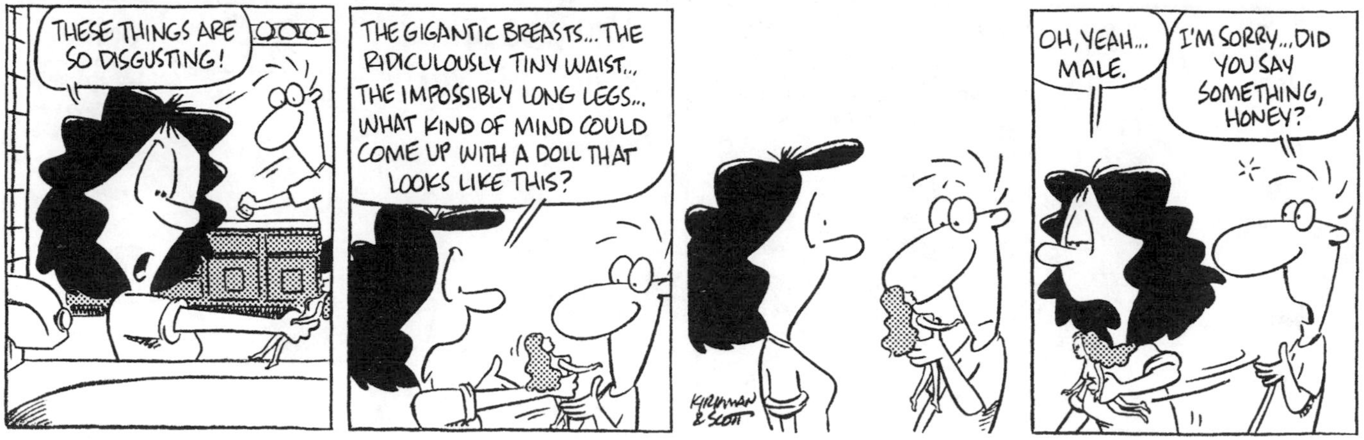
THESE THINGS ARE SO DISGUSTING!
THE GIGANTIC BREASTS... THE RIDICULOUSLY TINY WAIST... THE IMPOSSIBLY LONG LEGS... WHAT KIND OF MIND COULD COME UP WITH A DOLL THAT LOOKS LIKE THIS?
KIRKMAN & SCOTT
OH, YEAH... MALE.
I'M SORRY... DID YOU SAY SOMETHING, HONEY?

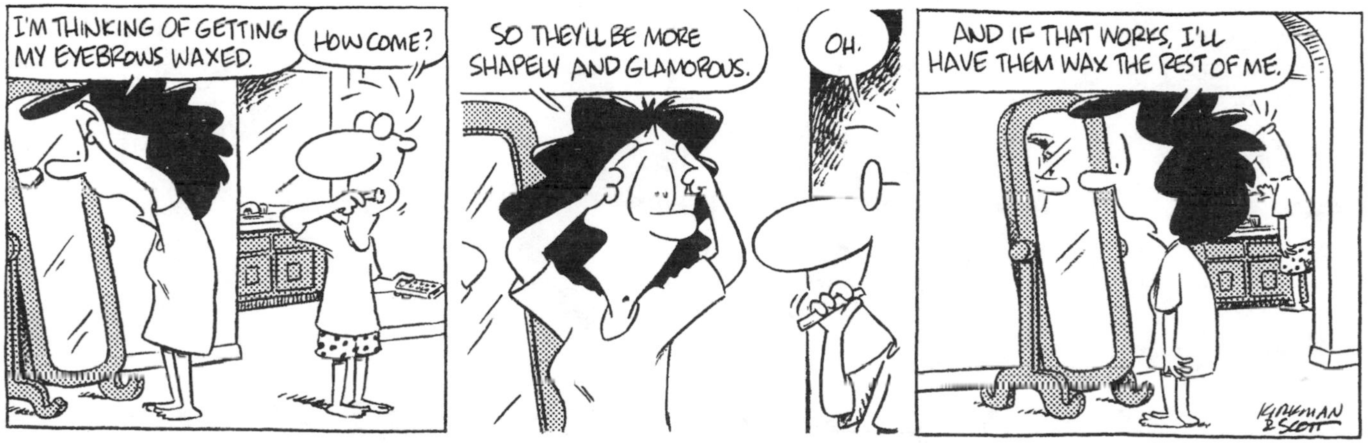
I'M THINKING OF GETTING MY EYEBROWS WAXED.
HOW COME?
SO THEY'LL BE MORE SHAPELY AND GLAMOROUS.
OH.
AND IF THAT WORKS, I'LL HAVE THEM WAX THE REST OF ME.
KIRKMAN & SCOTT

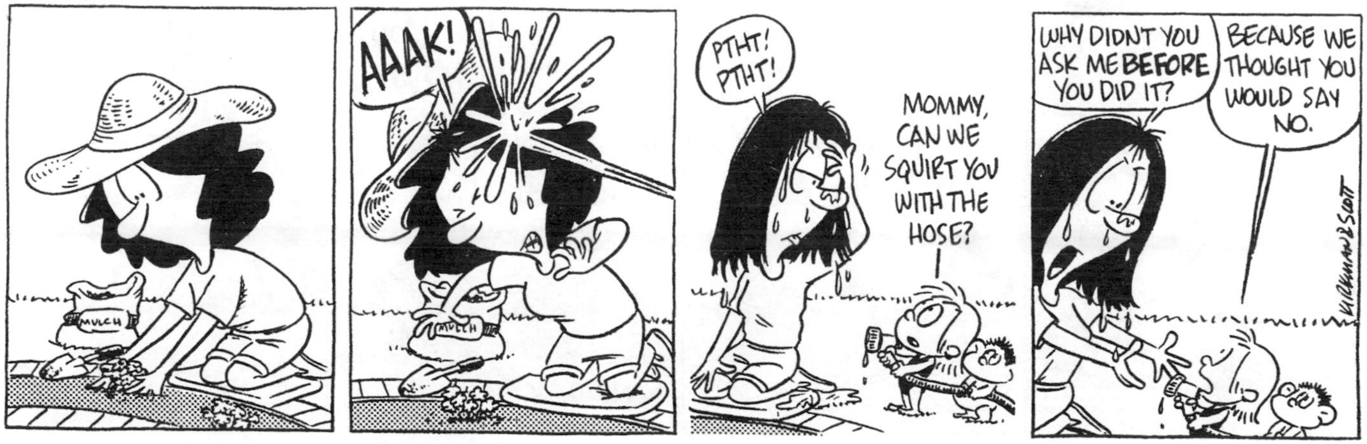
MULCH
AAAK!
PTHT! PTHT!
MOMMY, CAN WE SQUIRT YOU WITH THE HOSE?
WHY DIDN'T YOU ASK ME BEFORE YOU DID IT?
BECAUSE WE THOUGHT YOU WOULD SAY NO.
KIRKMAN & SCOTT

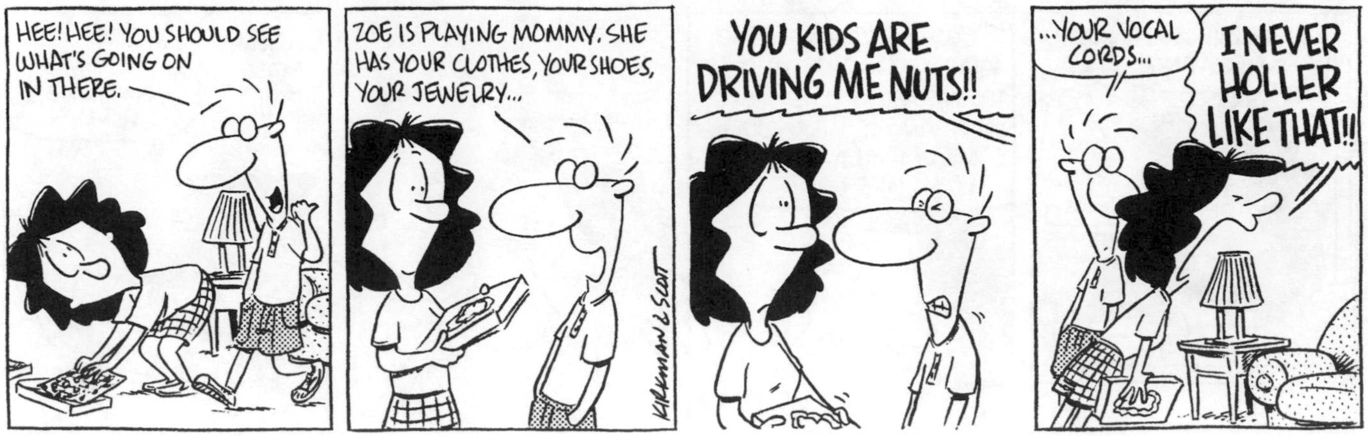
HEE! HEE! YOU SHOULD SEE WHAT'S GOING ON IN THERE.
ZOE IS PLAYING MOMMY. SHE HAS YOUR CLOTHES, YOUR SHOES, YOUR JEWELRY...
KIRKMAN & SCOTT
YOU KIDS ARE DRIVING ME NUTS!!
...YOUR VOCAL CORDS...
I NEVER HOLLER LIKE THAT!!

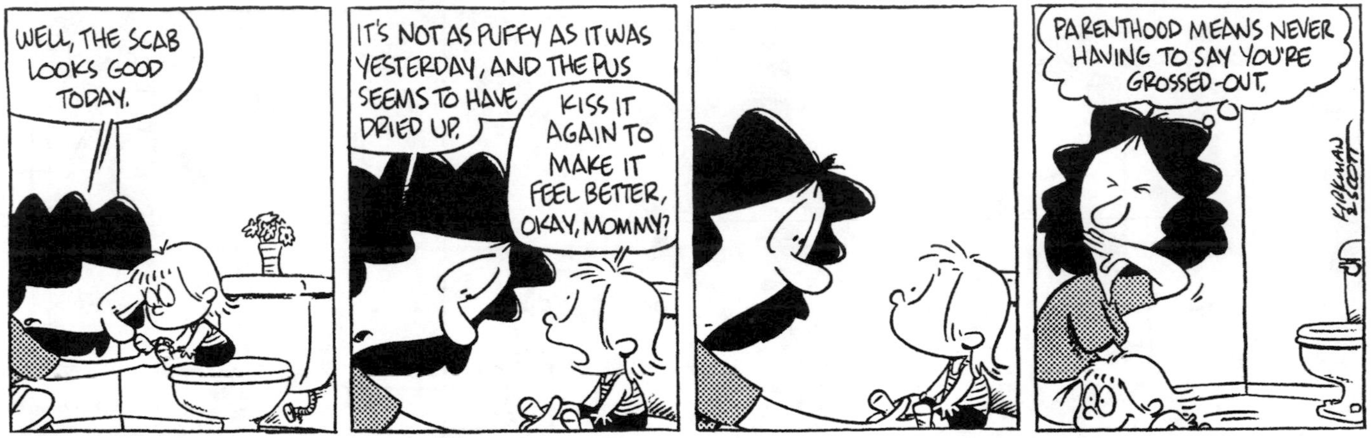
WELL, THE SCAB LOOKS GOOD TODAY.
IT'S NOT AS PUFFY AS IT WAS YESTERDAY, AND THE PUS SEEMS TO HAVE DRIED UP.
KISS IT AGAIN TO MAKE IT FEEL BETTER, OKAY, MOMMY?
PARENTHOOD MEANS NEVER HAVING TO SAY YOU'RE GROSSED-OUT.
KIRKMAN & SCOTT

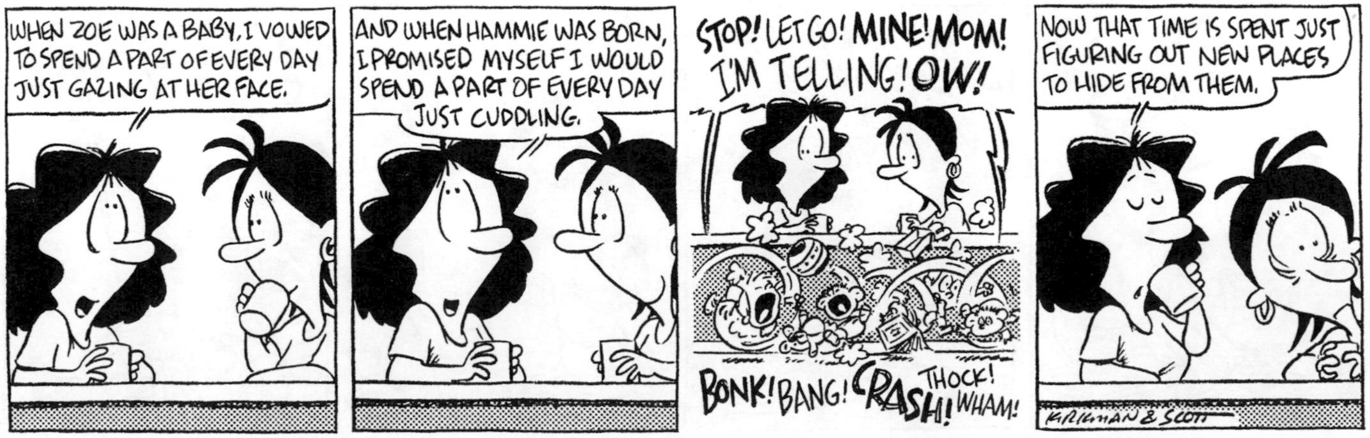
WHEN ZOE WAS A BABY, I VOWED TO SPEND A PART OF EVERY DAY JUST GAZING AT HER FACE.
AND WHEN HAMMIE WAS BORN, I PROMISED MYSELF I WOULD SPEND A PART OF EVERY DAY JUST CUDDLING.
STOP! LET GO! MINE! MOM! I'M TELLING! OW!
BONK! BANG! CRASH! THOCK! WHAM!
NOW THAT TIME IS SPENT JUST FIGURING OUT NEW PLACES TO HIDE FROM THEM.
KIRKMAN & SCOTT

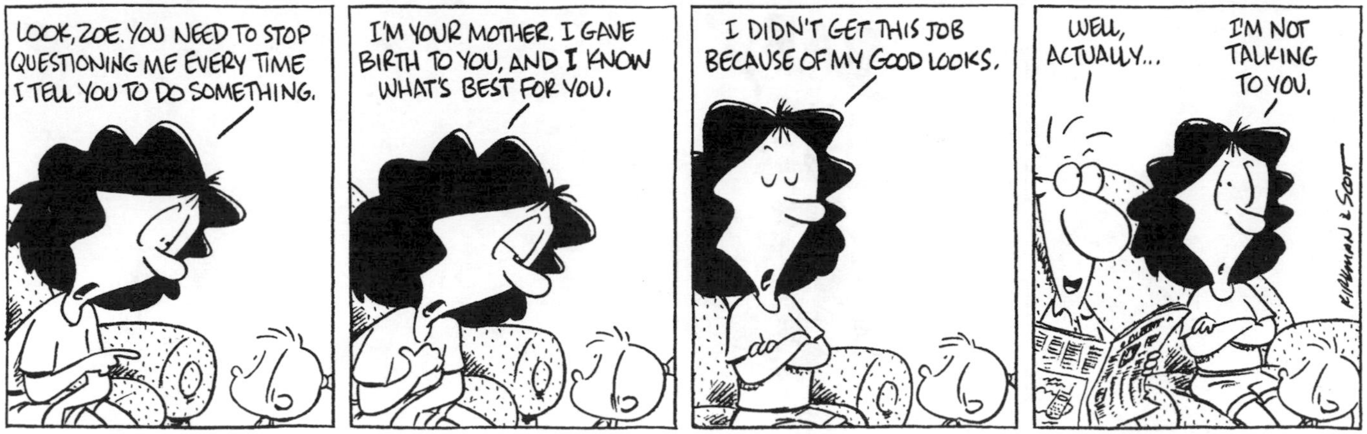
LOOK, ZOE. YOU NEED TO STOP QUESTIONING ME EVERY TIME I TELL YOU TO DO SOMETHING.
I'M YOUR MOTHER. I GAVE BIRTH TO YOU, AND I KNOW WHAT'S BEST FOR YOU.
I DIDN'T GET THIS JOB BECAUSE OF MY GOOD LOOKS.
WELL, ACTUALLY...
I'M NOT TALKING TO YOU.
KIRKMAN & SCOTT

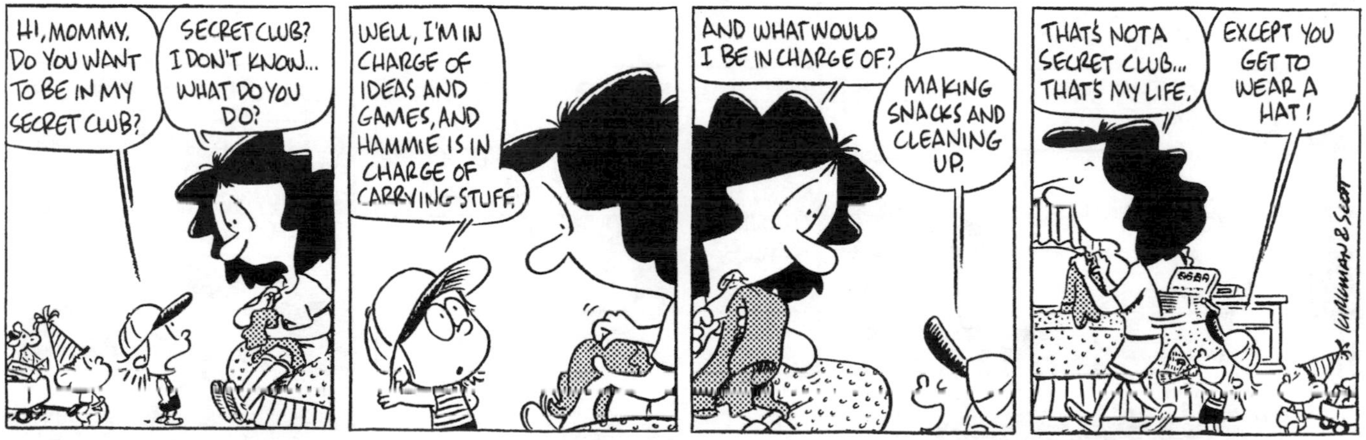
HI, MOMMY. DO YOU WANT TO BE IN MY SECRET CLUB?
SECRET CLUB? I DON'T KNOW... WHAT DO YOU DO?
WELL, I'M IN CHARGE OF IDEAS AND GAMES, AND HAMMIE IS IN CHARGE OF CARRYING STUFF.
AND WHAT WOULD I BE IN CHARGE OF?
MAKING SNACKS AND CLEANING UP.
THAT'S NOT A SECRET CLUB... THAT'S MY LIFE.
EXCEPT YOU GET TO WEAR A HAT!
KIRKMAN & SCOTT

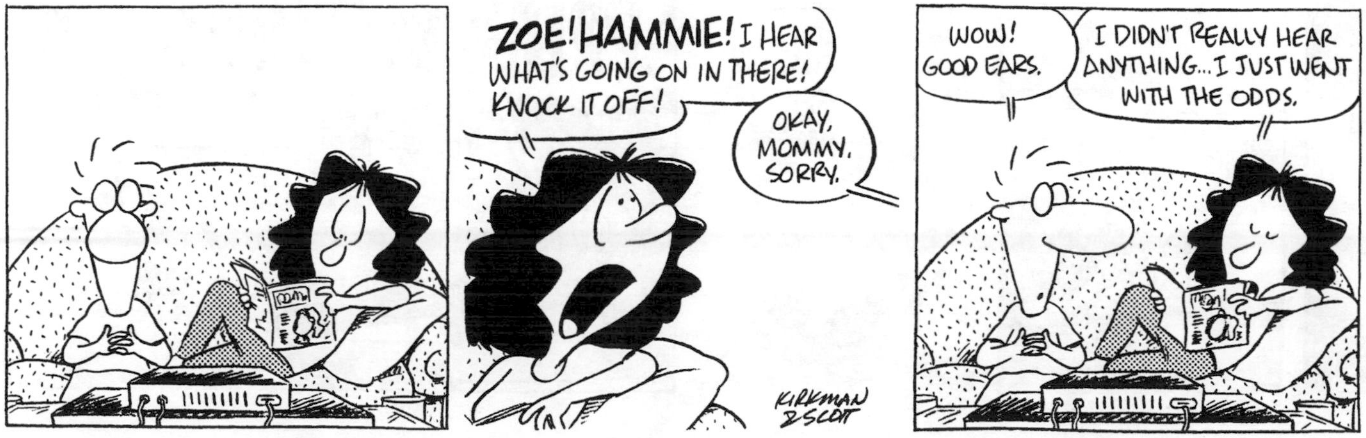
ZOE! HAMMIE! I HEAR WHAT'S GOING ON IN THERE! KNOCK IT OFF!
OKAY, MOMMY. SORRY.
KIRKMAN & SCOTT
WOW! GOOD EARS.
I DIDN'T REALLY HEAR ANYTHING... I JUST WENT WITH THE ODDS.

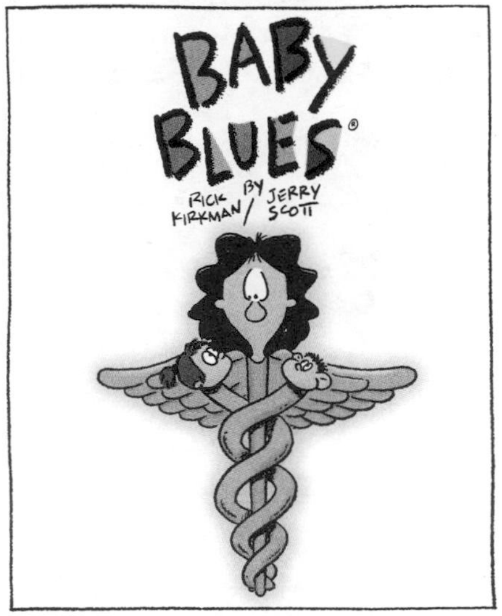
BABY BLUES®
BY RICK KIRKMAN / JERRY SCOTT

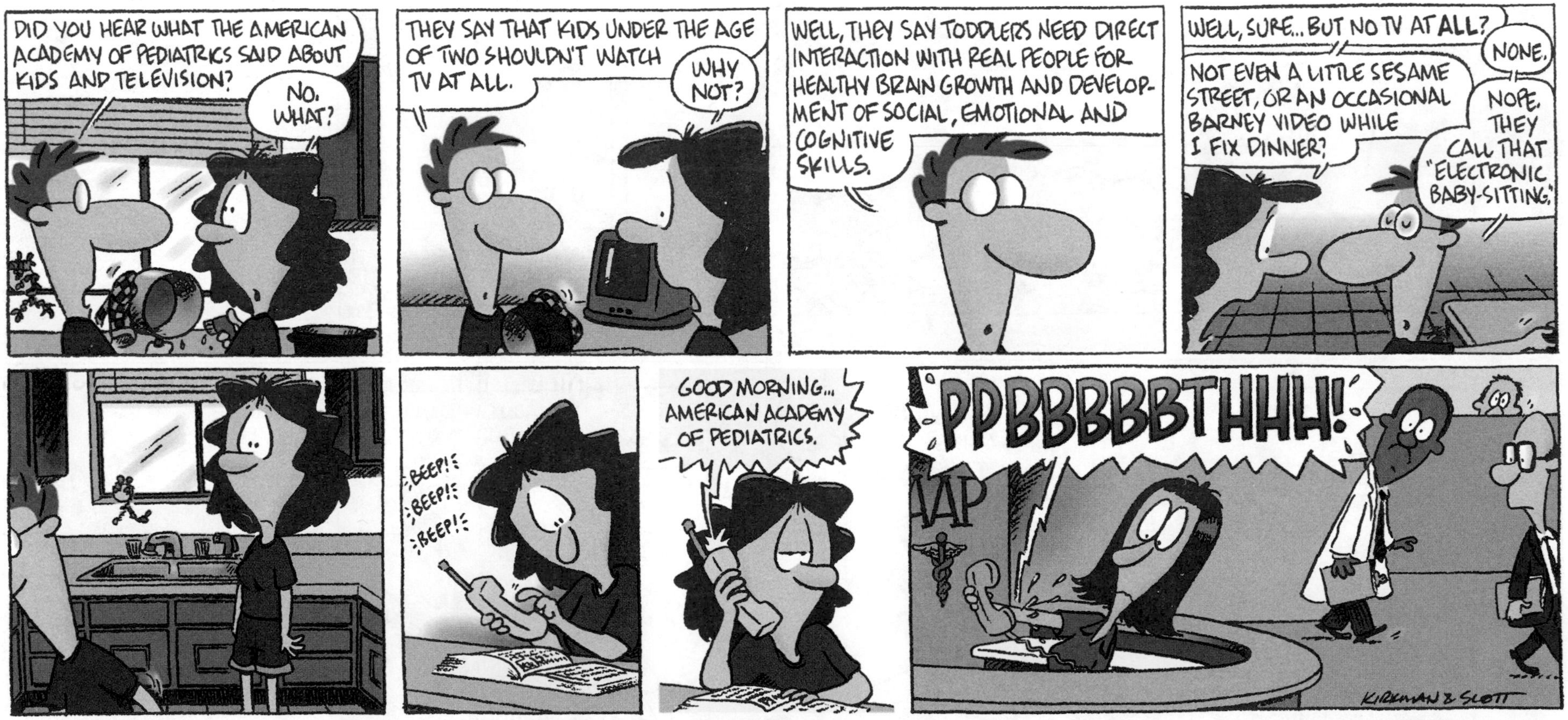
DID YOU HEAR WHAT THE AMERICAN ACADEMY OF PEDIATRICS SAID ABOUT KIDS AND TELEVISION?
NO. WHAT?
THEY SAY THAT KIDS UNDER THE AGE OF TWO SHOULDN'T WATCH TV AT ALL.
WHY NOT?
WELL, THEY SAY TODDLERS NEED DIRECT INTERACTION WITH REAL PEOPLE FOR HEALTHY BRAIN GROWTH AND DEVELOPMENT OF SOCIAL, EMOTIONAL AND COGNITIVE SKILLS.
WELL, SURE... BUT NO TV AT ALL?
NONE.
NOT EVEN A LITTLE SESAME STREET, OR AN OCCASIONAL BARNEY VIDEO WHILE I FIX DINNER?
NOPE. THEY CALL THAT "ELECTRONIC BABY-SITTING."
BEEP! BEEP! BEEP!
GOOD MORNING... AMERICAN ACADEMY OF PEDIATRICS.
PPBBBBBTHHH!
AAP
KIRKMAN & SCOTT

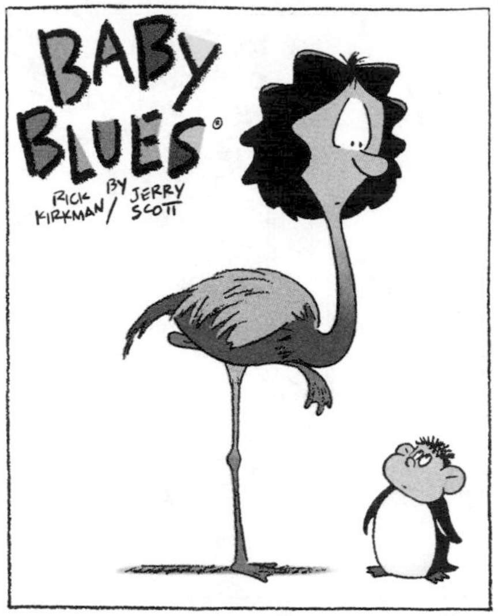
BABY BLUES®
BY RICK KIRKMAN / JERRY SCOTT

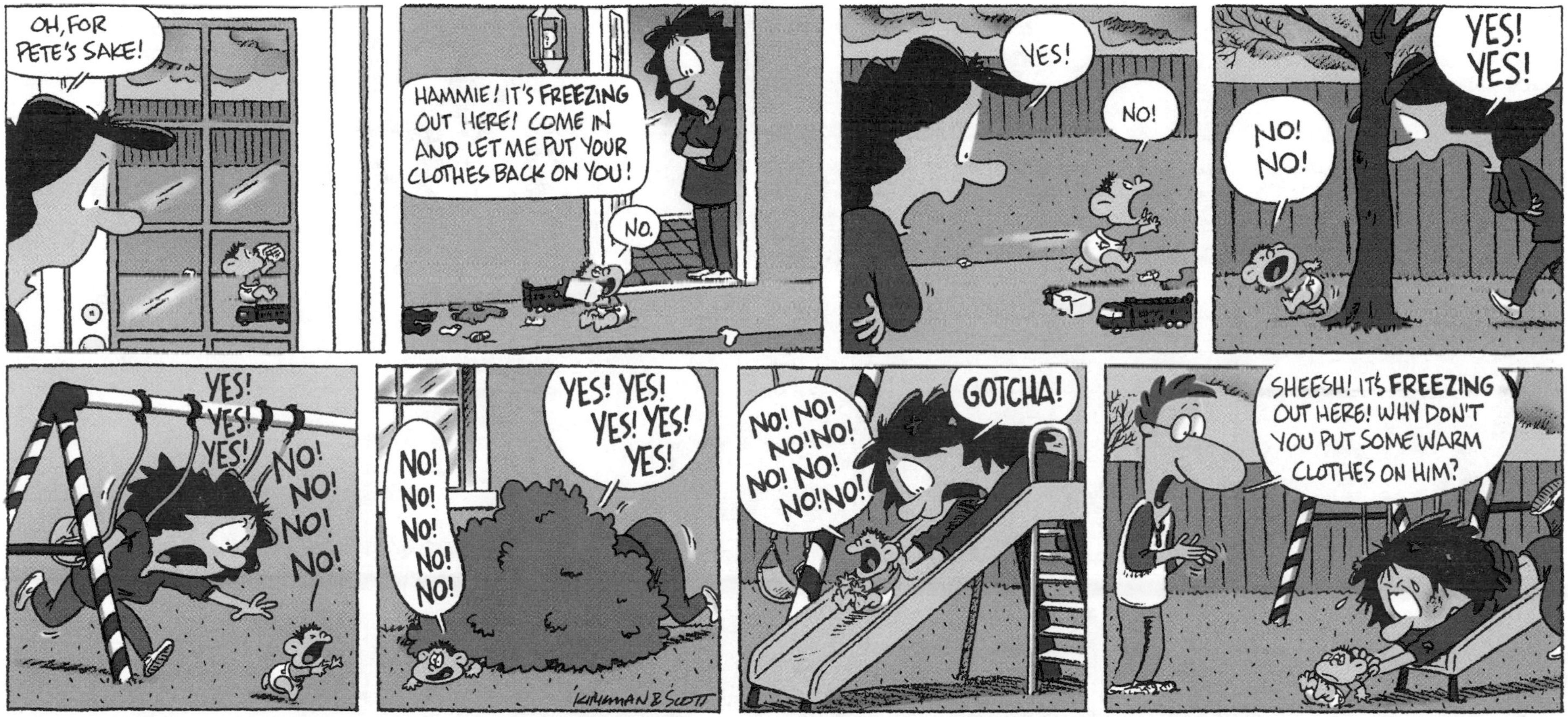
OH, FOR PETE'S SAKE!
HAMMIE! IT'S FREEZING OUT HERE! COME IN AND LET ME PUT YOUR CLOTHES BACK ON YOU!
NO.
YES!
NO!
YES! YES!
NO! NO!
YES! YES! YES!
NO! NO! NO! NO!
YES! YES! YES! YES! YES!
NO! NO! NO! NO! NO!
GOTCHA!
NO! NO! NO! NO! NO! NO! NO! NO!
SHEESH! IT'S FREEZING OUT HERE! WHY DON'T YOU PUT SOME WARM CLOTHES ON HIM?

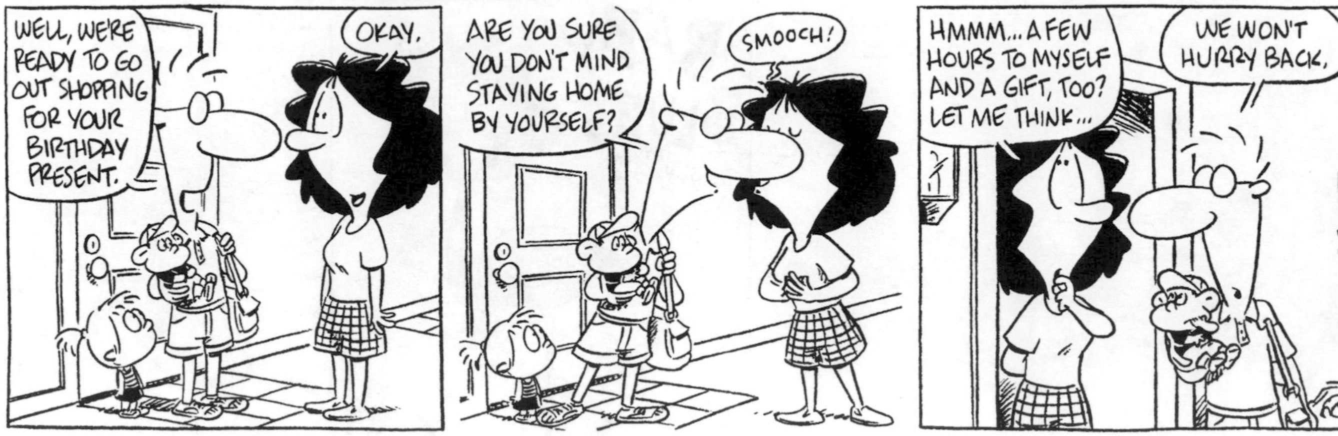
WELL, WE'RE READY TO GO OUT SHOPPING FOR YOUR BIRTHDAY PRESENT.
OKAY.
ARE YOU SURE YOU DON'T MIND STAYING HOME BY YOURSELF?
SMOOCH!
HMMM... A FEW HOURS TO MYSELF AND A GIFT, TOO? LET ME THINK...
WE WON'T HURRY BACK.
KIRKMAN & SCOTT

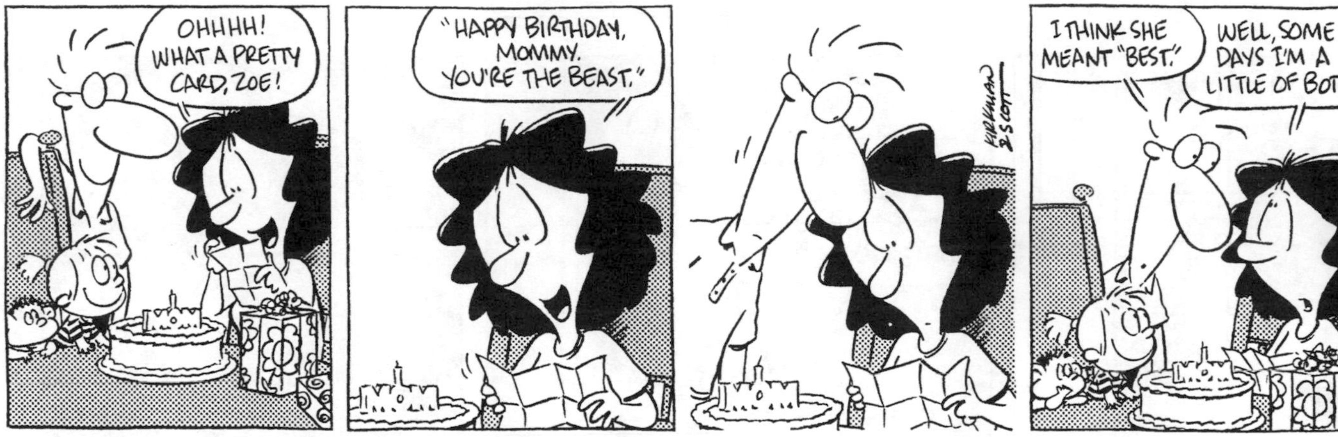
OHHHH! WHAT A PRETTY CARD, ZOE!
"HAPPY BIRTHDAY, MOMMY. YOU'RE THE BEAST."
KIRKMAN & SCOTT
I THINK SHE MEANT "BEST."
WELL, SOME DAYS I'M A LITTLE OF BOTH.

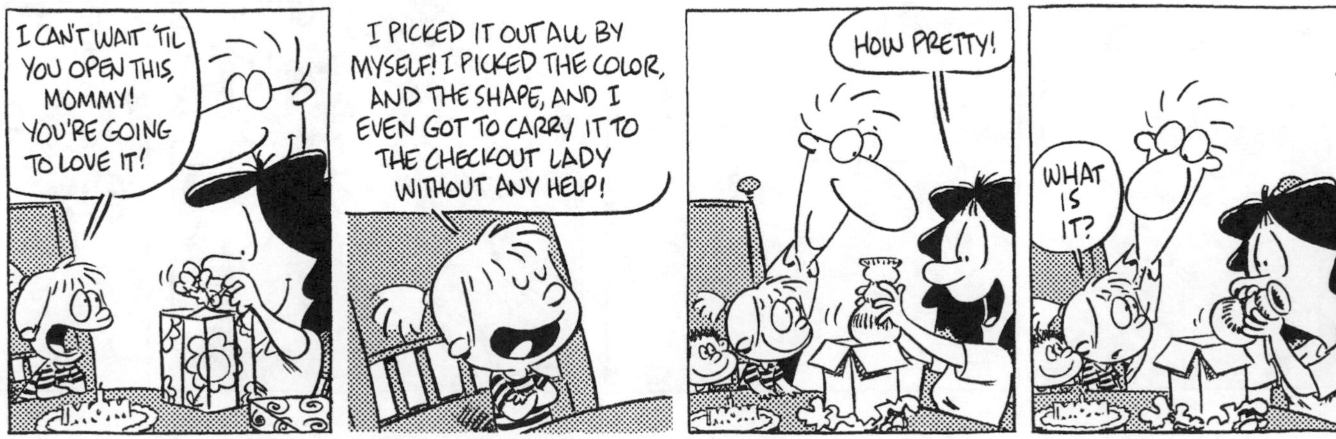
I CAN'T WAIT 'TIL YOU OPEN THIS, MOMMY! YOU'RE GOING TO LOVE IT!
I PICKED IT OUT ALL BY MYSELF! I PICKED THE COLOR, AND THE SHAPE, AND I EVEN GOT TO CARRY IT TO THE CHECKOUT LADY WITHOUT ANY HELP!
HOW PRETTY!
WHAT IS IT?
KIRKMAN & SCOTT

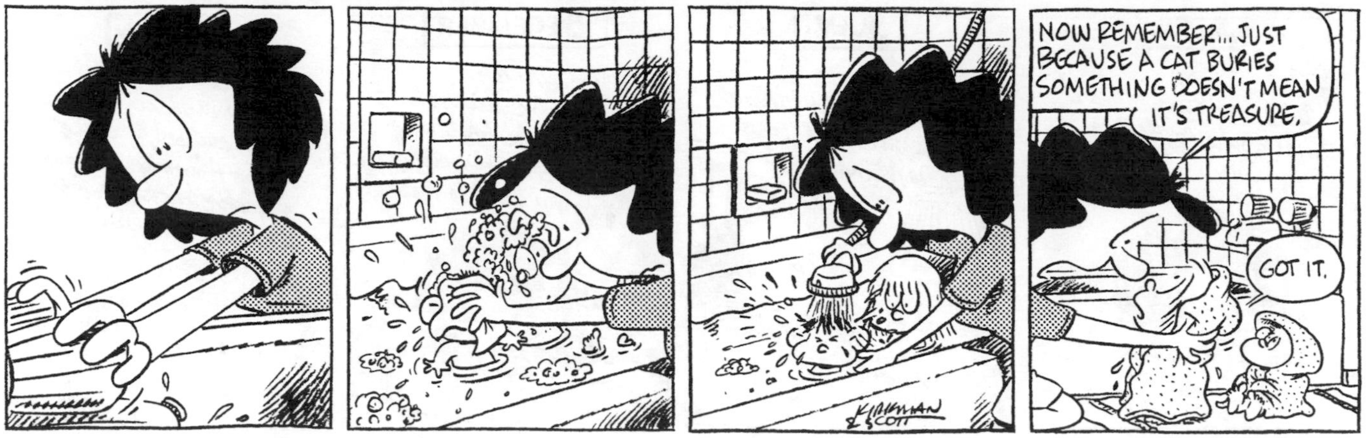

KIRKMAN & SCOTT
NOW REMEMBER... JUST BECAUSE A CAT BURIES SOMETHING DOESN'T MEAN IT'S TREASURE.
GOT IT.

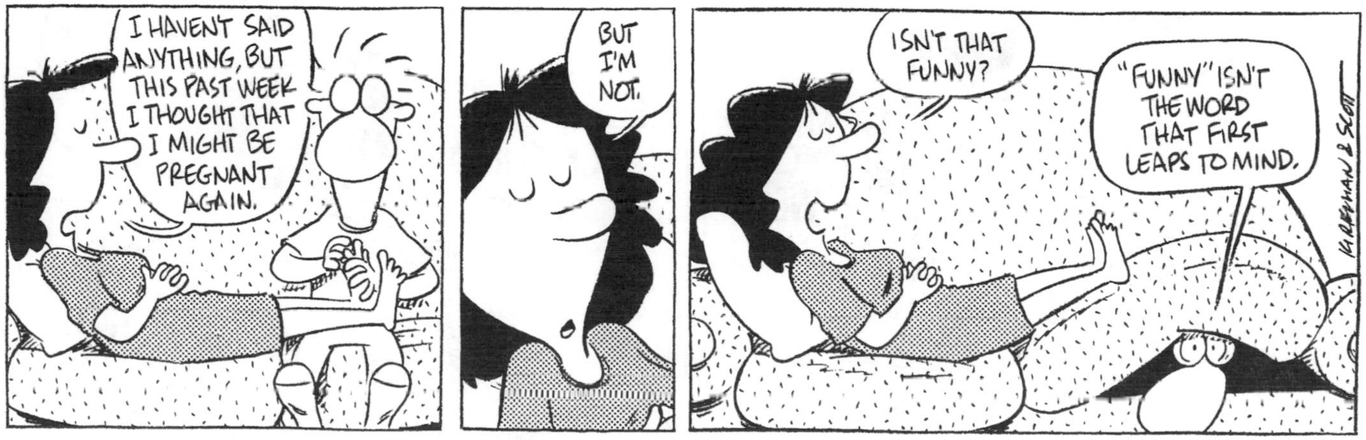

I HAVEN'T SAID ANYTHING, BUT THIS PAST WEEK I THOUGHT THAT I MIGHT BE PREGNANT AGAIN.
BUT I'M NOT.
ISN'T THAT FUNNY?
"FUNNY" ISN'T THE WORD THAT FIRST LEAPS TO MIND.
KIRKMAN & SCOTT

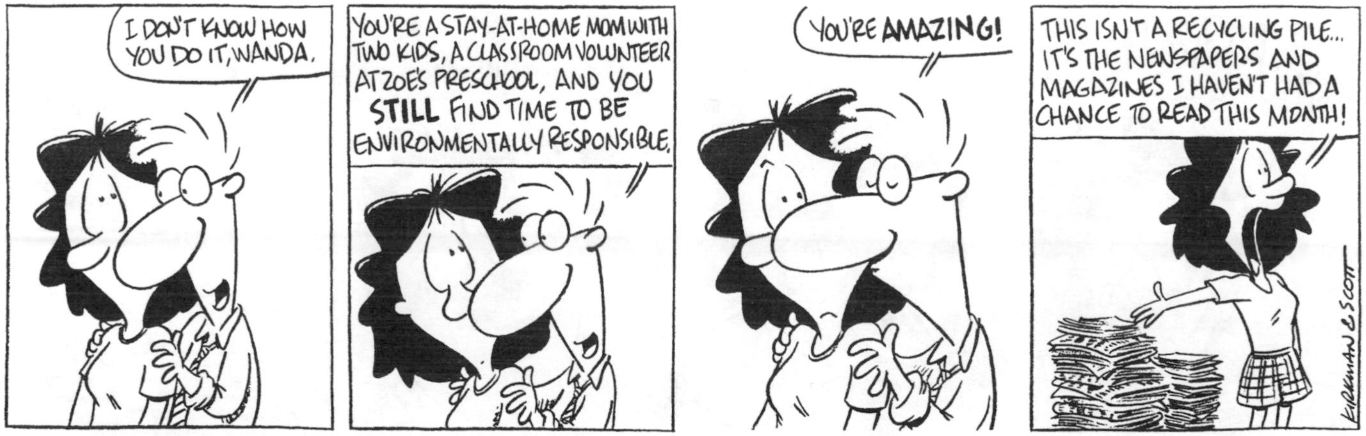

I DON'T KNOW HOW YOU DO IT, WANDA.
YOU'RE A STAY-AT-HOME MOM WITH TWO KIDS, A CLASSROOM VOLUNTEER AT ZOE'S PRESCHOOL, AND YOU STILL FIND TIME TO BE ENVIRONMENTALLY RESPONSIBLE.
YOU'RE AMAZING!
THIS ISN'T A RECYCLING PILE... IT'S THE NEWSPAPERS AND MAGAZINES I HAVEN'T HAD A CHANCE TO READ THIS MONTH!
KIRKMAN & SCOTT

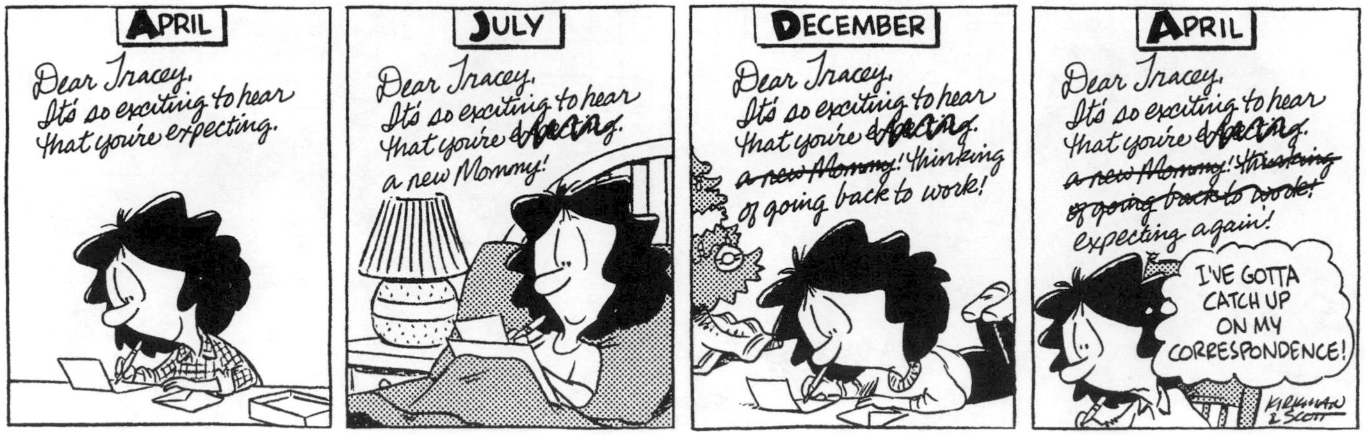
APRIL
Dear Tracey,
It's so exciting to hear that you're expecting.
JULY
Dear Tracey,
It's so exciting to hear that you're
a new Mommy!
DECEMBER
Dear Tracey,
It's so exciting to hear that you're
~~a new Mommy~~! Thinking of going back to work!
APRIL
Dear Tracey,
It's so exciting to hear that you're
~~a new Mommy! Thinking of going back to work!~~
expecting again!
I'VE GOTTA CATCH UP ON MY CORRESPONDENCE!
KIRKMAN & SCOTT

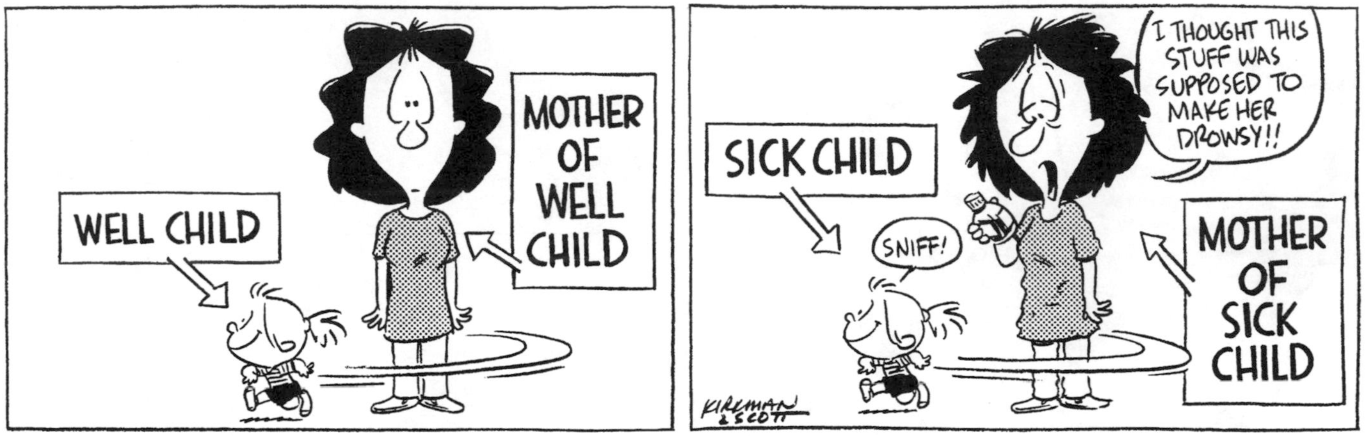
WELL CHILD
MOTHER OF WELL CHILD
SICK CHILD
SNIFF!
I THOUGHT THIS STUFF WAS SUPPOSED TO MAKE HER DROWSY!!
MOTHER OF SICK CHILD
KIRKMAN & SCOTT

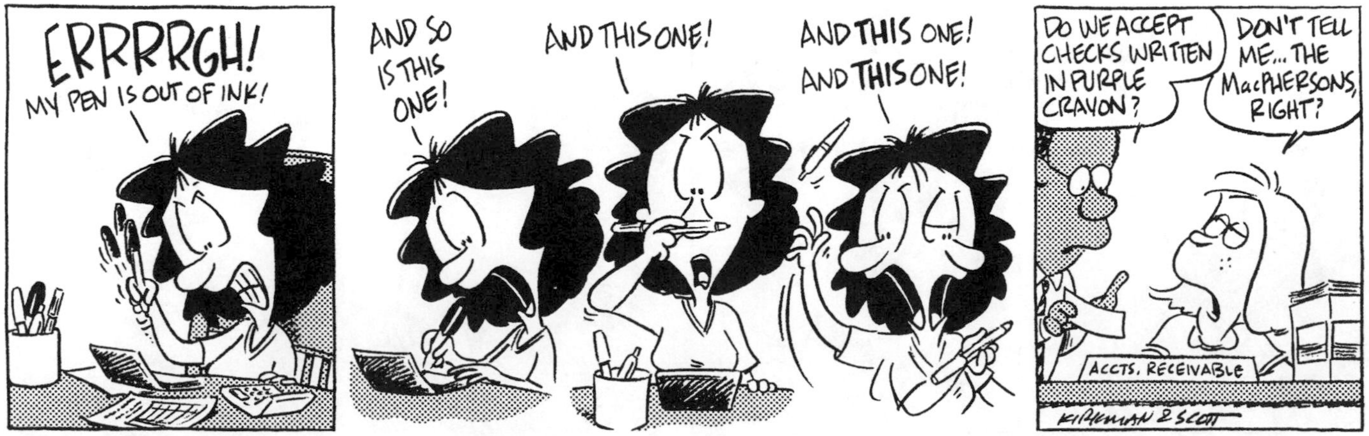
ERRRRGH!
MY PEN IS OUT OF INK!
AND SO IS THIS ONE!
AND THIS ONE!
AND THIS ONE! AND THIS ONE!
DO WE ACCEPT CHECKS WRITTEN IN PURPLE CRAYON?
DON'T TELL ME... THE MacPHERSONS, RIGHT?
ACCTS. RECEIVABLE
KIRKMAN & SCOTT

DARRYL

If kids got to pick their dads, guys like Darryl would be first-draft choices: not too slick, not too good-looking, and smart enough to have his priorities straight.

Darryl is into fatherhood for the long haul. He's a lifer. A guy who is so committed to his kids that he would rather be playing a bad game of Wiffle ball with them in the backyard on a Saturday morning than golfing with the guys. That is, if he knew any guys . . . or where a golf course was . . . and if the kids hadn't used his clubs to make a "bridge" over the big mud hole by the hose.

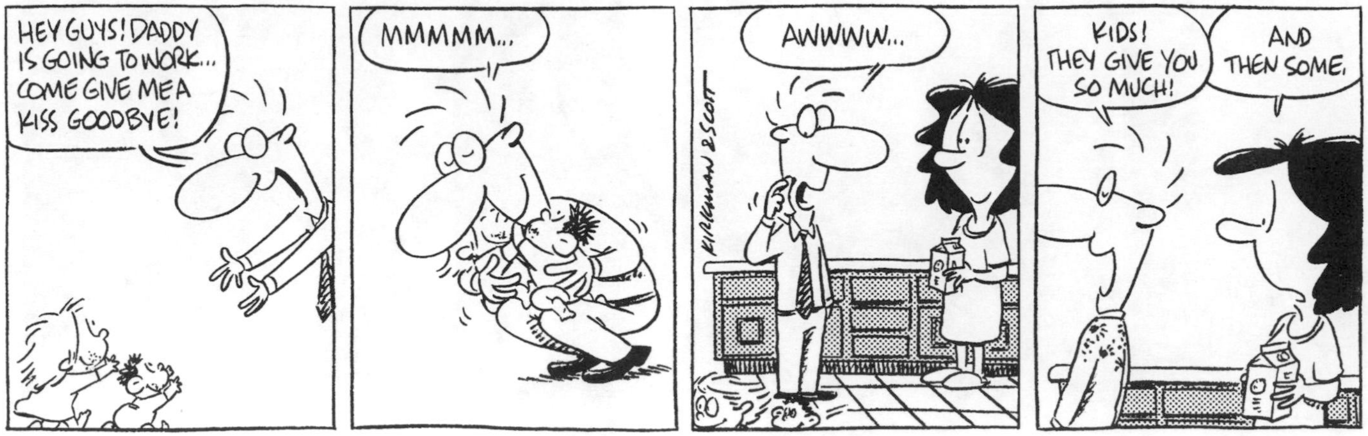
HEY GUYS! DADDY IS GOING TO WORK... COME GIVE ME A KISS GOODBYE!
MMMMM...
AWWWW...
KIDS! THEY GIVE YOU SO MUCH!
AND THEN SOME.

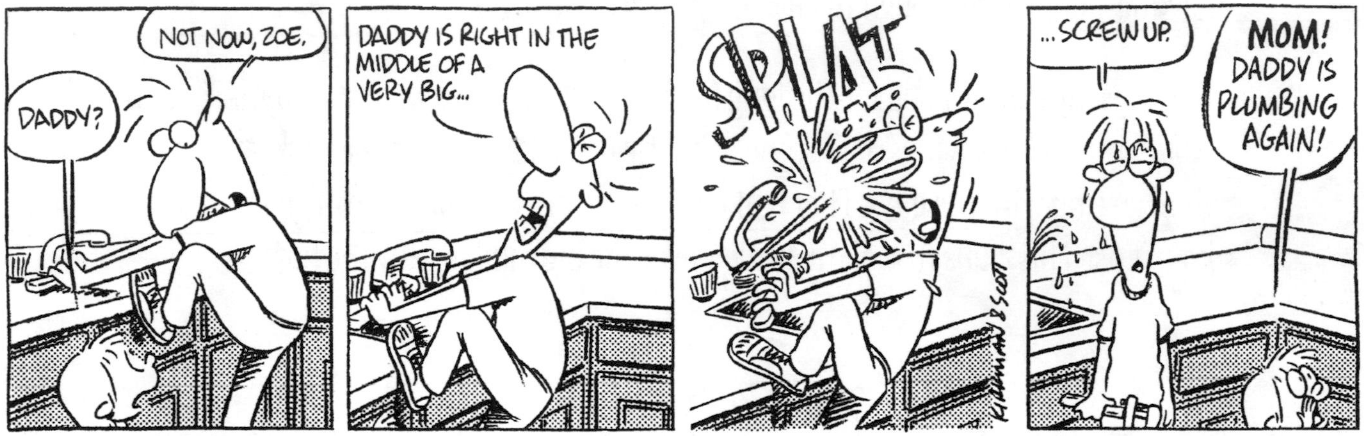
NOT NOW, ZOE.
DADDY?
DADDY IS RIGHT IN THE MIDDLE OF A VERY BIG...
SPLAT
...SCREW UP.
MOM! DADDY IS PLUMBING AGAIN!

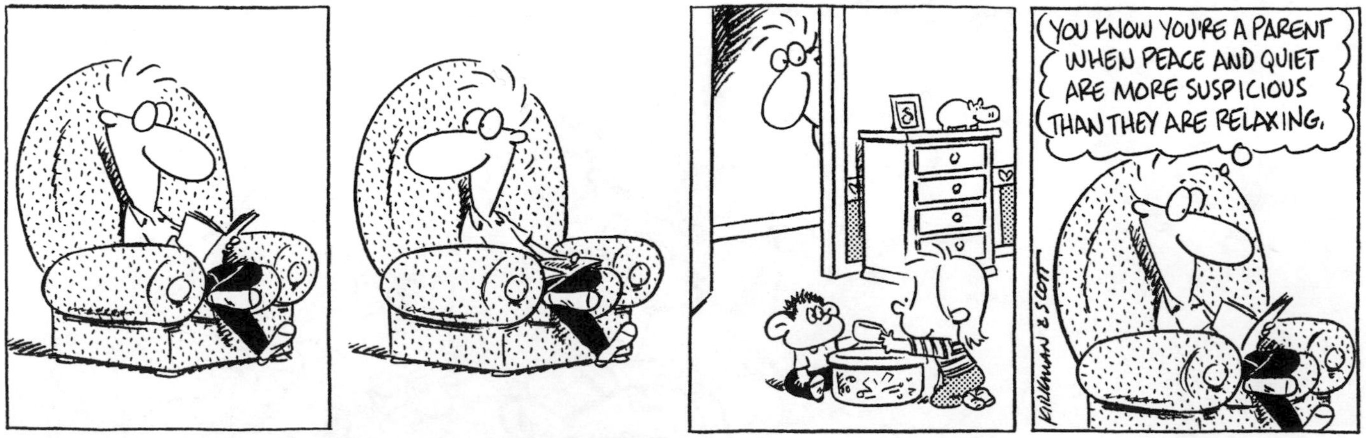
YOU KNOW YOU'RE A PARENT WHEN PEACE AND QUIET ARE MORE SUSPICIOUS THAN THEY ARE RELAXING.

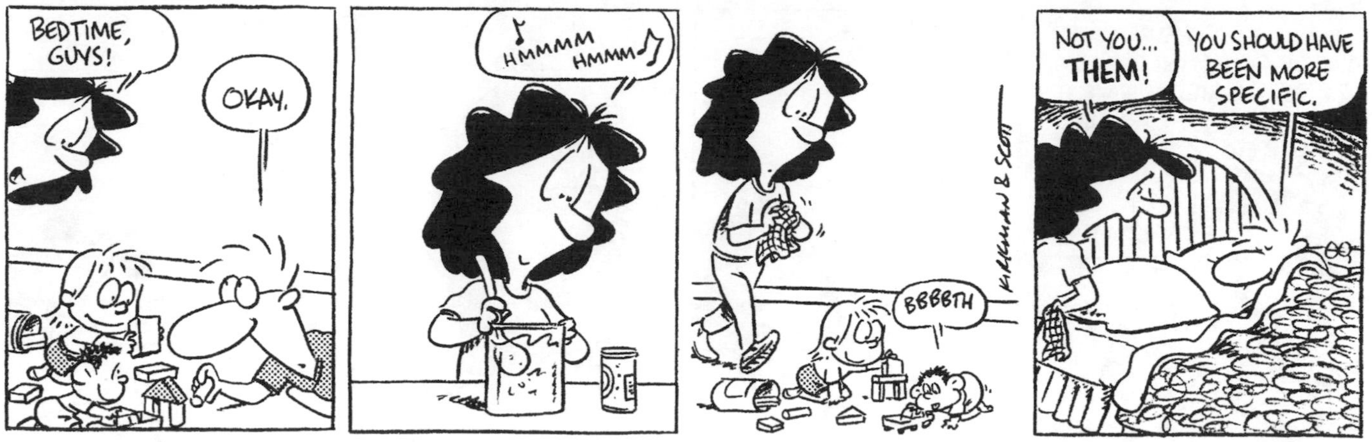
BEDTIME, GUYS!
OKAY.
HMMMM HMMM
BBBBTH
KIRKMAN & SCOTT
NOT YOU... THEM!
YOU SHOULD HAVE BEEN MORE SPECIFIC.

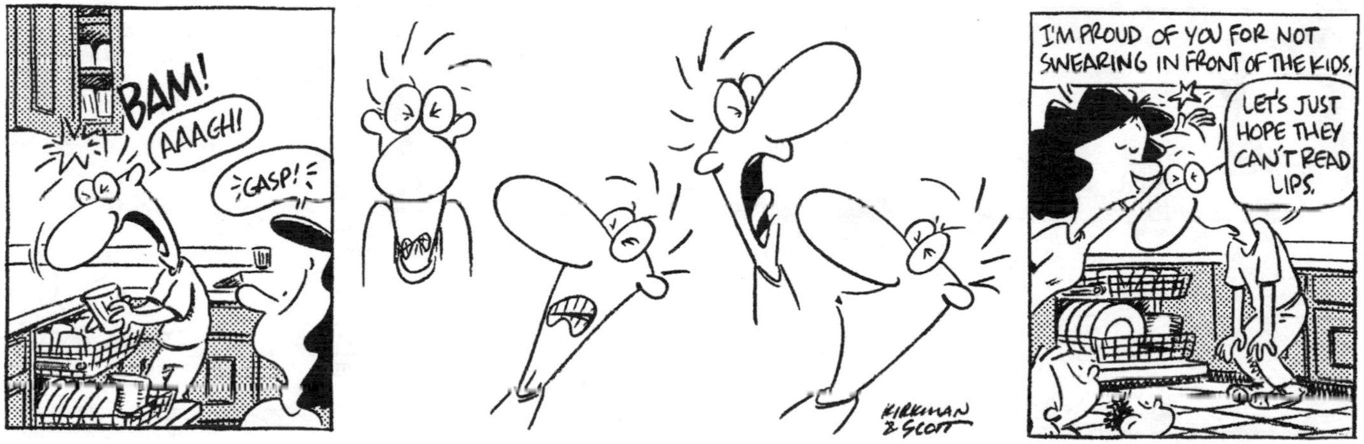
BAM!
AAAGH!
GASP!
KIRKMAN & SCOTT
I'M PROUD OF YOU FOR NOT SWEARING IN FRONT OF THE KIDS.
LET'S JUST HOPE THEY CAN'T READ LIPS.

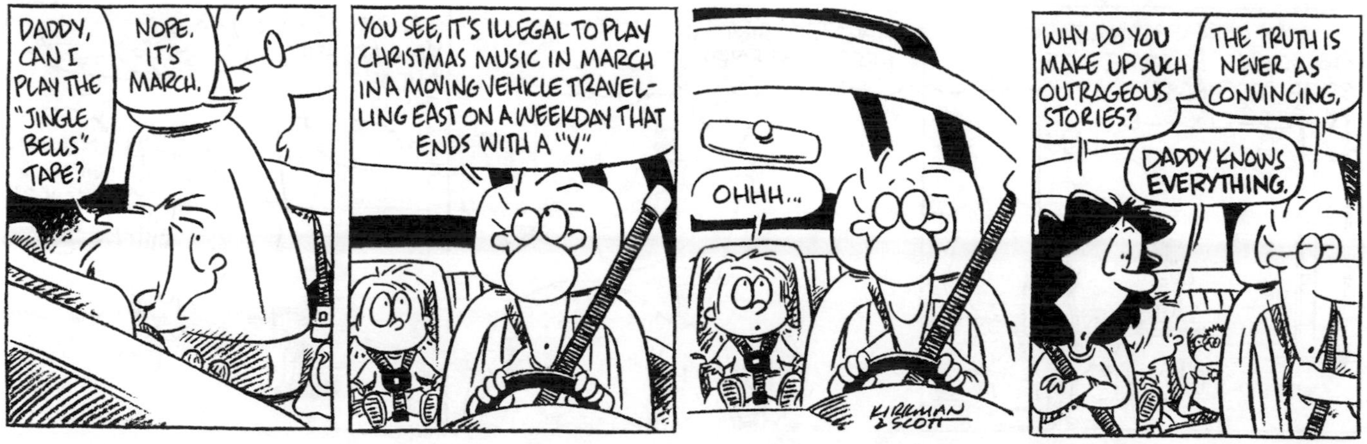
DADDY, CAN I PLAY THE "JINGLE BELLS" TAPE?
NOPE. IT'S MARCH.
YOU SEE, IT'S ILLEGAL TO PLAY CHRISTMAS MUSIC IN MARCH IN A MOVING VEHICLE TRAVELLING EAST ON A WEEKDAY THAT ENDS WITH A "Y."
OHHH...
KIRKMAN & SCOTT
WHY DO YOU MAKE UP SUCH OUTRAGEOUS STORIES?
THE TRUTH IS NEVER AS CONVINCING.
DADDY KNOWS EVERYTHING.

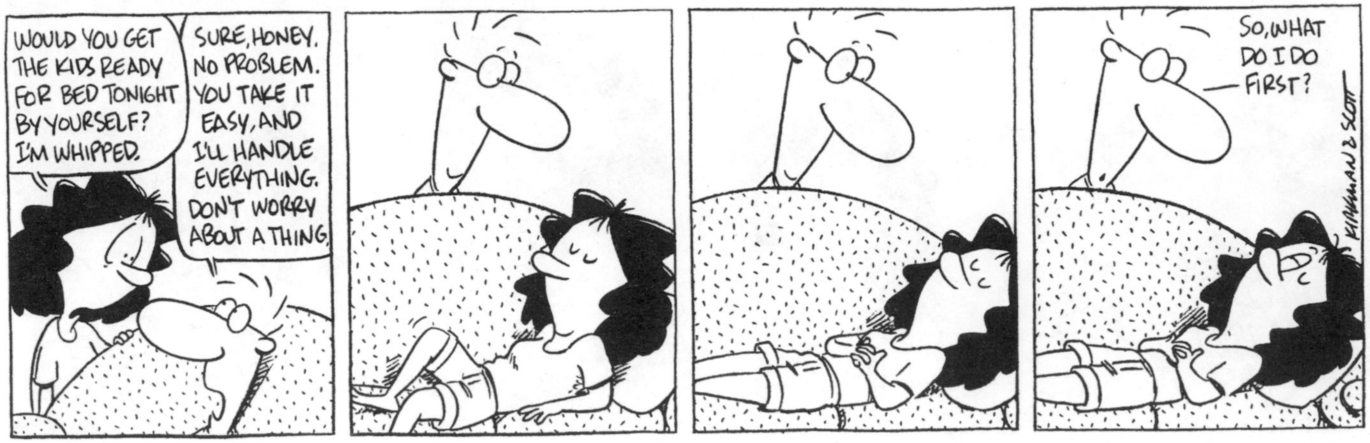
WOULD YOU GET THE KIDS READY FOR BED TONIGHT BY YOURSELF? I'M WHIPPED.
SURE, HONEY. NO PROBLEM. YOU TAKE IT EASY, AND I'LL HANDLE EVERYTHING. DON'T WORRY ABOUT A THING.
SO, WHAT DO I DO FIRST?
KIRKMAN & SCOTT

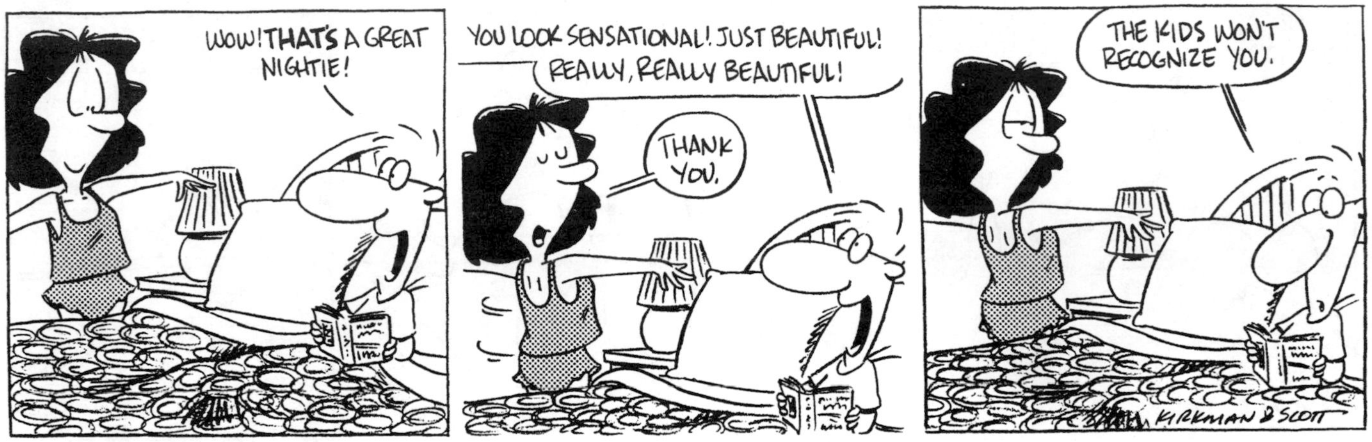
WOW! THAT'S A GREAT NIGHTIE!
YOU LOOK SENSATIONAL! JUST BEAUTIFUL! REALLY, REALLY BEAUTIFUL!
THANK YOU.
THE KIDS WON'T RECOGNIZE YOU.
KIRKMAN & SCOTT

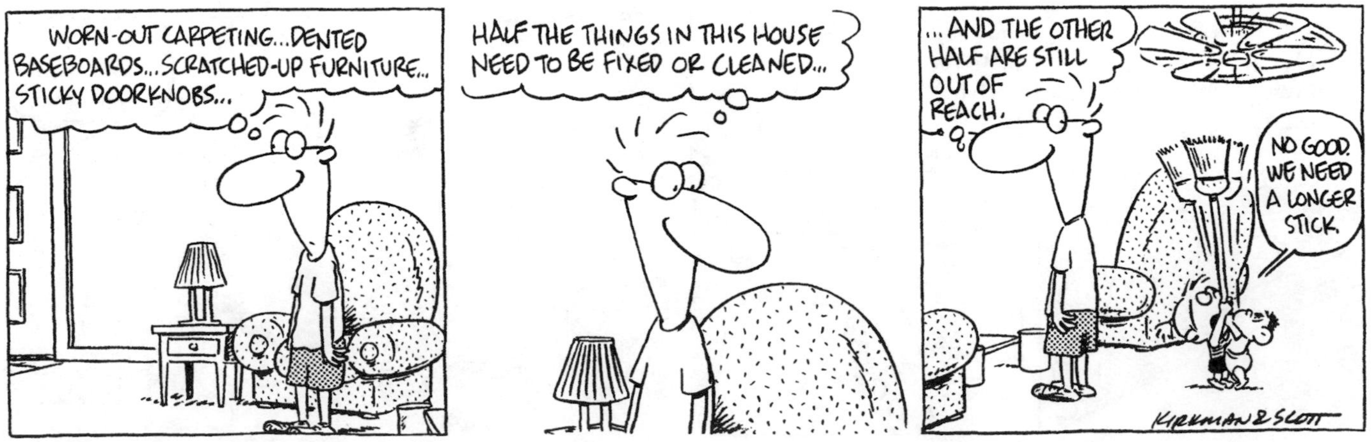
WORN-OUT CARPETING...DENTED BASEBOARDS...SCRATCHED-UP FURNITURE... STICKY DOORKNOBS...
HALF THE THINGS IN THIS HOUSE NEED TO BE FIXED OR CLEANED...
...AND THE OTHER HALF ARE STILL OUT OF REACH.
NO GOOD. WE NEED A LONGER STICK.
KIRKMAN & SCOTT

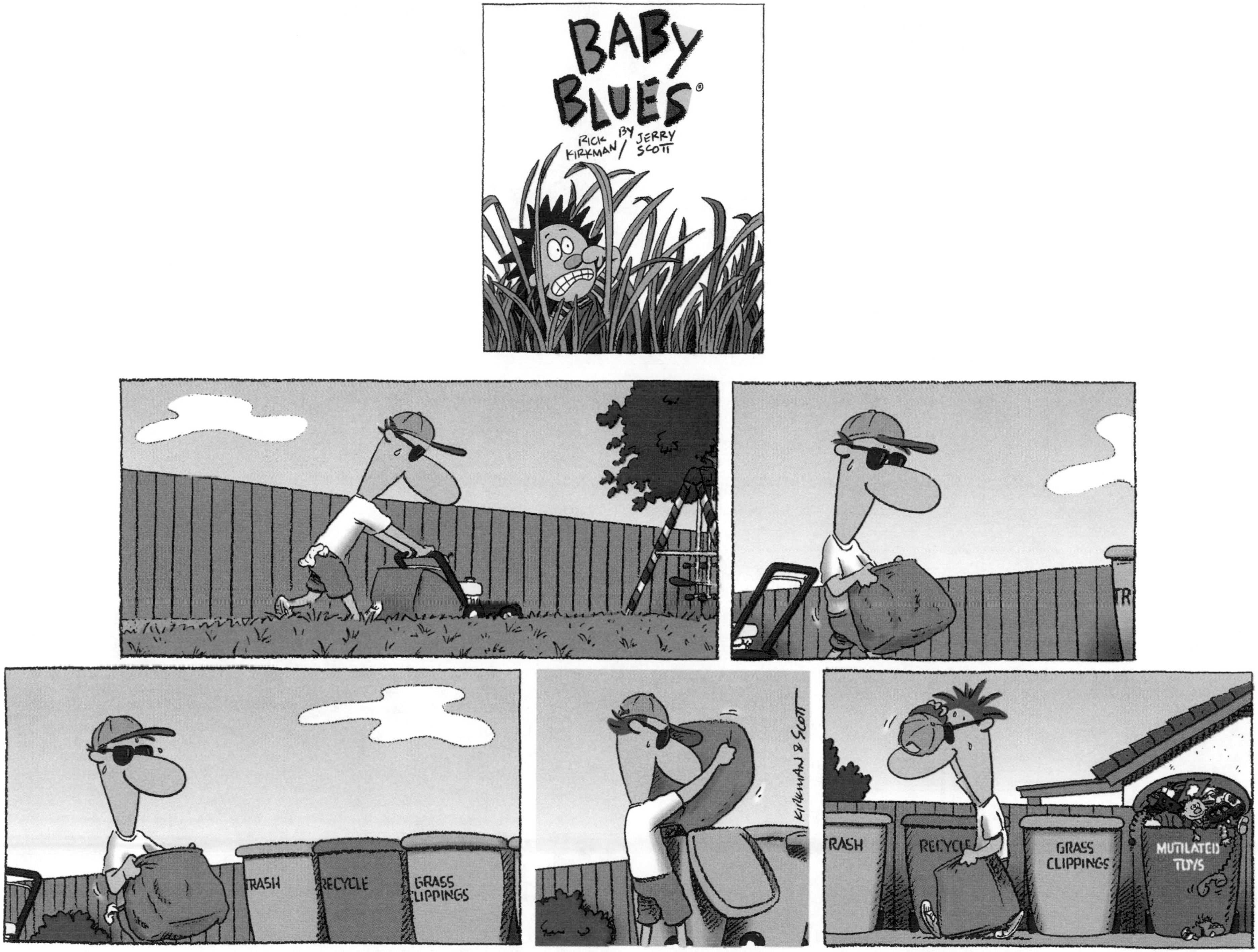
BABY BLUES®
BY RICK KIRKMAN / JERRY SCOTT
TRASH
RECYCLE
GRASS CLIPPINGS
KIRKMAN & SCOTT
TRASH
RECYCLE
GRASS CLIPPINGS
MUTILATED TOYS

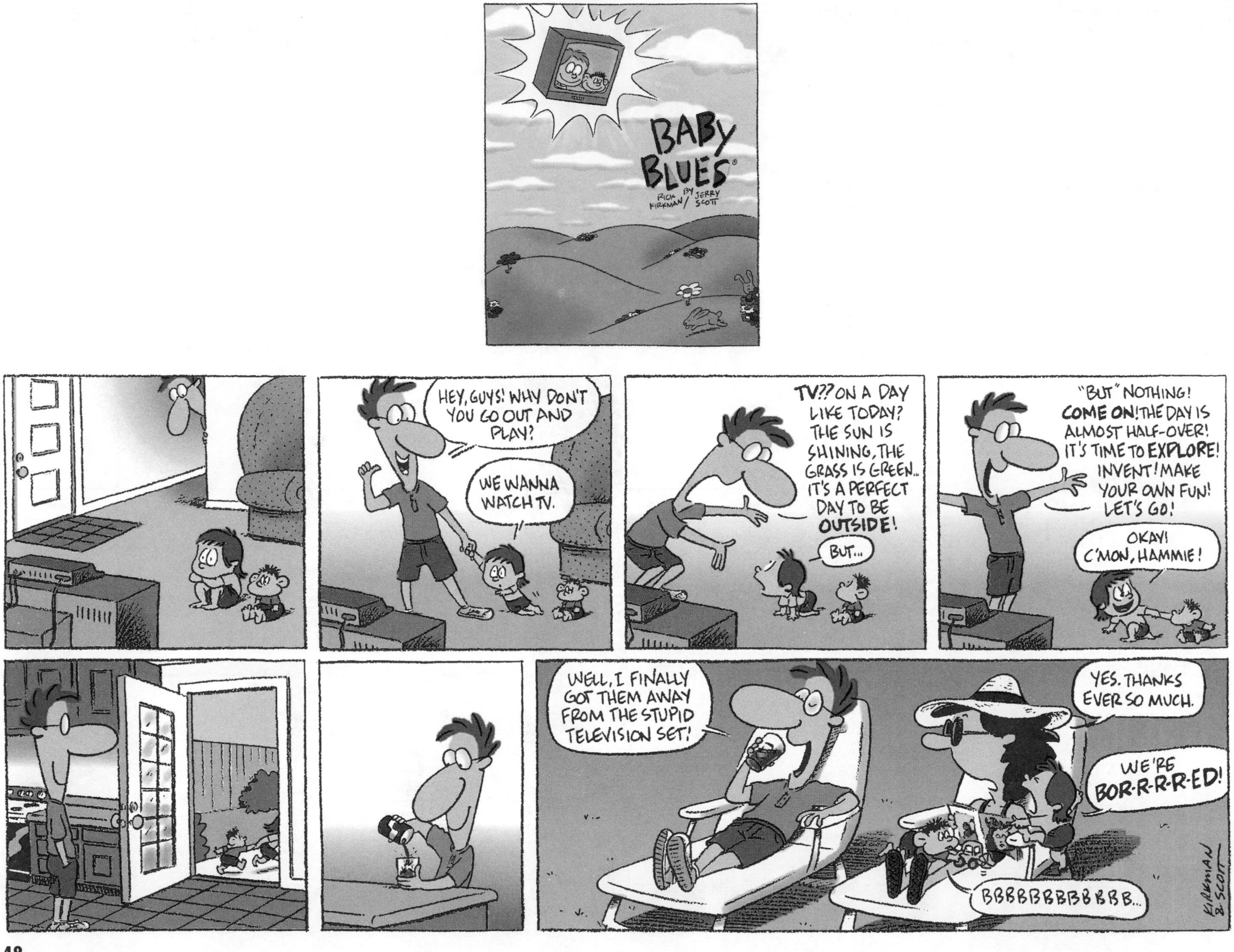
BABY BLUES®
BY RICK KIRKMAN / JERRY SCOTT
HEY, GUYS! WHY DON'T YOU GO OUT AND PLAY?
WE WANNA WATCH TV.
TV?? ON A DAY LIKE TODAY? THE SUN IS SHINING, THE GRASS IS GREEN... IT'S A PERFECT DAY TO BE OUTSIDE!
BUT...
"BUT" NOTHING! COME ON! THE DAY IS ALMOST HALF-OVER! IT'S TIME TO EXPLORE! INVENT! MAKE YOUR OWN FUN! LET'S GO!
OKAY! C'MON, HAMMIE!
WELL, I FINALLY GOT THEM AWAY FROM THE STUPID TELEVISION SET!
YES. THANKS EVER SO MUCH.
WE'RE BOR-R-R-R-ED!
BBBBBBBBBBBB...
KIRKMAN & SCOTT

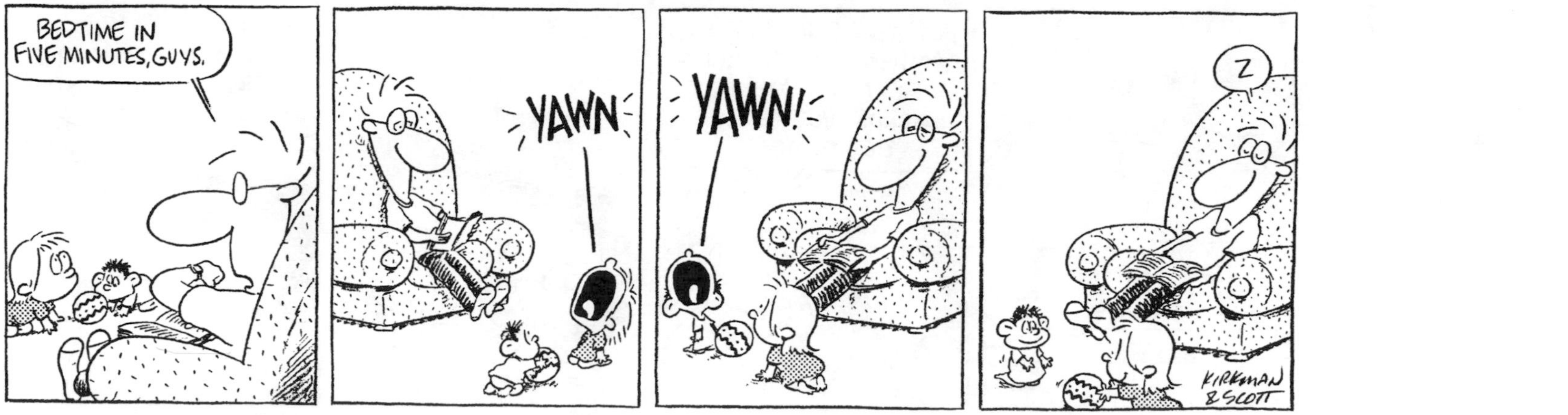
BEDTIME IN FIVE MINUTES, GUYS.
YAWN
YAWN!
Z
KIRKMAN & SCOTT

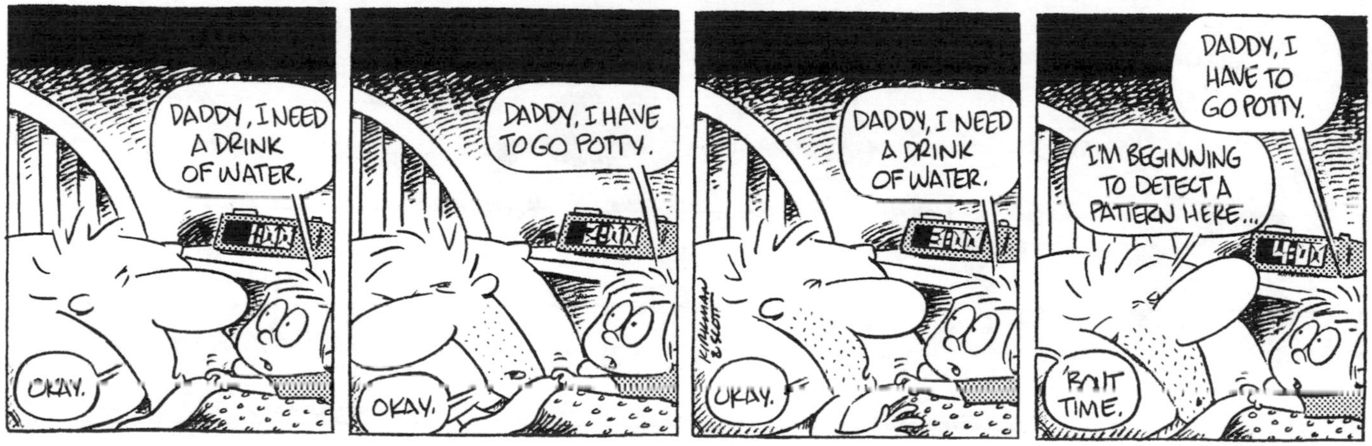
DADDY, I NEED A DRINK OF WATER.
OKAY.
DADDY, I HAVE TO GO POTTY.
OKAY.
KIRKMAN & SCOTT
DADDY, I NEED A DRINK OF WATER.
OKAY.
DADDY, I HAVE TO GO POTTY.
I'M BEGINNING TO DETECT A PATTERN HERE...
'BOUT TIME.

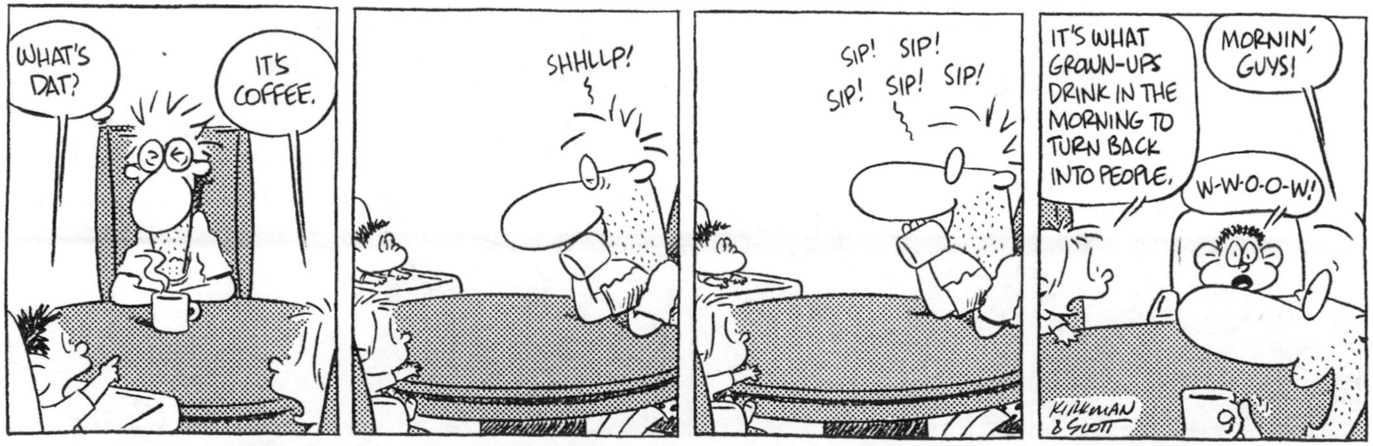
WHAT'S DAT?
IT'S COFFEE.
SHHLLP!
SIP! SIP! SIP! SIP! SIP!
IT'S WHAT GROWN-UPS DRINK IN THE MORNING TO TURN BACK INTO PEOPLE.
MORNIN', GUYS!
W-W-O-O-W!
KIRKMAN & SCOTT

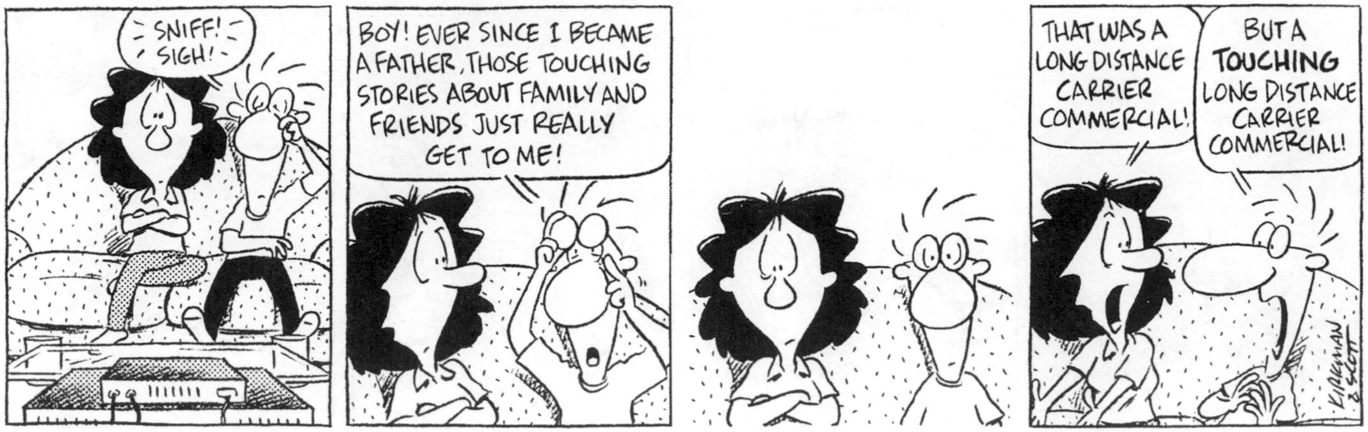
SNIFF! SIGH!
BOY! EVER SINCE I BECAME A FATHER, THOSE TOUCHING STORIES ABOUT FAMILY AND FRIENDS JUST REALLY GET TO ME!
THAT WAS A LONG DISTANCE CARRIER COMMERCIAL!
BUT A **TOUCHING** LONG DISTANCE CARRIER COMMERCIAL!
KIRKMAN & SCOTT

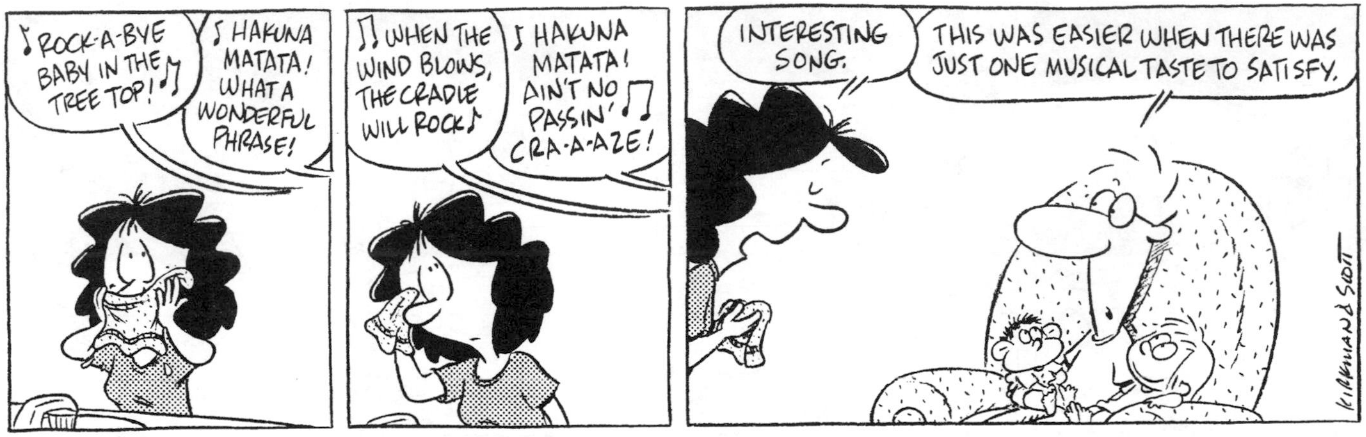
♪ ROCK-A-BYE BABY IN THE TREE TOP! ♫
♪ HAKUNA MATATA! WHAT A WONDERFUL PHRASE!
♫ WHEN THE WIND BLOWS, THE CRADLE WILL ROCK ♪
♪ HAKUNA MATATA! AIN'T NO PASSIN' CRA-A-AZE! ♫
INTERESTING SONG.
THIS WAS EASIER WHEN THERE WAS JUST ONE MUSICAL TASTE TO SATISFY.
KIRKMAN & SCOTT

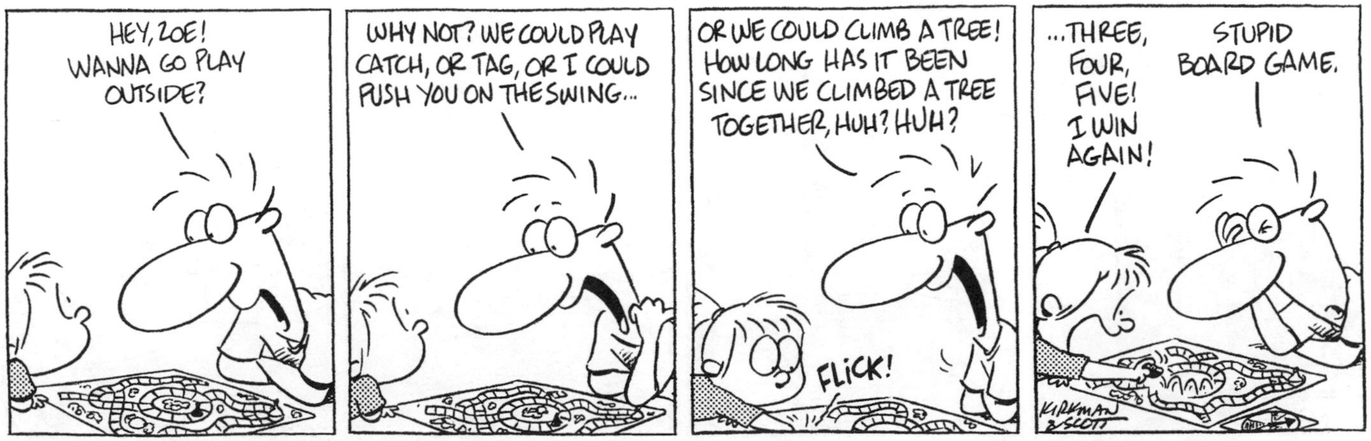
HEY, ZOE! WANNA GO PLAY OUTSIDE?
WHY NOT? WE COULD PLAY CATCH, OR TAG, OR I COULD PUSH YOU ON THE SWING...
OR WE COULD CLIMB A TREE! HOW LONG HAS IT BEEN SINCE WE CLIMBED A TREE TOGETHER, HUH? HUH?
FLICK!
...THREE, FOUR, FIVE! I WIN AGAIN!
STUPID BOARD GAME.
KIRKMAN & SCOTT

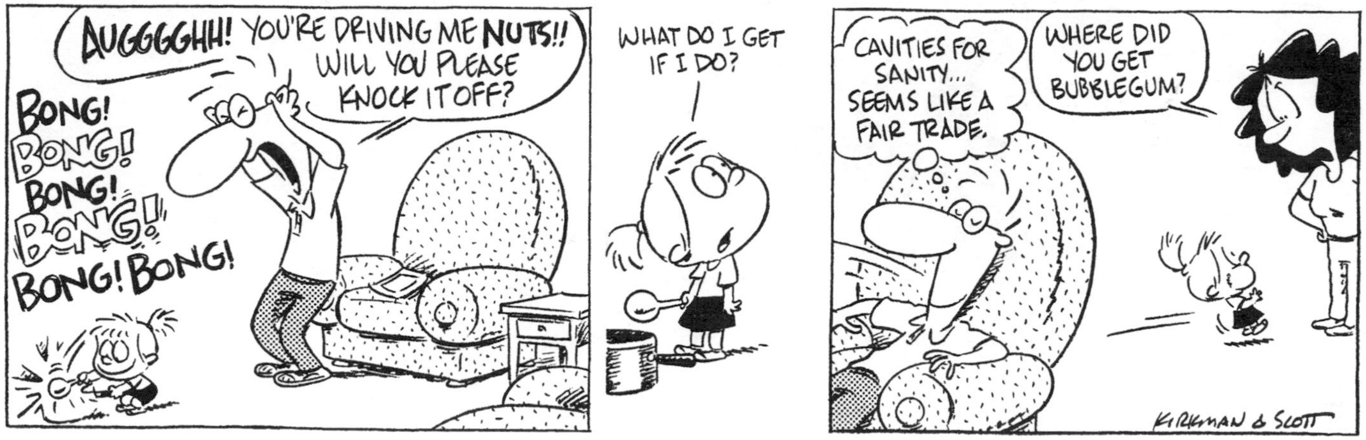
AUGGGGHH! YOU'RE DRIVING ME NUTS!! WILL YOU PLEASE KNOCK IT OFF?
BONG! BONG! BONG! BONG! BONG! BONG!
WHAT DO I GET IF I DO?
CAVITIES FOR SANITY... SEEMS LIKE A FAIR TRADE.
WHERE DID YOU GET BUBBLEGUM?
KIRKMAN & SCOTT

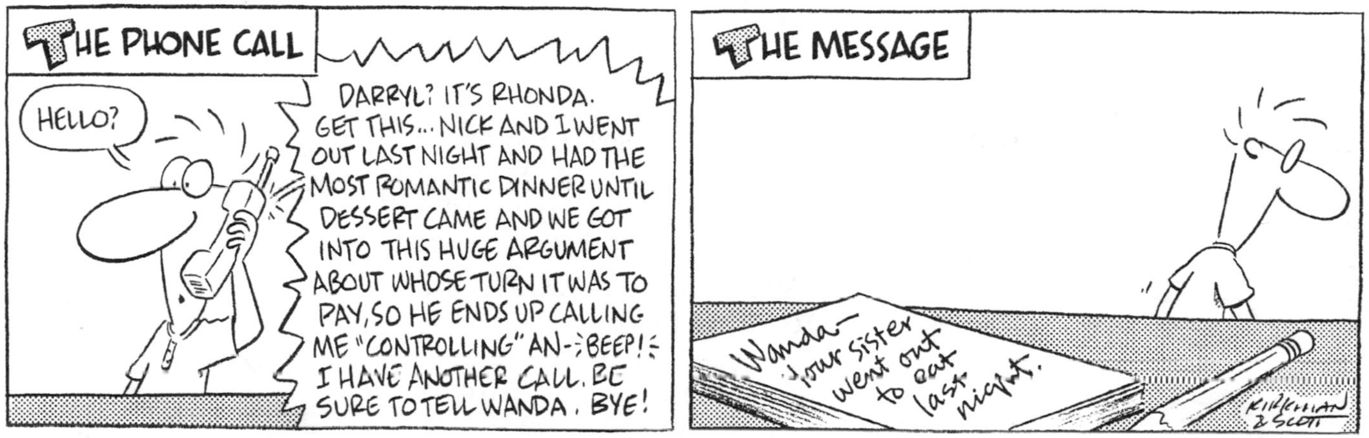
THE PHONE CALL
HELLO?
DARRYL? IT'S RHONDA. GET THIS... NICK AND I WENT OUT LAST NIGHT AND HAD THE MOST ROMANTIC DINNER UNTIL DESSERT CAME AND WE GOT INTO THIS HUGE ARGUMENT ABOUT WHOSE TURN IT WAS TO PAY, SO HE ENDS UP CALLING ME "CONTROLLING" AN- BEEP! I HAVE ANOTHER CALL. BE SURE TO TELL WANDA. BYE!
THE MESSAGE
Wanda— your sister went out to eat last night.
KIRKMAN & SCOTT

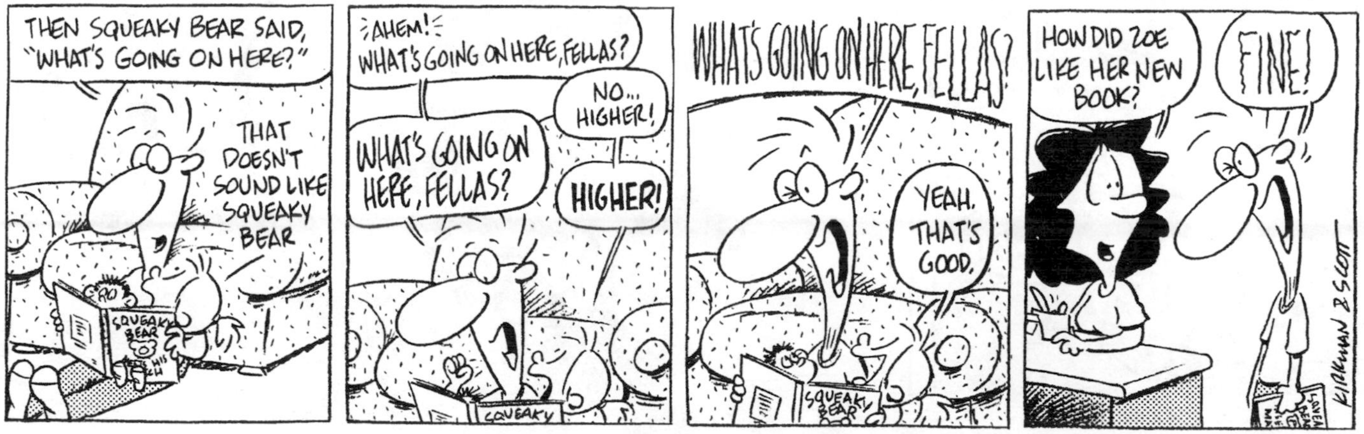
THEN SQUEAKY BEAR SAID, "WHAT'S GOING ON HERE?"
THAT DOESN'T SOUND LIKE SQUEAKY BEAR
SQUEAKY BEAR
AHEM! WHAT'S GOING ON HERE, FELLAS?
WHAT'S GOING ON HERE, FELLAS?
NO... HIGHER!
HIGHER!
WHAT'S GOING ON HERE, FELLAS?
YEAH. THAT'S GOOD.
HOW DID ZOE LIKE HER NEW BOOK?
FINE!
KIRKMAN & SCOTT

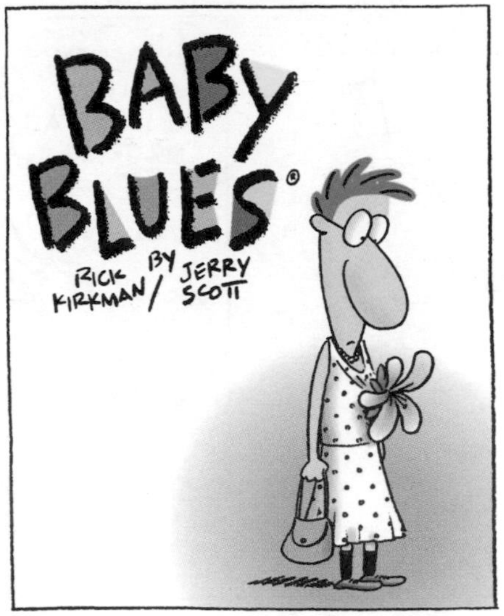
BABY BLUES®
BY RICK KIRKMAN / JERRY SCOTT

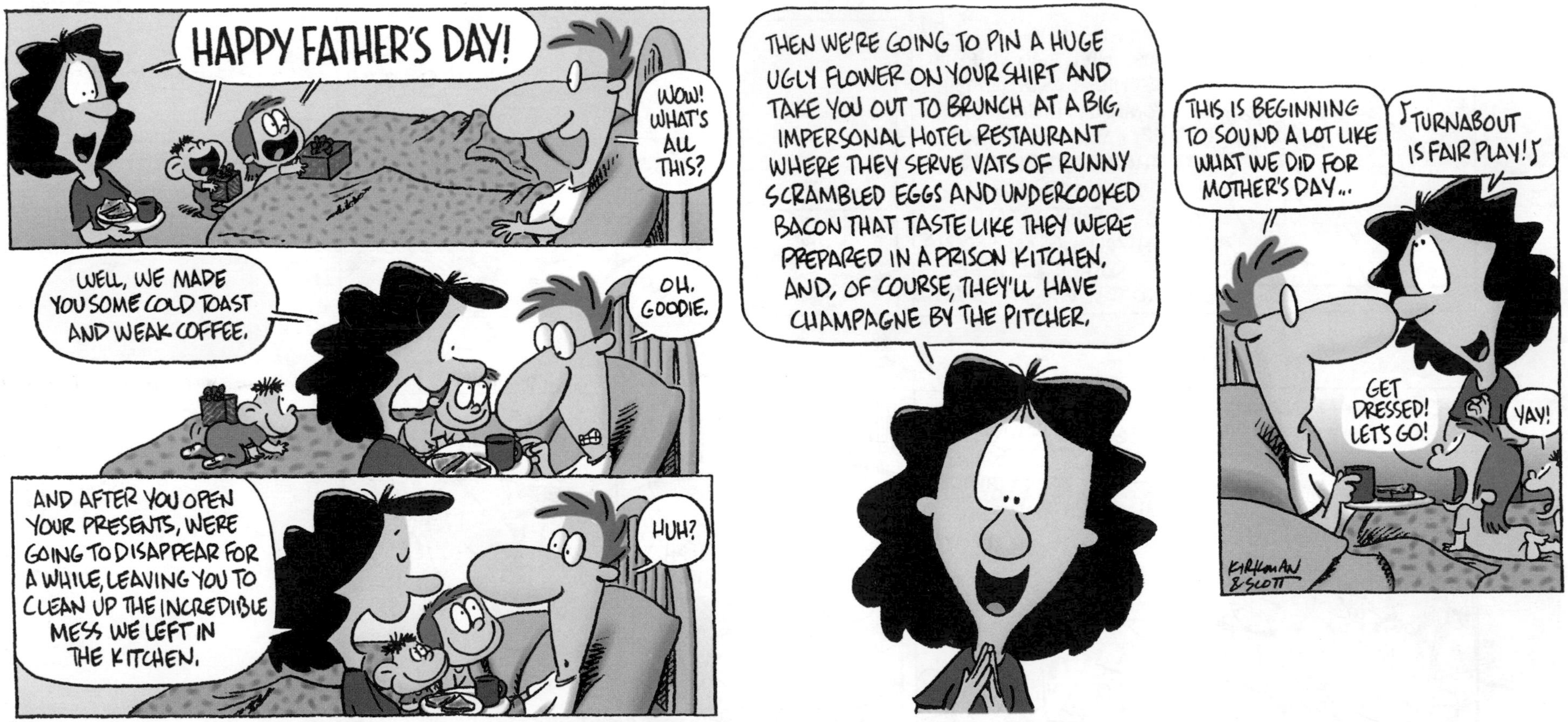
HAPPY FATHER'S DAY!
WOW! WHAT'S ALL THIS?
WELL, WE MADE YOU SOME COLD TOAST AND WEAK COFFEE.
OH. GOODIE.
AND AFTER YOU OPEN YOUR PRESENTS, WE'RE GOING TO DISAPPEAR FOR A WHILE, LEAVING YOU TO CLEAN UP THE INCREDIBLE MESS WE LEFT IN THE KITCHEN.
HUH?
THEN WE'RE GOING TO PIN A HUGE UGLY FLOWER ON YOUR SHIRT AND TAKE YOU OUT TO BRUNCH AT A BIG, IMPERSONAL HOTEL RESTAURANT WHERE THEY SERVE VATS OF RUNNY SCRAMBLED EGGS AND UNDERCOOKED BACON THAT TASTE LIKE THEY WERE PREPARED IN A PRISON KITCHEN. AND, OF COURSE, THEY'LL HAVE CHAMPAGNE BY THE PITCHER.
THIS IS BEGINNING TO SOUND A LOT LIKE WHAT WE DID FOR MOTHER'S DAY...
♪ TURNABOUT IS FAIR PLAY! ♪
GET DRESSED! LET'S GO!
YAY!
KIRKMAN & SCOTT

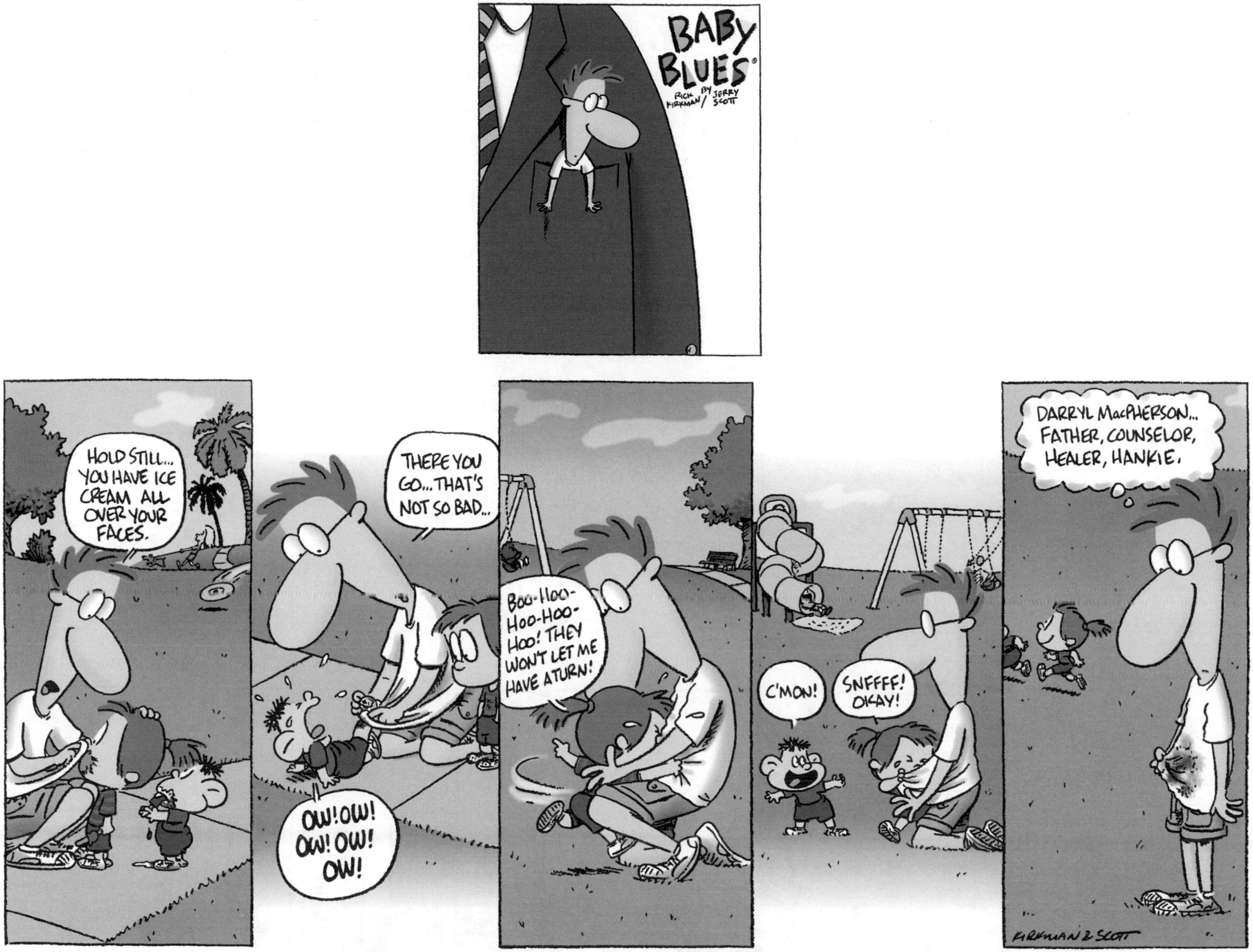
BABY BLUES®
BY RICK KIRKMAN / JERRY SCOTT
HOLD STILL... YOU HAVE ICE CREAM ALL OVER YOUR FACES.
THERE YOU GO... THAT'S NOT SO BAD...
OW! OW! OW! OW! OW!
BOO-HOO-HOO-HOO-HOO! THEY WON'T LET ME HAVE A TURN!
C'MON!
SNFFFF! OKAY!
DARRYL MacPHERSON... FATHER, COUNSELOR, HEALER, HANKIE.
KIRKMAN & SCOTT

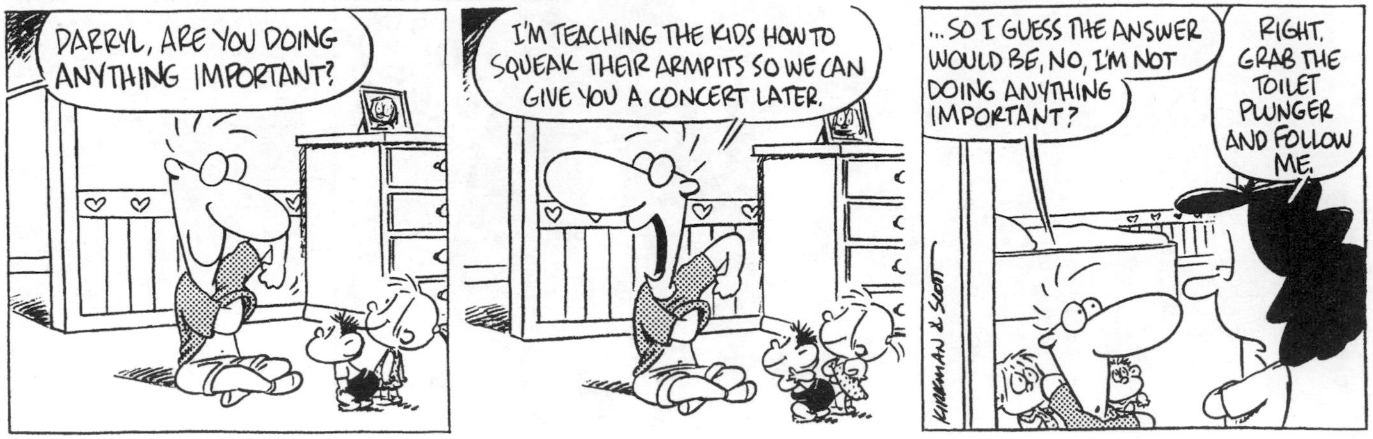
DARRYL, ARE YOU DOING ANYTHING IMPORTANT?
I'M TEACHING THE KIDS HOW TO SQUEAK THEIR ARMPITS SO WE CAN GIVE YOU A CONCERT LATER.
...SO I GUESS THE ANSWER WOULD BE, NO, I'M NOT DOING ANYTHING IMPORTANT?
RIGHT. GRAB THE TOILET PLUNGER AND FOLLOW ME.
KIRKMAN & SCOTT

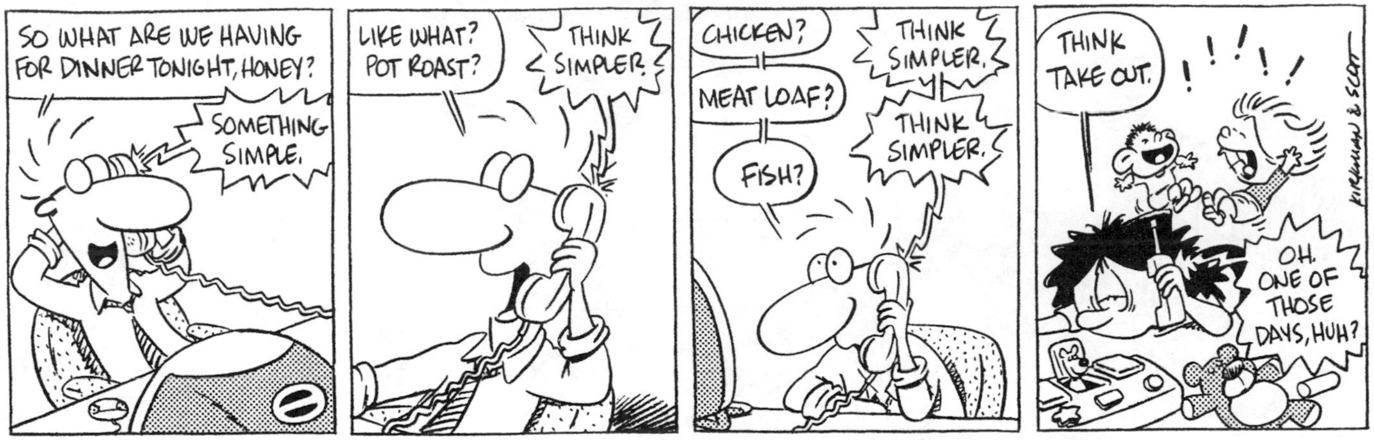
SO WHAT ARE WE HAVING FOR DINNER TONIGHT, HONEY?
SOMETHING SIMPLE.
LIKE WHAT? POT ROAST?
THINK SIMPLER.
CHICKEN?
MEAT LOAF?
FISH?
THINK SIMPLER.
THINK SIMPLER.
THINK TAKE OUT.
! ! ! ! !
OH. ONE OF THOSE DAYS, HUH?
KIRKMAN & SCOTT

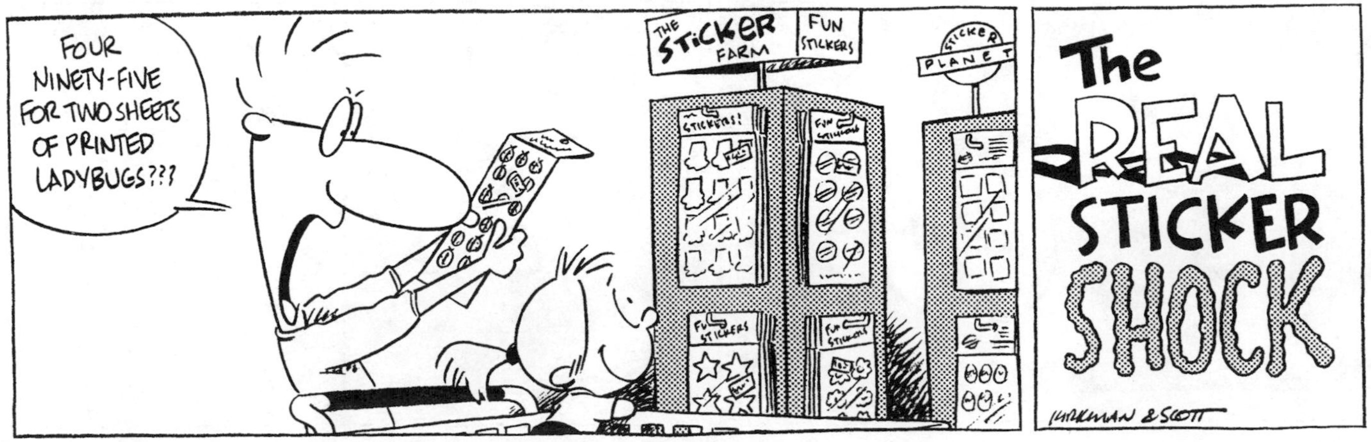
FOUR NINETY-FIVE FOR TWO SHEETS OF PRINTED LADYBUGS???
THE STICKER FARM
FUN STICKERS
STICKER PLANET
The REAL STICKER SHOCK
KIRKMAN & SCOTT

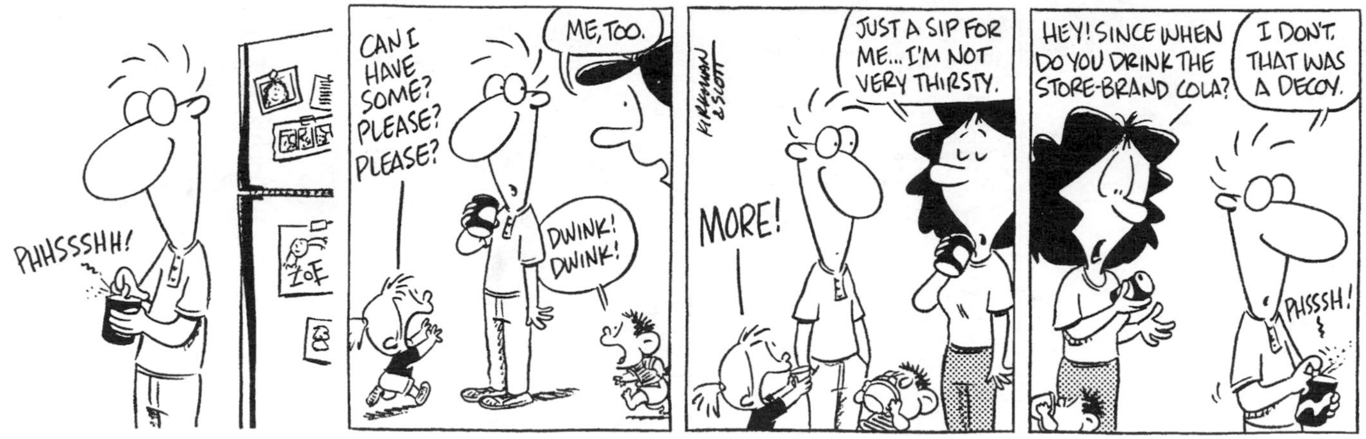
PHHSSSHH!
CAN I HAVE SOME? PLEASE? PLEASE?
ME, TOO.
DWINK! DWINK!
KIRKMAN & SCOTT
JUST A SIP FOR ME... I'M NOT VERY THIRSTY.
MORE!
HEY! SINCE WHEN DO YOU DRINK THE STORE-BRAND COLA?
I DON'T. THAT WAS A DECOY.
PHSSSH!

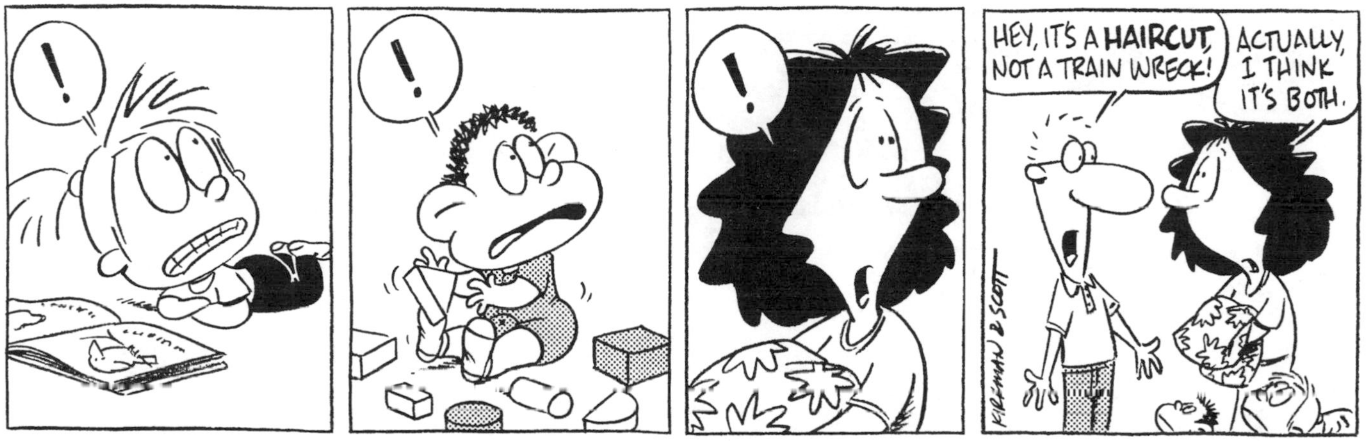
!
!
!
KIRKMAN & SCOTT
HEY, IT'S A **HAIRCUT**, NOT A TRAIN WRECK!
ACTUALLY, I THINK IT'S BOTH.

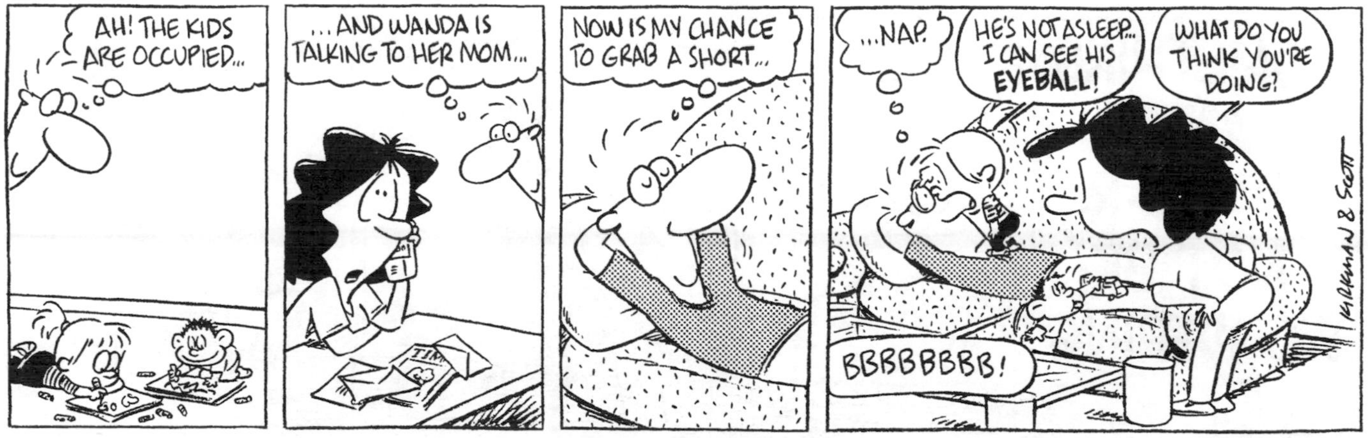
AH! THE KIDS ARE OCCUPIED...
...AND WANDA IS TALKING TO HER MOM...
NOW IS MY CHANCE TO GRAB A SHORT...
...NAP.
HE'S NOT ASLEEP... I CAN SEE HIS **EYEBALL**!
WHAT DO YOU THINK YOU'RE DOING?
BBBBBBBB!
KIRKMAN & SCOTT

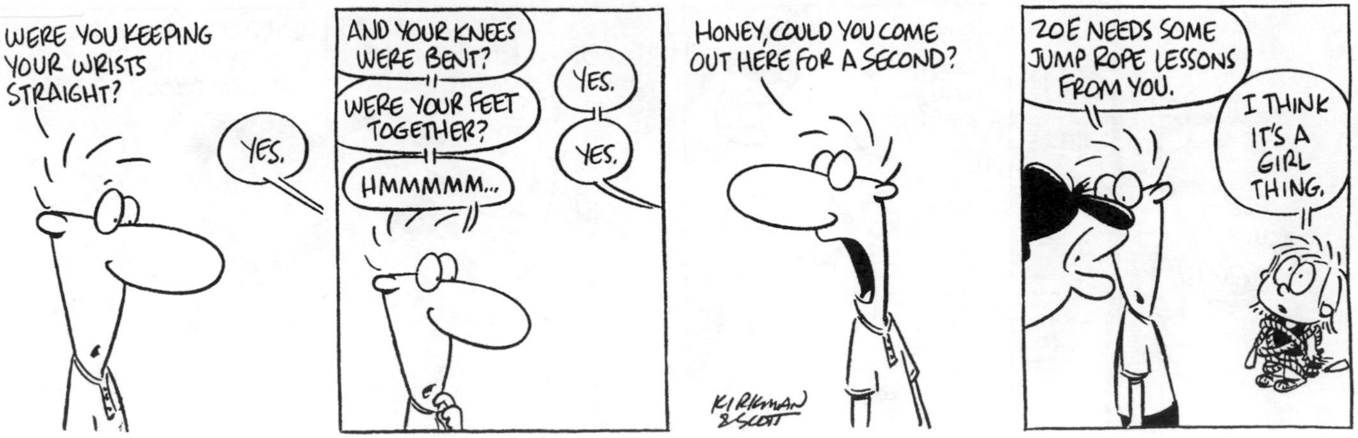
WERE YOU KEEPING YOUR WRISTS STRAIGHT?
YES.
AND YOUR KNEES WERE BENT?
WERE YOUR FEET TOGETHER?
HMMMMM...
YES.
YES.
HONEY, COULD YOU COME OUT HERE FOR A SECOND?
KIRKMAN & SCOTT
ZOE NEEDS SOME JUMP ROPE LESSONS FROM YOU.
I THINK IT'S A GIRL THING.

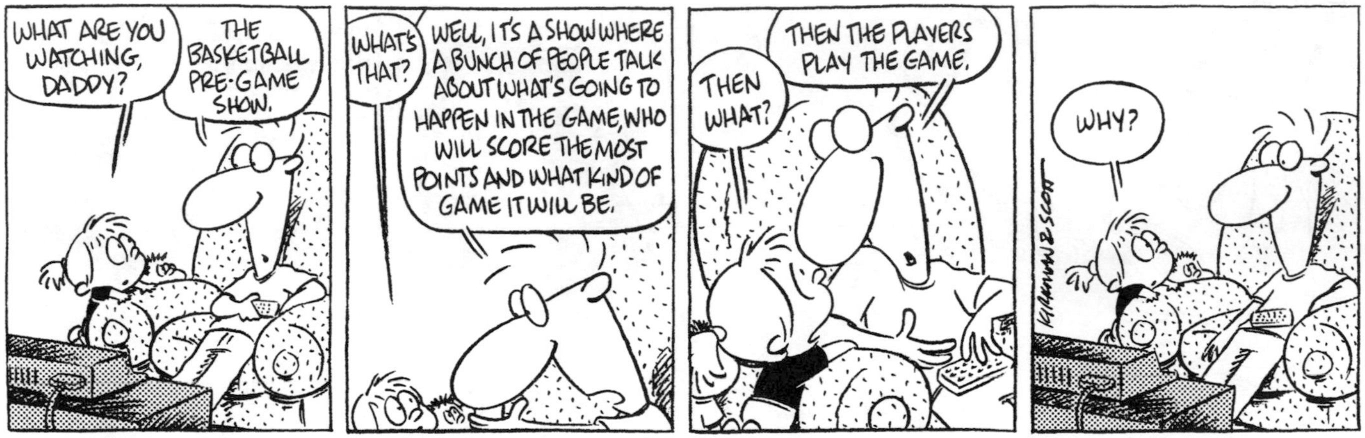
WHAT ARE YOU WATCHING, DADDY?
THE BASKETBALL PRE-GAME SHOW.
WHAT'S THAT?
WELL, IT'S A SHOW WHERE A BUNCH OF PEOPLE TALK ABOUT WHAT'S GOING TO HAPPEN IN THE GAME, WHO WILL SCORE THE MOST POINTS AND WHAT KIND OF GAME IT WILL BE.
THEN WHAT?
THEN THE PLAYERS PLAY THE GAME.
KIRKMAN & SCOTT
WHY?

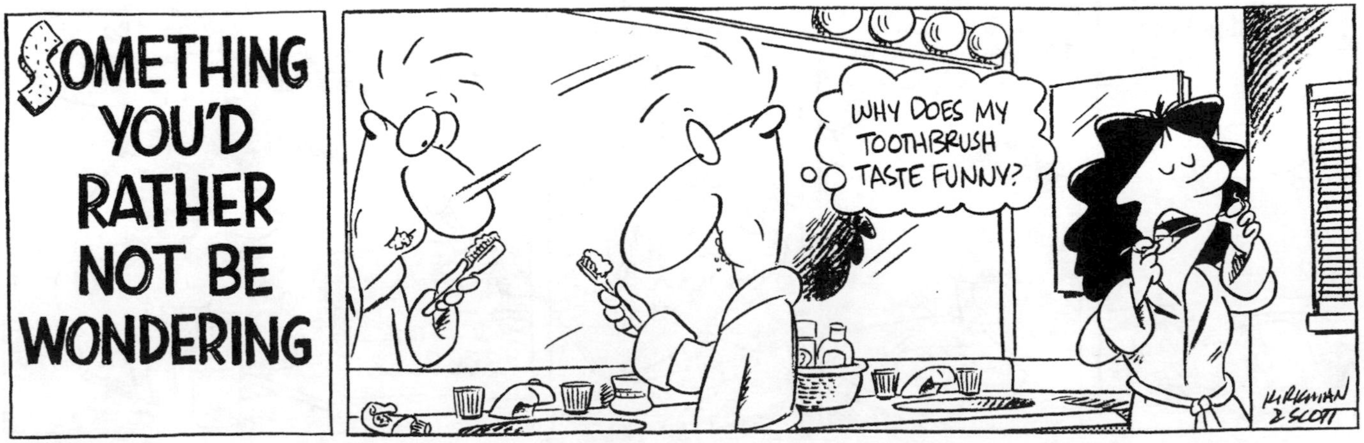
SOMETHING YOU'D RATHER NOT BE WONDERING
WHY DOES MY TOOTHBRUSH TASTE FUNNY?
KIRKMAN & SCOTT

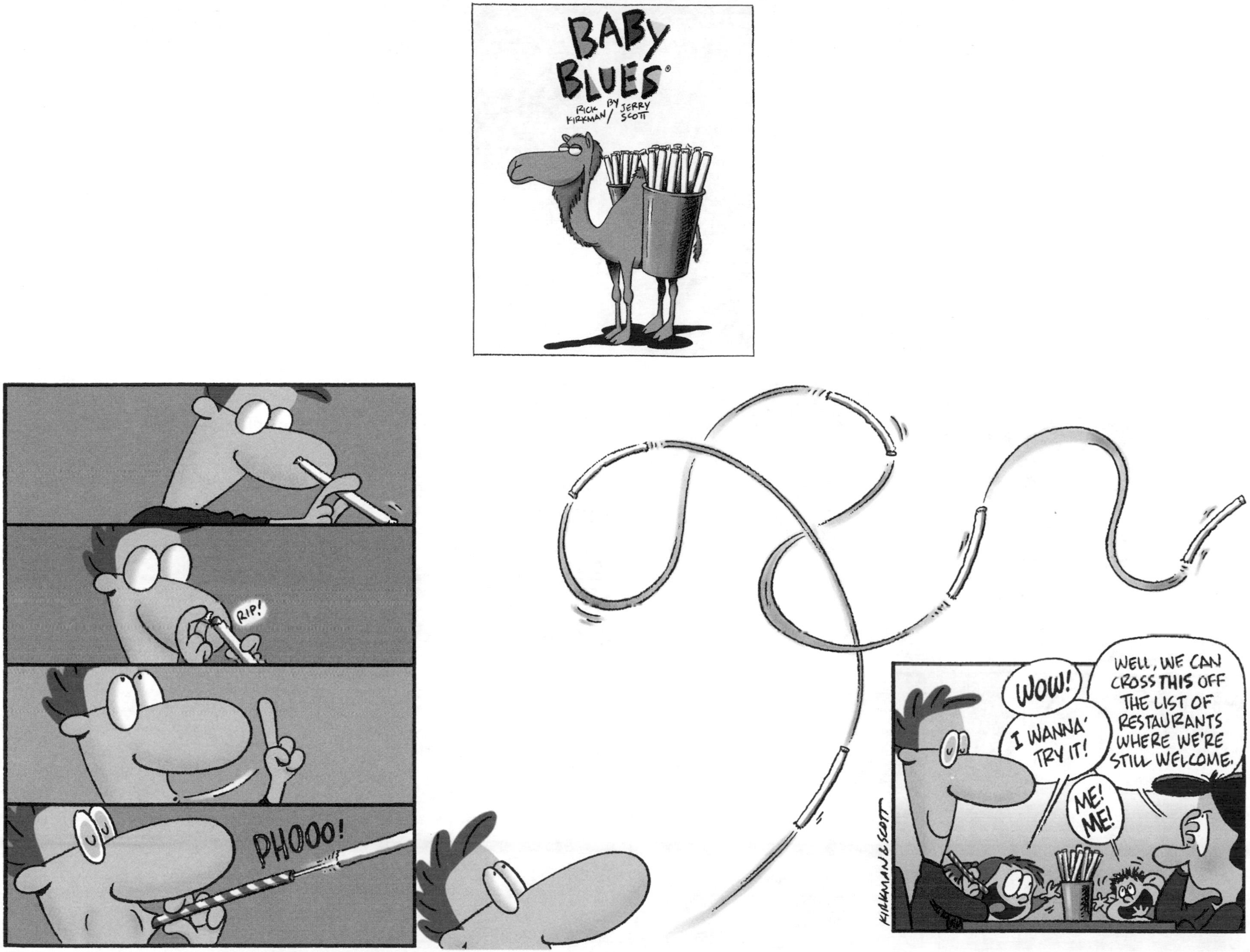
BABY BLUES®
BY RICK KIRKMAN / JERRY SCOTT
RIP!
PHOOO!
WOW!
I WANNA' TRY IT!
WELL, WE CAN CROSS THIS OFF THE LIST OF RESTAURANTS WHERE WE'RE STILL WELCOME.
ME! ME!
KIRKMAN & SCOTT

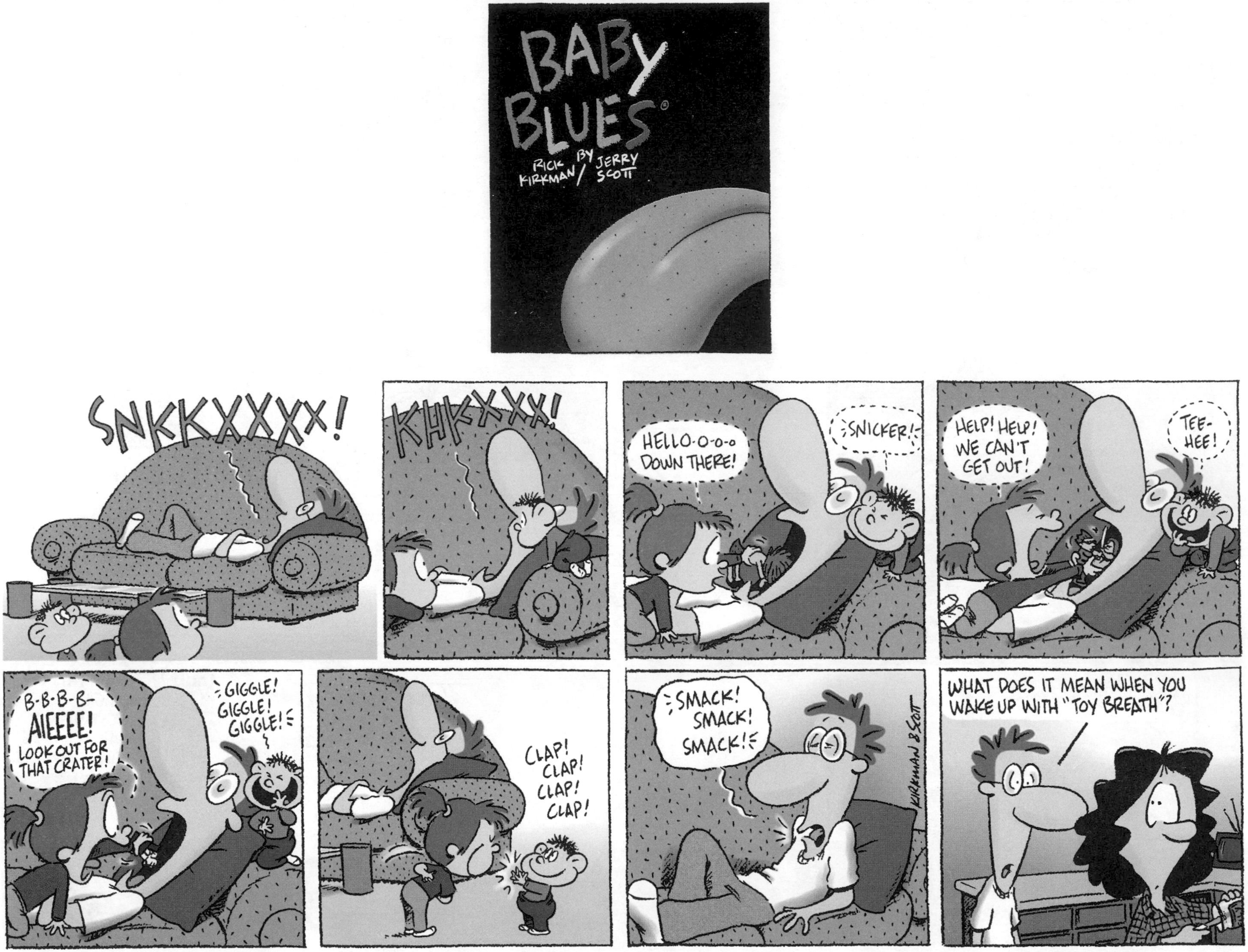
BABY BLUES®
BY RICK KIRKMAN / JERRY SCOTT
SNKKXXXX!
KHKXXX!
HELLO-O-O-O DOWN THERE!
SNICKER!
HELP! HELP! WE CAN'T GET OUT!
TEE-HEE!
B-B-B-B-AIEEEE! LOOK OUT FOR THAT CRATER!
GIGGLE! GIGGLE! GIGGLE!
CLAP! CLAP! CLAP! CLAP!
SMACK! SMACK! SMACK!
KIRKMAN & SCOTT
WHAT DOES IT MEAN WHEN YOU WAKE UP WITH "TOY BREATH"?

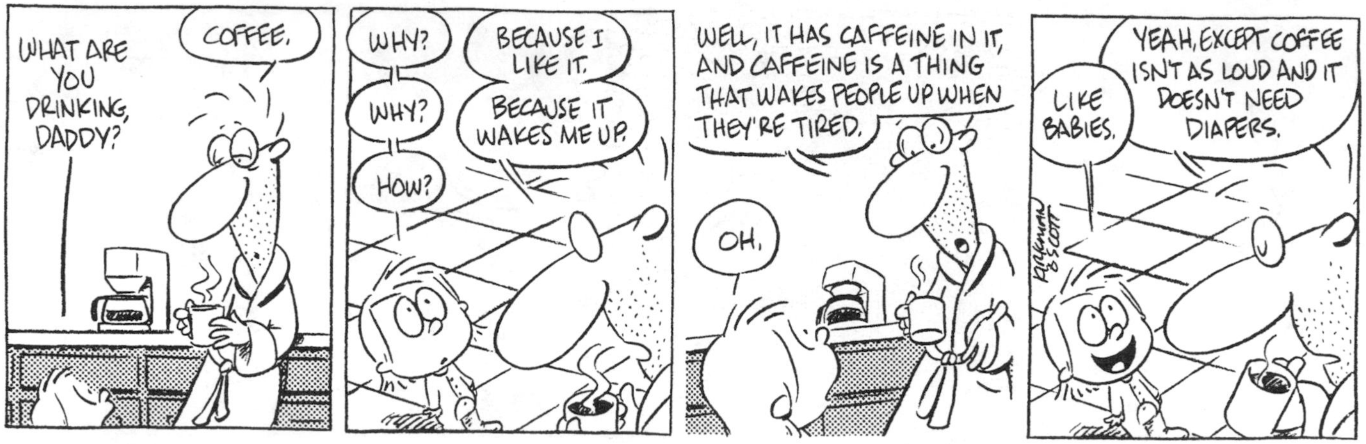
WHAT ARE YOU DRINKING, DADDY?
COFFEE.
WHY?
BECAUSE I LIKE IT.
WHY?
BECAUSE IT WAKES ME UP.
HOW?
WELL, IT HAS CAFFEINE IN IT, AND CAFFEINE IS A THING THAT WAKES PEOPLE UP WHEN THEY'RE TIRED.
OH.
LIKE BABIES.
YEAH, EXCEPT COFFEE ISN'T AS LOUD AND IT DOESN'T NEED DIAPERS.
KIRKMAN & SCOTT

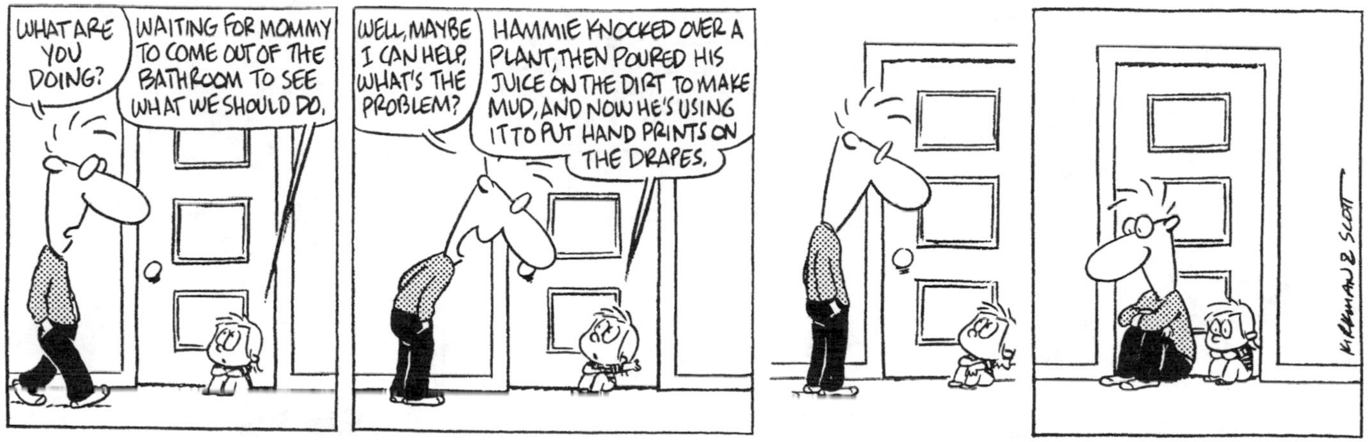
WHAT ARE YOU DOING?
WAITING FOR MOMMY TO COME OUT OF THE BATHROOM TO SEE WHAT WE SHOULD DO.
WELL, MAYBE I CAN HELP. WHAT'S THE PROBLEM?
HAMMIE KNOCKED OVER A PLANT, THEN POURED HIS JUICE ON THE DIRT TO MAKE MUD, AND NOW HE'S USING IT TO PUT HAND PRINTS ON THE DRAPES.
KIRKMAN & SCOTT

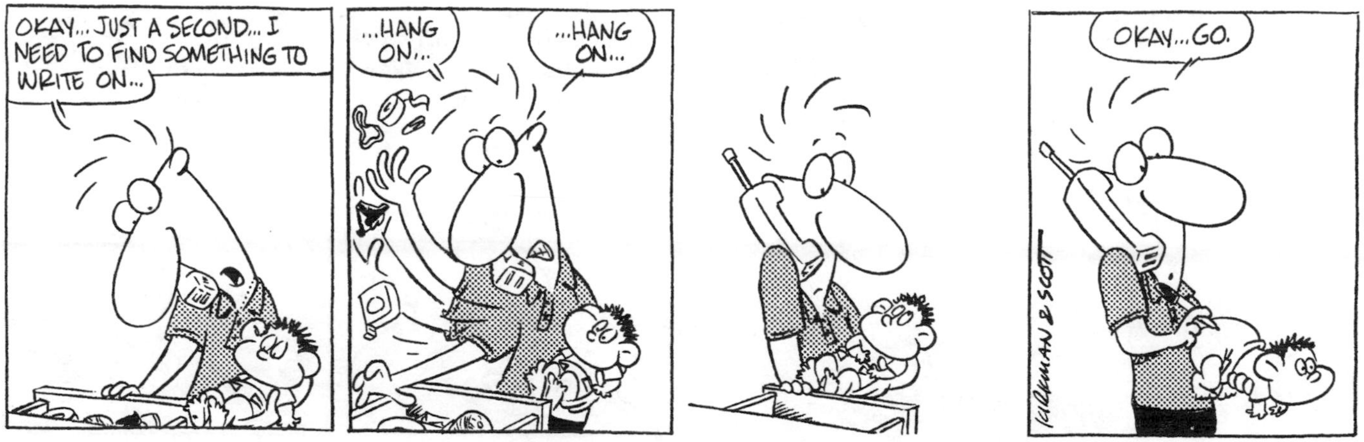
OKAY... JUST A SECOND... I NEED TO FIND SOMETHING TO WRITE ON...
...HANG ON...
...HANG ON...
KIRKMAN & SCOTT
OKAY... GO.

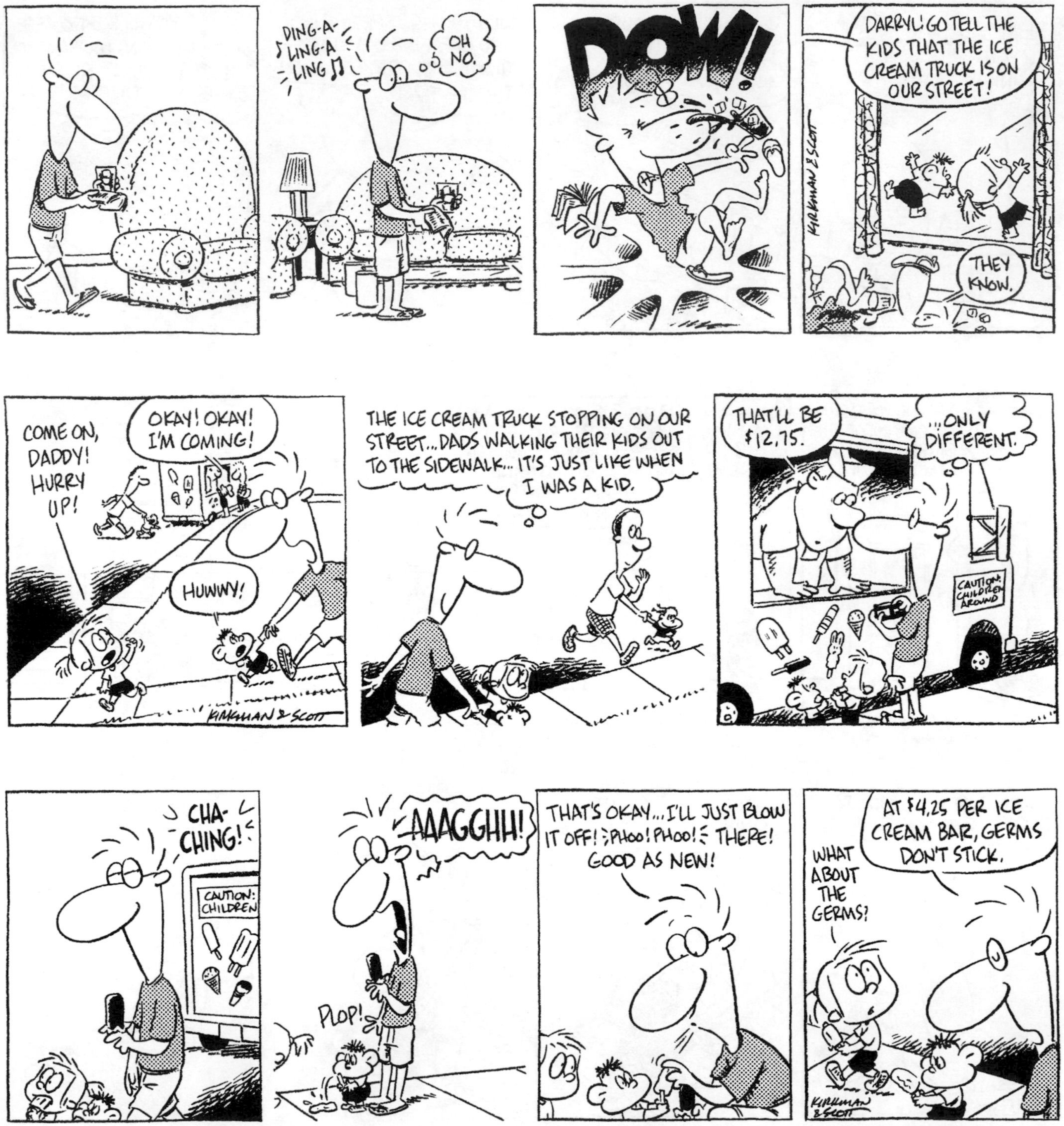
DING-A-LING-A LING
OH NO.
POW!
DARRYL! GO TELL THE KIDS THAT THE ICE CREAM TRUCK IS ON OUR STREET!
THEY KNOW.
KIRKMAN & SCOTT
COME ON, DADDY! HURRY UP!
OKAY! OKAY! I'M COMING!
HUWWY!
KIRKMAN & SCOTT
THE ICE CREAM TRUCK STOPPING ON OUR STREET... DADS WALKING THEIR KIDS OUT TO THE SIDEWALK... IT'S JUST LIKE WHEN I WAS A KID.
THAT'LL BE $12.75.
...ONLY DIFFERENT.
CAUTION: CHILDREN AROUND
CHA-CHING!
CAUTION: CHILDREN
AAAGGHH!
PLOP!
THAT'S OKAY... I'LL JUST BLOW IT OFF! PHOO! PHOO! THERE! GOOD AS NEW!
WHAT ABOUT THE GERMS?
AT $4.25 PER ICE CREAM BAR, GERMS DON'T STICK.
KIRKMAN & SCOTT

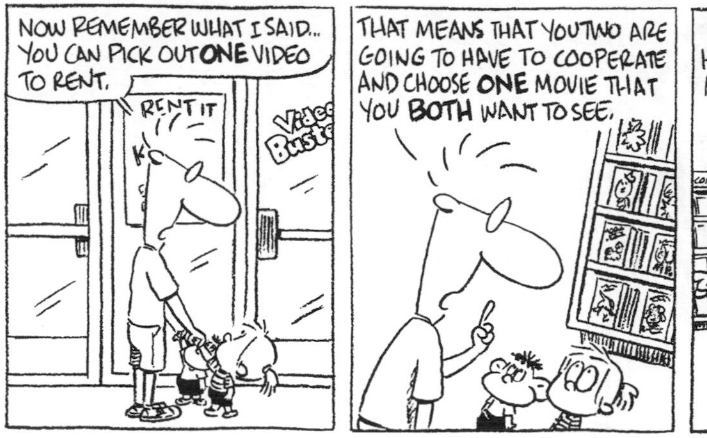
NOW REMEMBER WHAT I SAID... YOU CAN PICK OUT **ONE** VIDEO TO RENT.
RENT IT
THAT MEANS THAT YOU TWO ARE GOING TO HAVE TO COOPERATE AND CHOOSE **ONE** MOVIE THAT YOU **BOTH** WANT TO SEE.
I'M NOT WALKING OUT OF HERE WITH A WHOLE STACK OF MOVIES LIKE THE LAST TIME!
COMEDY
SIGH!
RENT IT NOW, KEEP IT FOR 3 DAYS!
KIRKMAN & SCOTT

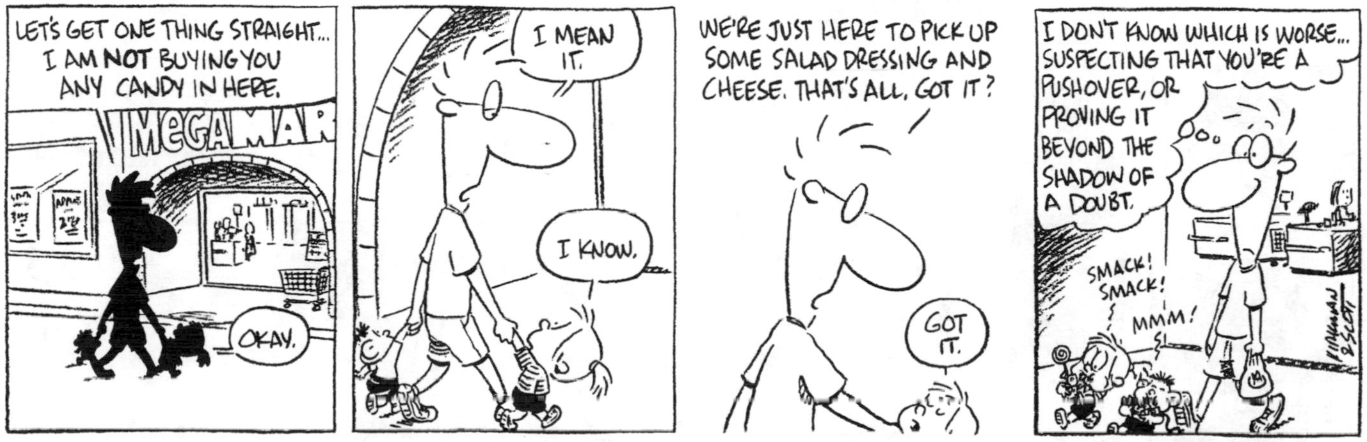
LET'S GET ONE THING STRAIGHT... I AM **NOT** BUYING YOU ANY CANDY IN HERE.
MEGAMAR
OKAY.
I MEAN IT.
I KNOW.
WE'RE JUST HERE TO PICK UP SOME SALAD DRESSING AND CHEESE. THAT'S ALL. GOT IT?
GOT IT.
I DON'T KNOW WHICH IS WORSE... SUSPECTING THAT YOU'RE A PUSHOVER, OR PROVING IT BEYOND THE SHADOW OF A DOUBT.
SMACK! SMACK!
MMM!
KIRKMAN & SCOTT

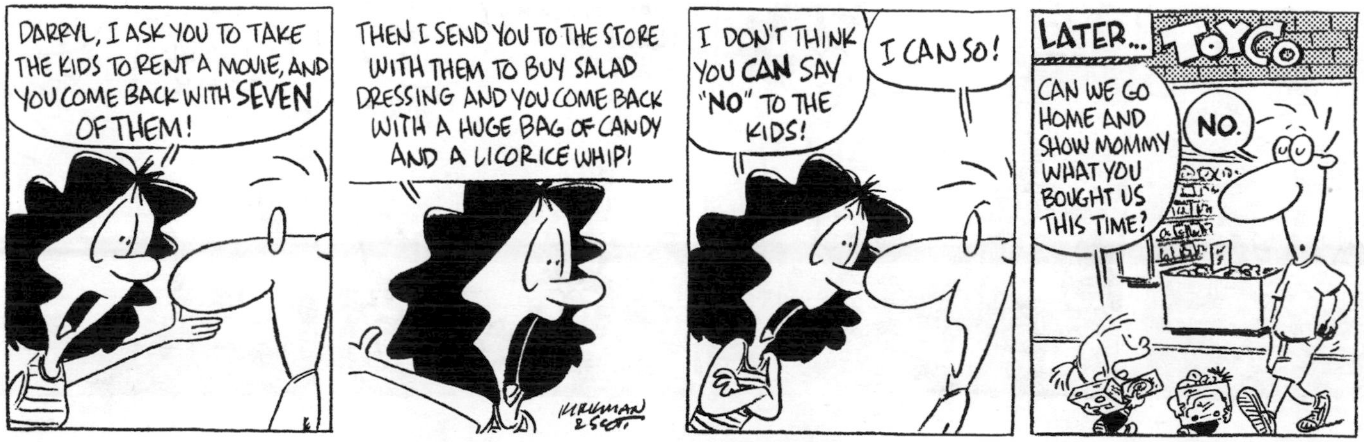
DARRYL, I ASK YOU TO TAKE THE KIDS TO RENT A MOVIE, AND YOU COME BACK WITH **SEVEN OF THEM**!
THEN I SEND YOU TO THE STORE WITH THEM TO BUY SALAD DRESSING AND YOU COME BACK WITH A HUGE BAG OF CANDY AND A LICORICE WHIP!
KIRKMAN & SCOTT
I DON'T THINK YOU **CAN** SAY "**NO**" TO THE KIDS!
I CAN SO!
LATER...
TOYCO
CAN WE GO HOME AND SHOW MOMMY WHAT YOU BOUGHT US THIS TIME?
NO.

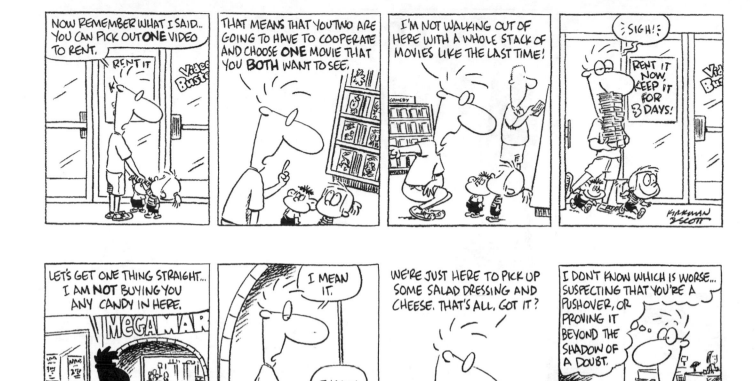

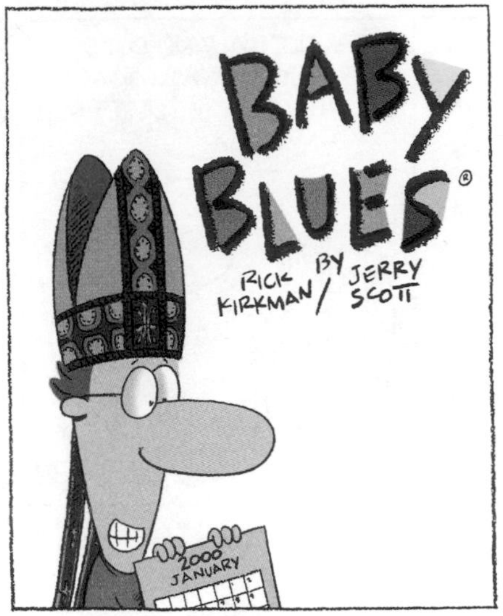
BABY BLUES®
BY RICK KIRKMAN / JERRY SCOTT
2000 JANUARY

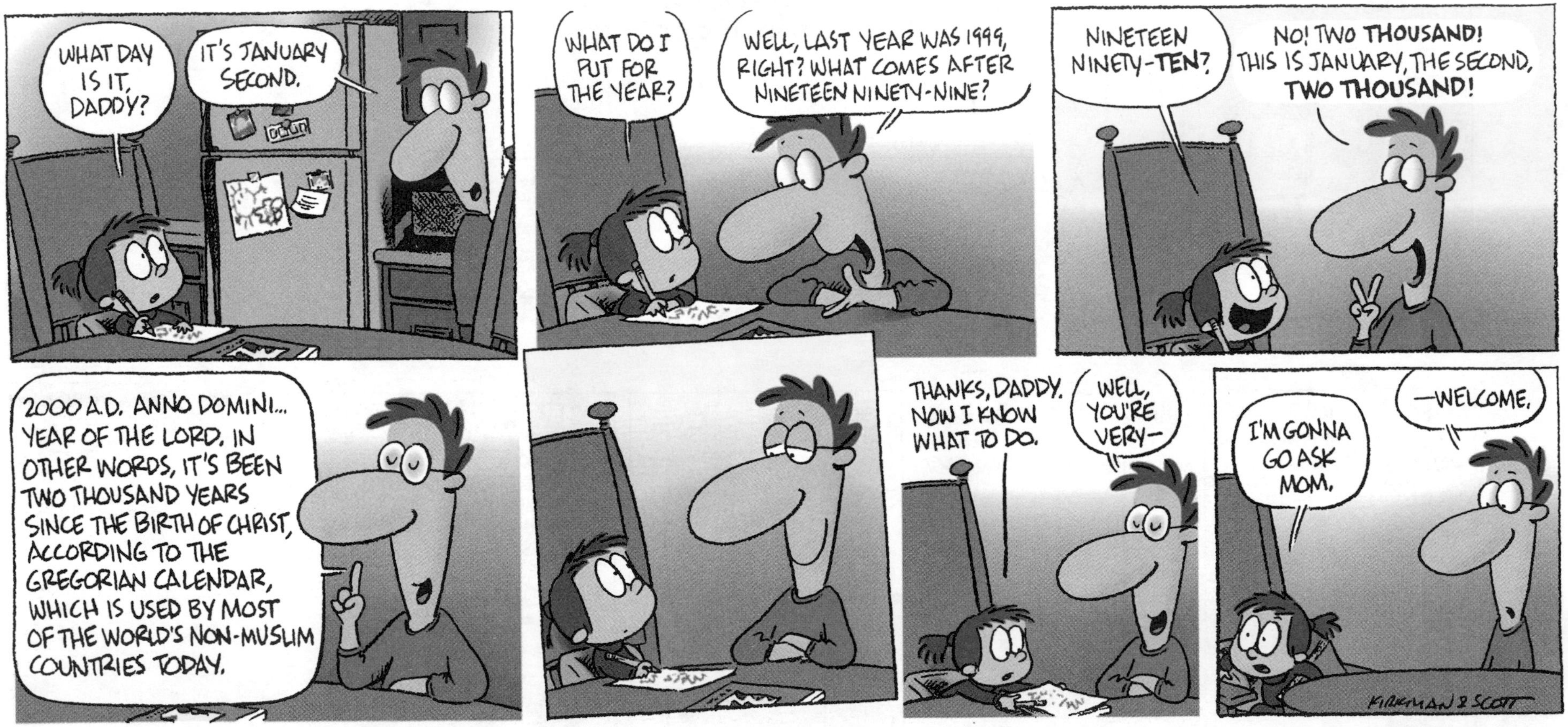
WHAT DAY IS IT, DADDY?
IT'S JANUARY SECOND.
WHAT DO I PUT FOR THE YEAR?
WELL, LAST YEAR WAS 1999, RIGHT? WHAT COMES AFTER NINETEEN NINETY-NINE?
NINETEEN NINETY-TEN?
NO! TWO THOUSAND! THIS IS JANUARY, THE SECOND, TWO THOUSAND!
2000 A.D. ANNO DOMINI... YEAR OF THE LORD. IN OTHER WORDS, IT'S BEEN TWO THOUSAND YEARS SINCE THE BIRTH OF CHRIST, ACCORDING TO THE GREGORIAN CALENDAR, WHICH IS USED BY MOST OF THE WORLD'S NON-MUSLIM COUNTRIES TODAY.
THANKS, DADDY. NOW I KNOW WHAT TO DO.
WELL, YOU'RE VERY—
I'M GONNA GO ASK MOM.
—WELCOME.
KIRKMAN & SCOTT

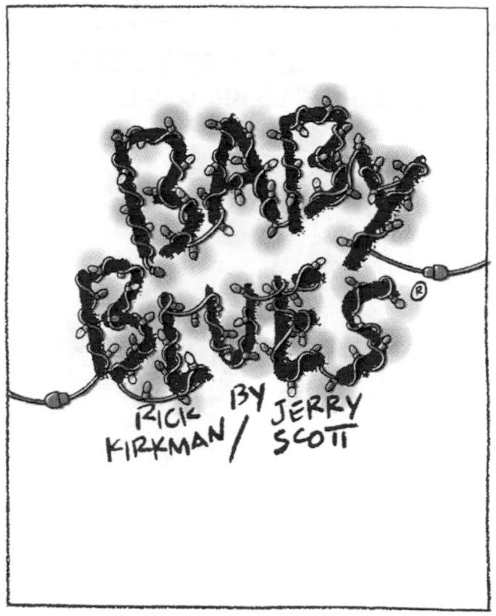
BABY BLUES®
BY
RICK KIRKMAN / JERRY SCOTT

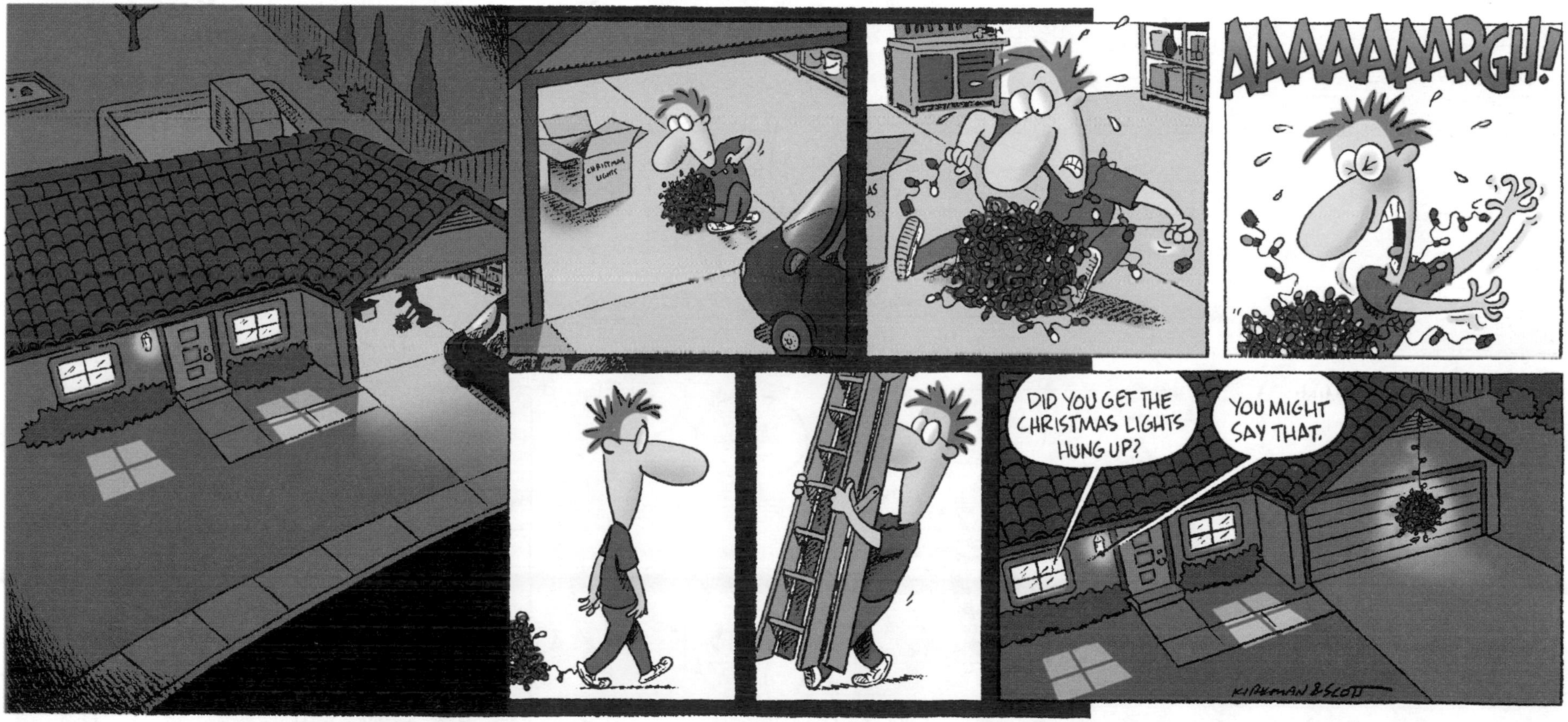
CHRISTMAS LIGHTS
AAAAAAARGH!
DID YOU GET THE CHRISTMAS LIGHTS HUNG UP?
YOU MIGHT SAY THAT.
KIRKMAN & SCOTT

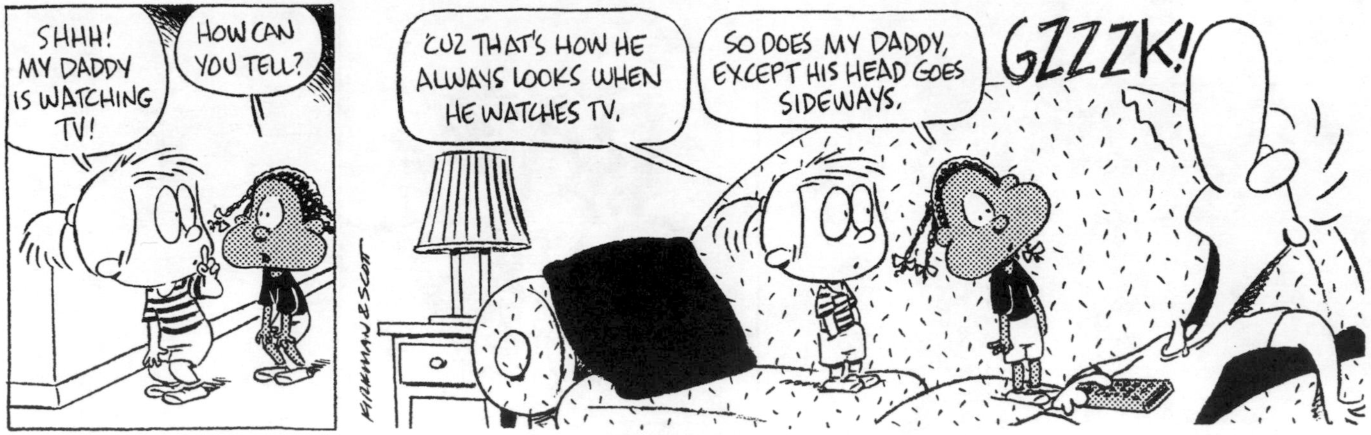
SHHH! MY DADDY IS WATCHING TV!
HOW CAN YOU TELL?
KIRKMAN & SCOTT
'CUZ THAT'S HOW HE ALWAYS LOOKS WHEN HE WATCHES TV.
SO DOES MY DADDY, EXCEPT HIS HEAD GOES SIDEWAYS.
GZZZK!

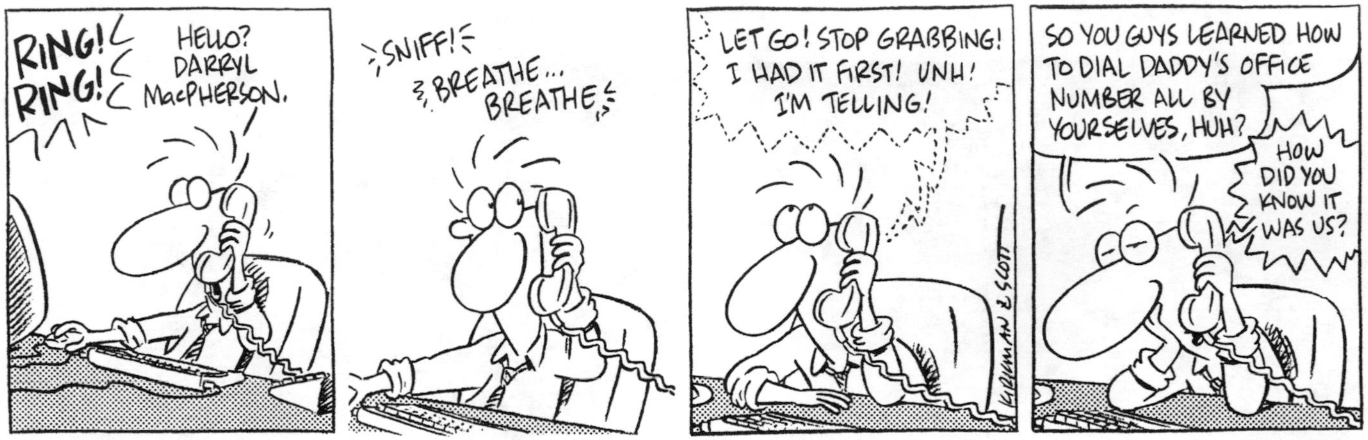
RING! RING!
HELLO? DARRYL MacPHERSON.
SNIFF!
BREATHE... BREATHE
LET GO! STOP GRABBING! I HAD IT FIRST! UNH! I'M TELLING!
KIRKMAN & SCOTT
SO YOU GUYS LEARNED HOW TO DIAL DADDY'S OFFICE NUMBER ALL BY YOURSELVES, HUH?
HOW DID YOU KNOW IT WAS US?

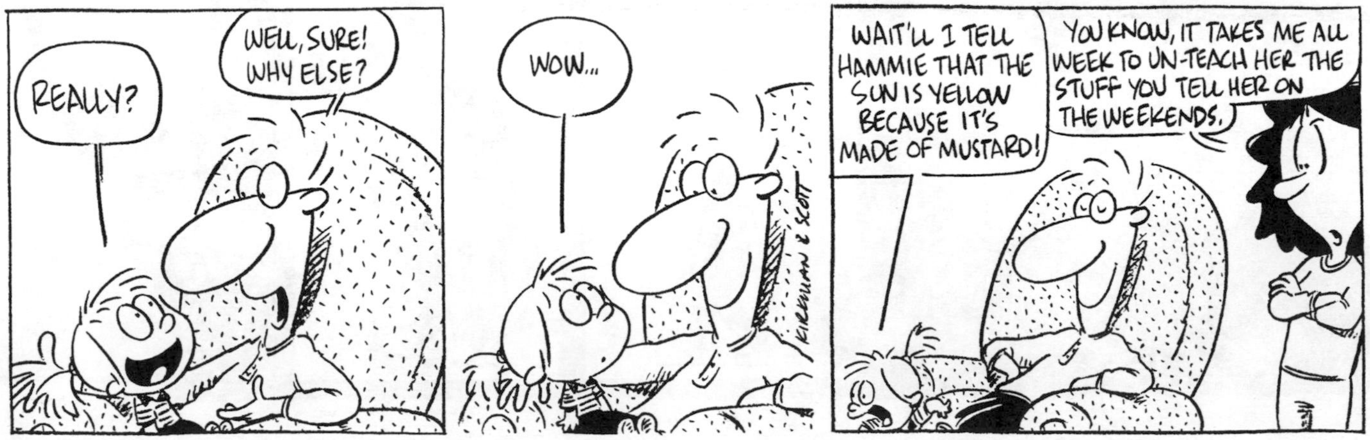
REALLY?
WELL, SURE! WHY ELSE?
WOW...
KIRKMAN & SCOTT
WAIT'LL I TELL HAMMIE THAT THE SUN IS YELLOW BECAUSE IT'S MADE OF MUSTARD!
YOU KNOW, IT TAKES ME ALL WEEK TO UN-TEACH HER THE STUFF YOU TELL HER ON THE WEEKENDS.

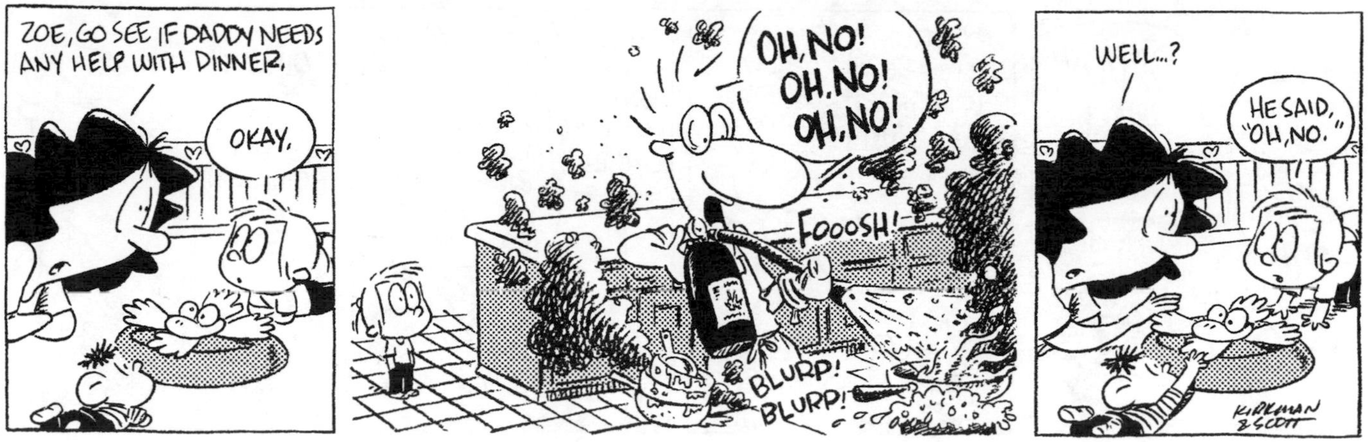
ZOE, GO SEE IF DADDY NEEDS ANY HELP WITH DINNER.
OKAY.
OH, NO! OH, NO! OH, NO!
FOOOSH!
BLURP! BLURP!
WELL...?
HE SAID, "OH, NO."
KIRKMAN & SCOTT

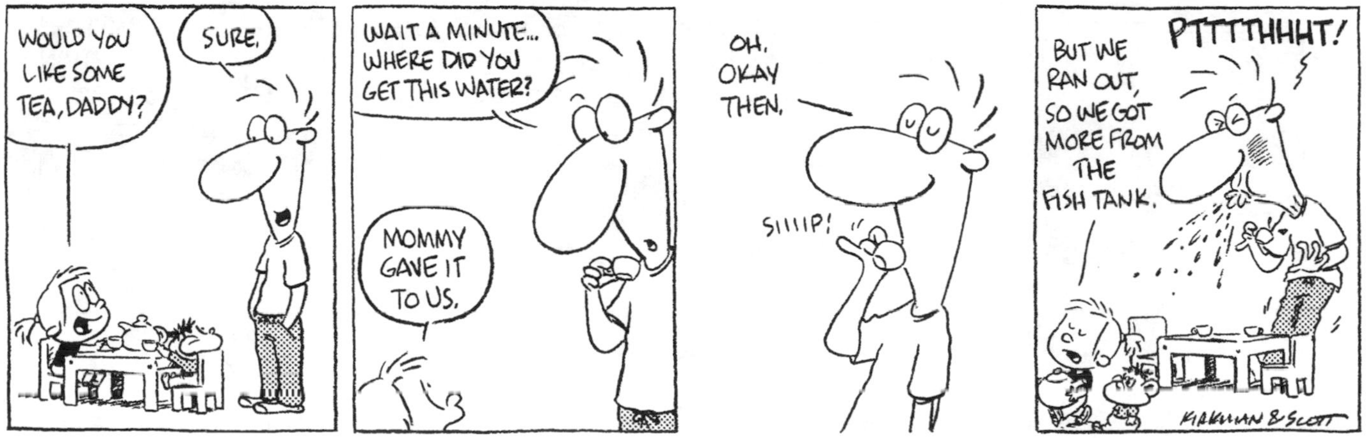
WOULD YOU LIKE SOME TEA, DADDY?
SURE.
WAIT A MINUTE... WHERE DID YOU GET THIS WATER?
MOMMY GAVE IT TO US.
OH. OKAY THEN.
SIIIIP!
BUT WE RAN OUT, SO WE GOT MORE FROM THE FISH TANK.
PTTTTHHHT!
KIRKMAN & SCOTT

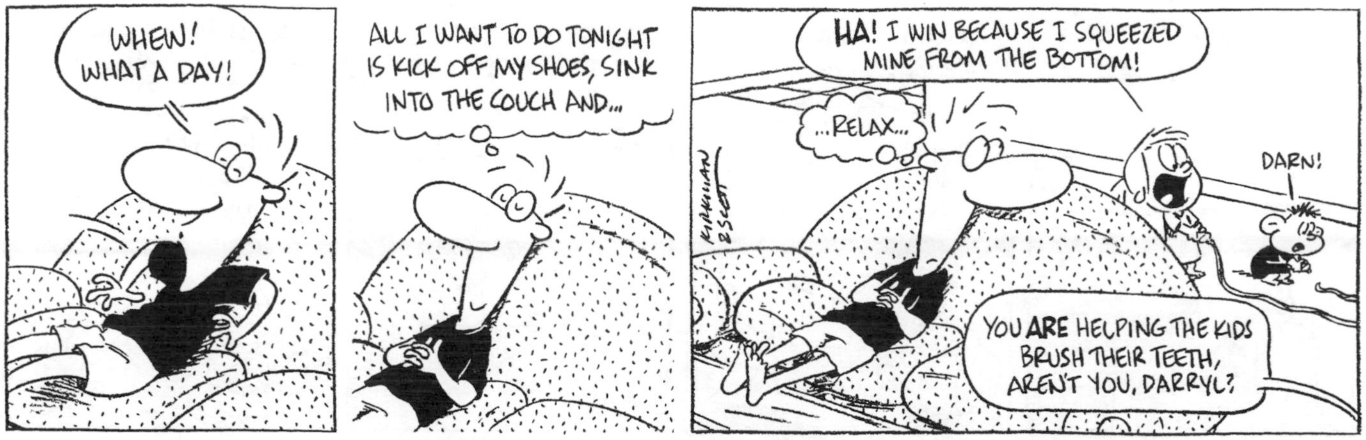
WHEW! WHAT A DAY!
ALL I WANT TO DO TONIGHT IS KICK OFF MY SHOES, SINK INTO THE COUCH AND...
KIRKMAN & SCOTT
...RELAX...
HA! I WIN BECAUSE I SQUEEZED MINE FROM THE BOTTOM!
DARN!
YOU ARE HELPING THE KIDS BRUSH THEIR TEETH, AREN'T YOU, DARRYL?

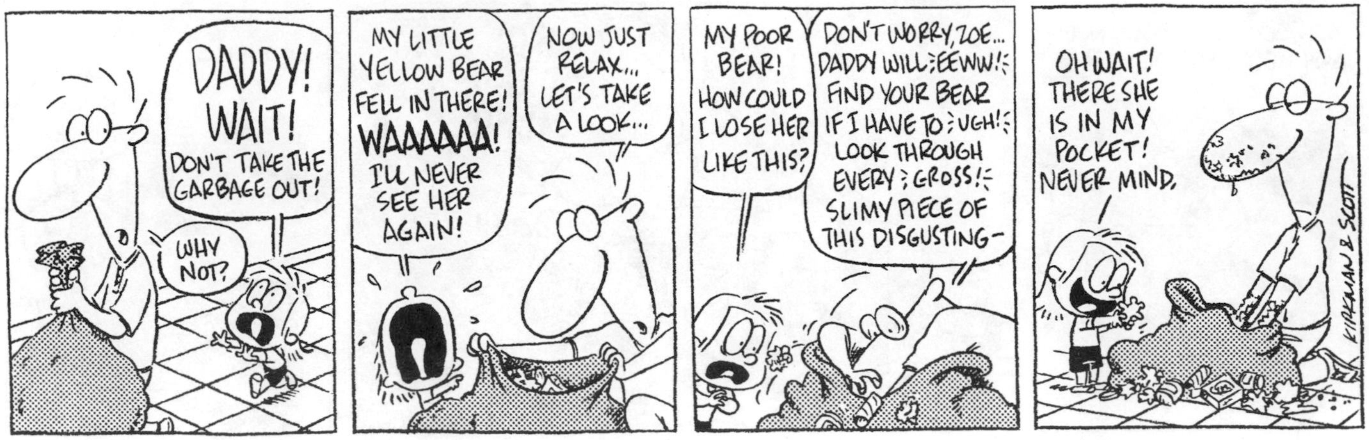
DADDY! WAIT! DON'T TAKE THE GARBAGE OUT!
WHY NOT?
MY LITTLE YELLOW BEAR FELL IN THERE! WAAAAAA! I'LL NEVER SEE HER AGAIN!
NOW JUST RELAX... LET'S TAKE A LOOK...
MY POOR BEAR! HOW COULD I LOSE HER LIKE THIS?
DON'T WORRY, ZOE... DADDY WILL EEWW! FIND YOUR BEAR IF I HAVE TO UGH! LOOK THROUGH EVERY GROSS! SLIMY PIECE OF THIS DISGUSTING—
OH WAIT! THERE SHE IS IN MY POCKET! NEVER MIND.
KIRKMAN & SCOTT

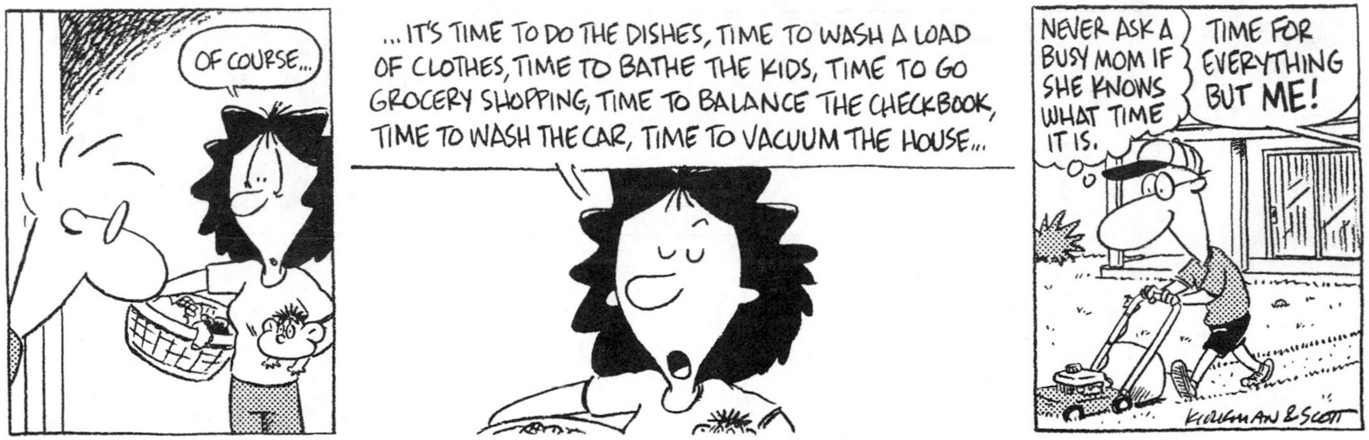
OF COURSE...
...IT'S TIME TO DO THE DISHES, TIME TO WASH A LOAD OF CLOTHES, TIME TO BATHE THE KIDS, TIME TO GO GROCERY SHOPPING, TIME TO BALANCE THE CHECKBOOK, TIME TO WASH THE CAR, TIME TO VACUUM THE HOUSE...
NEVER ASK A BUSY MOM IF SHE KNOWS WHAT TIME IT IS.
TIME FOR EVERYTHING BUT ME!
KIRKMAN & SCOTT

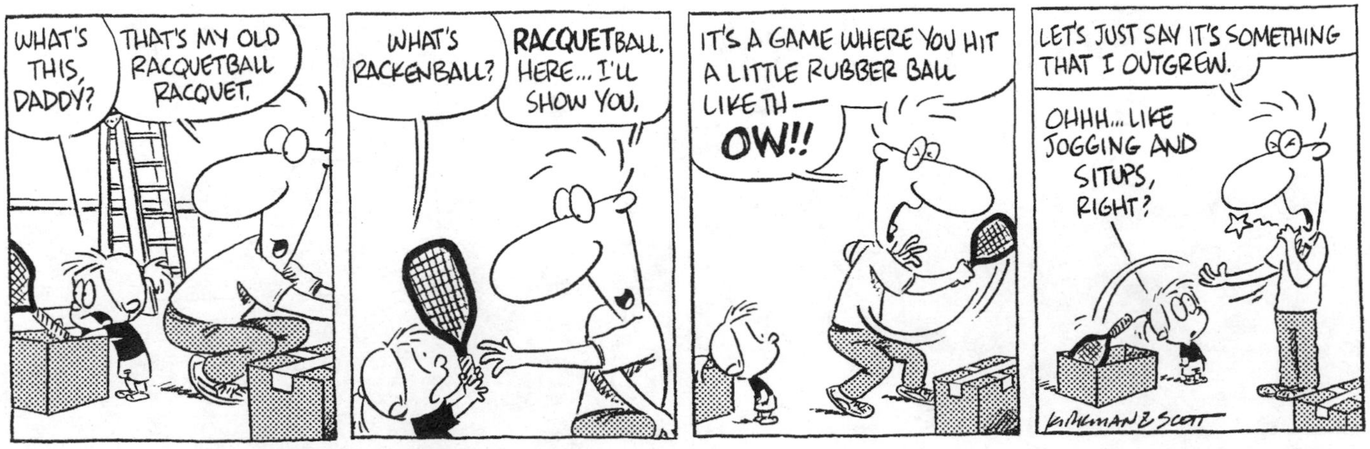
WHAT'S THIS, DADDY?
THAT'S MY OLD RACQUETBALL RACQUET.
WHAT'S RACKENBALL?
RACQUETBALL. HERE... I'LL SHOW YOU.
IT'S A GAME WHERE YOU HIT A LITTLE RUBBER BALL LIKE TH—
OW!!
LET'S JUST SAY IT'S SOMETHING THAT I OUTGREW.
OHHH... LIKE JOGGING AND SITUPS, RIGHT?
KIRKMAN & SCOTT

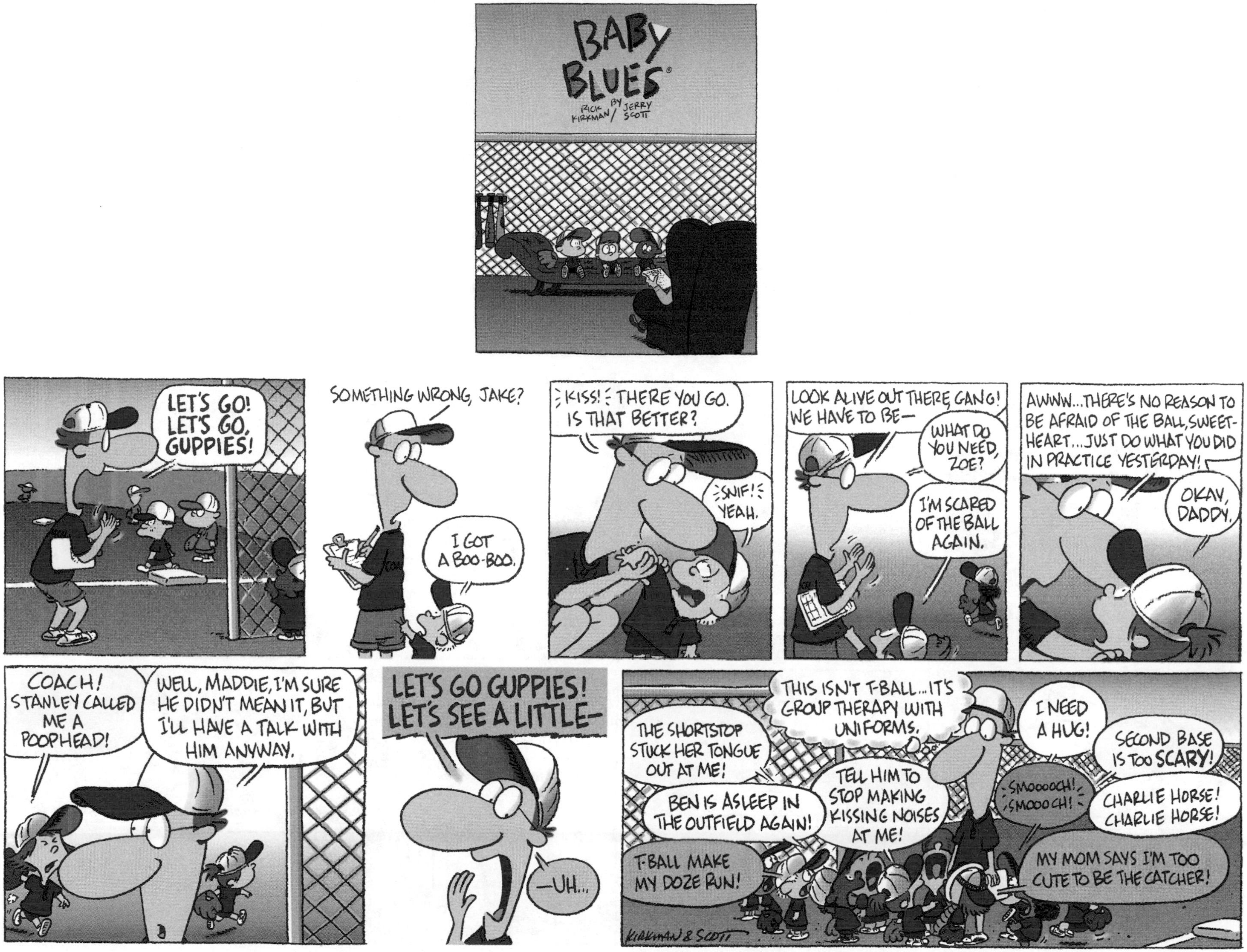
BABY BLUES®
BY RICK KIRKMAN / JERRY SCOTT
LET'S GO! LET'S GO, GUPPIES!
SOMETHING WRONG, JAKE?
I GOT A BOO-BOO.
KISS! THERE YOU GO. IS THAT BETTER?
SNIF! YEAH.
LOOK ALIVE OUT THERE, GANG! WE HAVE TO BE—
WHAT DO YOU NEED, ZOE?
I'M SCARED OF THE BALL AGAIN.
AWWW...THERE'S NO REASON TO BE AFRAID OF THE BALL, SWEETHEART...JUST DO WHAT YOU DID IN PRACTICE YESTERDAY!
OKAY, DADDY.
COACH! STANLEY CALLED ME A POOPHEAD!
WELL, MADDIE, I'M SURE HE DIDN'T MEAN IT, BUT I'LL HAVE A TALK WITH HIM ANYWAY.
LET'S GO GUPPIES! LET'S SEE A LITTLE—
—UH...
THIS ISN'T T-BALL...IT'S GROUP THERAPY WITH UNIFORMS.
THE SHORTSTOP STUCK HER TONGUE OUT AT ME!
I NEED A HUG!
SECOND BASE IS TOO SCARY!
BEN IS ASLEEP IN THE OUTFIELD AGAIN!
TELL HIM TO STOP MAKING KISSING NOISES AT ME!
SMOOOOCH! SMOOOCH!
CHARLIE HORSE! CHARLIE HORSE!
T-BALL MAKE MY DOZE RUN!
MY MOM SAYS I'M TOO CUTE TO BE THE CATCHER!
KIRKMAN & SCOTT

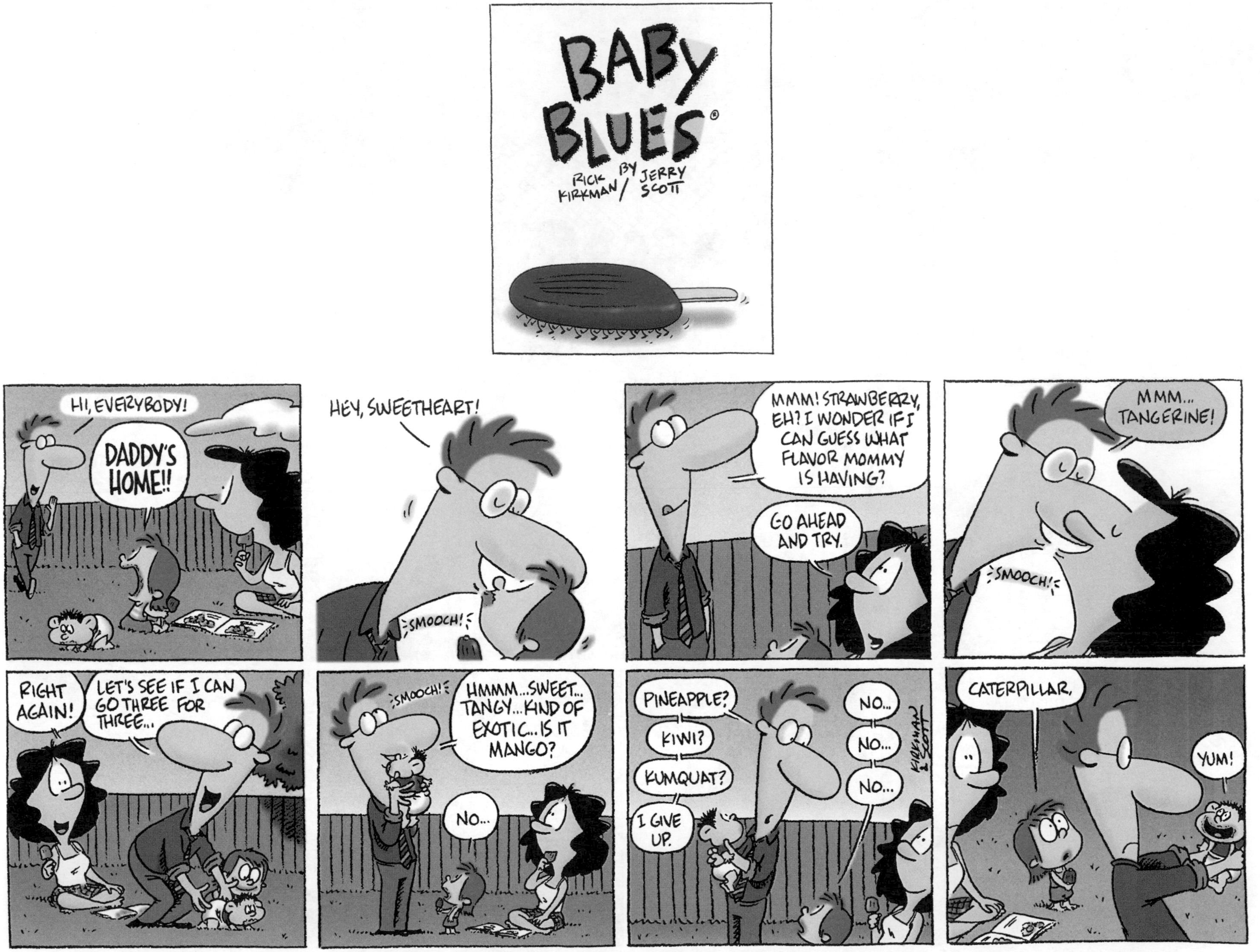
BABY BLUES®
BY RICK KIRKMAN / JERRY SCOTT
HI, EVERYBODY!
DADDY'S HOME!!
HEY, SWEETHEART!
SMOOCH!
MMM! STRAWBERRY, EH? I WONDER IF I CAN GUESS WHAT FLAVOR MOMMY IS HAVING?
GO AHEAD AND TRY.
MMM... TANGERINE!
SMOOCH!
RIGHT AGAIN!
LET'S SEE IF I CAN GO THREE FOR THREE...
SMOOCH!
HMMM...SWEET... TANGY...KIND OF EXOTIC...IS IT MANGO?
NO...
PINEAPPLE?
NO...
KIWI?
NO...
KUMQUAT?
NO...
I GIVE UP.
KIRKMAN & SCOTT
CATERPILLAR.
YUM!

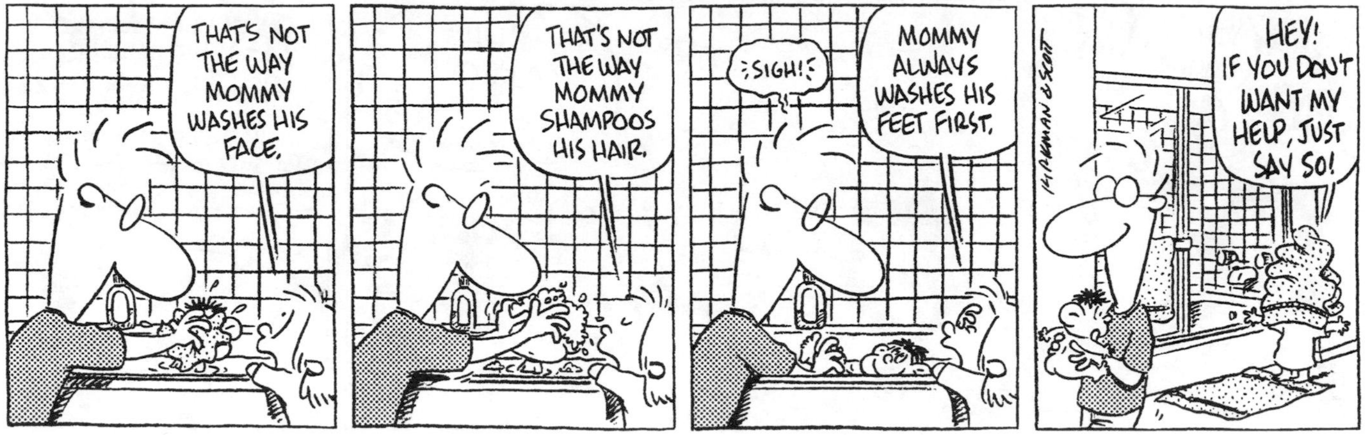
THAT'S NOT THE WAY MOMMY WASHES HIS FACE.
THAT'S NOT THE WAY MOMMY SHAMPOOS HIS HAIR.
SIGH!
MOMMY ALWAYS WASHES HIS FEET FIRST.
HEY! IF YOU DON'T WANT MY HELP, JUST SAY SO!

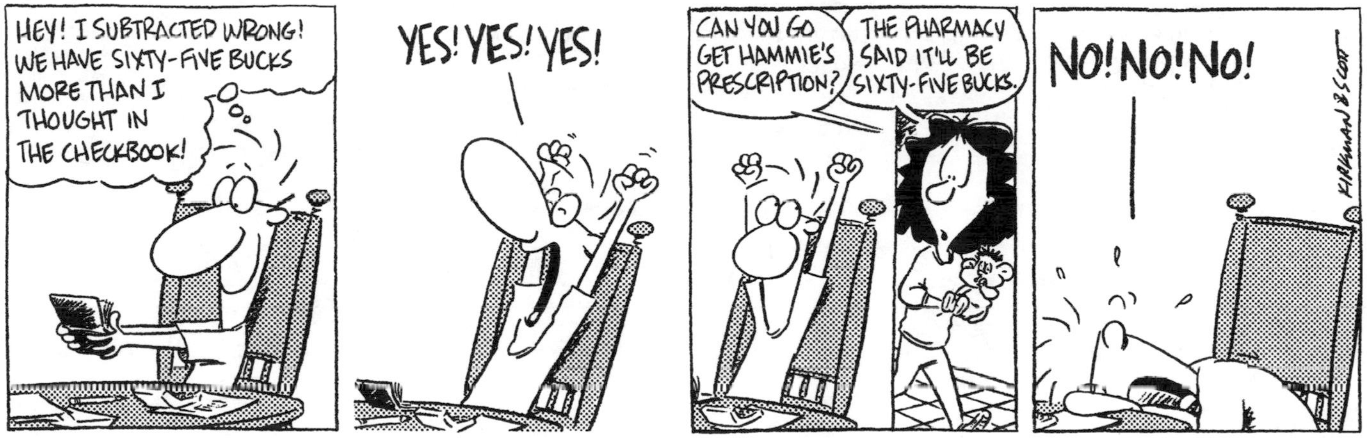
HEY! I SUBTRACTED WRONG! WE HAVE SIXTY-FIVE BUCKS MORE THAN I THOUGHT IN THE CHECKBOOK!
YES! YES! YES!
CAN YOU GO GET HAMMIE'S PRESCRIPTION?
THE PHARMACY SAID IT'LL BE SIXTY-FIVE BUCKS.
NO! NO! NO!

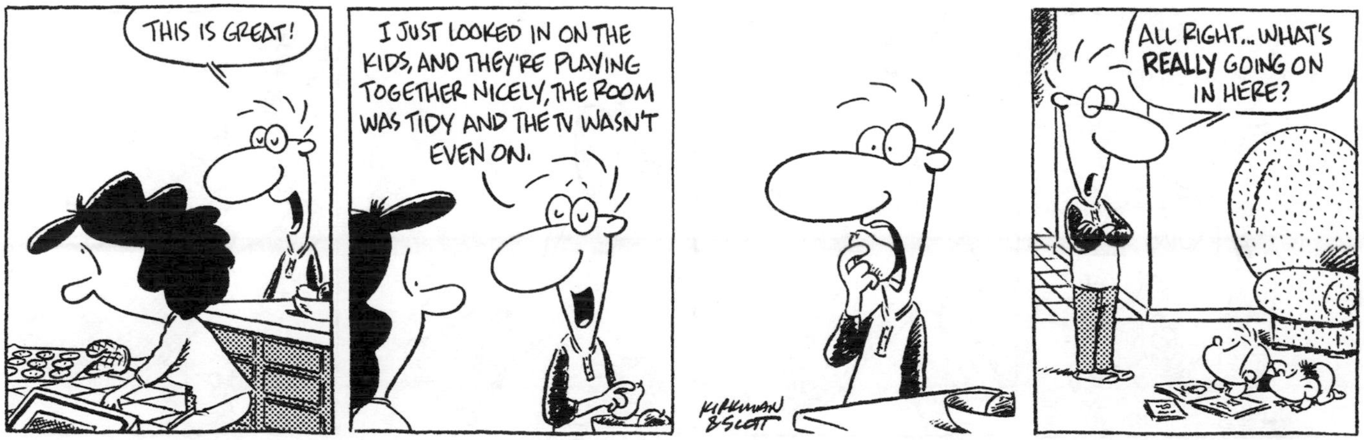
THIS IS GREAT!
I JUST LOOKED IN ON THE KIDS, AND THEY'RE PLAYING TOGETHER NICELY, THE ROOM WAS TIDY AND THE TV WASN'T EVEN ON.
ALL RIGHT... WHAT'S REALLY GOING ON IN HERE?

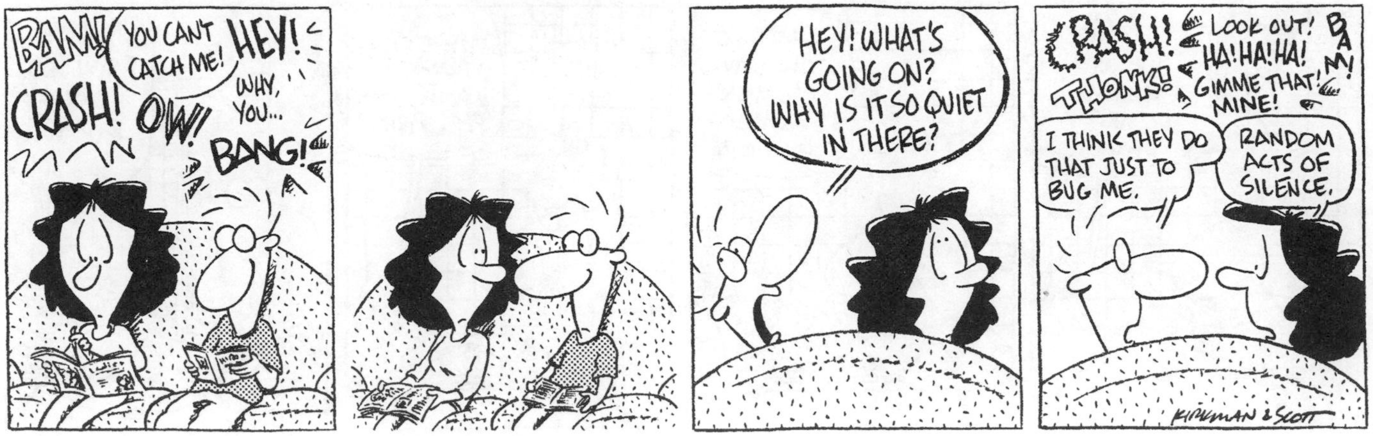
BAM!
YOU CAN'T CATCH ME!
HEY!
CRASH!
OW!
WHY, YOU...
BANG!
HEY! WHAT'S GOING ON? WHY IS IT SO QUIET IN THERE?
CRASH!
LOOK OUT!
HA! HA! HA!
BAM!
THONK!
GIMME THAT!
MINE!
I THINK THEY DO THAT JUST TO BUG ME.
RANDOM ACTS OF SILENCE.
KIRKMAN & SCOTT

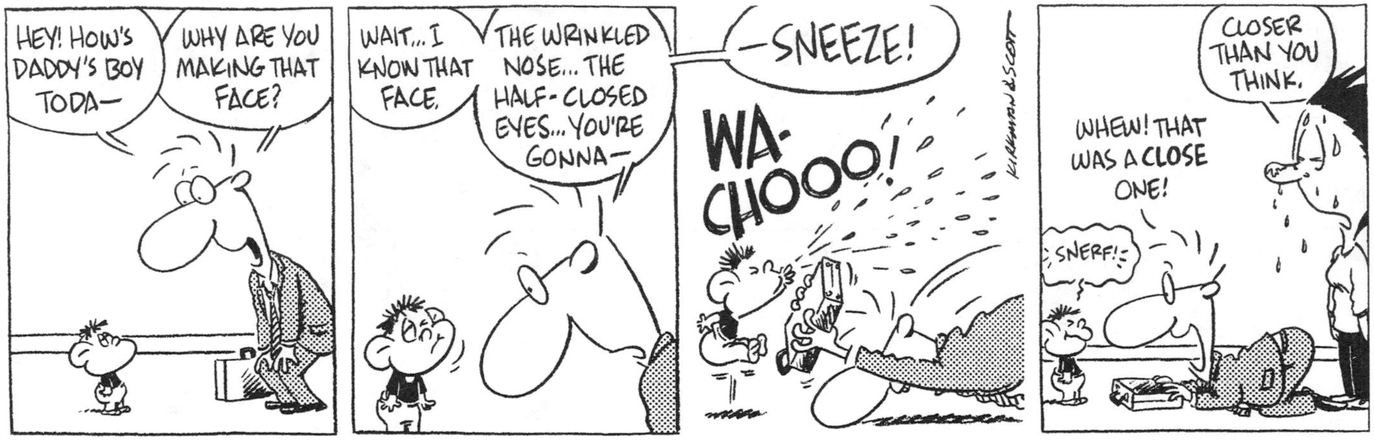
HEY! HOW'S DADDY'S BOY TODA—
WHY ARE YOU MAKING THAT FACE?
WAIT... I KNOW THAT FACE.
THE WRINKLED NOSE... THE HALF-CLOSED EYES... YOU'RE GONNA—
—SNEEZE!
WA-CHOOO!
KIRKMAN & SCOTT
WHEW! THAT WAS A CLOSE ONE!
SNERF!
CLOSER THAN YOU THINK.

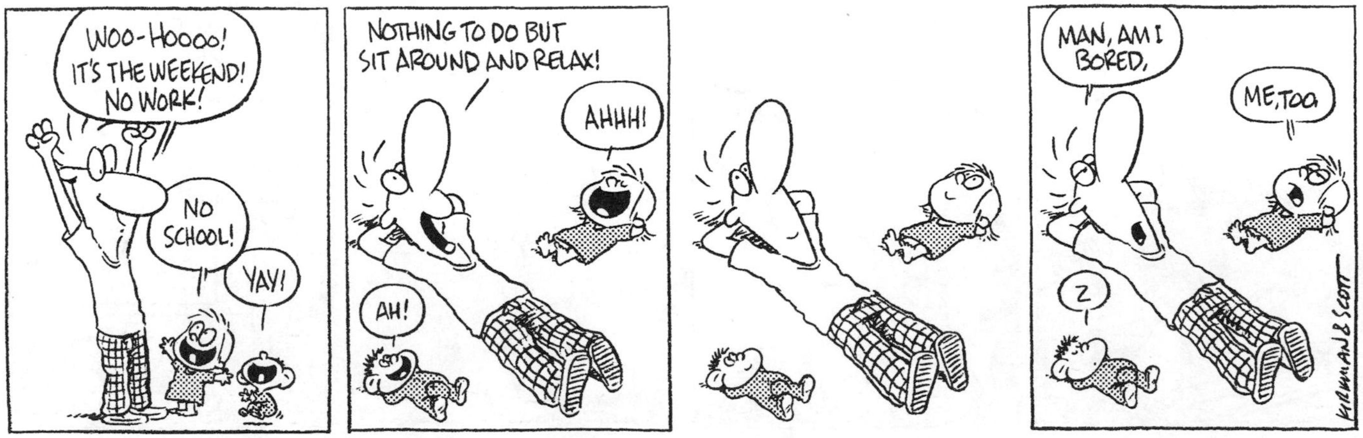
WOO-HOOOO! IT'S THE WEEKEND! NO WORK!
NO SCHOOL!
YAY!
NOTHING TO DO BUT SIT AROUND AND RELAX!
AHHH!
AH!
MAN, AM I BORED.
ME, TOO.
Z
KIRKMAN & SCOTT

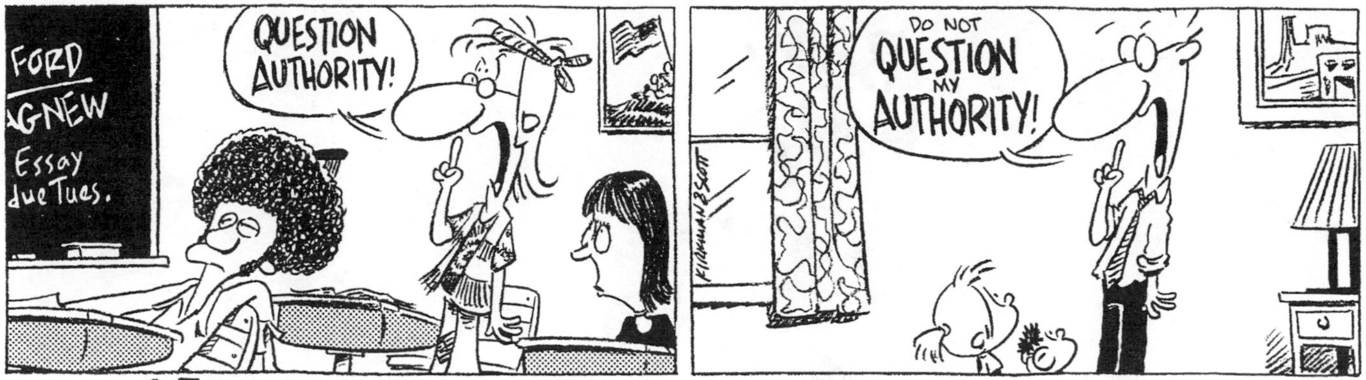
FORD
AGNEW
Essay due Tues.
QUESTION AUTHORITY!
KIRKMAN & SCOTT
DO NOT QUESTION MY AUTHORITY!

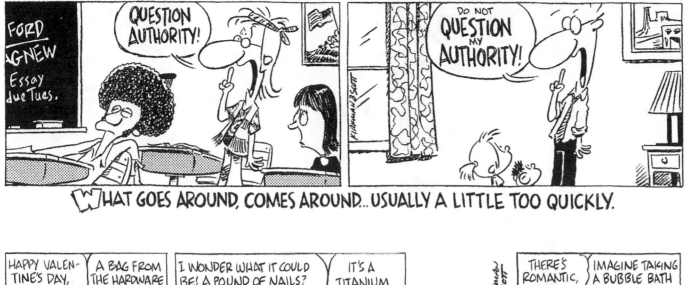

WHAT GOES AROUND, COMES AROUND... USUALLY A LITTLE TOO QUICKLY.

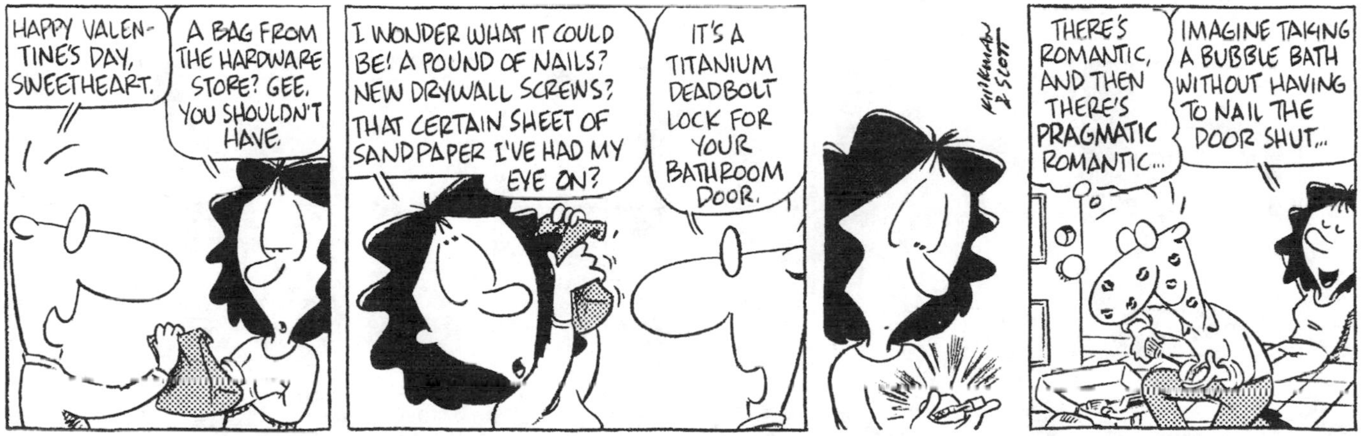
HAPPY VALENTINE'S DAY, SWEETHEART.
A BAG FROM THE HARDWARE STORE? GEE. YOU SHOULDN'T HAVE.
I WONDER WHAT IT COULD BE! A POUND OF NAILS? NEW DRYWALL SCREWS? THAT CERTAIN SHEET OF SANDPAPER I'VE HAD MY EYE ON?
IT'S A TITANIUM DEADBOLT LOCK FOR YOUR BATHROOM DOOR.
KIRKMAN & SCOTT
THERE'S ROMANTIC, AND THEN THERE'S PRAGMATIC ROMANTIC...
IMAGINE TAKING A BUBBLE BATH WITHOUT HAVING TO NAIL THE DOOR SHUT...

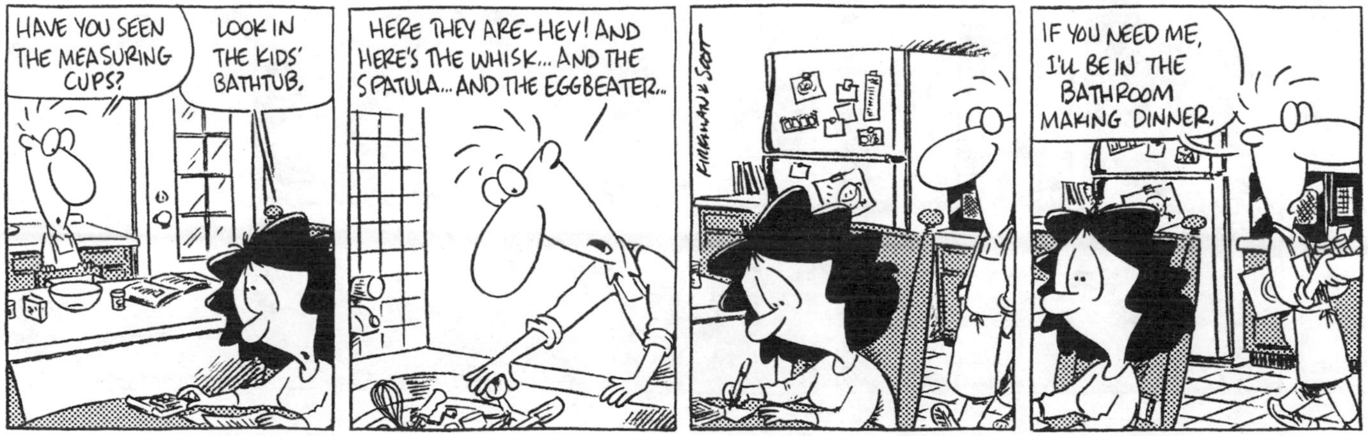
HAVE YOU SEEN THE MEASURING CUPS?
LOOK IN THE KIDS' BATHTUB.
HERE THEY ARE-HEY! AND HERE'S THE WHISK... AND THE SPATULA... AND THE EGGBEATER...
KIRKMAN & SCOTT
IF YOU NEED ME, I'LL BE IN THE BATHROOM MAKING DINNER.

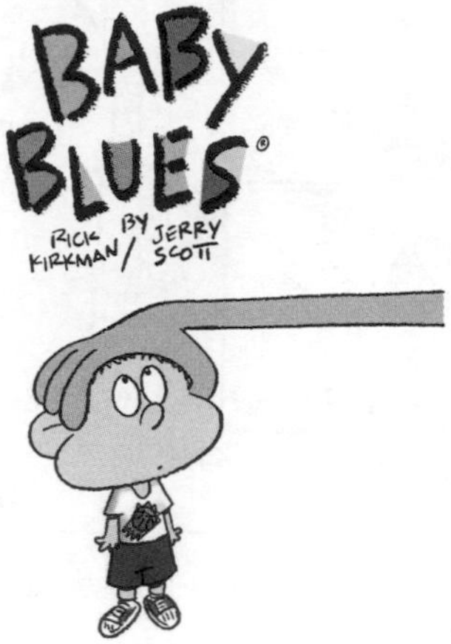
BABY BLUES®
RICK KIRKMAN / BY JERRY SCOTT

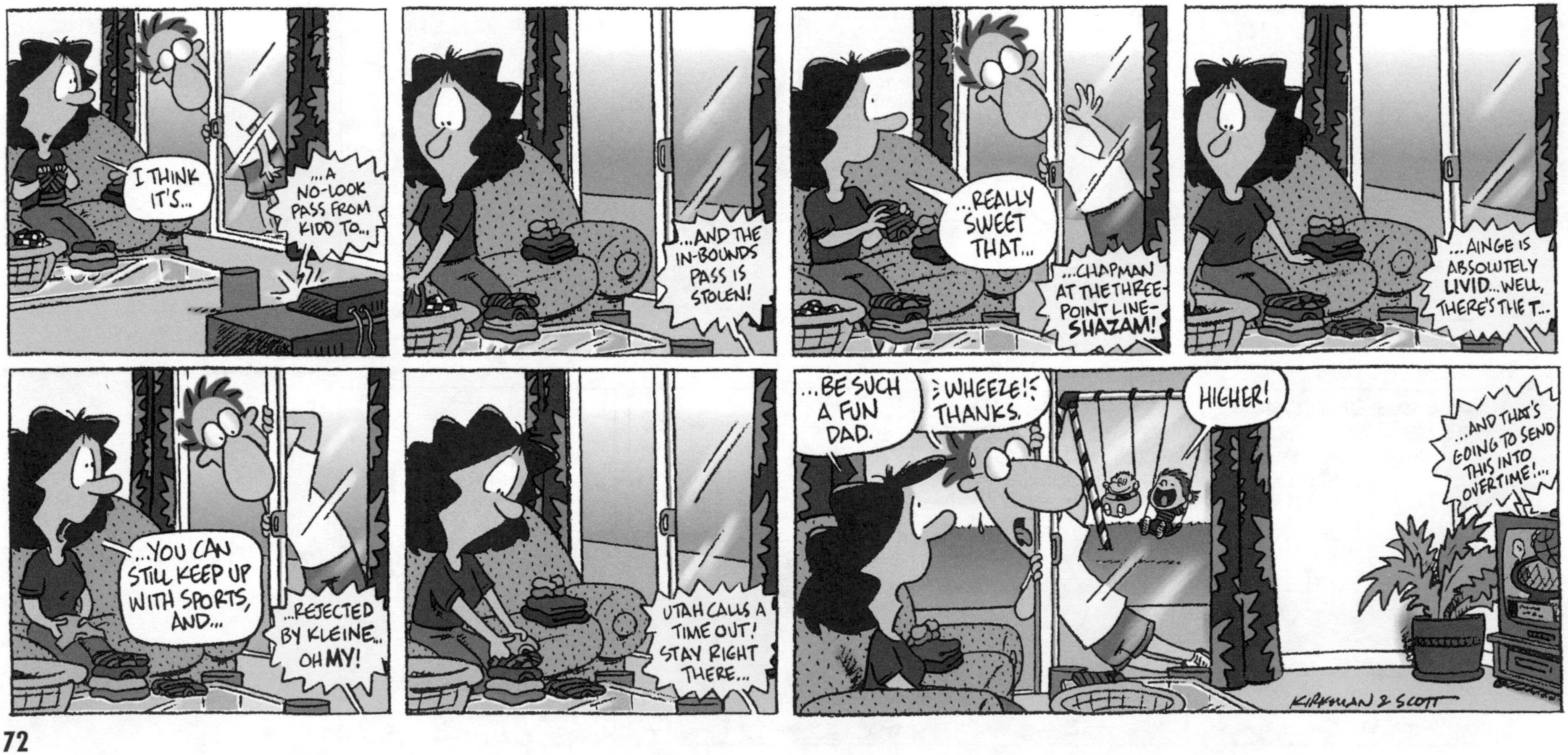
I THINK IT'S...
...A NO-LOOK PASS FROM KIDD TO...
...AND THE IN-BOUNDS PASS IS STOLEN!
...REALLY SWEET THAT...
...CHAPMAN AT THE THREE-POINT LINE-SHAZAM!
...AINGE IS ABSOLUTELY LIVID...WELL, THERE'S THE T...
...YOU CAN STILL KEEP UP WITH SPORTS, AND...
...REJECTED BY KLEINE... OH MY!
UTAH CALLS A TIME OUT! STAY RIGHT THERE...
...BE SUCH A FUN DAD.
WHEEZE! THANKS.
HIGHER!
...AND THAT'S GOING TO SEND THIS INTO OVERTIME!...
KIRKMAN & SCOTT

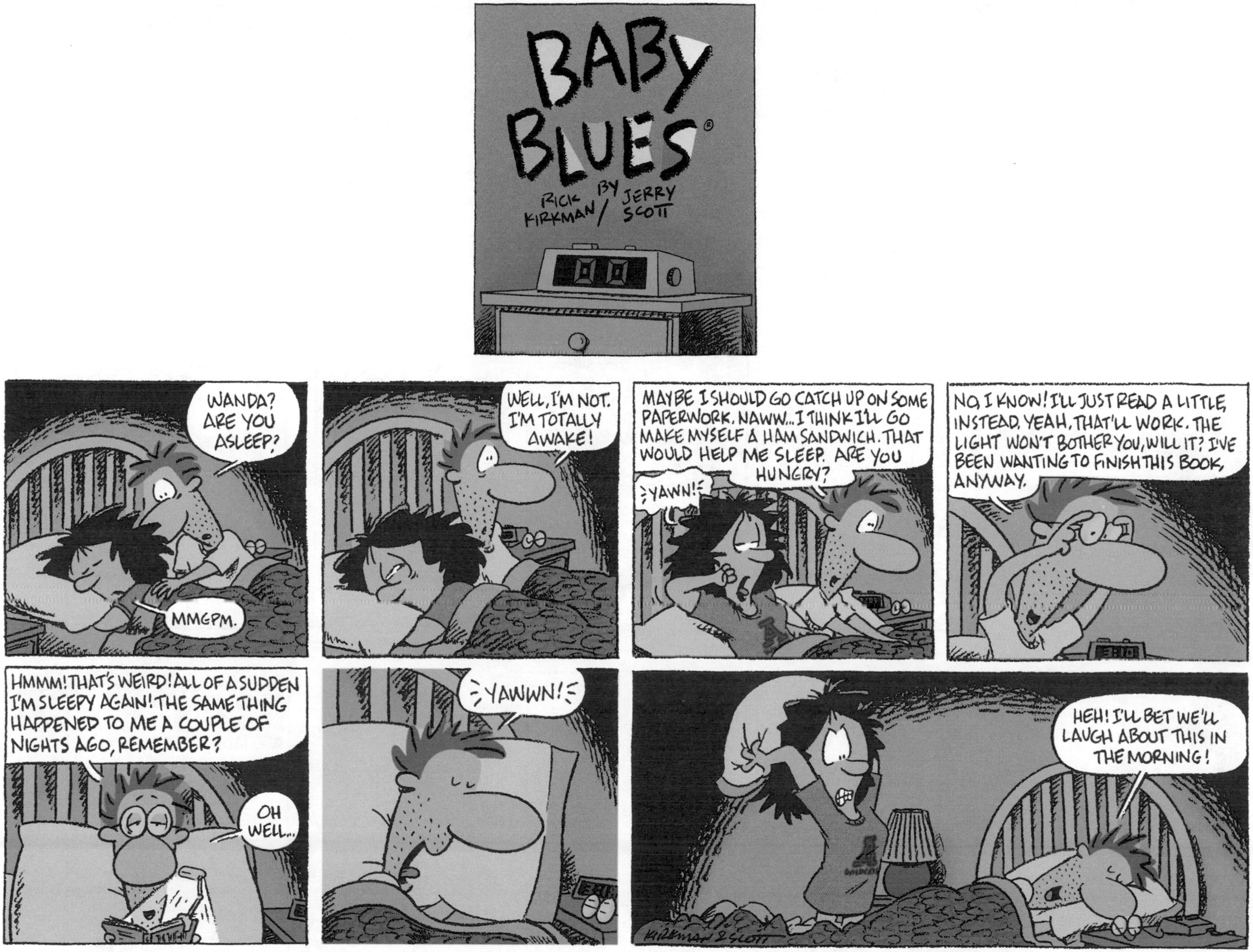
BABY BLUES®
BY RICK KIRKMAN / JERRY SCOTT
WANDA? ARE YOU ASLEEP?
MMGPM.
WELL, I'M NOT. I'M TOTALLY AWAKE!
MAYBE I SHOULD GO CATCH UP ON SOME PAPERWORK. NAWW... I THINK I'LL GO MAKE MYSELF A HAM SANDWICH. THAT WOULD HELP ME SLEEP. ARE YOU HUNGRY?
YAWN!
NO, I KNOW! I'LL JUST READ A LITTLE, INSTEAD. YEAH, THAT'LL WORK. THE LIGHT WON'T BOTHER YOU, WILL IT? I'VE BEEN WANTING TO FINISH THIS BOOK, ANYWAY.
HMMM! THAT'S WEIRD! ALL OF A SUDDEN I'M SLEEPY AGAIN! THE SAME THING HAPPENED TO ME A COUPLE OF NIGHTS AGO, REMEMBER?
OH WELL...
YAWWN!
HEH! I'LL BET WE'LL LAUGH ABOUT THIS IN THE MORNING!
KIRKMAN & SCOTT

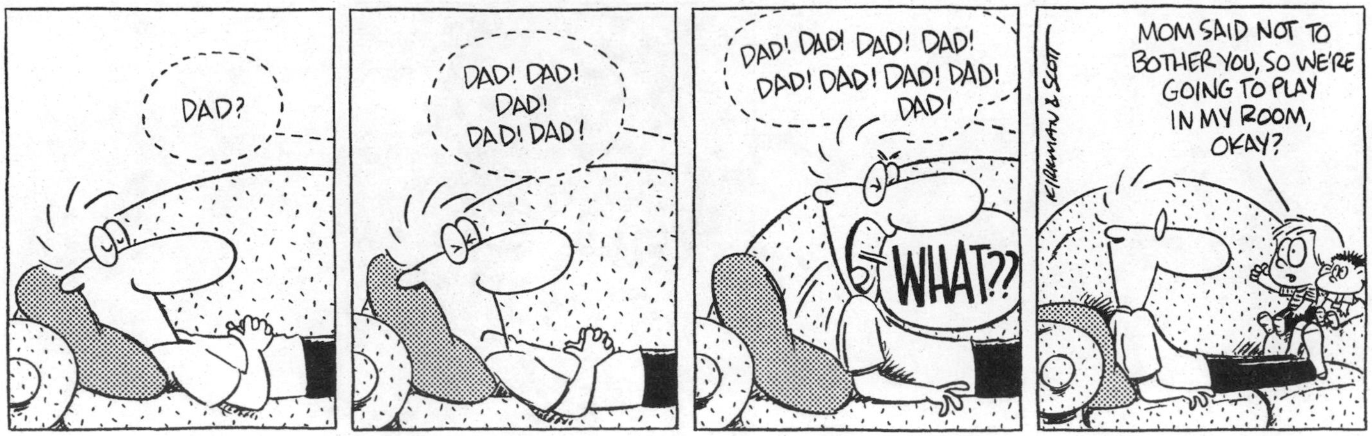
DAD?
DAD! DAD! DAD! DAD! DAD!
DAD! DAD! DAD! DAD! DAD! DAD! DAD! DAD! DAD!
WHAT??
KIRKMAN & SCOTT
MOM SAID NOT TO BOTHER YOU, SO WE'RE GOING TO PLAY IN MY ROOM, OKAY?

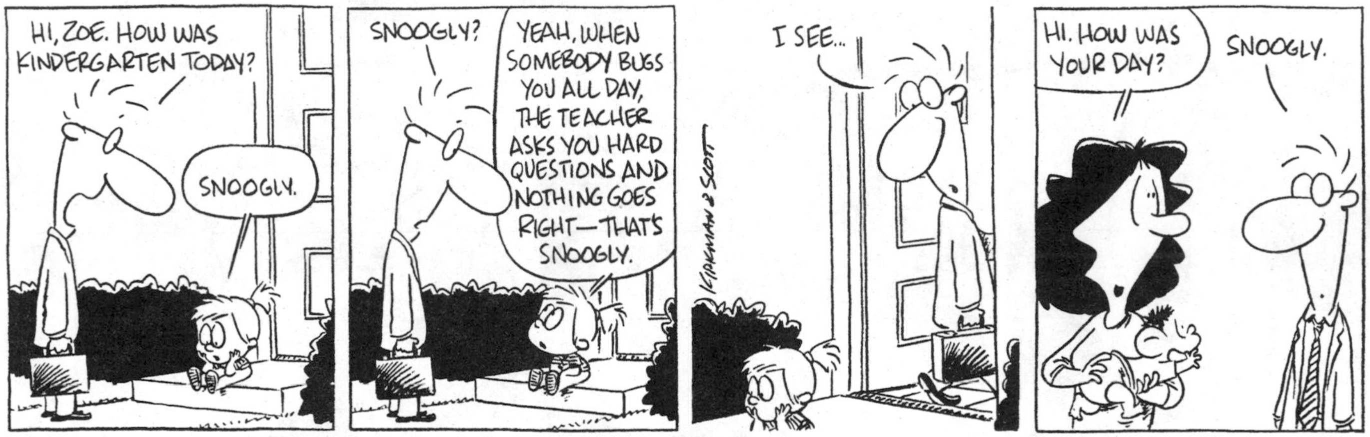
HI, ZOE. HOW WAS KINDERGARTEN TODAY?
SNOOGLY.
SNOOGLY?
YEAH, WHEN SOMEBODY BUGS YOU ALL DAY, THE TEACHER ASKS YOU HARD QUESTIONS AND NOTHING GOES RIGHT—THAT'S SNOOGLY.
KIRKMAN & SCOTT
I SEE...
HI. HOW WAS YOUR DAY?
SNOOGLY.

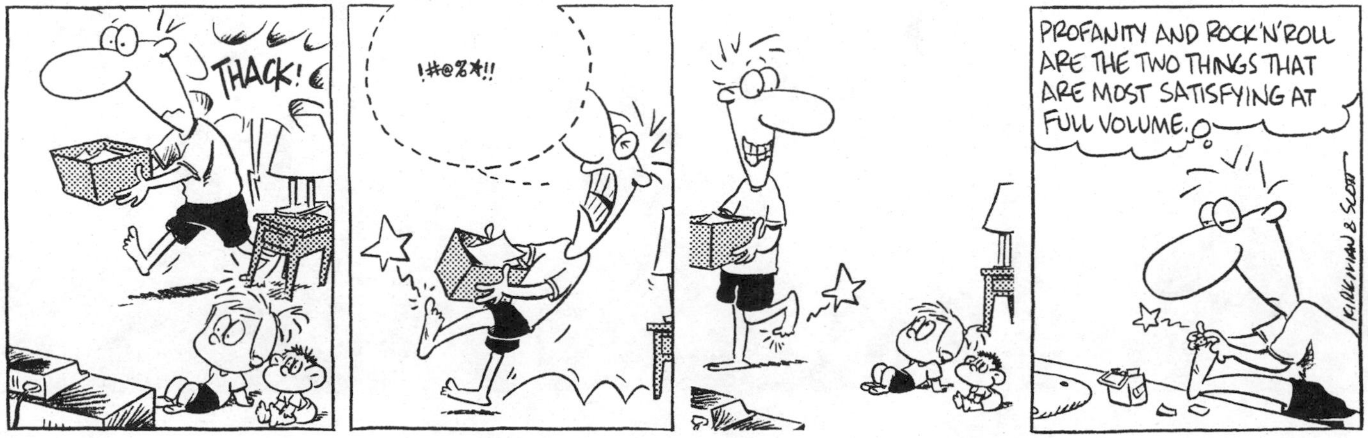
THACK!
!#@%*!!
PROFANITY AND ROCK'N'ROLL ARE THE TWO THINGS THAT ARE MOST SATISFYING AT FULL VOLUME.
KIRKMAN & SCOTT

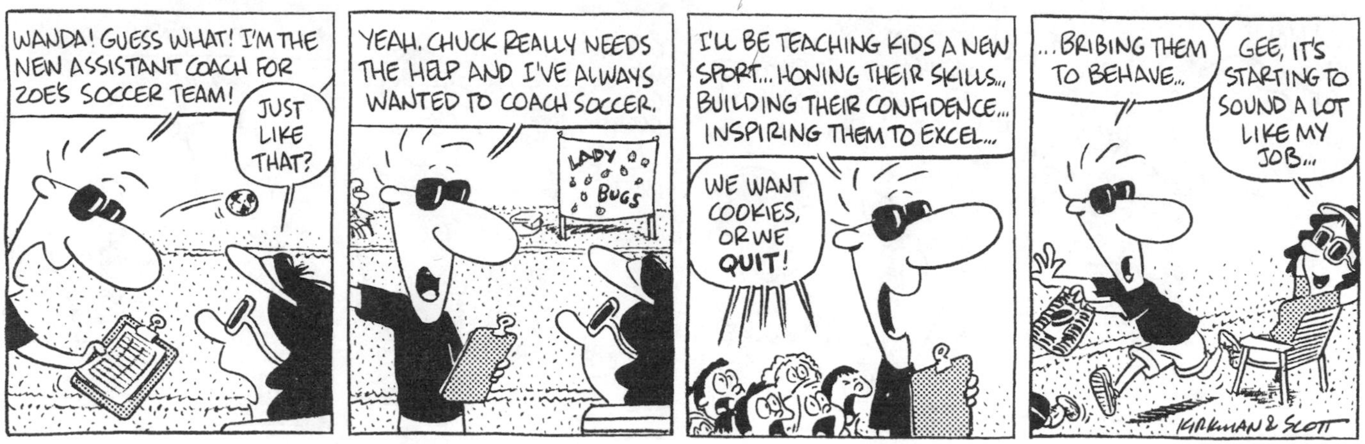
WANDA! GUESS WHAT! I'M THE NEW ASSISTANT COACH FOR ZOE'S SOCCER TEAM!
JUST LIKE THAT?
YEAH. CHUCK REALLY NEEDS THE HELP AND I'VE ALWAYS WANTED TO COACH SOCCER.
LADY BUGS
I'LL BE TEACHING KIDS A NEW SPORT... HONING THEIR SKILLS... BUILDING THEIR CONFIDENCE... INSPIRING THEM TO EXCEL...
WE WANT COOKIES, OR WE **QUIT**!
...BRIBING THEM TO BEHAVE...
GEE, IT'S STARTING TO SOUND A LOT LIKE MY JOB...
KIRKMAN & SCOTT

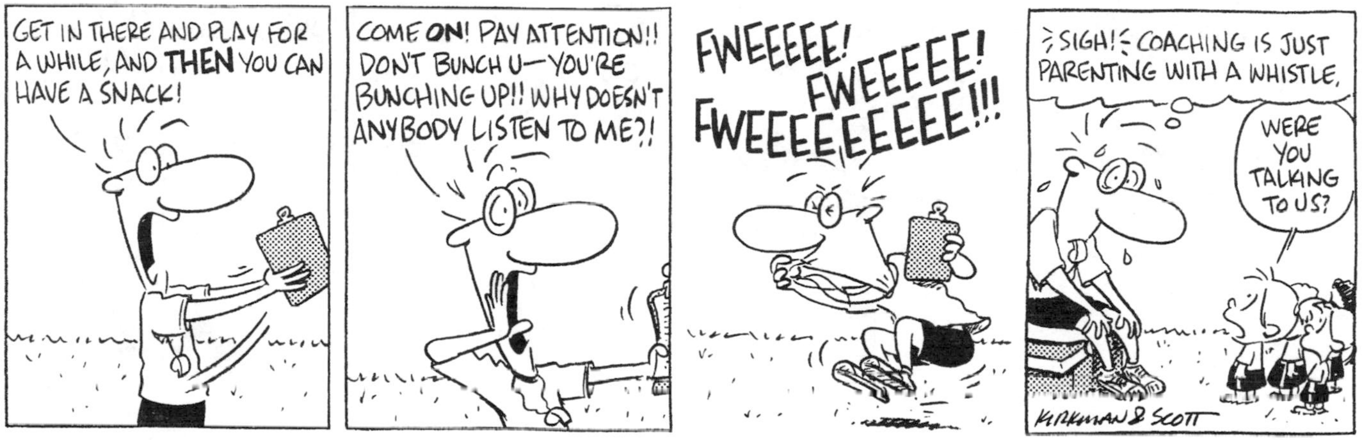
GET IN THERE AND PLAY FOR A WHILE, AND **THEN** YOU CAN HAVE A SNACK!
COME **ON**! PAY ATTENTION!! DON'T BUNCH U—YOU'RE BUNCHING UP!! WHY DOESN'T ANYBODY LISTEN TO ME?!
FWEEEEE! FWEEEEE! FWEEEEEEEEE!!!
SIGH! COACHING IS JUST PARENTING WITH A WHISTLE.
WERE YOU TALKING TO US?
KIRKMAN & SCOTT

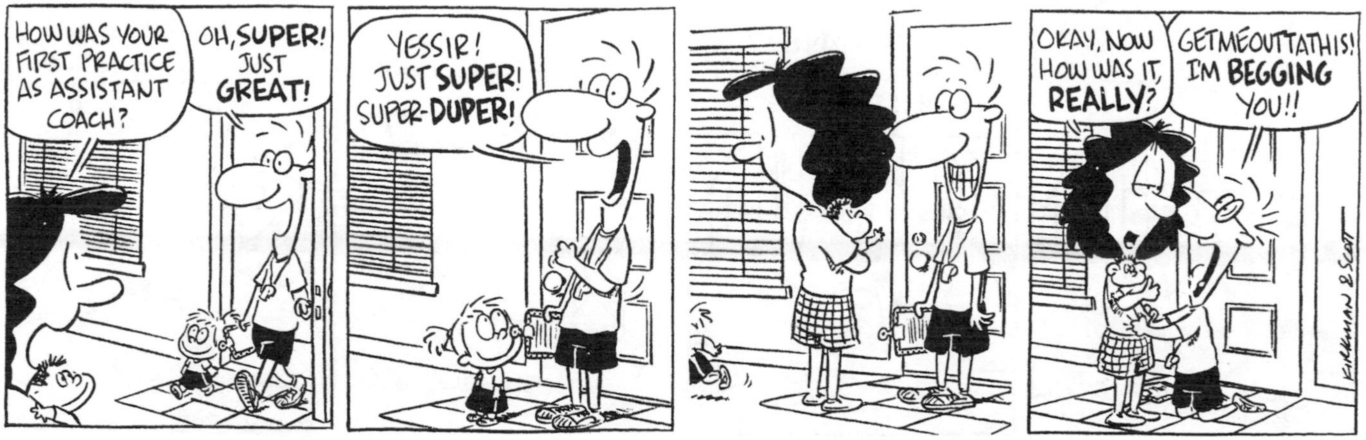
HOW WAS YOUR FIRST PRACTICE AS ASSISTANT COACH?
OH, **SUPER**! JUST **GREAT**!
YESSIR! JUST **SUPER**! SUPER-**DUPER**!
OKAY, NOW HOW WAS IT, **REALLY**?
GETMEOUTTATHIS! I'M **BEGGING** YOU!!
KIRKMAN & SCOTT

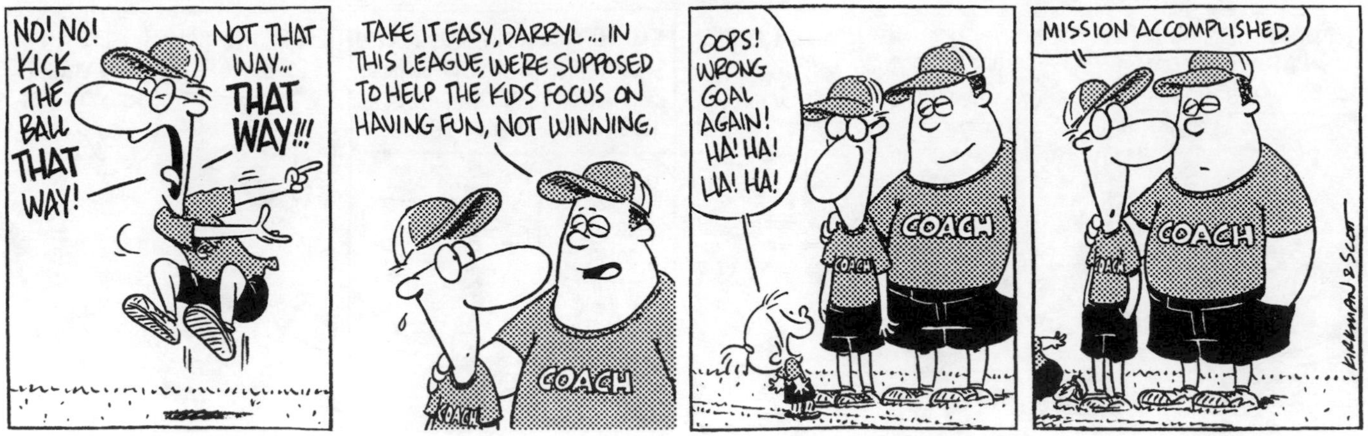

NO! NO! KICK THE BALL THAT WAY!
NOT THAT WAY... THAT WAY!!!
TAKE IT EASY, DARRYL... IN THIS LEAGUE, WE'RE SUPPOSED TO HELP THE KIDS FOCUS ON HAVING FUN, NOT WINNING.
COACH
COACH
OOPS! WRONG GOAL AGAIN! HA! HA! HA! HA!
COACH
COACH
MISSION ACCOMPLISHED.
COACH
KIRKMAN & SCOTT

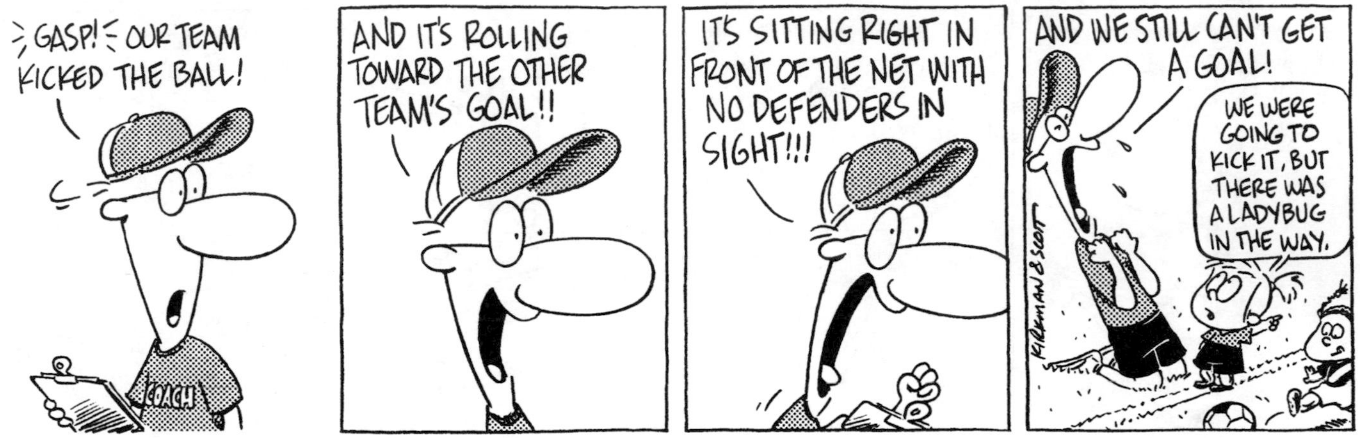

GASP! OUR TEAM KICKED THE BALL!
COACH
AND IT'S ROLLING TOWARD THE OTHER TEAM'S GOAL!!
IT'S SITTING RIGHT IN FRONT OF THE NET WITH NO DEFENDERS IN SIGHT!!!
AND WE STILL CAN'T GET A GOAL!
WE WERE GOING TO KICK IT, BUT THERE WAS A LADYBUG IN THE WAY.
KIRKMAN & SCOTT

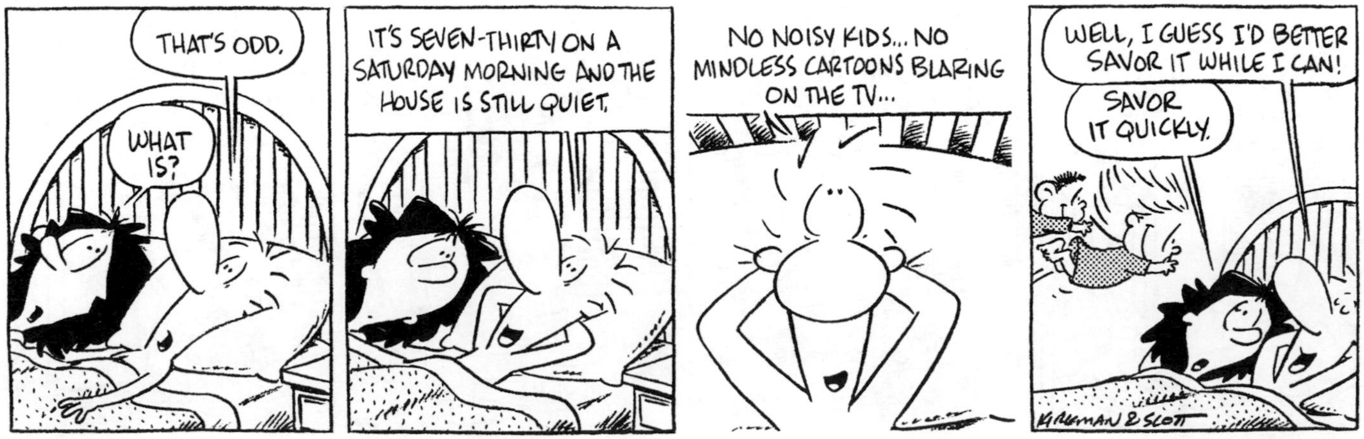

THAT'S ODD.
WHAT IS?
IT'S SEVEN-THIRTY ON A SATURDAY MORNING AND THE HOUSE IS STILL QUIET.
NO NOISY KIDS... NO MINDLESS CARTOONS BLARING ON THE TV...
WELL, I GUESS I'D BETTER SAVOR IT WHILE I CAN!
SAVOR IT QUICKLY.
KIRKMAN & SCOTT

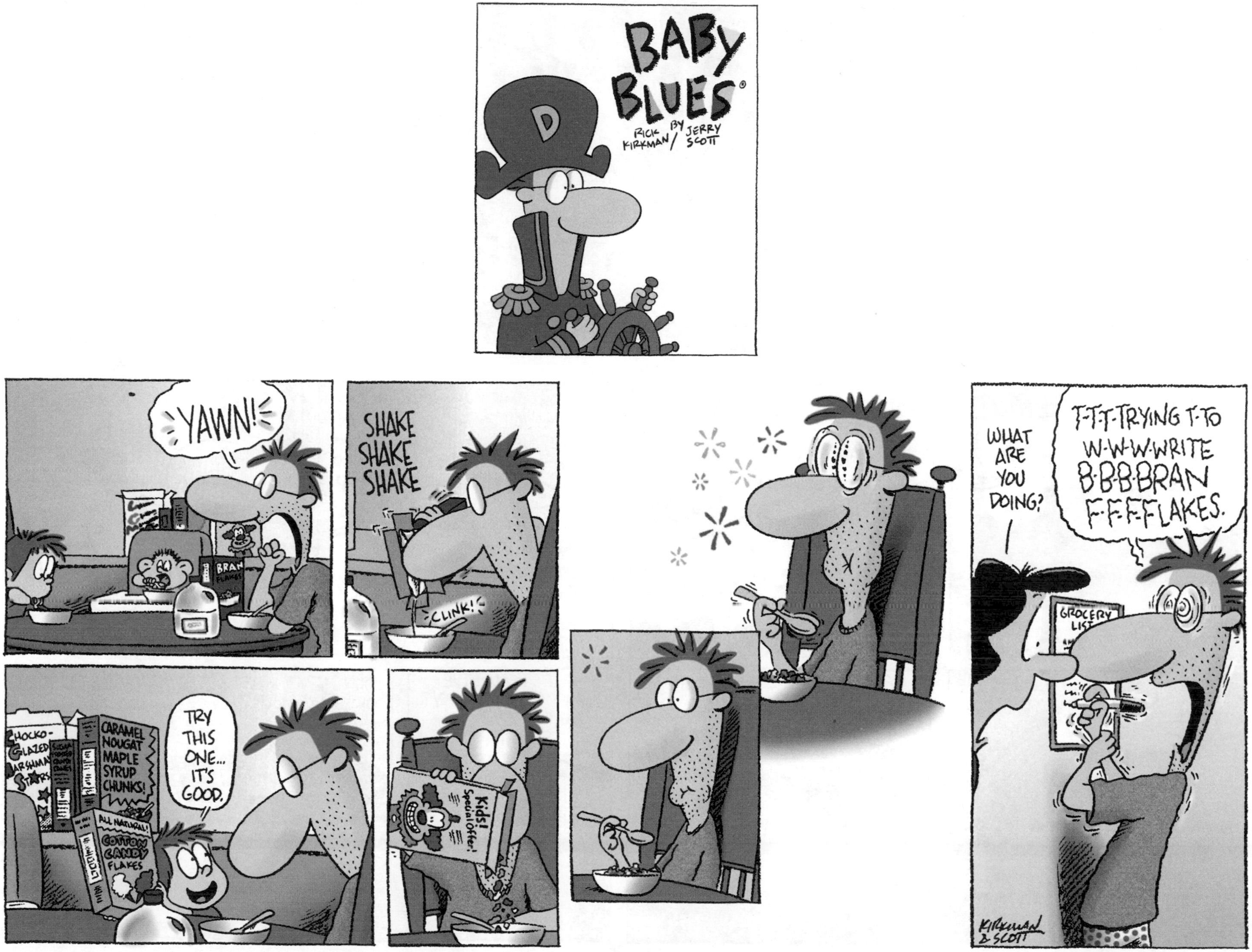
BABY BLUES®
BY RICK KIRKMAN / JERRY SCOTT
YAWN!
BRAN FLAKES
SHAKE SHAKE SHAKE
CLINK!
CARAMEL NOUGAT MAPLE SYRUP CHUNKS!
TRY THIS ONE... IT'S GOOD.
ALL NATURAL!
COTTON CANDY FLAKES
Kids! Special Offer!
WHAT ARE YOU DOING?
T-T-T-TRYING T-TO W-W-W-WRITE B-B-B-BRAN F-F-F-FLAKES.
GROCERY LIST
KIRKMAN & SCOTT

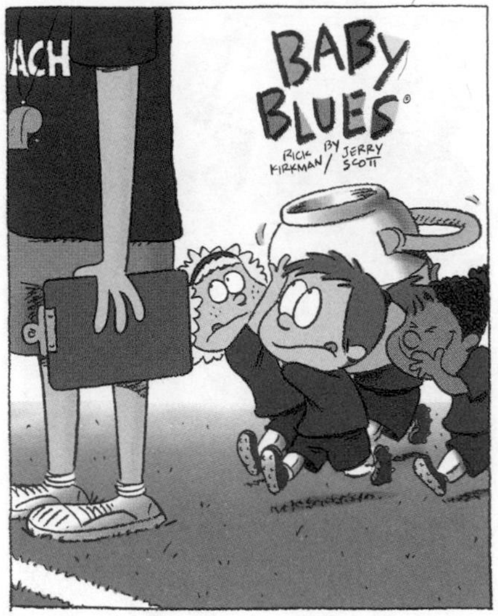
BABY BLUES®
BY RICK KIRKMAN / JERRY SCOTT

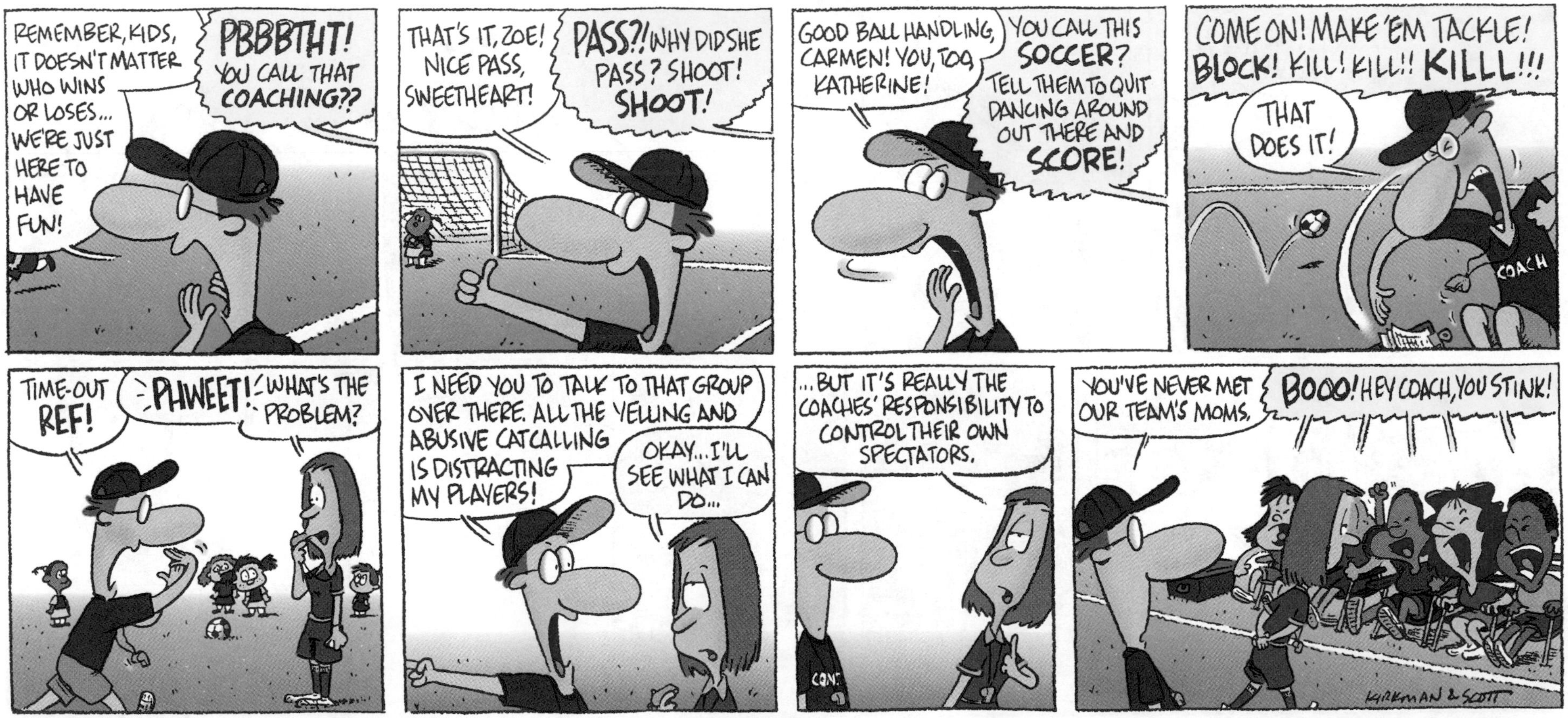
REMEMBER, KIDS, IT DOESN'T MATTER WHO WINS OR LOSES... WE'RE JUST HERE TO HAVE FUN!
PBBBTHT! YOU CALL THAT COACHING??
THAT'S IT, ZOE! NICE PASS, SWEETHEART!
PASS?! WHY DID SHE PASS? SHOOT! SHOOT!
GOOD BALL HANDLING, CARMEN! YOU, TOO, KATHERINE!
YOU CALL THIS SOCCER? TELL THEM TO QUIT DANCING AROUND OUT THERE AND SCORE!
COME ON! MAKE 'EM TACKLE! BLOCK! KILL! KILL!! KILLL!!!
THAT DOES IT!
COACH
TIME-OUT REF!
PHWEET!
WHAT'S THE PROBLEM?
I NEED YOU TO TALK TO THAT GROUP OVER THERE. ALL THE YELLING AND ABUSIVE CATCALLING IS DISTRACTING MY PLAYERS!
OKAY... I'LL SEE WHAT I CAN DO...
...BUT IT'S REALLY THE COACHES' RESPONSIBILITY TO CONTROL THEIR OWN SPECTATORS.
YOU'VE NEVER MET OUR TEAM'S MOMS.
BOOO! HEY COACH, YOU STINK!
KIRKMAN & SCOTT

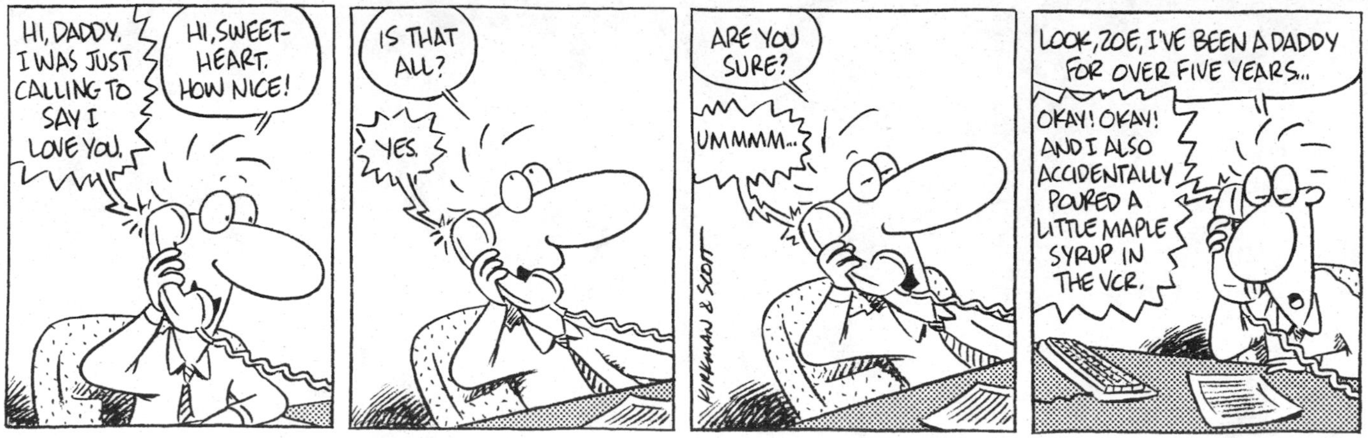
HI, DADDY. I WAS JUST CALLING TO SAY I LOVE YOU.
HI, SWEETHEART. HOW NICE!
IS THAT ALL?
YES.
ARE YOU SURE?
UMMMM...
KIRKMAN & SCOTT
LOOK, ZOE, I'VE BEEN A DADDY FOR OVER FIVE YEARS...
OKAY! OKAY! AND I ALSO ACCIDENTALLY POURED A LITTLE MAPLE SYRUP IN THE VCR.

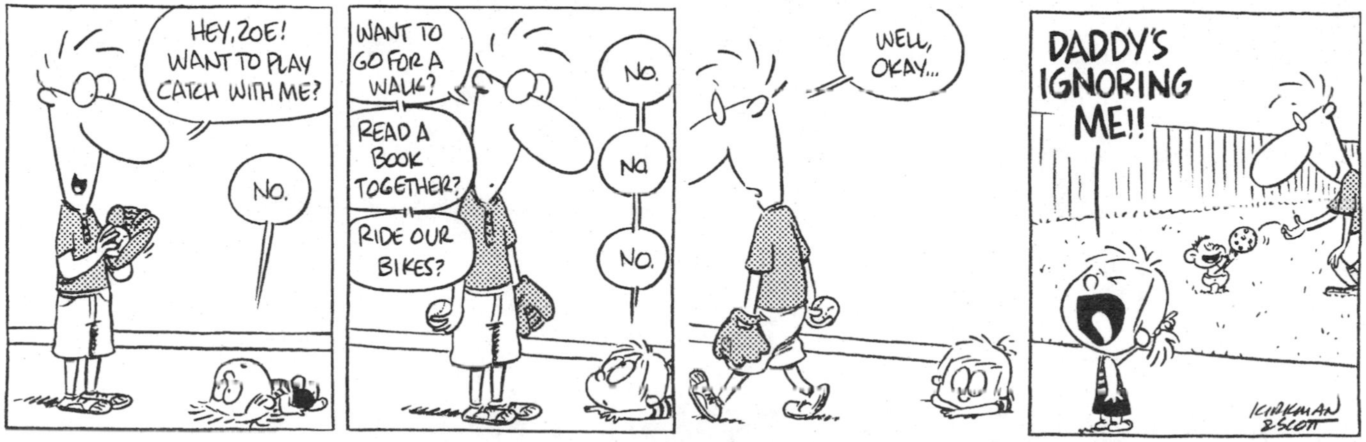
HEY, ZOE! WANT TO PLAY CATCH WITH ME?
NO.
WANT TO GO FOR A WALK?
NO.
READ A BOOK TOGETHER?
NO.
RIDE OUR BIKES?
NO.
WELL, OKAY...
DADDY'S IGNORING ME!!
KIRKMAN & SCOTT

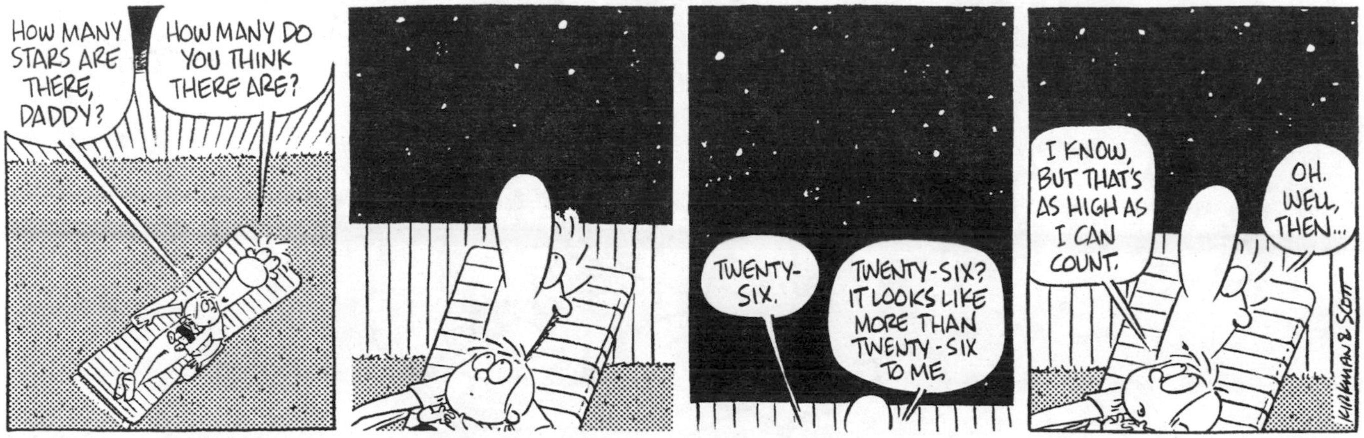
HOW MANY STARS ARE THERE, DADDY?
HOW MANY DO YOU THINK THERE ARE?
TWENTY-SIX.
TWENTY-SIX? IT LOOKS LIKE MORE THAN TWENTY-SIX TO ME.
I KNOW, BUT THAT'S AS HIGH AS I CAN COUNT.
OH. WELL, THEN...
KIRKMAN & SCOTT

PARENTING

"There are times when parenthood seems like nothing but feeding the mouth that bites you." —Peter de Vries

Parenting may not be the most glamorous job in the world, but it's definitely the most rewarding. BWAA-HA-HA-HA-HA-HA!! Get real. Being a ridiculously highly paid fat cat with stock options, bonuses, and a jet would be the most rewarding job in the world. What Darryl and Wanda and the rest of us who are parents have are the most important jobs in the world. Raising kids to become decent human beings is a full-time, all-consuming, extravagantly expensive, hilarious, heart-breaking, frustrating, and joyous experience that few of us would trade for anything. Well, almost anything. That jet sounded pretty good. . . .

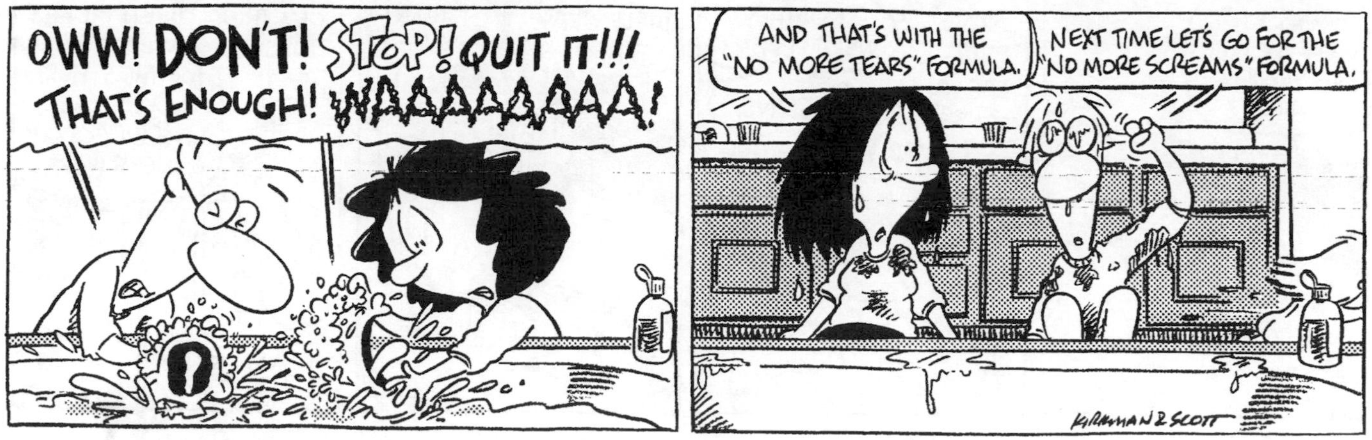
OWW! DON'T! STOP! QUIT IT!!! THAT'S ENOUGH! WAAAAAAAA!
AND THAT'S WITH THE "NO MORE TEARS" FORMULA.
NEXT TIME LET'S GO FOR THE "NO MORE SCREAMS" FORMULA.
KIRKMAN & SCOTT

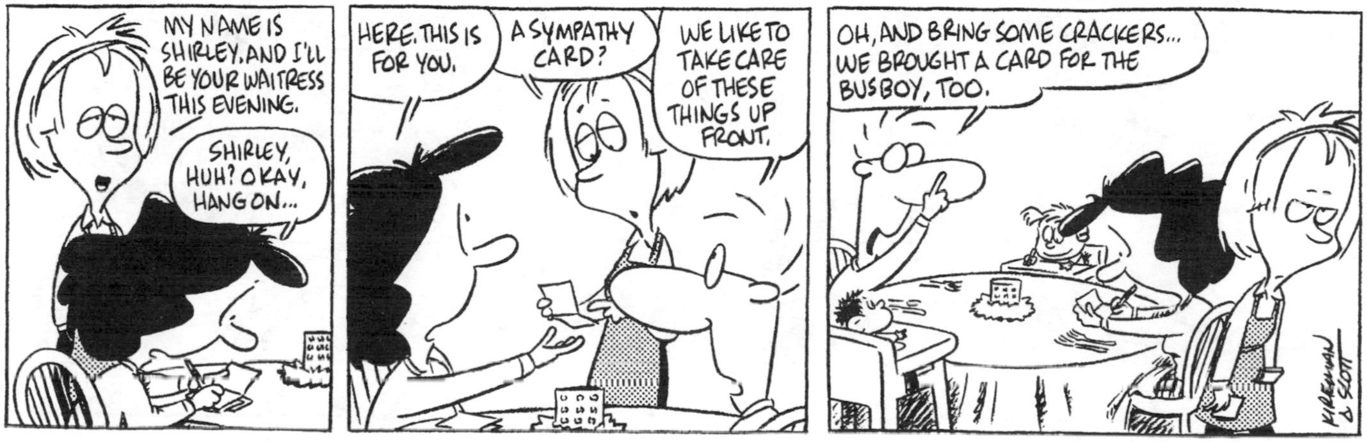
MY NAME IS SHIRLEY, AND I'LL BE YOUR WAITRESS THIS EVENING.
SHIRLEY, HUH? OKAY, HANG ON...
HERE. THIS IS FOR YOU.
A SYMPATHY CARD?
WE LIKE TO TAKE CARE OF THESE THINGS UP FRONT.
OH, AND BRING SOME CRACKERS... WE BROUGHT A CARD FOR THE BUSBOY, TOO.
KIRKMAN & SCOTT

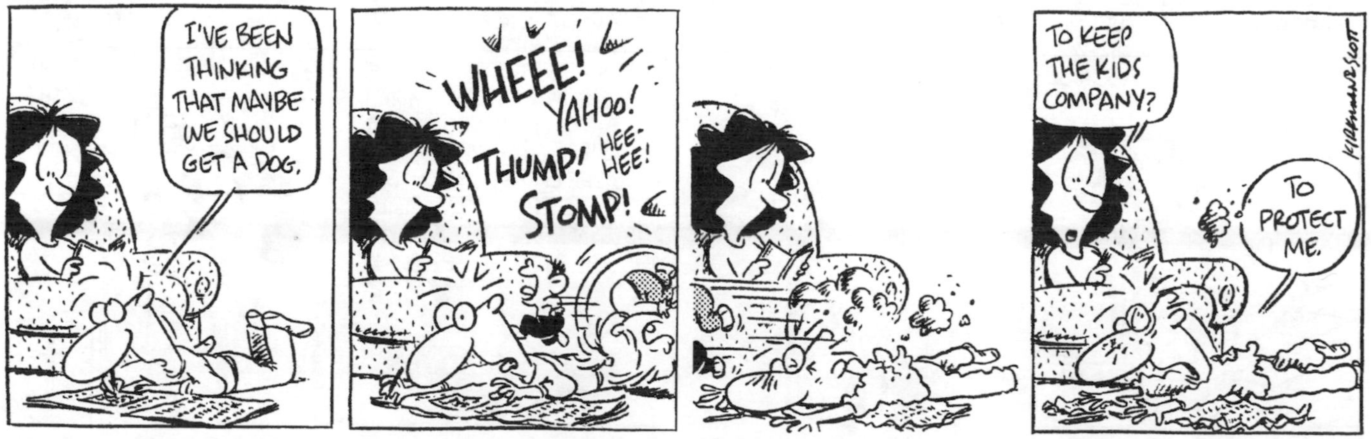
I'VE BEEN THINKING THAT MAYBE WE SHOULD GET A DOG.
WHEEE!
YAHOO!
THUMP!
HEE-HEE!
STOMP!
KIRKMAN & SCOTT
TO KEEP THE KIDS COMPANY?
TO PROTECT ME.

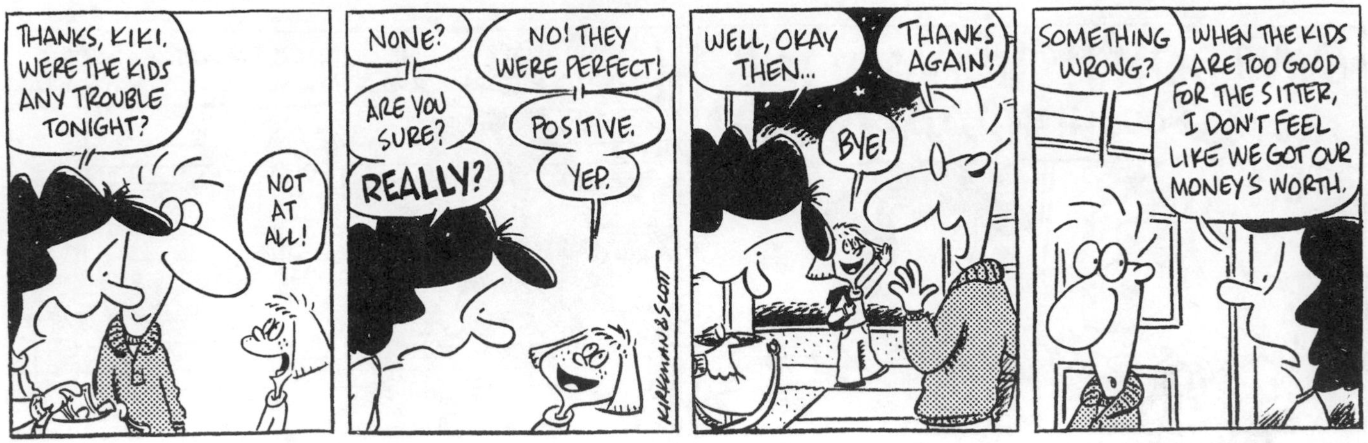
THANKS, KIKI. WERE THE KIDS ANY TROUBLE TONIGHT?
NOT AT ALL!
NONE?
NO! THEY WERE PERFECT!
ARE YOU SURE?
POSITIVE.
REALLY?
YEP.
KIRKMAN & SCOTT
WELL, OKAY THEN...
THANKS AGAIN!
BYE!
SOMETHING WRONG?
WHEN THE KIDS ARE TOO GOOD FOR THE SITTER, I DON'T FEEL LIKE WE GOT OUR MONEY'S WORTH.

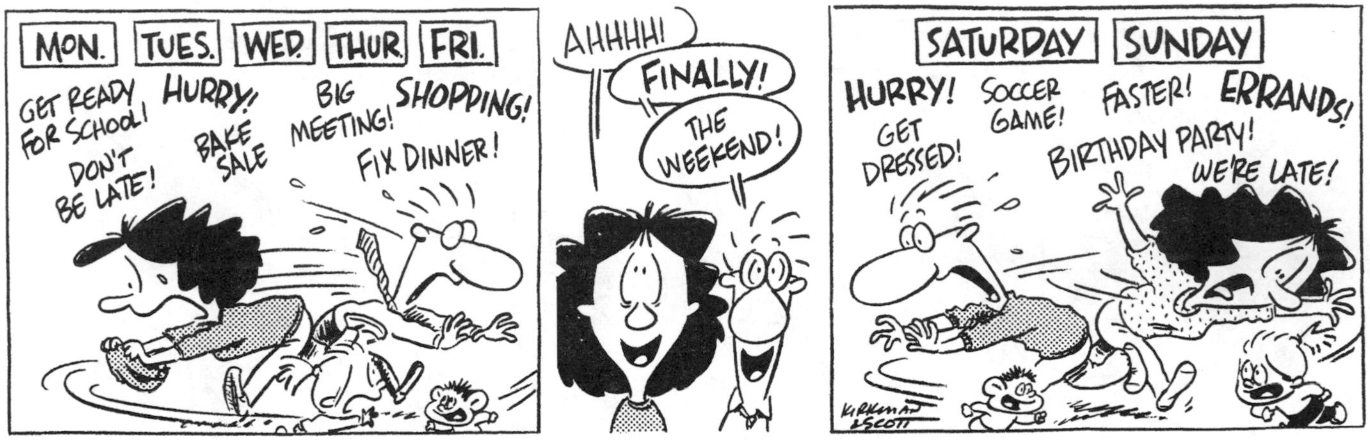
MON.
TUES.
WED.
THUR.
FRI.
GET READY FOR SCHOOL!
HURRY!
BIG MEETING!
SHOPPING!
DON'T BE LATE!
BAKE SALE
FIX DINNER!
AHHHH!
FINALLY!
THE WEEKEND!
SATURDAY
SUNDAY
HURRY!
SOCCER GAME!
FASTER!
ERRANDS!
GET DRESSED!
BIRTHDAY PARTY!
WE'RE LATE!
KIRKMAN & SCOTT

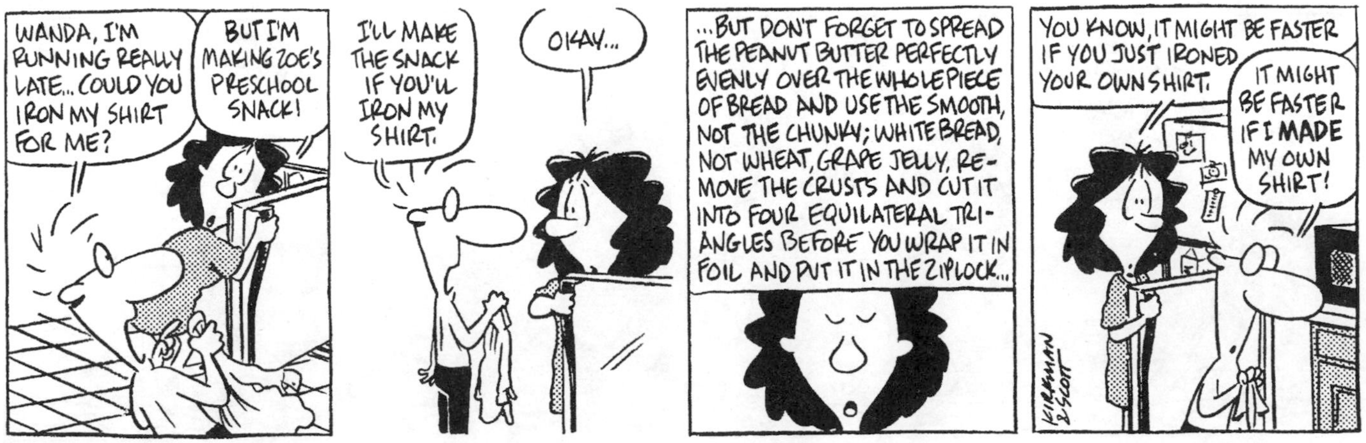
WANDA, I'M RUNNING REALLY LATE... COULD YOU IRON MY SHIRT FOR ME?
BUT I'M MAKING ZOE'S PRESCHOOL SNACK!
I'LL MAKE THE SNACK IF YOU'LL IRON MY SHIRT.
OKAY...
...BUT DON'T FORGET TO SPREAD THE PEANUT BUTTER PERFECTLY EVENLY OVER THE WHOLE PIECE OF BREAD AND USE THE SMOOTH, NOT THE CHUNKY; WHITE BREAD, NOT WHEAT, GRAPE JELLY, REMOVE THE CRUSTS AND CUT IT INTO FOUR EQUILATERAL TRIANGLES BEFORE YOU WRAP IT IN FOIL AND PUT IT IN THE ZIPLOCK...
YOU KNOW, IT MIGHT BE FASTER IF YOU JUST IRONED YOUR OWN SHIRT.
IT MIGHT BE FASTER IF I MADE MY OWN SHIRT!
KIRKMAN & SCOTT

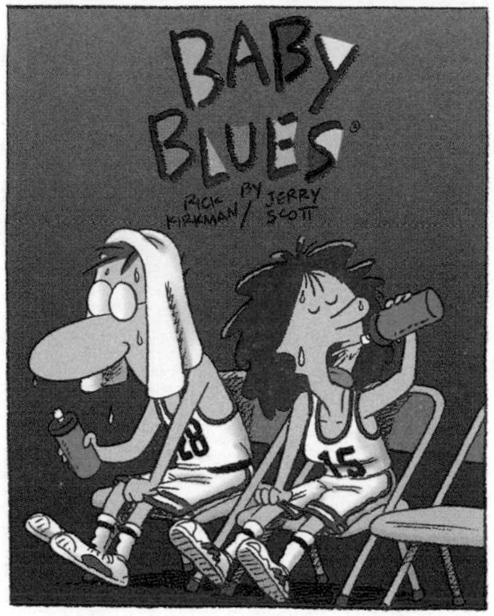
BABY BLUES®
BY RICK KIRKMAN / JERRY SCOTT

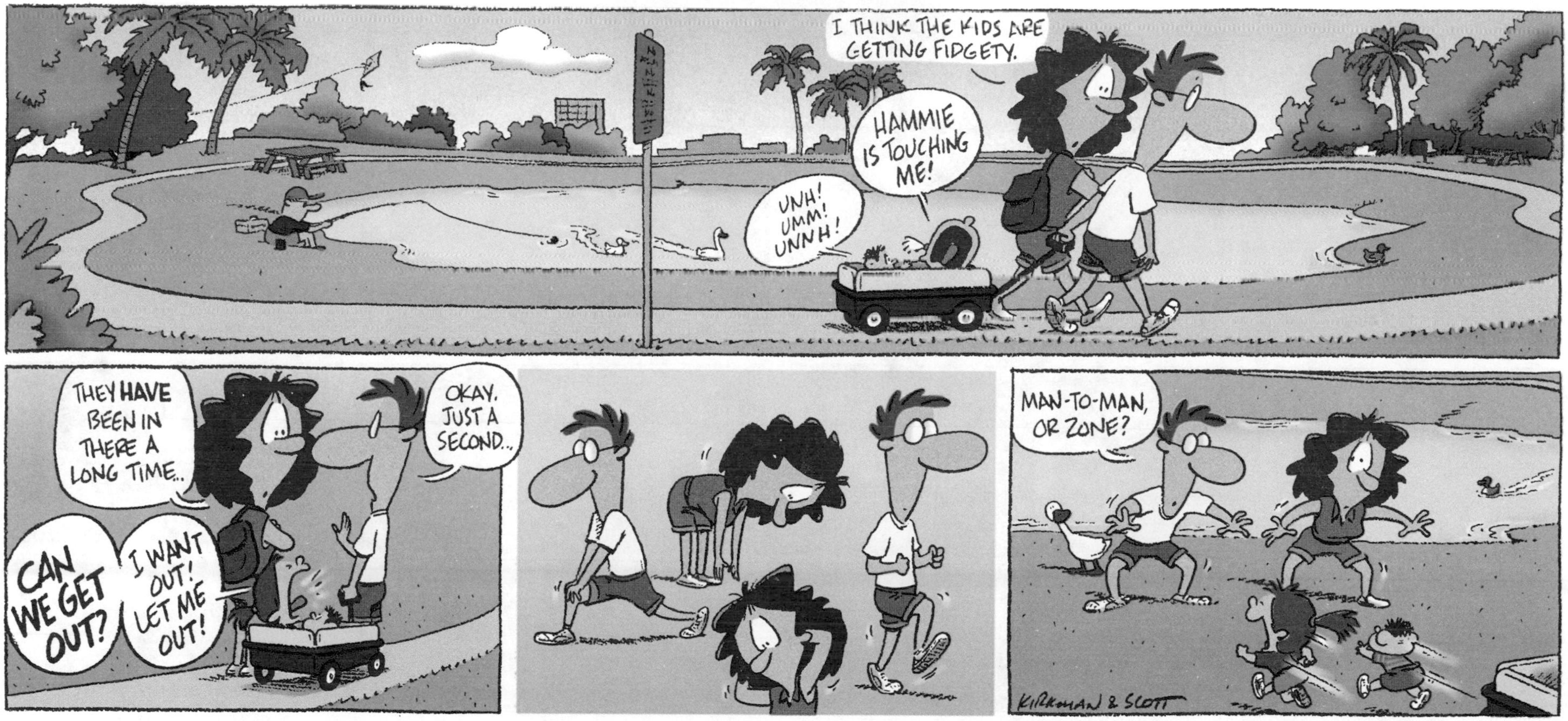
I THINK THE KIDS ARE GETTING FIDGETY.
HAMMIE IS TOUCHING ME!
UNH! UMM! UNNH!
THEY HAVE BEEN IN THERE A LONG TIME...
OKAY. JUST A SECOND...
CAN WE GET OUT?
I WANT OUT! LET ME OUT!
MAN-TO-MAN, OR ZONE?
KIRKMAN & SCOTT

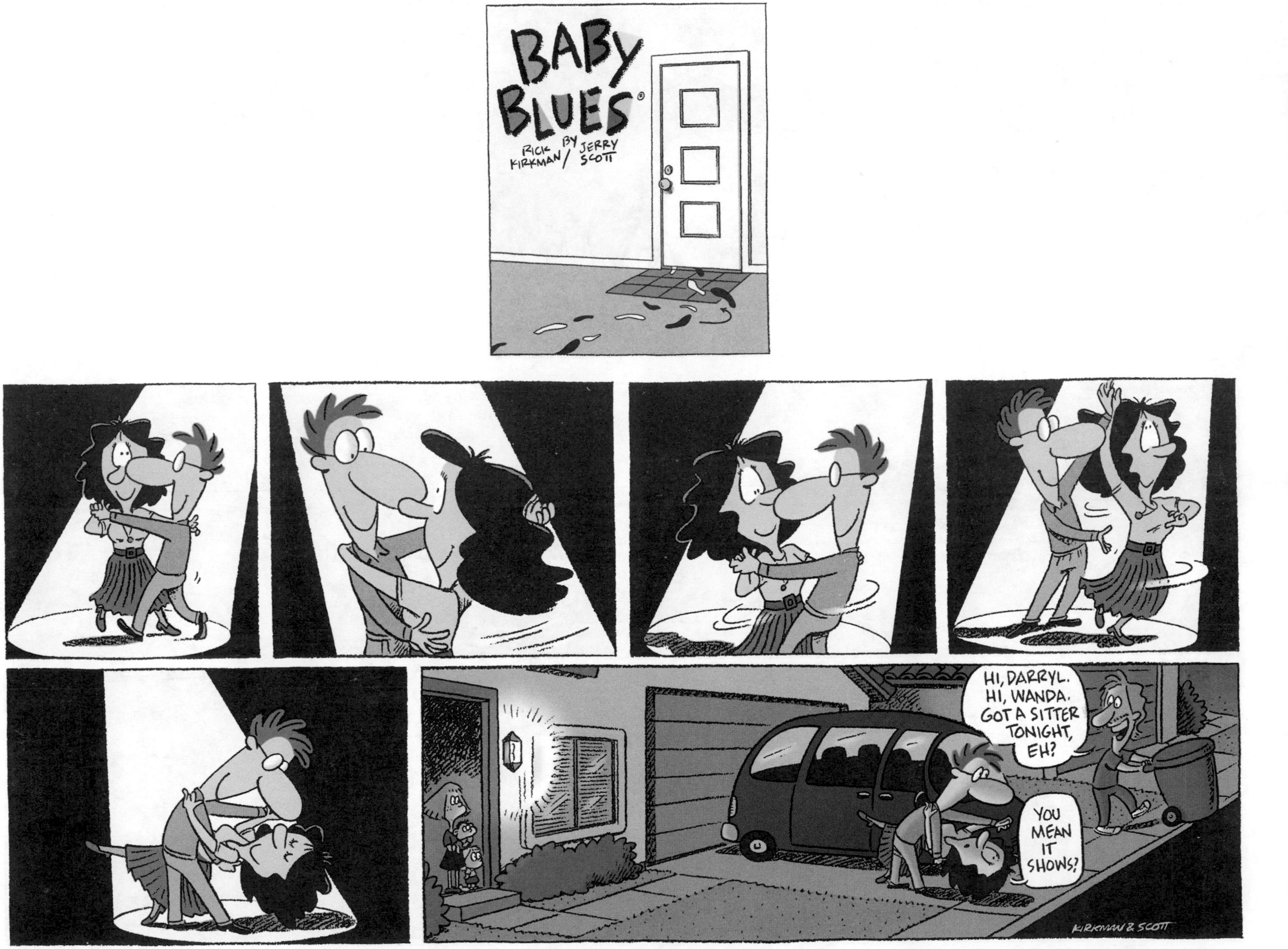
BABY BLUES®
BY RICK KIRKMAN / JERRY SCOTT
HI, DARRYL. HI, WANDA. GOT A SITTER TONIGHT, EH?
YOU MEAN IT SHOWS?
KIRKMAN & SCOTT

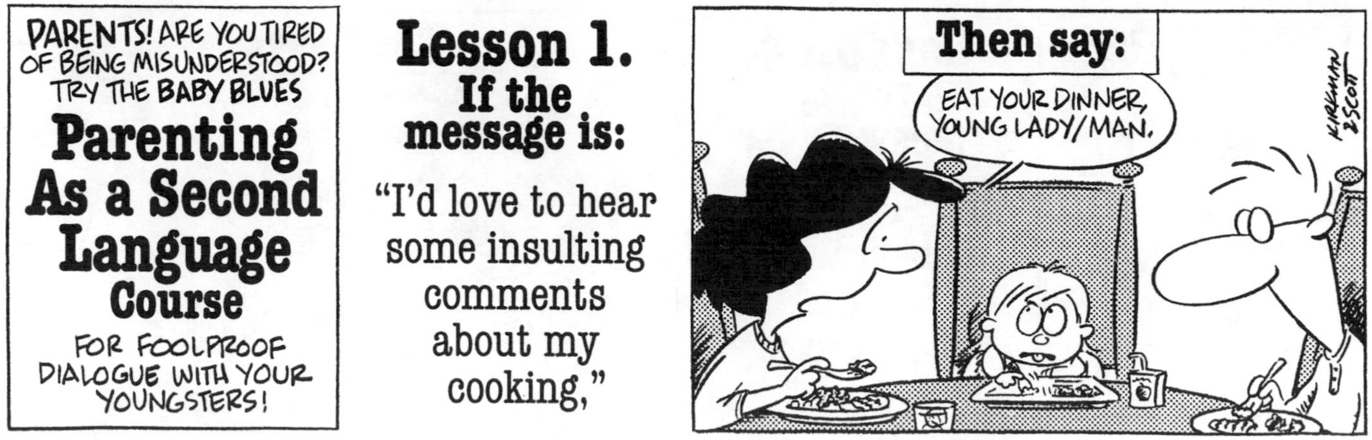
PARENTS! ARE YOU TIRED OF BEING MISUNDERSTOOD? TRY THE BABY BLUES
Parenting As a Second Language Course
FOR FOOLPROOF DIALOGUE WITH YOUR YOUNGSTERS!
Lesson 1.
If the message is:
"I'd love to hear some insulting comments about my cooking,"
Then say:
EAT YOUR DINNER, YOUNG LADY/MAN.
KIRKMAN & SCOTT

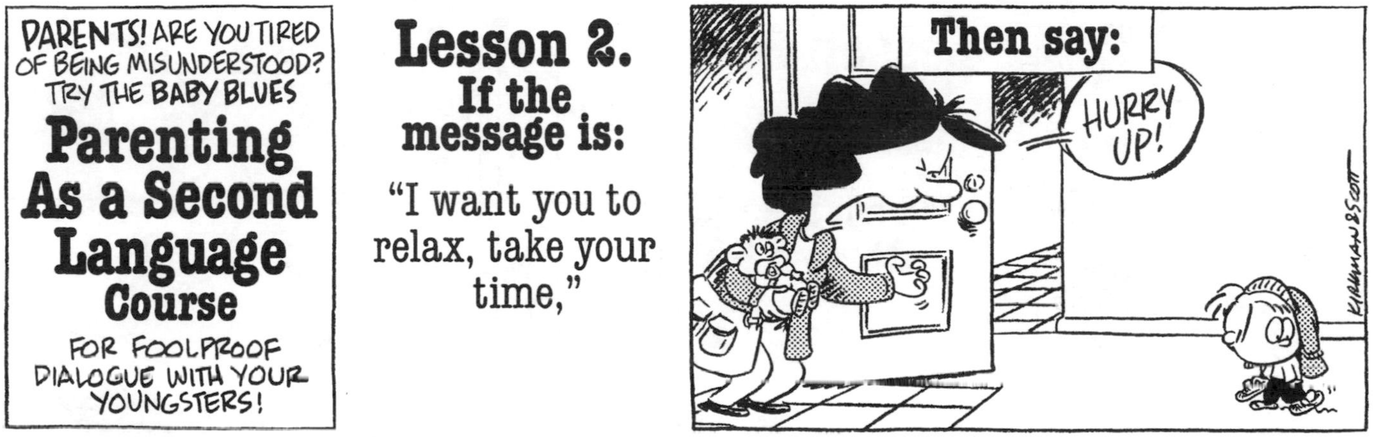
PARENTS! ARE YOU TIRED OF BEING MISUNDERSTOOD? TRY THE BABY BLUES
Parenting As a Second Language Course
FOR FOOLPROOF DIALOGUE WITH YOUR YOUNGSTERS!
Lesson 2.
If the message is:
"I want you to relax, take your time,"
Then say:
HURRY UP!
KIRKMAN & SCOTT

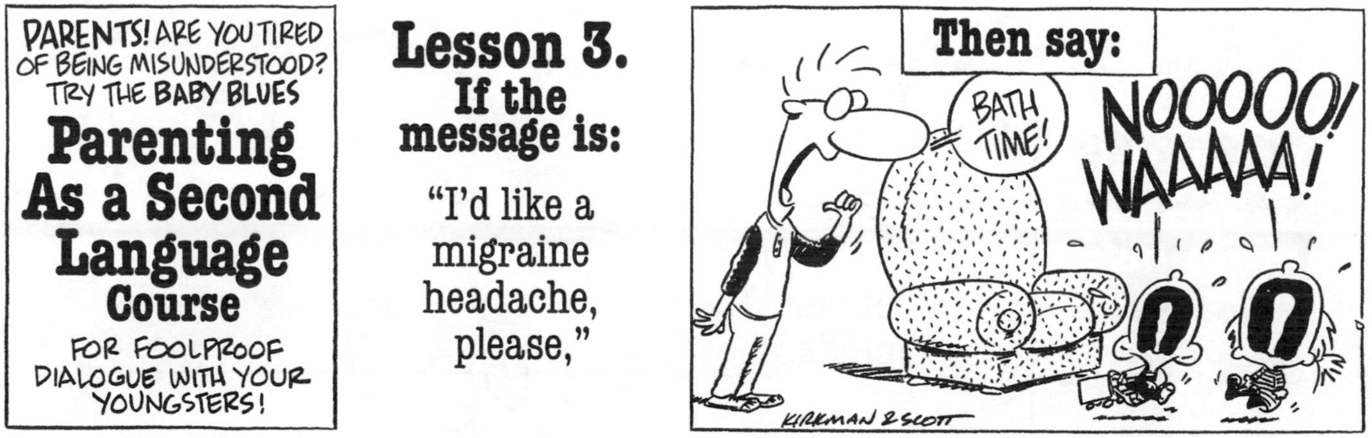
PARENTS! ARE YOU TIRED OF BEING MISUNDERSTOOD? TRY THE BABY BLUES
Parenting As a Second Language Course
FOR FOOLPROOF DIALOGUE WITH YOUR YOUNGSTERS!
Lesson 3.
If the message is:
"I'd like a migraine headache, please,"
Then say:
BATH TIME!
NOOOOO! WAAAAA!
KIRKMAN & SCOTT

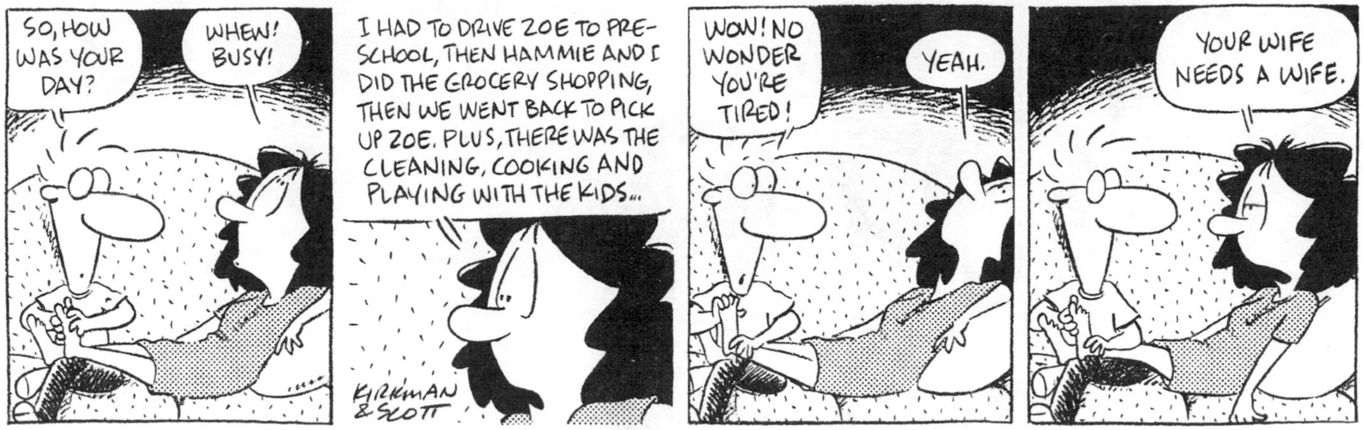

SO, HOW WAS YOUR DAY?
WHEW! BUSY!
I HAD TO DRIVE ZOE TO PRE-SCHOOL, THEN HAMMIE AND I DID THE GROCERY SHOPPING, THEN WE WENT BACK TO PICK UP ZOE. PLUS, THERE WAS THE CLEANING, COOKING AND PLAYING WITH THE KIDS...
KIRKMAN & SCOTT
WOW! NO WONDER YOU'RE TIRED!
YEAH.
YOUR WIFE NEEDS A WIFE.

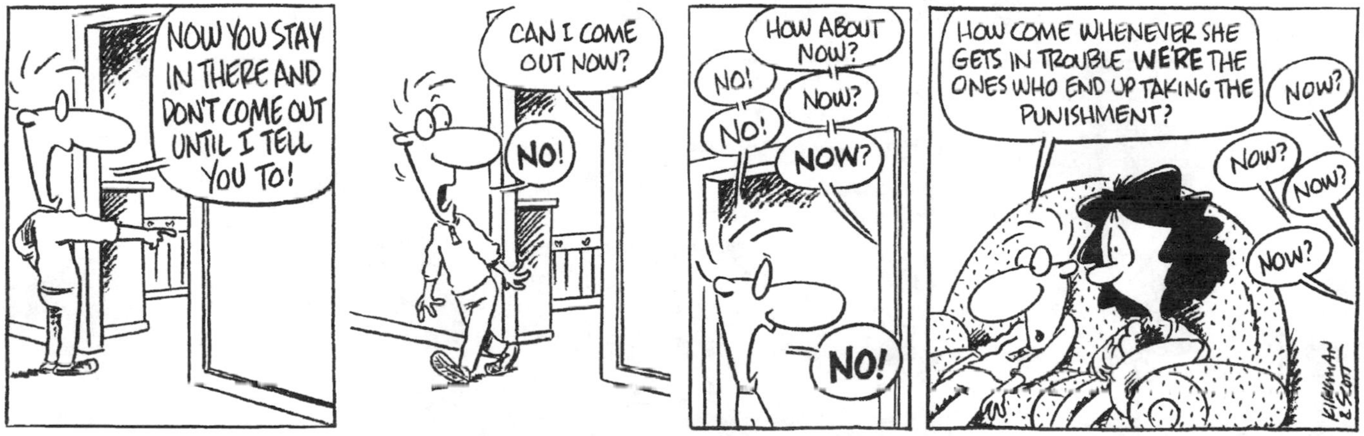

NOW YOU STAY IN THERE AND DON'T COME OUT UNTIL I TELL YOU TO!
CAN I COME OUT NOW?
NO!
HOW ABOUT NOW?
NO!
NOW?
NO!
NOW?
NO!
HOW COME WHENEVER SHE GETS IN TROUBLE **WE'RE** THE ONES WHO END UP TAKING THE PUNISHMENT?
NOW?
NOW?
NOW?
NOW?
KIRKMAN & SCOTT

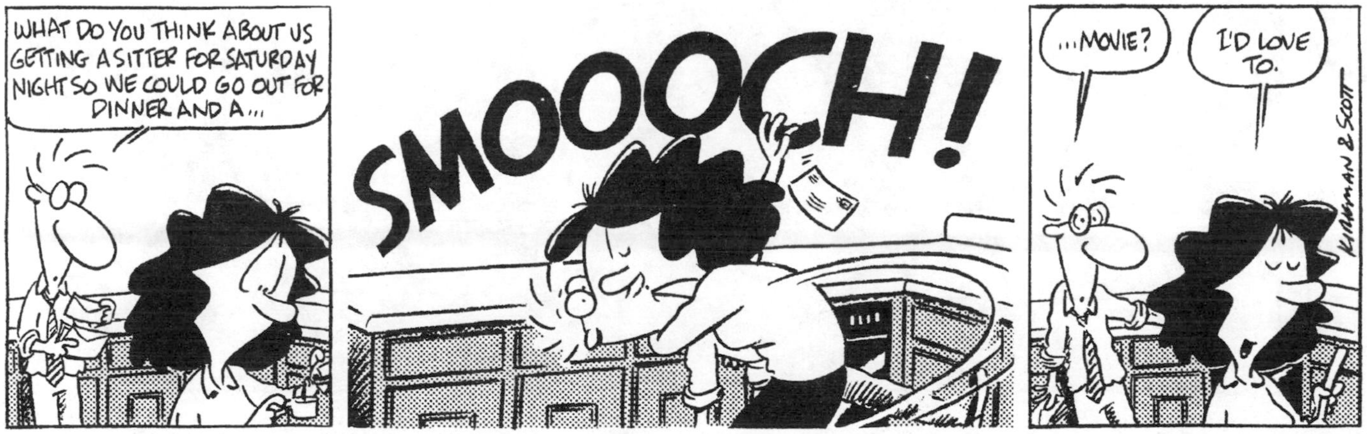

WHAT DO YOU THINK ABOUT US GETTING A SITTER FOR SATURDAY NIGHT SO WE COULD GO OUT FOR DINNER AND A...
SMOOOCH!
...MOVIE?
I'D LOVE TO.
KIRKMAN & SCOTT

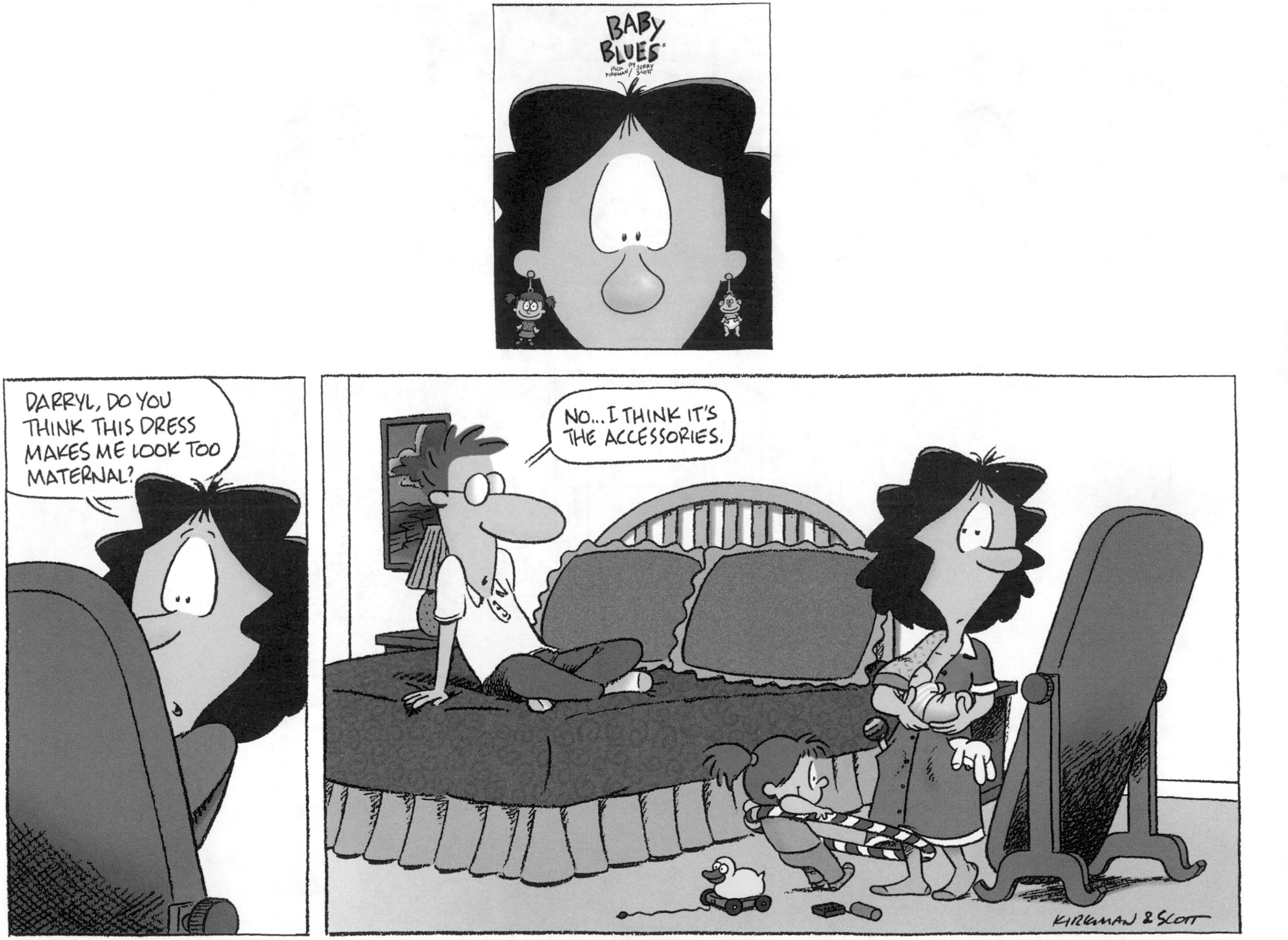
BABY BLUES®
BY RICK KIRKMAN / JERRY SCOTT
DARRYL, DO YOU THINK THIS DRESS MAKES ME LOOK TOO MATERNAL?
NO... I THINK IT'S THE ACCESSORIES.
KIRKMAN & SCOTT

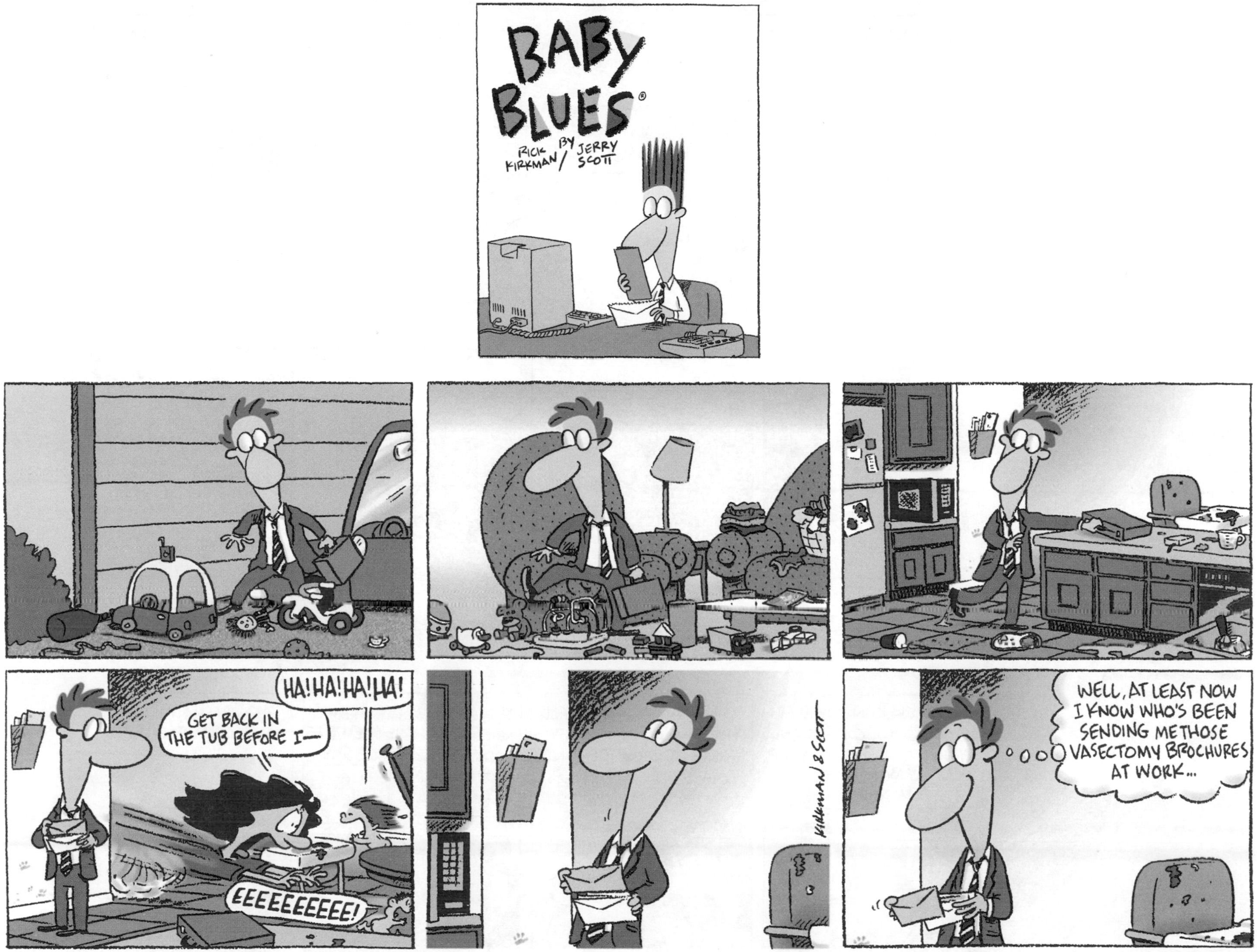
BABY BLUES®
BY RICK KIRKMAN / JERRY SCOTT
GET BACK IN THE TUB BEFORE I—
HA!HA!HA!HA!
EEEEEEEEEE!
KIRKMAN & SCOTT
WELL, AT LEAST NOW I KNOW WHO'S BEEN SENDING ME THOSE VASECTOMY BROCHURES AT WORK...

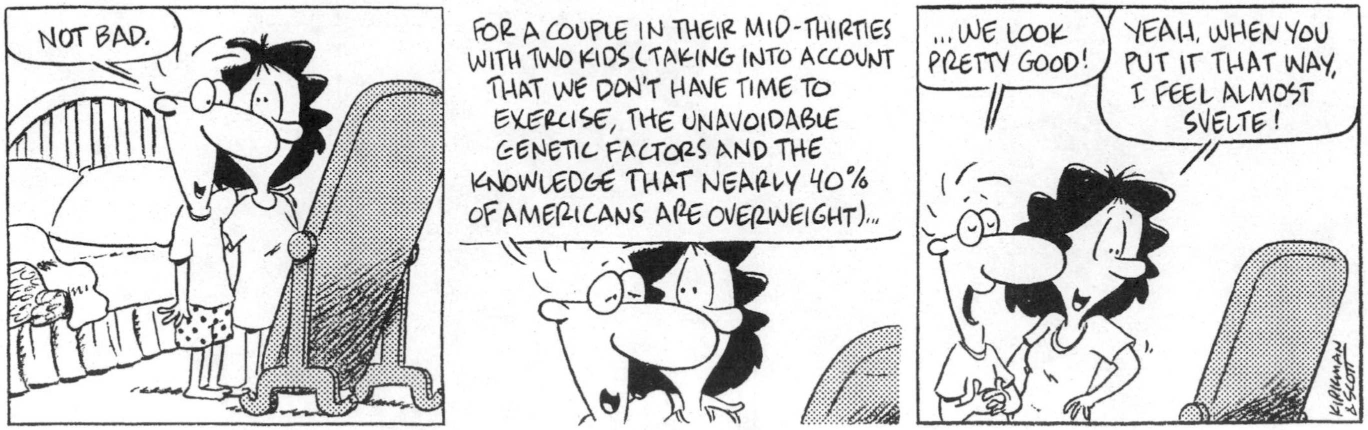
NOT BAD.
FOR A COUPLE IN THEIR MID-THIRTIES WITH TWO KIDS (TAKING INTO ACCOUNT THAT WE DON'T HAVE TIME TO EXERCISE, THE UNAVOIDABLE GENETIC FACTORS AND THE KNOWLEDGE THAT NEARLY 40% OF AMERICANS ARE OVERWEIGHT)...
...WE LOOK PRETTY GOOD!
YEAH, WHEN YOU PUT IT THAT WAY, I FEEL ALMOST SVELTE!
KIRKMAN & SCOTT

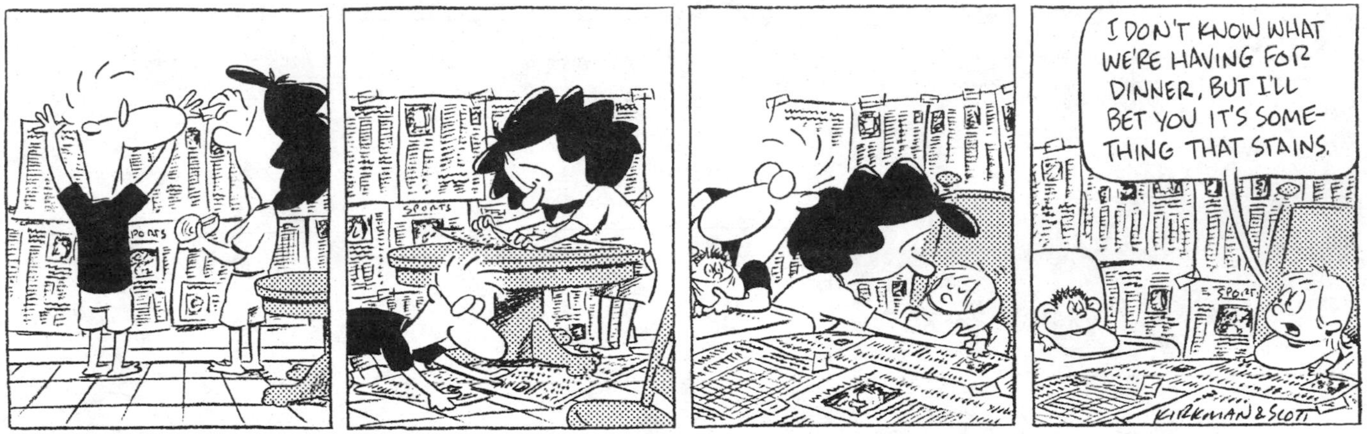
I DON'T KNOW WHAT WE'RE HAVING FOR DINNER, BUT I'LL BET YOU IT'S SOMETHING THAT STAINS.
KIRKMAN & SCOTT

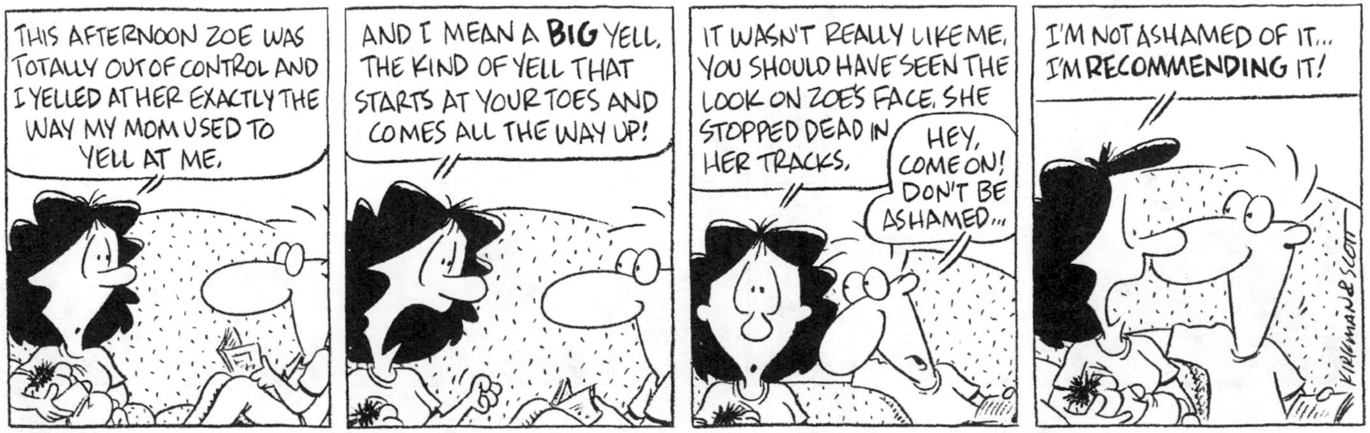
THIS AFTERNOON ZOE WAS TOTALLY OUT OF CONTROL AND I YELLED AT HER EXACTLY THE WAY MY MOM USED TO YELL AT ME.
AND I MEAN A **BIG** YELL. THE KIND OF YELL THAT STARTS AT YOUR TOES AND COMES ALL THE WAY UP!
IT WASN'T REALLY LIKE ME. YOU SHOULD HAVE SEEN THE LOOK ON ZOE'S FACE. SHE STOPPED DEAD IN HER TRACKS.
HEY, COME ON! DON'T BE ASHAMED...
I'M NOT ASHAMED OF IT... I'M **RECOMMENDING** IT!
KIRKMAN & SCOTT

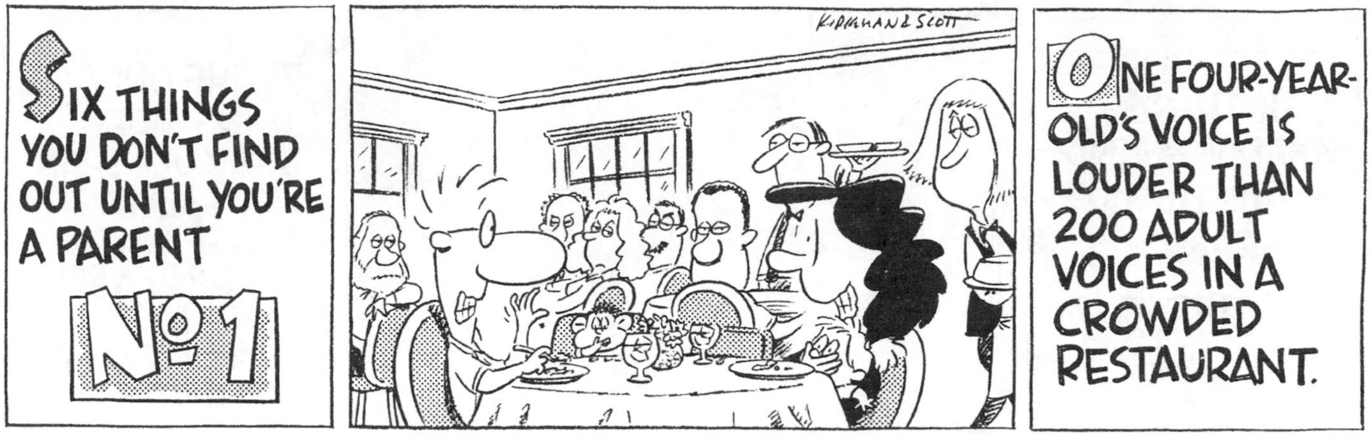
SIX THINGS YOU DON'T FIND OUT UNTIL YOU'RE A PARENT
No. 1
KIRKMAN & SCOTT
ONE FOUR-YEAR-OLD'S VOICE IS LOUDER THAN 200 ADULT VOICES IN A CROWDED RESTAURANT.

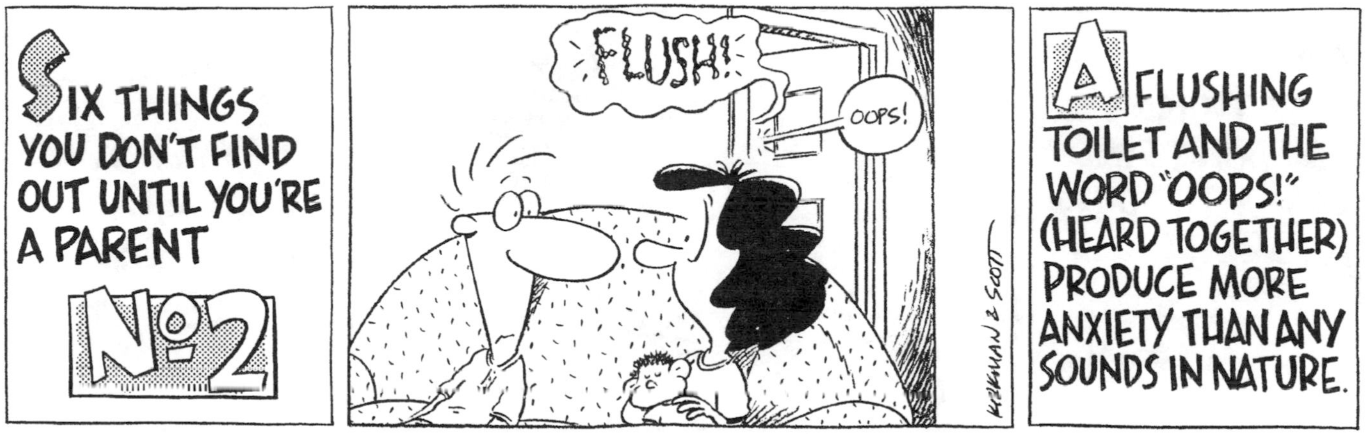
SIX THINGS YOU DON'T FIND OUT UNTIL YOU'RE A PARENT
No. 2
FLUSH!
OOPS!
KIRKMAN & SCOTT
A FLUSHING TOILET AND THE WORD "OOPS!" (HEARD TOGETHER) PRODUCE MORE ANXIETY THAN ANY SOUNDS IN NATURE.

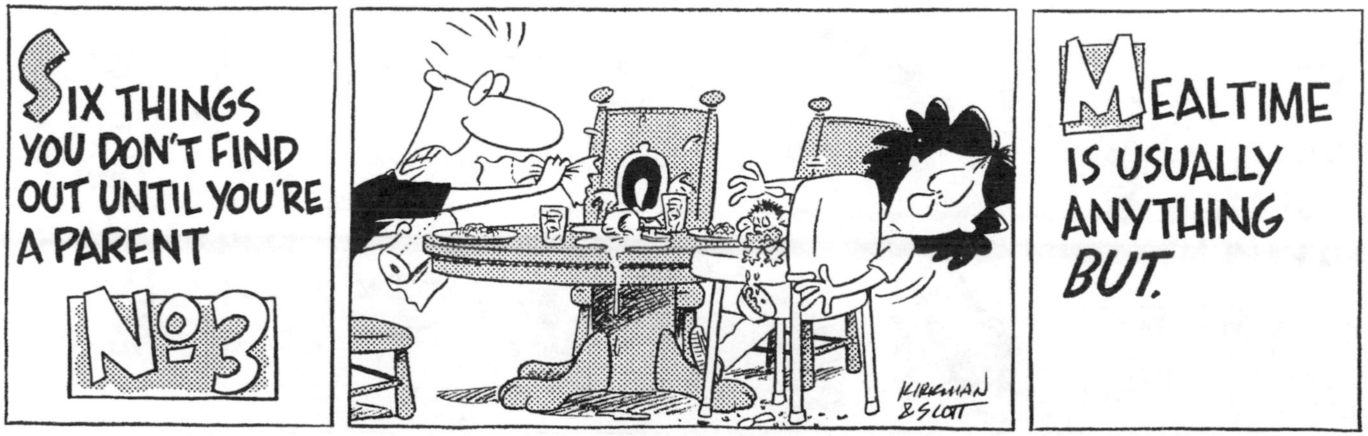
SIX THINGS YOU DON'T FIND OUT UNTIL YOU'RE A PARENT
No. 3
KIRKMAN & SCOTT
MEALTIME IS USUALLY ANYTHING BUT.

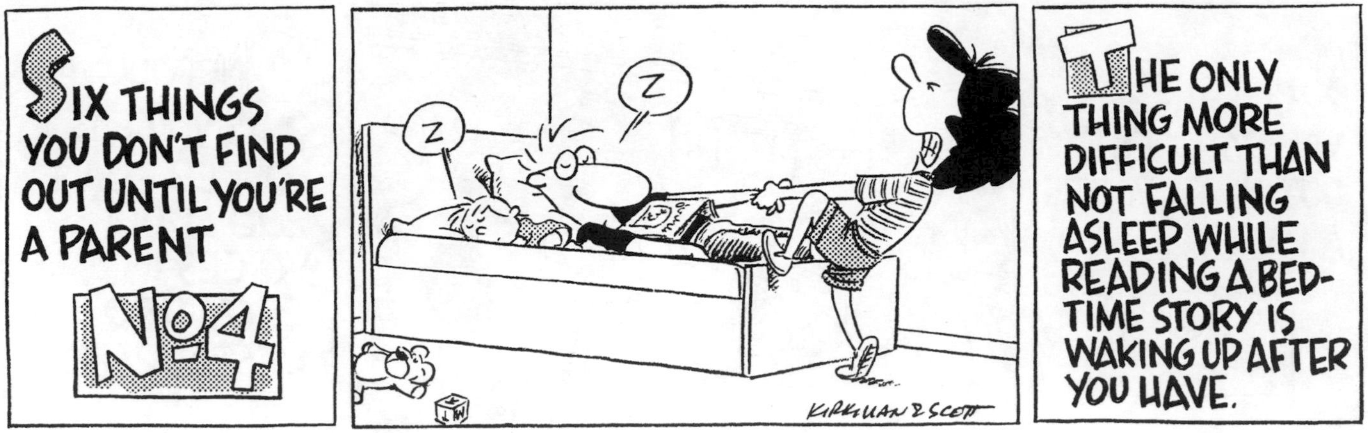
SIX THINGS YOU DON'T FIND OUT UNTIL YOU'RE A PARENT
No. 4
Z
Z
KIRKMAN & SCOTT
THE ONLY THING MORE DIFFICULT THAN NOT FALLING ASLEEP WHILE READING A BED-TIME STORY IS WAKING UP AFTER YOU HAVE.

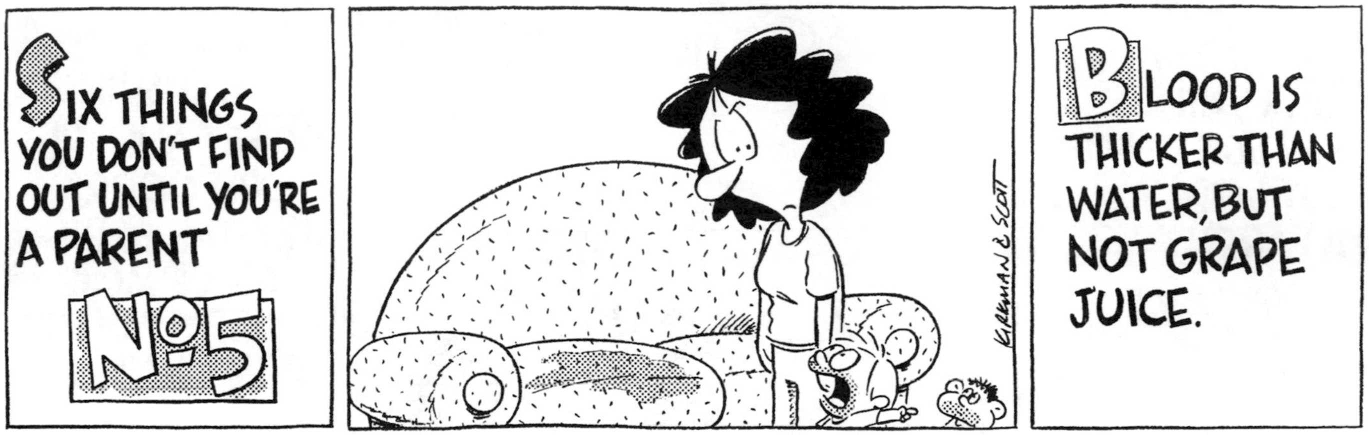
SIX THINGS YOU DON'T FIND OUT UNTIL YOU'RE A PARENT
No. 5
KIRKMAN & SCOTT
BLOOD IS THICKER THAN WATER, BUT NOT GRAPE JUICE.

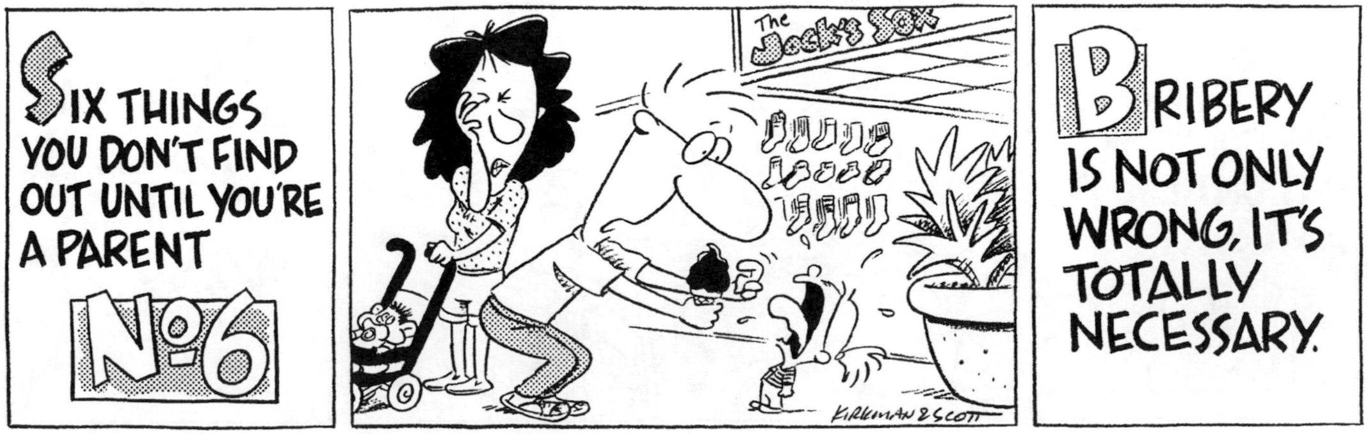
SIX THINGS YOU DON'T FIND OUT UNTIL YOU'RE A PARENT
No. 6
The Jock's Sox
KIRKMAN & SCOTT
BRIBERY IS NOT ONLY WRONG, IT'S TOTALLY NECESSARY.

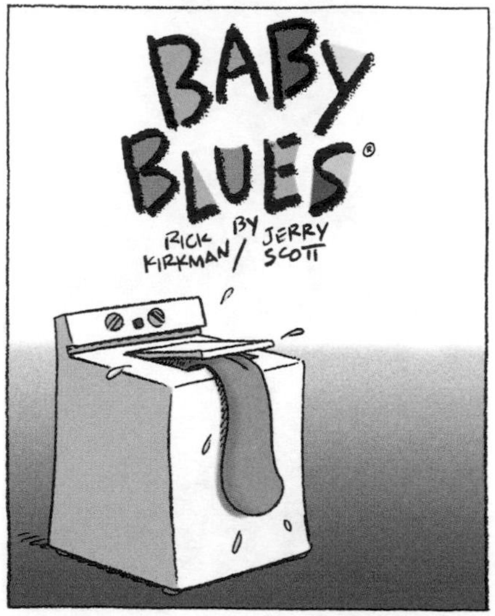
BABY BLUES®
BY
RICK KIRKMAN / JERRY SCOTT

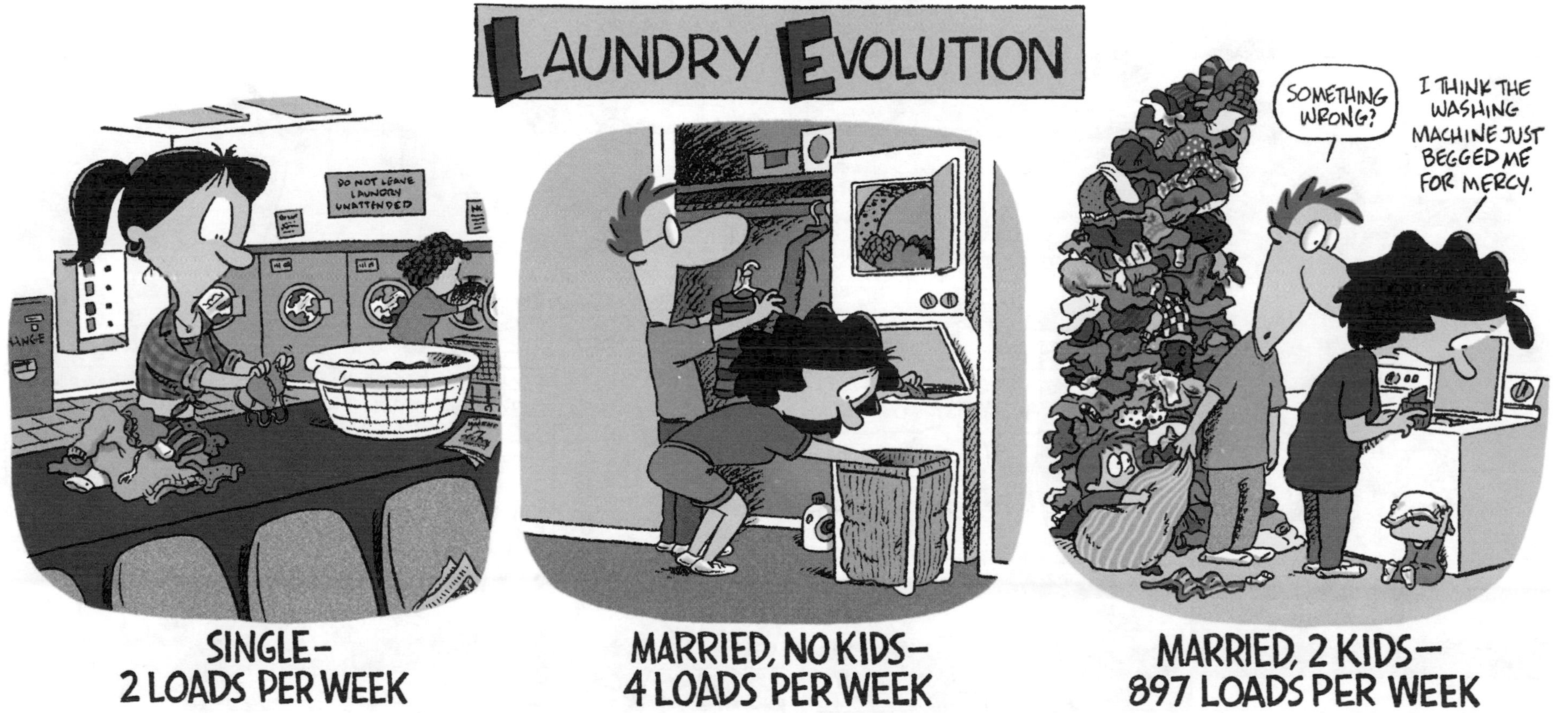
LAUNDRY EVOLUTION
DO NOT LEAVE LAUNDRY UNATTENDED
SINGLE—
2 LOADS PER WEEK
MARRIED, NO KIDS—
4 LOADS PER WEEK
SOMETHING WRONG?
I THINK THE WASHING MACHINE JUST BEGGED ME FOR MERCY.
MARRIED, 2 KIDS—
897 LOADS PER WEEK

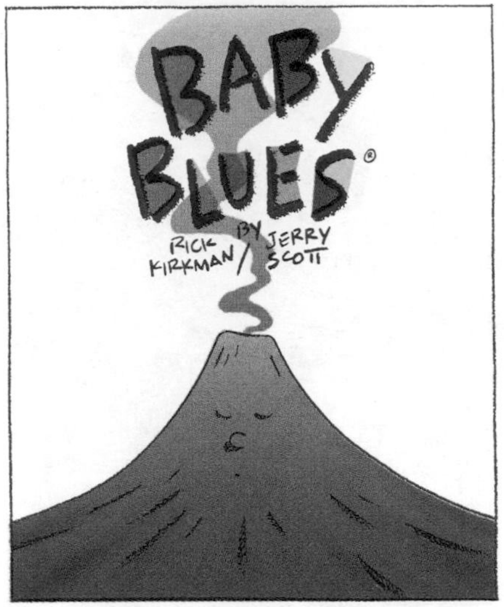
BABY BLUES®
BY RICK KIRKMAN / JERRY SCOTT

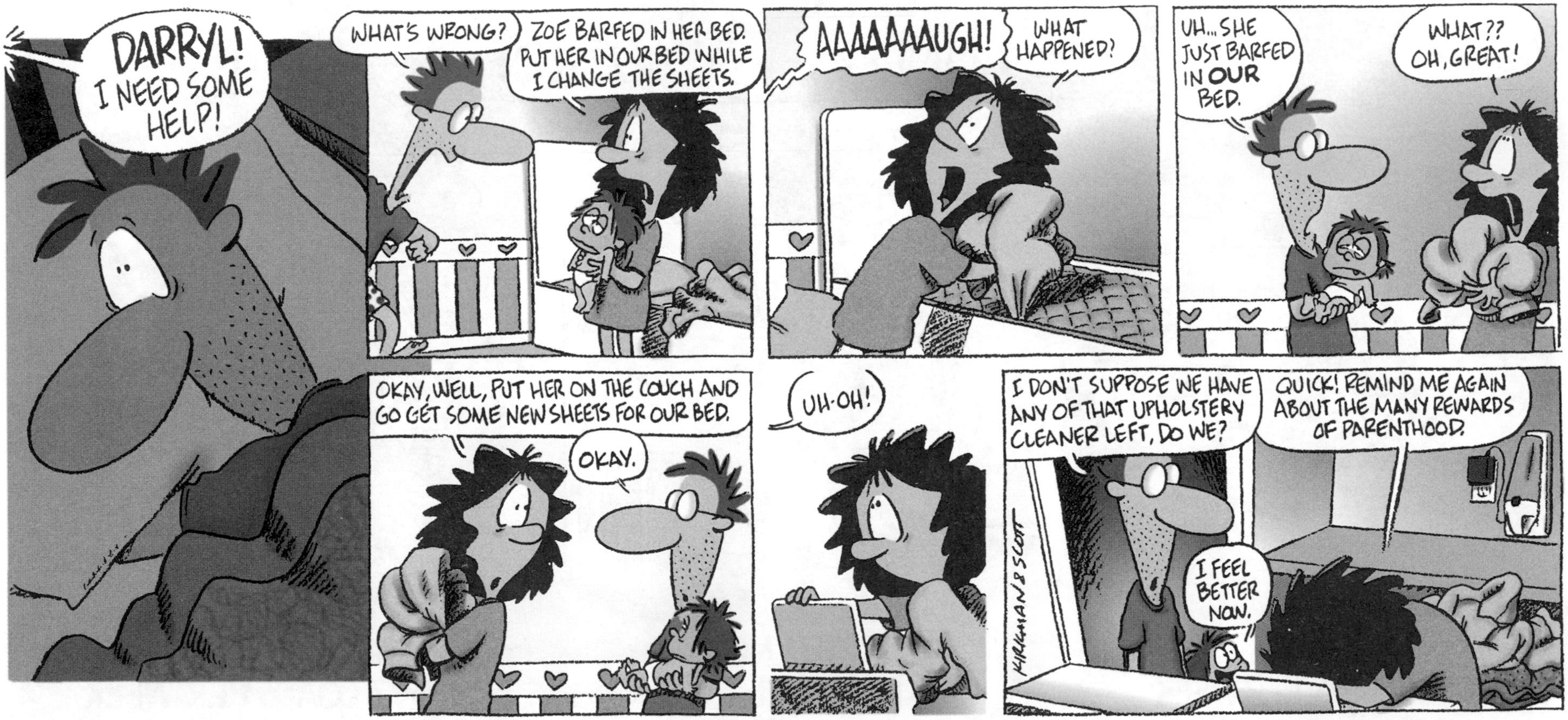
DARRYL! I NEED SOME HELP!
WHAT'S WRONG?
ZOE BARFED IN HER BED. PUT HER IN OUR BED WHILE I CHANGE THE SHEETS.
AAAAAAAUGH!
WHAT HAPPENED?
UH... SHE JUST BARFED IN **OUR** BED.
WHAT?? OH, GREAT!
OKAY, WELL, PUT HER ON THE COUCH AND GO GET SOME NEW SHEETS FOR OUR BED.
OKAY.
UH-OH!
KIRKMAN & SCOTT
I DON'T SUPPOSE WE HAVE ANY OF THAT UPHOLSTERY CLEANER LEFT, DO WE?
QUICK! REMIND ME AGAIN ABOUT THE MANY REWARDS OF PARENTHOOD.
I FEEL BETTER NOW.

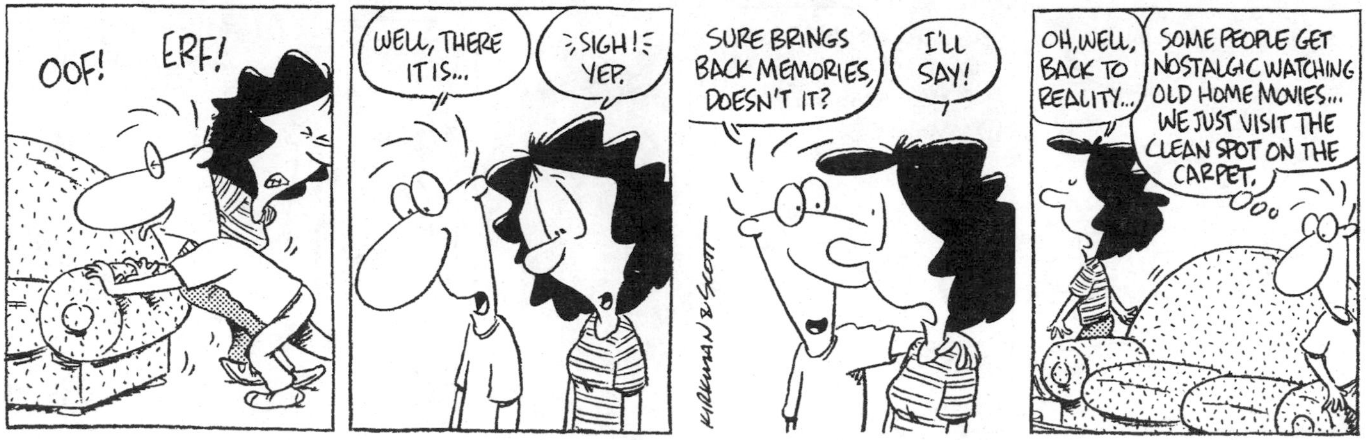
OOF!
ERF!
WELL, THERE IT IS...
SIGH! YEP.
SURE BRINGS BACK MEMORIES, DOESN'T IT?
I'LL SAY!
KIRKMAN & SCOTT
OH, WELL, BACK TO REALITY...
SOME PEOPLE GET NOSTALGIC WATCHING OLD HOME MOVIES... WE JUST VISIT THE CLEAN SPOT ON THE CARPET.

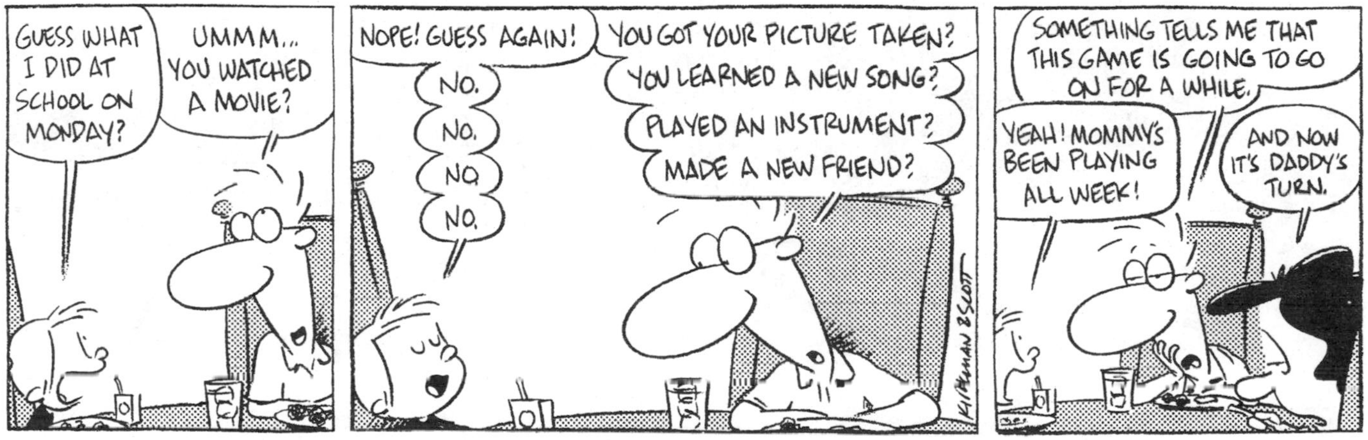
GUESS WHAT I DID AT SCHOOL ON MONDAY?
UMMM... YOU WATCHED A MOVIE?
NOPE! GUESS AGAIN!
YOU GOT YOUR PICTURE TAKEN?
NO.
YOU LEARNED A NEW SONG?
NO.
PLAYED AN INSTRUMENT?
NO.
MADE A NEW FRIEND?
NO.
KIRKMAN & SCOTT
SOMETHING TELLS ME THAT THIS GAME IS GOING TO GO ON FOR A WHILE.
YEAH! MOMMY'S BEEN PLAYING ALL WEEK!
AND NOW IT'S DADDY'S TURN.

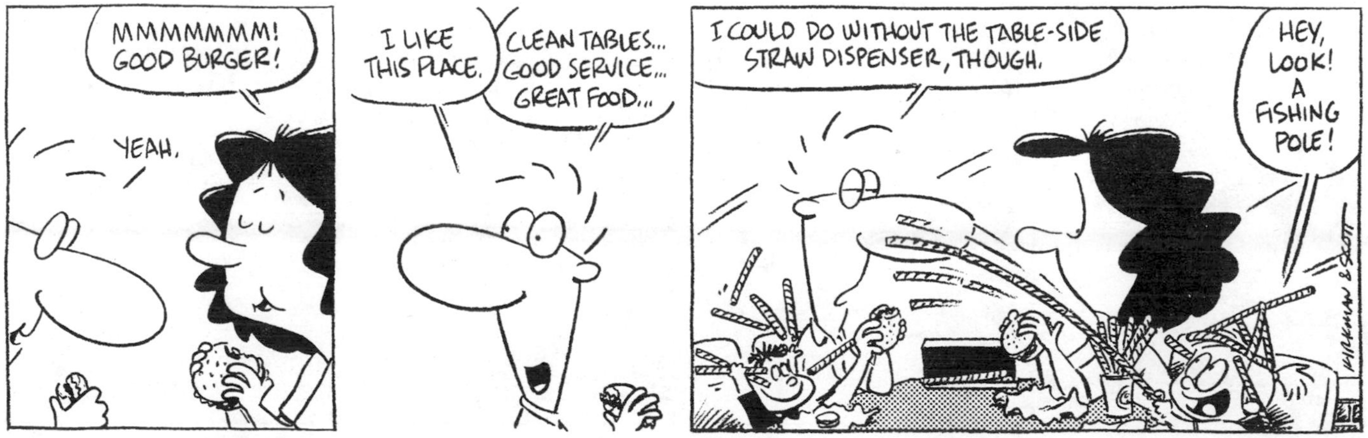
MMMMMMMM! GOOD BURGER!
YEAH.
I LIKE THIS PLACE.
CLEAN TABLES... GOOD SERVICE... GREAT FOOD...
I COULD DO WITHOUT THE TABLE-SIDE STRAW DISPENSER, THOUGH.
HEY, LOOK! A FISHING POLE!
KIRKMAN & SCOTT

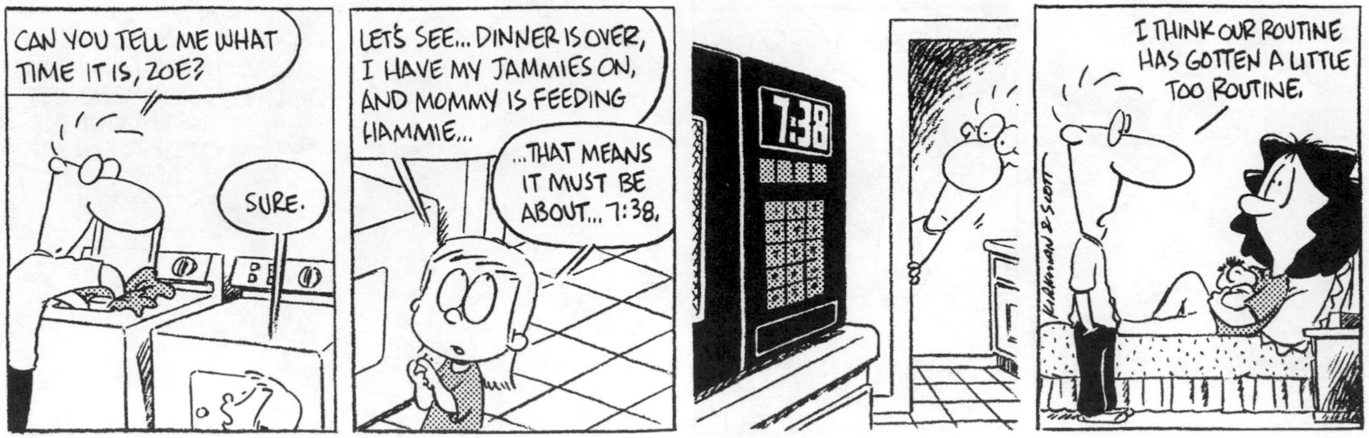
CAN YOU TELL ME WHAT TIME IT IS, ZOE?
SURE.
LET'S SEE... DINNER IS OVER, I HAVE MY JAMMIES ON, AND MOMMY IS FEEDING HAMMIE...
...THAT MEANS IT MUST BE ABOUT... 7:38.
7:38
I THINK OUR ROUTINE HAS GOTTEN A LITTLE TOO ROUTINE.
KIRKMAN & SCOTT

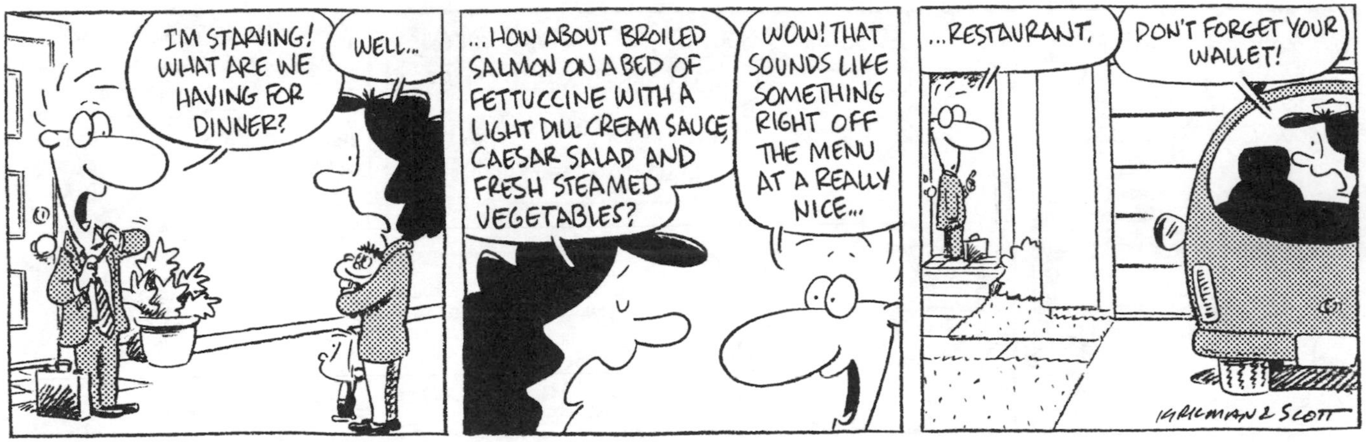
I'M STARVING! WHAT ARE WE HAVING FOR DINNER?
WELL...
...HOW ABOUT BROILED SALMON ON A BED OF FETTUCCINE WITH A LIGHT DILL CREAM SAUCE, CAESAR SALAD AND FRESH STEAMED VEGETABLES?
WOW! THAT SOUNDS LIKE SOMETHING RIGHT OFF THE MENU AT A REALLY NICE...
...RESTAURANT.
DON'T FORGET YOUR WALLET!
KIRKMAN & SCOTT

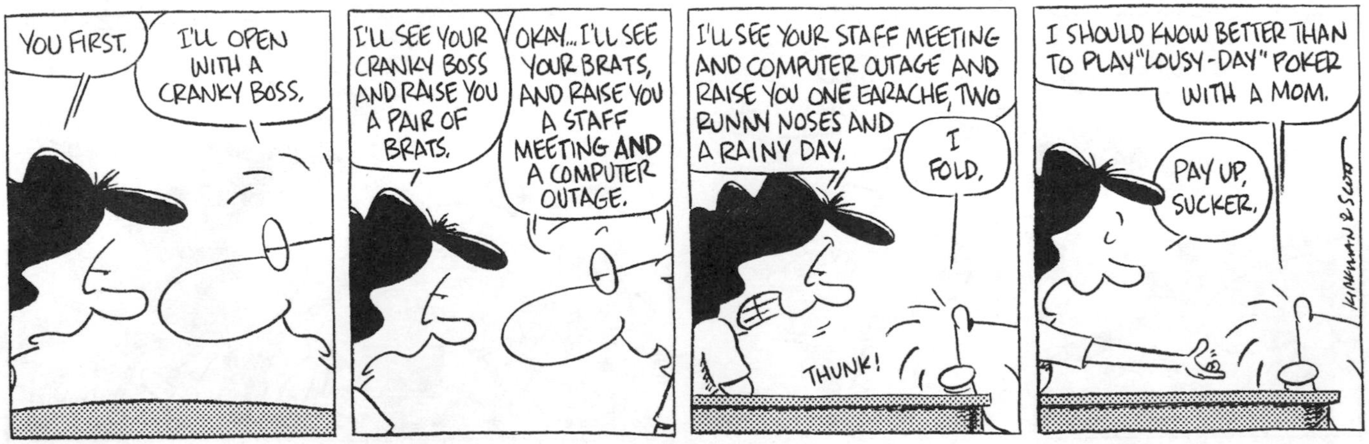
YOU FIRST.
I'LL OPEN WITH A CRANKY BOSS.
I'LL SEE YOUR CRANKY BOSS AND RAISE YOU A PAIR OF BRATS.
OKAY... I'LL SEE YOUR BRATS, AND RAISE YOU A STAFF MEETING AND A COMPUTER OUTAGE.
I'LL SEE YOUR STAFF MEETING AND COMPUTER OUTAGE AND RAISE YOU ONE EARACHE, TWO RUNNY NOSES AND A RAINY DAY.
I FOLD.
THUNK!
I SHOULD KNOW BETTER THAN TO PLAY "LOUSY-DAY" POKER WITH A MOM.
PAY UP, SUCKER.
KIRKMAN & SCOTT

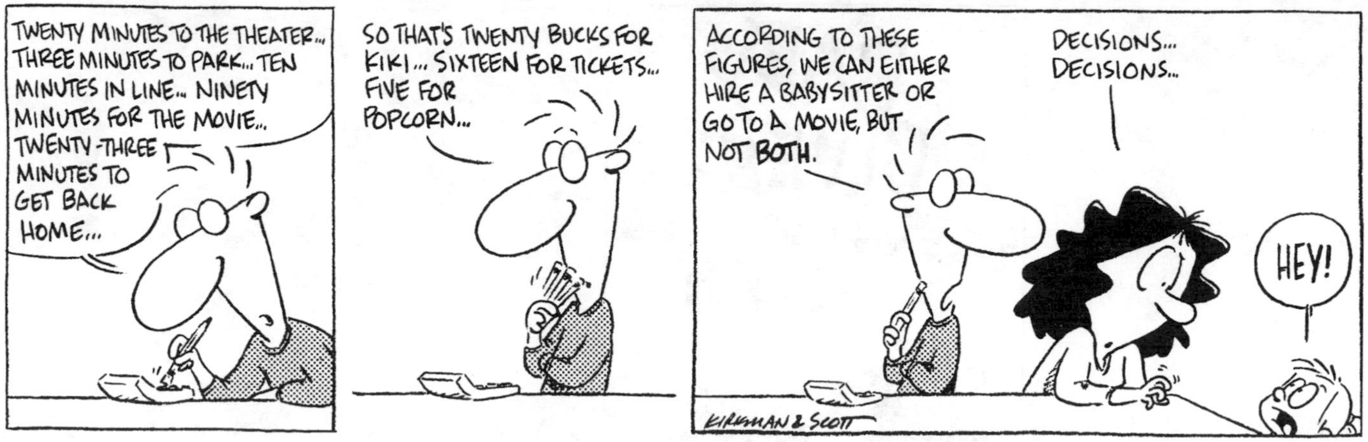
TWENTY MINUTES TO THE THEATER... THREE MINUTES TO PARK... TEN MINUTES IN LINE... NINETY MINUTES FOR THE MOVIE... TWENTY-THREE MINUTES TO GET BACK HOME...
SO THAT'S TWENTY BUCKS FOR KIKI... SIXTEEN FOR TICKETS... FIVE FOR POPCORN...
ACCORDING TO THESE FIGURES, WE CAN EITHER HIRE A BABYSITTER OR GO TO A MOVIE, BUT NOT BOTH.
DECISIONS... DECISIONS...
HEY!
KIRKMAN & SCOTT

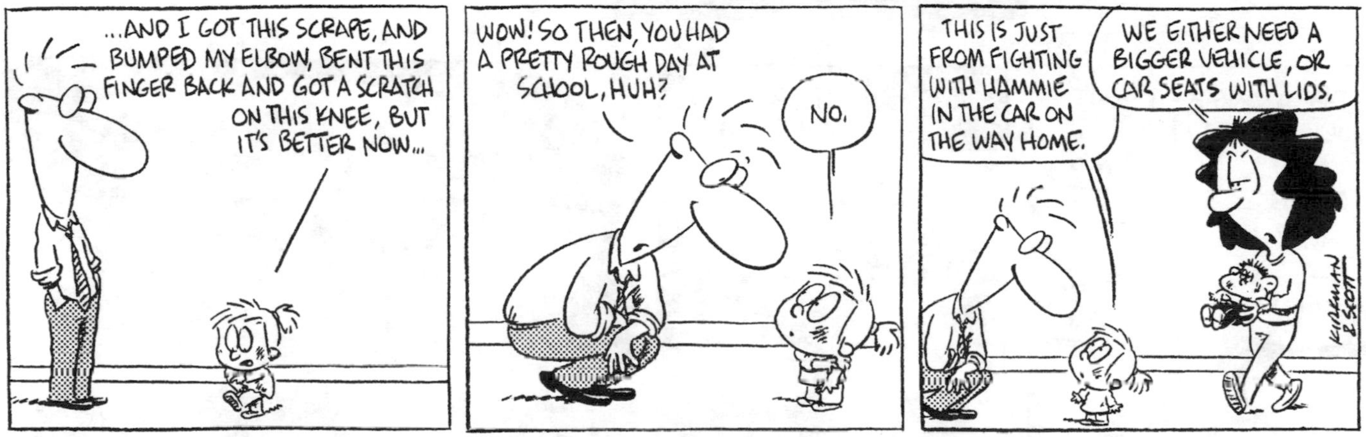
...AND I GOT THIS SCRAPE, AND BUMPED MY ELBOW, BENT THIS FINGER BACK AND GOT A SCRATCH ON THIS KNEE, BUT IT'S BETTER NOW...
WOW! SO THEN, YOU HAD A PRETTY ROUGH DAY AT SCHOOL, HUH?
NO.
THIS IS JUST FROM FIGHTING WITH HAMMIE IN THE CAR ON THE WAY HOME.
WE EITHER NEED A BIGGER VEHICLE, OR CAR SEATS WITH LIDS.
KIRKMAN & SCOTT

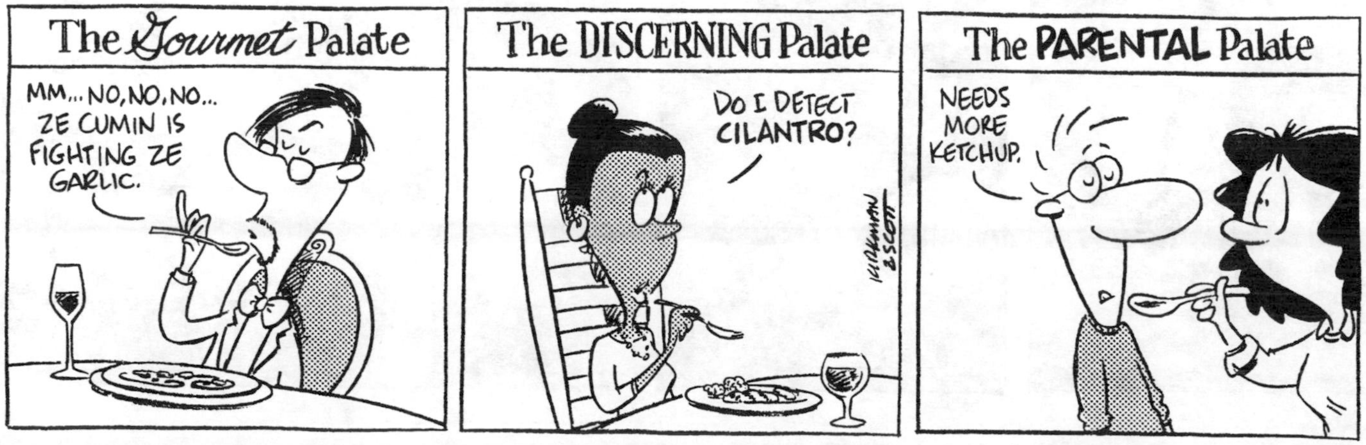
The Gourmet Palate
MM... NO, NO, NO... ZE CUMIN IS FIGHTING ZE GARLIC.
The DISCERNING Palate
DO I DETECT CILANTRO?
KIRKMAN & SCOTT
The PARENTAL Palate
NEEDS MORE KETCHUP.

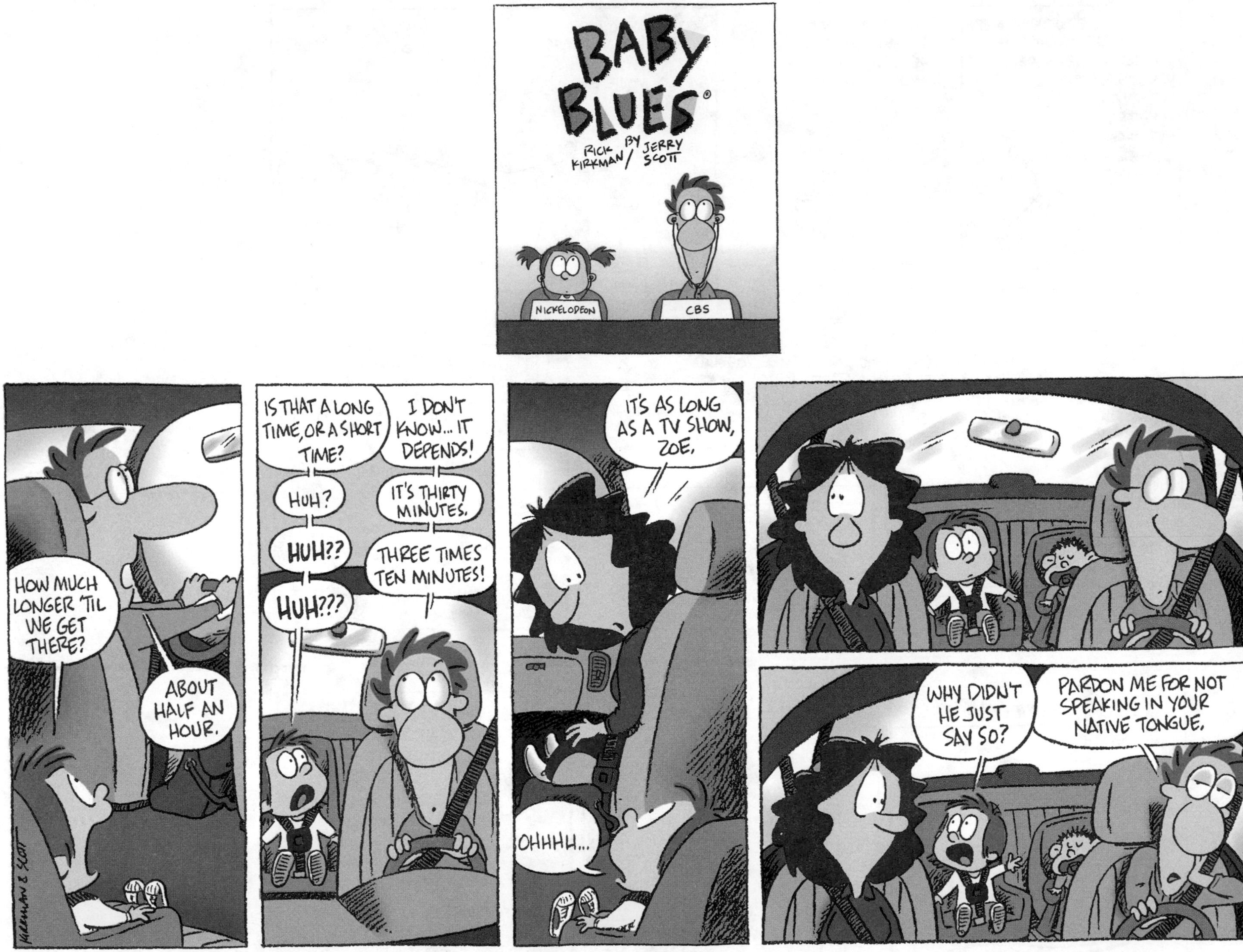
BABY BLUES®
BY RICK KIRKMAN / JERRY SCOTT
NICKELODEON
CBS
HOW MUCH LONGER 'TIL WE GET THERE?
ABOUT HALF AN HOUR.
KIRKMAN & SCOTT
IS THAT A LONG TIME, OR A SHORT TIME?
I DON'T KNOW... IT DEPENDS!
HUH?
IT'S THIRTY MINUTES.
HUH??
THREE TIMES TEN MINUTES!
HUH???
IT'S AS LONG AS A TV SHOW, ZOE.
OHHHH...
WHY DIDN'T HE JUST SAY SO?
PARDON ME FOR NOT SPEAKING IN YOUR NATIVE TONGUE.

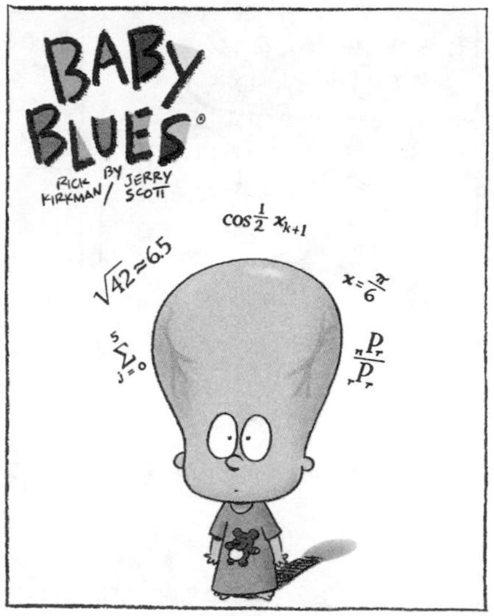
BABY BLUES®
RICK KIRKMAN / BY JERRY SCOTT
$\cos\frac{1}{2}x_{k+1}$
$\sqrt{42}=6.5$
$x=\frac{\pi}{6}$

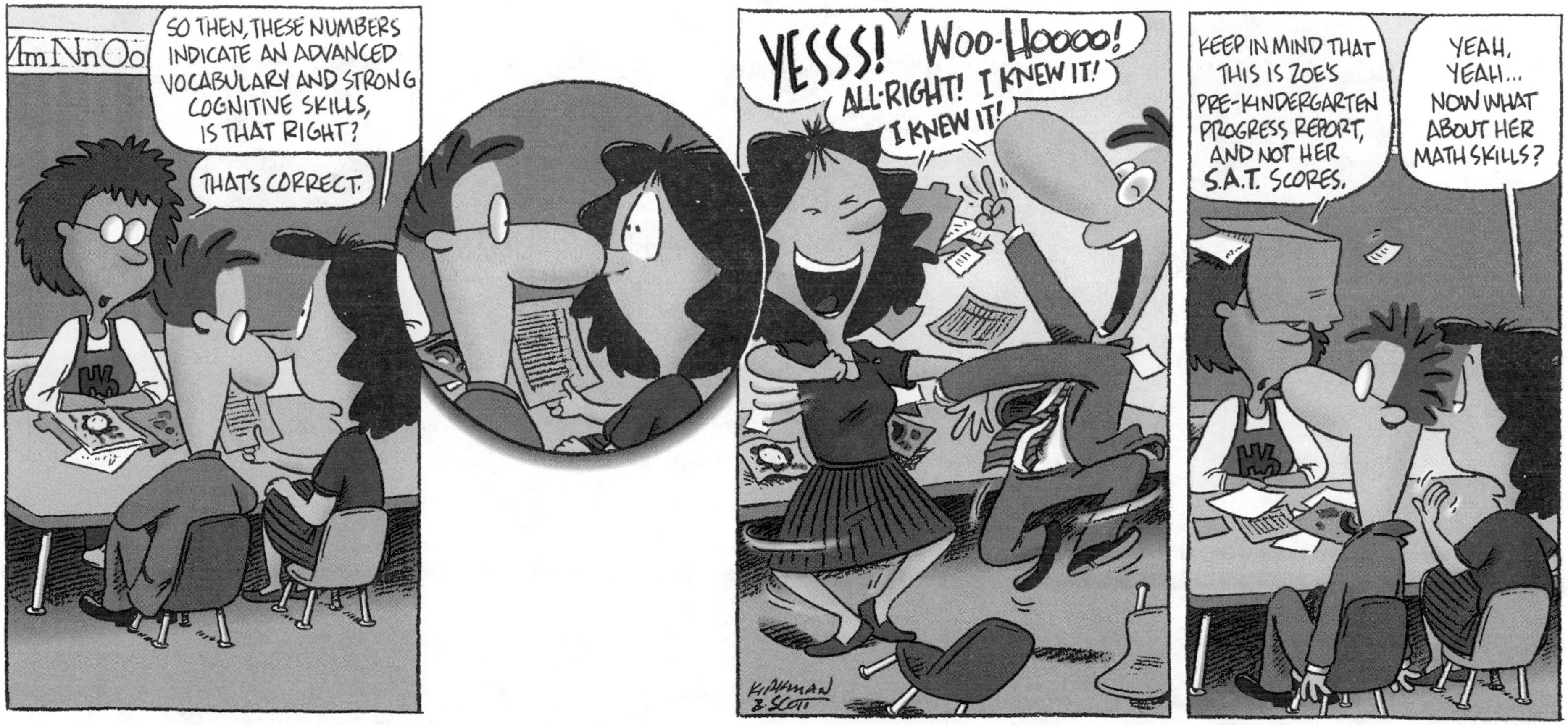
MmNnOo
SO THEN, THESE NUMBERS INDICATE AN ADVANCED VOCABULARY AND STRONG COGNITIVE SKILLS, IS THAT RIGHT?
THAT'S CORRECT.
YESSS!
WOO-HOOOO!
ALL-RIGHT! I KNEW IT!
I KNEW IT!
KIRKMAN & SCOTT
KEEP IN MIND THAT THIS IS ZOE'S PRE-KINDERGARTEN PROGRESS REPORT, AND NOT HER S.A.T. SCORES.
YEAH, YEAH... NOW WHAT ABOUT HER MATH SKILLS?

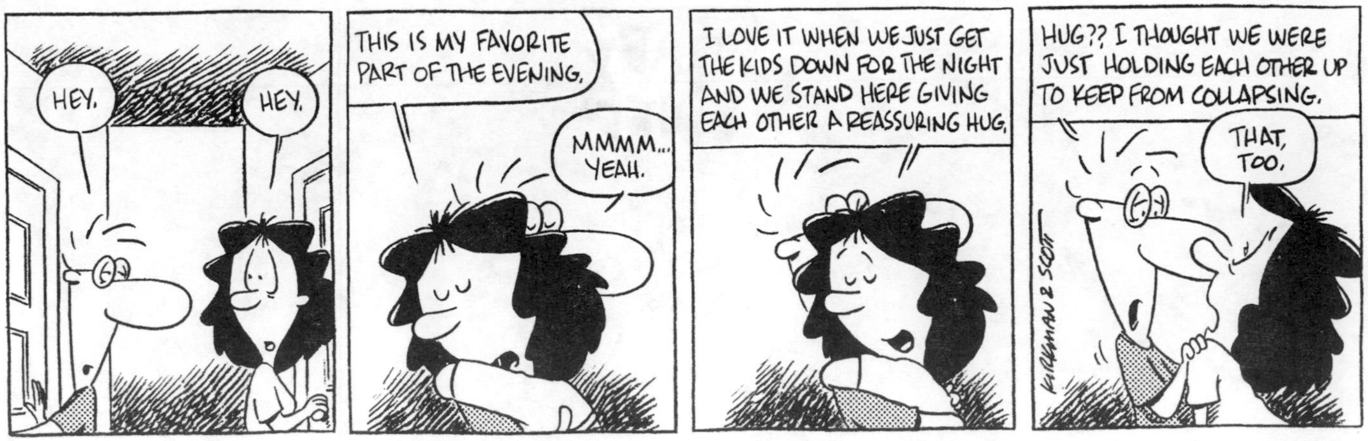
HEY.
HEY.
THIS IS MY FAVORITE PART OF THE EVENING.
MMMM... YEAH.
I LOVE IT WHEN WE JUST GET THE KIDS DOWN FOR THE NIGHT AND WE STAND HERE GIVING EACH OTHER A REASSURING HUG.
HUG?? I THOUGHT WE WERE JUST HOLDING EACH OTHER UP TO KEEP FROM COLLAPSING.
THAT, TOO.
KIRKMAN & SCOTT

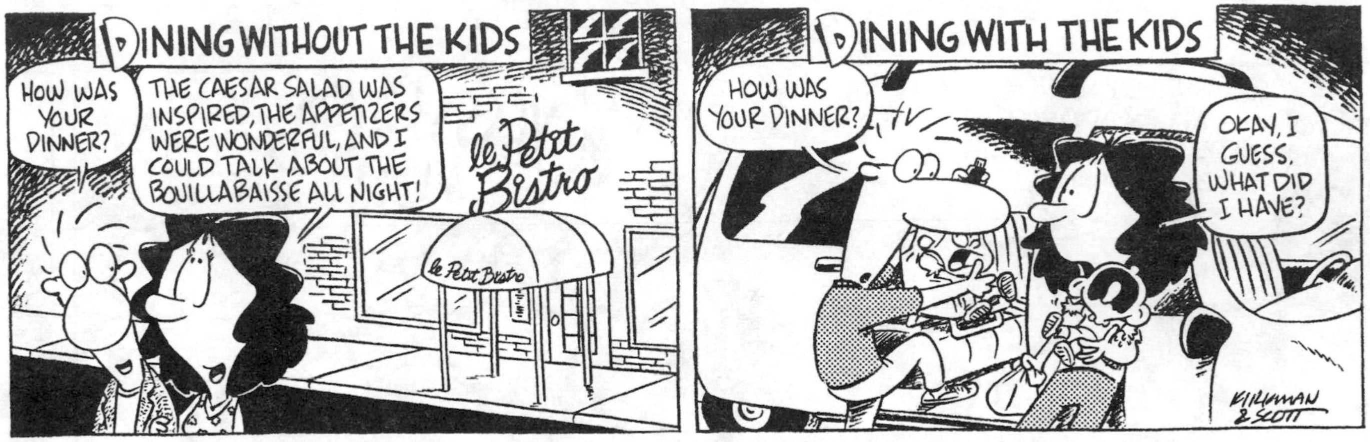
DINING WITHOUT THE KIDS
HOW WAS YOUR DINNER?
THE CAESAR SALAD WAS INSPIRED, THE APPETIZERS WERE WONDERFUL, AND I COULD TALK ABOUT THE BOUILLABAISSE ALL NIGHT!
le Petit Bistro
le Petit Bistro
DINING WITH THE KIDS
HOW WAS YOUR DINNER?
OKAY, I GUESS. WHAT DID I HAVE?
KIRKMAN & SCOTT

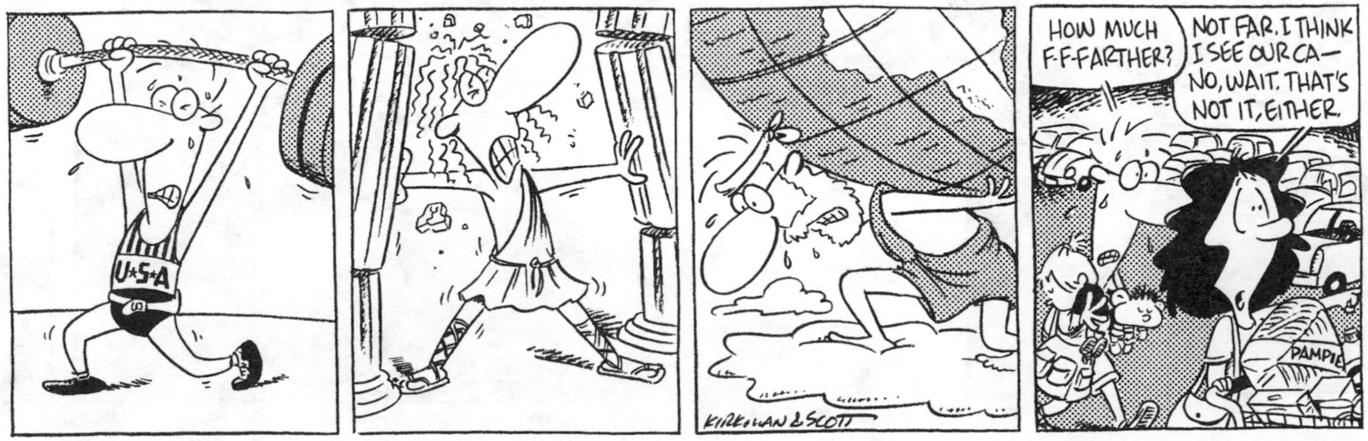
U*S*A
KIRKMAN & SCOTT
HOW MUCH F-F-FARTHER?
NOT FAR. I THINK I SEE OUR CA— NO, WAIT. THAT'S NOT IT, EITHER.
PAMPIE

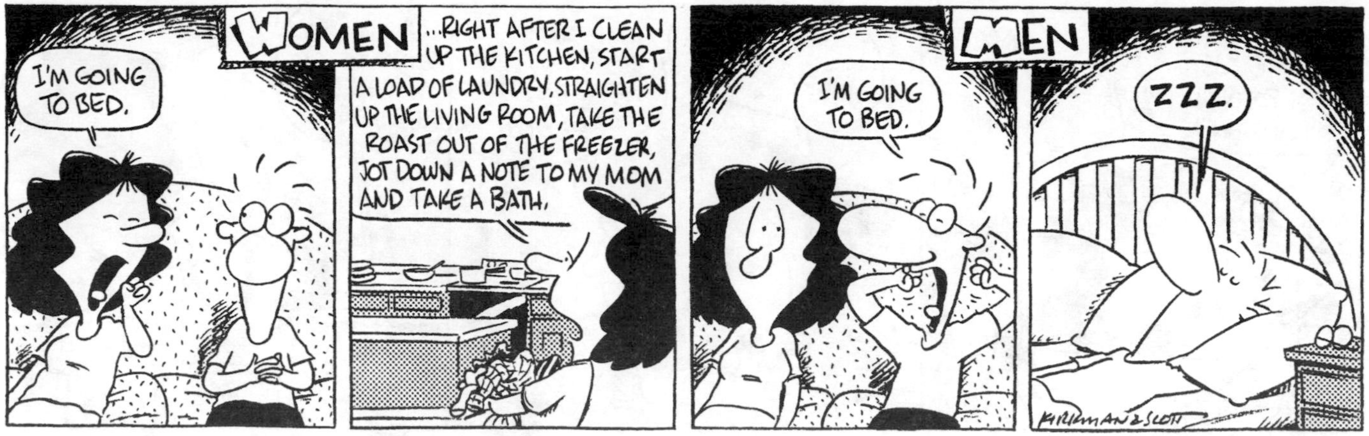
WOMEN
I'M GOING TO BED.
...RIGHT AFTER I CLEAN UP THE KITCHEN, START A LOAD OF LAUNDRY, STRAIGHTEN UP THE LIVING ROOM, TAKE THE ROAST OUT OF THE FREEZER, JOT DOWN A NOTE TO MY MOM AND TAKE A BATH.
MEN
I'M GOING TO BED.
ZZZ.
KIRKMAN & SCOTT

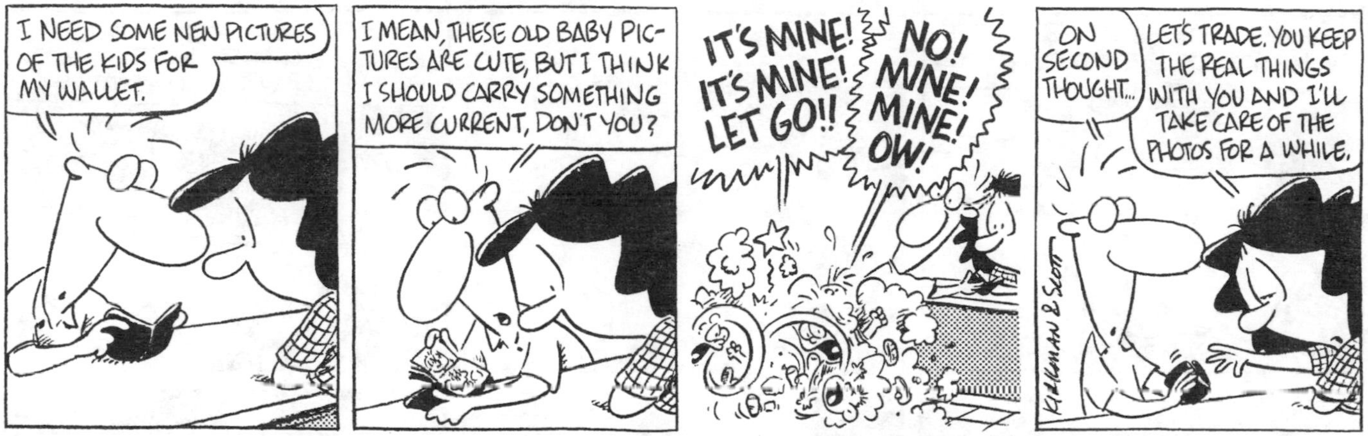
I NEED SOME NEW PICTURES OF THE KIDS FOR MY WALLET.
I MEAN, THESE OLD BABY PICTURES ARE CUTE, BUT I THINK I SHOULD CARRY SOMETHING MORE CURRENT, DON'T YOU?
IT'S MINE! IT'S MINE! LET GO!!
NO! MINE! MINE! OW!
ON SECOND THOUGHT...
LET'S TRADE. YOU KEEP THE REAL THINGS WITH YOU AND I'LL TAKE CARE OF THE PHOTOS FOR A WHILE.
KIRKMAN & SCOTT

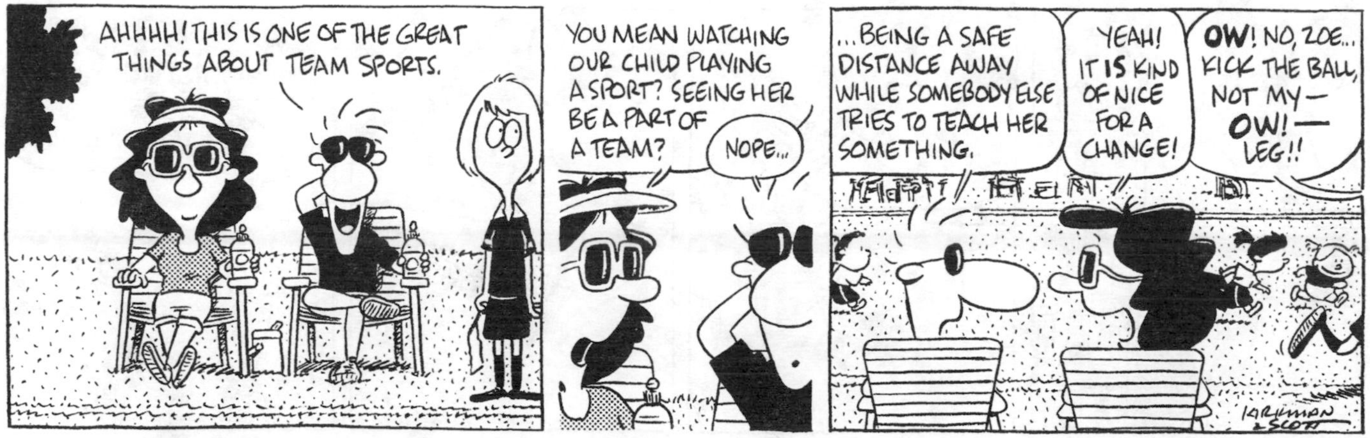
AHHHH! THIS IS ONE OF THE GREAT THINGS ABOUT TEAM SPORTS.
YOU MEAN WATCHING OUR CHILD PLAYING A SPORT? SEEING HER BE A PART OF A TEAM?
NOPE...
...BEING A SAFE DISTANCE AWAY WHILE SOMEBODY ELSE TRIES TO TEACH HER SOMETHING.
YEAH! IT IS KIND OF NICE FOR A CHANGE!
OW! NO, ZOE... KICK THE BALL, NOT MY— OW!— LEG!!
KIRKMAN & SCOTT

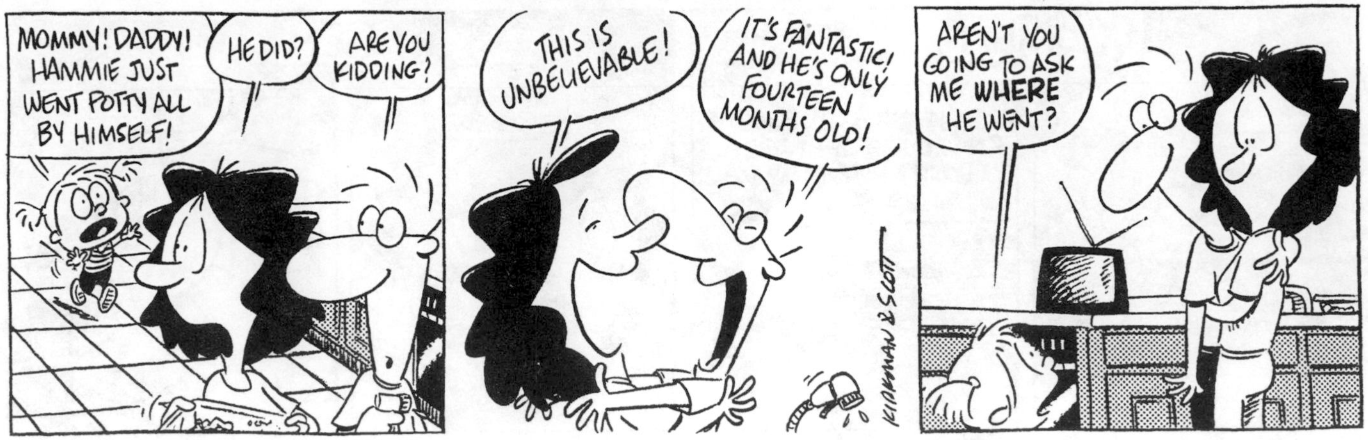
MOMMY! DADDY! HAMMIE JUST WENT POTTY ALL BY HIMSELF!
HE DID?
ARE YOU KIDDING?
THIS IS UNBELIEVABLE!
IT'S FANTASTIC! AND HE'S ONLY FOURTEEN MONTHS OLD!
KIRKMAN & SCOTT
AREN'T YOU GOING TO ASK ME WHERE HE WENT?

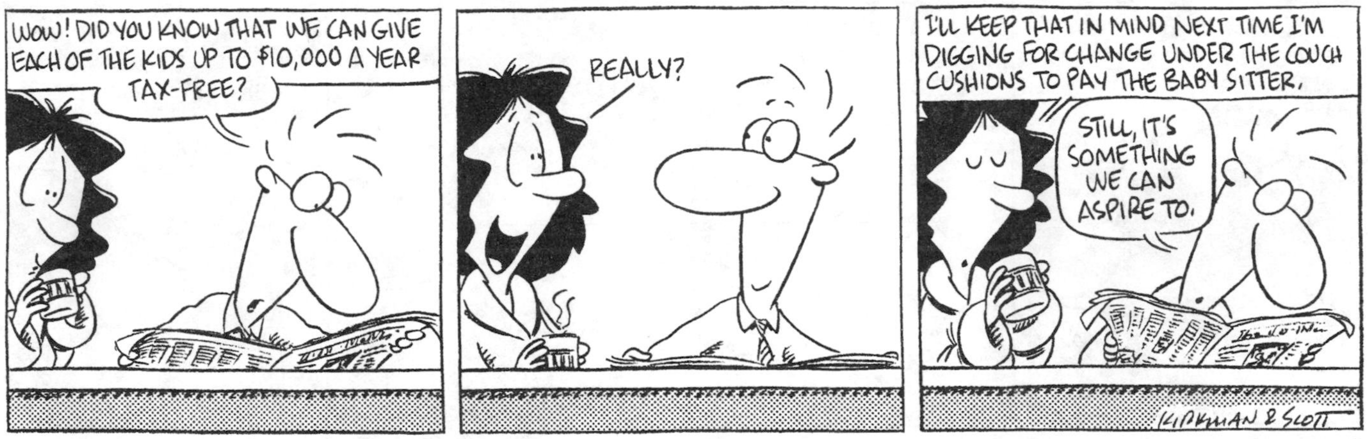
WOW! DID YOU KNOW THAT WE CAN GIVE EACH OF THE KIDS UP TO $10,000 A YEAR TAX-FREE?
REALLY?
I'LL KEEP THAT IN MIND NEXT TIME I'M DIGGING FOR CHANGE UNDER THE COUCH CUSHIONS TO PAY THE BABY SITTER.
STILL, IT'S SOMETHING WE CAN ASPIRE TO.
KIRKMAN & SCOTT

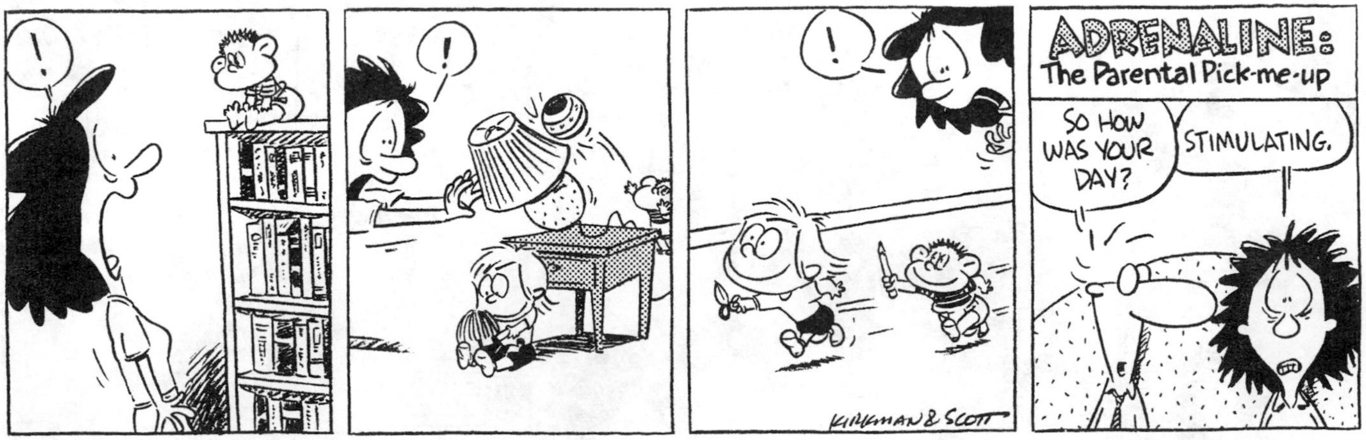
!
!
!
KIRKMAN & SCOTT
ADRENALINE:
The Parental Pick-me-up
SO HOW WAS YOUR DAY?
STIMULATING.

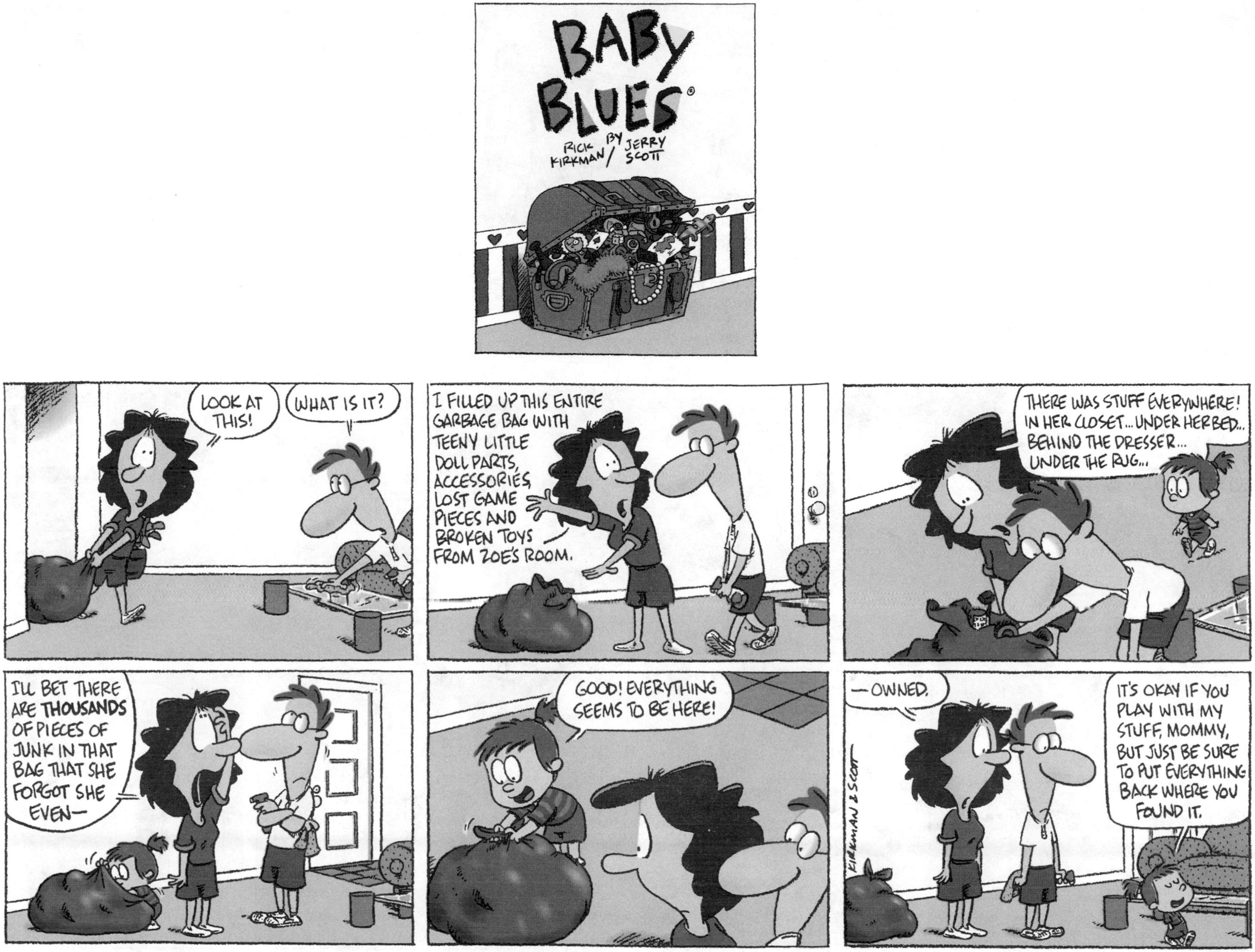
BABY BLUES®
RICK KIRKMAN / BY JERRY SCOTT
LOOK AT THIS!
WHAT IS IT?
I FILLED UP THIS ENTIRE GARBAGE BAG WITH TEENY LITTLE DOLL PARTS, ACCESSORIES, LOST GAME PIECES AND BROKEN TOYS FROM ZOE'S ROOM.
THERE WAS STUFF EVERYWHERE! IN HER CLOSET... UNDER HER BED... BEHIND THE DRESSER... UNDER THE RUG...
I'LL BET THERE ARE **THOUSANDS** OF PIECES OF JUNK IN THAT BAG THAT SHE FORGOT SHE EVEN—
GOOD! EVERYTHING SEEMS TO BE HERE!
—OWNED.
KIRKMAN & SCOTT
IT'S OKAY IF YOU PLAY WITH MY STUFF, MOMMY, BUT JUST BE SURE TO PUT EVERYTHING BACK WHERE YOU FOUND IT.

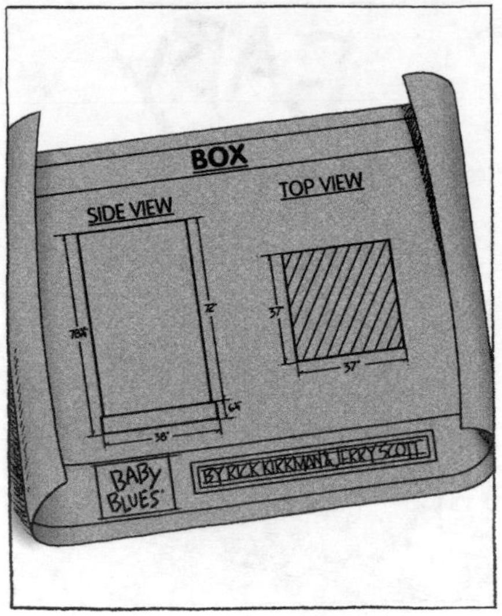
BOX
SIDE VIEW
TOP VIEW
BABY BLUES
BY RICK KIRKMAN & JERRY SCOTT

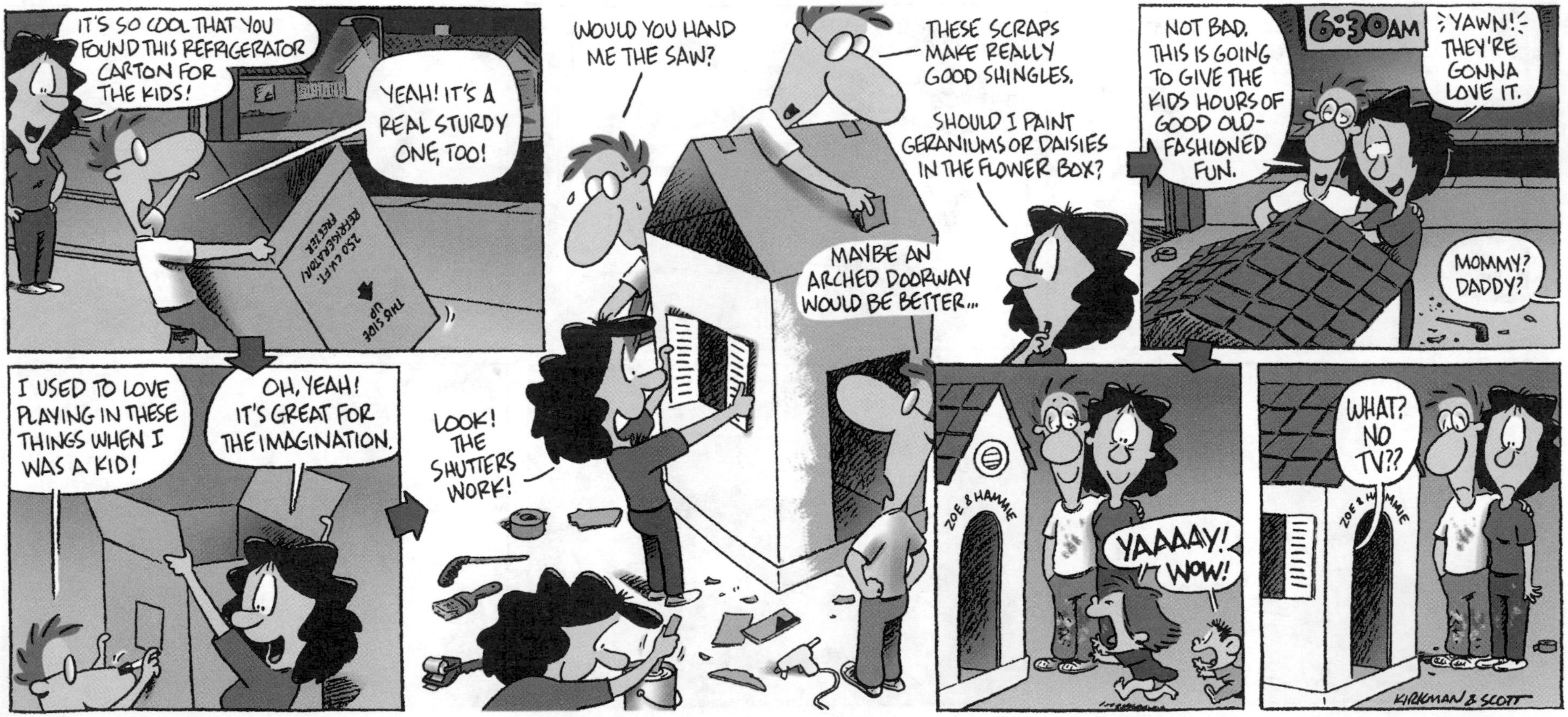
IT'S SO COOL THAT YOU FOUND THIS REFRIGERATOR CARTON FOR THE KIDS!
YEAH! IT'S A REAL STURDY ONE, TOO!
I USED TO LOVE PLAYING IN THESE THINGS WHEN I WAS A KID!
OH, YEAH! IT'S GREAT FOR THE IMAGINATION.
WOULD YOU HAND ME THE SAW?
THESE SCRAPS MAKE REALLY GOOD SHINGLES.
SHOULD I PAINT GERANIUMS OR DAISIES IN THE FLOWER BOX?
MAYBE AN ARCHED DOORWAY WOULD BE BETTER...
LOOK! THE SHUTTERS WORK!
6:30AM
NOT BAD. THIS IS GOING TO GIVE THE KIDS HOURS OF GOOD OLD-FASHIONED FUN.
YAWN! THEY'RE GONNA LOVE IT.
MOMMY? DADDY?
ZOE & HAMMIE
YAAAAY!
WOW!
WHAT? NO TV??
KIRKMAN & SCOTT

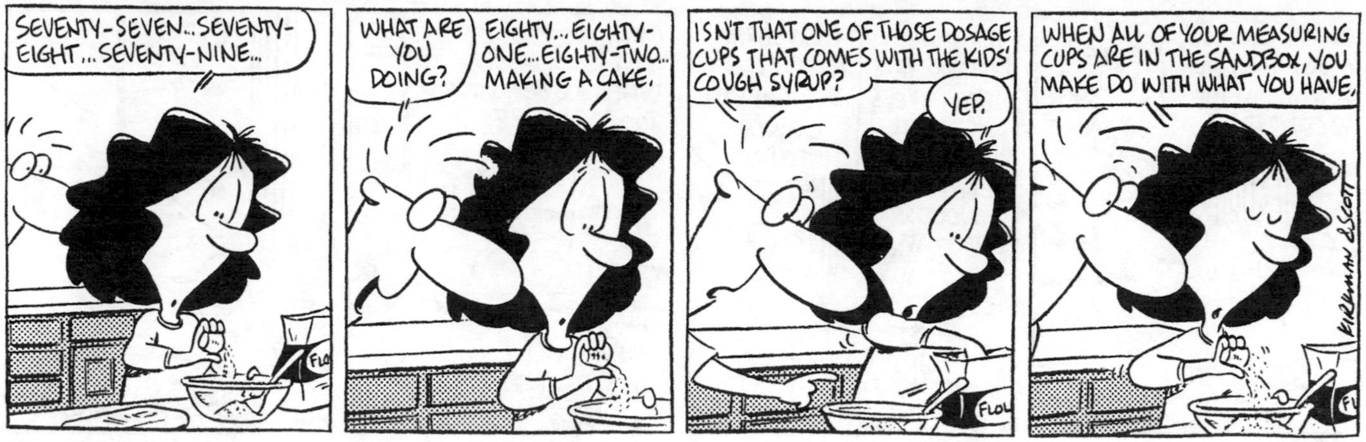
SEVENTY-SEVEN... SEVENTY-EIGHT... SEVENTY-NINE...
WHAT ARE YOU DOING?
EIGHTY... EIGHTY-ONE... EIGHTY-TWO... MAKING A CAKE.
ISN'T THAT ONE OF THOSE DOSAGE CUPS THAT COMES WITH THE KIDS' COUGH SYRUP?
YEP.
WHEN ALL OF YOUR MEASURING CUPS ARE IN THE SANDBOX, YOU MAKE DO WITH WHAT YOU HAVE.
KIRKMAN & SCOTT

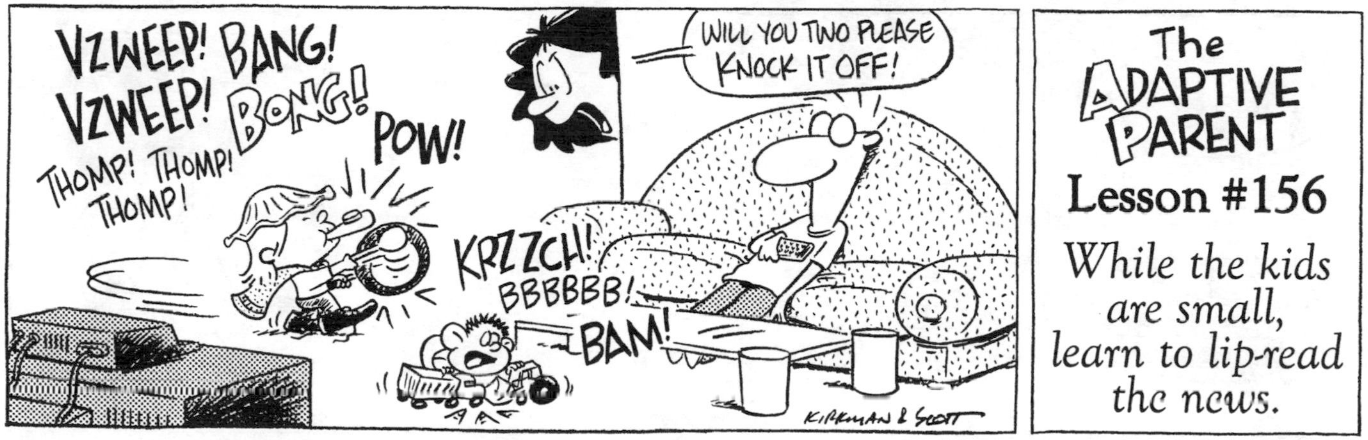
VZWEEP! VZWEEP!
BANG!
BONG!
POW!
THOMP! THOMP! THOMP!
KRZZCH!
BBBBBB!
BAM!
WILL YOU TWO PLEASE KNOCK IT OFF!
KIRKMAN & SCOTT
The ADAPTIVE PARENT
Lesson #156
While the kids are small, learn to lip-read the news.

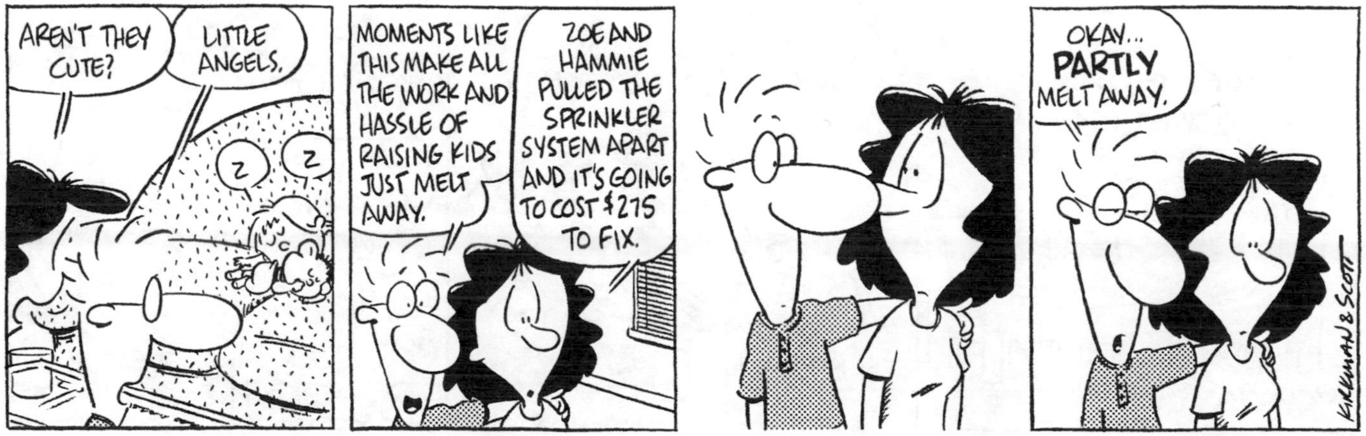
AREN'T THEY CUTE?
LITTLE ANGELS.
Z Z
MOMENTS LIKE THIS MAKE ALL THE WORK AND HASSLE OF RAISING KIDS JUST MELT AWAY.
ZOE AND HAMMIE PULLED THE SPRINKLER SYSTEM APART AND IT'S GOING TO COST $275 TO FIX.
OKAY... PARTLY MELT AWAY.
KIRKMAN & SCOTT

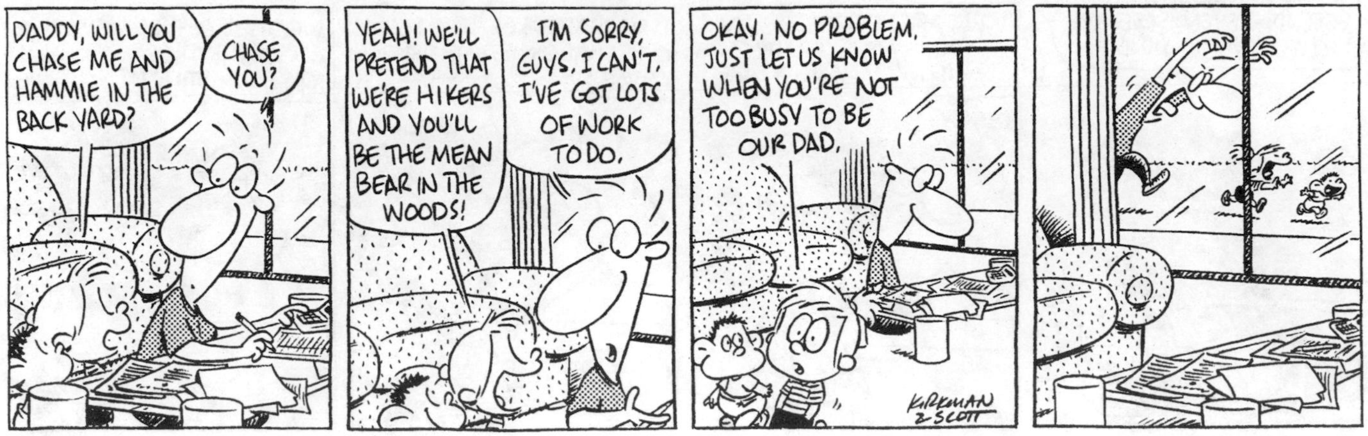
DADDY, WILL YOU CHASE ME AND HAMMIE IN THE BACK YARD?
CHASE YOU?
YEAH! WE'LL PRETEND THAT WE'RE HIKERS AND YOU'LL BE THE MEAN BEAR IN THE WOODS!
I'M SORRY, GUYS. I CAN'T. I'VE GOT LOTS OF WORK TO DO.
OKAY. NO PROBLEM. JUST LET US KNOW WHEN YOU'RE NOT TOO BUSY TO BE OUR DAD.
KIRKMAN & SCOTT

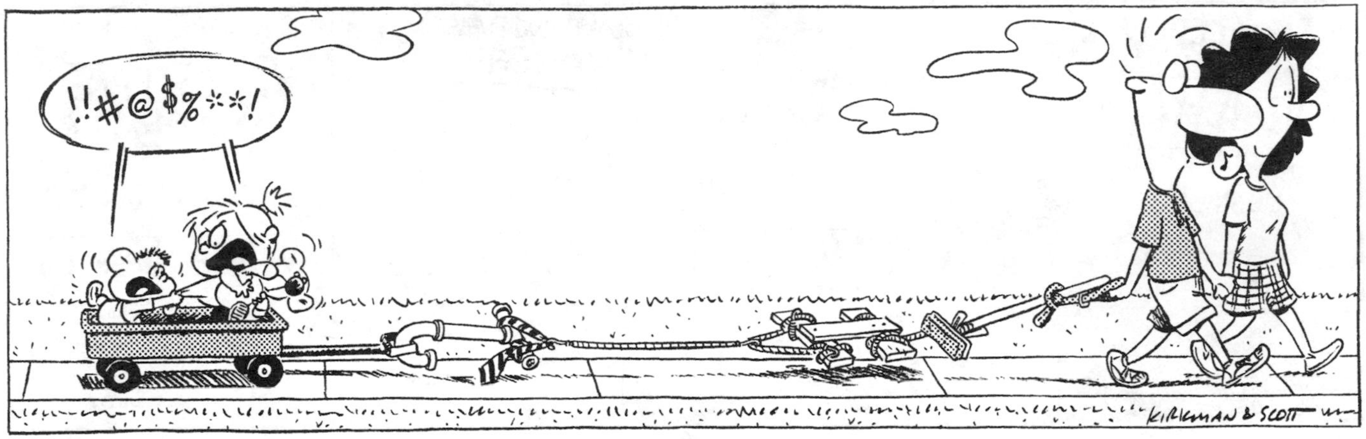
!!#@$%**!
KIRKMAN & SCOTT

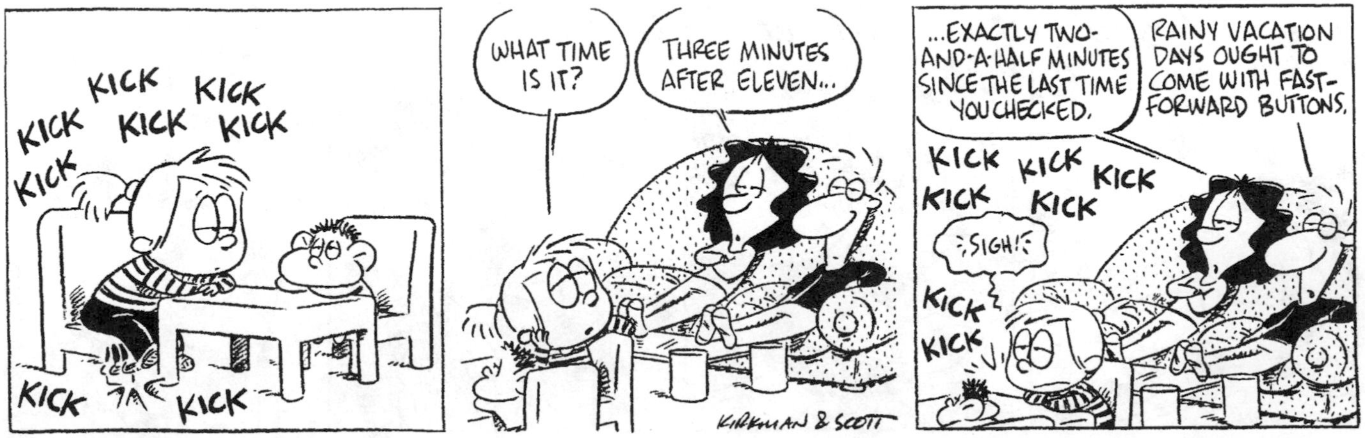
KICK KICK KICK KICK KICK KICK KICK KICK
WHAT TIME IS IT?
THREE MINUTES AFTER ELEVEN...
...EXACTLY TWO-AND-A-HALF MINUTES SINCE THE LAST TIME YOU CHECKED.
RAINY VACATION DAYS OUGHT TO COME WITH FAST-FORWARD BUTTONS.
KICK KICK KICK KICK KICK
SIGH!
KICK KICK
KIRKMAN & SCOTT

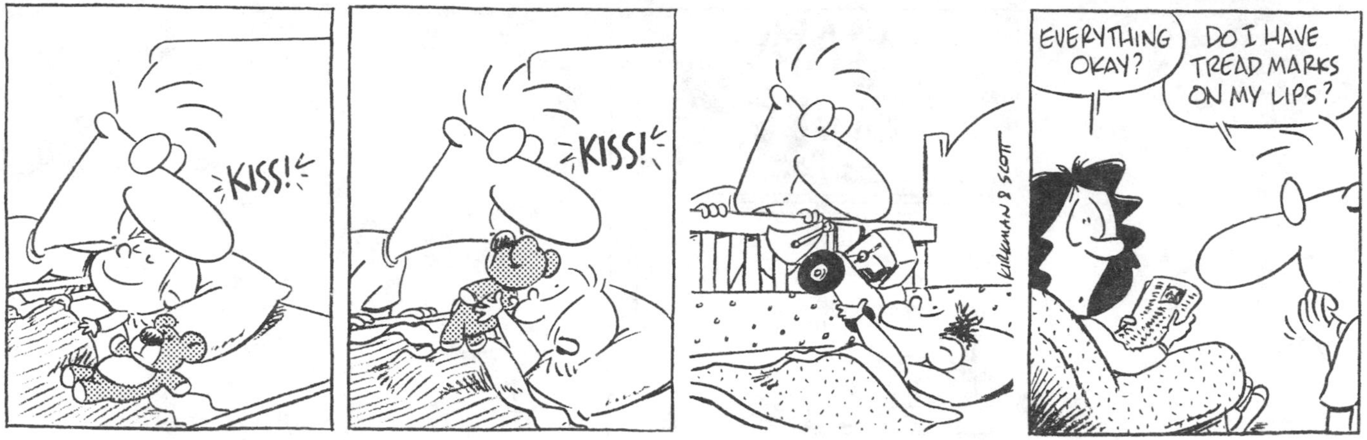
KISS!
KISS!
KIRKMAN & SCOTT
EVERYTHING OKAY?
DO I HAVE TREAD MARKS ON MY LIPS?

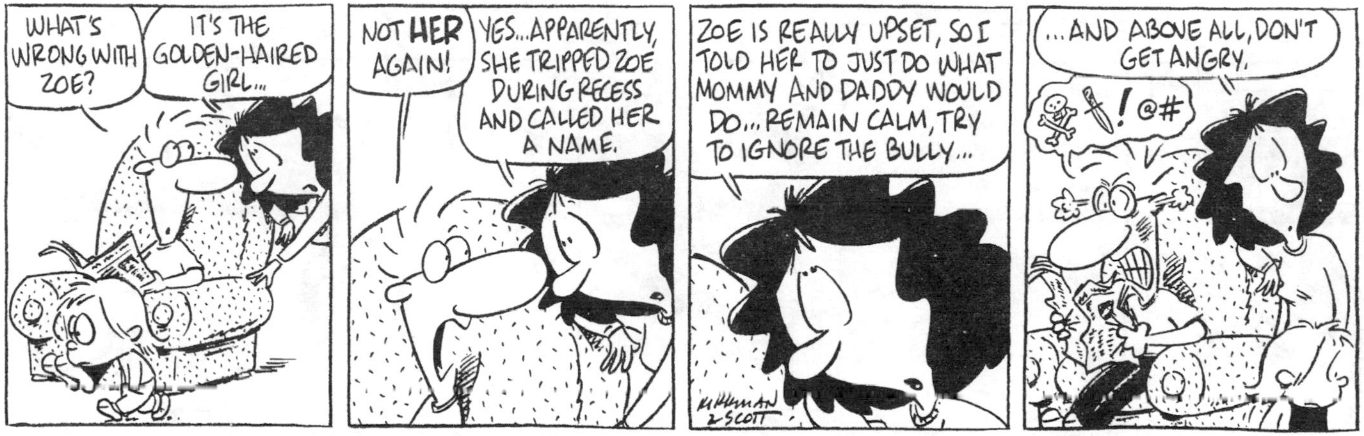
WHAT'S WRONG WITH ZOE?
IT'S THE GOLDEN-HAIRED GIRL...
NOT HER AGAIN!
YES...APPARENTLY, SHE TRIPPED ZOE DURING RECESS AND CALLED HER A NAME.
ZOE IS REALLY UPSET, SO I TOLD HER TO JUST DO WHAT MOMMY AND DADDY WOULD DO... REMAIN CALM, TRY TO IGNORE THE BULLY...
KIRKMAN & SCOTT
...AND ABOVE ALL, DON'T GET ANGRY.
!@#

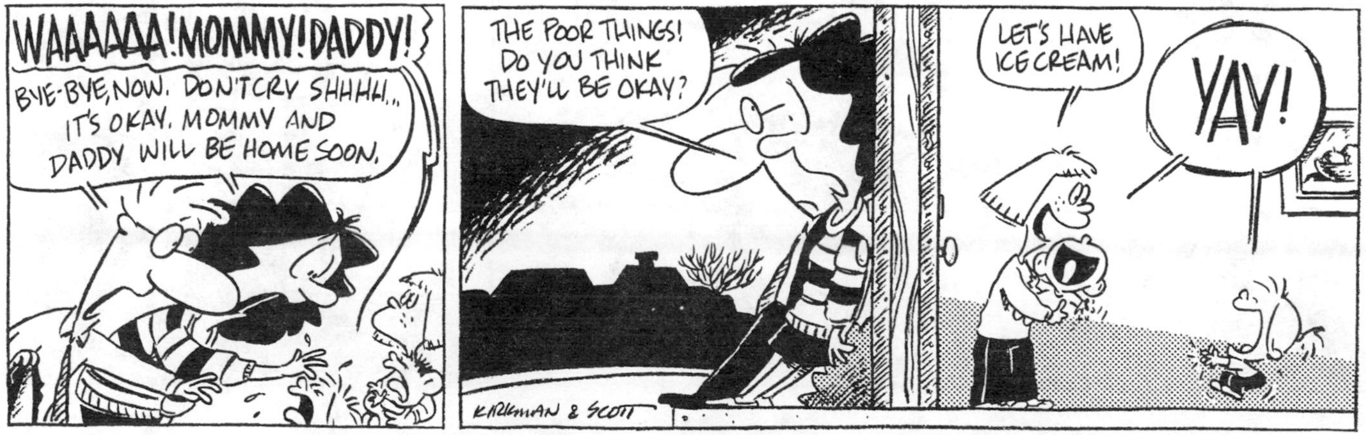
WAAAAAA! MOMMY! DADDY!
BYE-BYE, NOW. DON'T CRY SHHHH... IT'S OKAY. MOMMY AND DADDY WILL BE HOME SOON.
THE POOR THINGS! DO YOU THINK THEY'LL BE OKAY?
LET'S HAVE ICE CREAM!
YAY!
KIRKMAN & SCOTT

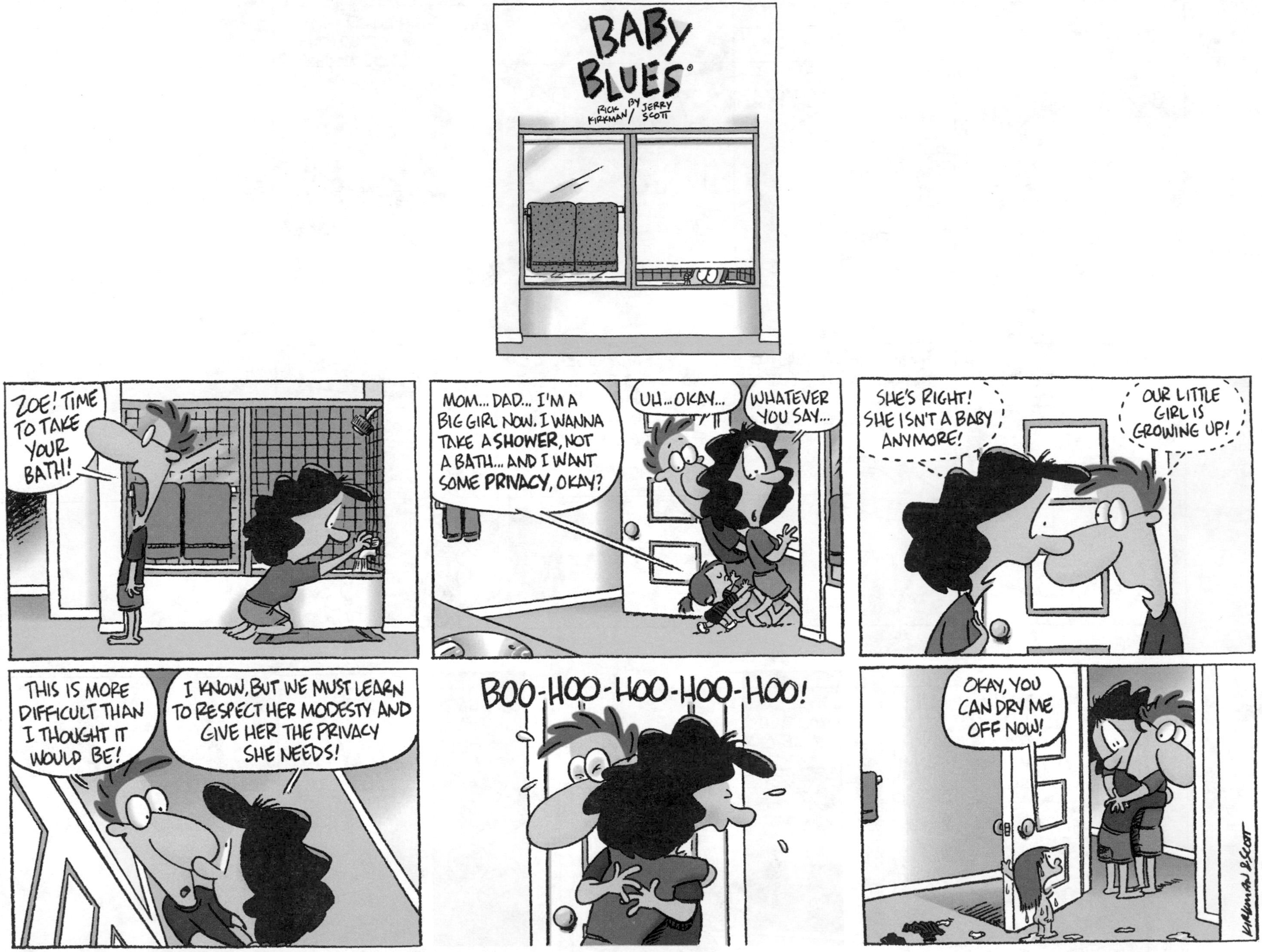
BABY BLUES®
BY RICK KIRKMAN / JERRY SCOTT
ZOE! TIME TO TAKE YOUR BATH!
MOM... DAD... I'M A BIG GIRL NOW. I WANNA TAKE A SHOWER, NOT A BATH... AND I WANT SOME PRIVACY, OKAY?
UH...OKAY...
WHATEVER YOU SAY...
SHE'S RIGHT! SHE ISN'T A BABY ANYMORE!
OUR LITTLE GIRL IS GROWING UP!
THIS IS MORE DIFFICULT THAN I THOUGHT IT WOULD BE!
I KNOW, BUT WE MUST LEARN TO RESPECT HER MODESTY AND GIVE HER THE PRIVACY SHE NEEDS!
BOO-HOO-HOO-HOO-HOO!
OKAY, YOU CAN DRY ME OFF NOW!
KIRKMAN & SCOTT

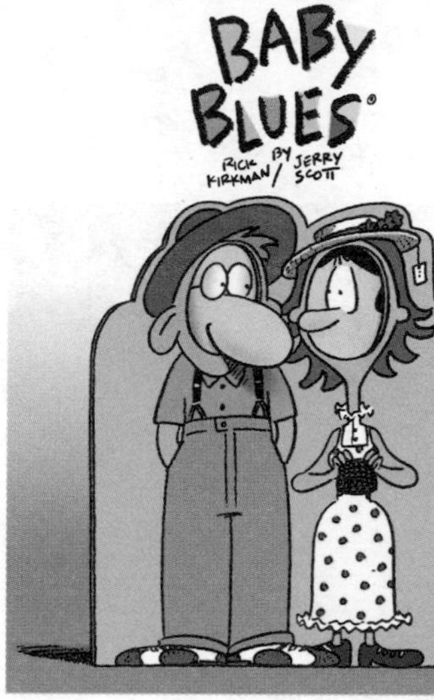
BABY BLUES®
BY RICK KIRKMAN / JERRY SCOTT

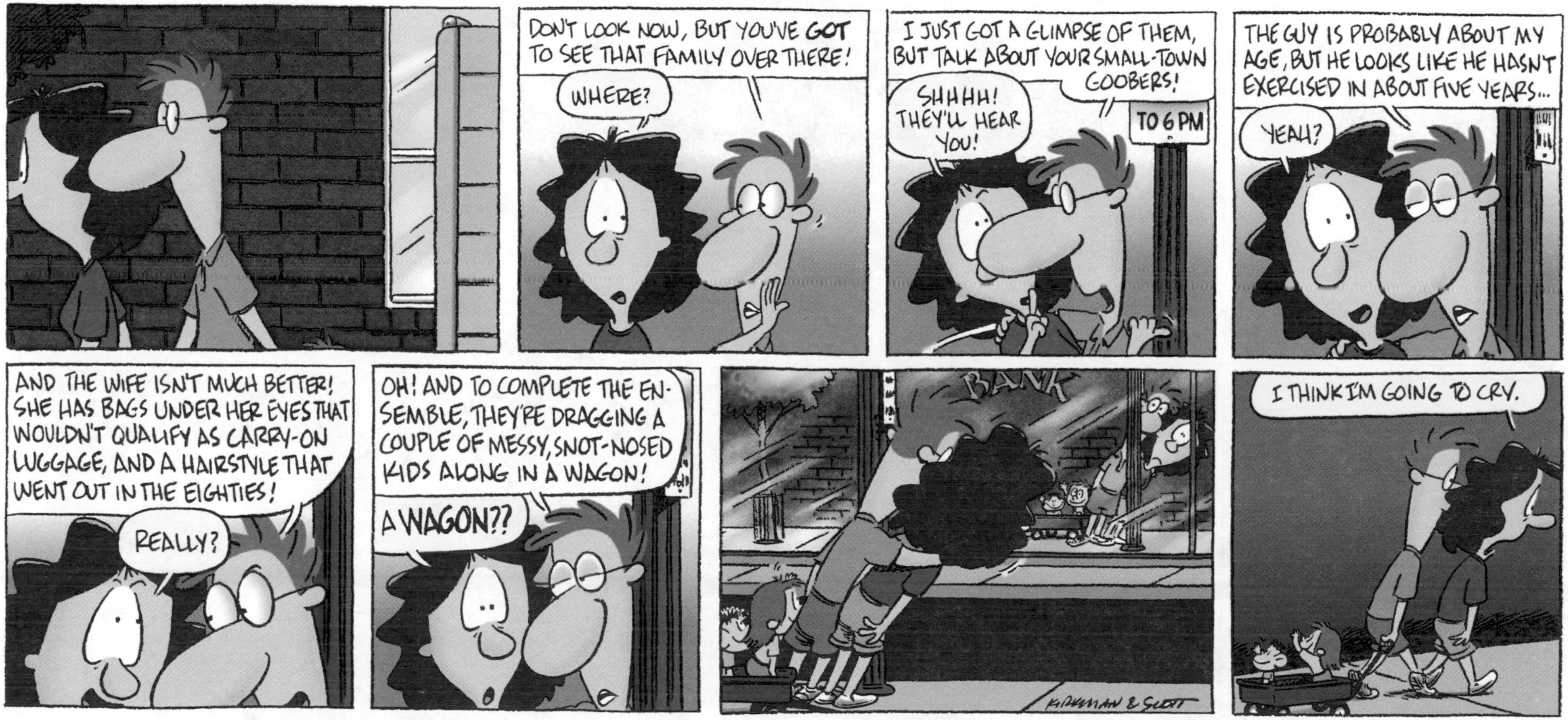
DON'T LOOK NOW, BUT YOU'VE GOT TO SEE THAT FAMILY OVER THERE!
WHERE?
I JUST GOT A GLIMPSE OF THEM, BUT TALK ABOUT YOUR SMALL-TOWN GOOBERS!
SHHHH! THEY'LL HEAR YOU!
TO 6 PM
THE GUY IS PROBABLY ABOUT MY AGE, BUT HE LOOKS LIKE HE HASN'T EXERCISED IN ABOUT FIVE YEARS...
YEAH?
AND THE WIFE ISN'T MUCH BETTER! SHE HAS BAGS UNDER HER EYES THAT WOULDN'T QUALIFY AS CARRY-ON LUGGAGE, AND A HAIRSTYLE THAT WENT OUT IN THE EIGHTIES!
REALLY?
OH! AND TO COMPLETE THE EN-SEMBLE, THEY'RE DRAGGING A COUPLE OF MESSY, SNOT-NOSED KIDS ALONG IN A WAGON!
A WAGON??
BANK
KIRKMAN & SCOTT
I THINK I'M GOING TO CRY.

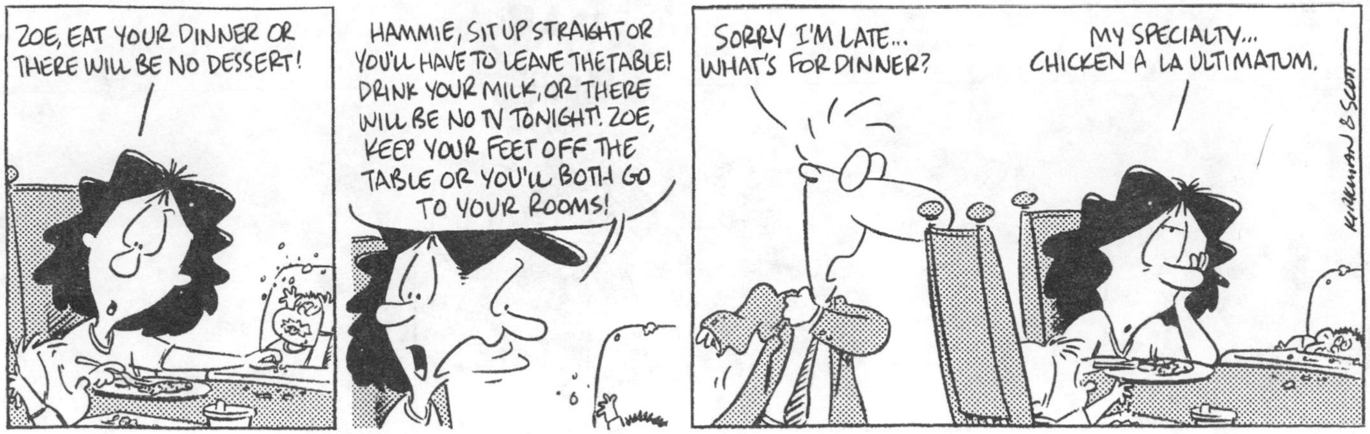
ZOE, EAT YOUR DINNER OR THERE WILL BE NO DESSERT!
HAMMIE, SIT UP STRAIGHT OR YOU'LL HAVE TO LEAVE THE TABLE! DRINK YOUR MILK, OR THERE WILL BE NO TV TONIGHT! ZOE, KEEP YOUR FEET OFF THE TABLE OR YOU'LL BOTH GO TO YOUR ROOMS!
SORRY I'M LATE... WHAT'S FOR DINNER?
MY SPECIALTY... CHICKEN A LA ULTIMATUM.
KIRKMAN & SCOTT

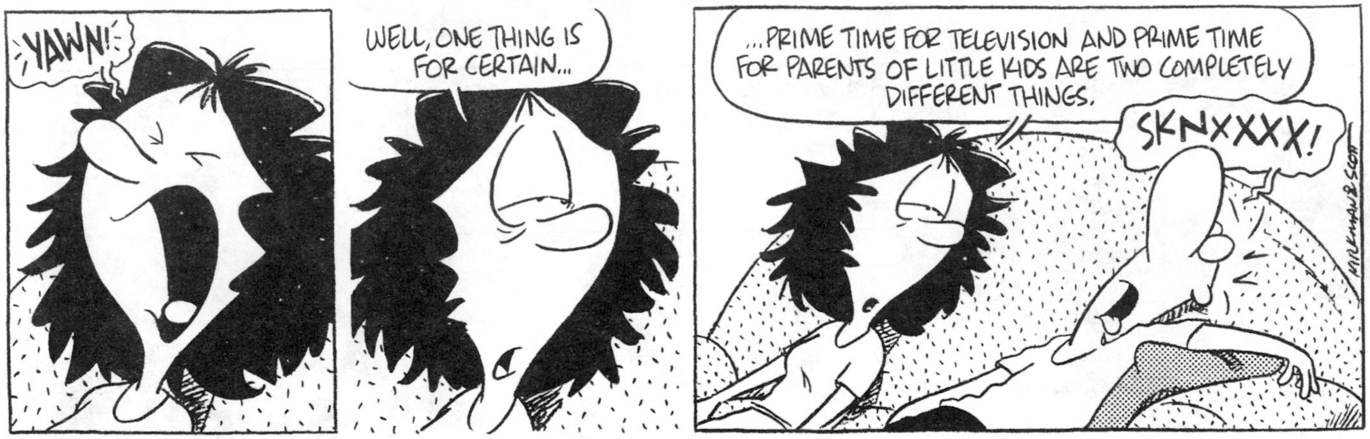
YAWN!
WELL, ONE THING IS FOR CERTAIN...
...PRIME TIME FOR TELEVISION AND PRIME TIME FOR PARENTS OF LITTLE KIDS ARE TWO COMPLETELY DIFFERENT THINGS.
SKNXXXX!

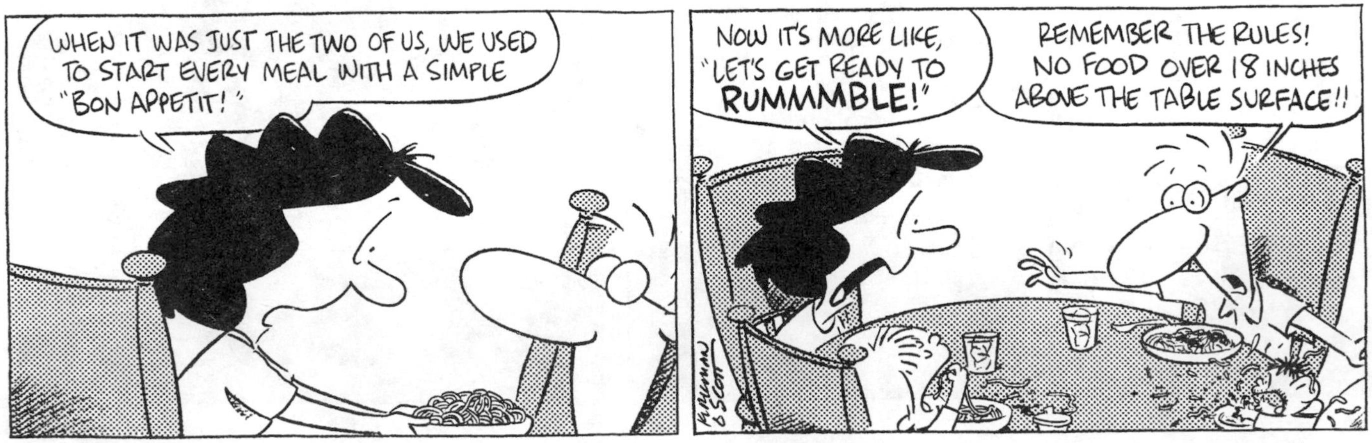
WHEN IT WAS JUST THE TWO OF US, WE USED TO START EVERY MEAL WITH A SIMPLE "BON APPETIT!"
NOW IT'S MORE LIKE, "LET'S GET READY TO RUMMMBLE!"
REMEMBER THE RULES! NO FOOD OVER 18 INCHES ABOVE THE TABLE SURFACE!!

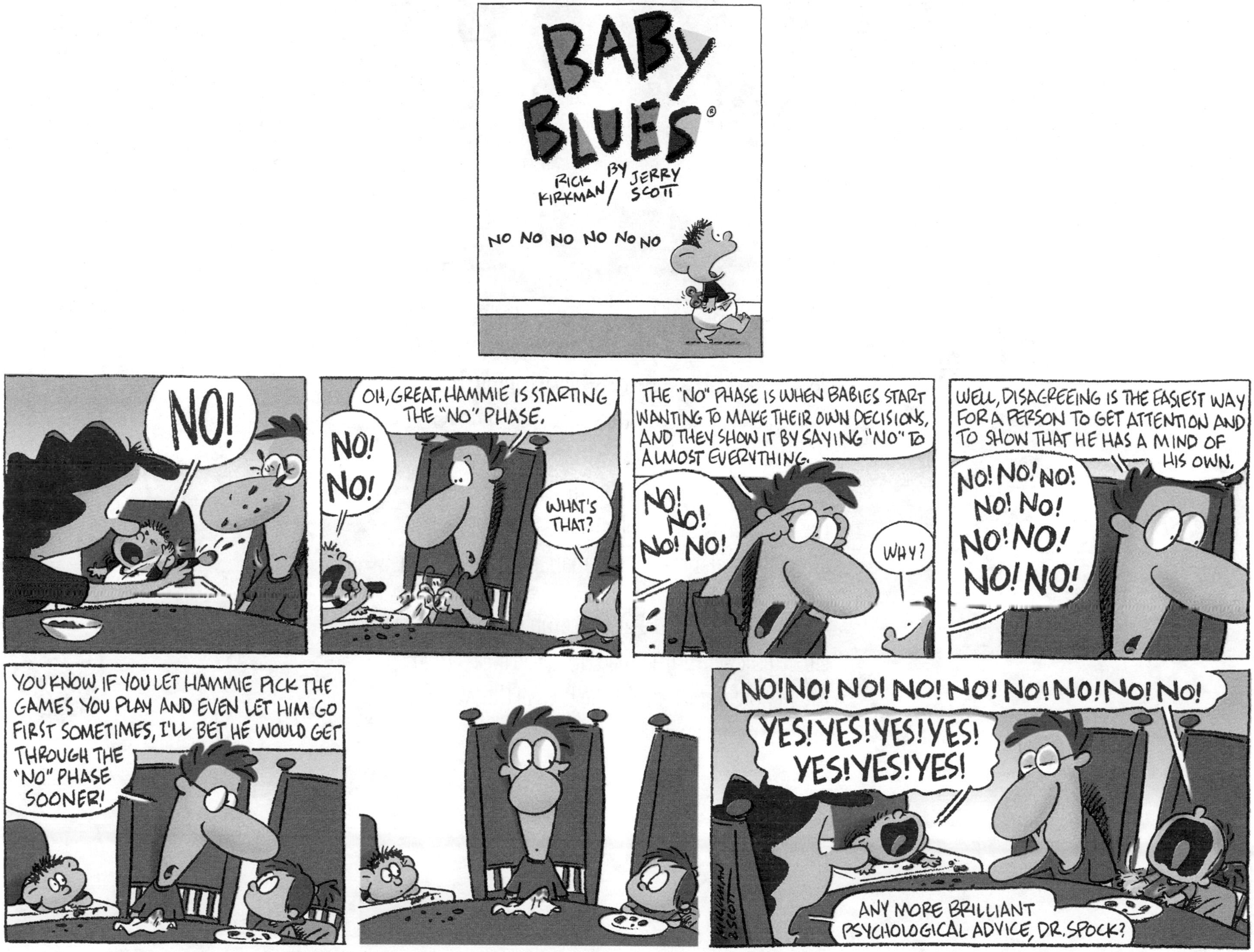
BABY BLUES®
BY RICK KIRKMAN / JERRY SCOTT
NO NO NO NO NO NO
NO!
OH, GREAT. HAMMIE IS STARTING THE "NO" PHASE.
NO! NO!
WHAT'S THAT?
THE "NO" PHASE IS WHEN BABIES START WANTING TO MAKE THEIR OWN DECISIONS, AND THEY SHOW IT BY SAYING "NO" TO ALMOST EVERYTHING.
NO! NO! NO! NO!
WHY?
WELL, DISAGREEING IS THE EASIEST WAY FOR A PERSON TO GET ATTENTION AND TO SHOW THAT HE HAS A MIND OF HIS OWN.
NO! NO! NO! NO! NO! NO! NO! NO! NO!
YOU KNOW, IF YOU LET HAMMIE PICK THE GAMES YOU PLAY AND EVEN LET HIM GO FIRST SOMETIMES, I'LL BET HE WOULD GET THROUGH THE "NO" PHASE SOONER!
NO! NO! NO! NO! NO! NO! NO! NO! NO!
YES! YES! YES! YES! YES! YES! YES!
ANY MORE BRILLIANT PSYCHOLOGICAL ADVICE, DR. SPOCK?
KIRKMAN & SCOTT

ZOE

Zoe was the firstborn and therefore charged with the responsibility of breaking in the parents. She's done a good job, too, successfully weaning them from such vices as free time and quiet moments together as a couple. Now with a little brother in the house, she has been able to let him take over the day-to-day monopolizing of Mom and Dad's attention and moved into a management position.

A natural leader and a gifted complainer, Zoe has earned the self-proclaimed title of "Princess High 'n' Mighty Big-Shot Told-You-So Boss of the World," and she wears it proudly.

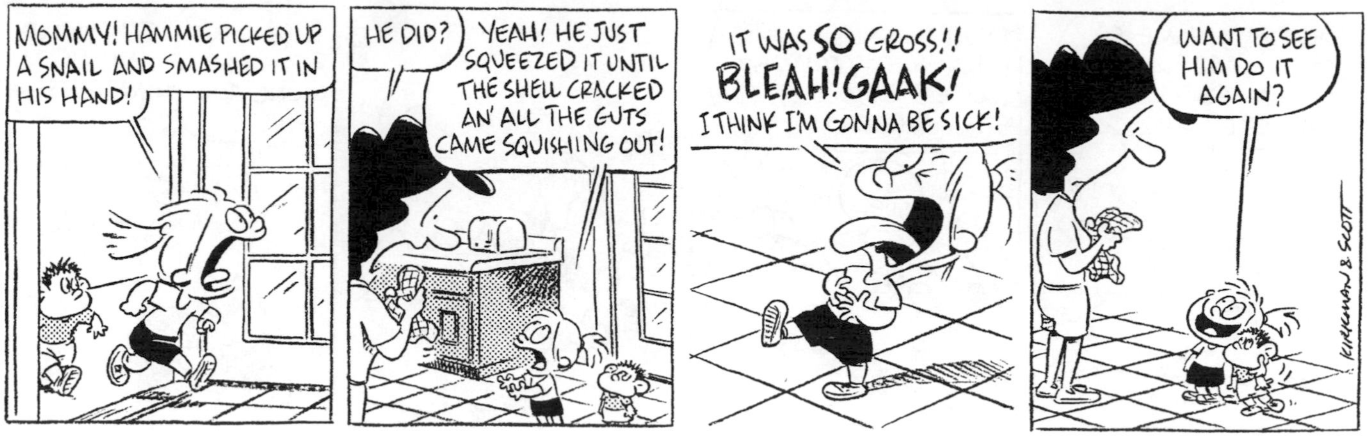
MOMMY! HAMMIE PICKED UP A SNAIL AND SMASHED IT IN HIS HAND!
HE DID?
YEAH! HE JUST SQUEEZED IT UNTIL THE SHELL CRACKED AN' ALL THE GUTS CAME SQUISHING OUT!
IT WAS SO GROSS!! BLEAH! GAAK! I THINK I'M GONNA BE SICK!
WANT TO SEE HIM DO IT AGAIN?
KIRKMAN & SCOTT

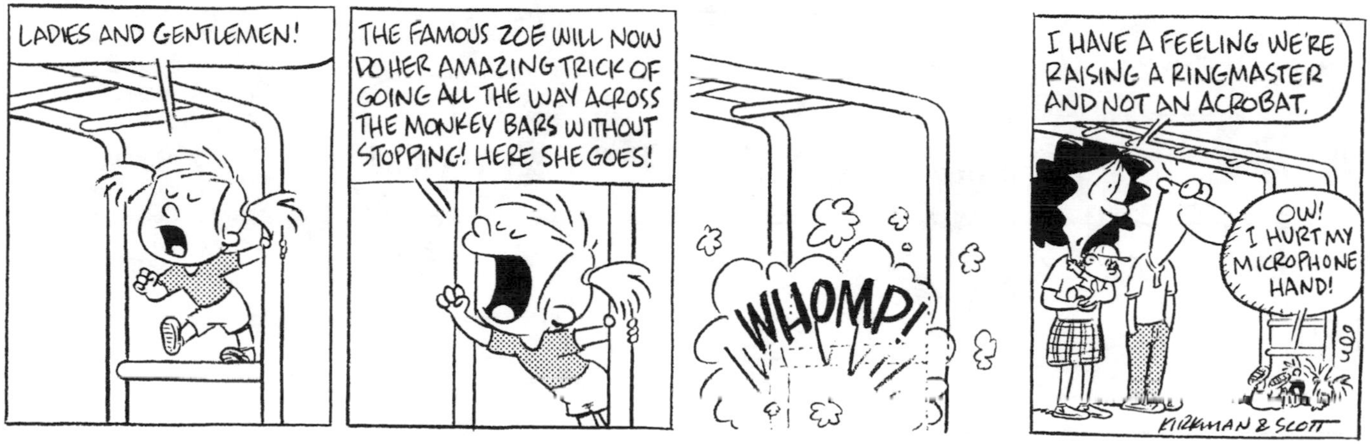
LADIES AND GENTLEMEN!
THE FAMOUS ZOE WILL NOW DO HER AMAZING TRICK OF GOING ALL THE WAY ACROSS THE MONKEY BARS WITHOUT STOPPING! HERE SHE GOES!
WHOMP!
I HAVE A FEELING WE'RE RAISING A RINGMASTER AND NOT AN ACROBAT.
OW! I HURT MY MICROPHONE HAND!
KIRKMAN & SCOTT

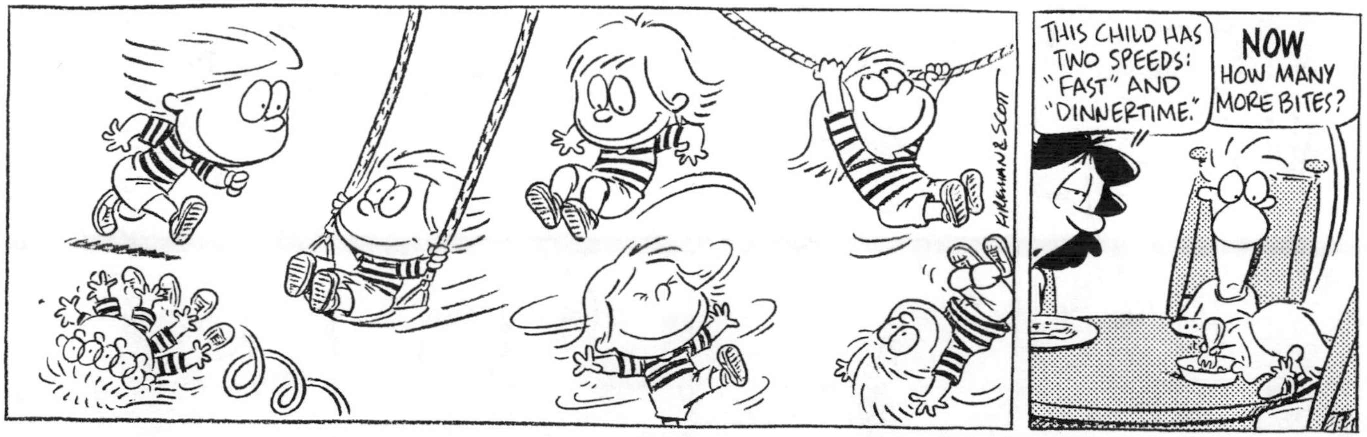
KIRKMAN & SCOTT
THIS CHILD HAS TWO SPEEDS: "FAST" AND "DINNERTIME."
NOW HOW MANY MORE BITES?

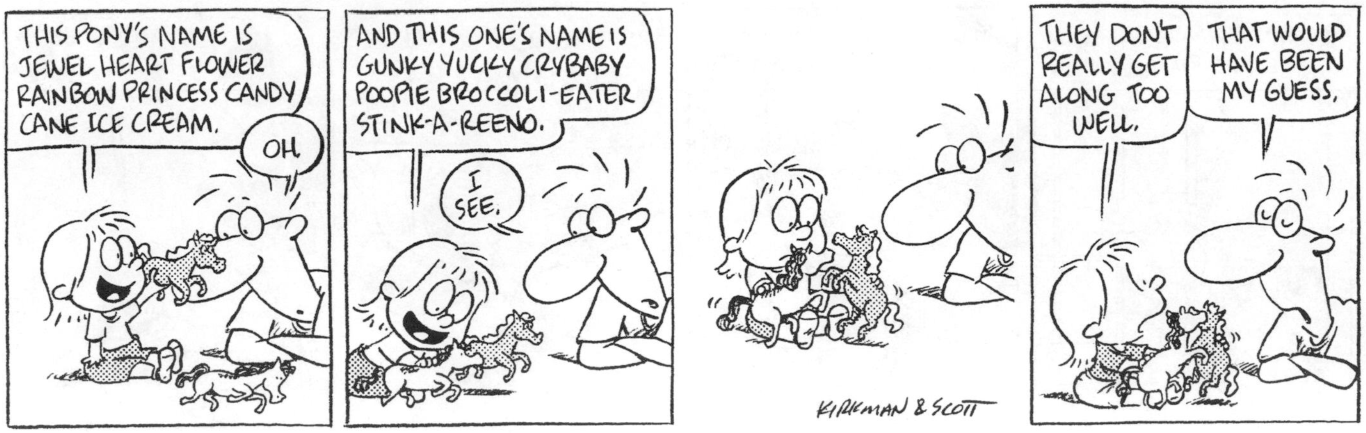
THIS PONY'S NAME IS JEWEL HEART FLOWER RAINBOW PRINCESS CANDY CANE ICE CREAM.
OH.
AND THIS ONE'S NAME IS GUNKY YUCKY CRYBABY POOPIE BROCCOLI-EATER STINK-A-REENO.
I SEE.
THEY DON'T REALLY GET ALONG TOO WELL.
THAT WOULD HAVE BEEN MY GUESS.
KIRKMAN & SCOTT

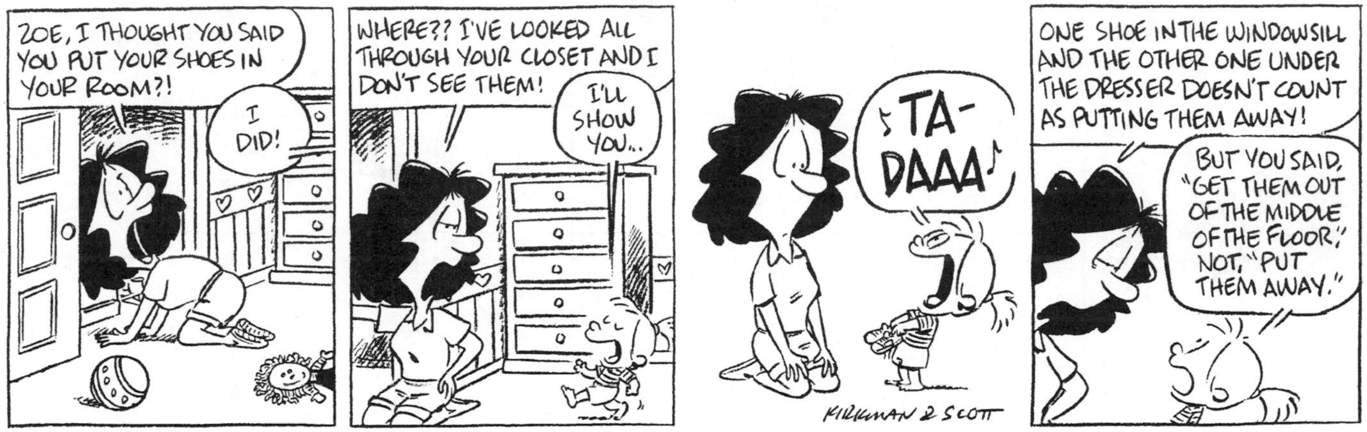
ZOE, I THOUGHT YOU SAID YOU PUT YOUR SHOES IN YOUR ROOM?!
I DID!
WHERE?? I'VE LOOKED ALL THROUGH YOUR CLOSET AND I DON'T SEE THEM!
I'LL SHOW YOU...
TA-DAAA
ONE SHOE IN THE WINDOWSILL AND THE OTHER ONE UNDER THE DRESSER DOESN'T COUNT AS PUTTING THEM AWAY!
BUT YOU SAID, "GET THEM OUT OF THE MIDDLE OF THE FLOOR," NOT, "PUT THEM AWAY."
KIRKMAN & SCOTT

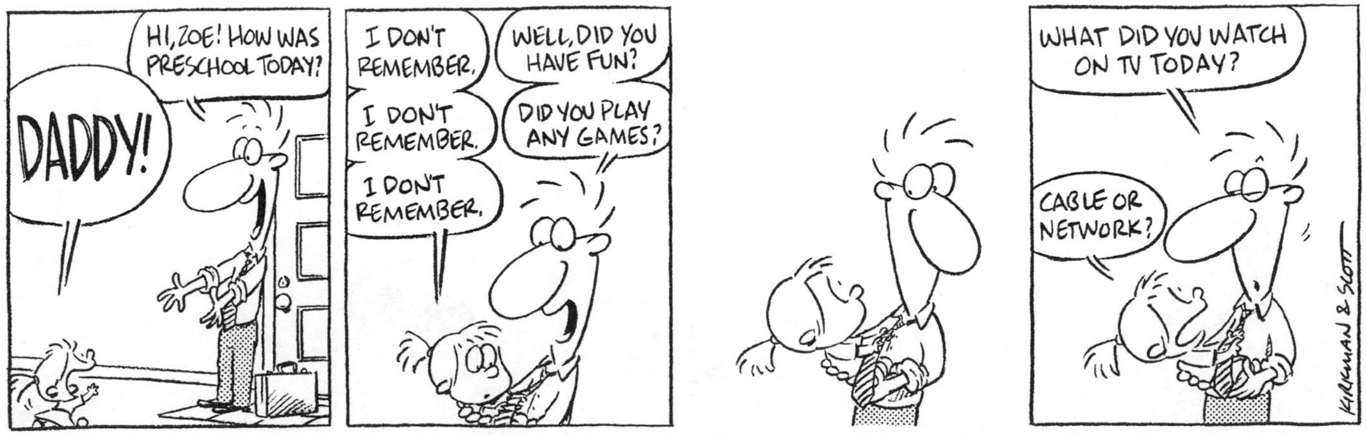
DADDY!
HI, ZOE! HOW WAS PRESCHOOL TODAY?
I DON'T REMEMBER.
WELL, DID YOU HAVE FUN?
I DON'T REMEMBER.
DID YOU PLAY ANY GAMES?
I DON'T REMEMBER.
WHAT DID YOU WATCH ON TV TODAY?
CABLE OR NETWORK?
KIRKMAN & SCOTT

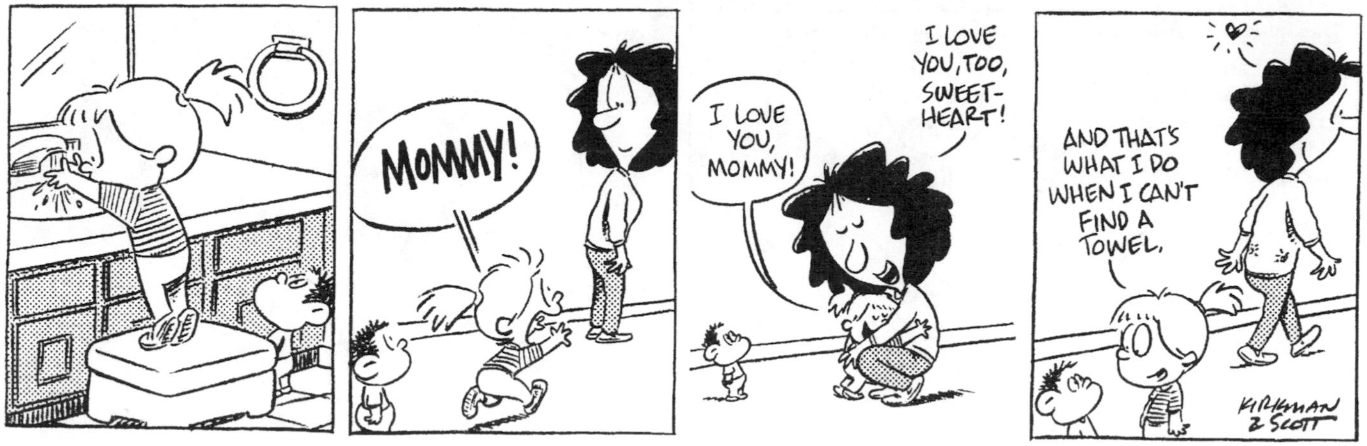
MOMMY!
I LOVE YOU, MOMMY!
I LOVE YOU, TOO, SWEET-HEART!
AND THAT'S WHAT I DO WHEN I CAN'T FIND A TOWEL.
KIRKMAN & SCOTT

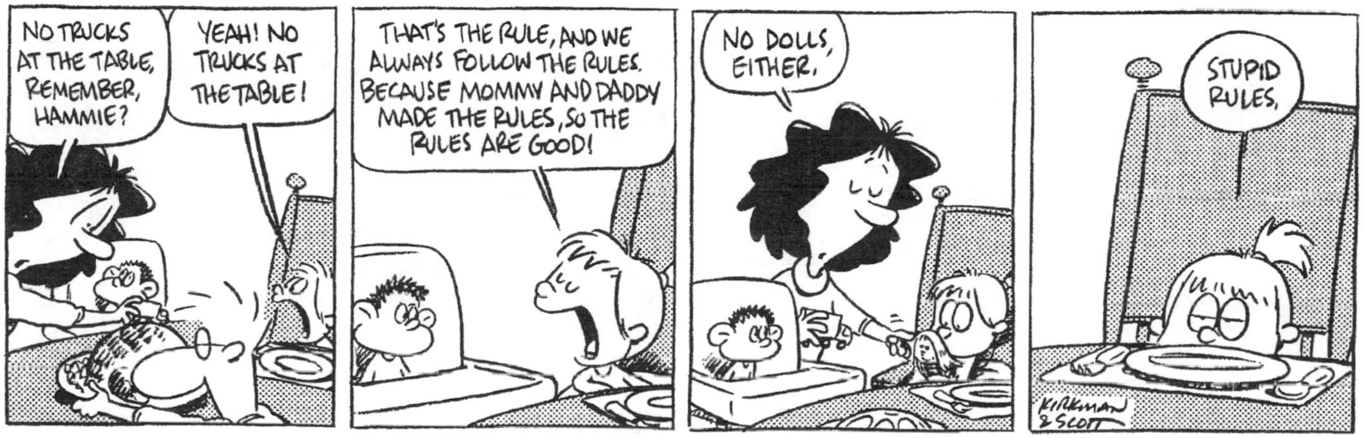
NO TRUCKS AT THE TABLE, REMEMBER, HAMMIE?
YEAH! NO TRUCKS AT THE TABLE!
THAT'S THE RULE, AND WE ALWAYS FOLLOW THE RULES. BECAUSE MOMMY AND DADDY MADE THE RULES, SO THE RULES ARE GOOD!
NO DOLLS, EITHER.
STUPID RULES.
KIRKMAN & SCOTT

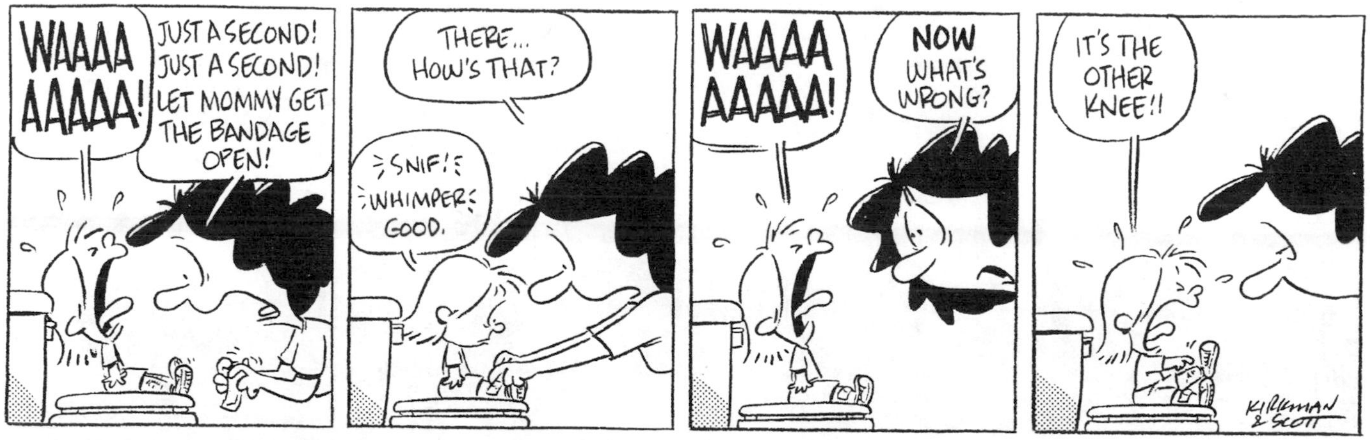
WAAAA AAAAA!
JUST A SECOND! JUST A SECOND! LET MOMMY GET THE BANDAGE OPEN!
THERE... HOW'S THAT?
SNIF! WHIMPER GOOD.
WAAAA AAAAA!
NOW WHAT'S WRONG?
IT'S THE OTHER KNEE!!
KIRKMAN & SCOTT

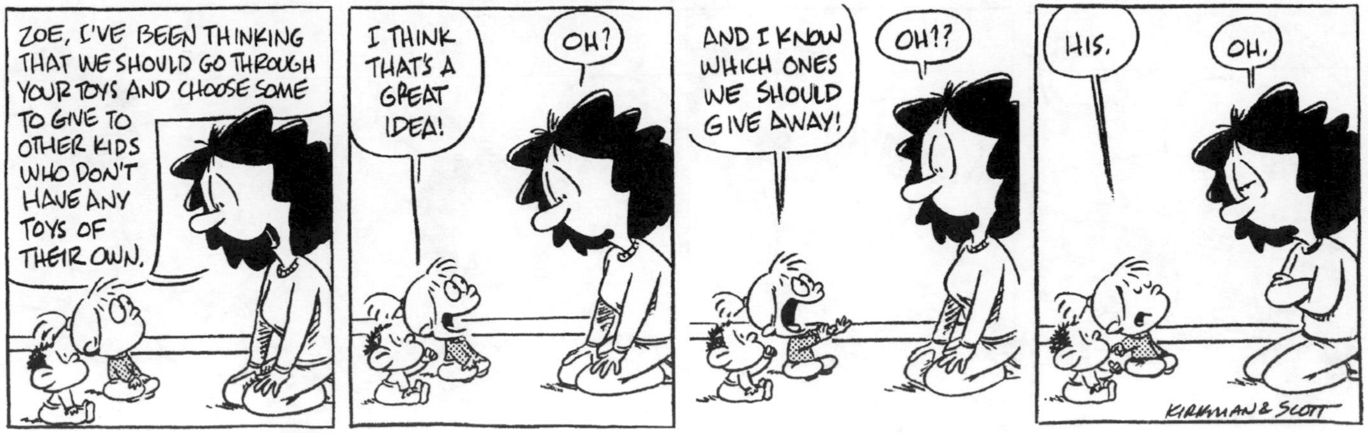
ZOE, I'VE BEEN THINKING THAT WE SHOULD GO THROUGH YOUR TOYS AND CHOOSE SOME TO GIVE TO OTHER KIDS WHO DON'T HAVE ANY TOYS OF THEIR OWN.
I THINK THAT'S A GREAT IDEA!
OH?
AND I KNOW WHICH ONES WE SHOULD GIVE AWAY!
OH!?
HIS.
OH.
KIRKMAN & SCOTT

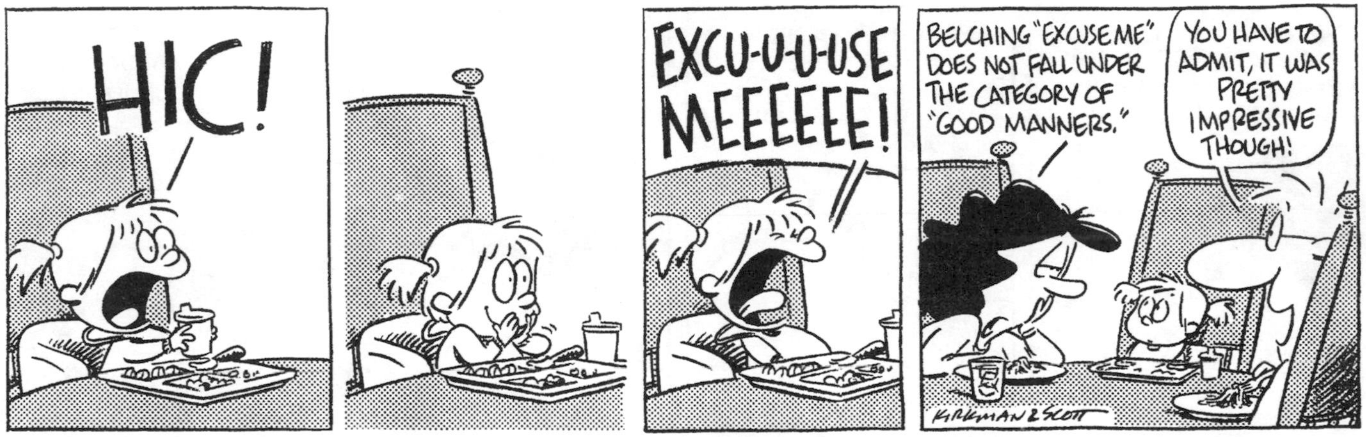
HIC!
EXCU-U-U-USE MEEEEEE!
BELCHING "EXCUSE ME" DOES NOT FALL UNDER THE CATEGORY OF "GOOD MANNERS."
YOU HAVE TO ADMIT, IT WAS PRETTY IMPRESSIVE THOUGH!
KIRKMAN & SCOTT

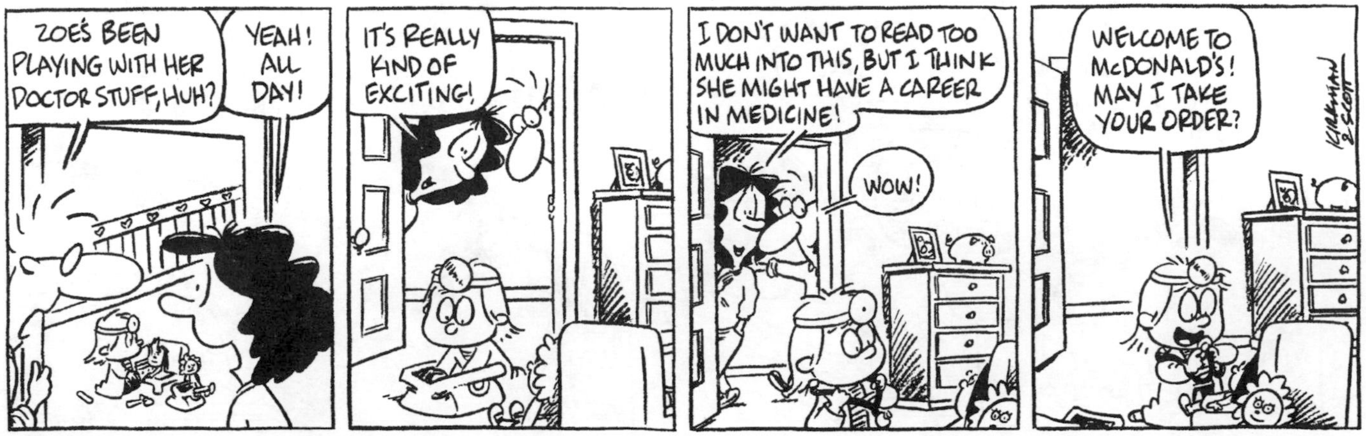
ZOE'S BEEN PLAYING WITH HER DOCTOR STUFF, HUH?
YEAH! ALL DAY!
IT'S REALLY KIND OF EXCITING!
I DON'T WANT TO READ TOO MUCH INTO THIS, BUT I THINK SHE MIGHT HAVE A CAREER IN MEDICINE!
WOW!
WELCOME TO McDONALD'S! MAY I TAKE YOUR ORDER?
KIRKMAN & SCOTT

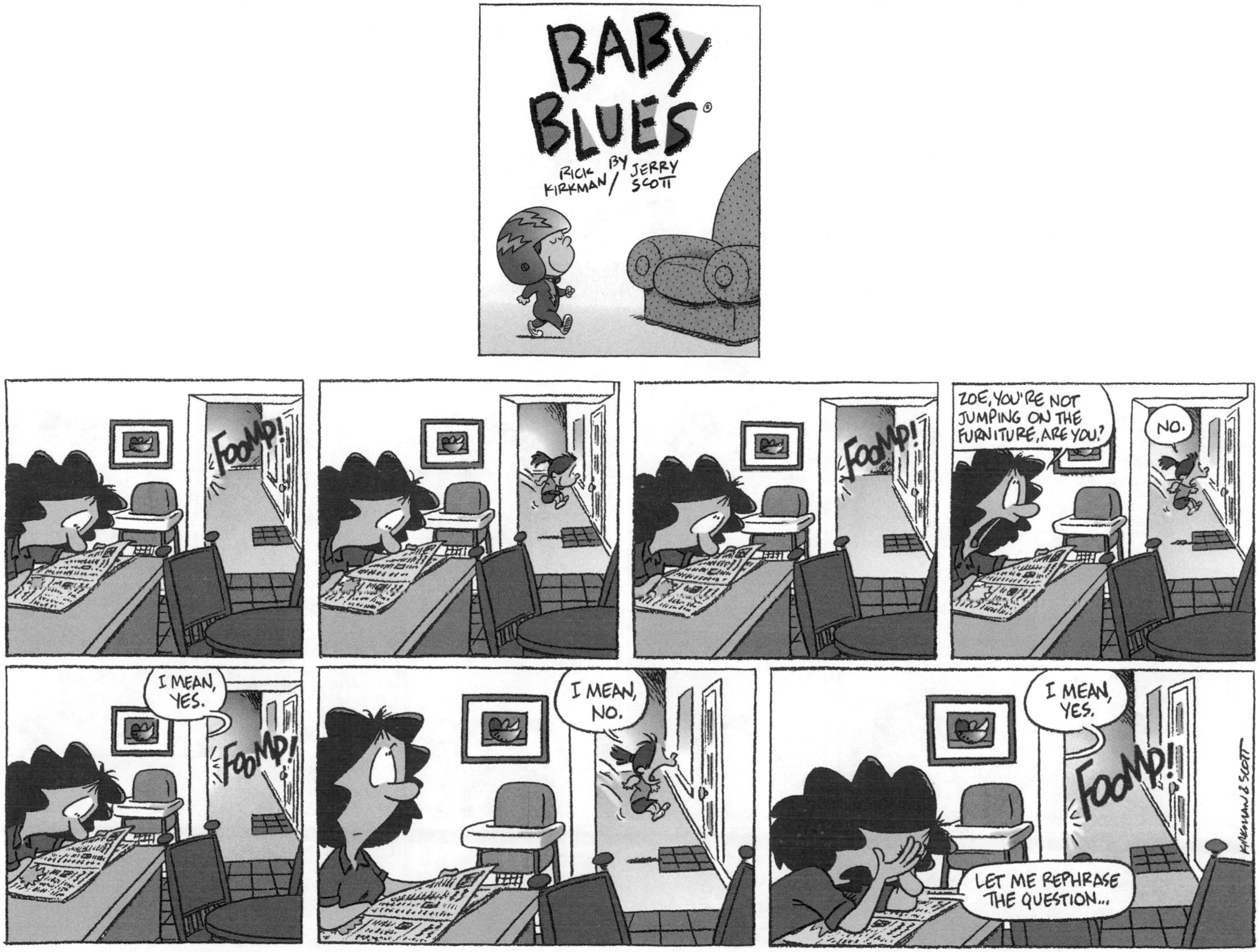
BABY BLUES®
BY RICK KIRKMAN / JERRY SCOTT
FOOMP!
FOOMP!
ZOE, YOU'RE NOT JUMPING ON THE FURNITURE, ARE YOU?
NO.
I MEAN, YES.
FOOMP!
I MEAN, NO.
I MEAN, YES.
FOOMP!
LET ME REPHRASE THE QUESTION...
KIRKMAN & SCOTT

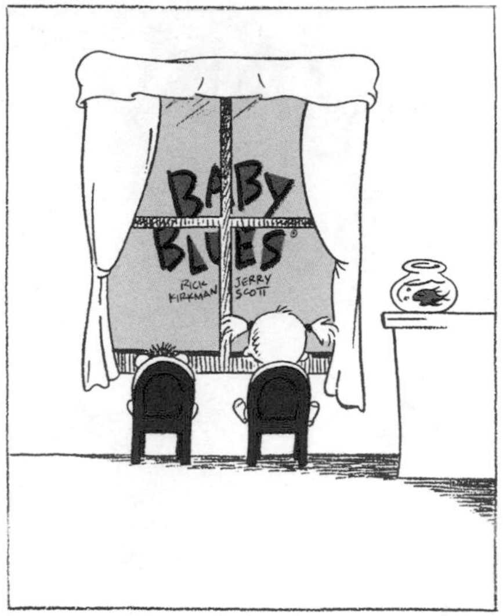
BABY BLUES®
RICK KIRKMAN
JERRY SCOTT

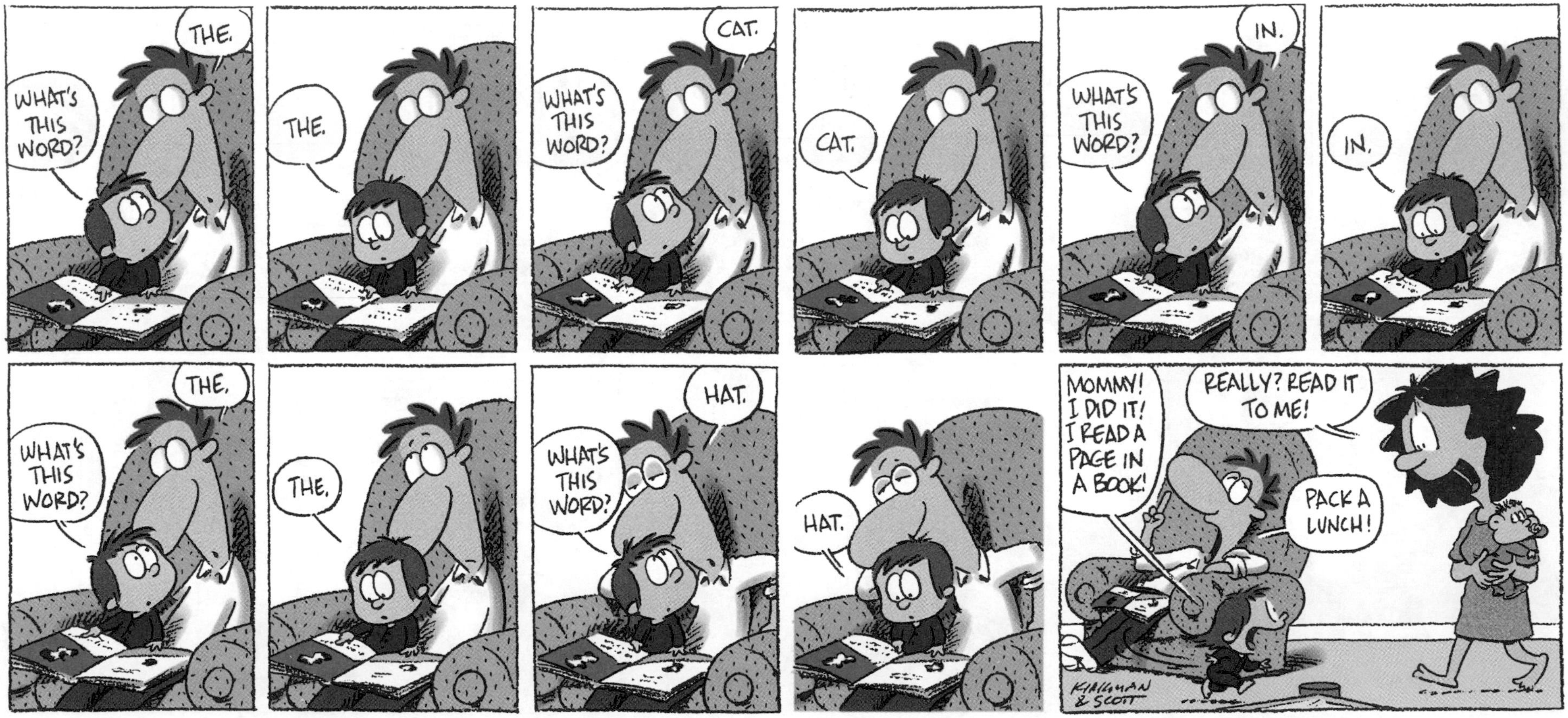
WHAT'S THIS WORD?
THE.
THE.
WHAT'S THIS WORD?
CAT.
CAT.
WHAT'S THIS WORD?
IN.
IN.
WHAT'S THIS WORD?
THE.
THE.
WHAT'S THIS WORD?
HAT.
HAT.
MOMMY! I DID IT! I READ A PAGE IN A BOOK!
REALLY? READ IT TO ME!
PACK A LUNCH!
KIRKMAN & SCOTT

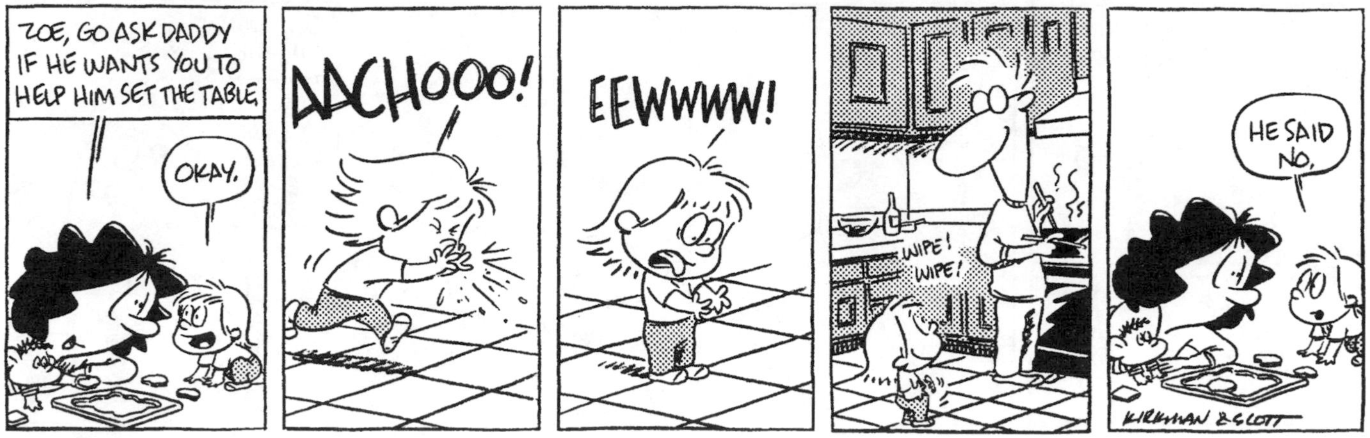
ZOE, GO ASK DADDY IF HE WANTS YOU TO HELP HIM SET THE TABLE.
OKAY.
AACHOOO!
EEWWWW!
WIPE! WIPE!
HE SAID NO.
KIRKMAN & SCOTT

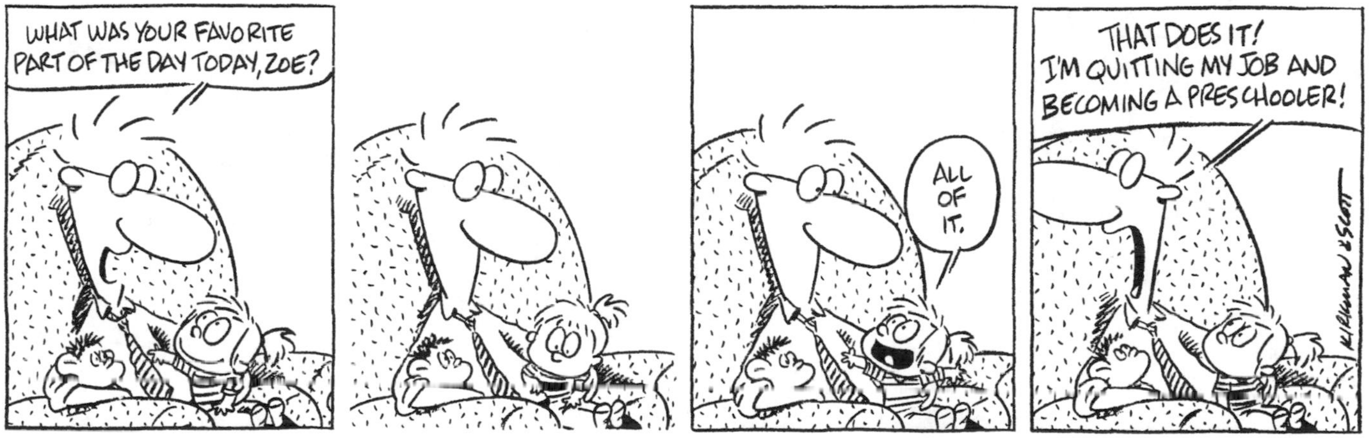
WHAT WAS YOUR FAVORITE PART OF THE DAY TODAY, ZOE?
ALL OF IT.
THAT DOES IT! I'M QUITTING MY JOB AND BECOMING A PRESCHOOLER!
KIRKMAN & SCOTT

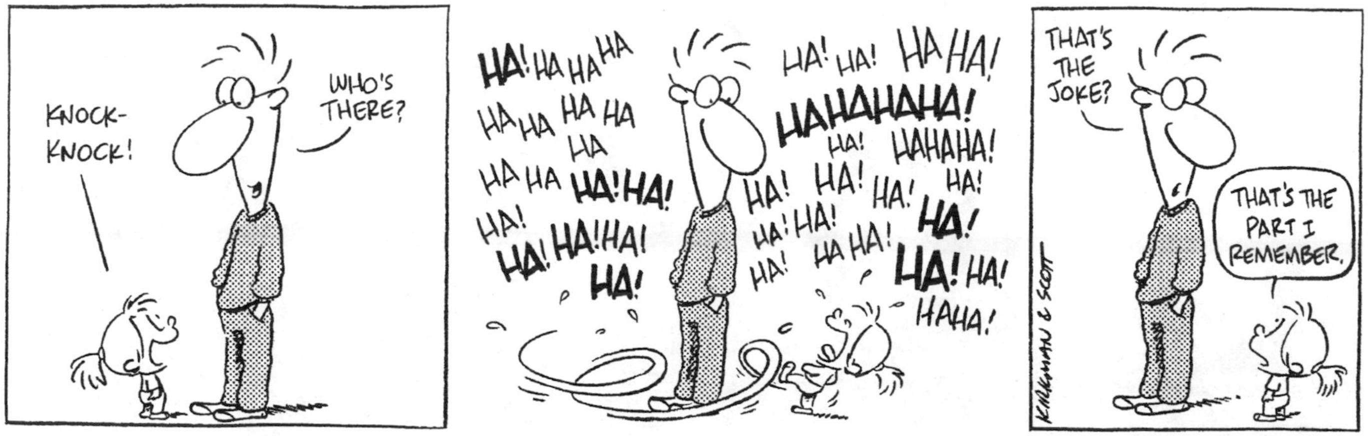
KNOCK-KNOCK!
WHO'S THERE?
HA! HA HA HA HA HA HA HA HA HA HA HA HA HA HA! HA! HA! HA! HA! HA! HA! HA!
HA! HA! HA HA! HAHAHAHA! HA! HAHAHA! HA! HA! HA! HA! HA! HA! HA! HA! HA HA! HA! HA! HA! HAHA!
KIRKMAN & SCOTT
THAT'S THE JOKE?
THAT'S THE PART I REMEMBER.

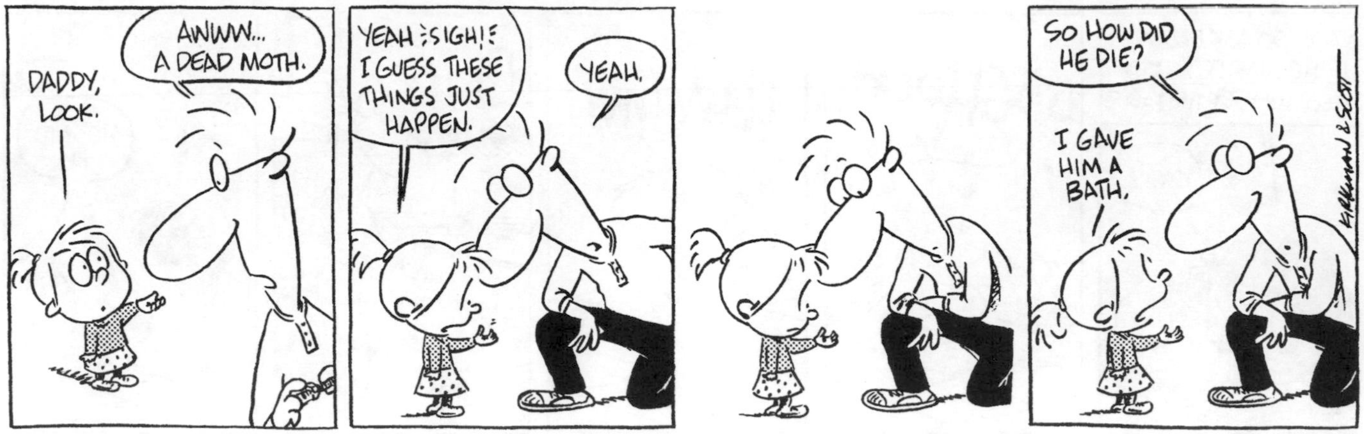
DADDY, LOOK.
AWWW... A DEAD MOTH.
YEAH ;SIGH!; I GUESS THESE THINGS JUST HAPPEN.
YEAH.
SO HOW DID HE DIE?
I GAVE HIM A BATH.
KIRKMAN & SCOTT

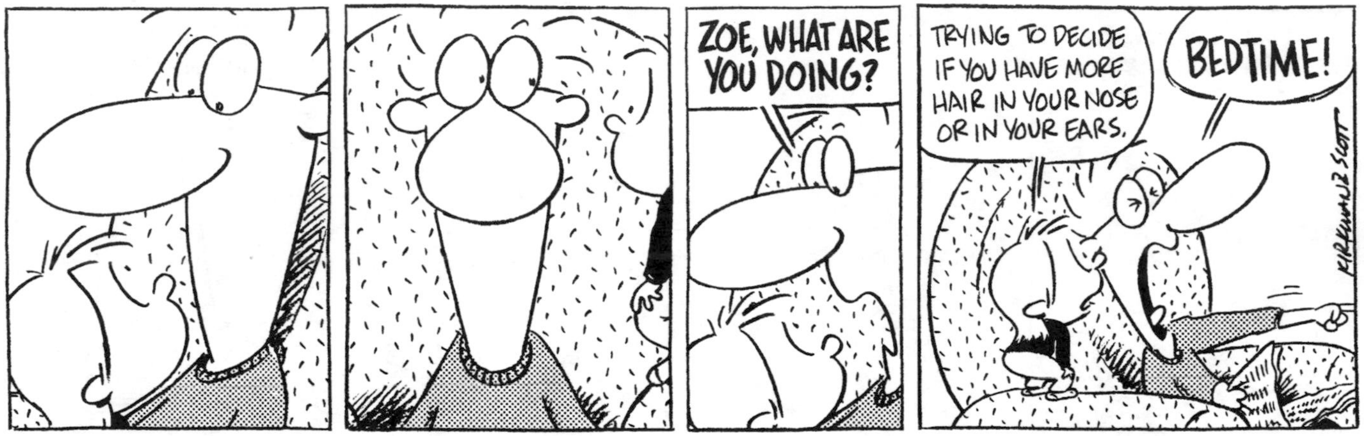
ZOE, WHAT ARE YOU DOING?
TRYING TO DECIDE IF YOU HAVE MORE HAIR IN YOUR NOSE OR IN YOUR EARS.
BEDTIME!
KIRKMAN & SCOTT

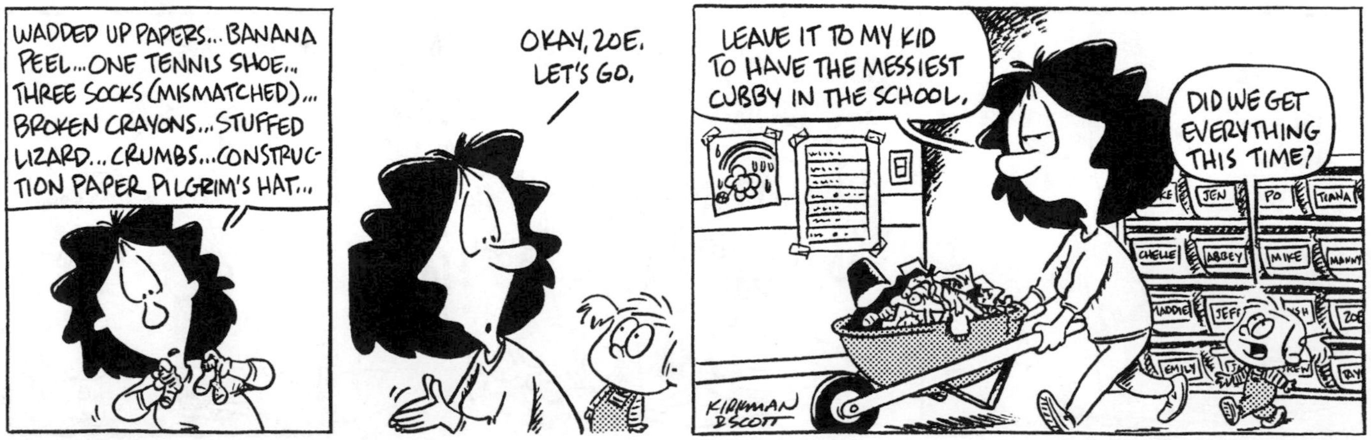
WADDED UP PAPERS... BANANA PEEL... ONE TENNIS SHOE... THREE SOCKS (MISMATCHED)... BROKEN CRAYONS... STUFFED LIZARD... CRUMBS... CONSTRUCTION PAPER PILGRIM'S HAT...
OKAY, ZOE. LET'S GO.
LEAVE IT TO MY KID TO HAVE THE MESSIEST CUBBY IN THE SCHOOL.
DID WE GET EVERYTHING THIS TIME?
JEN
PO
TIANA
CHELLE
ABBEY
MIKE
MANNY
MADDIE
JEFF
ZOE
EMILY
KIRKMAN & SCOTT

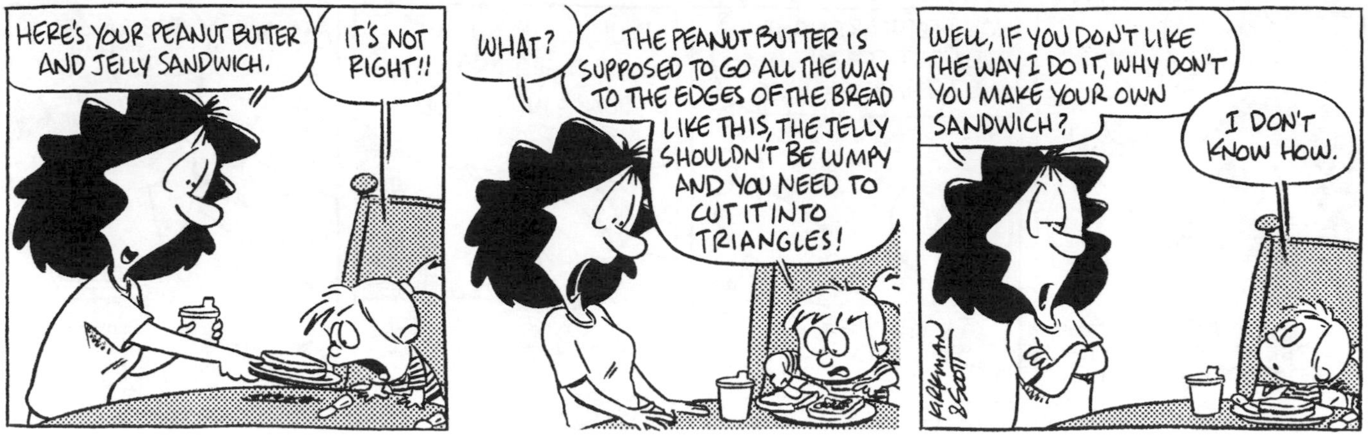
HERE'S YOUR PEANUT BUTTER AND JELLY SANDWICH.
IT'S NOT RIGHT!!
WHAT?
THE PEANUT BUTTER IS SUPPOSED TO GO ALL THE WAY TO THE EDGES OF THE BREAD LIKE THIS, THE JELLY SHOULDN'T BE LUMPY AND YOU NEED TO CUT IT INTO TRIANGLES!
KIRKMAN & SCOTT
WELL, IF YOU DON'T LIKE THE WAY I DO IT, WHY DON'T YOU MAKE YOUR OWN SANDWICH?
I DON'T KNOW HOW.

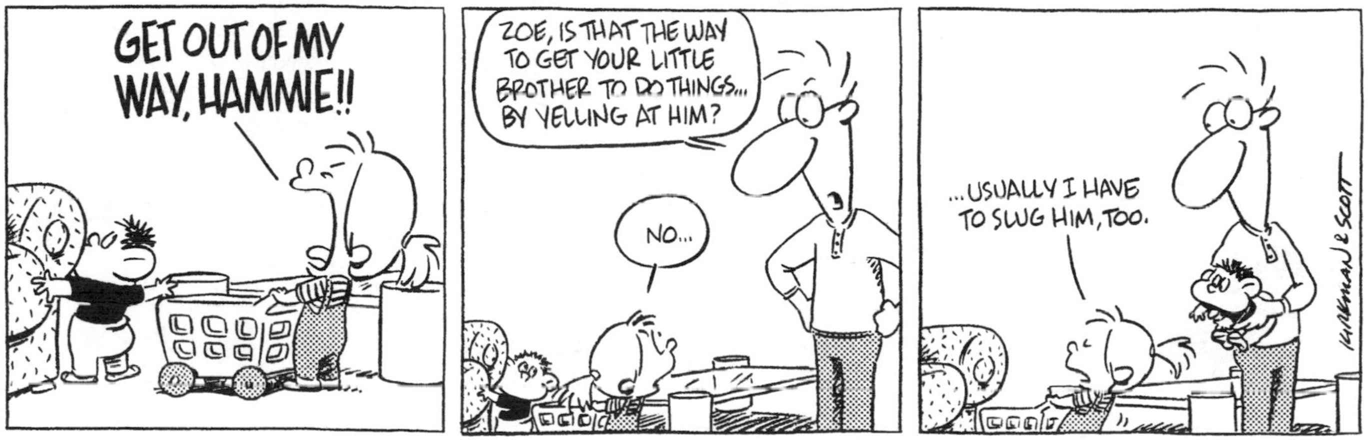
GET OUT OF MY WAY, HAMMIE!!
ZOE, IS THAT THE WAY TO GET YOUR LITTLE BROTHER TO DO THINGS... BY YELLING AT HIM?
NO...
...USUALLY I HAVE TO SLUG HIM, TOO.
KIRKMAN & SCOTT

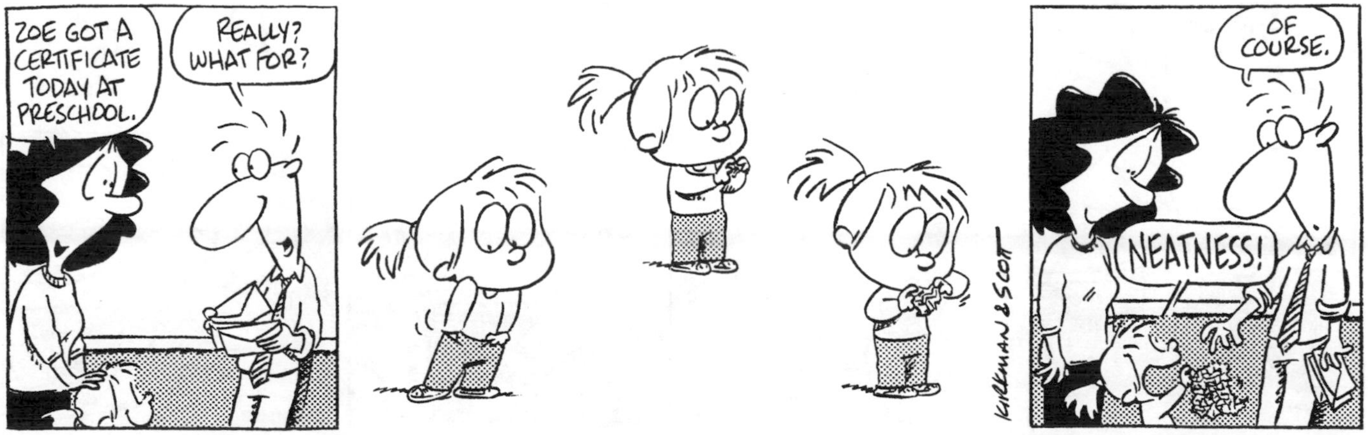
ZOE GOT A CERTIFICATE TODAY AT PRESCHOOL.
REALLY? WHAT FOR?
KIRKMAN & SCOTT
OF COURSE.
NEATNESS!

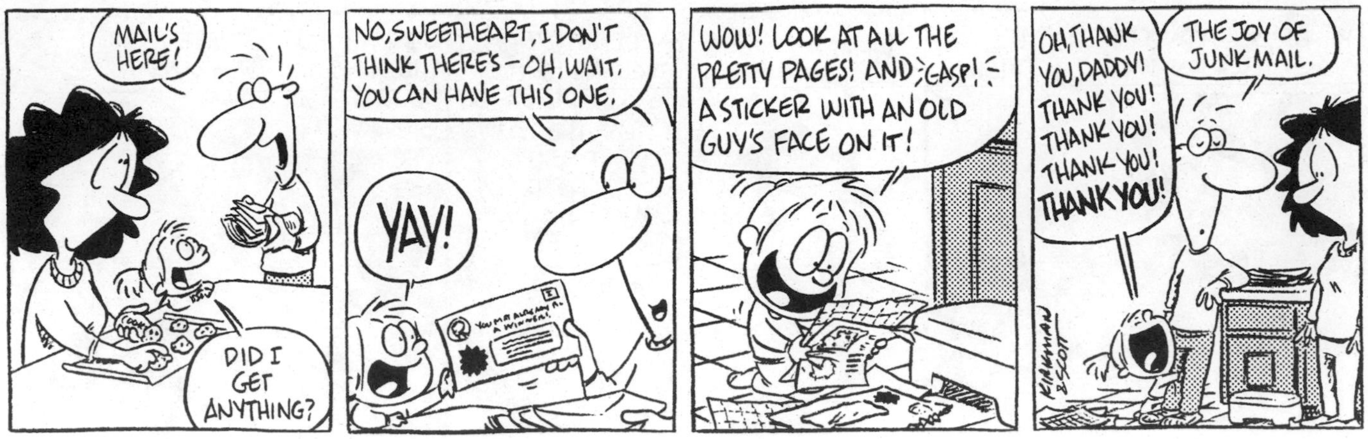
MAIL'S HERE!
DID I GET ANYTHING?
NO, SWEETHEART, I DON'T THINK THERE'S – OH, WAIT. YOU CAN HAVE THIS ONE.
YAY!
WOW! LOOK AT ALL THE PRETTY PAGES! AND ;GASP!; A STICKER WITH AN OLD GUY'S FACE ON IT!
OH, THANK YOU, DADDY! THANK YOU! THANK YOU! THANK YOU! THANK YOU!
THE JOY OF JUNK MAIL.
KIRKMAN & SCOTT

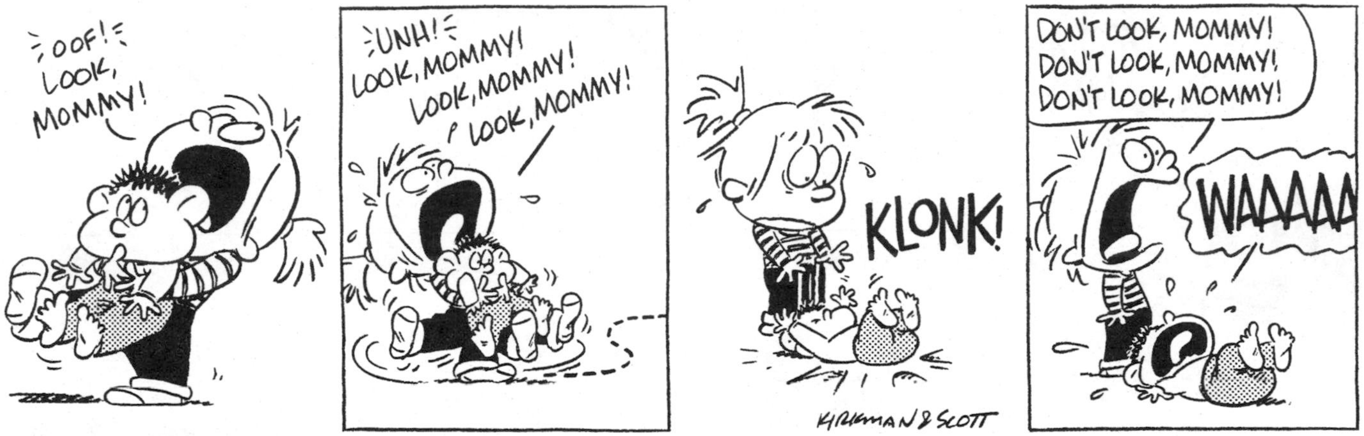
;OOF!; LOOK, MOMMY!
;UNH!; LOOK, MOMMY! LOOK, MOMMY! LOOK, MOMMY!
KLONK!
KIRKMAN & SCOTT
DON'T LOOK, MOMMY! DON'T LOOK, MOMMY! DON'T LOOK, MOMMY!
WAAAAA

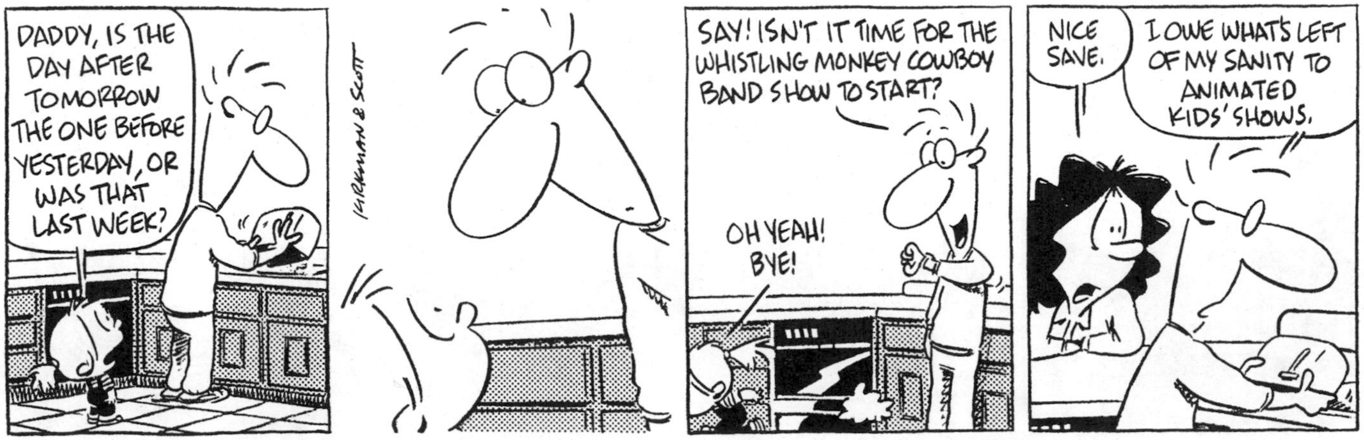
DADDY, IS THE DAY AFTER TOMORROW THE ONE BEFORE YESTERDAY, OR WAS THAT LAST WEEK?
KIRKMAN & SCOTT
SAY! ISN'T IT TIME FOR THE WHISTLING MONKEY COWBOY BAND SHOW TO START?
OH YEAH! BYE!
NICE SAVE.
I OWE WHAT'S LEFT OF MY SANITY TO ANIMATED KIDS' SHOWS.

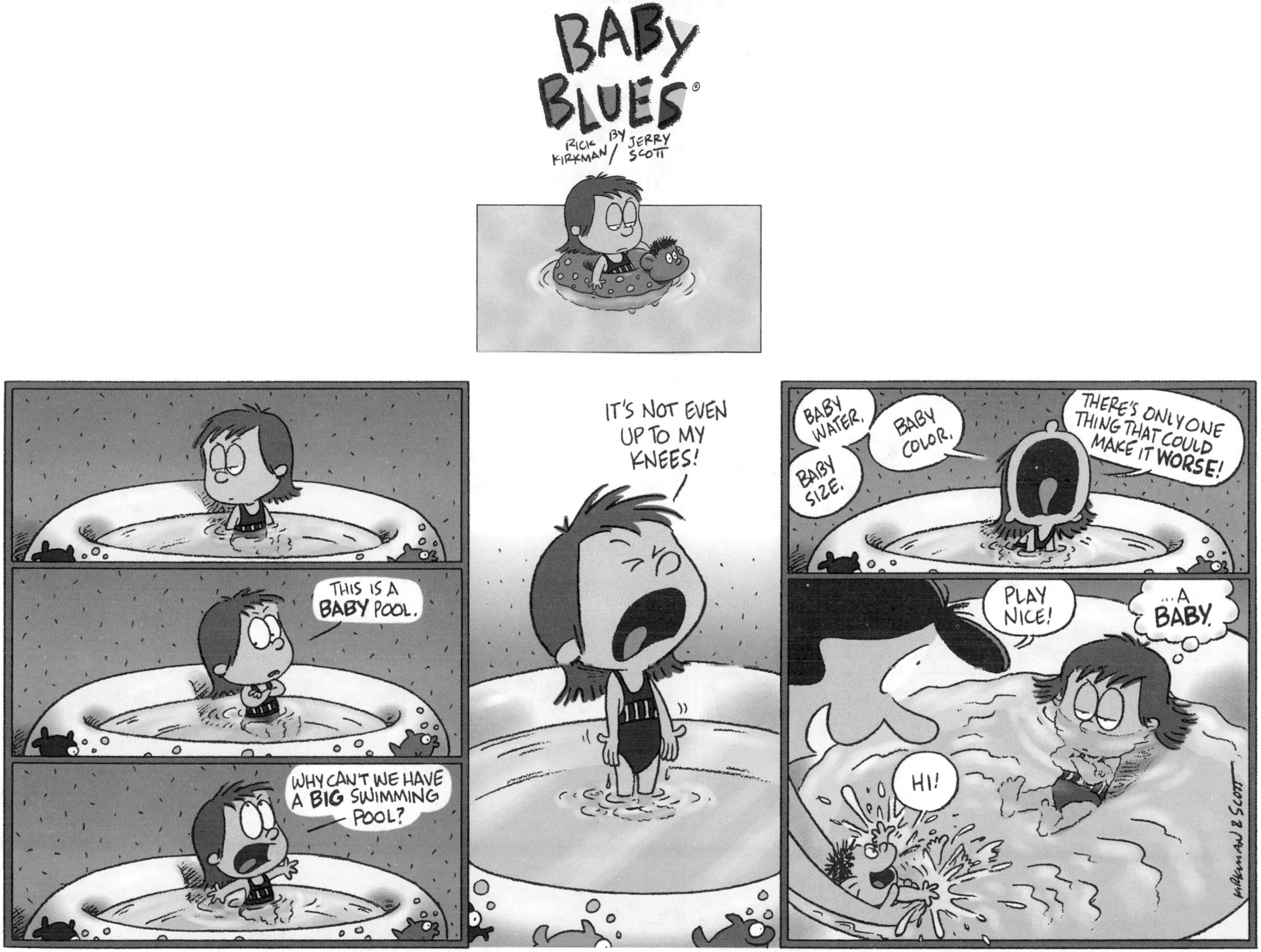
BABY BLUES®
BY RICK KIRKMAN / JERRY SCOTT
THIS IS A BABY POOL.
WHY CAN'T WE HAVE A BIG SWIMMING POOL?
IT'S NOT EVEN UP TO MY KNEES!
BABY WATER.
BABY SIZE.
BABY COLOR.
THERE'S ONLY ONE THING THAT COULD MAKE IT WORSE!
PLAY NICE!
...A BABY.
HI!
KIRKMAN & SCOTT

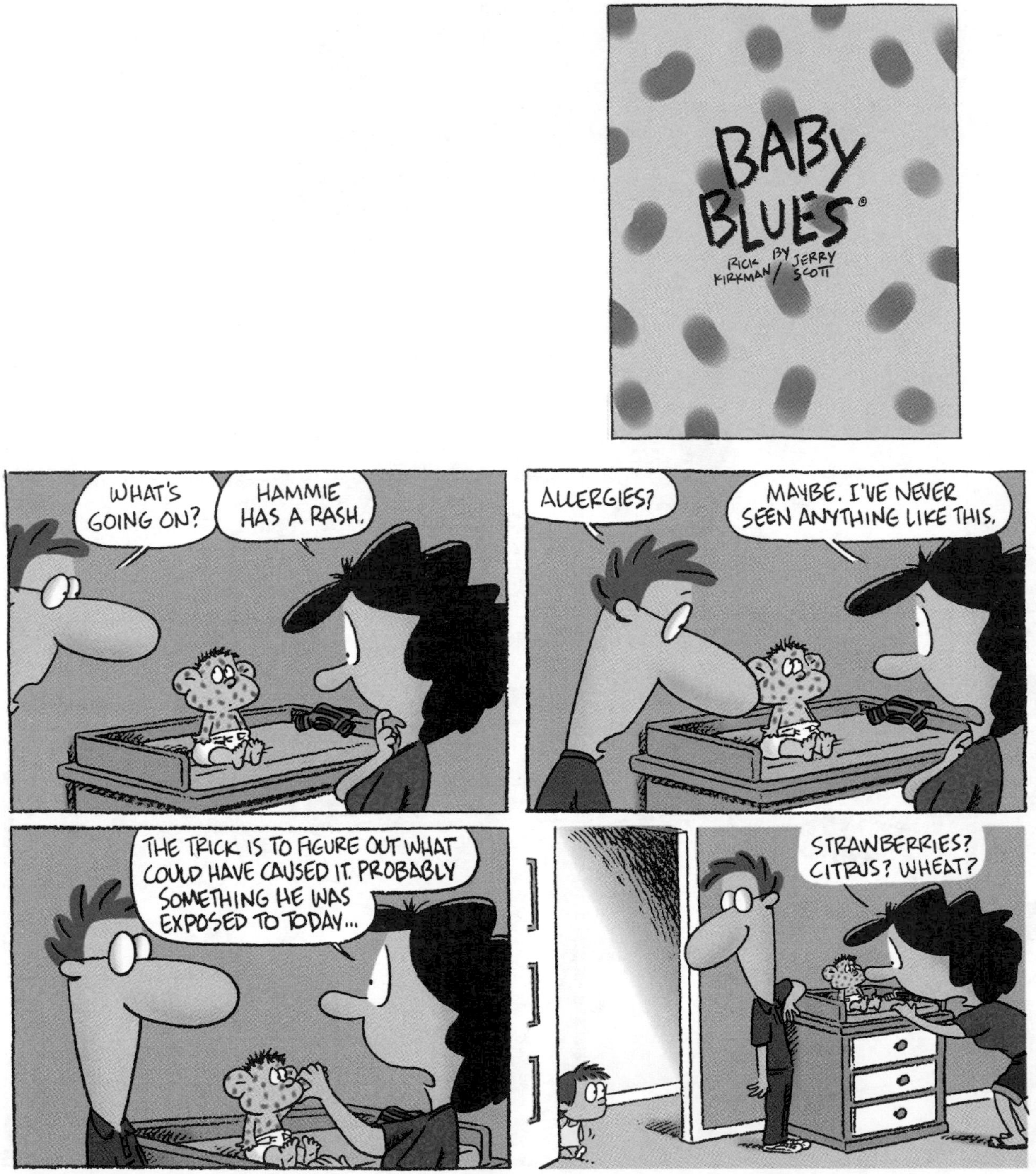

BABY BLUES®
BY RICK KIRKMAN / JERRY SCOTT
WHAT'S GOING ON?
HAMMIE HAS A RASH.
ALLERGIES?
MAYBE. I'VE NEVER SEEN ANYTHING LIKE THIS.
HE'S NEVER BEEN ALLERGIC TO ANYTHING BEFORE, HAS HE?
NO, BUT KIDS CAN DEVELOP ALLERGIES AT ANYTIME.
THE TRICK IS TO FIGURE OUT WHAT COULD HAVE CAUSED IT. PROBABLY SOMETHING HE WAS EXPOSED TO TODAY...
STRAWBERRIES? CITRUS? WHEAT?
SIBLING.
DOT...DOT.. DOT... DOT... DOT...
KIRKMAN & SCOTT

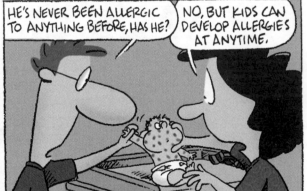

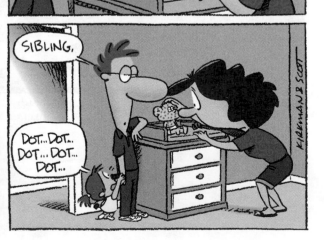

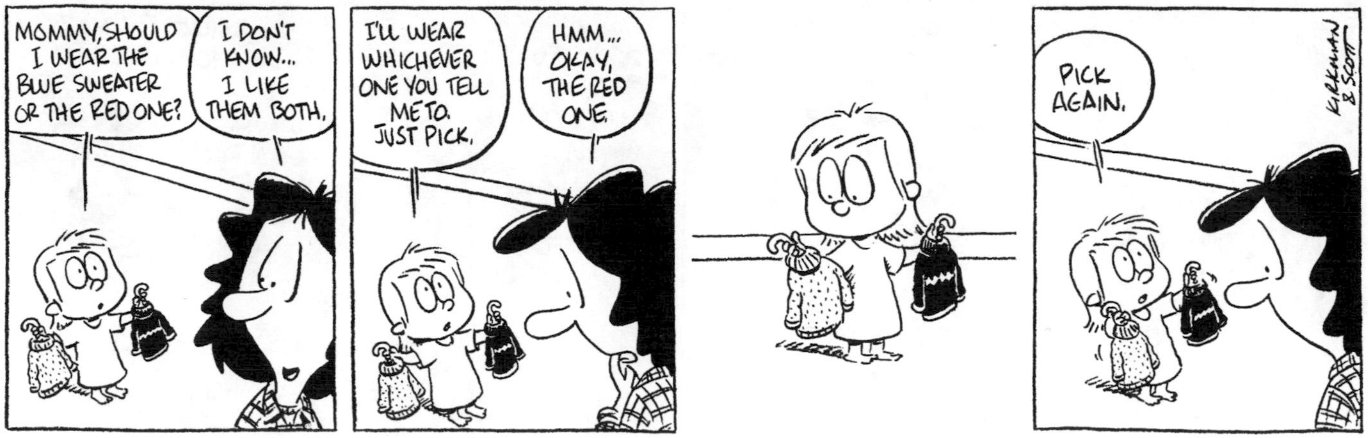
MOMMY, SHOULD I WEAR THE BLUE SWEATER OR THE RED ONE?
I DON'T KNOW... I LIKE THEM BOTH.
I'LL WEAR WHICHEVER ONE YOU TELL ME TO. JUST PICK.
HMM... OKAY, THE RED ONE.
PICK AGAIN.
KIRKMAN & SCOTT

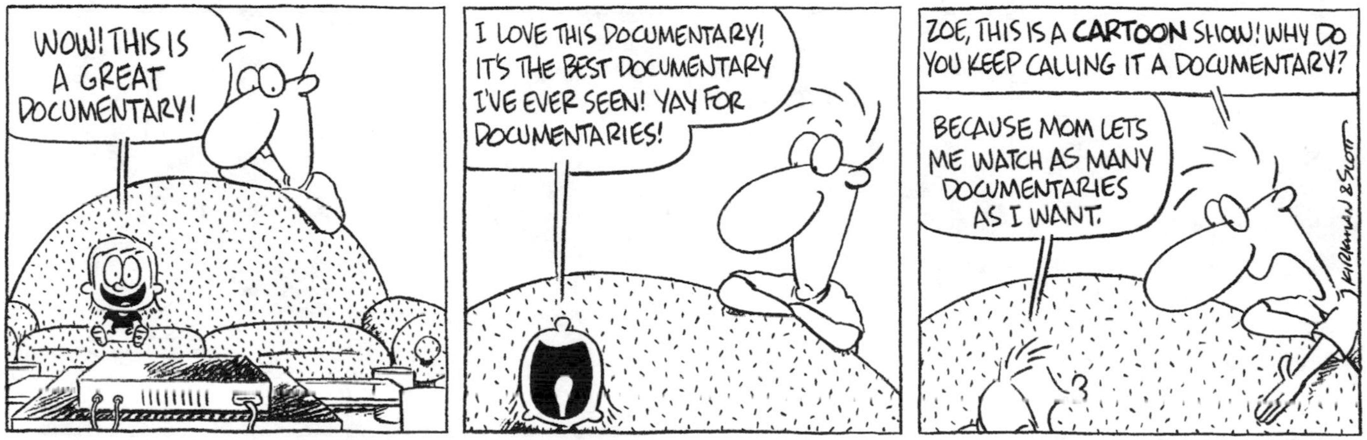
WOW! THIS IS A GREAT DOCUMENTARY!
I LOVE THIS DOCUMENTARY! IT'S THE BEST DOCUMENTARY I'VE EVER SEEN! YAY FOR DOCUMENTARIES!
ZOE, THIS IS A CARTOON SHOW! WHY DO YOU KEEP CALLING IT A DOCUMENTARY?
BECAUSE MOM LETS ME WATCH AS MANY DOCUMENTARIES AS I WANT.
KIRKMAN & SCOTT

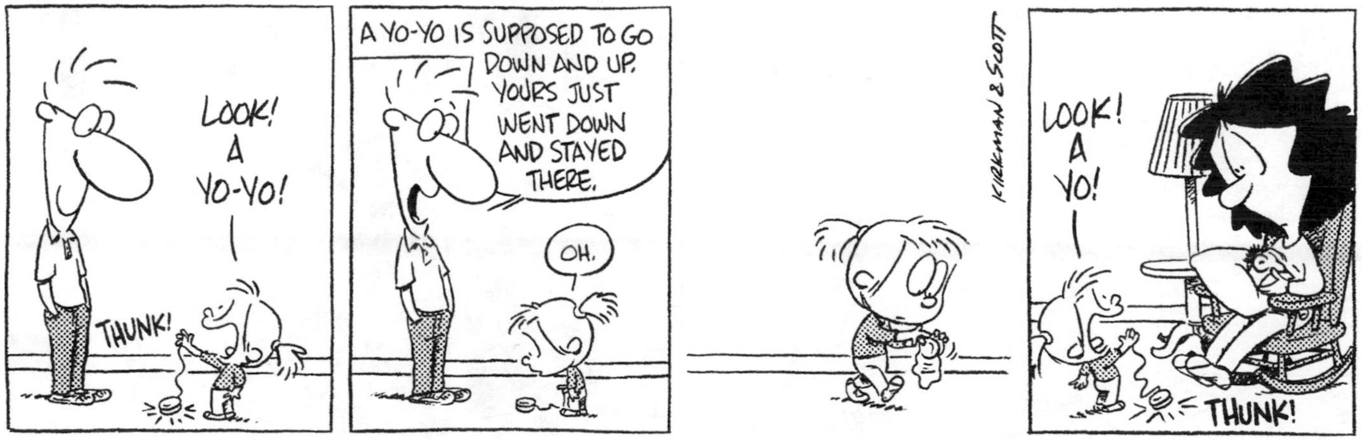
LOOK! A YO-YO!
THUNK!
A YO-YO IS SUPPOSED TO GO DOWN AND UP. YOURS JUST WENT DOWN AND STAYED THERE.
OH.
KIRKMAN & SCOTT
LOOK! A YO!
THUNK!

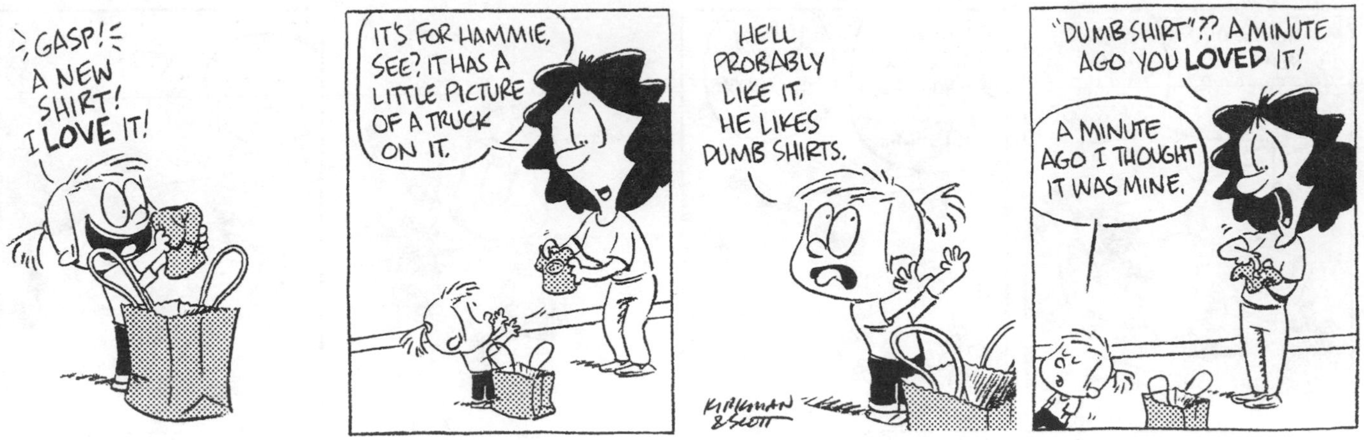
GASP! A NEW SHIRT! I **LOVE** IT!
IT'S FOR HAMMIE. SEE? IT HAS A LITTLE PICTURE OF A TRUCK ON IT.
HE'LL PROBABLY LIKE IT. HE LIKES DUMB SHIRTS.
"DUMB SHIRT"?? A MINUTE AGO YOU **LOVED** IT!
A MINUTE AGO I THOUGHT IT WAS MINE.
KIRKMAN & SCOTT

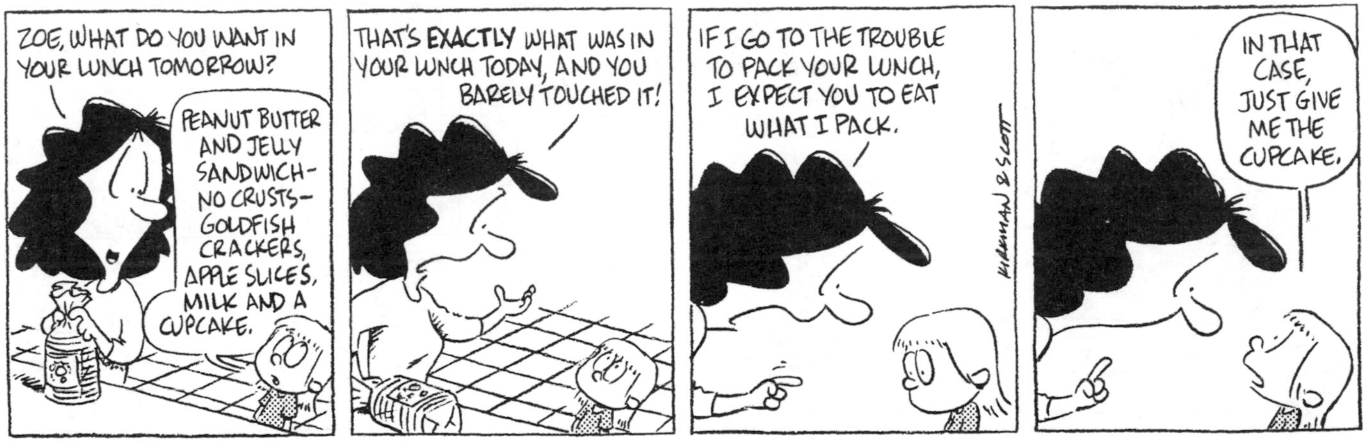
ZOE, WHAT DO YOU WANT IN YOUR LUNCH TOMORROW?
PEANUT BUTTER AND JELLY SANDWICH- NO CRUSTS- GOLDFISH CRACKERS, APPLE SLICES, MILK AND A CUPCAKE.
THAT'S **EXACTLY** WHAT WAS IN YOUR LUNCH TODAY, AND YOU BARELY TOUCHED IT!
IF I GO TO THE TROUBLE TO PACK YOUR LUNCH, I EXPECT YOU TO EAT WHAT I PACK.
KIRKMAN & SCOTT
IN THAT CASE, JUST GIVE ME THE CUPCAKE.

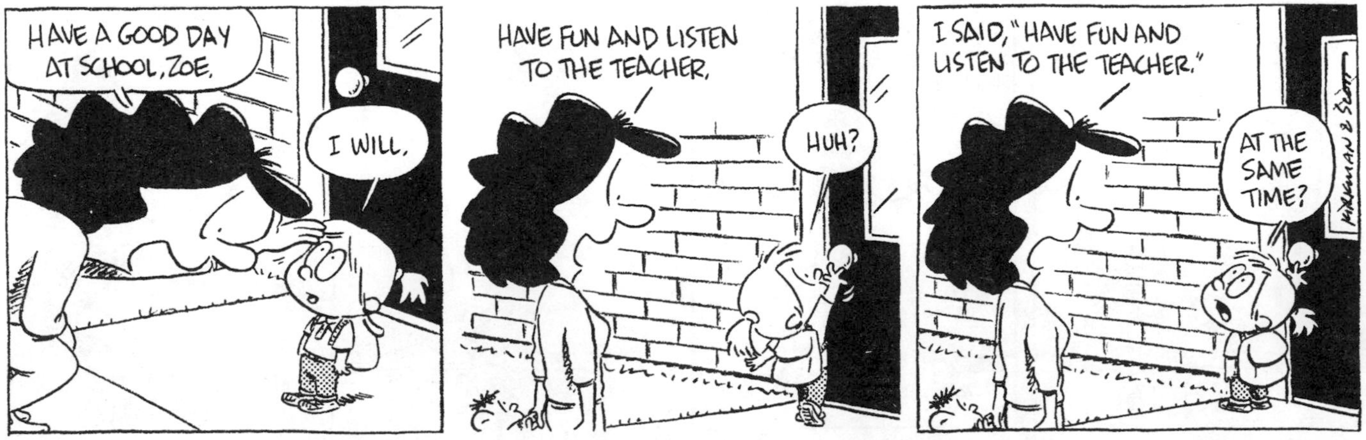
HAVE A GOOD DAY AT SCHOOL, ZOE.
I WILL.
HAVE FUN AND LISTEN TO THE TEACHER.
HUH?
I SAID, "HAVE FUN AND LISTEN TO THE TEACHER."
AT THE SAME TIME?
KIRKMAN & SCOTT

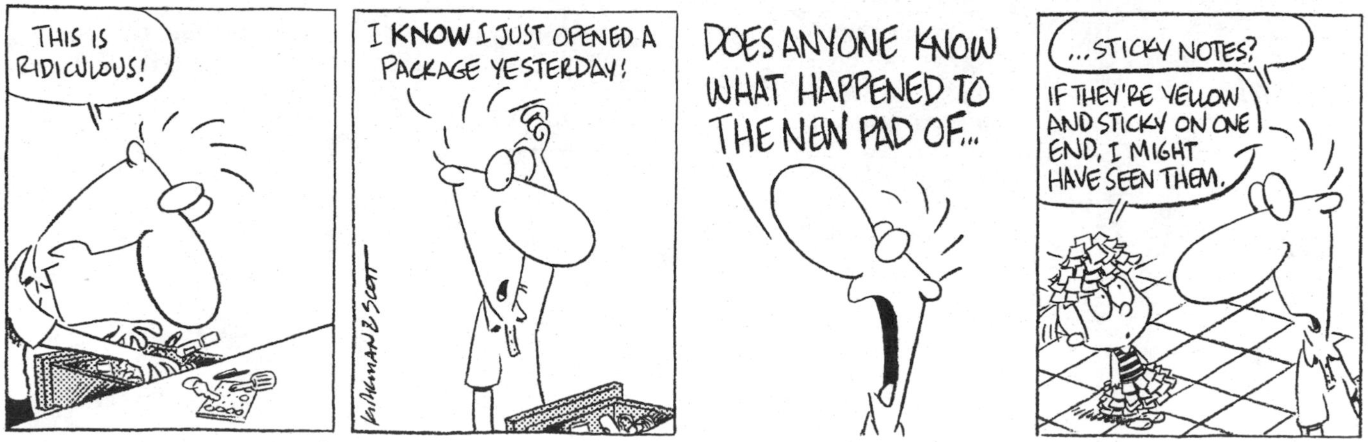
THIS IS RIDICULOUS!
I KNOW I JUST OPENED A PACKAGE YESTERDAY!
DOES ANYONE KNOW WHAT HAPPENED TO THE NEW PAD OF...
...STICKY NOTES?
IF THEY'RE YELLOW AND STICKY ON ONE END, I MIGHT HAVE SEEN THEM.

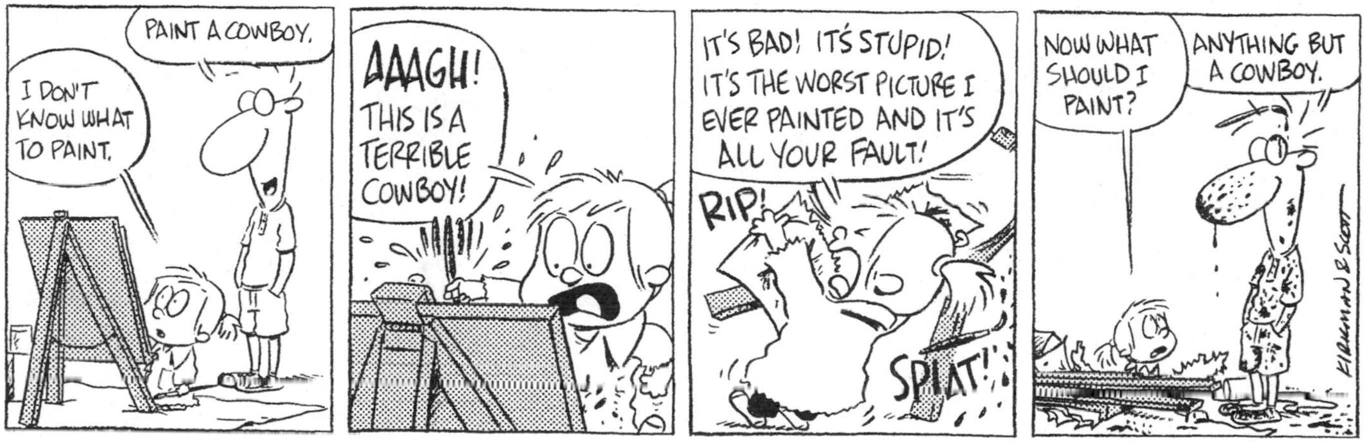
PAINT A COWBOY.
I DON'T KNOW WHAT TO PAINT.
AAAGH! THIS IS A TERRIBLE COWBOY!
IT'S BAD! IT'S STUPID! IT'S THE WORST PICTURE I EVER PAINTED AND IT'S ALL YOUR FAULT!
RIP!
SPLAT!
NOW WHAT SHOULD I PAINT?
ANYTHING BUT A COWBOY.

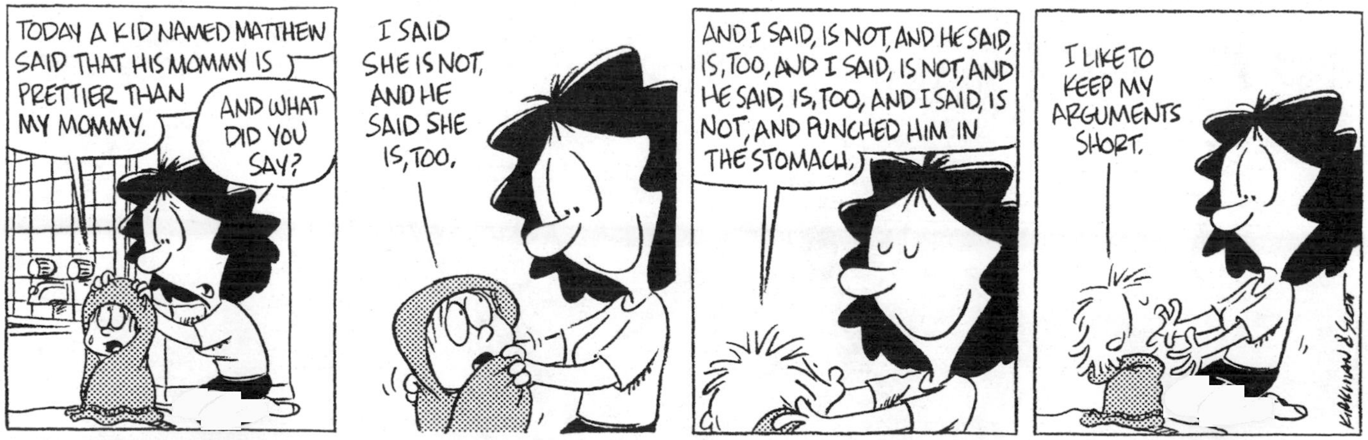
TODAY A KID NAMED MATTHEW SAID THAT HIS MOMMY IS PRETTIER THAN MY MOMMY.
AND WHAT DID YOU SAY?
I SAID SHE IS NOT, AND HE SAID SHE IS, TOO,
AND I SAID, IS NOT, AND HE SAID, IS, TOO, AND I SAID, IS NOT, AND HE SAID, IS, TOO, AND I SAID, IS NOT, AND PUNCHED HIM IN THE STOMACH.
I LIKE TO KEEP MY ARGUMENTS SHORT.

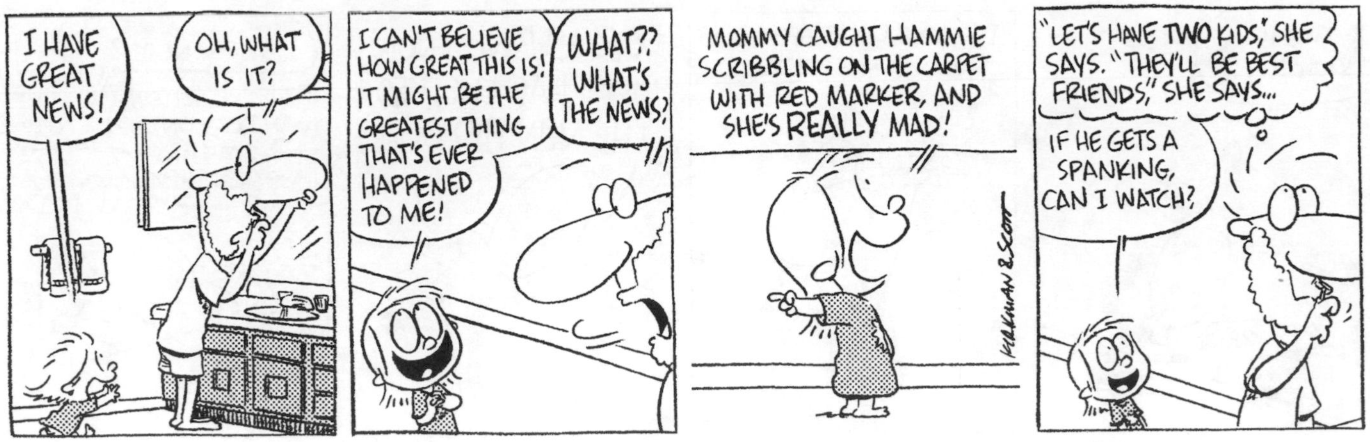
I HAVE GREAT NEWS!
OH, WHAT IS IT?
I CAN'T BELIEVE HOW GREAT THIS IS! IT MIGHT BE THE GREATEST THING THAT'S EVER HAPPENED TO ME!
WHAT?? WHAT'S THE NEWS?
MOMMY CAUGHT HAMMIE SCRIBBLING ON THE CARPET WITH RED MARKER, AND SHE'S REALLY MAD!
KIRKMAN & SCOTT
"LET'S HAVE TWO KIDS," SHE SAYS. "THEY'LL BE BEST FRIENDS," SHE SAYS...
IF HE GETS A SPANKING, CAN I WATCH?

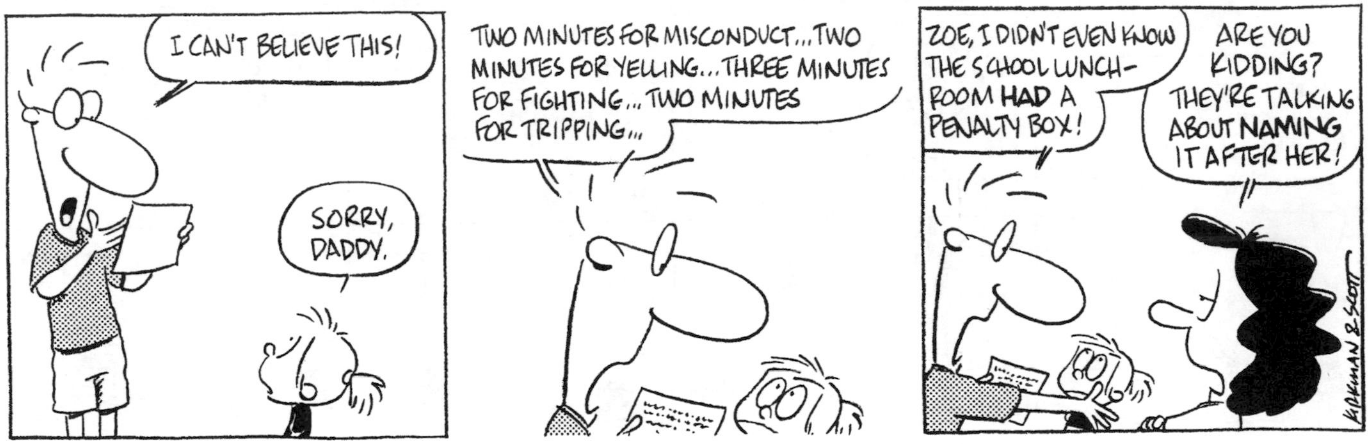
I CAN'T BELIEVE THIS!
SORRY, DADDY.
TWO MINUTES FOR MISCONDUCT... TWO MINUTES FOR YELLING... THREE MINUTES FOR FIGHTING... TWO MINUTES FOR TRIPPING...
ZOE, I DIDN'T EVEN KNOW THE SCHOOL LUNCH-ROOM HAD A PENALTY BOX!
ARE YOU KIDDING? THEY'RE TALKING ABOUT NAMING IT AFTER HER!
KIRKMAN & SCOTT

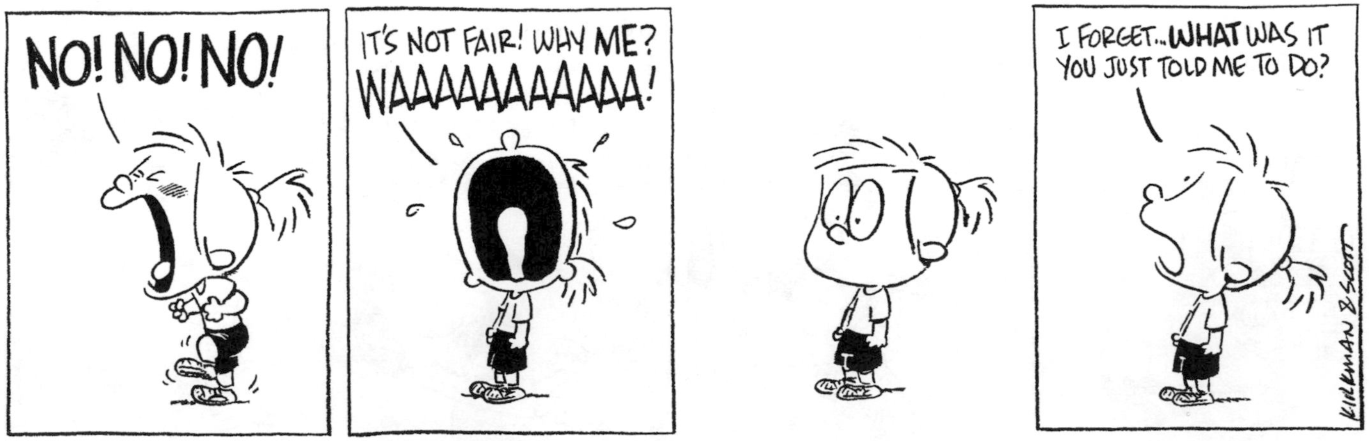
NO! NO! NO!
IT'S NOT FAIR! WHY ME? WAAAAAAAAAAA!
I FORGET... WHAT WAS IT YOU JUST TOLD ME TO DO?
KIRKMAN & SCOTT

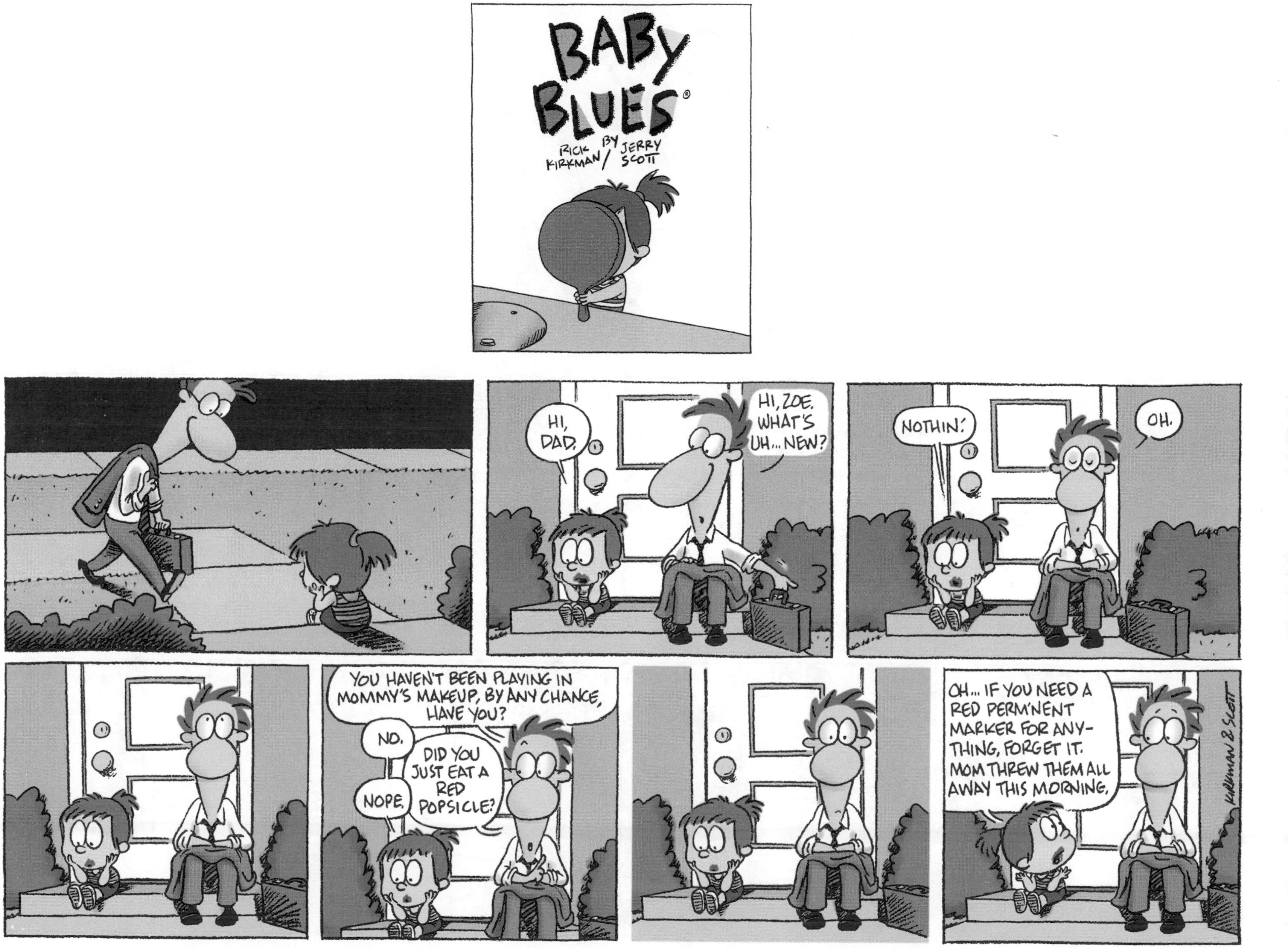
BABY BLUES®
BY RICK KIRKMAN / JERRY SCOTT
HI, DAD.
HI, ZOE. WHAT'S UH... NEW?
NOTHIN'.
OH.
YOU HAVEN'T BEEN PLAYING IN MOMMY'S MAKEUP, BY ANY CHANCE, HAVE YOU?
NO.
DID YOU JUST EAT A RED POPSICLE?
NOPE.
OH... IF YOU NEED A RED PERM'NENT MARKER FOR ANYTHING, FORGET IT. MOM THREW THEM ALL AWAY THIS MORNING.
KIRKMAN & SCOTT

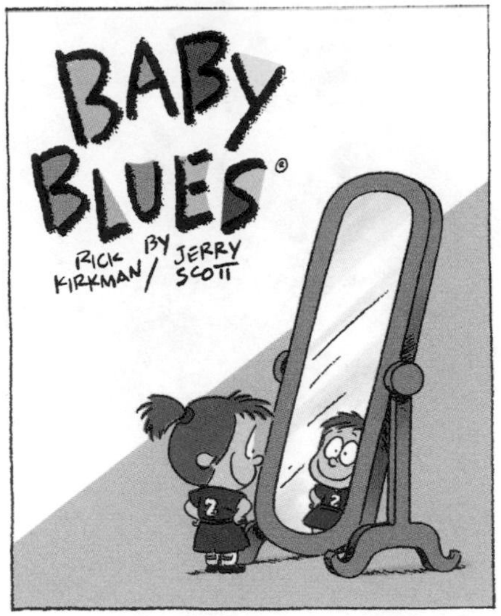
BABY BLUES®
BY
RICK KIRKMAN / JERRY SCOTT

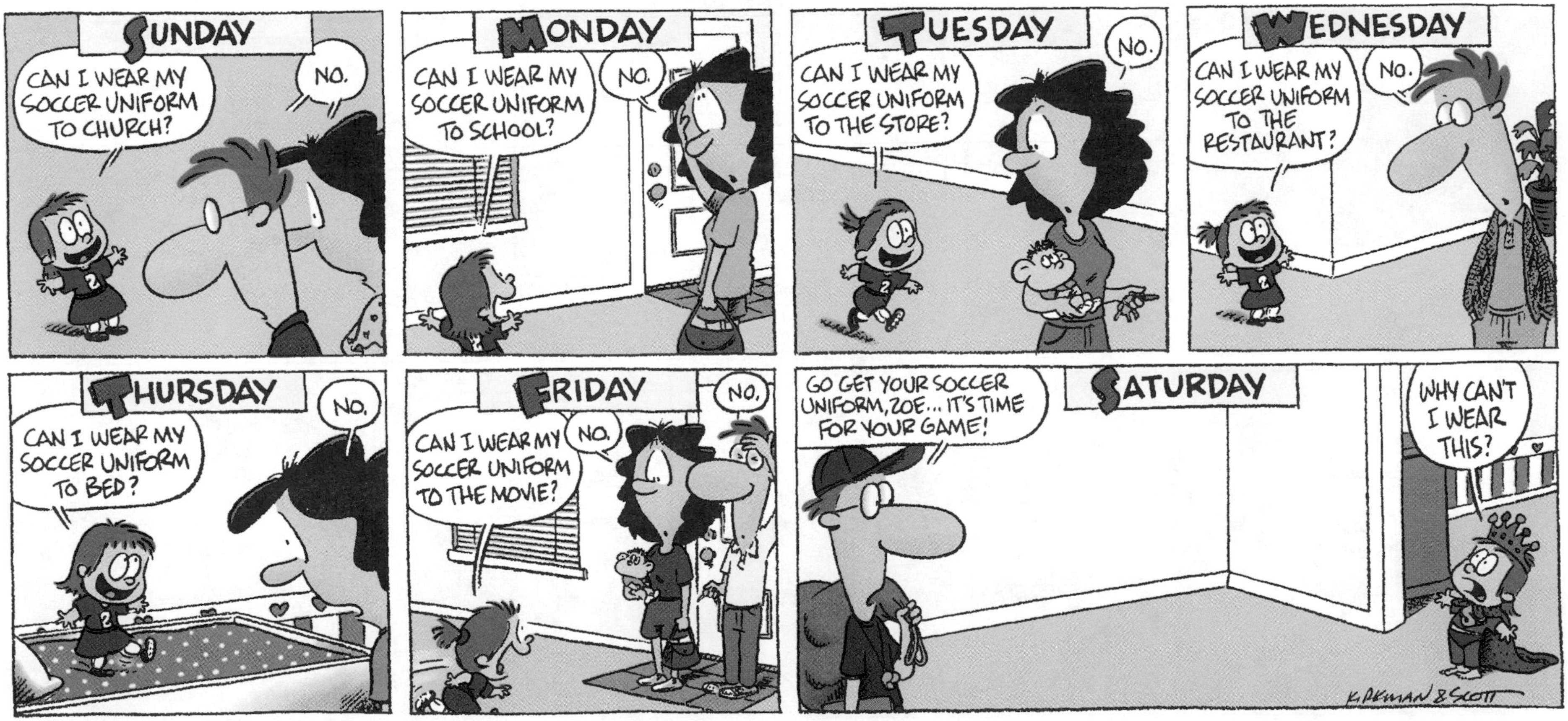
SUNDAY
CAN I WEAR MY SOCCER UNIFORM TO CHURCH?
NO.
MONDAY
CAN I WEAR MY SOCCER UNIFORM TO SCHOOL?
NO.
TUESDAY
CAN I WEAR MY SOCCER UNIFORM TO THE STORE?
NO.
WEDNESDAY
CAN I WEAR MY SOCCER UNIFORM TO THE RESTAURANT?
NO.
THURSDAY
CAN I WEAR MY SOCCER UNIFORM TO BED?
NO.
FRIDAY
CAN I WEAR MY SOCCER UNIFORM TO THE MOVIE?
NO.
NO.
SATURDAY
GO GET YOUR SOCCER UNIFORM, ZOE... IT'S TIME FOR YOUR GAME!
WHY CAN'T I WEAR THIS?
KIRKMAN & SCOTT

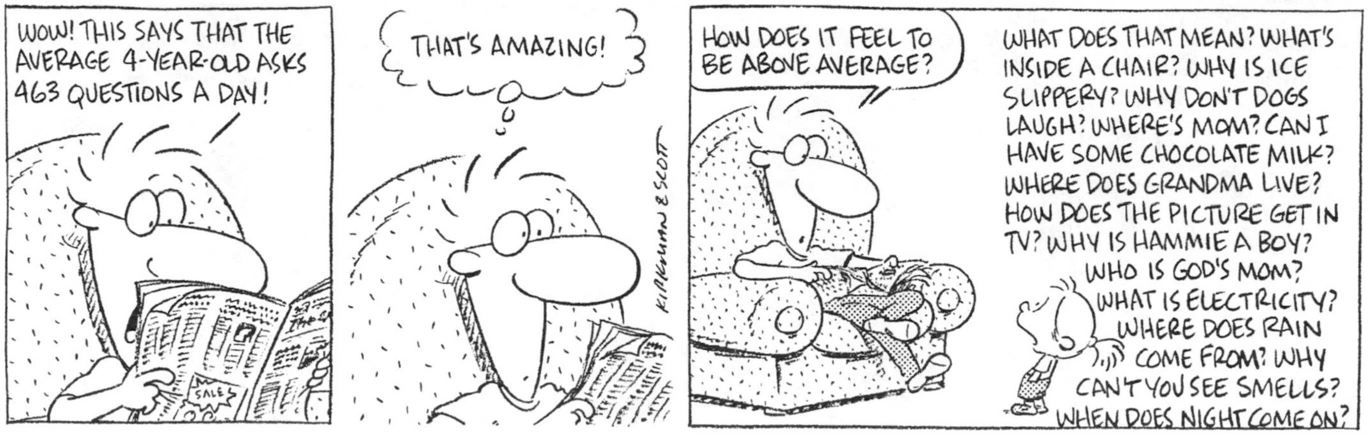
WOW! THIS SAYS THAT THE AVERAGE 4-YEAR-OLD ASKS 463 QUESTIONS A DAY!
THAT'S AMAZING!
KIRKMAN & SCOTT
HOW DOES IT FEEL TO BE ABOVE AVERAGE?
WHAT DOES THAT MEAN? WHAT'S INSIDE A CHAIR? WHY IS ICE SLIPPERY? WHY DON'T DOGS LAUGH? WHERE'S MOM? CAN I HAVE SOME CHOCOLATE MILK? WHERE DOES GRANDMA LIVE? HOW DOES THE PICTURE GET IN TV? WHY IS HAMMIE A BOY? WHO IS GOD'S MOM? WHAT IS ELECTRICITY? WHERE DOES RAIN COME FROM? WHY CAN'T YOU SEE SMELLS? WHEN DOES NIGHT COME ON?

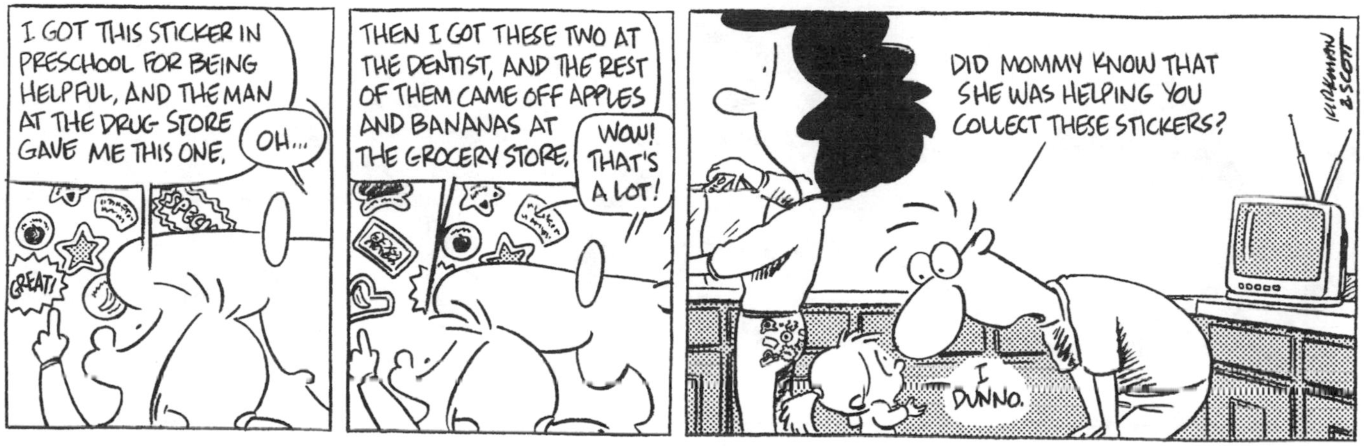
I GOT THIS STICKER IN PRESCHOOL FOR BEING HELPFUL, AND THE MAN AT THE DRUG STORE GAVE ME THIS ONE.
OH...
GREAT!
THEN I GOT THESE TWO AT THE DENTIST, AND THE REST OF THEM CAME OFF APPLES AND BANANAS AT THE GROCERY STORE.
WOW! THAT'S A LOT!
KIRKMAN & SCOTT
DID MOMMY KNOW THAT SHE WAS HELPING YOU COLLECT THESE STICKERS?
I DUNNO.

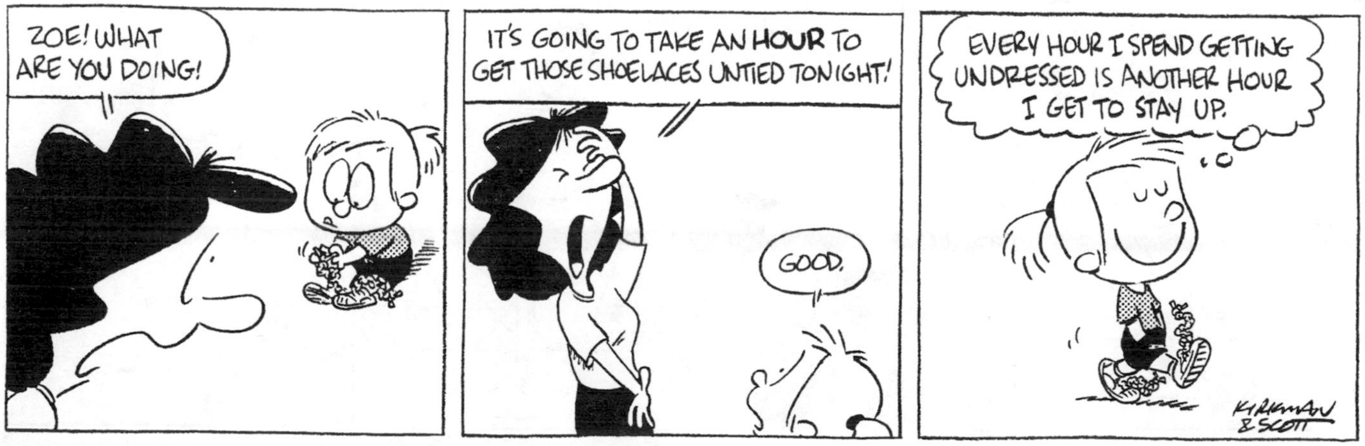
ZOE! WHAT ARE YOU DOING!
IT'S GOING TO TAKE AN **HOUR** TO GET THOSE SHOELACES UNTIED TONIGHT!
GOOD.
EVERY HOUR I SPEND GETTING UNDRESSED IS ANOTHER HOUR I GET TO STAY UP.
KIRKMAN & SCOTT

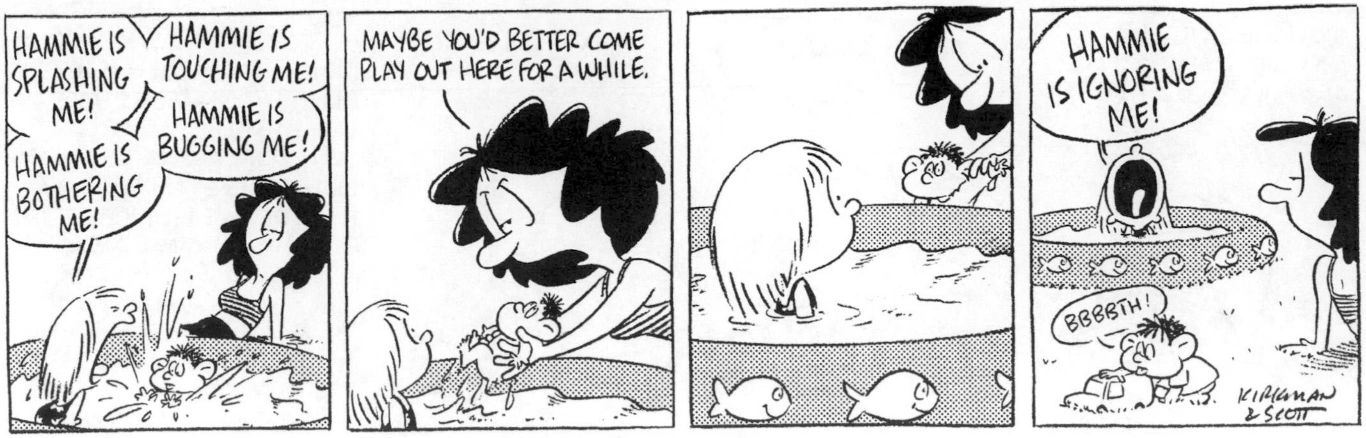
HAMMIE IS SPLASHING ME!
HAMMIE IS TOUCHING ME!
HAMMIE IS BOTHERING ME!
HAMMIE IS BUGGING ME!
MAYBE YOU'D BETTER COME PLAY OUT HERE FOR A WHILE.
HAMMIE IS IGNORING ME!
BBBBTH!
KIRKMAN & SCOTT

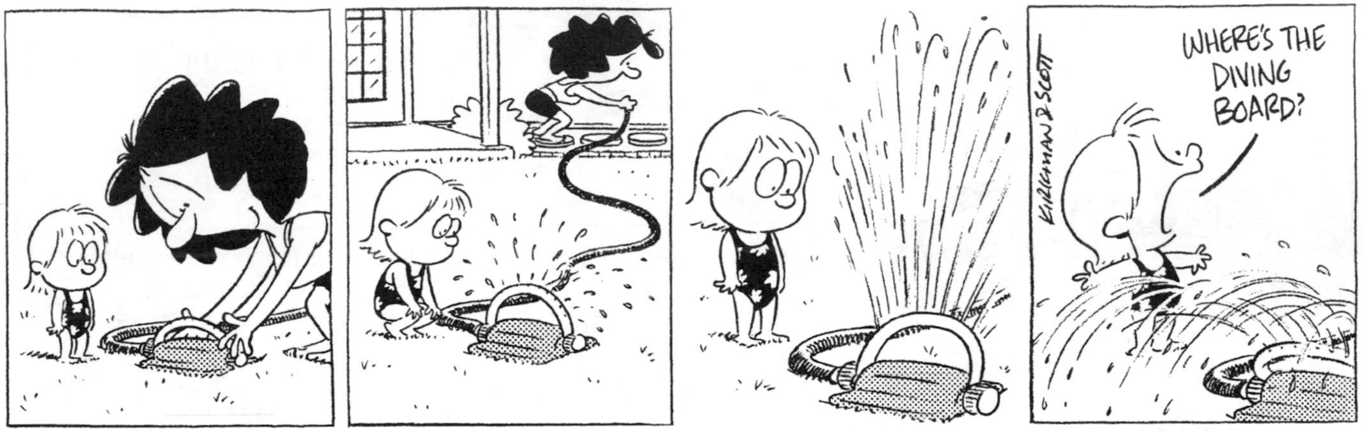
KIRKMAN & SCOTT
WHERE'S THE DIVING BOARD?

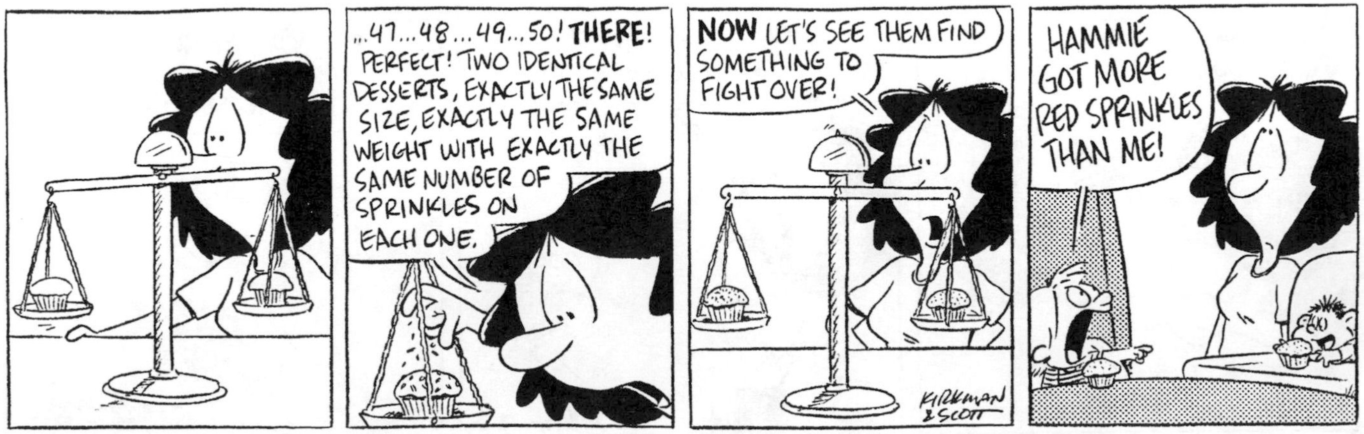
...47...48...49...50! THERE! PERFECT! TWO IDENTICAL DESSERTS, EXACTLY THE SAME SIZE, EXACTLY THE SAME WEIGHT WITH EXACTLY THE SAME NUMBER OF SPRINKLES ON EACH ONE.
NOW LET'S SEE THEM FIND SOMETHING TO FIGHT OVER!
KIRKMAN & SCOTT
HAMMIE GOT MORE RED SPRINKLES THAN ME!

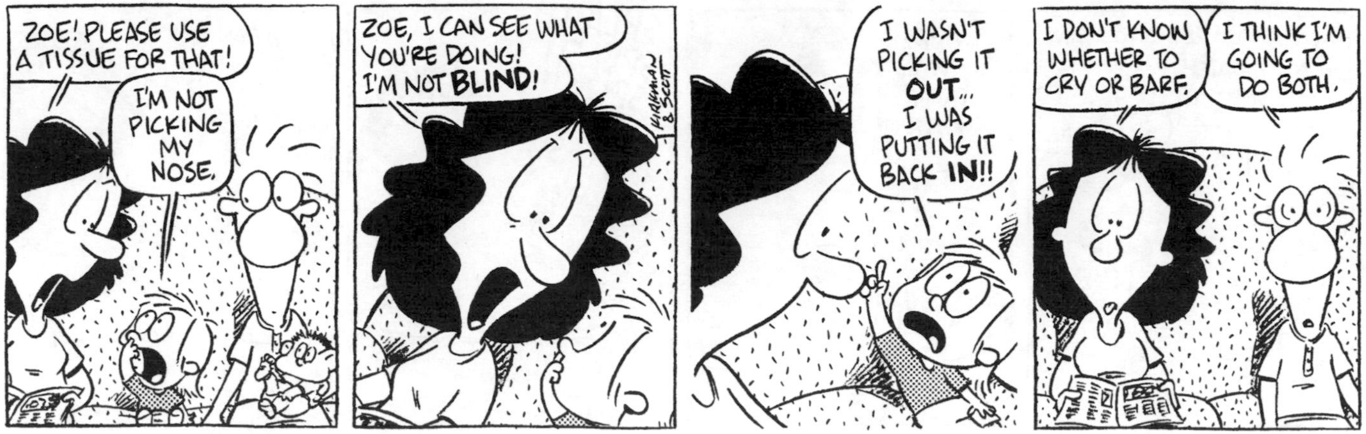

ZOE! PLEASE USE A TISSUE FOR THAT!
I'M NOT PICKING MY NOSE.
ZOE, I CAN SEE WHAT YOU'RE DOING! I'M NOT **BLIND**!
KIRKMAN & SCOTT
I WASN'T PICKING IT **OUT**... I WAS PUTTING IT BACK **IN**!!
I DON'T KNOW WHETHER TO CRY OR BARF.
I THINK I'M GOING TO DO BOTH.

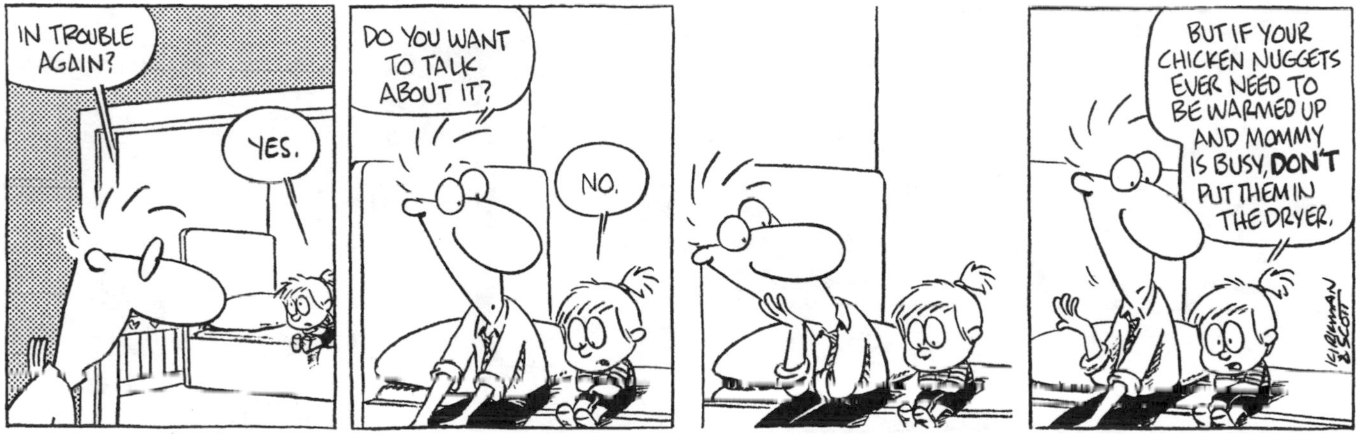

IN TROUBLE AGAIN?
YES.
DO YOU WANT TO TALK ABOUT IT?
NO.
BUT IF YOUR CHICKEN NUGGETS EVER NEED TO BE WARMED UP AND MOMMY IS BUSY, **DON'T** PUT THEM IN THE DRYER.
KIRKMAN & SCOTT

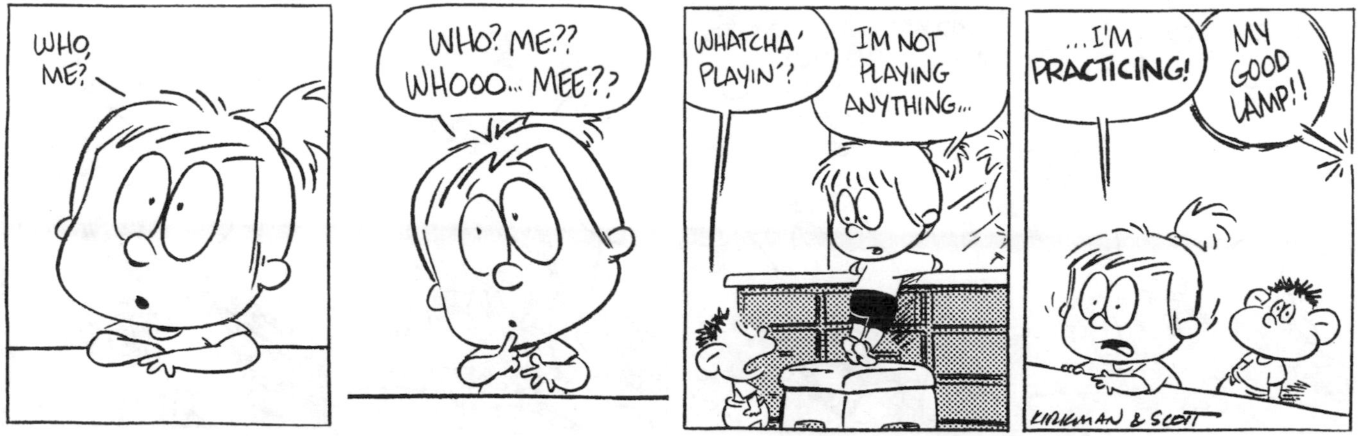

WHO, ME?
WHO? ME?? WHOOO... MEE??
WHATCHA' PLAYIN'?
I'M NOT PLAYING ANYTHING...
...I'M **PRACTICING**!
MY GOOD LAMP!!
KIRKMAN & SCOTT

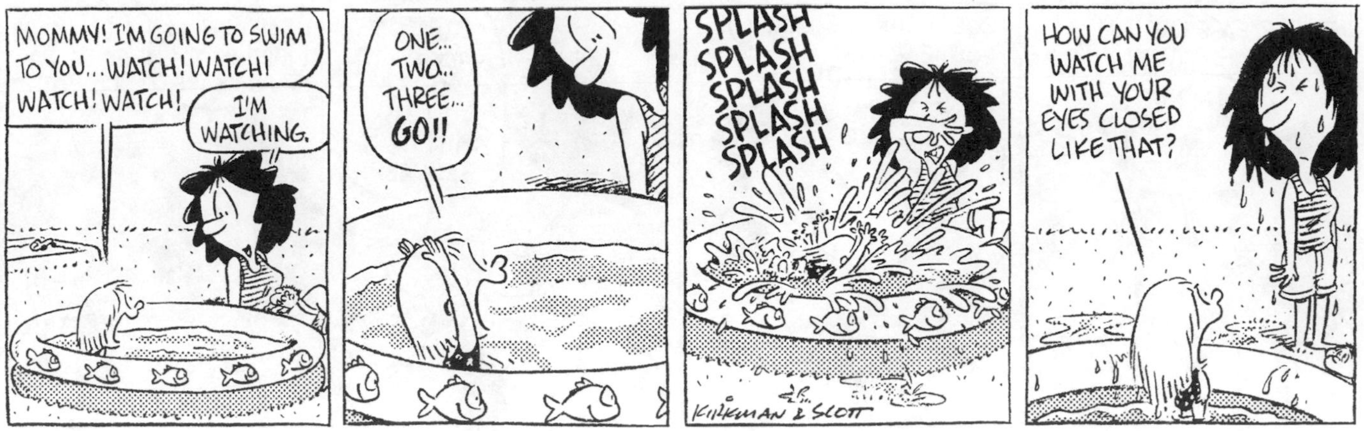
MOMMY! I'M GOING TO SWIM TO YOU...WATCH! WATCH! WATCH! WATCH!
I'M WATCHING.
ONE... TWO... THREE... GO!!
SPLASH SPLASH SPLASH SPLASH SPLASH
KIRKMAN & SCOTT
HOW CAN YOU WATCH ME WITH YOUR EYES CLOSED LIKE THAT?

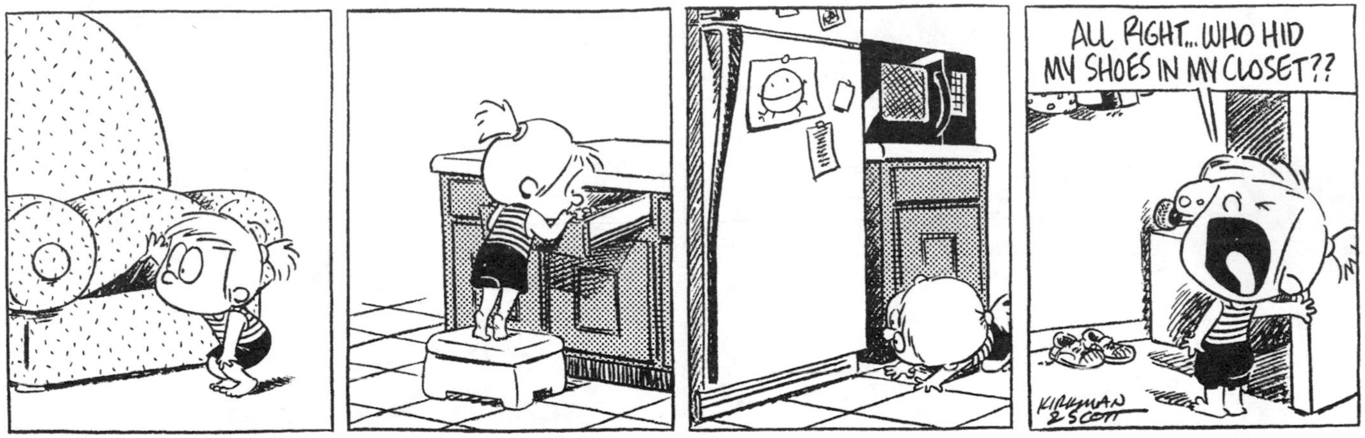
ALL RIGHT...WHO HID MY SHOES IN MY CLOSET??
KIRKMAN & SCOTT

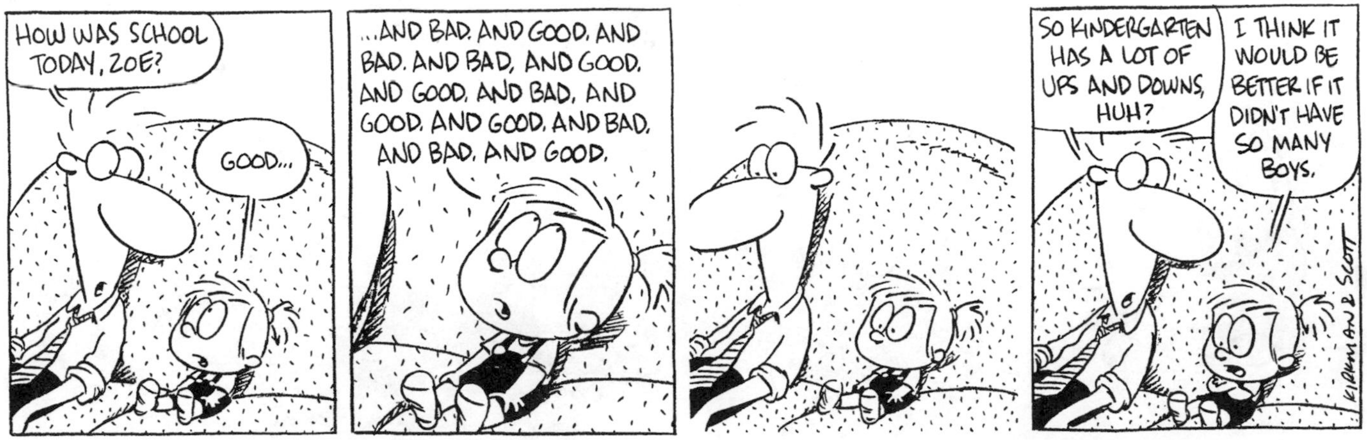
HOW WAS SCHOOL TODAY, ZOE?
GOOD...
...AND BAD. AND GOOD. AND BAD. AND BAD, AND GOOD. AND GOOD. AND BAD, AND GOOD. AND GOOD. AND BAD, AND BAD. AND GOOD.
SO KINDERGARTEN HAS A LOT OF UPS AND DOWNS, HUH?
I THINK IT WOULD BE BETTER IF IT DIDN'T HAVE SO MANY BOYS.
KIRKMAN & SCOTT

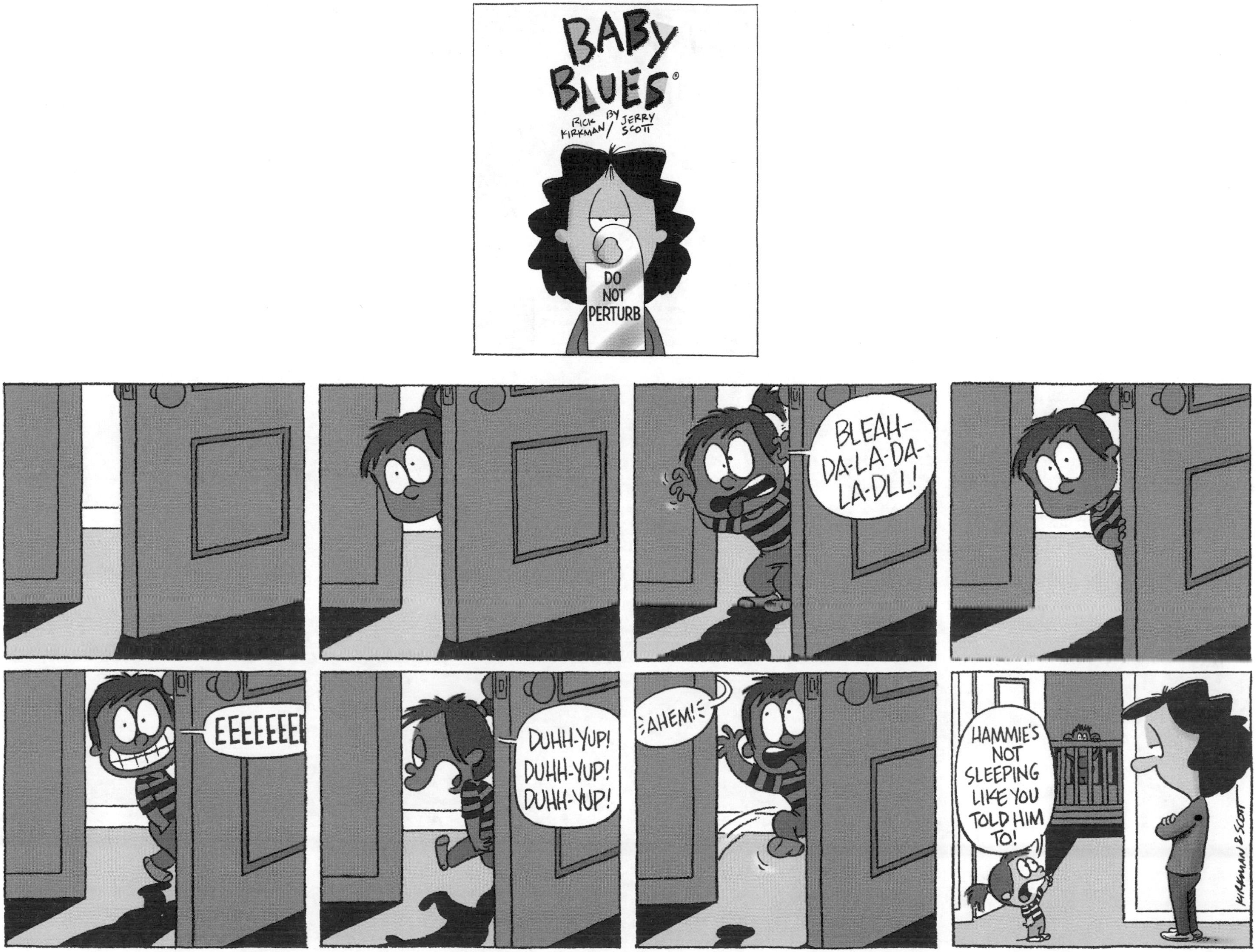
BABY BLUES®
BY RICK KIRKMAN / JERRY SCOTT
DO NOT PERTURB
BLEAH-DA-LA-DA-LA-DLL!
EEEEEEEE
DUHH-YUP! DUHH-YUP! DUHH-YUP!
AHEM!
HAMMIE'S NOT SLEEPING LIKE YOU TOLD HIM TO!
KIRKMAN & SCOTT

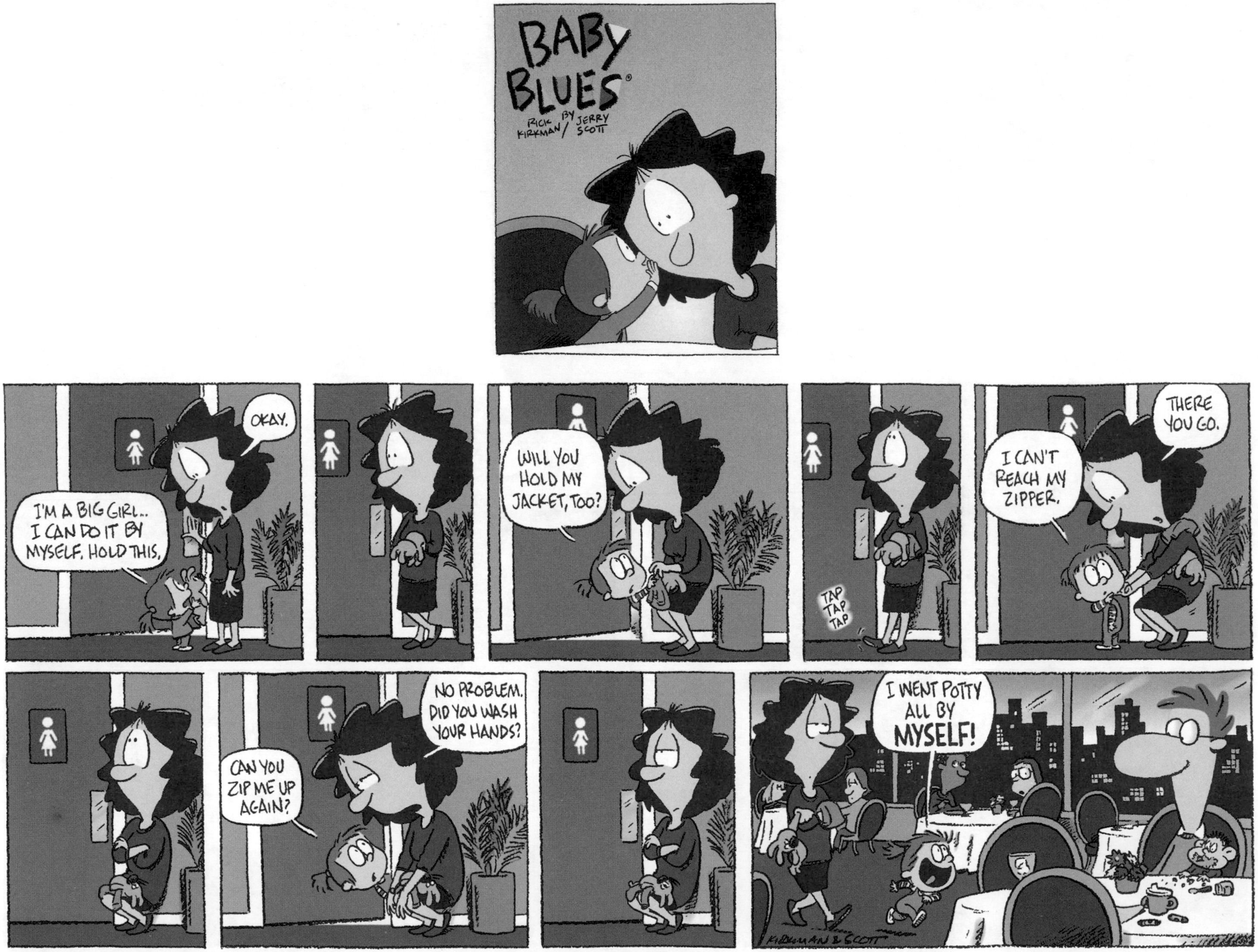
BABY BLUES®
BY RICK KIRKMAN / JERRY SCOTT
OKAY.
I'M A BIG GIRL.. I CAN DO IT BY MYSELF. HOLD THIS.
WILL YOU HOLD MY JACKET, TOO?
TAP TAP TAP
THERE YOU GO.
I CAN'T REACH MY ZIPPER.
NO PROBLEM. DID YOU WASH YOUR HANDS?
CAN YOU ZIP ME UP AGAIN?
I WENT POTTY ALL BY MYSELF!
KIRKMAN & SCOTT

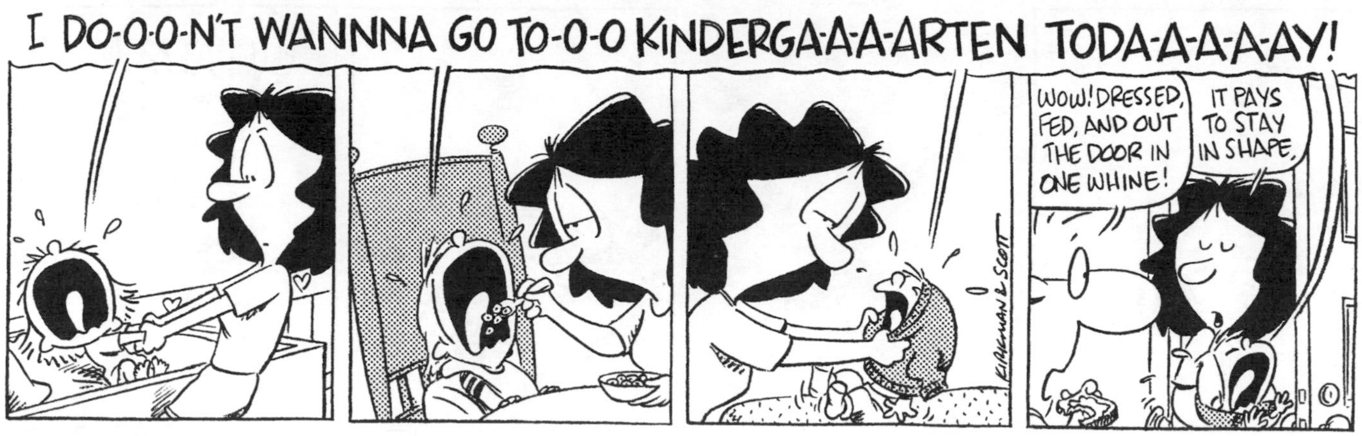
I DO-O-O-N'T WANNA GO TO-O-O KINDERGA-A-A-ARTEN TODA-A-A-A-AY!
WOW! DRESSED, FED, AND OUT THE DOOR IN ONE WHINE!
IT PAYS TO STAY IN SHAPE.

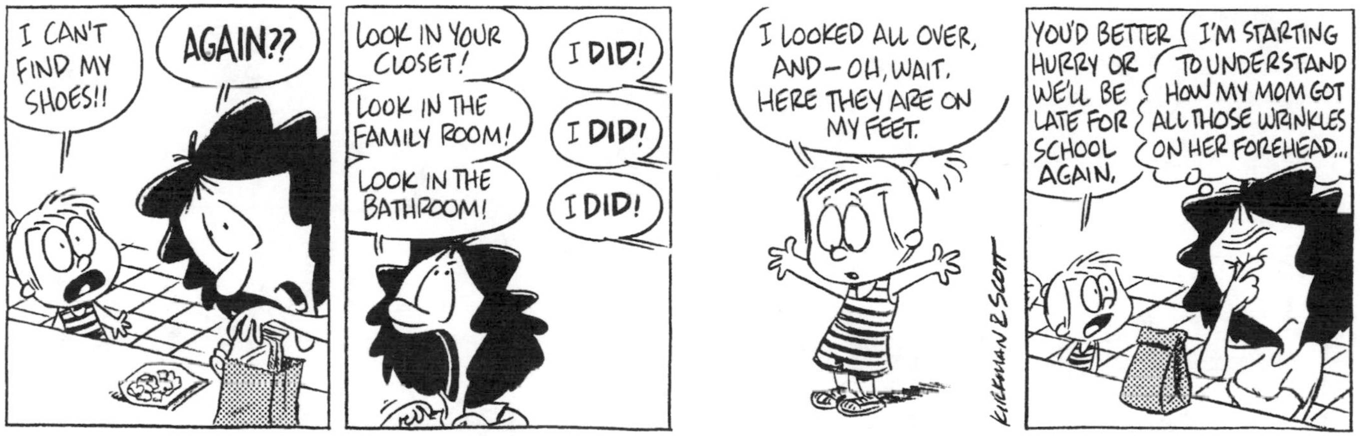
I CAN'T FIND MY SHOES!!
AGAIN??
LOOK IN YOUR CLOSET!
I DID!
LOOK IN THE FAMILY ROOM!
I DID!
LOOK IN THE BATHROOM!
I DID!
I LOOKED ALL OVER, AND – OH, WAIT. HERE THEY ARE ON MY FEET.
YOU'D BETTER HURRY OR WE'LL BE LATE FOR SCHOOL AGAIN.
I'M STARTING TO UNDERSTAND HOW MY MOM GOT ALL THOSE WRINKLES ON HER FOREHEAD...

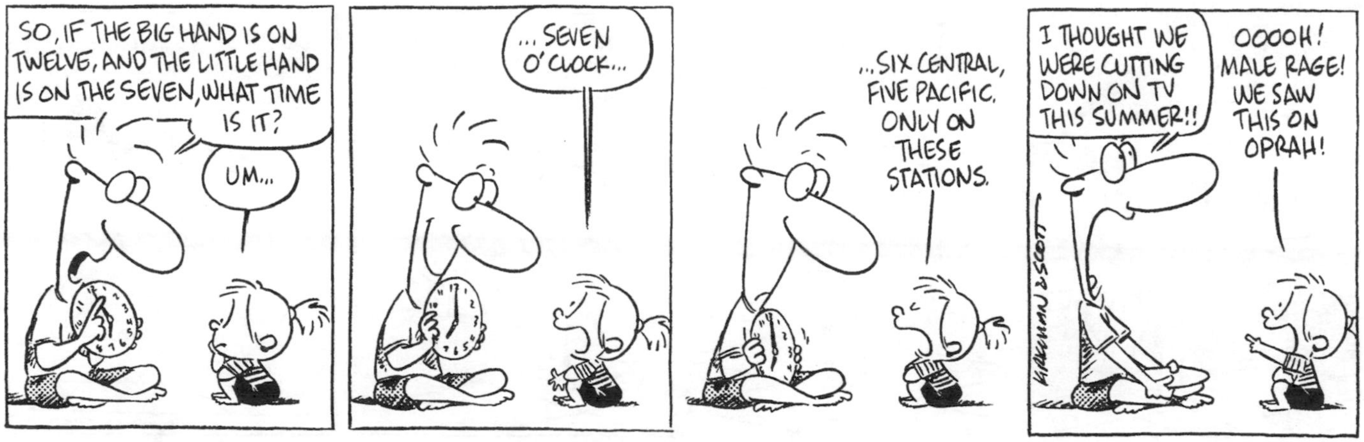
SO, IF THE BIG HAND IS ON TWELVE, AND THE LITTLE HAND IS ON THE SEVEN, WHAT TIME IS IT?
UM...
...SEVEN O'CLOCK...
...SIX CENTRAL, FIVE PACIFIC. ONLY ON THESE STATIONS.
I THOUGHT WE WERE CUTTING DOWN ON TV THIS SUMMER!!
OOOOH! MALE RAGE! WE SAW THIS ON OPRAH!

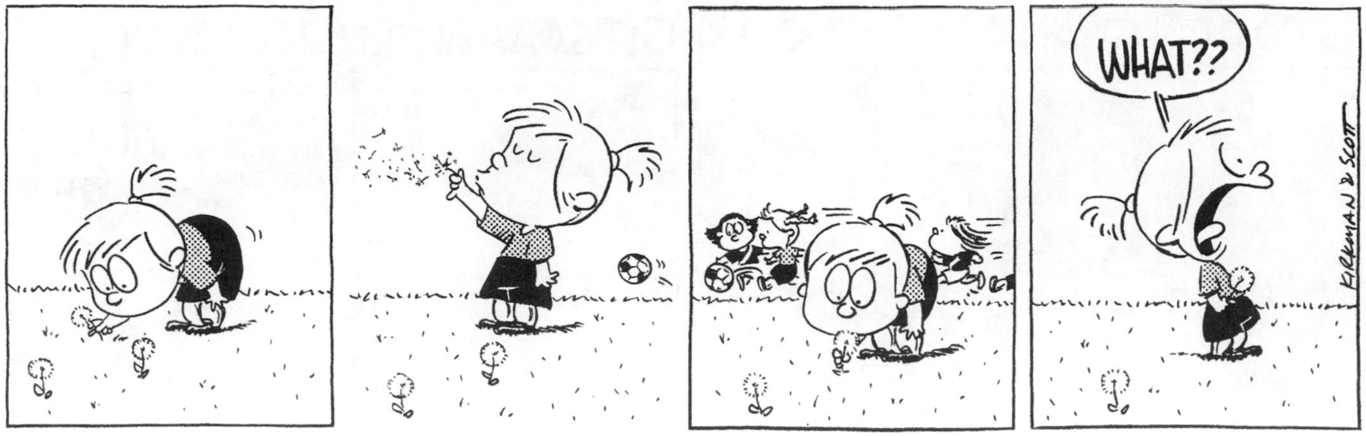
WHAT??
KIRKMAN & SCOTT

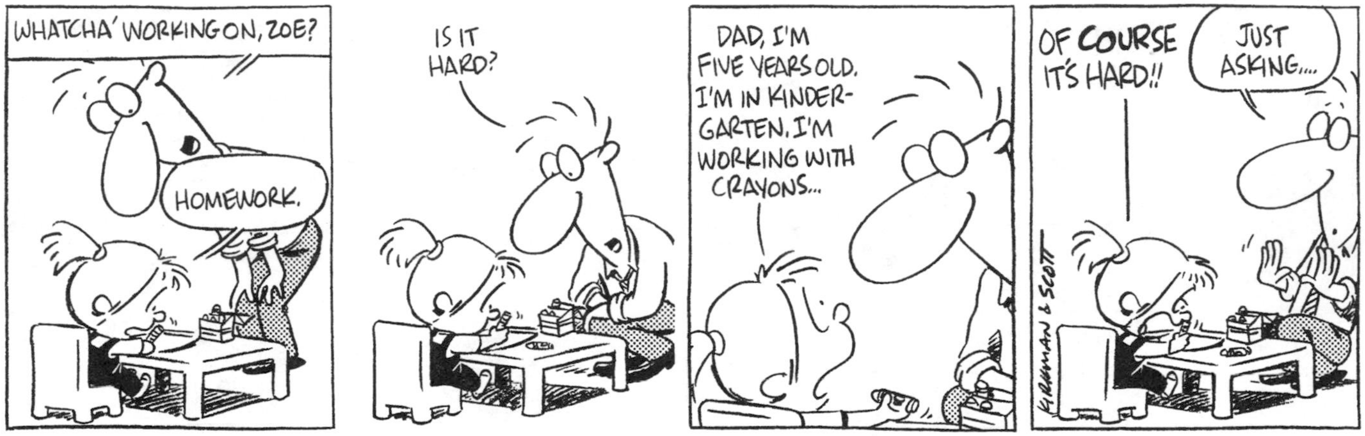
WHATCHA' WORKING ON, ZOE?
HOMEWORK.
IS IT HARD?
DAD, I'M FIVE YEARS OLD. I'M IN KINDER-GARTEN. I'M WORKING WITH CRAYONS...
KIRKMAN & SCOTT
OF COURSE IT'S HARD!!
JUST ASKING....

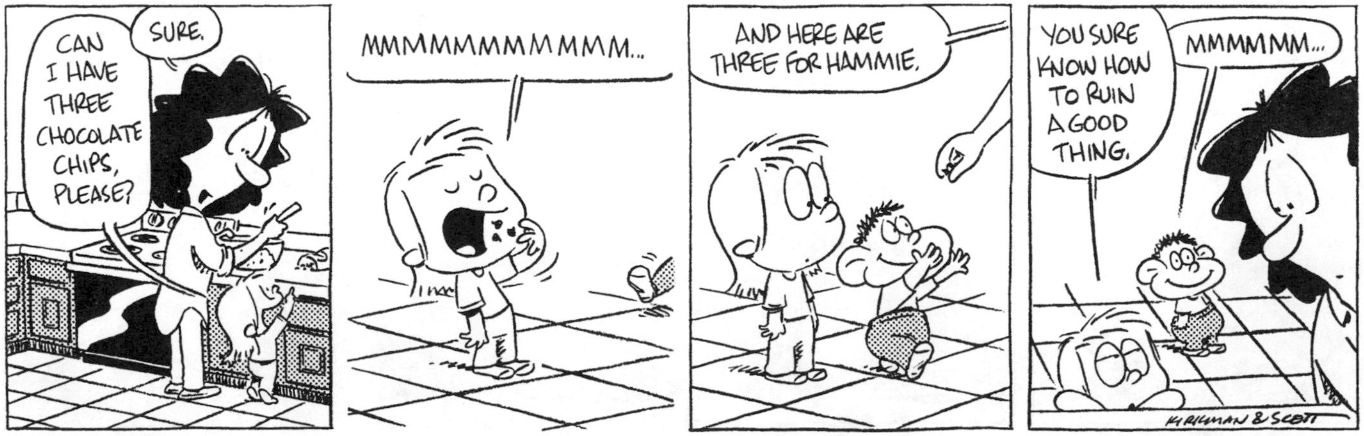
CAN I HAVE THREE CHOCOLATE CHIPS, PLEASE?
SURE.
MMMMMMMMMMM...
AND HERE ARE THREE FOR HAMMIE.
YOU SURE KNOW HOW TO RUIN A GOOD THING.
MMMMMM...
KIRKMAN & SCOTT

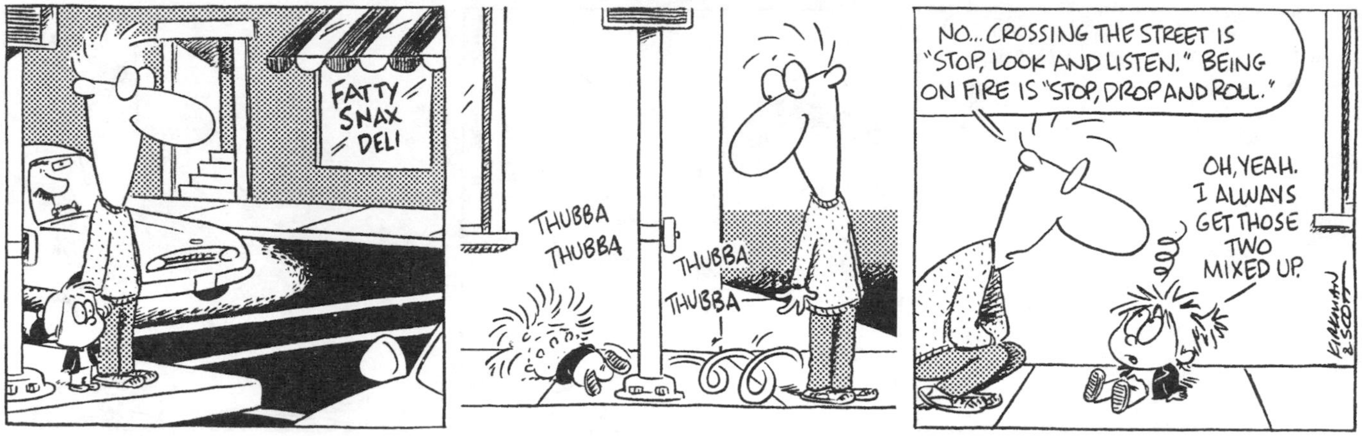
FATTY SNAX DELI
THUBBA THUBBA
THUBBA THUBBA
NO... CROSSING THE STREET IS "STOP, LOOK AND LISTEN." BEING ON FIRE IS "STOP, DROP AND ROLL."
OH, YEAH. I ALWAYS GET THOSE TWO MIXED UP.
KIRKMAN & SCOTT

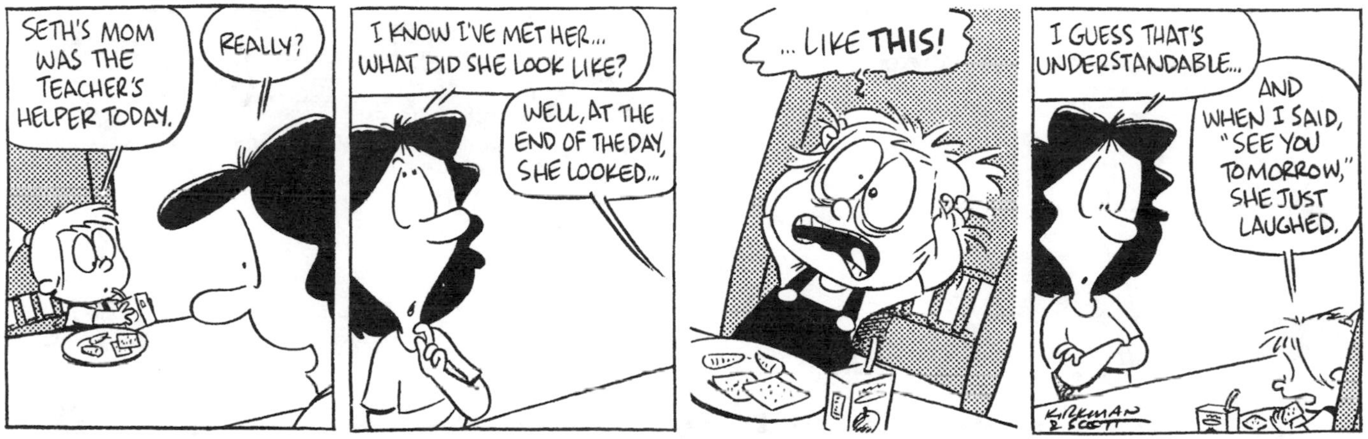
SETH'S MOM WAS THE TEACHER'S HELPER TODAY.
REALLY?
I KNOW I'VE MET HER... WHAT DID SHE LOOK LIKE?
WELL, AT THE END OF THE DAY, SHE LOOKED...
... LIKE **THIS!**
I GUESS THAT'S UNDERSTANDABLE...
AND WHEN I SAID, "SEE YOU TOMORROW," SHE JUST LAUGHED.
KIRKMAN & SCOTT

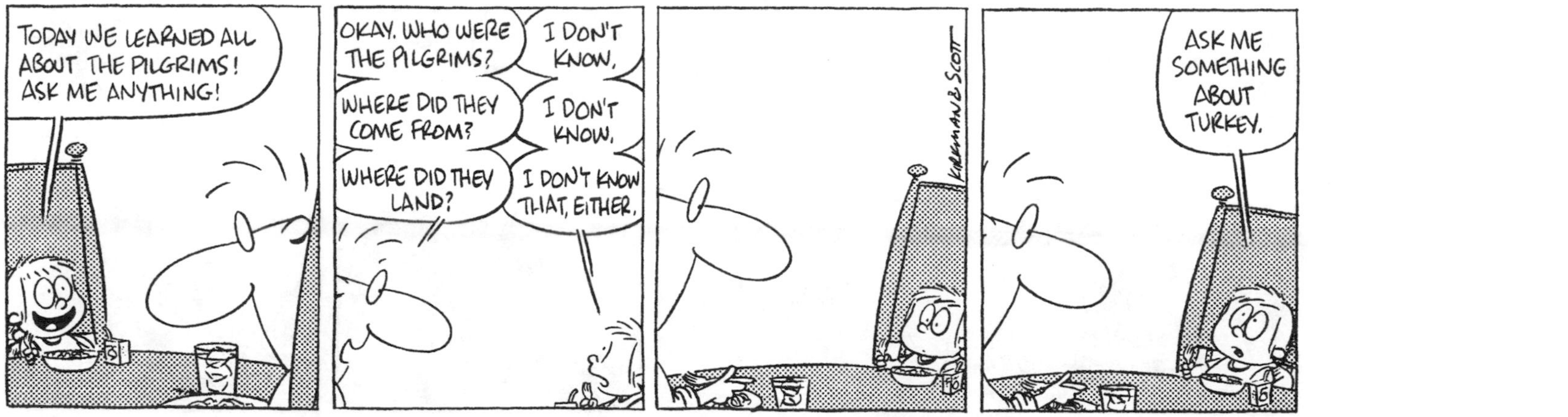
TODAY WE LEARNED ALL ABOUT THE PILGRIMS! ASK ME ANYTHING!
OKAY. WHO WERE THE PILGRIMS?
I DON'T KNOW.
WHERE DID THEY COME FROM?
I DON'T KNOW.
WHERE DID THEY LAND?
I DON'T KNOW THAT, EITHER.
KIRKMAN & SCOTT
ASK ME SOMETHING ABOUT TURKEY.

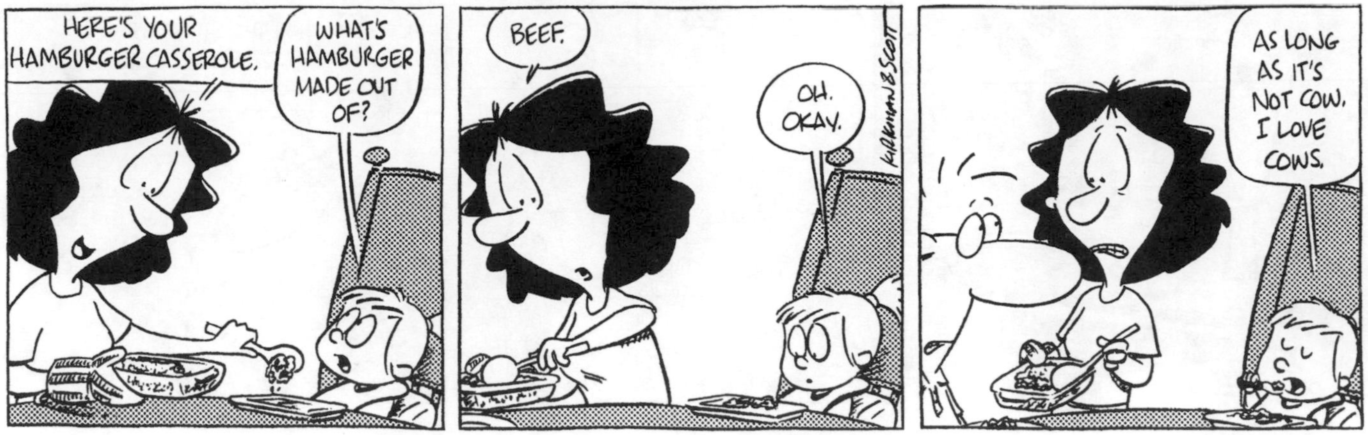
HERE'S YOUR HAMBURGER CASSEROLE.
WHAT'S HAMBURGER MADE OUT OF?
BEEF.
OH. OKAY.
AS LONG AS IT'S NOT COW. I LOVE COWS.

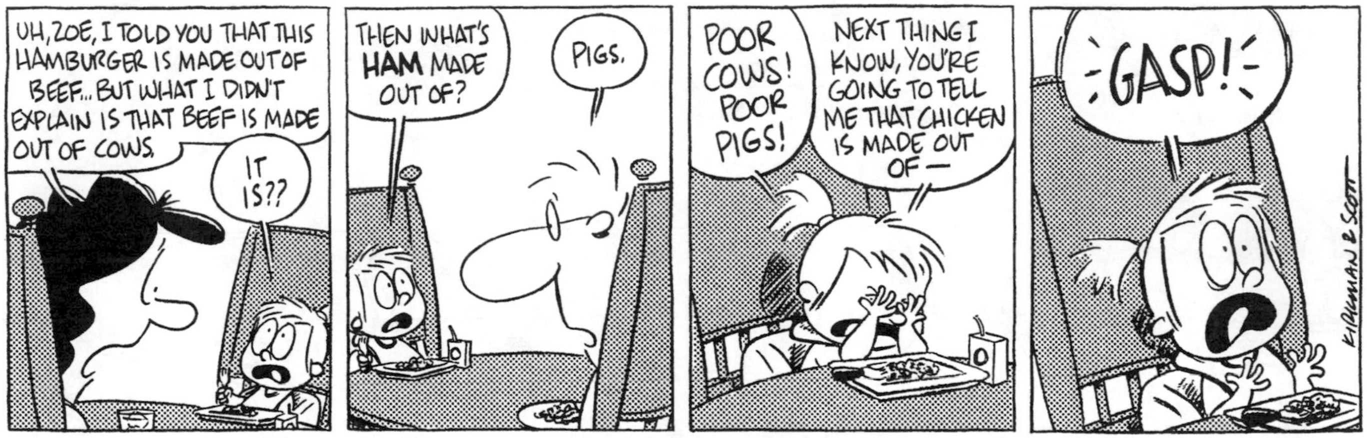
UH, ZOE, I TOLD YOU THAT THIS HAMBURGER IS MADE OUT OF BEEF... BUT WHAT I DIDN'T EXPLAIN IS THAT BEEF IS MADE OUT OF COWS.
IT IS??
THEN WHAT'S HAM MADE OUT OF?
PIGS.
POOR COWS! POOR PIGS!
NEXT THING I KNOW, YOU'RE GOING TO TELL ME THAT CHICKEN IS MADE OUT OF—
GASP!

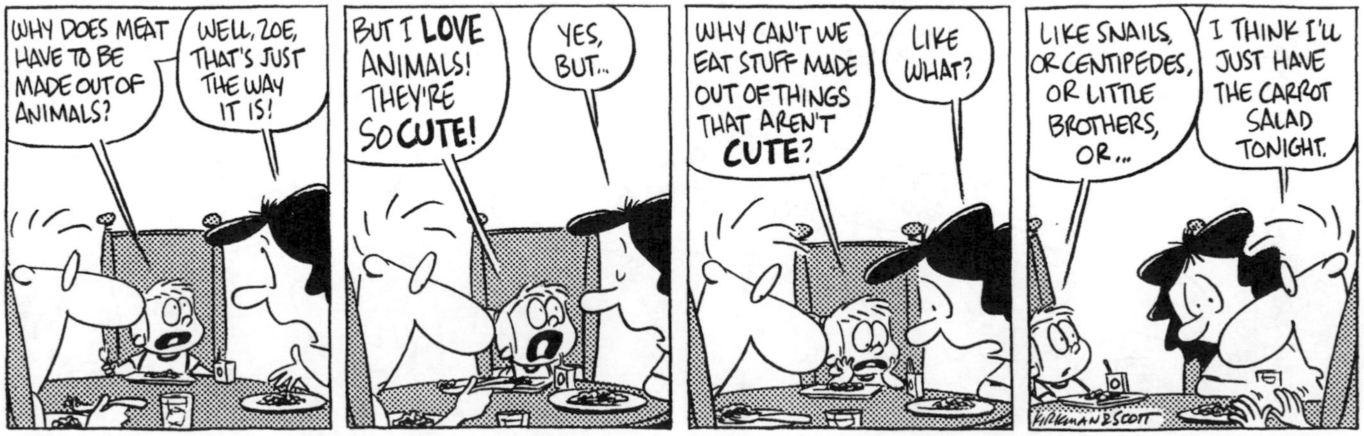
WHY DOES MEAT HAVE TO BE MADE OUT OF ANIMALS?
WELL, ZOE, THAT'S JUST THE WAY IT IS!
BUT I LOVE ANIMALS! THEY'RE SO CUTE!
YES, BUT...
WHY CAN'T WE EAT STUFF MADE OUT OF THINGS THAT AREN'T CUTE?
LIKE WHAT?
LIKE SNAILS, OR CENTIPEDES, OR LITTLE BROTHERS, OR...
I THINK I'LL JUST HAVE THE CARROT SALAD TONIGHT.

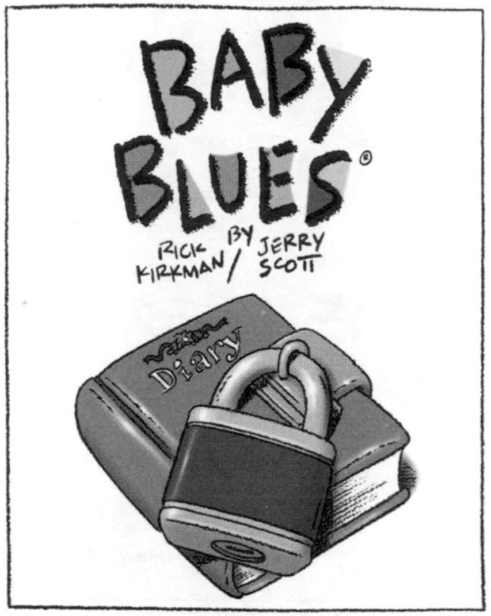
BABY BLUES®
BY RICK KIRKMAN / JERRY SCOTT
Diary

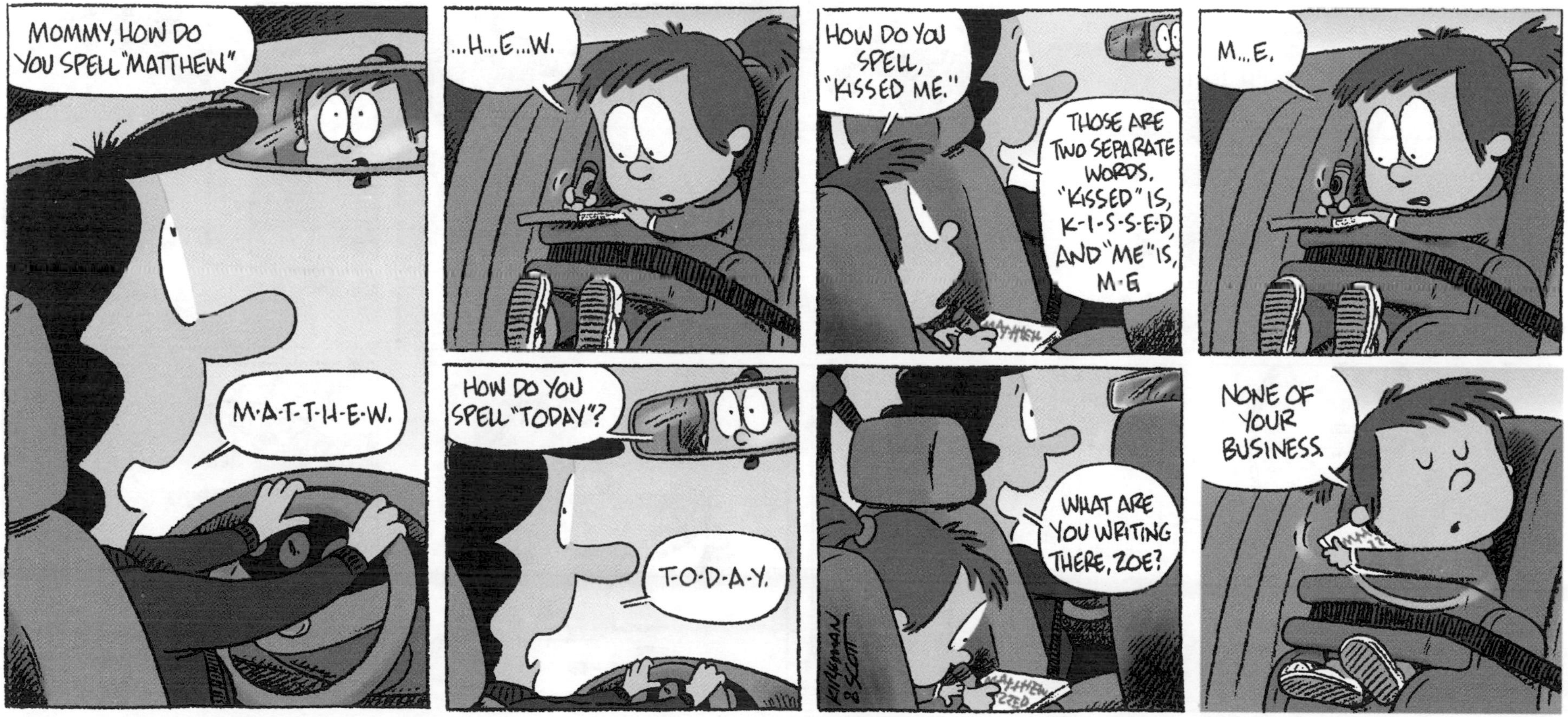
MOMMY, HOW DO YOU SPELL "MATTHEW."
M-A-T-T-H-E-W.
...H...E...W.
HOW DO YOU SPELL, "KISSED ME."
THOSE ARE TWO SEPARATE WORDS. "KISSED" IS, K-I-S-S-E-D, AND "ME" IS, M-E
M...E.
HOW DO YOU SPELL "TODAY"?
T-O-D-A-Y.
WHAT ARE YOU WRITING THERE, ZOE?
KIRKMAN & SCOTT
NONE OF YOUR BUSINESS.

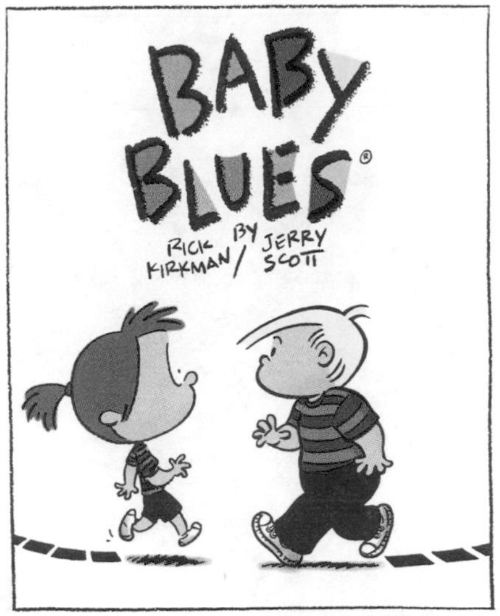
BABY BLUES®
BY
RICK KIRKMAN / JERRY SCOTT

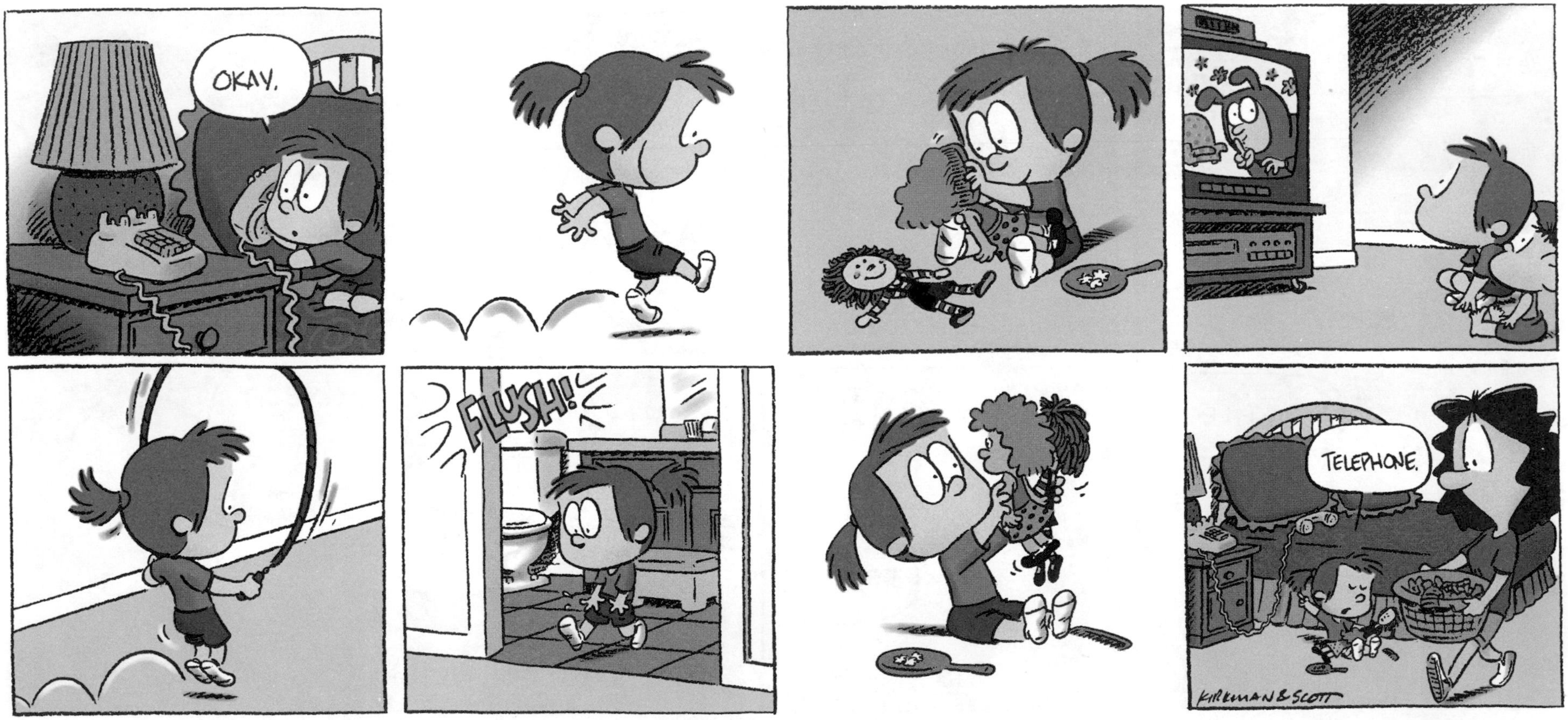
OKAY.
FLUSH!
TELEPHONE.
KIRKMAN&SCOTT

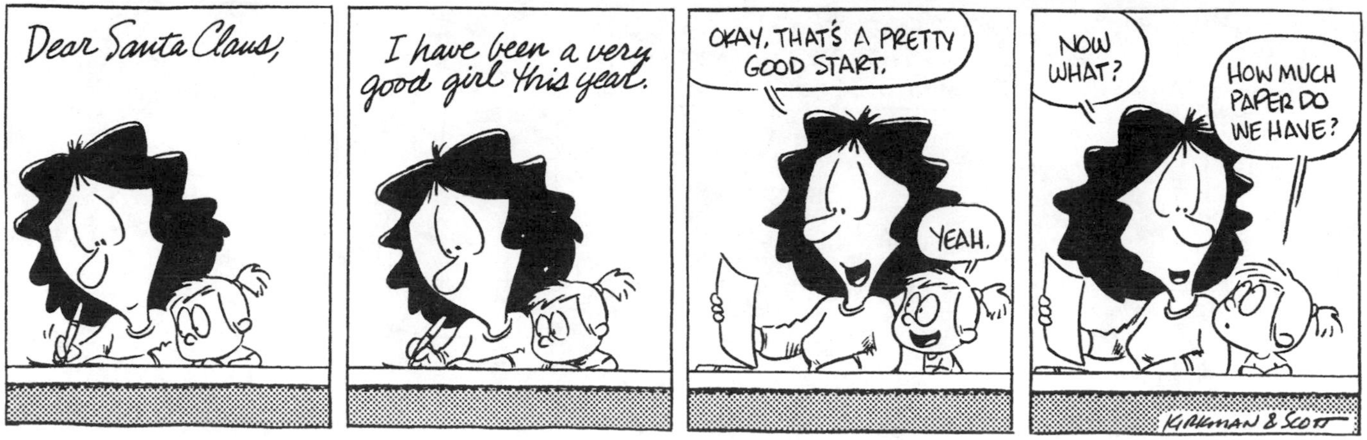
Dear Santa Claus,
I have been a very good girl this year.
OKAY, THAT'S A PRETTY GOOD START.
YEAH.
NOW WHAT?
HOW MUCH PAPER DO WE HAVE?
KIRKMAN & SCOTT

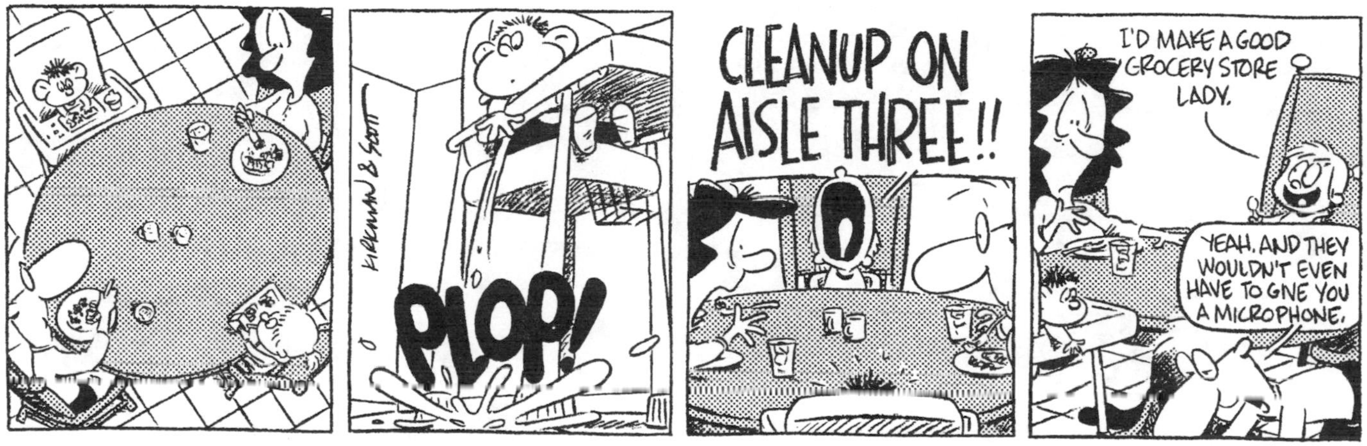
KIRKMAN & SCOTT
PLOP!
CLEANUP ON AISLE THREE!!
I'D MAKE A GOOD GROCERY STORE LADY.
YEAH. AND THEY WOULDN'T EVEN HAVE TO GIVE YOU A MICROPHONE.

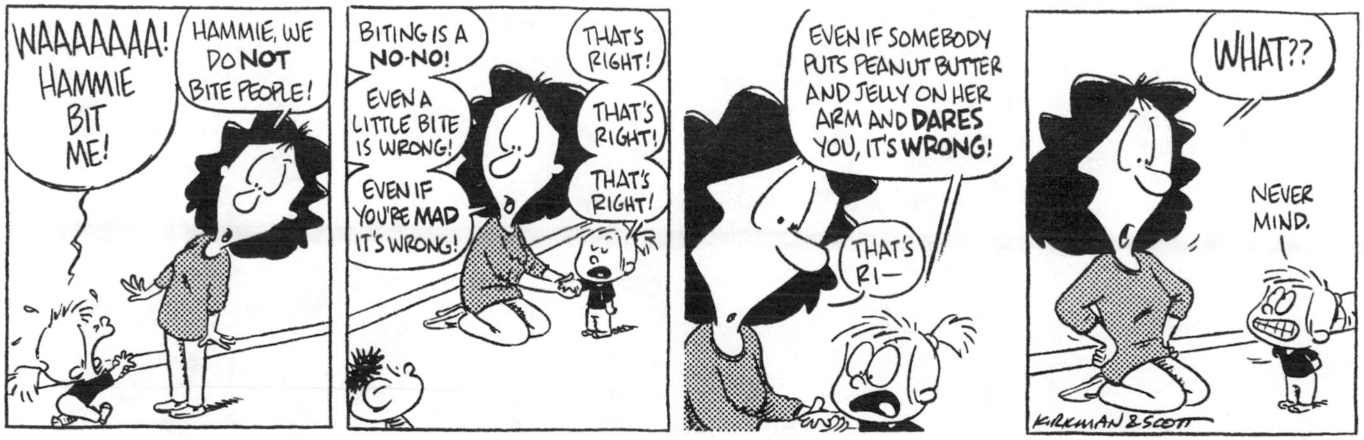
WAAAAAAA! HAMMIE BIT ME!
HAMMIE, WE DO NOT BITE PEOPLE!
BITING IS A NO-NO!
THAT'S RIGHT!
EVEN A LITTLE BITE IS WRONG!
THAT'S RIGHT!
EVEN IF YOU'RE MAD IT'S WRONG!
THAT'S RIGHT!
EVEN IF SOMEBODY PUTS PEANUT BUTTER AND JELLY ON HER ARM AND DARES YOU, IT'S WRONG!
THAT'S RI—
WHAT??
NEVER MIND.
KIRKMAN & SCOTT

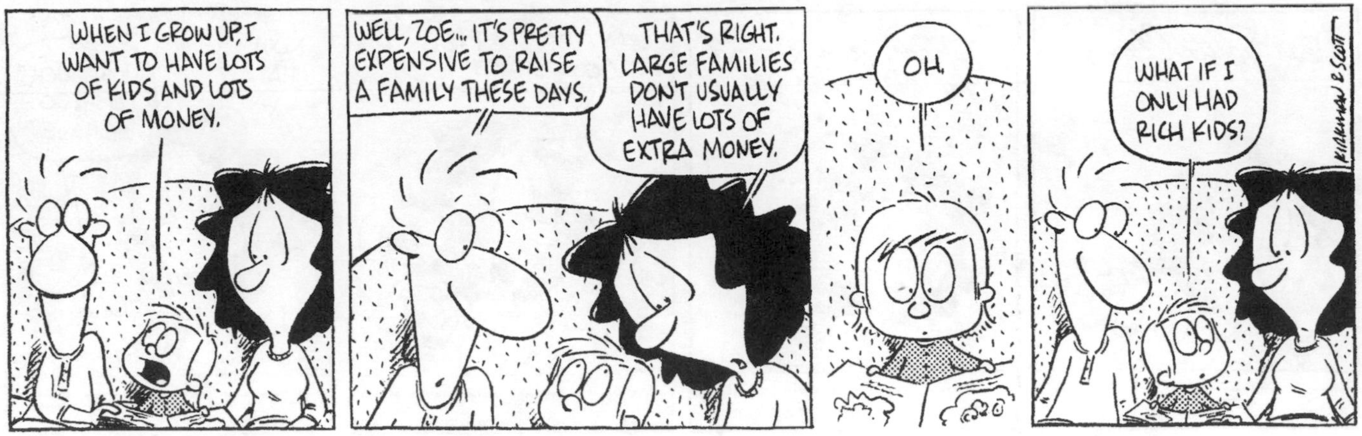
WHEN I GROW UP, I WANT TO HAVE LOTS OF KIDS AND LOTS OF MONEY.
WELL, ZOE... IT'S PRETTY EXPENSIVE TO RAISE A FAMILY THESE DAYS.
THAT'S RIGHT. LARGE FAMILIES DON'T USUALLY HAVE LOTS OF EXTRA MONEY.
OH.
WHAT IF I ONLY HAD RICH KIDS?
KIRKMAN & SCOTT

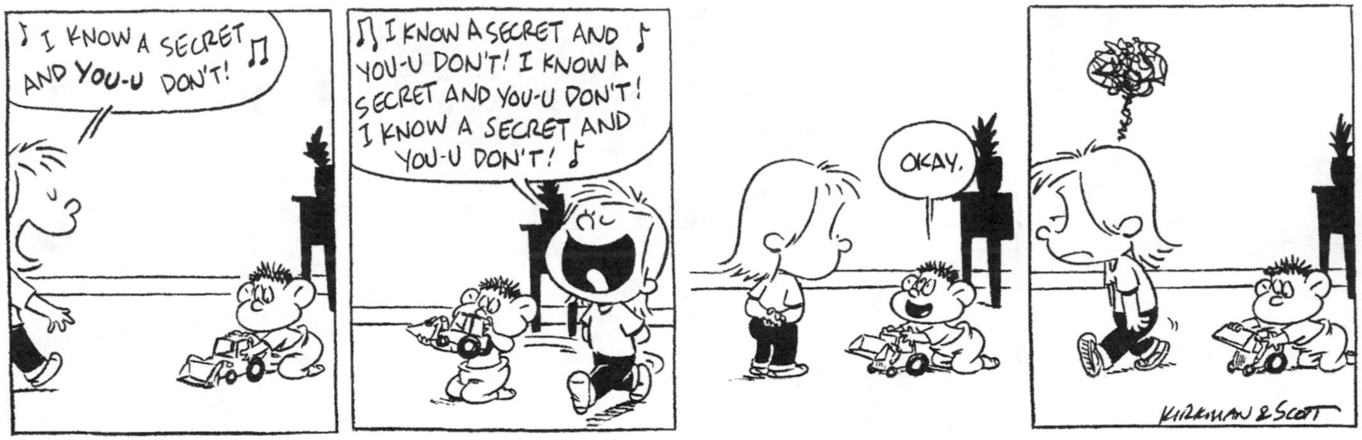
♪ I KNOW A SECRET AND YOU-U DON'T! ♫
♫ I KNOW A SECRET AND YOU-U DON'T! I KNOW A SECRET AND YOU-U DON'T! I KNOW A SECRET AND YOU-U DON'T! ♪
OKAY.
KIRKMAN & SCOTT

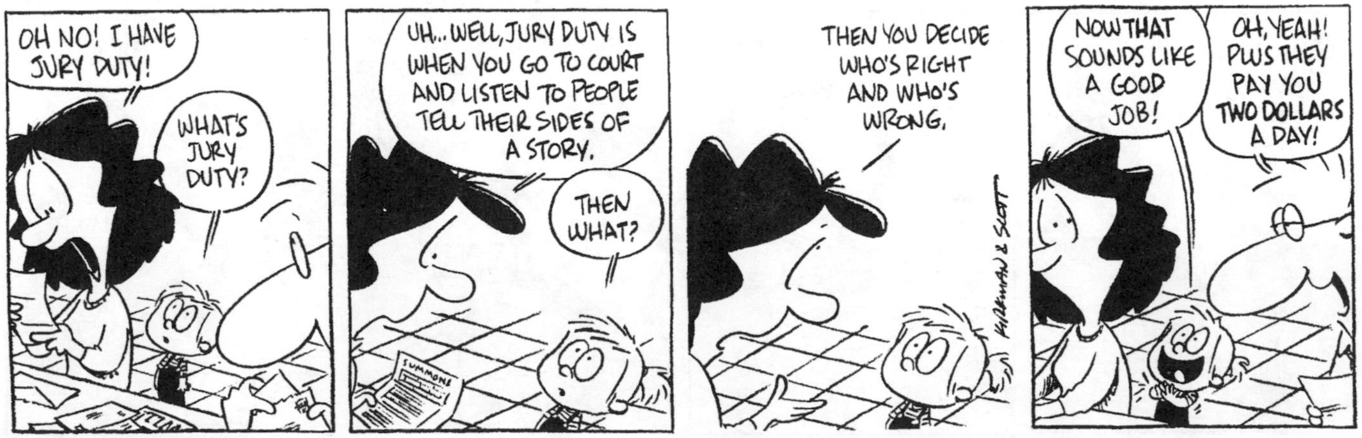
OH NO! I HAVE JURY DUTY!
WHAT'S JURY DUTY?
UH... WELL, JURY DUTY IS WHEN YOU GO TO COURT AND LISTEN TO PEOPLE TELL THEIR SIDES OF A STORY.
THEN WHAT?
THEN YOU DECIDE WHO'S RIGHT AND WHO'S WRONG.
KIRKMAN & SCOTT
NOW THAT SOUNDS LIKE A GOOD JOB!
OH, YEAH! PLUS THEY PAY YOU TWO DOLLARS A DAY!

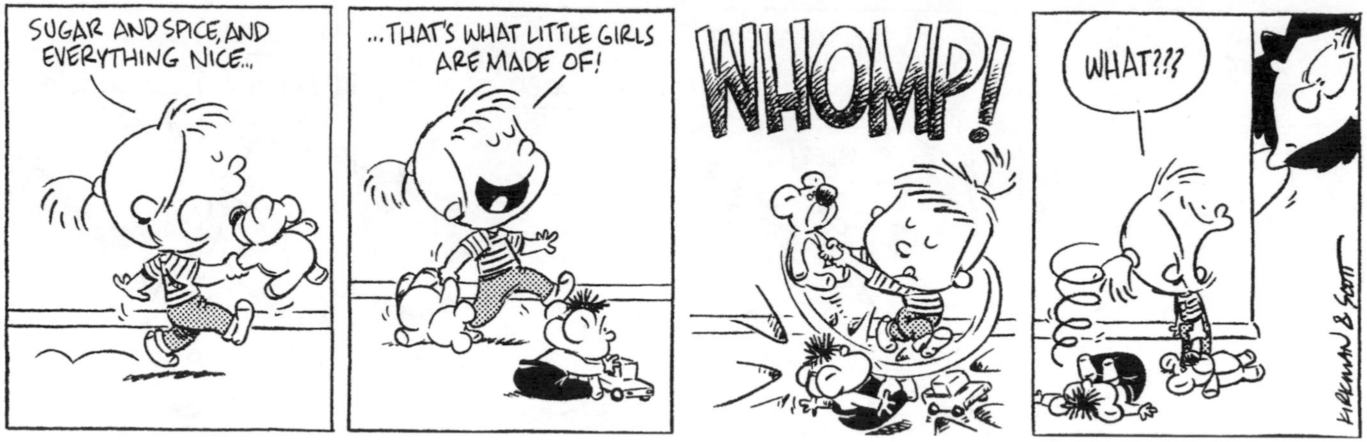
SUGAR AND SPICE, AND EVERYTHING NICE...
...THAT'S WHAT LITTLE GIRLS ARE MADE OF!
WHOMP!
WHAT???
KIRKMAN & SCOTT

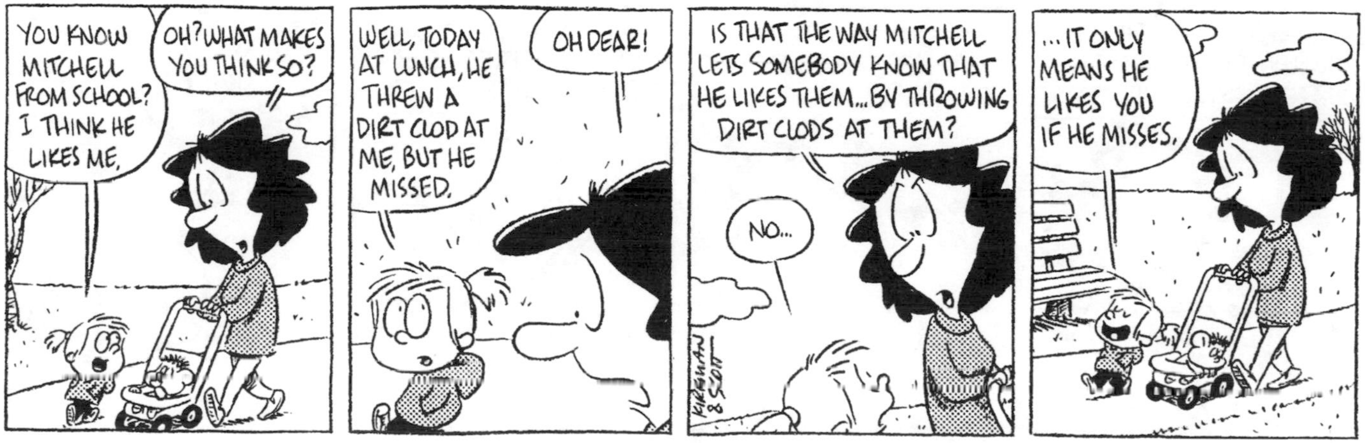
YOU KNOW MITCHELL FROM SCHOOL? I THINK HE LIKES ME.
OH? WHAT MAKES YOU THINK SO?
WELL, TODAY AT LUNCH, HE THREW A DIRT CLOD AT ME, BUT HE MISSED.
OH DEAR!
KIRKMAN & SCOTT
IS THAT THE WAY MITCHELL LETS SOMEBODY KNOW THAT HE LIKES THEM... BY THROWING DIRT CLODS AT THEM?
NO...
...IT ONLY MEANS HE LIKES YOU IF HE MISSES.

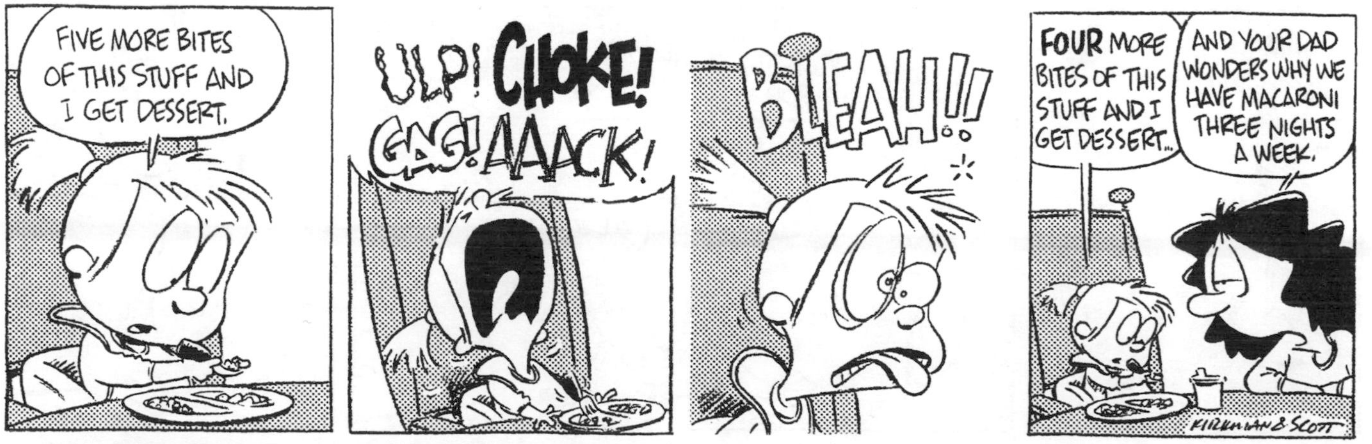
FIVE MORE BITES OF THIS STUFF AND I GET DESSERT.
ULP! CHOKE!
GAG! AAACK!
BLEAH!!!
FOUR MORE BITES OF THIS STUFF AND I GET DESSERT...
AND YOUR DAD WONDERS WHY WE HAVE MACARONI THREE NIGHTS A WEEK.
KIRKMAN & SCOTT

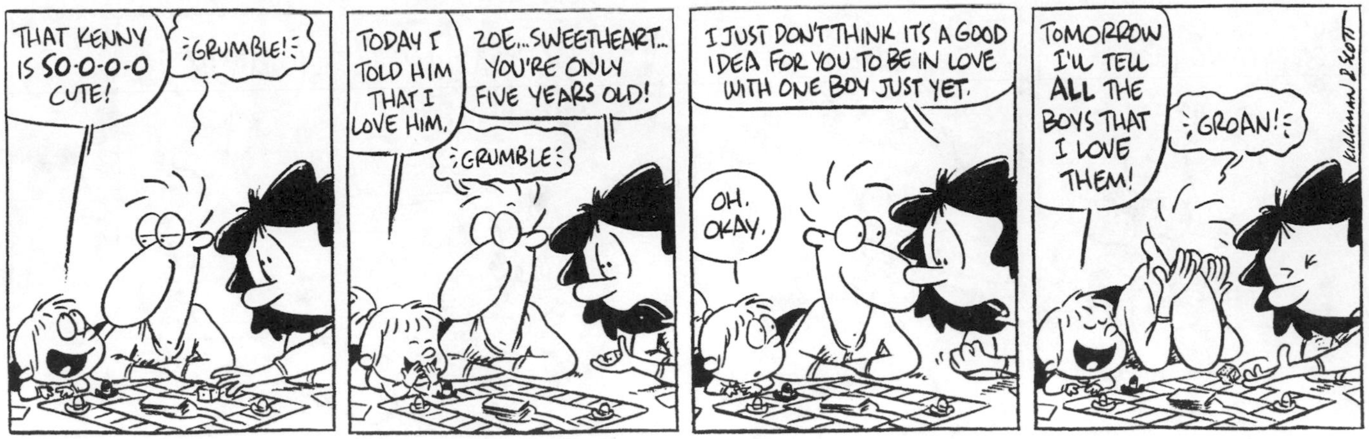
THAT KENNY IS SO-O-O-O CUTE!
GRUMBLE!
TODAY I TOLD HIM THAT I LOVE HIM.
ZOE...SWEETHEART... YOU'RE ONLY FIVE YEARS OLD!
GRUMBLE
I JUST DON'T THINK IT'S A GOOD IDEA FOR YOU TO BE IN LOVE WITH ONE BOY JUST YET.
OH. OKAY.
TOMORROW I'LL TELL ALL THE BOYS THAT I LOVE THEM!
GROAN!
KIRKMAN & SCOTT

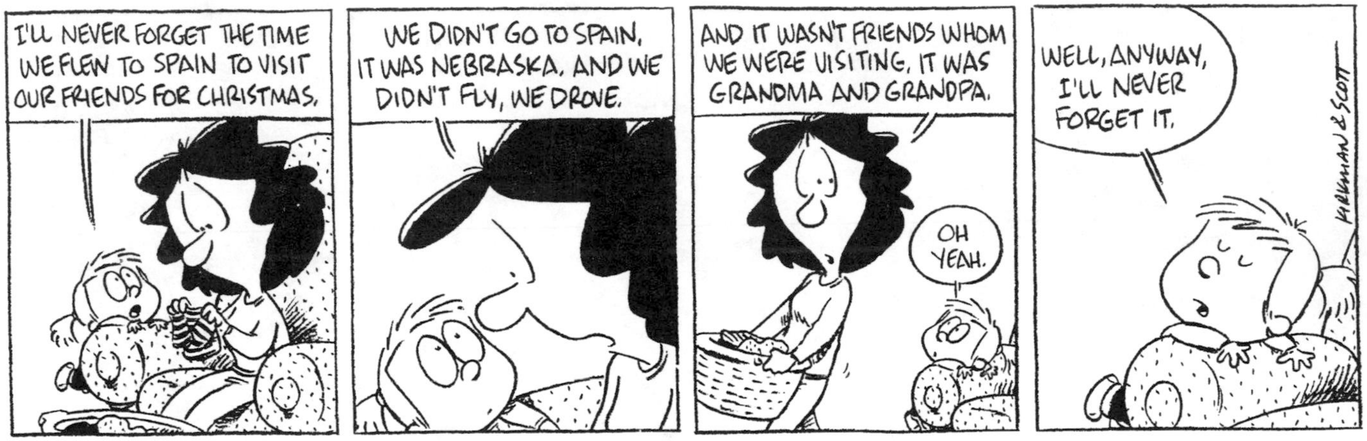
I'LL NEVER FORGET THE TIME WE FLEW TO SPAIN TO VISIT OUR FRIENDS FOR CHRISTMAS.
WE DIDN'T GO TO SPAIN. IT WAS NEBRASKA. AND WE DIDN'T FLY, WE DROVE.
AND IT WASN'T FRIENDS WHOM WE WERE VISITING. IT WAS GRANDMA AND GRANDPA.
OH YEAH.
WELL, ANYWAY, I'LL NEVER FORGET IT.
KIRKMAN & SCOTT

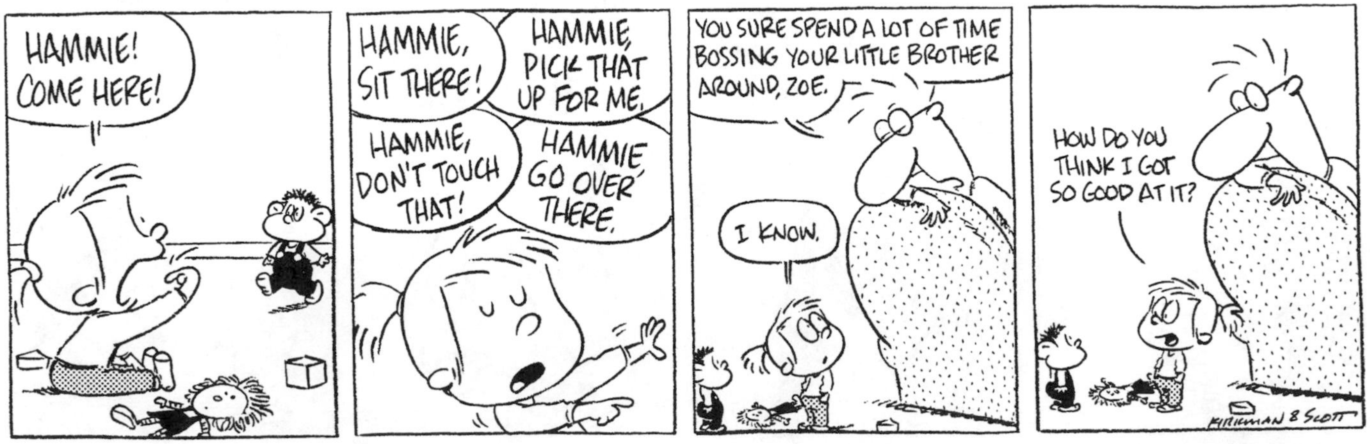
HAMMIE! COME HERE!
HAMMIE, SIT THERE!
HAMMIE, PICK THAT UP FOR ME.
HAMMIE, DON'T TOUCH THAT!
HAMMIE GO OVER THERE.
YOU SURE SPEND A LOT OF TIME BOSSING YOUR LITTLE BROTHER AROUND, ZOE.
I KNOW.
HOW DO YOU THINK I GOT SO GOOD AT IT?
KIRKMAN & SCOTT

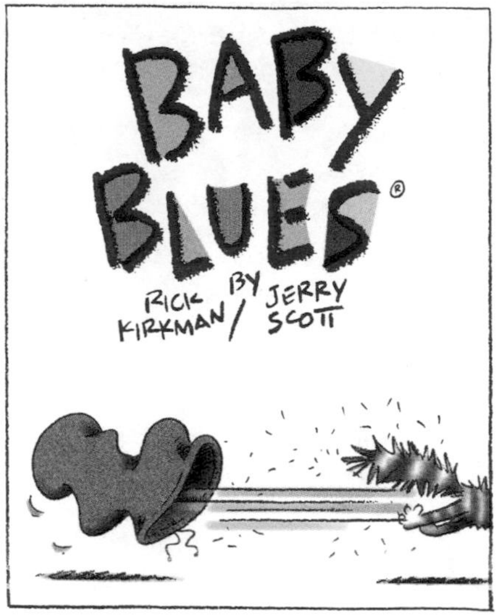
BABY BLUES®
BY RICK KIRKMAN / JERRY SCOTT

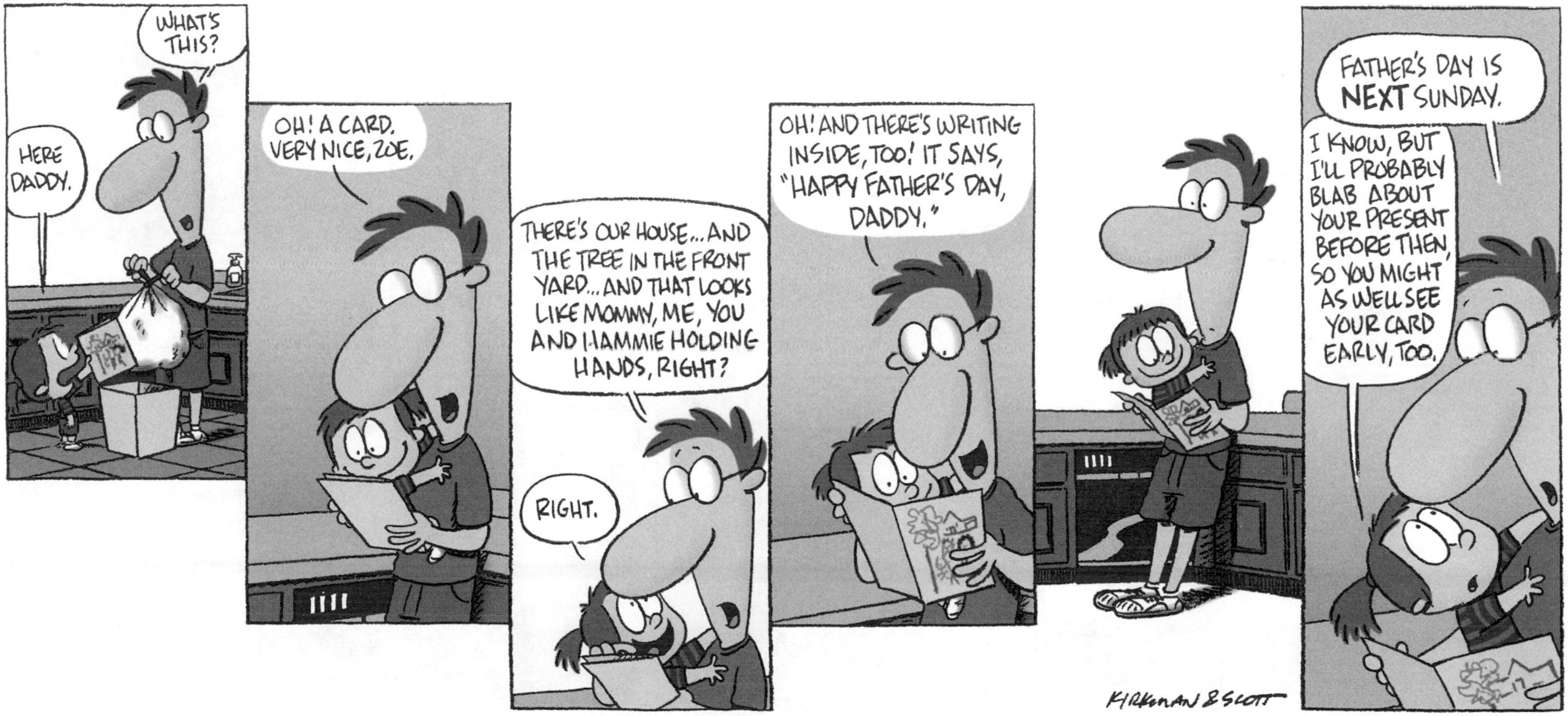
WHAT'S THIS?
HERE DADDY.
OH! A CARD. VERY NICE, ZOE.
THERE'S OUR HOUSE... AND THE TREE IN THE FRONT YARD... AND THAT LOOKS LIKE MOMMY, ME, YOU AND HAMMIE HOLDING HANDS, RIGHT?
RIGHT.
OH! AND THERE'S WRITING INSIDE, TOO! IT SAYS, "HAPPY FATHER'S DAY, DADDY."
FATHER'S DAY IS NEXT SUNDAY.
I KNOW, BUT I'LL PROBABLY BLAB ABOUT YOUR PRESENT BEFORE THEN, SO YOU MIGHT AS WELL SEE YOUR CARD EARLY, TOO.
KIRKMAN & SCOTT

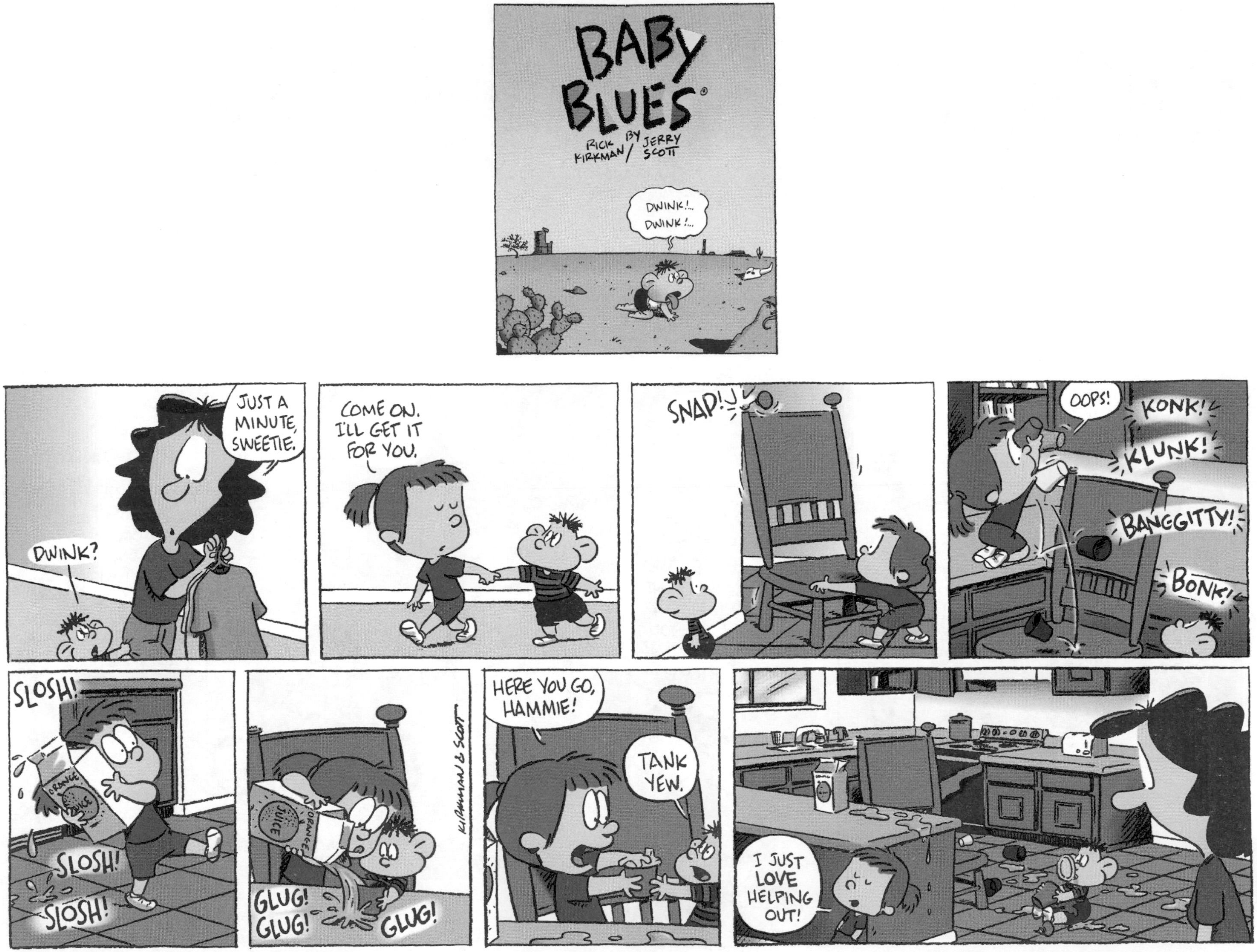
BABY BLUES®
BY RICK KIRKMAN / JERRY SCOTT
DWINK!... DWINK!...
JUST A MINUTE, SWEETIE.
DWINK?
COME ON. I'LL GET IT FOR YOU.
SNAP!
OOPS!
KONK!
KLUNK!
BANGGITTY!
BONK!
SLOSH!
SLOSH!
SLOSH!
ORANGE JUICE
GLUG! GLUG!
GLUG!
KIRKMAN & SCOTT
HERE YOU GO, HAMMIE!
TANK YEW.
I JUST LOVE HELPING OUT!

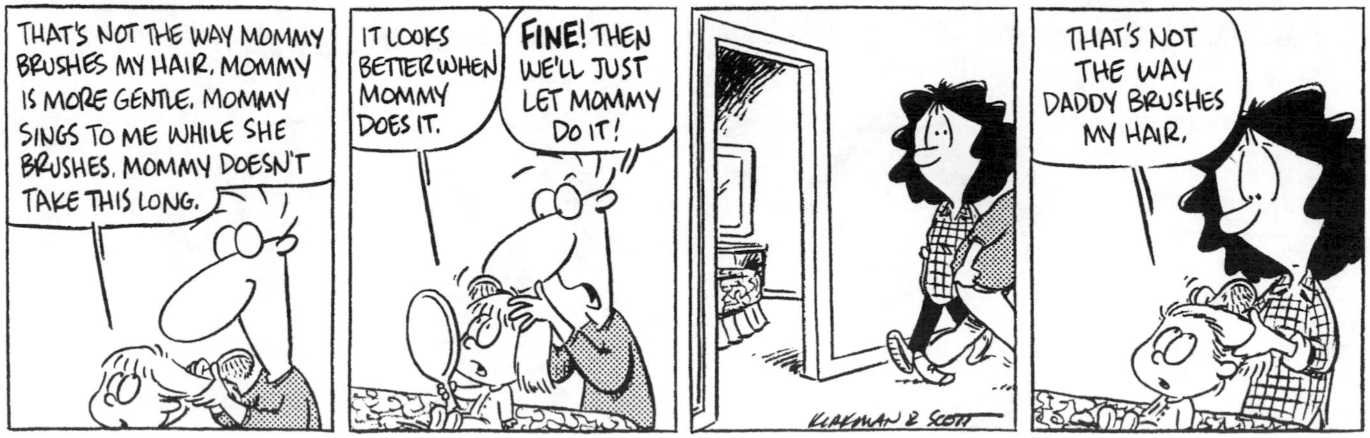
THAT'S NOT THE WAY MOMMY BRUSHES MY HAIR. MOMMY IS MORE GENTLE. MOMMY SINGS TO ME WHILE SHE BRUSHES. MOMMY DOESN'T TAKE THIS LONG.
IT LOOKS BETTER WHEN MOMMY DOES IT.
FINE! THEN WE'LL JUST LET MOMMY DO IT!
KIRKMAN & SCOTT
THAT'S NOT THE WAY DADDY BRUSHES MY HAIR.

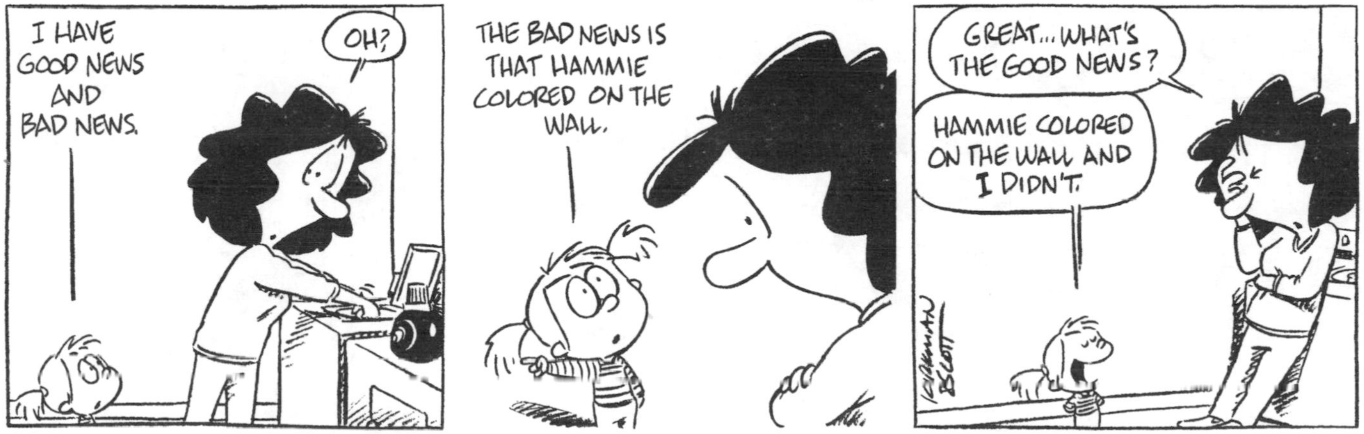
I HAVE GOOD NEWS AND BAD NEWS.
OH?
THE BAD NEWS IS THAT HAMMIE COLORED ON THE WALL.
GREAT... WHAT'S THE GOOD NEWS?
HAMMIE COLORED ON THE WALL AND I DIDN'T.
KIRKMAN & SCOTT

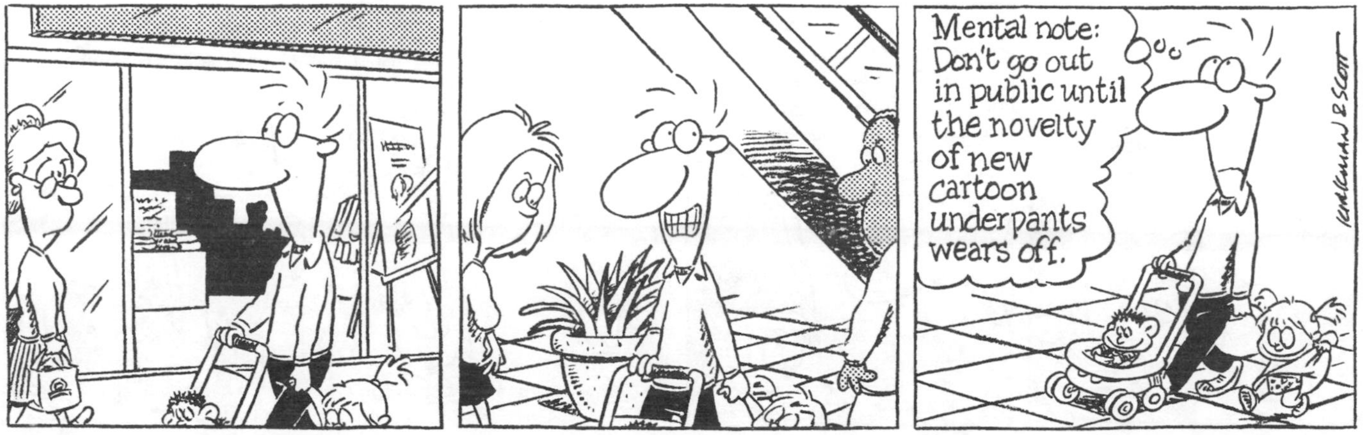
Mental note: Don't go out in public until the novelty of new cartoon underpants wears off.
KIRKMAN & SCOTT

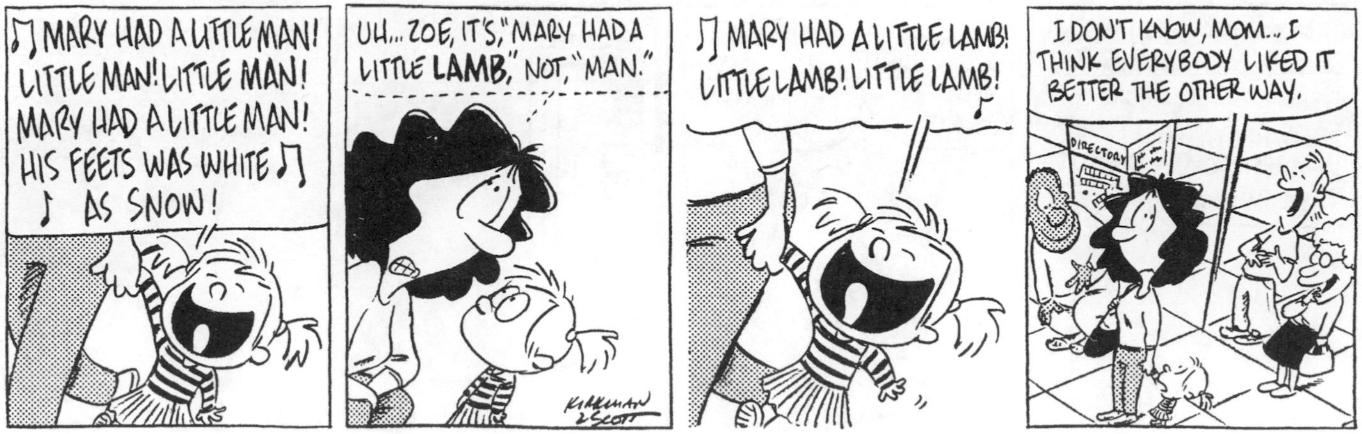
MARY HAD A LITTLE MAN! LITTLE MAN! LITTLE MAN! MARY HAD A LITTLE MAN! HIS FEETS WAS WHITE AS SNOW!
UH... ZOE, IT'S, "MARY HAD A LITTLE LAMB," NOT, "MAN."
MARY HAD A LITTLE LAMB! LITTLE LAMB! LITTLE LAMB!
I DON'T KNOW, MOM... I THINK EVERYBODY LIKED IT BETTER THE OTHER WAY.

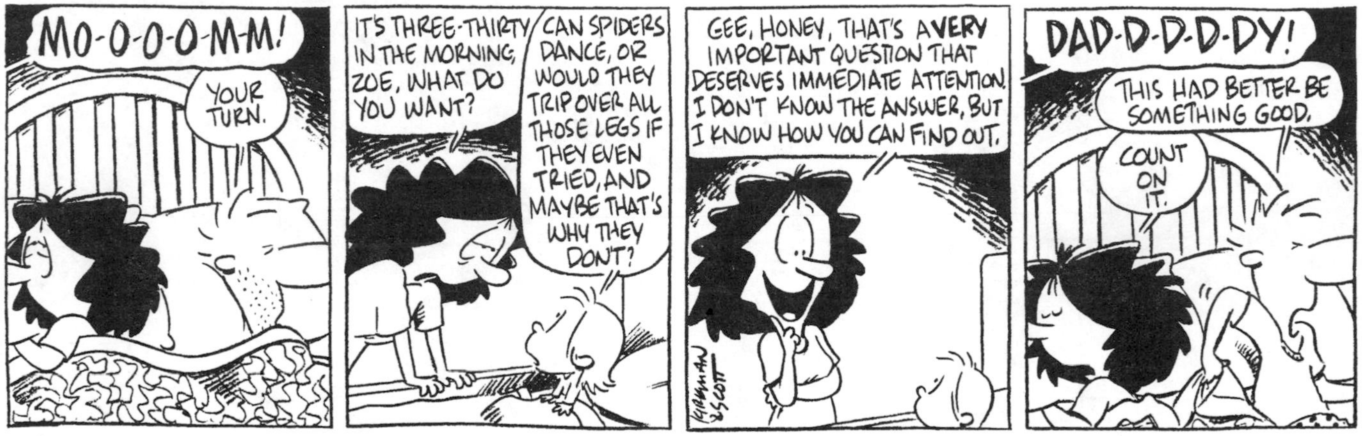
MO-O-O-O-M-M!
YOUR TURN.
IT'S THREE-THIRTY IN THE MORNING, ZOE, WHAT DO YOU WANT?
CAN SPIDERS DANCE, OR WOULD THEY TRIP OVER ALL THOSE LEGS IF THEY EVEN TRIED, AND MAYBE THAT'S WHY THEY DON'T?
GEE, HONEY, THAT'S A VERY IMPORTANT QUESTION THAT DESERVES IMMEDIATE ATTENTION. I DON'T KNOW THE ANSWER, BUT I KNOW HOW YOU CAN FIND OUT.
DAD-D-D-D-DY!
THIS HAD BETTER BE SOMETHING GOOD.
COUNT ON IT.

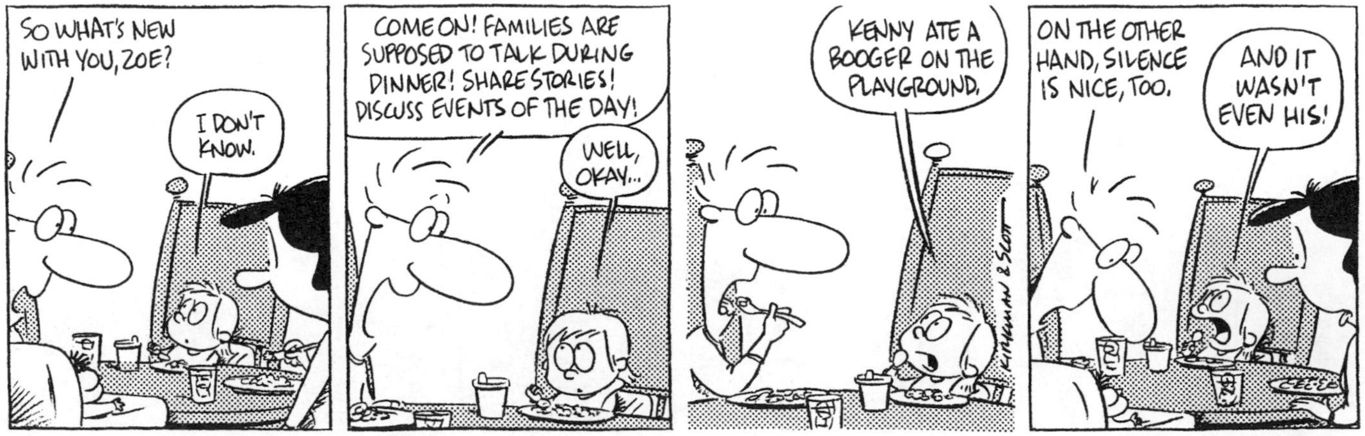
SO WHAT'S NEW WITH YOU, ZOE?
I DON'T KNOW.
COME ON! FAMILIES ARE SUPPOSED TO TALK DURING DINNER! SHARE STORIES! DISCUSS EVENTS OF THE DAY!
WELL, OKAY...
KENNY ATE A BOOGER ON THE PLAYGROUND.
ON THE OTHER HAND, SILENCE IS NICE, TOO.
AND IT WASN'T EVEN HIS!

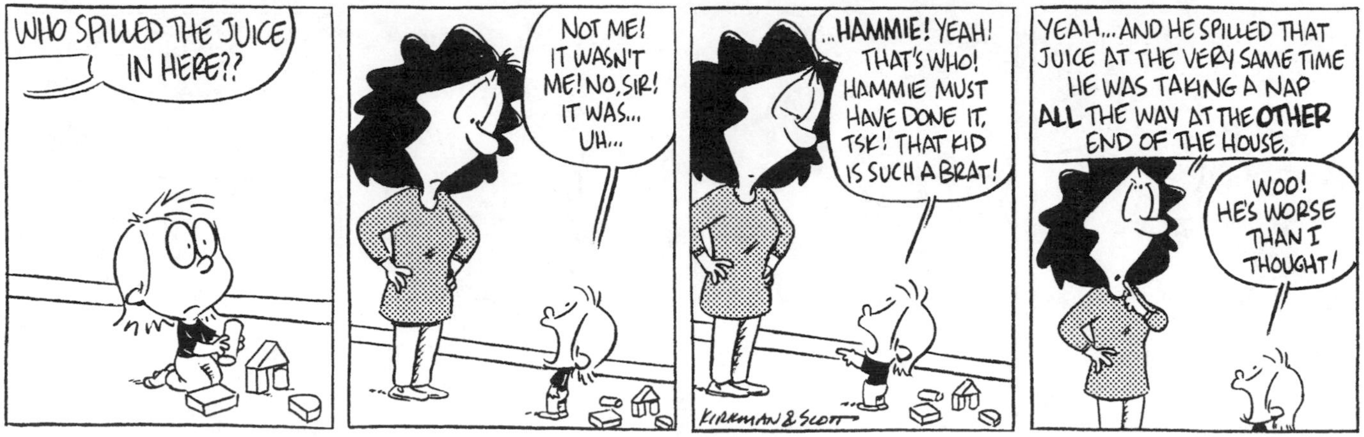
WHO SPILLED THE JUICE IN HERE??
NOT ME! IT WASN'T ME! NO, SIR! IT WAS... UH...
...HAMMIE! YEAH! THAT'S WHO! HAMMIE MUST HAVE DONE IT. TSK! THAT KID IS SUCH A BRAT!
KIRKMAN & SCOTT
YEAH... AND HE SPILLED THAT JUICE AT THE VERY SAME TIME HE WAS TAKING A NAP ALL THE WAY AT THE OTHER END OF THE HOUSE.
WOO! HE'S WORSE THAN I THOUGHT!

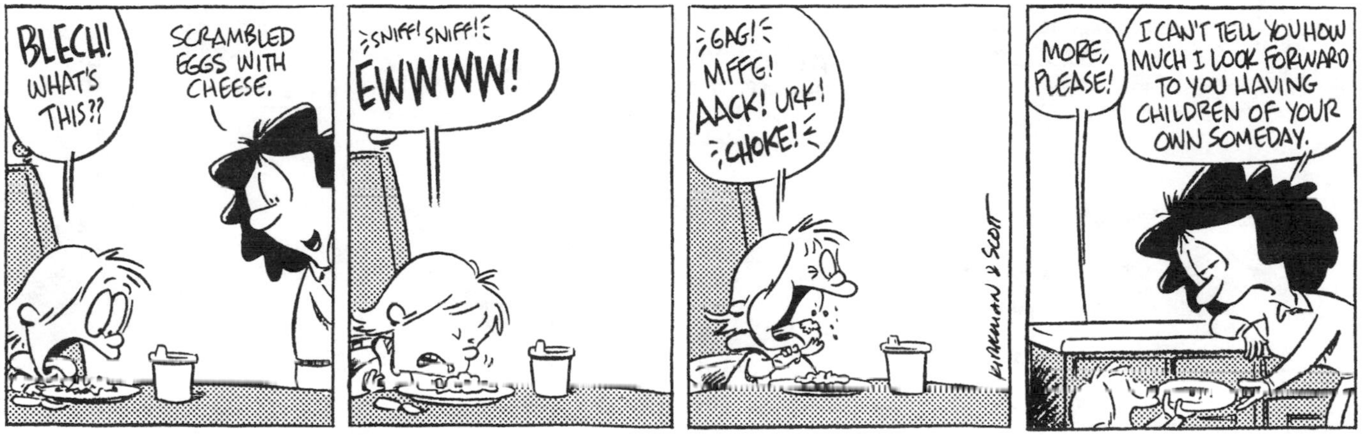
BLECH! WHAT'S THIS??
SCRAMBLED EGGS WITH CHEESE.
SNIFF! SNIFF!
EWWWW!
GAG! MFFG! AACK! URK! CHOKE!
KIRKMAN & SCOTT
MORE, PLEASE!
I CAN'T TELL YOU HOW MUCH I LOOK FORWARD TO YOU HAVING CHILDREN OF YOUR OWN SOMEDAY.

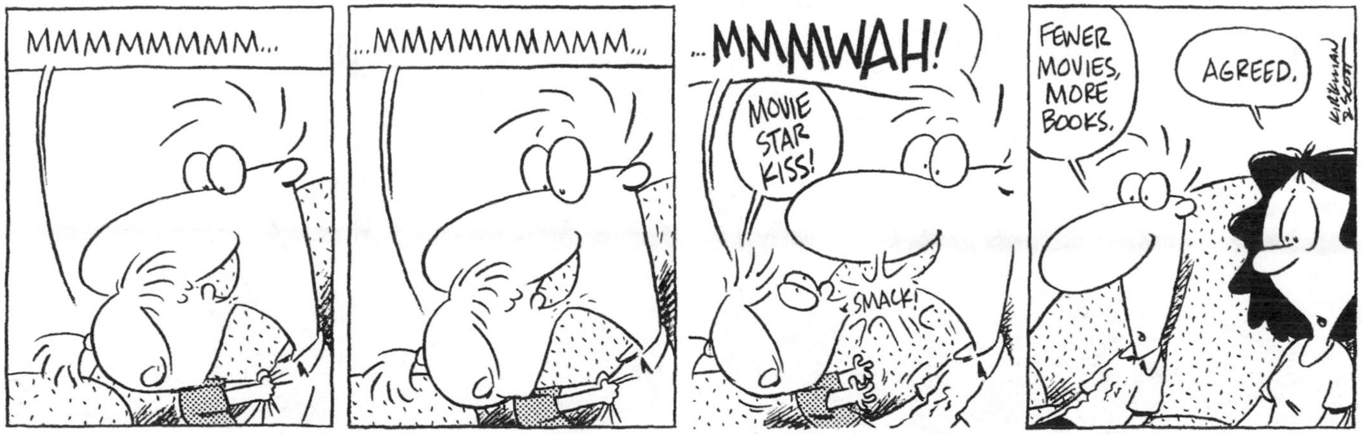
MMMMMMMM...
...MMMMMMMMM...
...MMMWAH!
MOVIE STAR KISS!
SMACK!
FEWER MOVIES, MORE BOOKS.
AGREED.
KIRKMAN & SCOTT

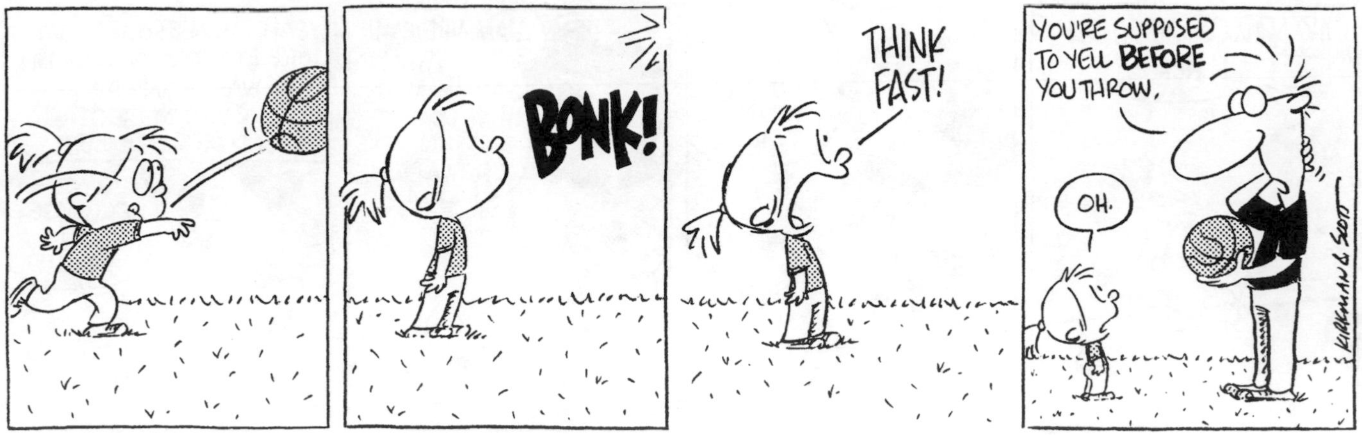
BONK!
THINK FAST!
YOU'RE SUPPOSED TO YELL BEFORE YOU THROW.
OH.
KIRKMAN & SCOTT

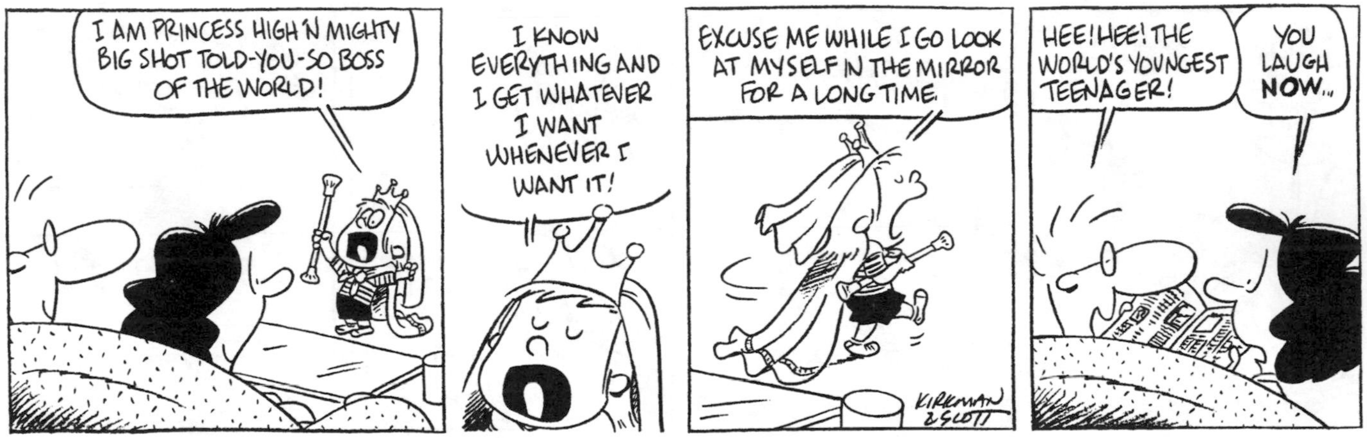
I AM PRINCESS HIGH 'N MIGHTY BIG SHOT TOLD-YOU-SO BOSS OF THE WORLD!
I KNOW EVERYTHING AND I GET WHATEVER I WANT WHENEVER I WANT IT!
EXCUSE ME WHILE I GO LOOK AT MYSELF IN THE MIRROR FOR A LONG TIME.
KIRKMAN & SCOTT
HEE! HEE! THE WORLD'S YOUNGEST TEENAGER!
YOU LAUGH NOW...

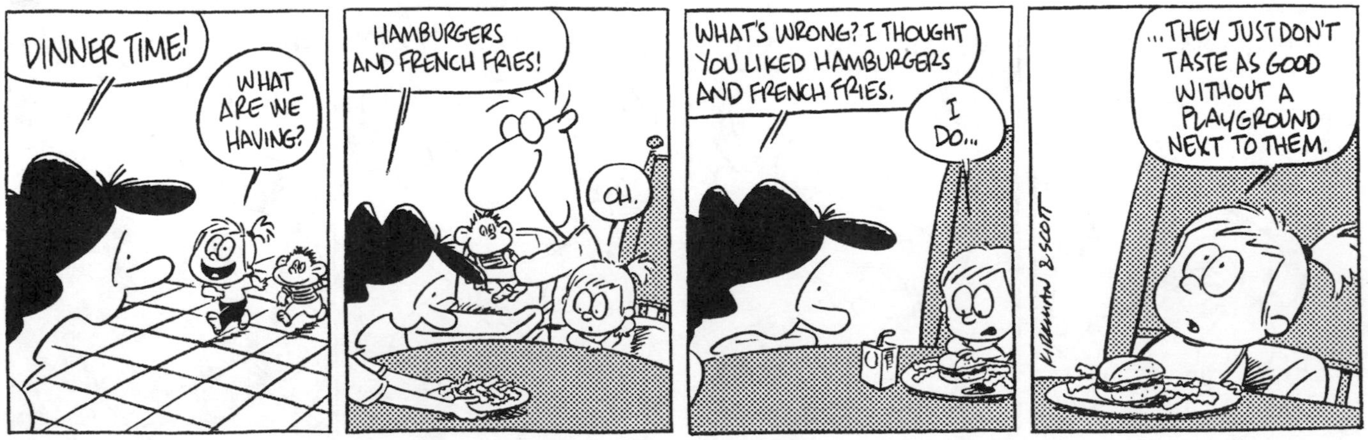
DINNER TIME!
WHAT ARE WE HAVING?
HAMBURGERS AND FRENCH FRIES!
OH.
WHAT'S WRONG? I THOUGHT YOU LIKED HAMBURGERS AND FRENCH FRIES.
I DO...
KIRKMAN & SCOTT
...THEY JUST DON'T TASTE AS GOOD WITHOUT A PLAYGROUND NEXT TO THEM.

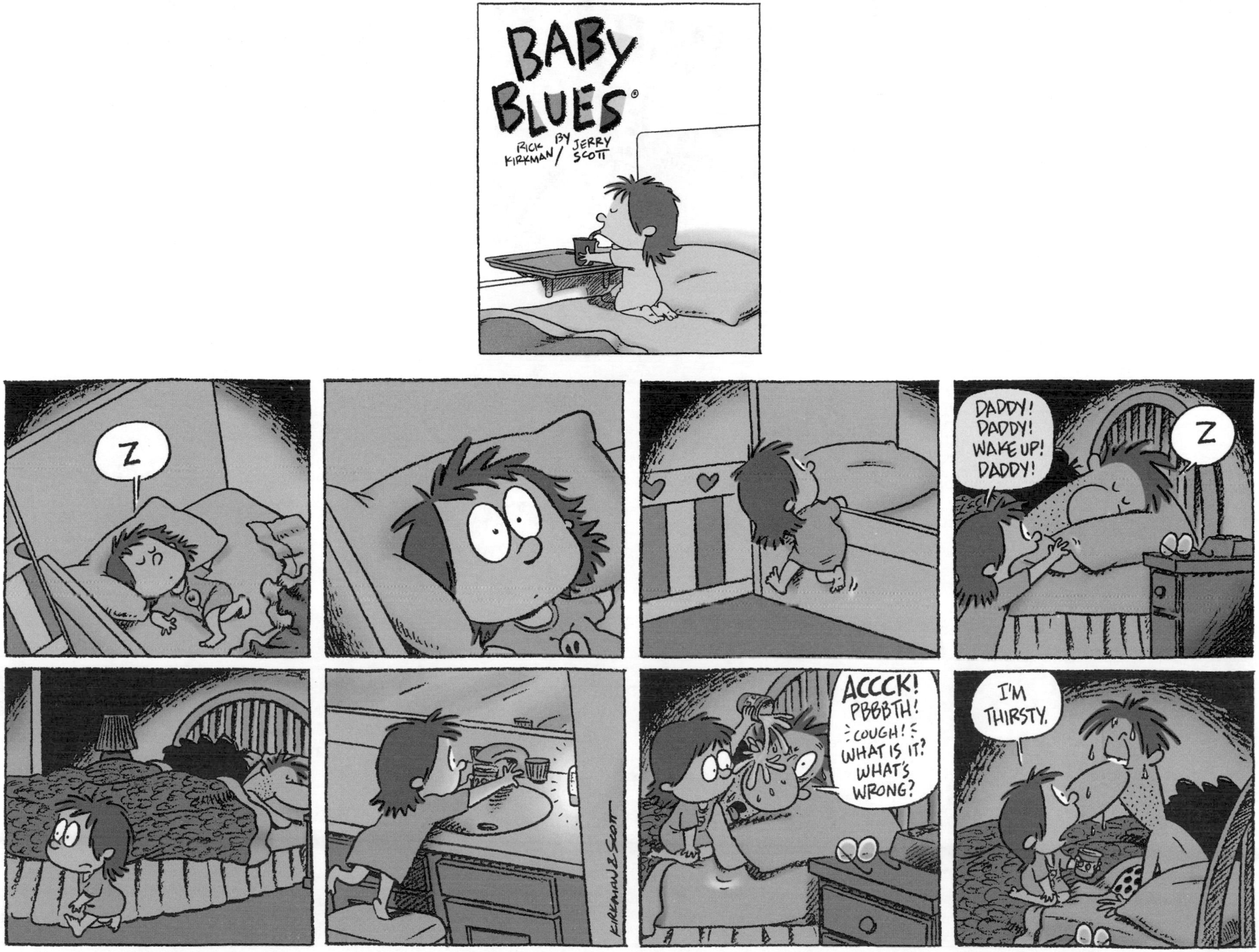
BABY BLUES®
BY RICK KIRKMAN / JERRY SCOTT
Z
DADDY! DADDY! WAKE UP! DADDY!
Z
KIRKMAN & SCOTT
ACCCK! PBBBTH! COUGH! WHAT IS IT? WHAT'S WRONG?
I'M THIRSTY.

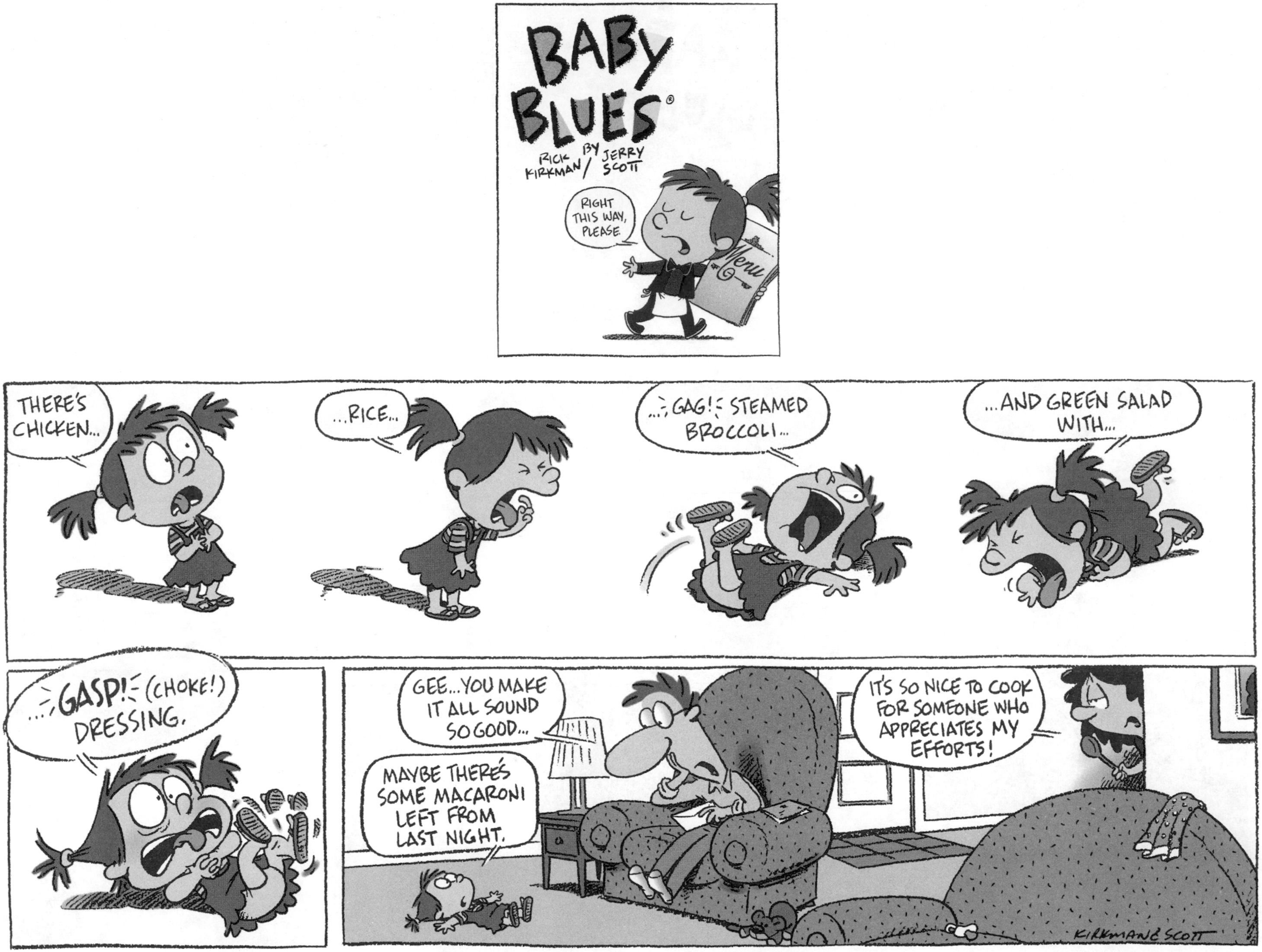
BABY BLUES®
BY RICK KIRKMAN / JERRY SCOTT
RIGHT THIS WAY, PLEASE.
Menu
THERE'S CHICKEN...
...RICE...
...GAG! STEAMED BROCCOLI...
...AND GREEN SALAD WITH...
...GASP! (CHOKE!) DRESSING.
GEE...YOU MAKE IT ALL SOUND SO GOOD...
MAYBE THERE'S SOME MACARONI LEFT FROM LAST NIGHT.
IT'S SO NICE TO COOK FOR SOMEONE WHO APPRECIATES MY EFFORTS!
KIRKMAN & SCOTT

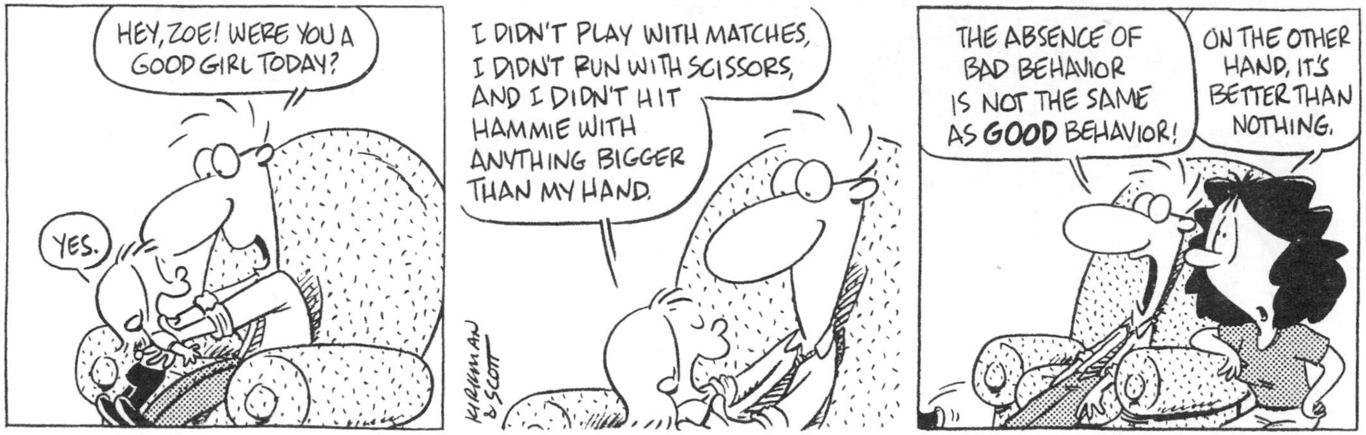
HEY, ZOE! WERE YOU A GOOD GIRL TODAY?
YES.
I DIDN'T PLAY WITH MATCHES, I DIDN'T RUN WITH SCISSORS, AND I DIDN'T HIT HAMMIE WITH ANYTHING BIGGER THAN MY HAND.
KIRKMAN & SCOTT
THE ABSENCE OF BAD BEHAVIOR IS NOT THE SAME AS GOOD BEHAVIOR!
ON THE OTHER HAND, IT'S BETTER THAN NOTHING.

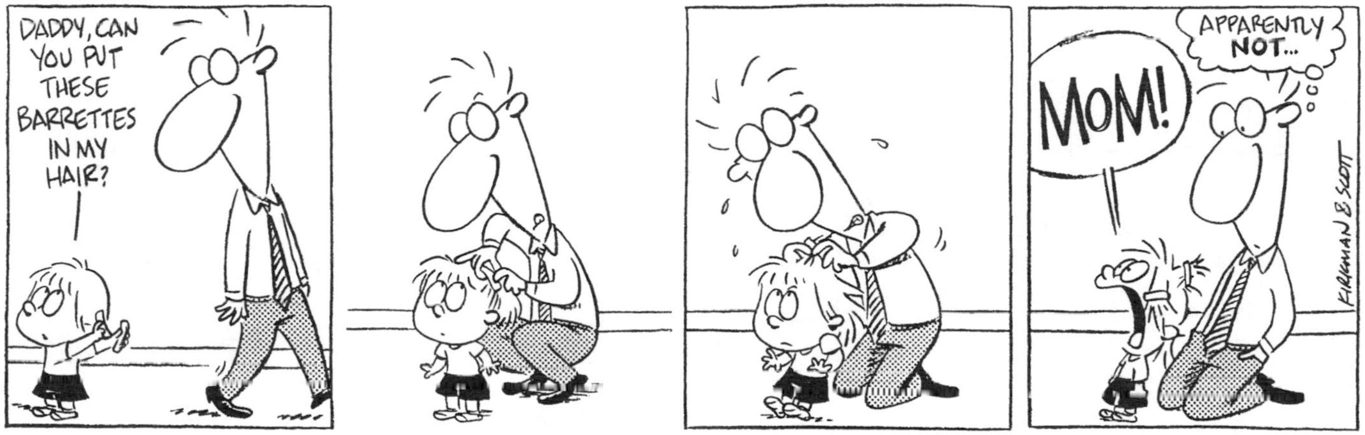
DADDY, CAN YOU PUT THESE BARRETTES IN MY HAIR?
MOM!
APPARENTLY NOT...
KIRKMAN & SCOTT

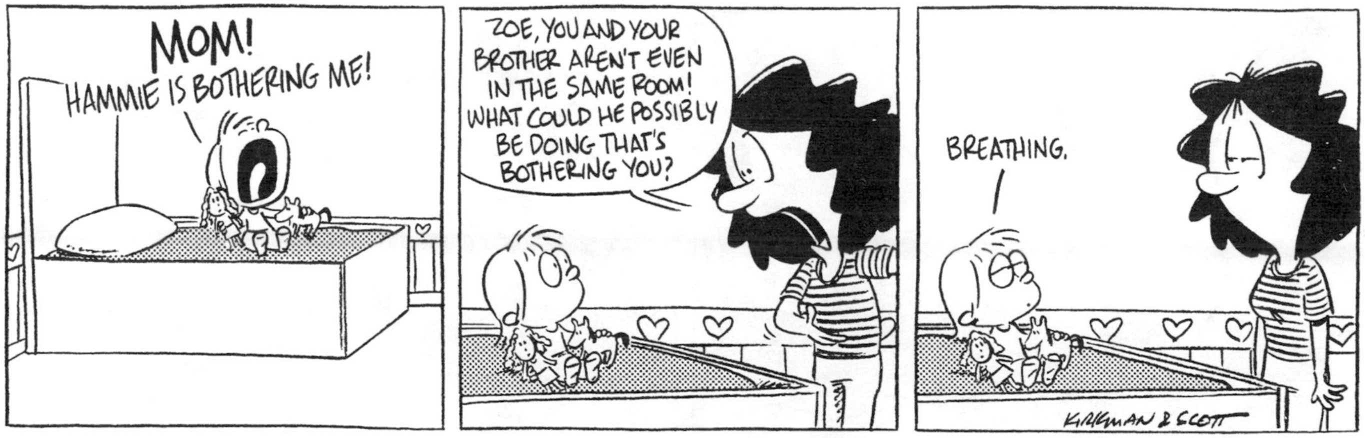
MOM! HAMMIE IS BOTHERING ME!
ZOE, YOU AND YOUR BROTHER AREN'T EVEN IN THE SAME ROOM! WHAT COULD HE POSSIBLY BE DOING THAT'S BOTHERING YOU?
BREATHING.
KIRKMAN & SCOTT

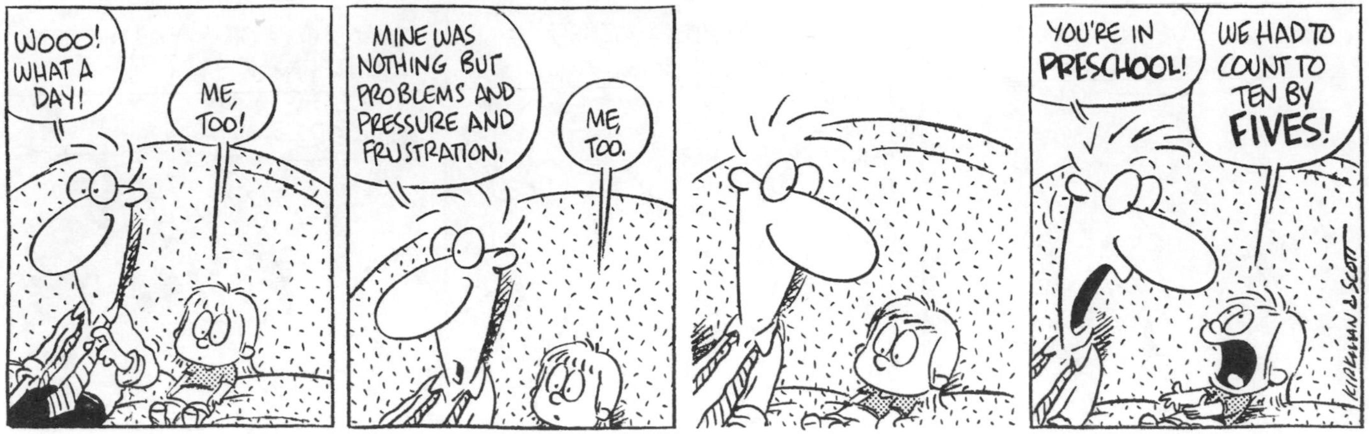

WOOO! WHAT A DAY!
ME, TOO!
MINE WAS NOTHING BUT PROBLEMS AND PRESSURE AND FRUSTRATION.
ME, TOO.
YOU'RE IN PRESCHOOL!
WE HAD TO COUNT TO TEN BY FIVES!
KIRKMAN & SCOTT

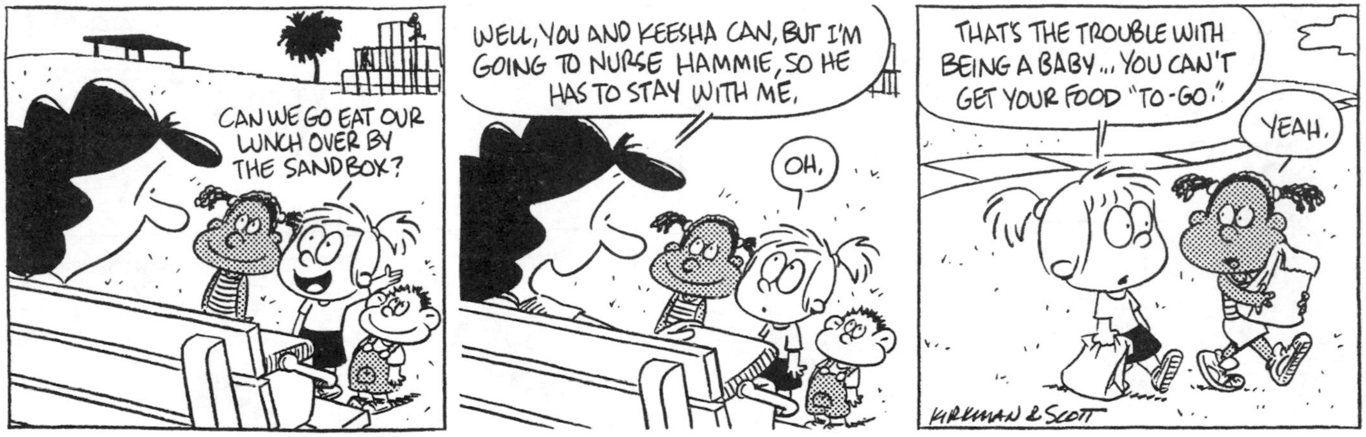

CAN WE GO EAT OUR LUNCH OVER BY THE SANDBOX?
WELL, YOU AND KEESHA CAN, BUT I'M GOING TO NURSE HAMMIE, SO HE HAS TO STAY WITH ME.
OH.
THAT'S THE TROUBLE WITH BEING A BABY... YOU CAN'T GET YOUR FOOD "TO-GO."
YEAH.
KIRKMAN & SCOTT

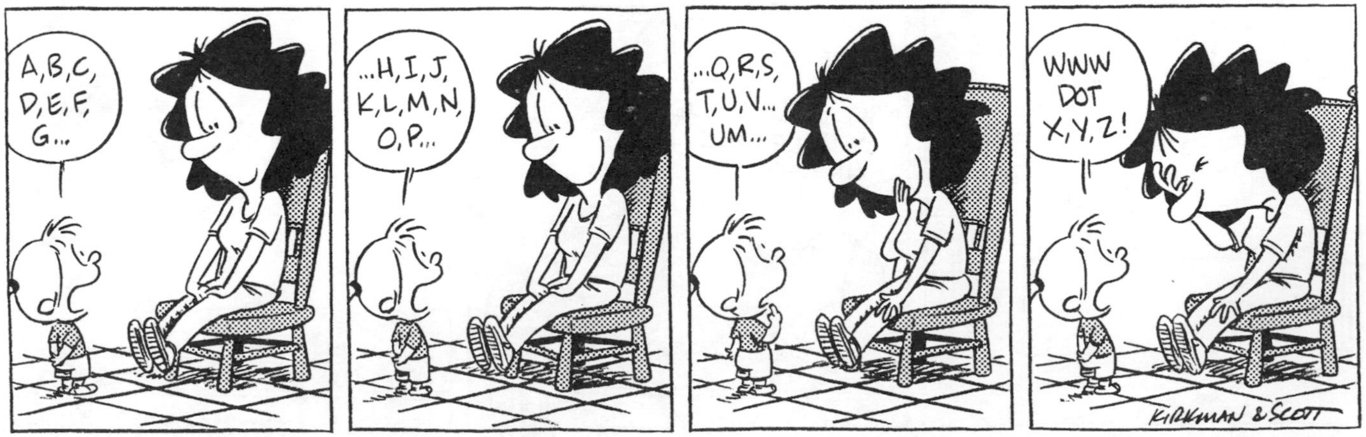

A, B, C, D, E, F, G...
...H, I, J, K, L, M, N, O, P...
...Q, R, S, T, U, V... UM...
WWW DOT X, Y, Z!
KIRKMAN & SCOTT

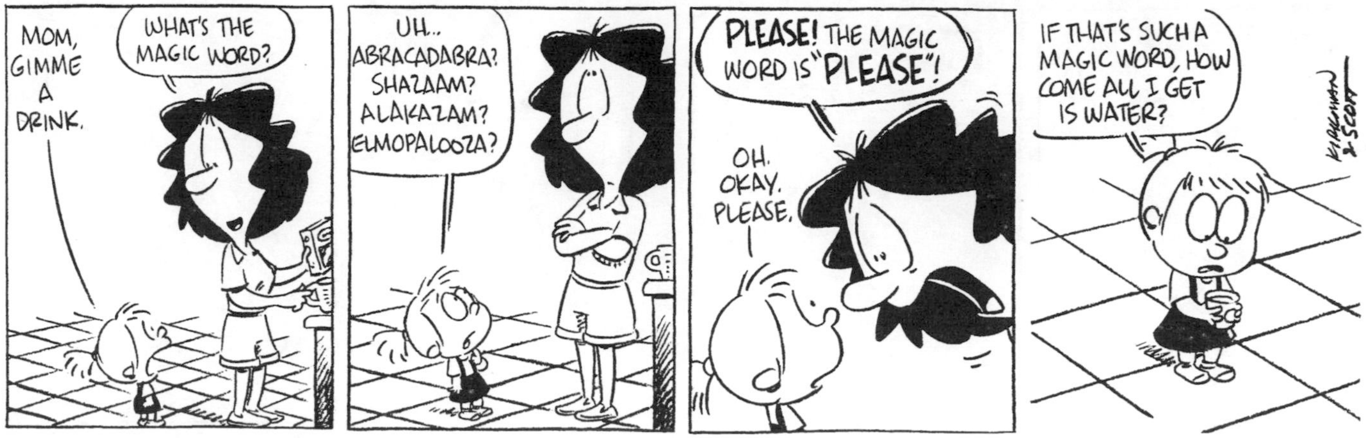
MOM, GIMME A DRINK.
WHAT'S THE MAGIC WORD?
UH... ABRACADABRA? SHAZAAM? ALAKAZAM? ELMOPALOOZA?
PLEASE! THE MAGIC WORD IS "PLEASE"!
OH. OKAY. PLEASE.
IF THAT'S SUCH A MAGIC WORD, HOW COME ALL I GET IS WATER?
KIRKMAN & SCOTT

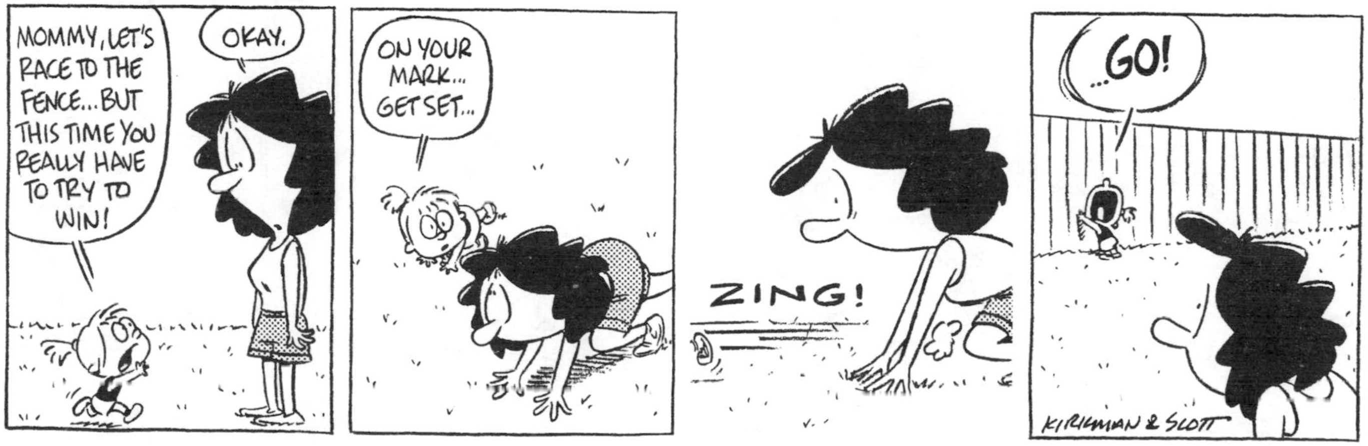
MOMMY, LET'S RACE TO THE FENCE... BUT THIS TIME YOU REALLY HAVE TO TRY TO WIN!
OKAY.
ON YOUR MARK... GET SET...
ZING!
...GO!
KIRKMAN & SCOTT

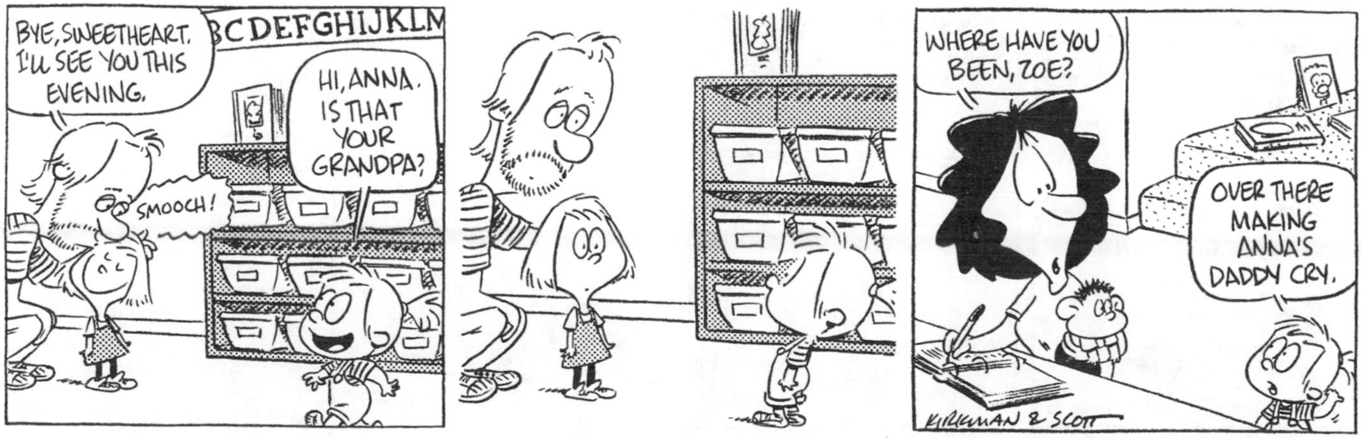
BYE, SWEETHEART. I'LL SEE YOU THIS EVENING.
SMOOCH!
HI, ANNA. IS THAT YOUR GRANDPA?
WHERE HAVE YOU BEEN, ZOE?
OVER THERE MAKING ANNA'S DADDY CRY.
KIRKMAN & SCOTT

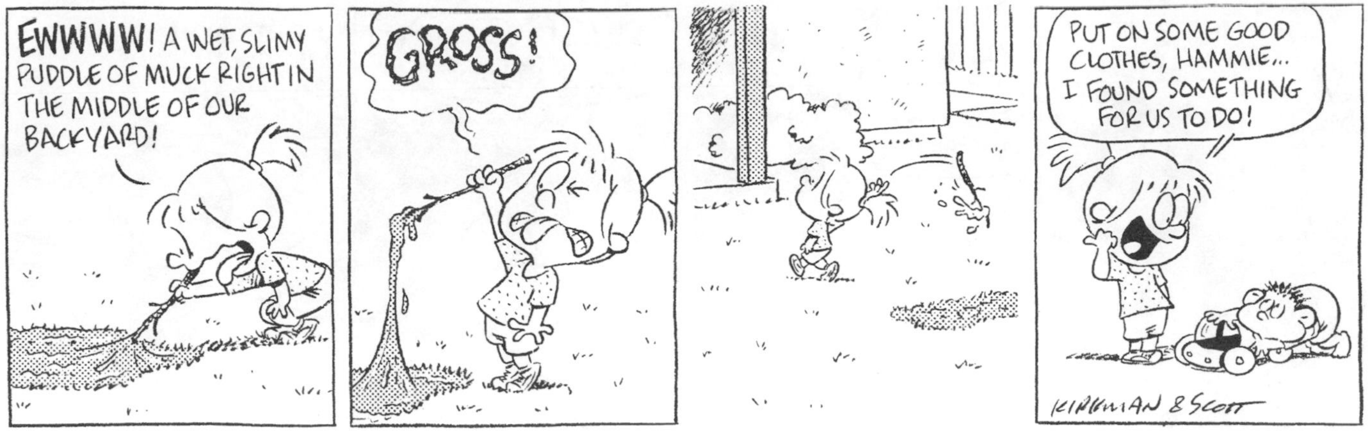
EWWWW! A WET, SLIMY PUDDLE OF MUCK RIGHT IN THE MIDDLE OF OUR BACKYARD!
GROSS!
PUT ON SOME GOOD CLOTHES, HAMMIE... I FOUND SOMETHING FOR US TO DO!
KIRKMAN & SCOTT

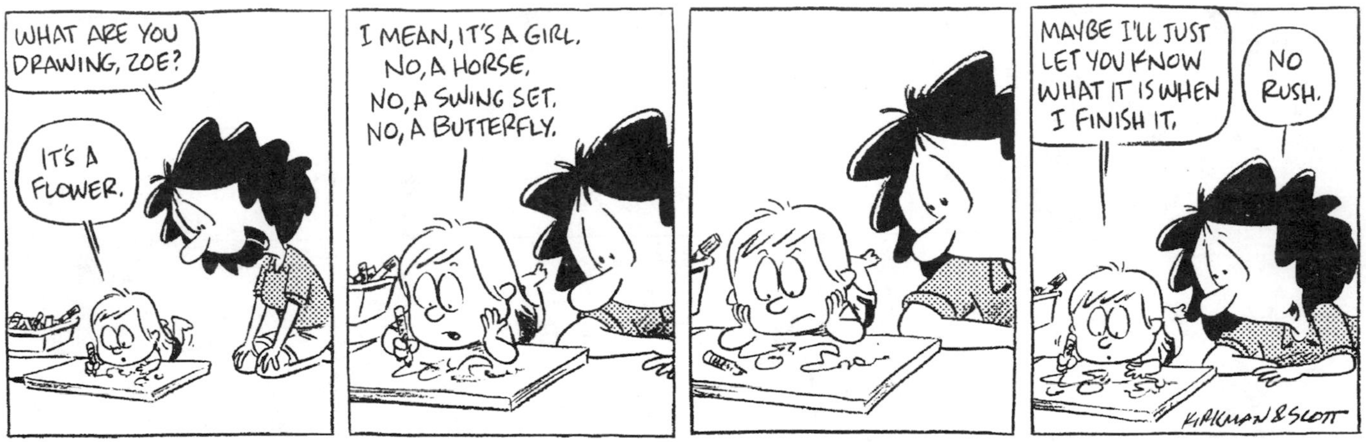
WHAT ARE YOU DRAWING, ZOE?
IT'S A FLOWER.
I MEAN, IT'S A GIRL. NO, A HORSE. NO, A SWING SET. NO, A BUTTERFLY.
MAYBE I'LL JUST LET YOU KNOW WHAT IT IS WHEN I FINISH IT.
NO RUSH.
KIRKMAN & SCOTT

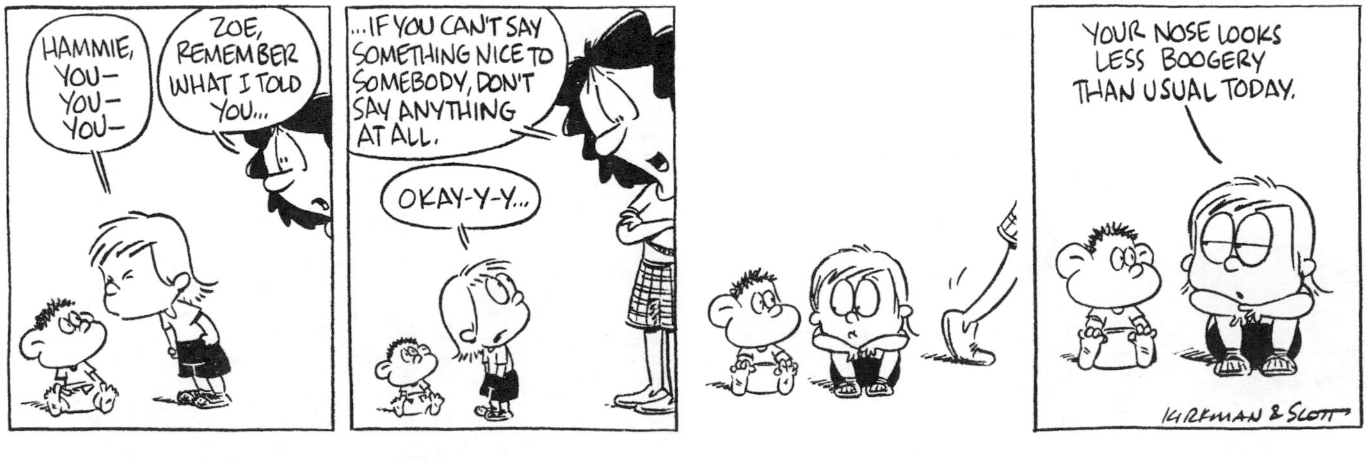
HAMMIE, YOU— YOU— YOU— YOU—
ZOE, REMEMBER WHAT I TOLD YOU...
...IF YOU CAN'T SAY SOMETHING NICE TO SOMEBODY, DON'T SAY ANYTHING AT ALL.
OKAY-Y-Y...
YOUR NOSE LOOKS LESS BOOGERY THAN USUAL TODAY.
KIRKMAN & SCOTT

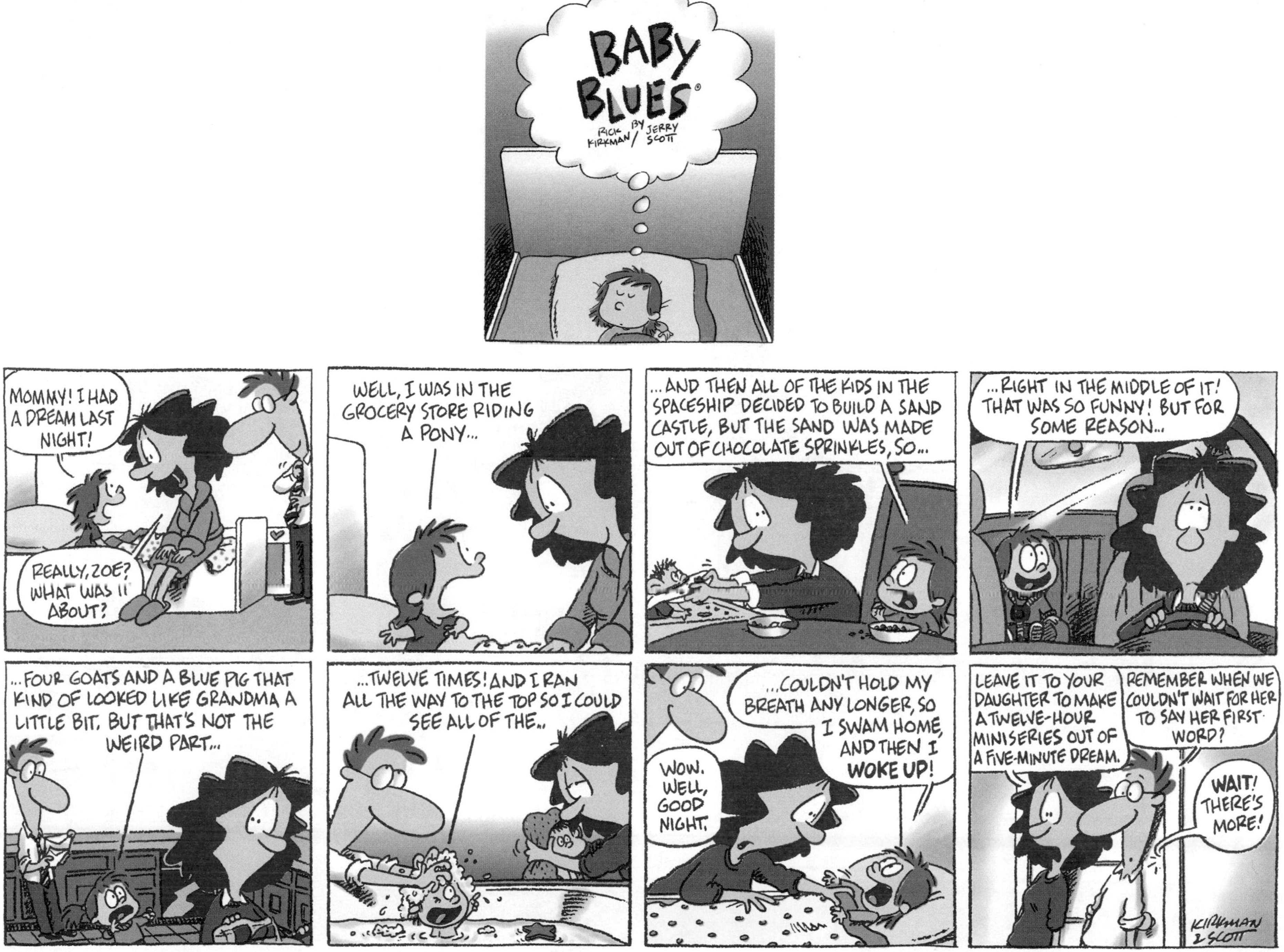
BABY BLUES®
BY RICK KIRKMAN / JERRY SCOTT
MOMMY! I HAD A DREAM LAST NIGHT!
REALLY, ZOE? WHAT WAS IT ABOUT?
WELL, I WAS IN THE GROCERY STORE RIDING A PONY...
...AND THEN ALL OF THE KIDS IN THE SPACESHIP DECIDED TO BUILD A SAND CASTLE, BUT THE SAND WAS MADE OUT OF CHOCOLATE SPRINKLES, SO...
...RIGHT IN THE MIDDLE OF IT! THAT WAS SO FUNNY! BUT FOR SOME REASON...
...FOUR GOATS AND A BLUE PIG THAT KIND OF LOOKED LIKE GRANDMA A LITTLE BIT. BUT THAT'S NOT THE WEIRD PART...
...TWELVE TIMES! AND I RAN ALL THE WAY TO THE TOP SO I COULD SEE ALL OF THE...
...COULDN'T HOLD MY BREATH ANY LONGER, SO I SWAM HOME, AND THEN I WOKE UP!
WOW. WELL, GOOD NIGHT.
LEAVE IT TO YOUR DAUGHTER TO MAKE A TWELVE-HOUR MINISERIES OUT OF A FIVE-MINUTE DREAM.
REMEMBER WHEN WE COULDN'T WAIT FOR HER TO SAY HER FIRST WORD?
WAIT! THERE'S MORE!
KIRKMAN & SCOTT

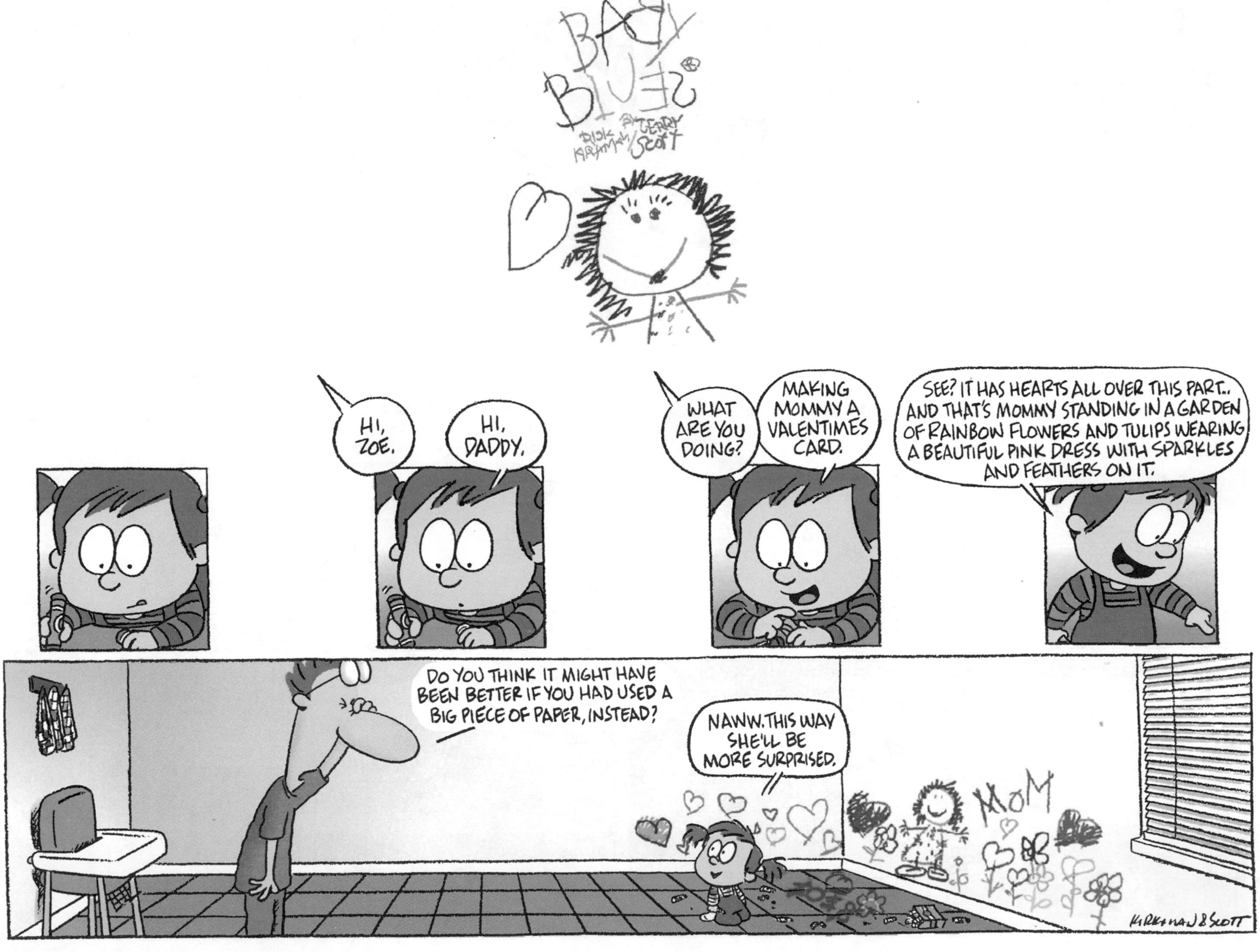
BABY BLUES®
BY RICK KIRKMAN / JERRY SCOTT
HI, ZOE.
HI, DADDY.
WHAT ARE YOU DOING?
MAKING MOMMY A VALENTIMES CARD.
SEE? IT HAS HEARTS ALL OVER THIS PART.. AND THAT'S MOMMY STANDING IN A GARDEN OF RAINBOW FLOWERS AND TULIPS WEARING A BEAUTIFUL PINK DRESS WITH SPARKLES AND FEATHERS ON IT.
DO YOU THINK IT MIGHT HAVE BEEN BETTER IF YOU HAD USED A BIG PIECE OF PAPER, INSTEAD?
NAWW. THIS WAY SHE'LL BE MORE SURPRISED.
MOM
KIRKMAN & SCOTT

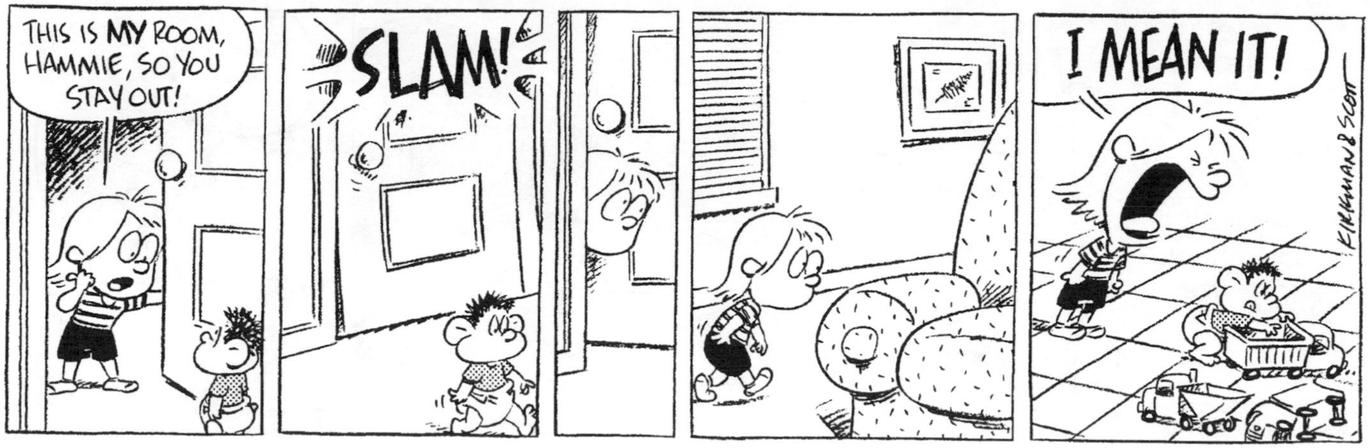
THIS IS MY ROOM, HAMMIE, SO YOU STAY OUT!
SLAM!
I MEAN IT!
KIRKMAN & SCOTT

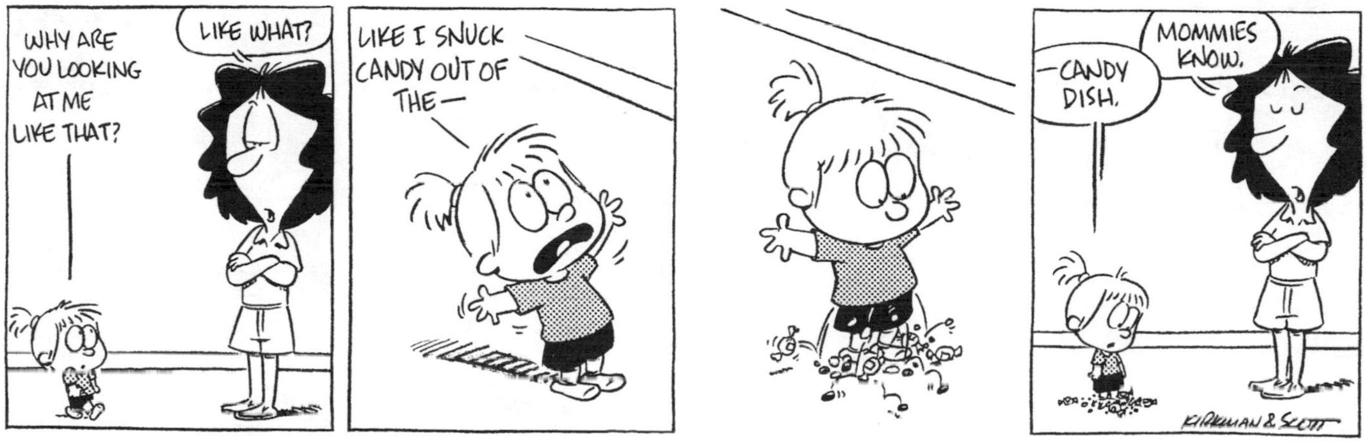
WHY ARE YOU LOOKING AT ME LIKE THAT?
LIKE WHAT?
LIKE I SNUCK CANDY OUT OF THE—
—CANDY DISH.
MOMMIES KNOW.
KIRKMAN & SCOTT

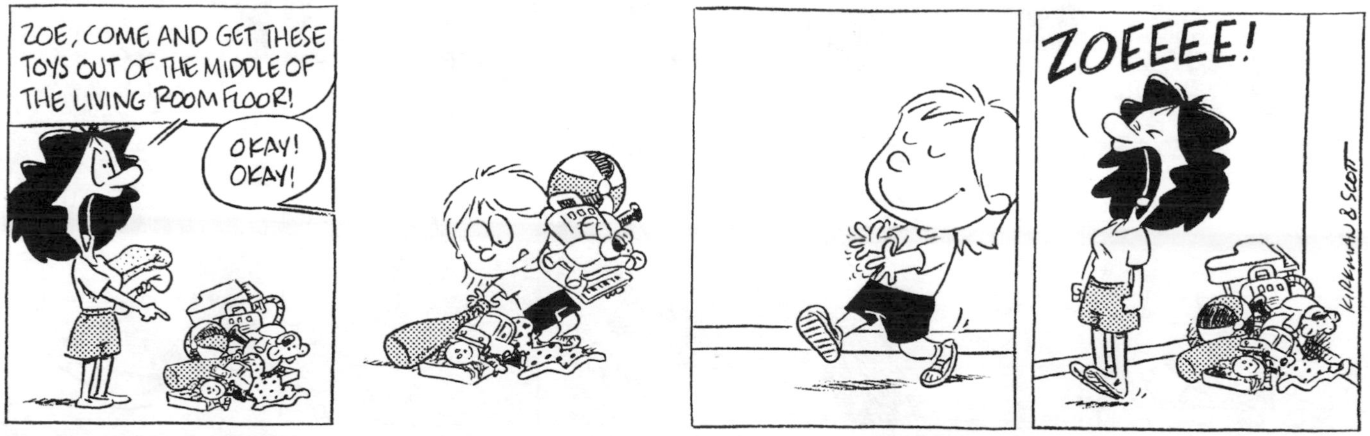
ZOE, COME AND GET THESE TOYS OUT OF THE MIDDLE OF THE LIVING ROOM FLOOR!
OKAY! OKAY!
ZOEEEE!
KIRKMAN & SCOTT

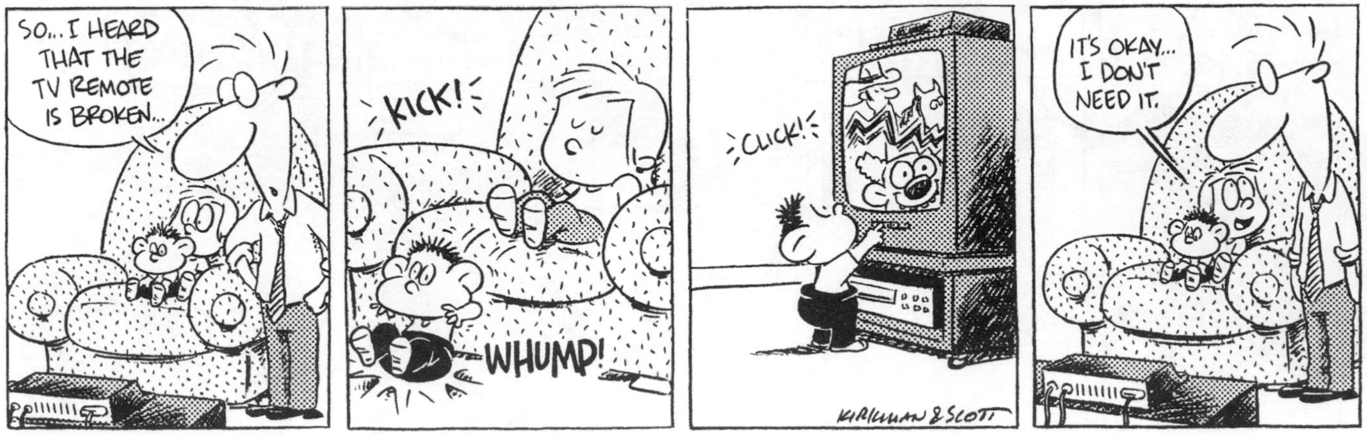
SO... I HEARD THAT THE TV REMOTE IS BROKEN...
KICK!
WHUMP!
CLICK!
KIRKMAN & SCOTT
IT'S OKAY... I DON'T NEED IT.

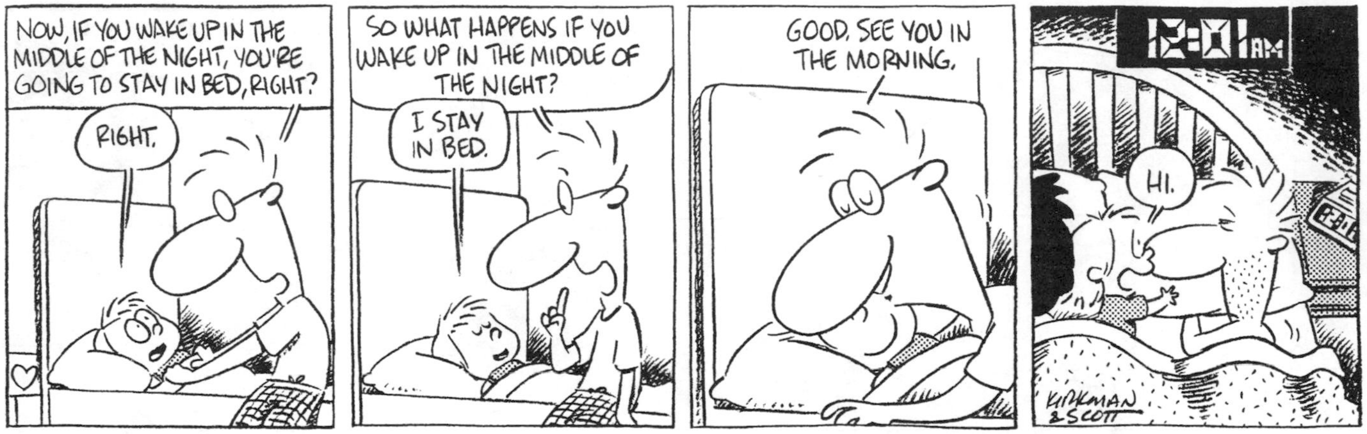
NOW, IF YOU WAKE UP IN THE MIDDLE OF THE NIGHT, YOU'RE GOING TO STAY IN BED, RIGHT?
RIGHT.
SO WHAT HAPPENS IF YOU WAKE UP IN THE MIDDLE OF THE NIGHT?
I STAY IN BED.
GOOD. SEE YOU IN THE MORNING.
12:01 AM
HI.
KIRKMAN & SCOTT

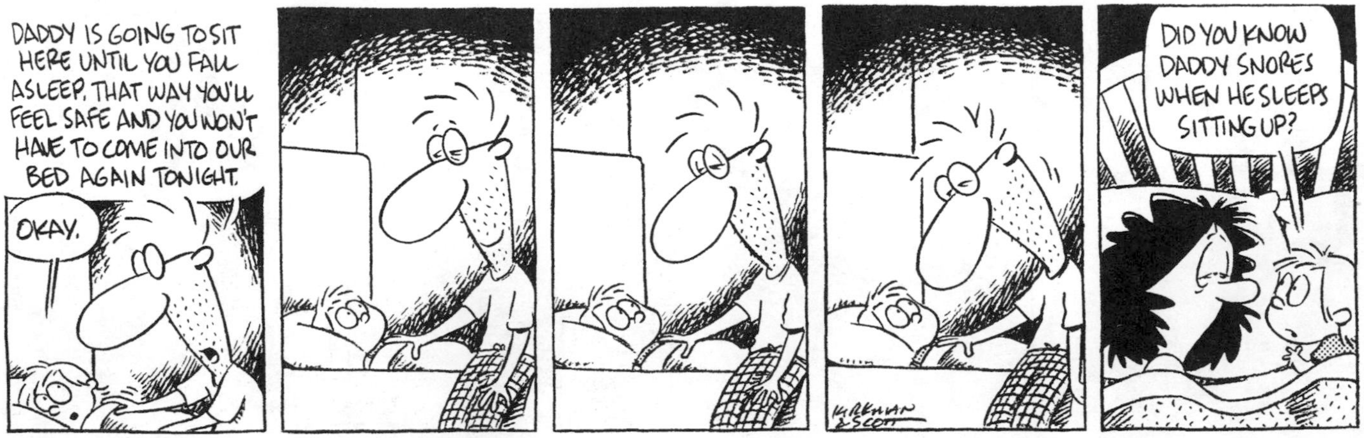
DADDY IS GOING TO SIT HERE UNTIL YOU FALL ASLEEP. THAT WAY YOU'LL FEEL SAFE AND YOU WON'T HAVE TO COME INTO OUR BED AGAIN TONIGHT.
OKAY.
KIRKMAN & SCOTT
DID YOU KNOW DADDY SNORES WHEN HE SLEEPS SITTING UP?

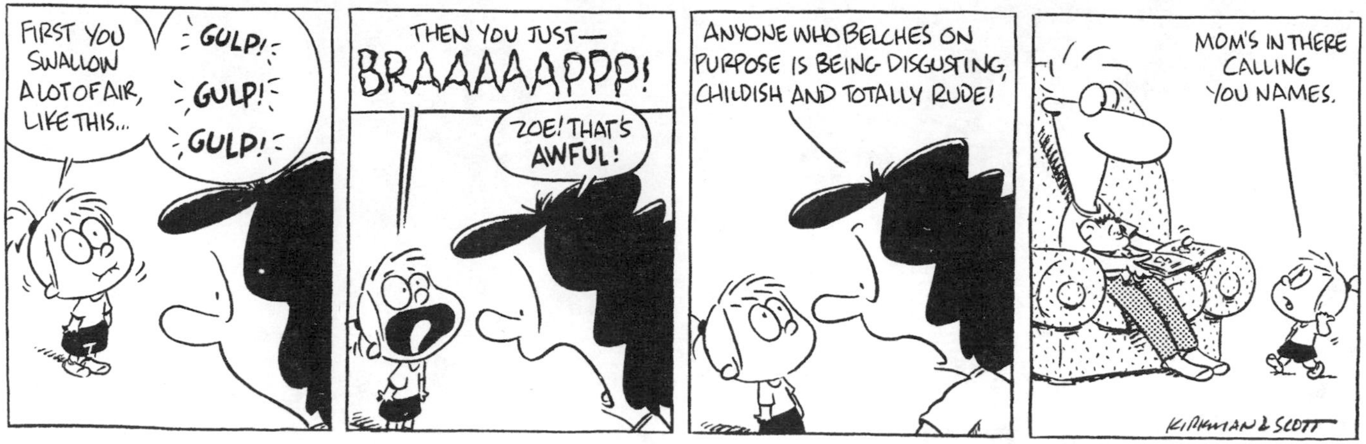
FIRST YOU SWALLOW A LOT OF AIR, LIKE THIS...
GULP! GULP! GULP!
THEN YOU JUST—
BRAAAAAPPP!
ZOE! THAT'S AWFUL!
ANYONE WHO BELCHES ON PURPOSE IS BEING DISGUSTING, CHILDISH AND TOTALLY RUDE!
MOM'S IN THERE CALLING YOU NAMES.
KIRKMAN & SCOTT

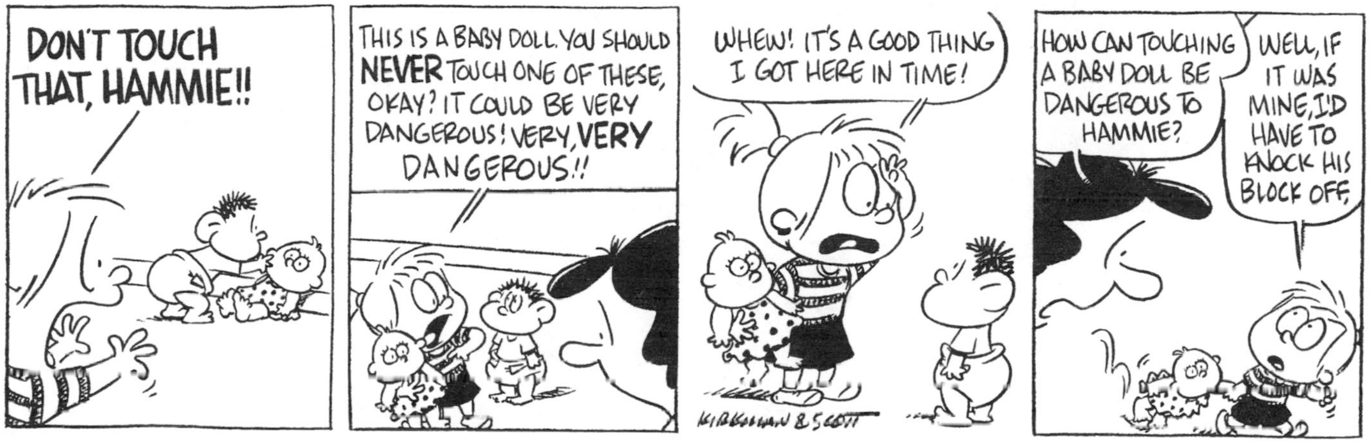
DON'T TOUCH THAT, HAMMIE!!
THIS IS A BABY DOLL. YOU SHOULD NEVER TOUCH ONE OF THESE, OKAY? IT COULD BE VERY DANGEROUS! VERY, VERY DANGEROUS!!
WHEW! IT'S A GOOD THING I GOT HERE IN TIME!
HOW CAN TOUCHING A BABY DOLL BE DANGEROUS TO HAMMIE?
WELL, IF IT WAS MINE, I'D HAVE TO KNOCK HIS BLOCK OFF.

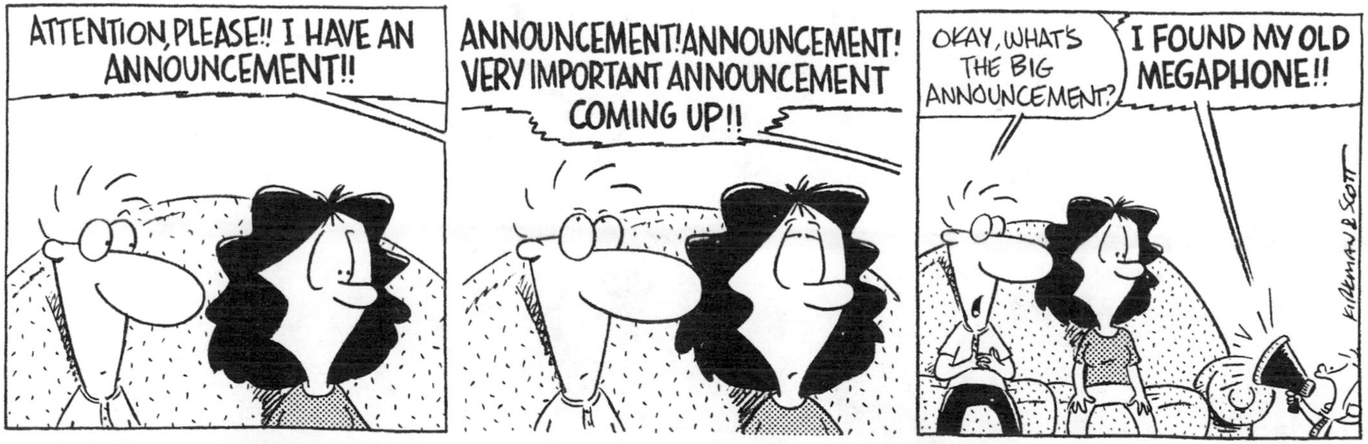
ATTENTION, PLEASE!! I HAVE AN ANNOUNCEMENT!!
ANNOUNCEMENT! ANNOUNCEMENT! VERY IMPORTANT ANNOUNCEMENT COMING UP!!
OKAY, WHAT'S THE BIG ANNOUNCEMENT?
I FOUND MY OLD MEGAPHONE!!
KIRKMAN & SCOTT

HAMMIE

Trucks, tractors, earthmovers, backhoes...generally speaking, it's heavy equipment that dominates Hammie's thoughts. Which is no big surprise when you consider that his first word was "bulldozer."

Second banana to his big sister, Zoe, Hammie sometimes has to struggle to match her pace. Quieter by nature, stubborn by necessity, he is bravely managing to hold his own in the dog-eat-dog world of this sibling relationship.

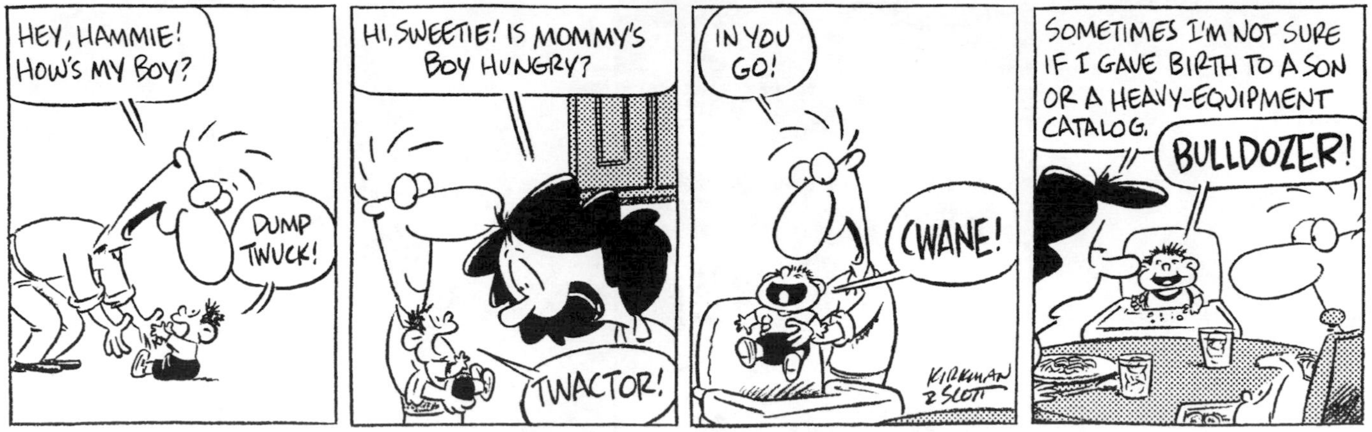
HEY, HAMMIE! HOW'S MY BOY?
DUMP TWUCK!
HI, SWEETIE! IS MOMMY'S BOY HUNGRY?
TWACTOR!
IN YOU GO!
CWANE!
KIRKMAN & SCOTT
SOMETIMES I'M NOT SURE IF I GAVE BIRTH TO A SON OR A HEAVY-EQUIPMENT CATALOG.
BULLDOZER!

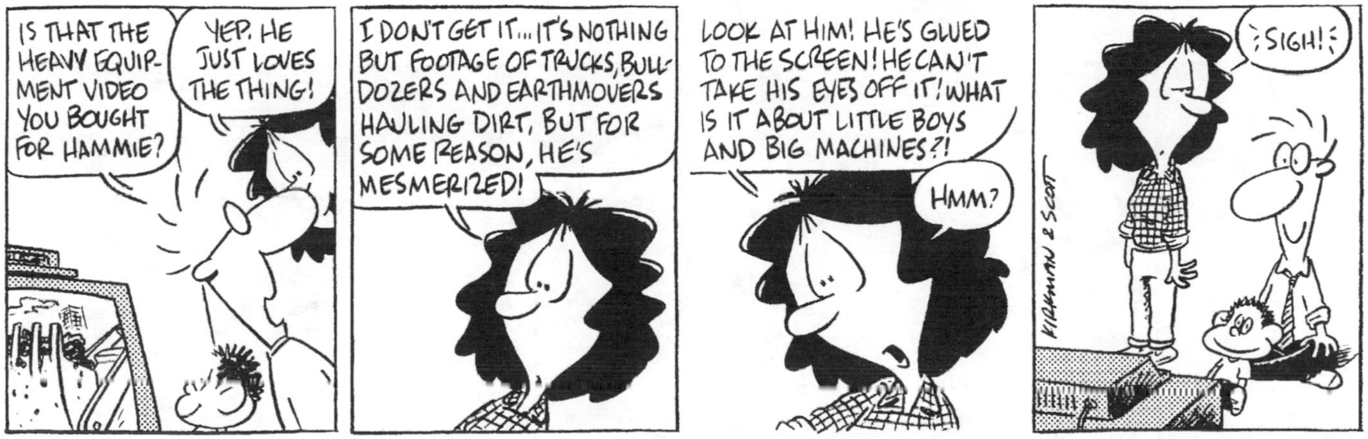
IS THAT THE HEAVY EQUIPMENT VIDEO YOU BOUGHT FOR HAMMIE?
YEP. HE JUST LOVES THE THING!
I DON'T GET IT... IT'S NOTHING BUT FOOTAGE OF TRUCKS, BULLDOZERS AND EARTHMOVERS HAULING DIRT, BUT FOR SOME REASON, HE'S MESMERIZED!
LOOK AT HIM! HE'S GLUED TO THE SCREEN! HE CAN'T TAKE HIS EYES OFF IT! WHAT IS IT ABOUT LITTLE BOYS AND BIG MACHINES?!
HMM?
KIRKMAN & SCOTT
SIGH!

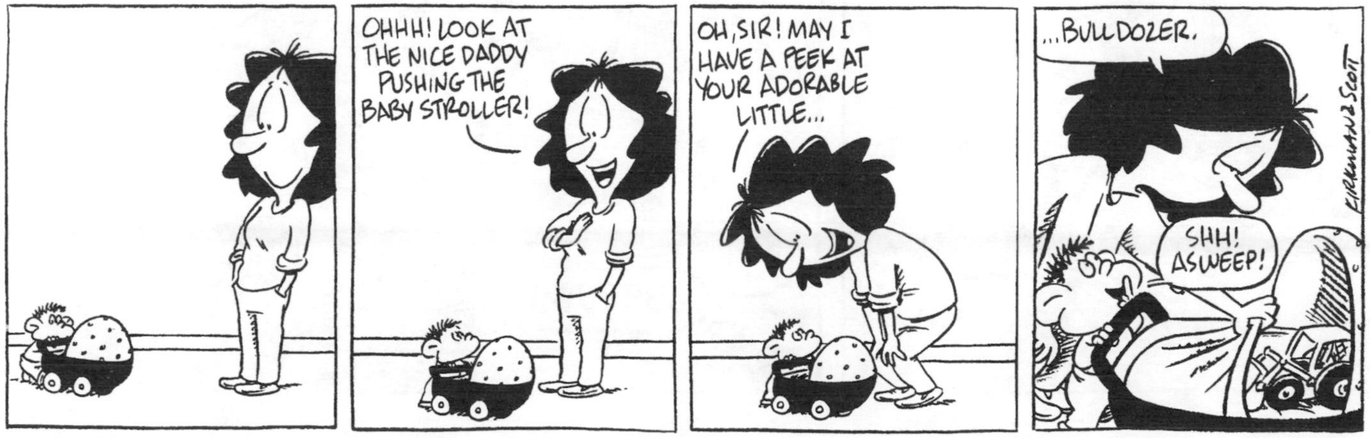
OHHH! LOOK AT THE NICE DADDY PUSHING THE BABY STROLLER!
OH, SIR! MAY I HAVE A PEEK AT YOUR ADORABLE LITTLE...
...BULLDOZER.
SHH! ASWEEP!
KIRKMAN & SCOTT

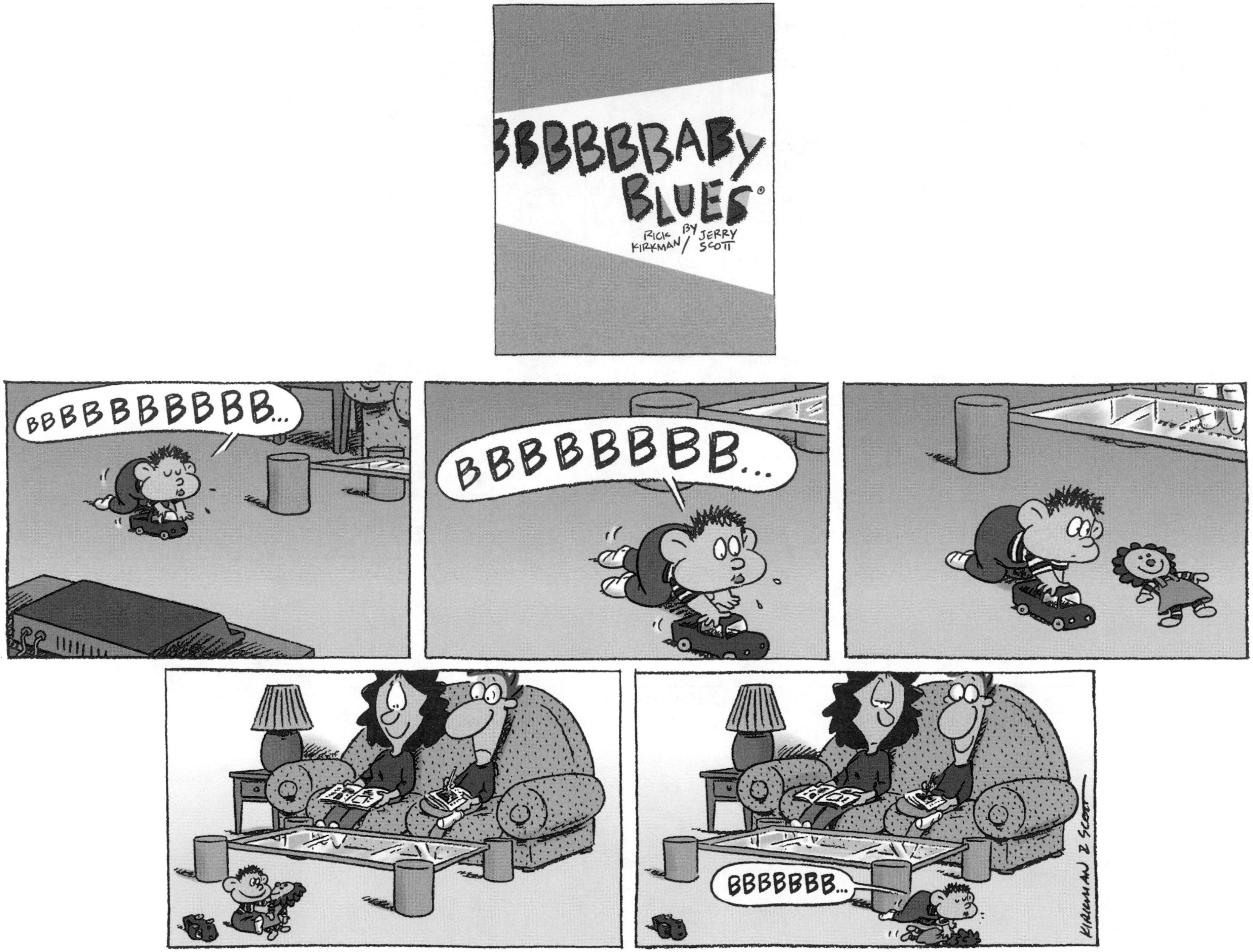
BBBBBBABY BLUES®
BY RICK KIRKMAN / JERRY SCOTT
BBBBBBBBBB...
BBBBBBBBB...
BBBBBBB...
KIRKMAN & SCOTT

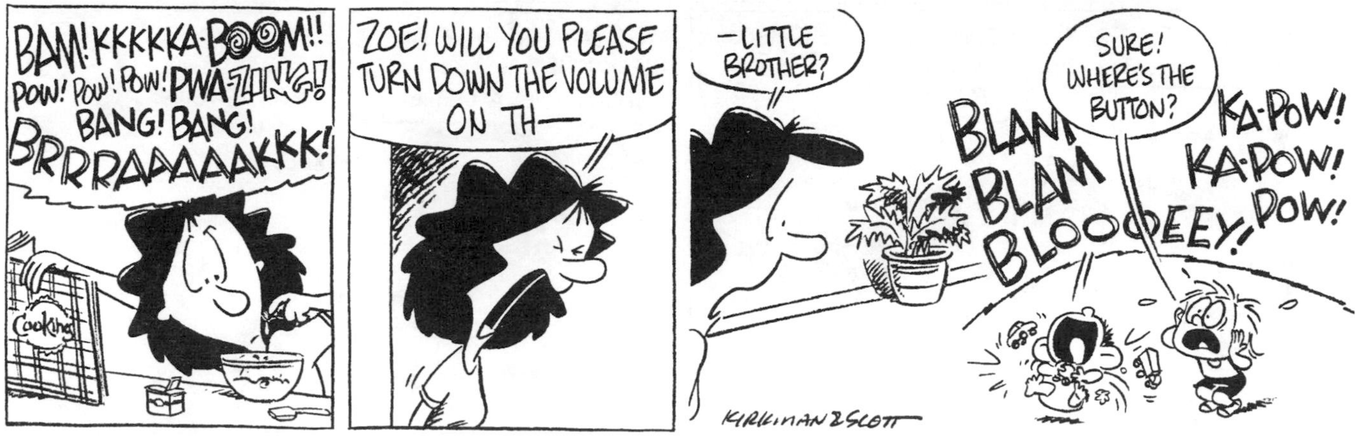
BAM! KKKKKA-BOOM!!
POW! POW! POW! PWA-ZING!
BANG! BANG!
BRRRAAAAAKKK!
COOKING
ZOE! WILL YOU PLEASE TURN DOWN THE VOLUME ON TH—
—LITTLE BROTHER?
SURE! WHERE'S THE BUTTON?
BLAM BLAM BLOOOEEY!
KA-POW! KA-POW! POW!
KIRKMAN & SCOTT

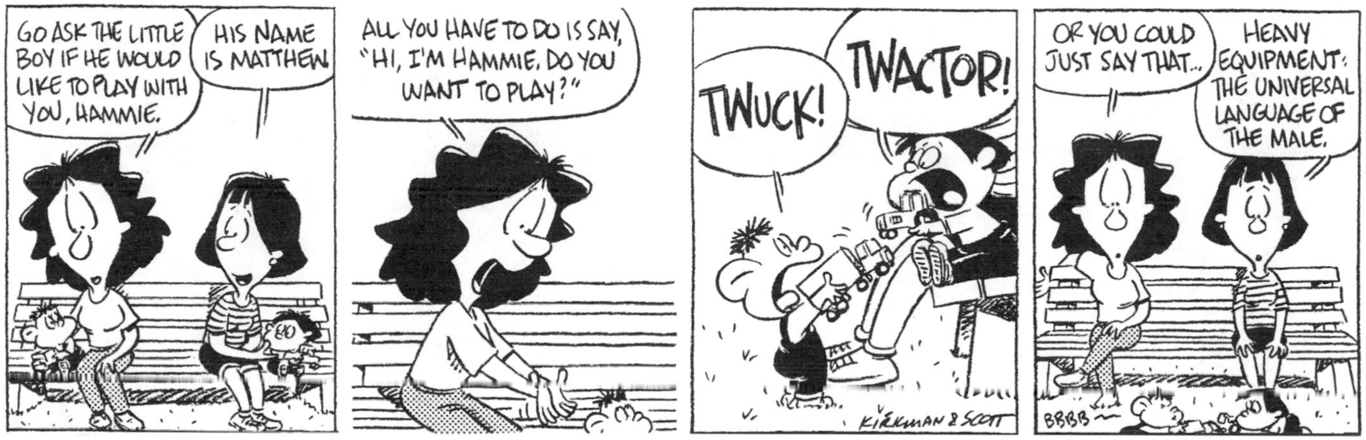
GO ASK THE LITTLE BOY IF HE WOULD LIKE TO PLAY WITH YOU, HAMMIE.
HIS NAME IS MATTHEW.
ALL YOU HAVE TO DO IS SAY, "HI, I'M HAMMIE. DO YOU WANT TO PLAY?"
TWUCK!
TWACTOR!
KIRKMAN & SCOTT
OR YOU COULD JUST SAY THAT...
HEAVY EQUIPMENT: THE UNIVERSAL LANGUAGE OF THE MALE.
BBBB~

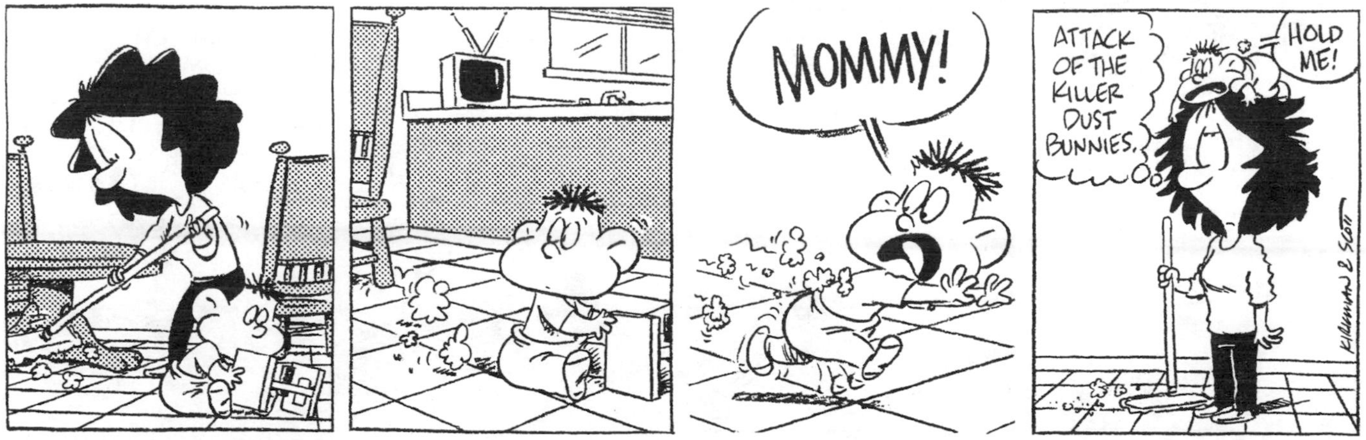
MOMMY!
ATTACK OF THE KILLER DUST BUNNIES.
HOLD ME!
KIRKMAN & SCOTT

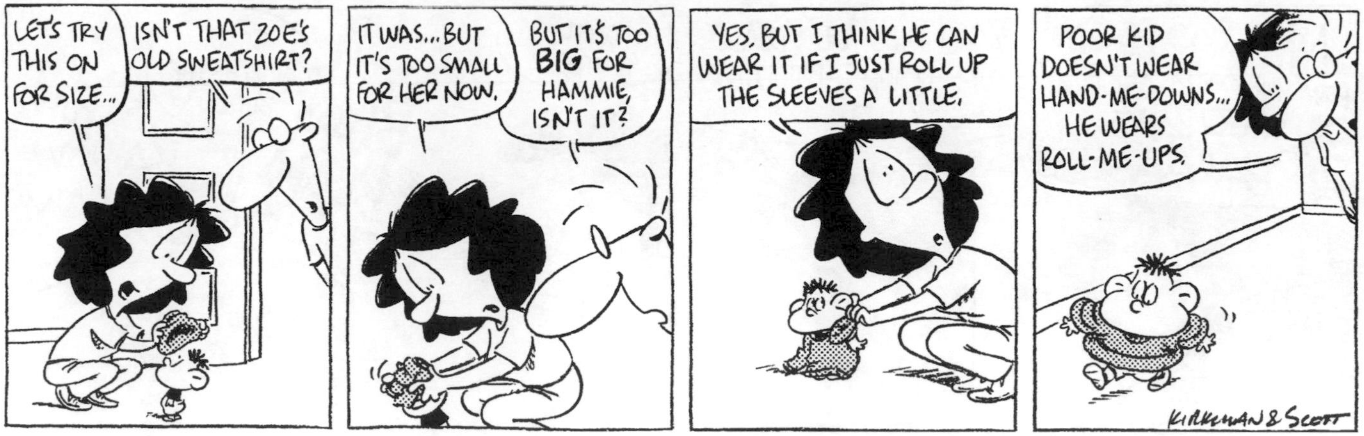
LET'S TRY THIS ON FOR SIZE...
ISN'T THAT ZOE'S OLD SWEATSHIRT?
IT WAS... BUT IT'S TOO SMALL FOR HER NOW.
BUT IT'S TOO BIG FOR HAMMIE, ISN'T IT?
YES, BUT I THINK HE CAN WEAR IT IF I JUST ROLL UP THE SLEEVES A LITTLE.
POOR KID DOESN'T WEAR HAND-ME-DOWNS... HE WEARS ROLL-ME-UPS.
KIRKMAN & SCOTT

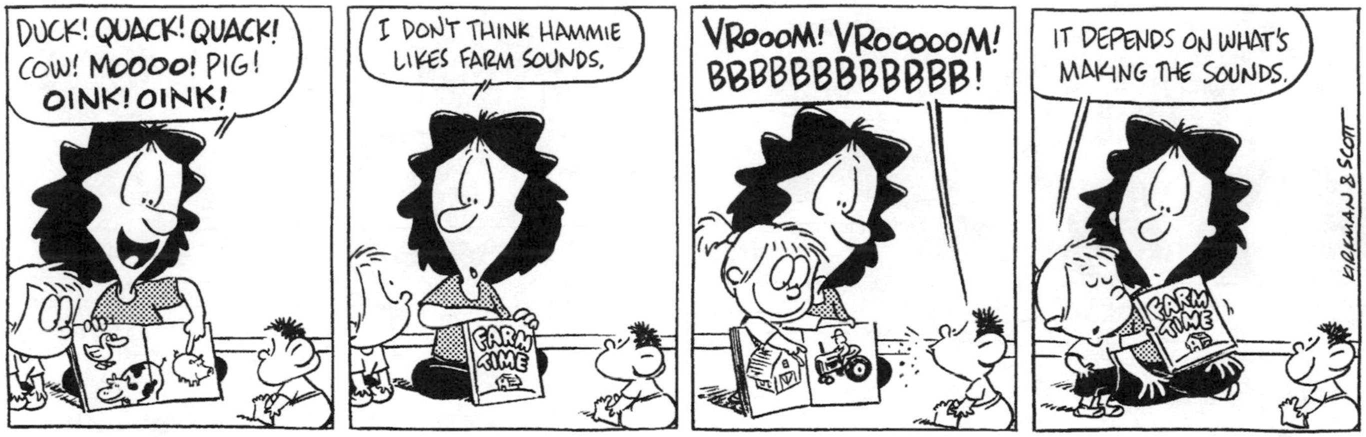
DUCK! QUACK! QUACK! COW! MOOOO! PIG! OINK! OINK!
FARM TIME
I DON'T THINK HAMMIE LIKES FARM SOUNDS.
FARM TIME
VROOOM! VROOOOOOM! BBBBBBBBBBBB!
IT DEPENDS ON WHAT'S MAKING THE SOUNDS.
FARM TIME
KIRKMAN & SCOTT

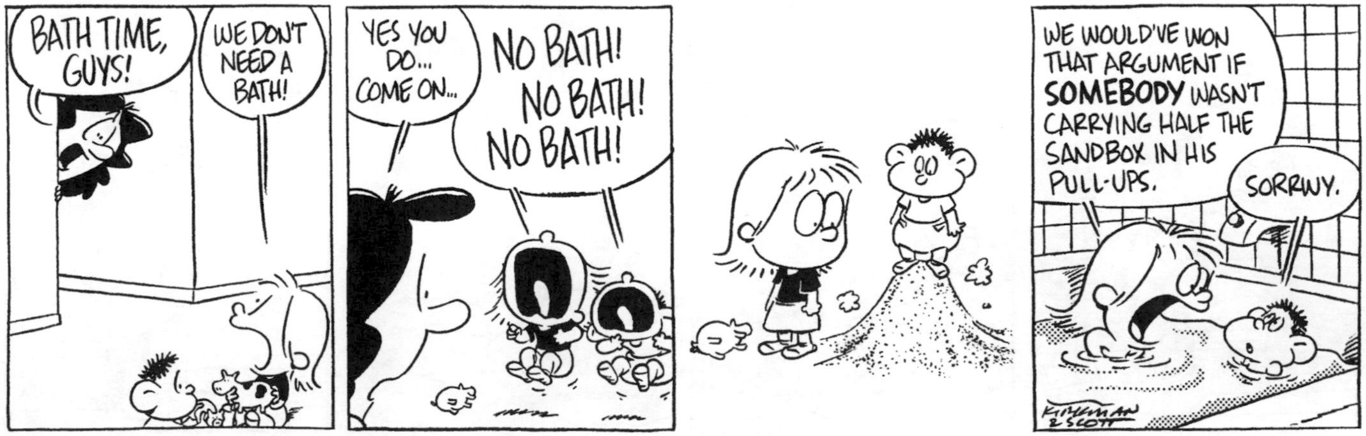
BATH TIME, GUYS!
WE DON'T NEED A BATH!
YES YOU DO... COME ON...
NO BATH! NO BATH! NO BATH!
WE WOULD'VE WON THAT ARGUMENT IF SOMEBODY WASN'T CARRYING HALF THE SANDBOX IN HIS PULL-UPS.
SORRWY.
KIRKMAN & SCOTT

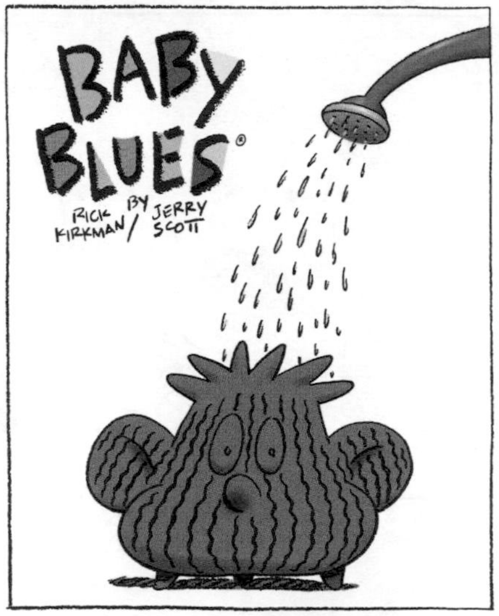
BABY BLUES®
BY RICK KIRKMAN / JERRY SCOTT

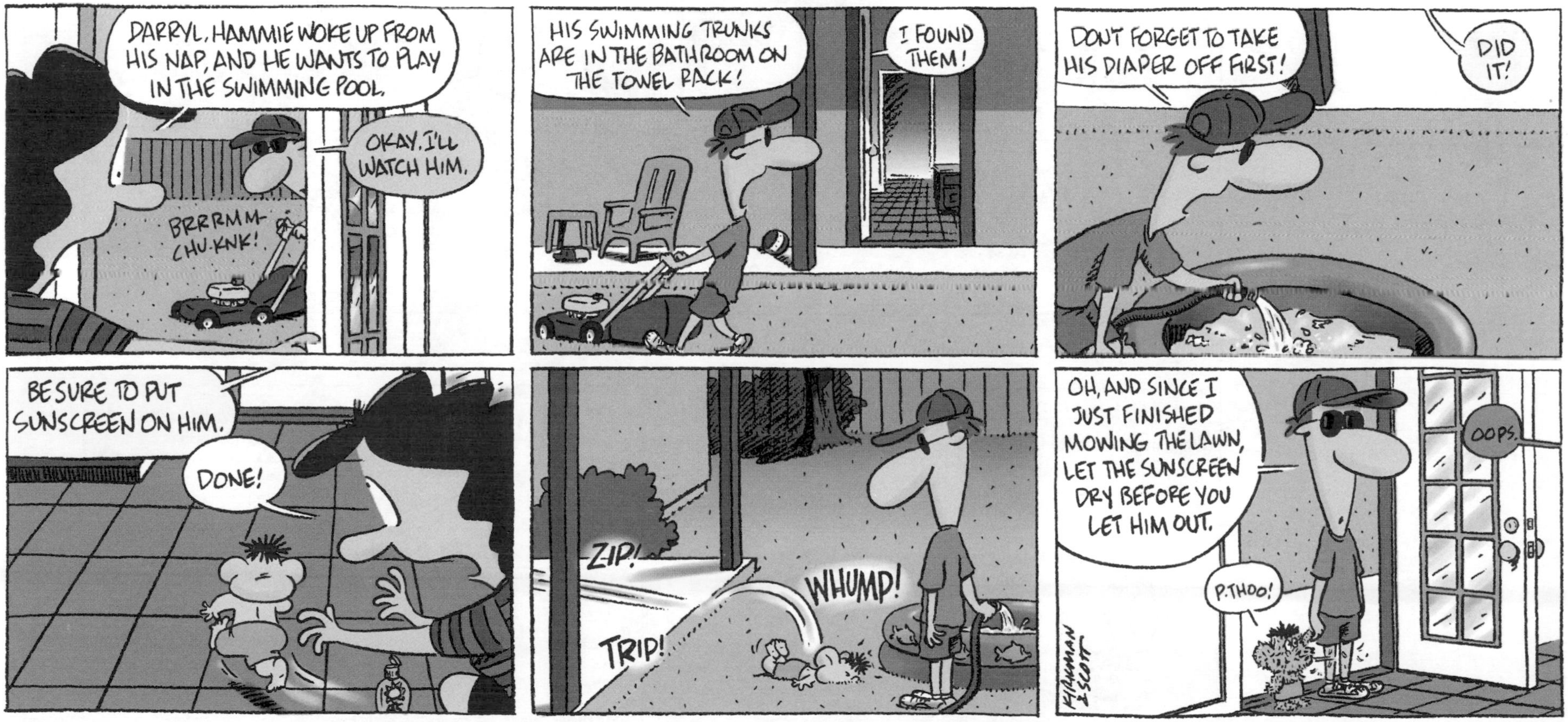
DARRYL, HAMMIE WOKE UP FROM HIS NAP, AND HE WANTS TO PLAY IN THE SWIMMING POOL.
OKAY. I'LL WATCH HIM.
BRRRMM-CHU-KNK!
HIS SWIMMING TRUNKS ARE IN THE BATHROOM ON THE TOWEL RACK!
I FOUND THEM!
DON'T FORGET TO TAKE HIS DIAPER OFF FIRST!
DID IT!
BE SURE TO PUT SUNSCREEN ON HIM.
DONE!
ZIP!
TRIP!
WHUMP!
OH, AND SINCE I JUST FINISHED MOWING THE LAWN, LET THE SUNSCREEN DRY BEFORE YOU LET HIM OUT.
OOPS.
P-THOO!
KIRKMAN & SCOTT

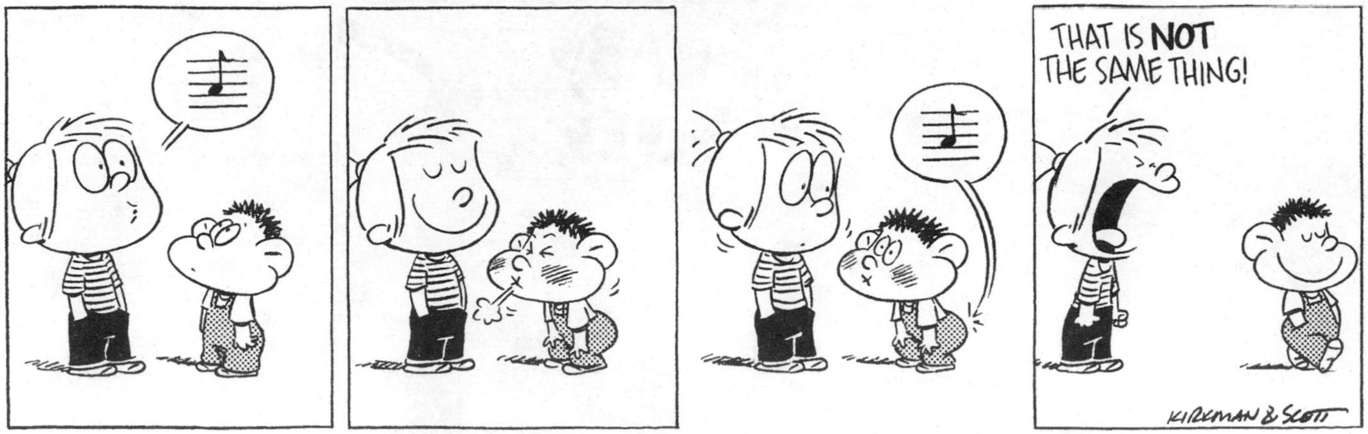
THAT IS **NOT** THE SAME THING!
KIRKMAN & SCOTT

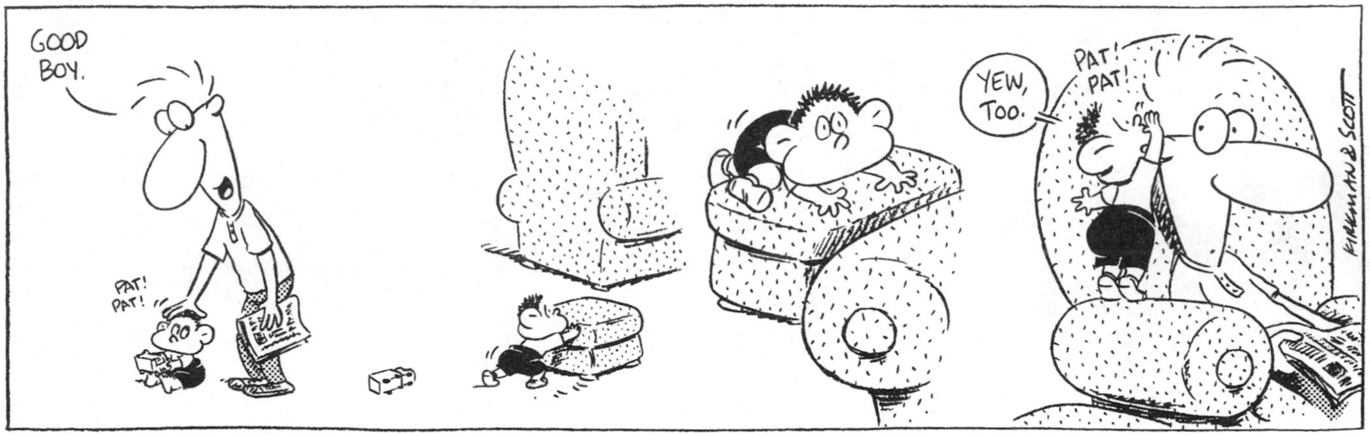
GOOD BOY.
PAT! PAT!
YEW, TOO.
PAT! PAT!
KIRKMAN & SCOTT

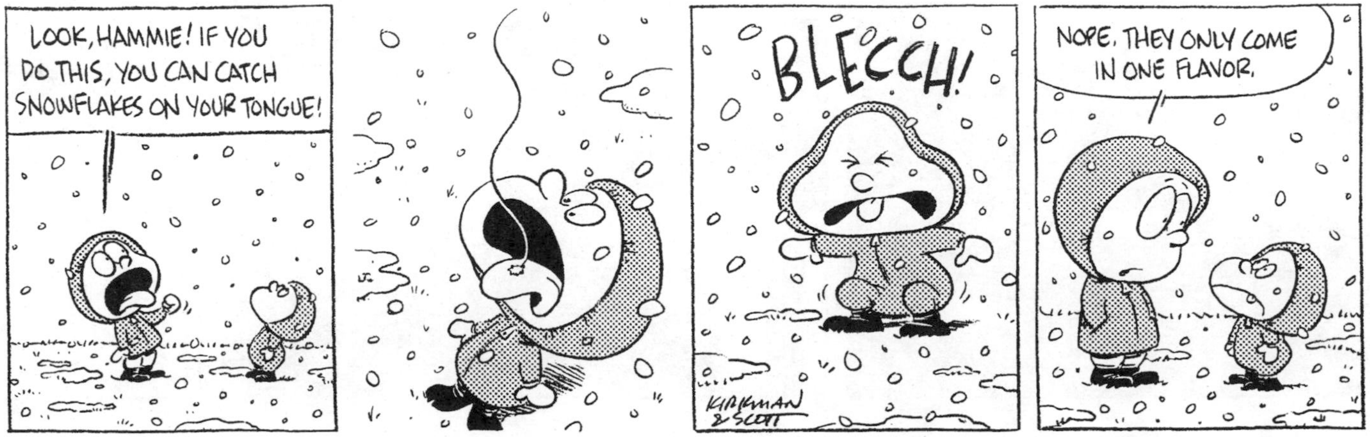
LOOK, HAMMIE! IF YOU DO THIS, YOU CAN CATCH SNOWFLAKES ON YOUR TONGUE!
BLECCH!
KIRKMAN & SCOTT
NOPE. THEY ONLY COME IN ONE FLAVOR.

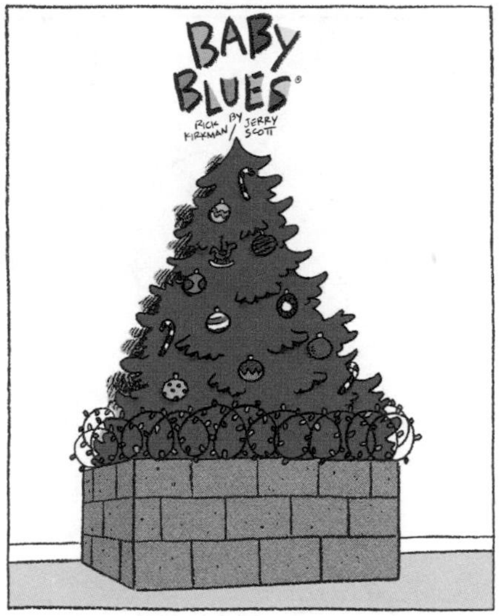
BABY BLUES
RICK KIRKMAN / BY JERRY SCOTT

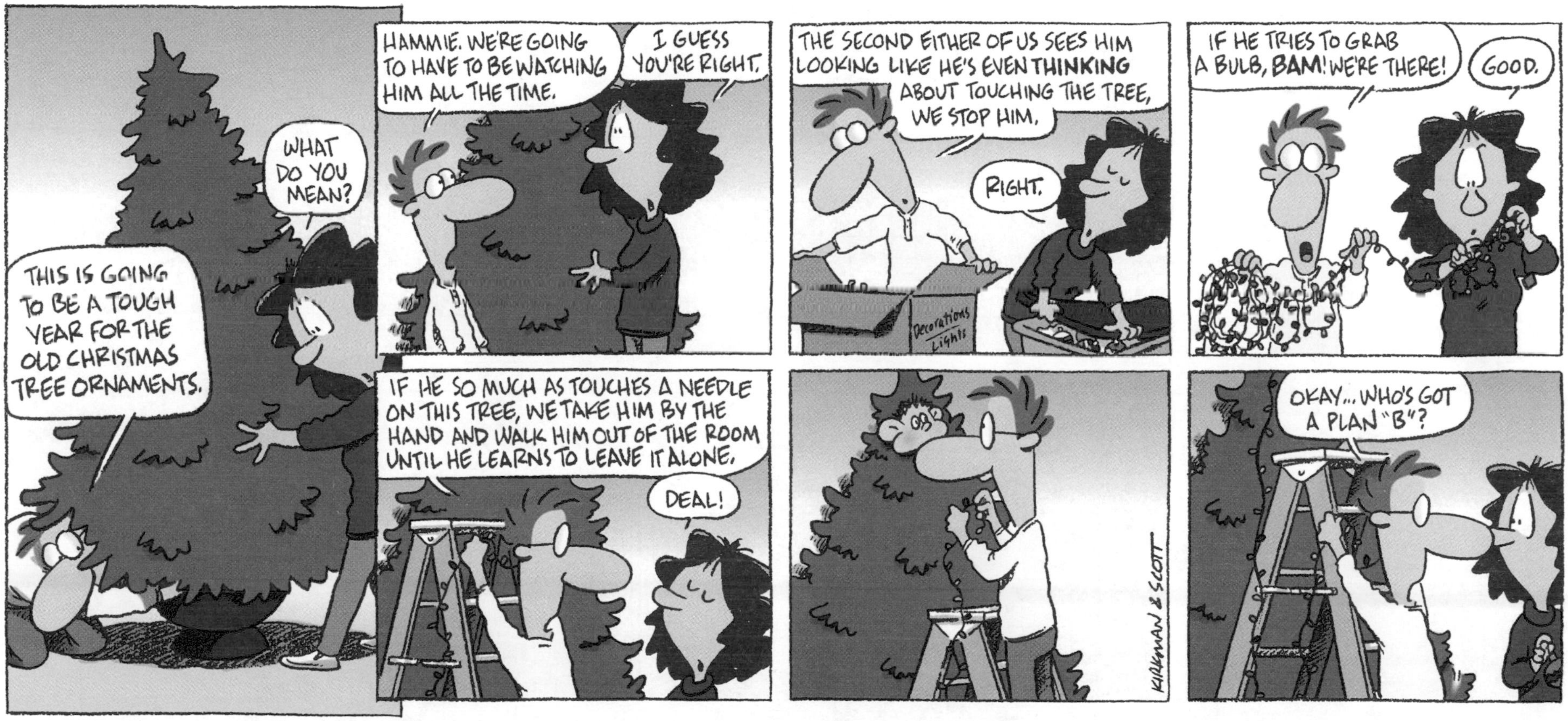
THIS IS GOING TO BE A TOUGH YEAR FOR THE OLD CHRISTMAS TREE ORNAMENTS.
WHAT DO YOU MEAN?
HAMMIE. WE'RE GOING TO HAVE TO BE WATCHING HIM ALL THE TIME.
I GUESS YOU'RE RIGHT.
THE SECOND EITHER OF US SEES HIM LOOKING LIKE HE'S EVEN **THINKING** ABOUT TOUCHING THE TREE, WE STOP HIM.
RIGHT.
Decorations Lights
IF HE TRIES TO GRAB A BULB, **BAM!** WE'RE THERE!
GOOD.
IF HE SO MUCH AS TOUCHES A NEEDLE ON THIS TREE, WE TAKE HIM BY THE HAND AND WALK HIM OUT OF THE ROOM UNTIL HE LEARNS TO LEAVE IT ALONE.
DEAL!
KIRKMAN & SCOTT
OKAY... WHO'S GOT A PLAN "B"?

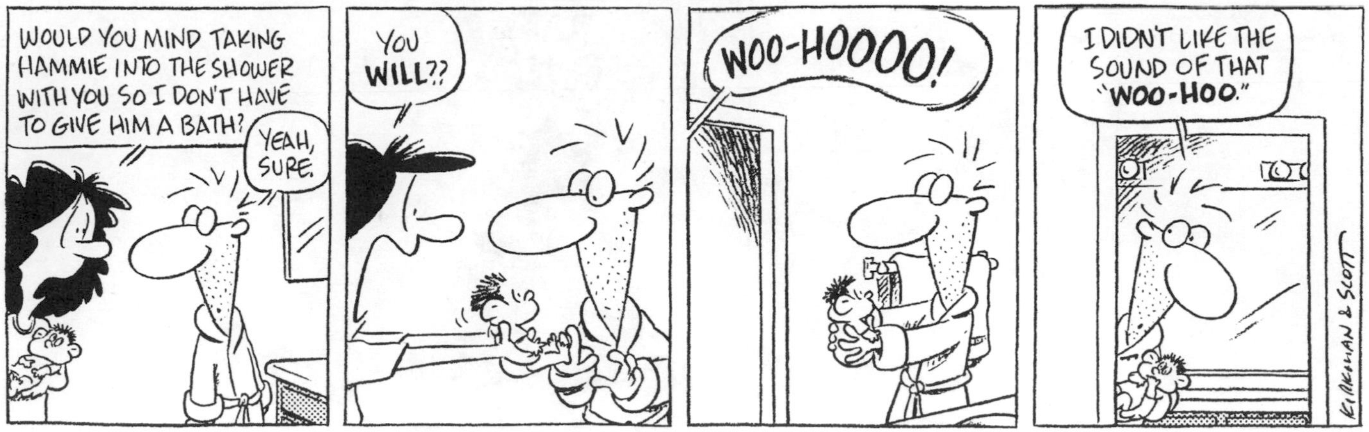
WOULD YOU MIND TAKING HAMMIE INTO THE SHOWER WITH YOU SO I DON'T HAVE TO GIVE HIM A BATH?
YEAH, SURE.
YOU WILL??
WOO-HOOOO!
I DIDN'T LIKE THE SOUND OF THAT "WOO-HOO."
KIRKMAN & SCOTT

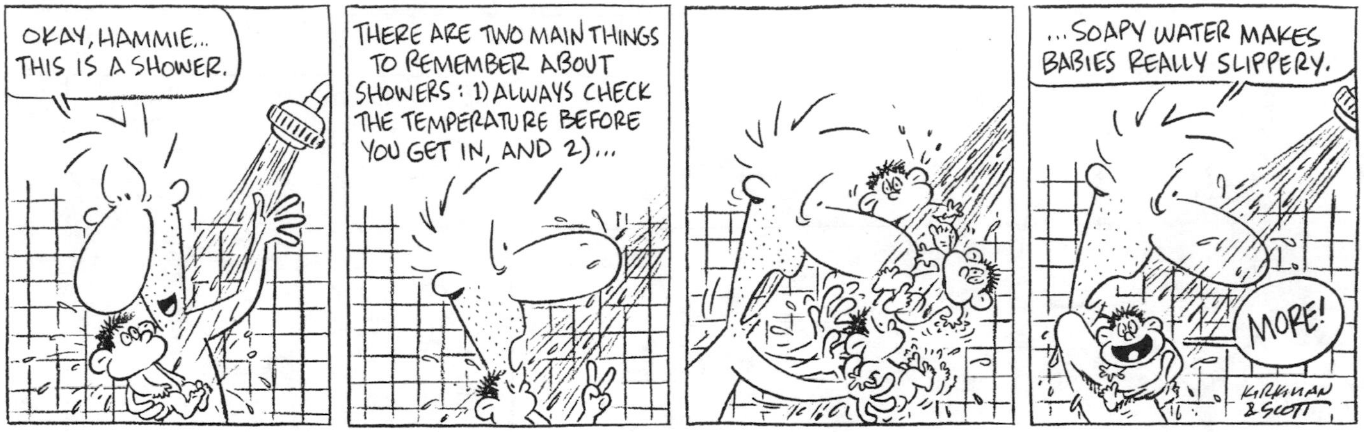
OKAY, HAMMIE... THIS IS A SHOWER.
THERE ARE TWO MAIN THINGS TO REMEMBER ABOUT SHOWERS: 1) ALWAYS CHECK THE TEMPERATURE BEFORE YOU GET IN, AND 2)...
...SOAPY WATER MAKES BABIES REALLY SLIPPERY.
MORE!
KIRKMAN & SCOTT

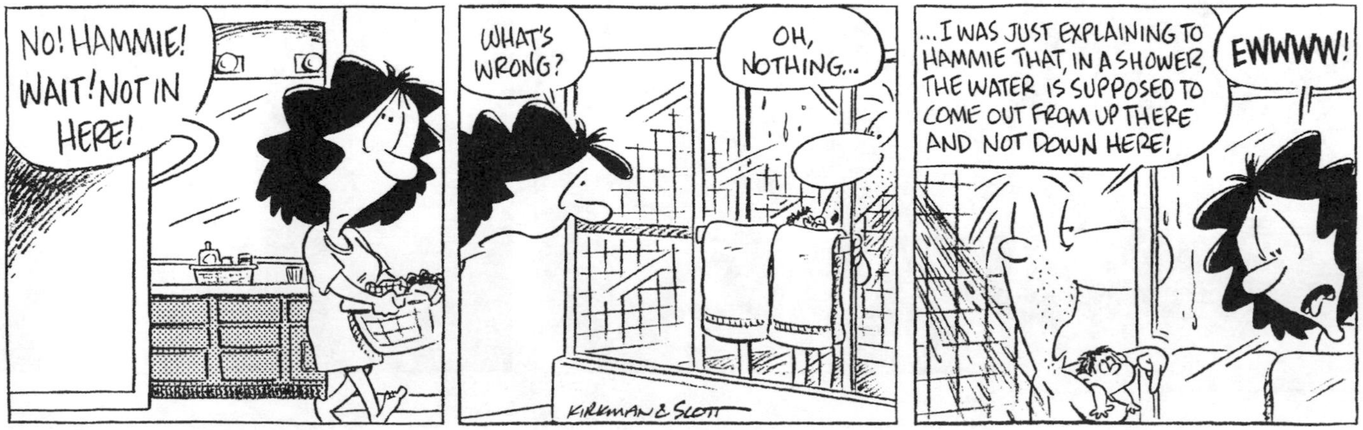
NO! HAMMIE! WAIT! NOT IN HERE!
WHAT'S WRONG?
OH, NOTHING...
KIRKMAN & SCOTT
...I WAS JUST EXPLAINING TO HAMMIE THAT, IN A SHOWER, THE WATER IS SUPPOSED TO COME OUT FROM UP THERE AND NOT DOWN HERE!
EWWWW!

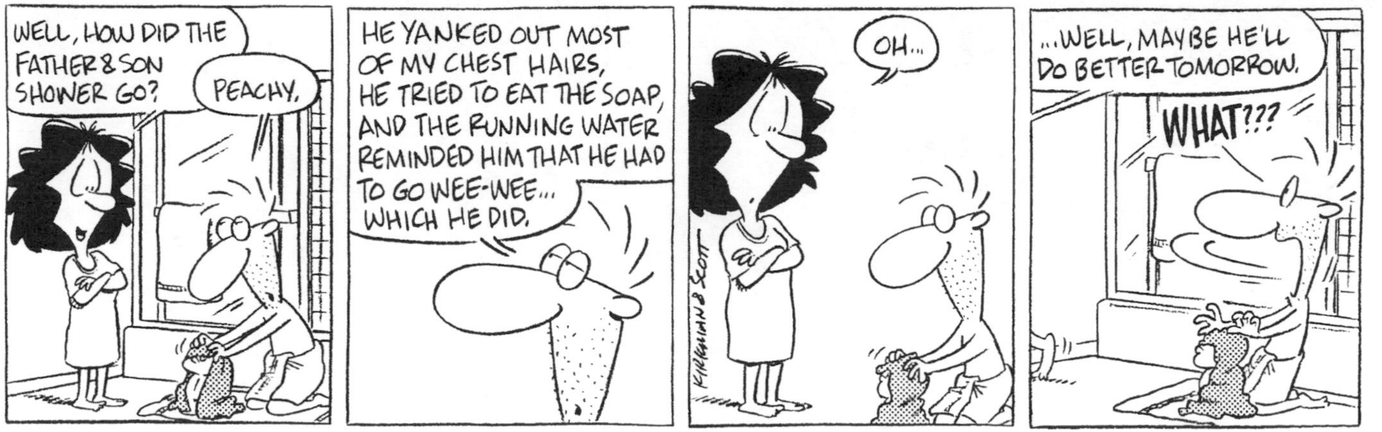
WELL, HOW DID THE FATHER & SON SHOWER GO?
PEACHY.
HE YANKED OUT MOST OF MY CHEST HAIRS, HE TRIED TO EAT THE SOAP, AND THE RUNNING WATER REMINDED HIM THAT HE HAD TO GO WEE-WEE... WHICH HE DID.
OH...
KIRKMAN & SCOTT
...WELL, MAYBE HE'LL DO BETTER TOMORROW.
WHAT???

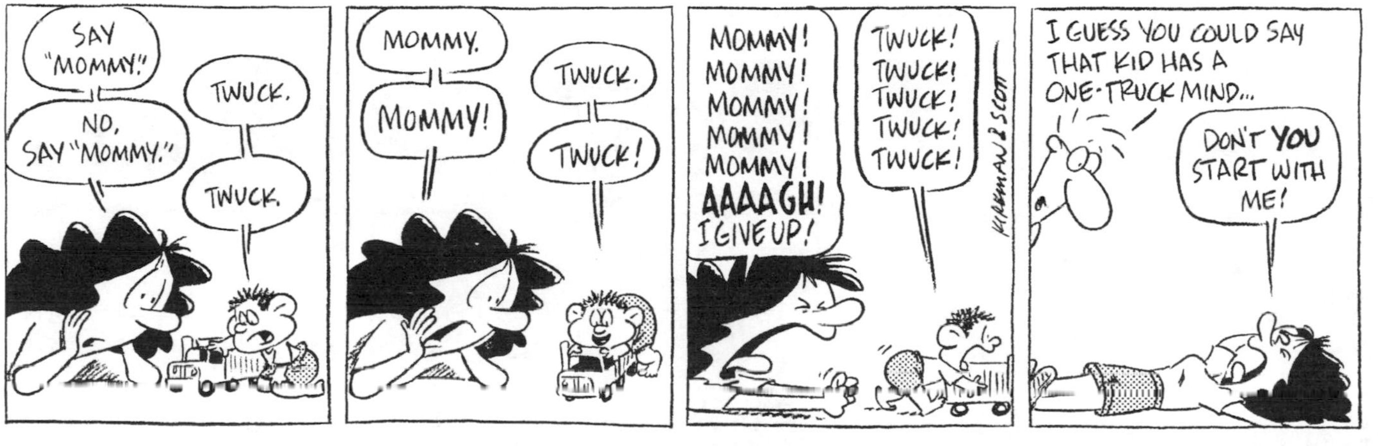
SAY "MOMMY."
TWUCK.
NO, SAY "MOMMY."
TWUCK.
MOMMY.
MOMMY!
TWUCK.
TWUCK!
MOMMY! MOMMY! MOMMY! MOMMY! MOMMY! AAAAGH! I GIVE UP!
TWUCK! TWUCK! TWUCK! TWUCK! TWUCK!
KIRKMAN & SCOTT
I GUESS YOU COULD SAY THAT KID HAS A ONE-TRUCK MIND...
DON'T YOU START WITH ME!

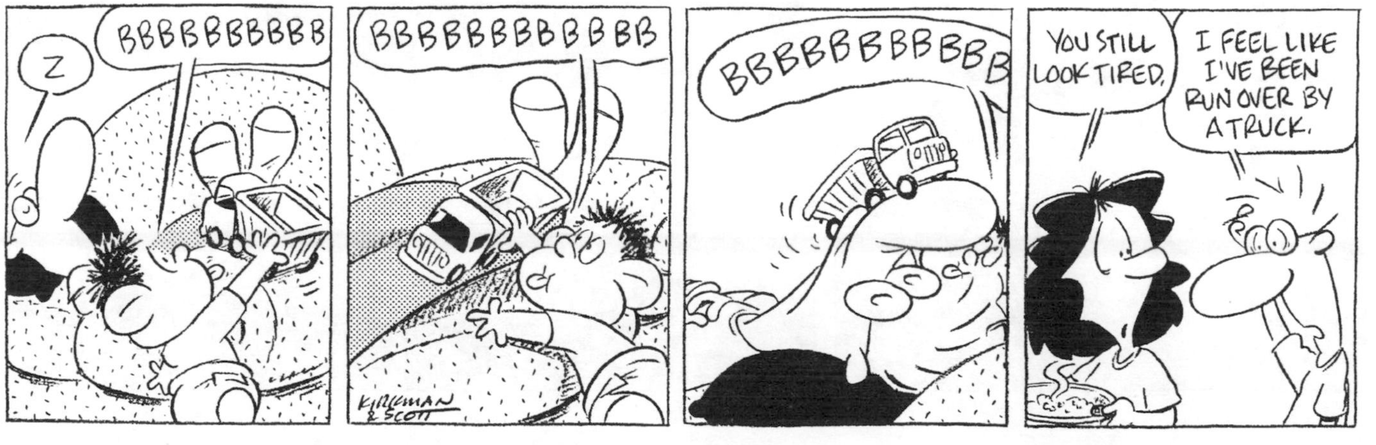
Z
BBBBBBBBBB
BBBBBBBBBBBB
KIRKMAN & SCOTT
BBBBBBBBBBB
YOU STILL LOOK TIRED.
I FEEL LIKE I'VE BEEN RUN OVER BY A TRUCK.

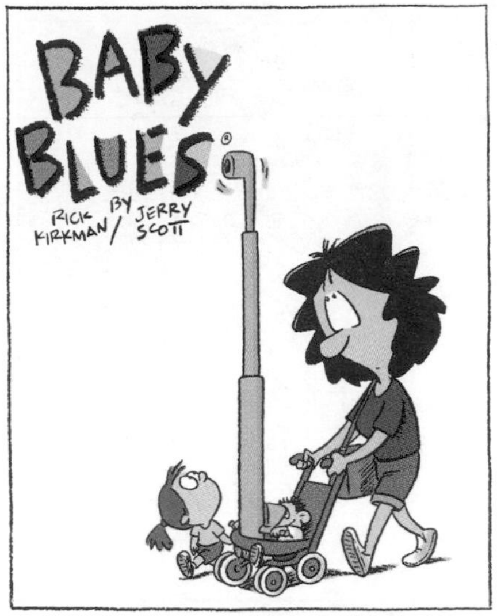
BABY BLUES®
BY RICK KIRKMAN / JERRY SCOTT

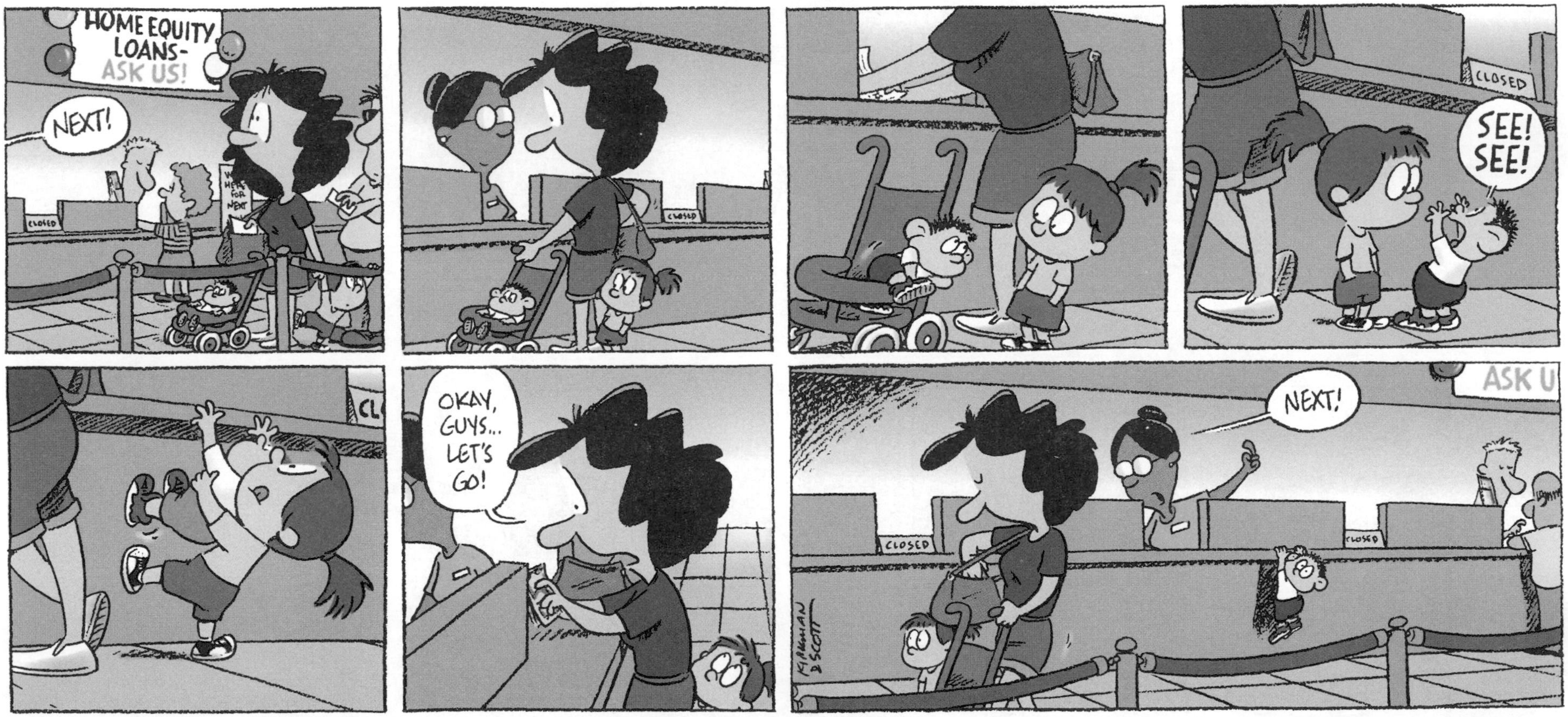
HOME EQUITY LOANS- ASK US!
NEXT!
CLOSED
CLOSED
CLOSED
SEE! SEE!
OKAY, GUYS... LET'S GO!
NEXT!
CLOSED
CLOSED
KIRKMAN & SCOTT

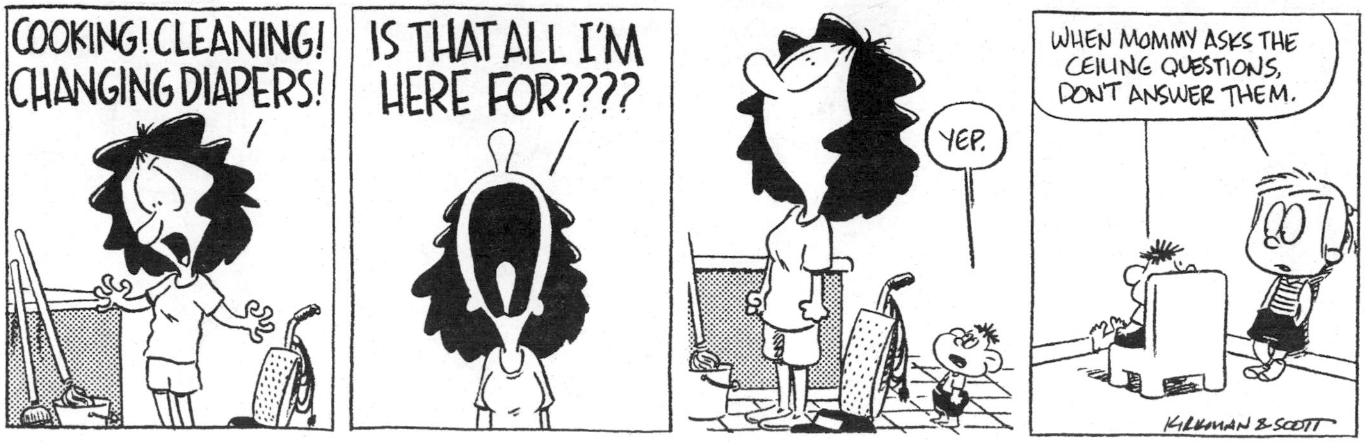
COOKING! CLEANING! CHANGING DIAPERS!
IS THAT ALL I'M HERE FOR????
YEP.
WHEN MOMMY ASKS THE CEILING QUESTIONS, DON'T ANSWER THEM.
KIRKMAN & SCOTT

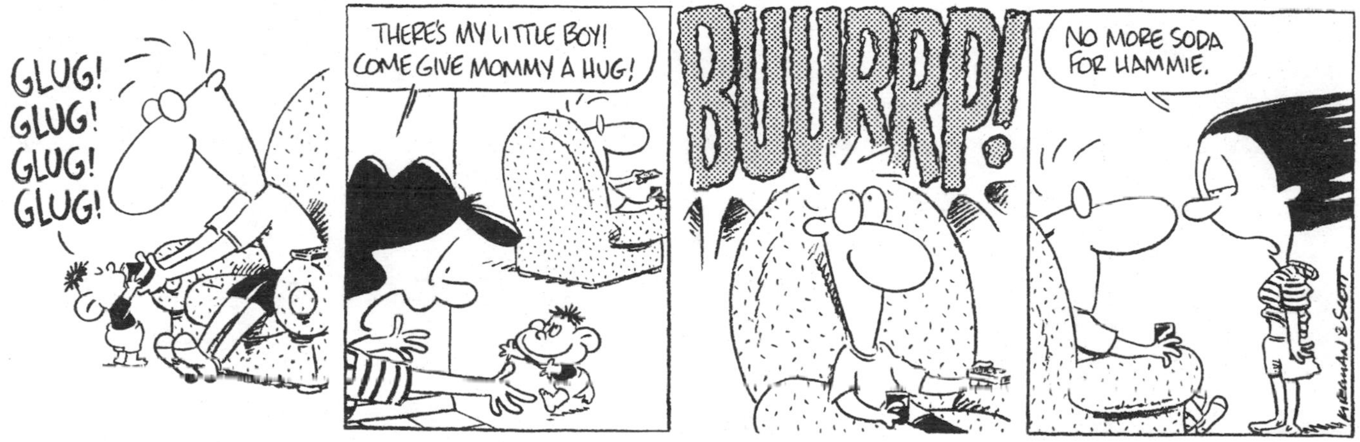
GLUG! GLUG! GLUG! GLUG!
THERE'S MY LITTLE BOY! COME GIVE MOMMY A HUG!
BUURRP!
NO MORE SODA FOR HAMMIE.
KIRKMAN & SCOTT

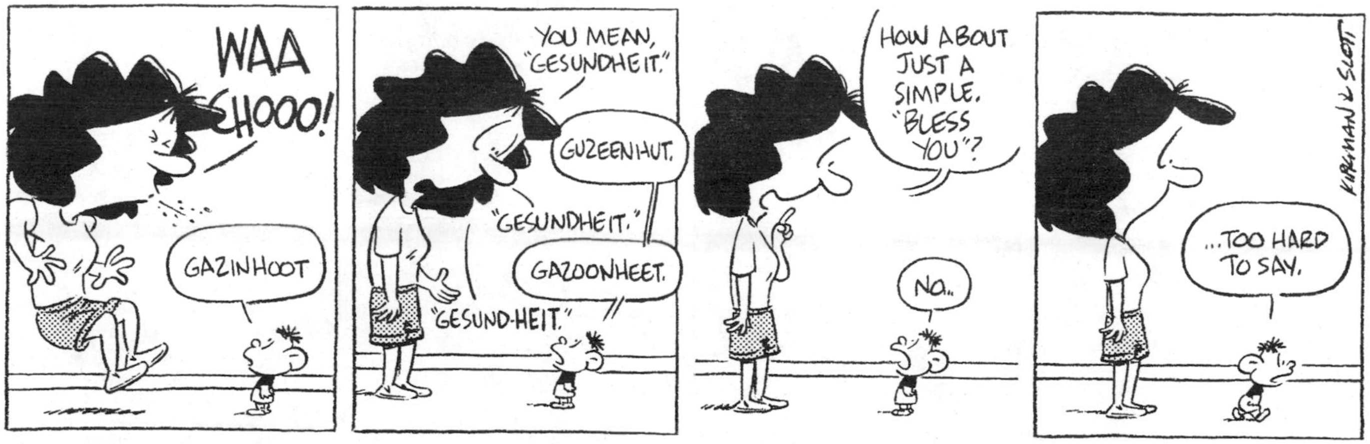
WAA CHOOO!
GAZINHOOT
YOU MEAN, "GESUNDHEIT."
GUZEENHUT.
"GESUNDHEIT."
GAZOONHEET.
"GESUND-HEIT."
HOW ABOUT JUST A SIMPLE, "BLESS YOU"?
NO..
...TOO HARD TO SAY.
KIRKMAN & SCOTT

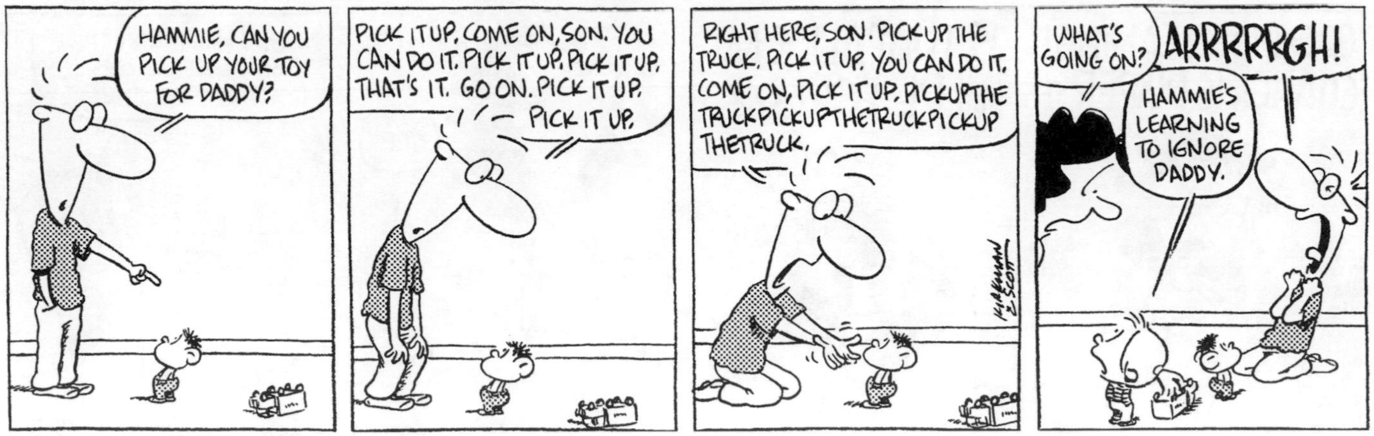
HAMMIE, CAN YOU PICK UP YOUR TOY FOR DADDY?
PICK IT UP. COME ON, SON. YOU CAN DO IT. PICK IT UP. PICK IT UP. THAT'S IT. GO ON. PICK IT UP.
PICK IT UP.
RIGHT HERE, SON. PICK UP THE TRUCK. PICK IT UP. YOU CAN DO IT. COME ON, PICK IT UP. PICKUPTHE TRUCKPICKUPTHETRUCKPICKUP THETRUCK.
KIRKMAN & SCOTT
WHAT'S GOING ON?
ARRRRRGH!
HAMMIE'S LEARNING TO IGNORE DADDY.

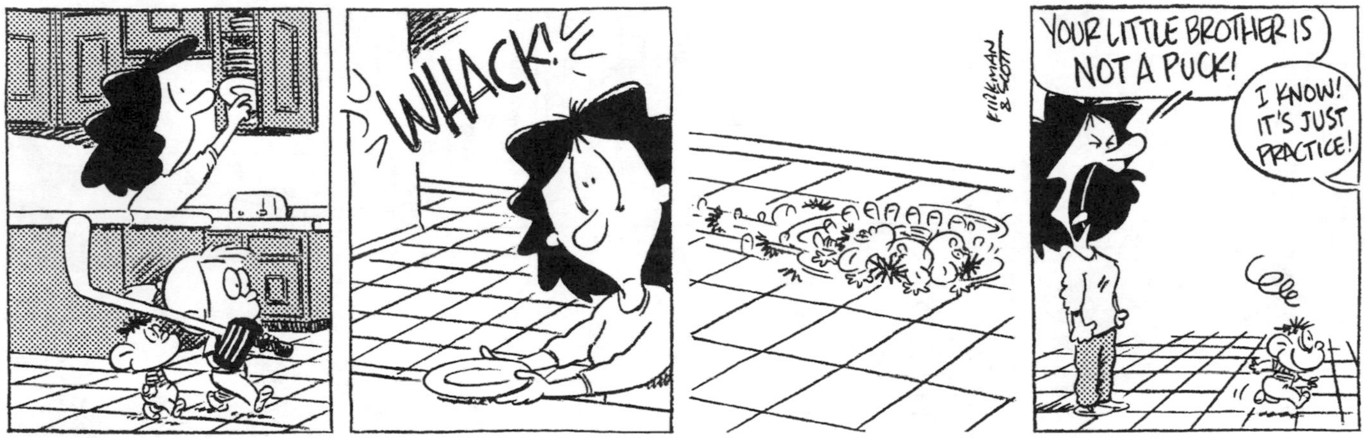
WHACK!
KIRKMAN & SCOTT
YOUR LITTLE BROTHER IS NOT A PUCK!
I KNOW! IT'S JUST PRACTICE!

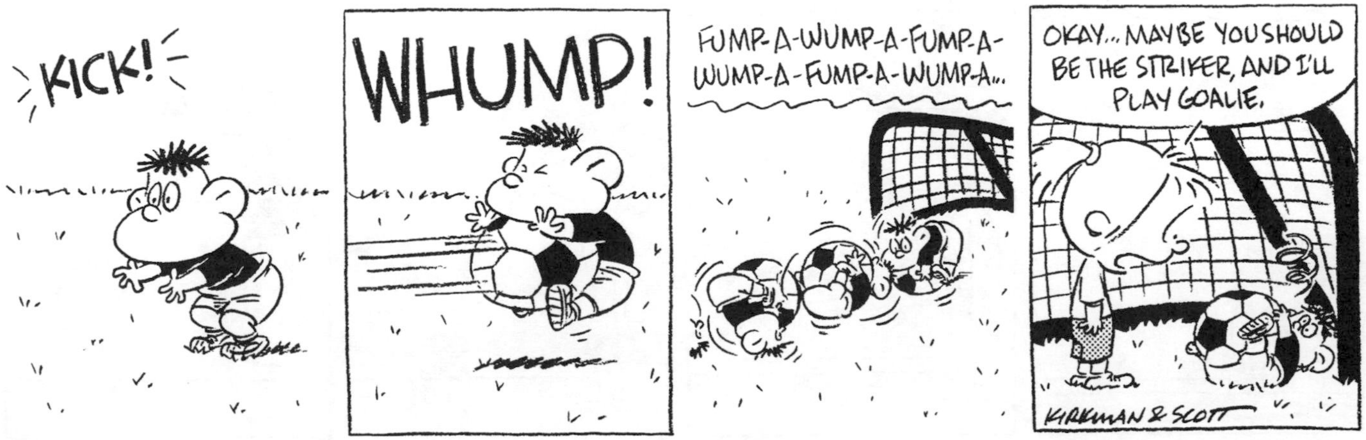
KICK!
WHUMP!
FUMP-A-WUMP-A-FUMP-A-WUMP-A-FUMP-A-WUMP-A...
OKAY... MAYBE YOU SHOULD BE THE STRIKER, AND I'LL PLAY GOALIE.
KIRKMAN & SCOTT

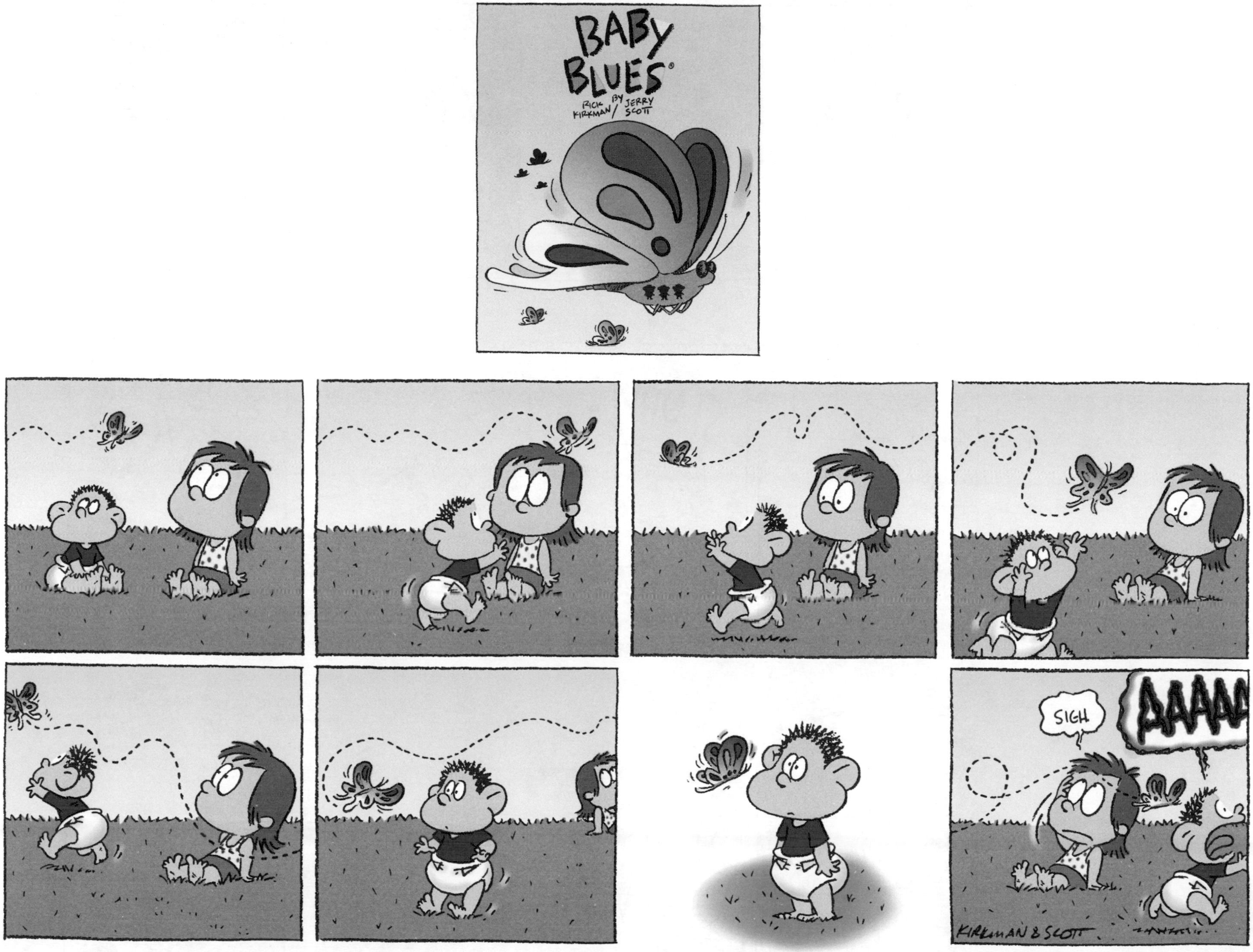
BABY BLUES®
BY RICK KIRKMAN / JERRY SCOTT
SIGH
AAAA
KIRKMAN & SCOTT

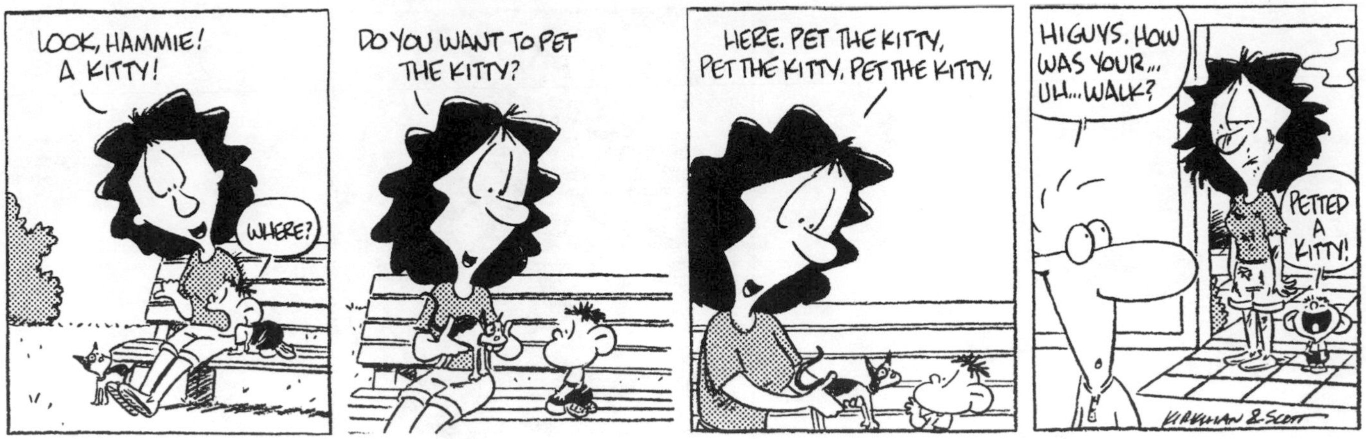
LOOK, HAMMIE! A KITTY!
WHERE?
DO YOU WANT TO PET THE KITTY?
HERE. PET THE KITTY, PET THE KITTY. PET THE KITTY.
HI GUYS. HOW WAS YOUR... UH... WALK?
PETTED A KITTY!
KIRKMAN & SCOTT

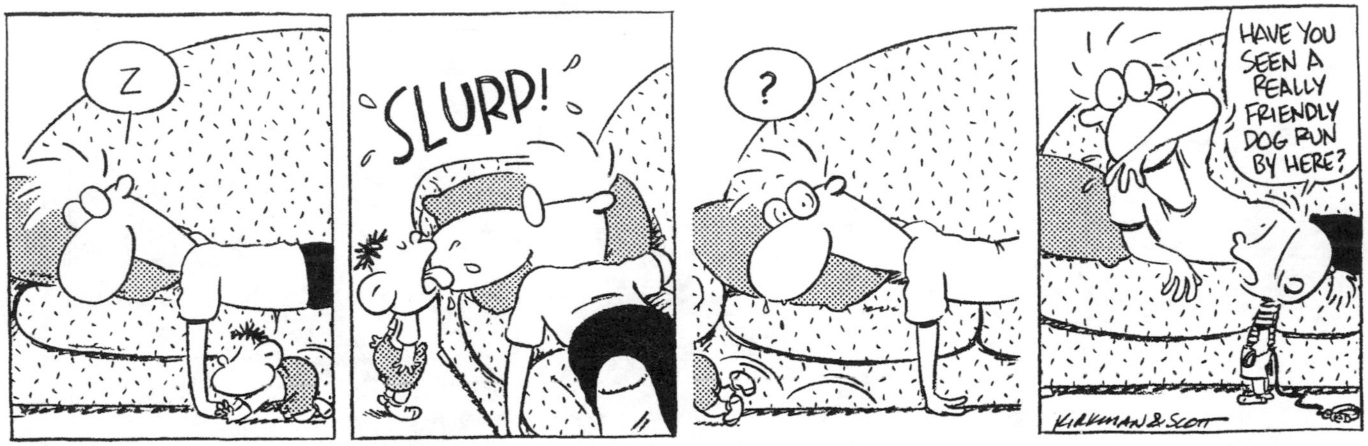
Z
SLURP!
?
HAVE YOU SEEN A REALLY FRIENDLY DOG RUN BY HERE?
KIRKMAN & SCOTT

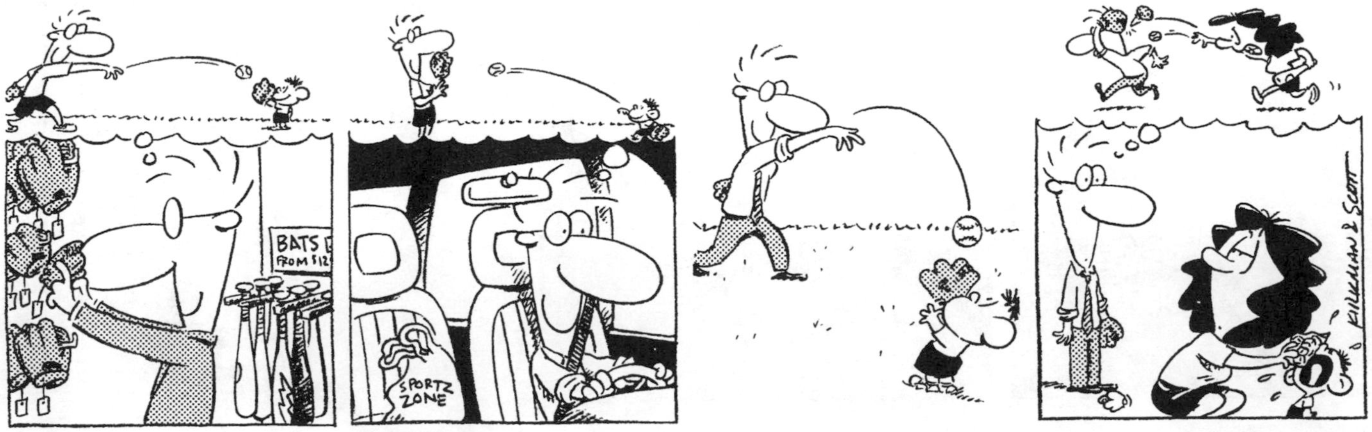
BATS
SPORTZ ZONE
KIRKMAN & SCOTT

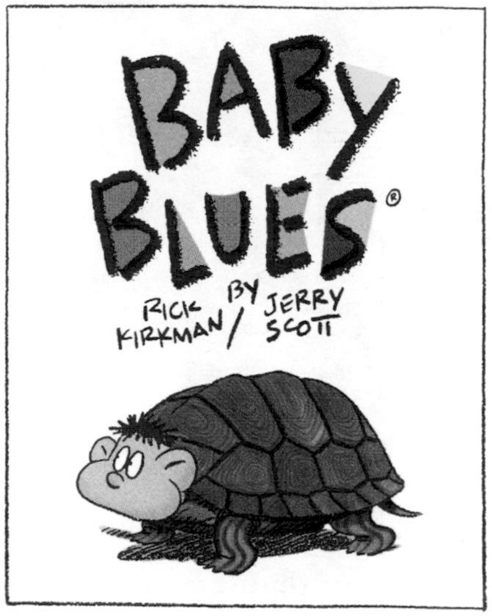
BABY BLUES®
BY RICK KIRKMAN / JERRY SCOTT

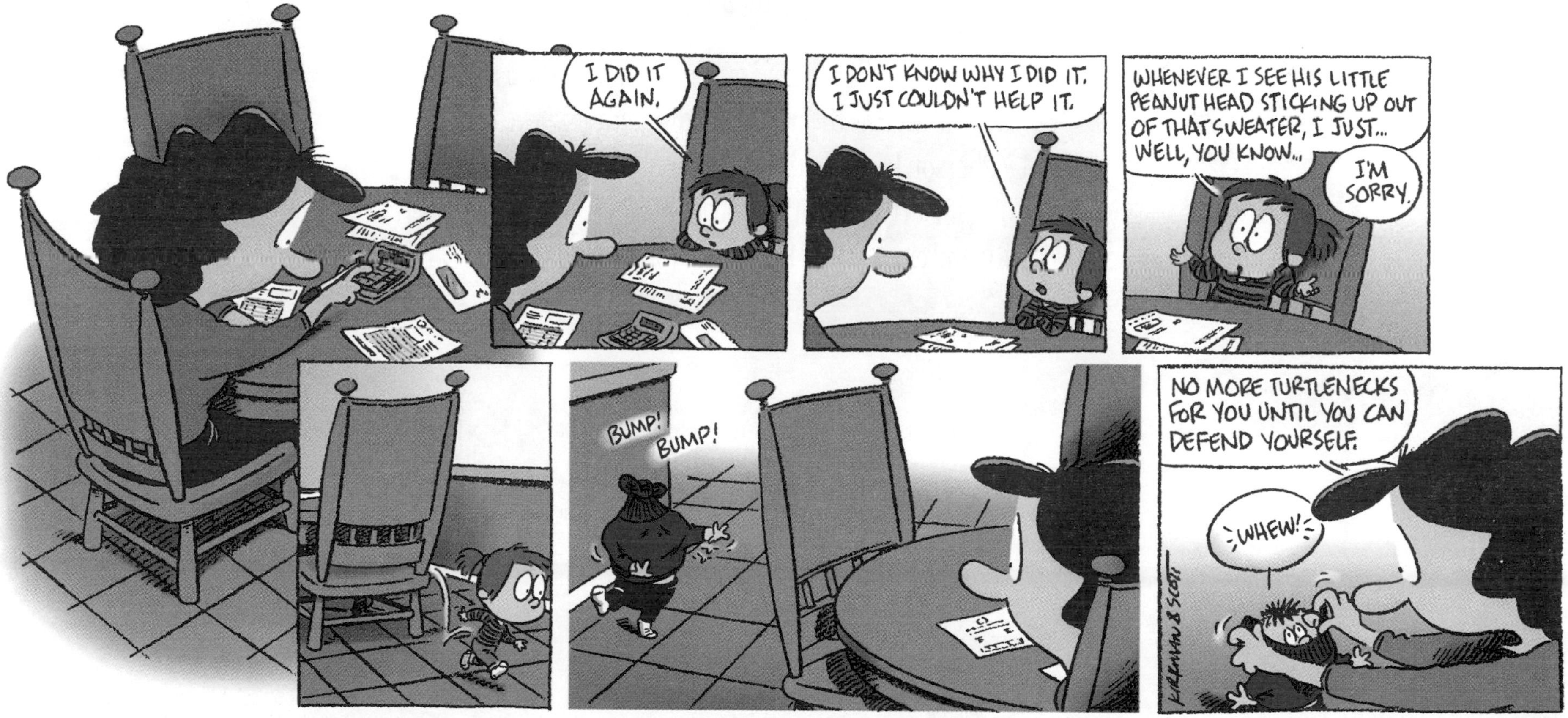
I DID IT AGAIN.
I DON'T KNOW WHY I DID IT. I JUST COULDN'T HELP IT.
WHENEVER I SEE HIS LITTLE PEANUT HEAD STICKING UP OUT OF THAT SWEATER, I JUST... WELL, YOU KNOW...
I'M SORRY.
BUMP! BUMP!
NO MORE TURTLENECKS FOR YOU UNTIL YOU CAN DEFEND YOURSELF.
WHEW!
KIRKMAN & SCOTT

SIBS

Bonnie and Clyde, Masters and Johnson, Rowan and Martin, and Zoe and Hammie. Sometimes it takes a great partnership to accomplish great things.

Ever since Hammie arrived on the scene, the atmosphere—as well as the math—is different in the MacPherson household. The teams are now even. It's two against two. Maturity and skill matched against youth and energy. God help Darryl and Wanda.

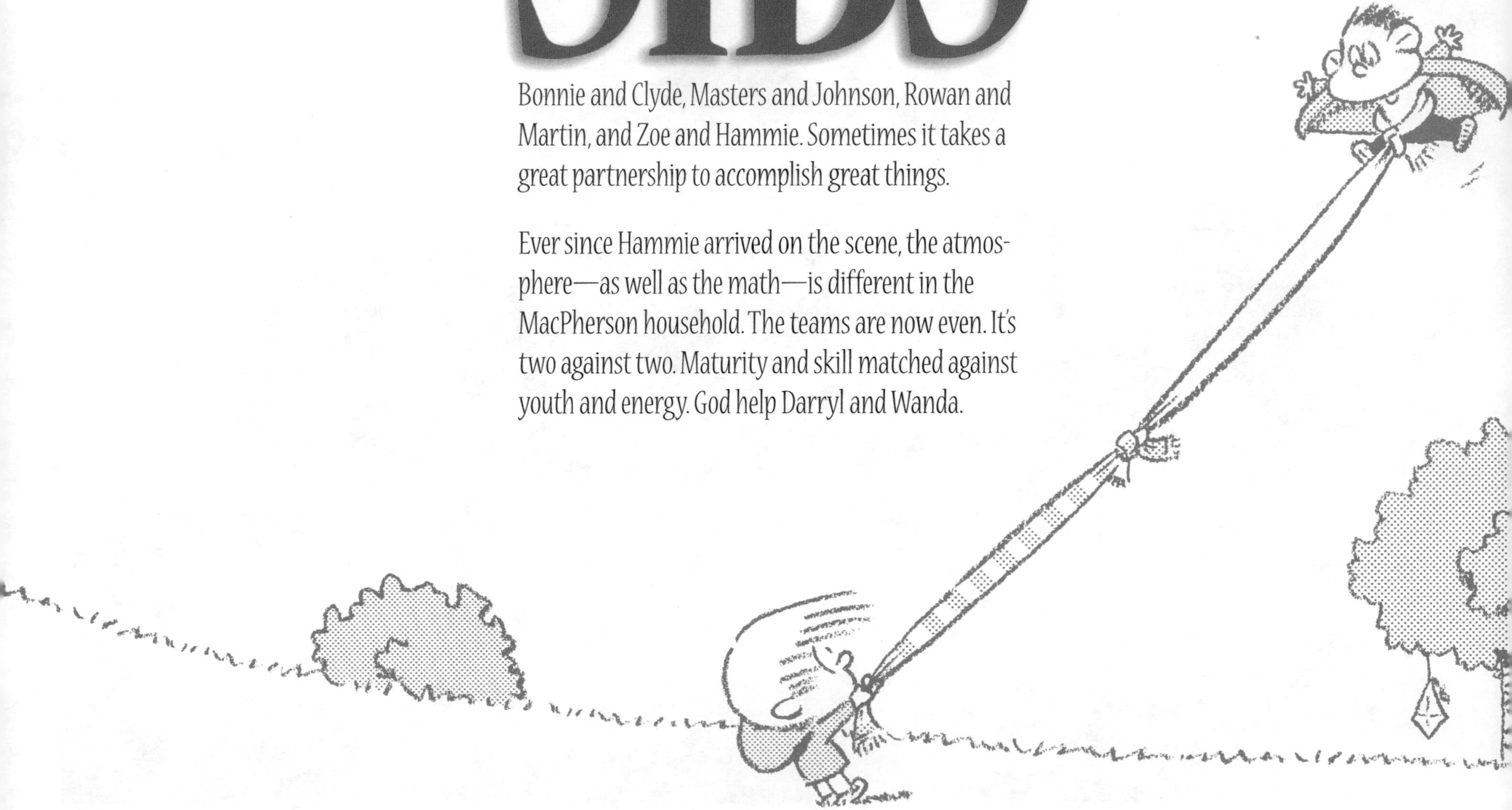

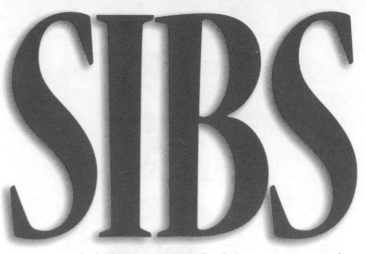

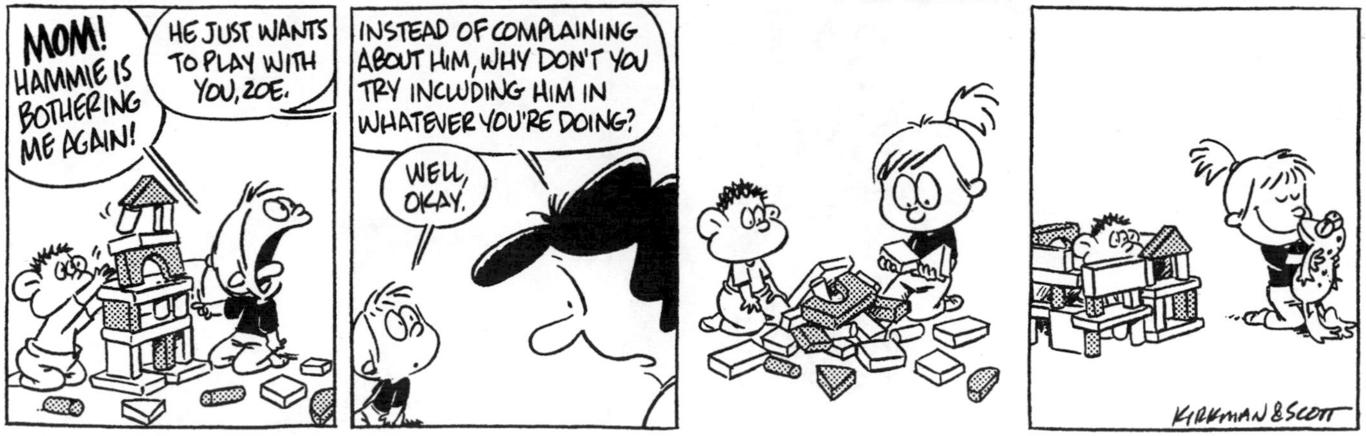
MOM! HAMMIE IS BOTHERING ME AGAIN!
HE JUST WANTS TO PLAY WITH YOU, ZOE.
INSTEAD OF COMPLAINING ABOUT HIM, WHY DON'T YOU TRY INCLUDING HIM IN WHATEVER YOU'RE DOING?
WELL, OKAY.
KIRKMAN & SCOTT

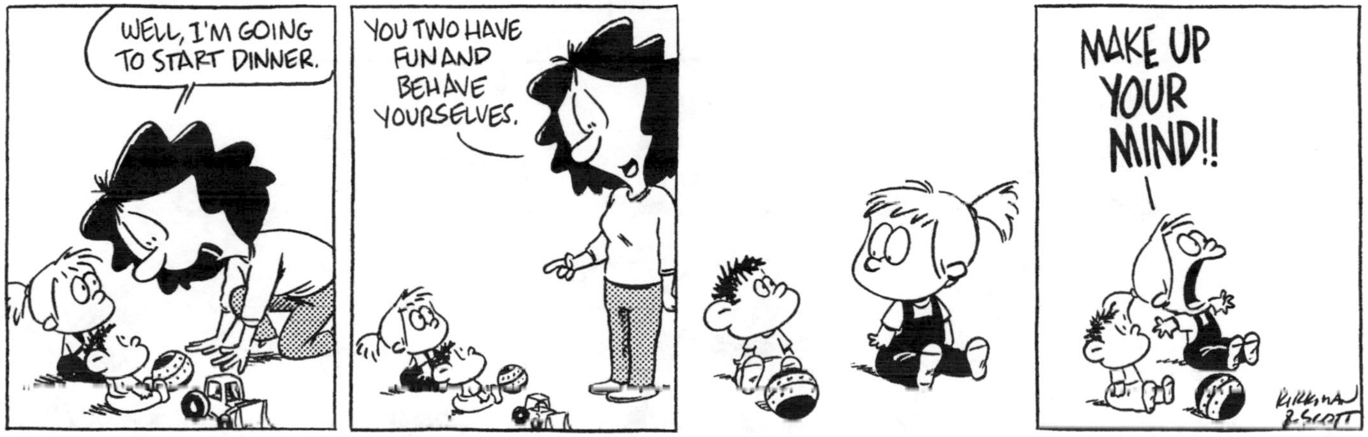
WELL, I'M GOING TO START DINNER.
YOU TWO HAVE FUN AND BEHAVE YOURSELVES.
MAKE UP YOUR MIND!!
KIRKMAN & SCOTT

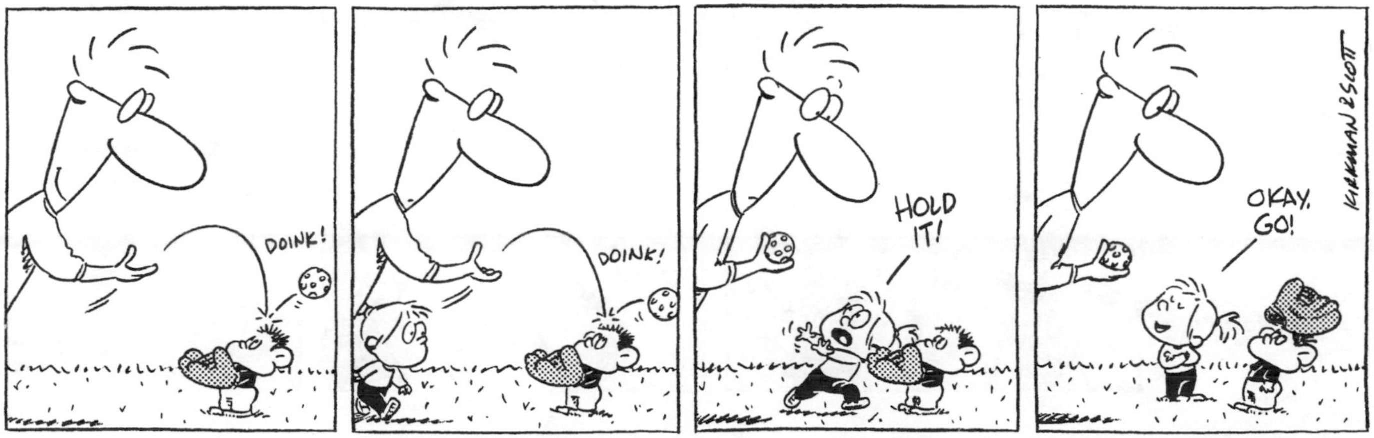
DOINK!
DOINK!
HOLD IT!
OKAY. GO!
KIRKMAN & SCOTT

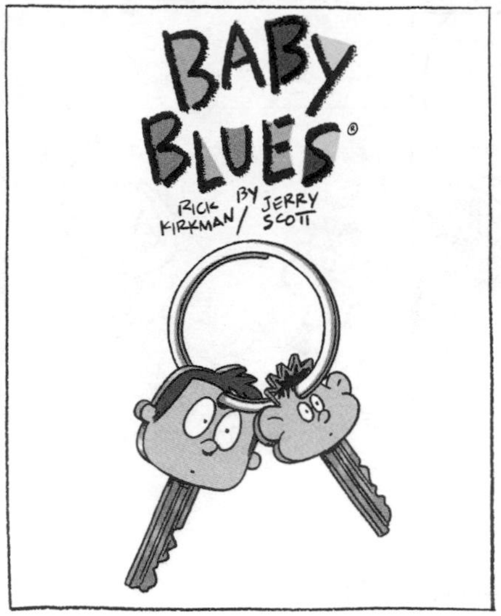
BABY BLUES®
BY RICK KIRKMAN / JERRY SCOTT

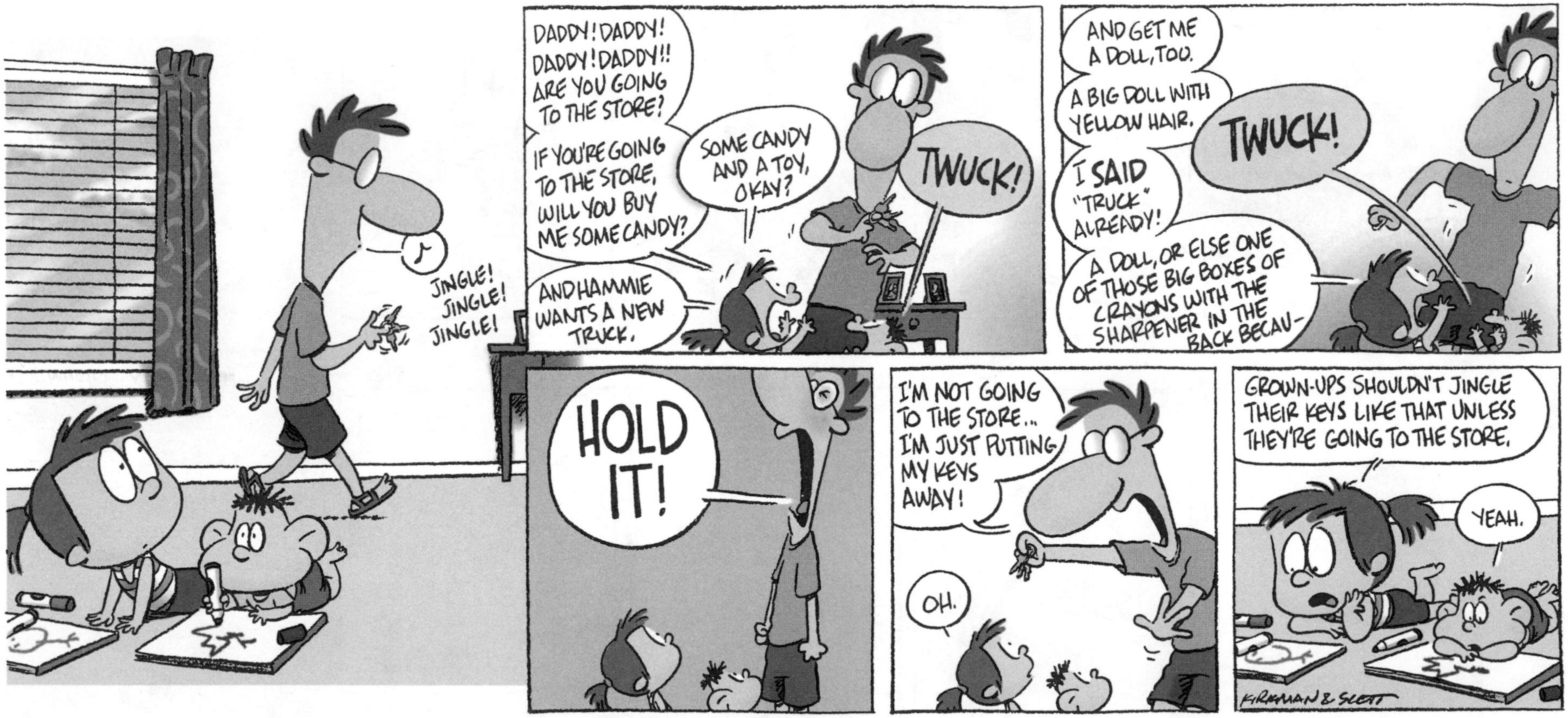
JINGLE! JINGLE! JINGLE!
DADDY! DADDY! DADDY! DADDY!! ARE YOU GOING TO THE STORE?
IF YOU'RE GOING TO THE STORE, WILL YOU BUY ME SOME CANDY?
SOME CANDY AND A TOY, OKAY?
AND HAMMIE WANTS A NEW TRUCK.
TWUCK!
AND GET ME A DOLL, TOO.
A BIG DOLL WITH YELLOW HAIR.
TWUCK!
I SAID "TRUCK" ALREADY!
A DOLL, OR ELSE ONE OF THOSE BIG BOXES OF CRAYONS WITH THE SHARPENER IN THE BACK BECAU–
HOLD IT!
I'M NOT GOING TO THE STORE... I'M JUST PUTTING MY KEYS AWAY!
OH.
GROWN-UPS SHOULDN'T JINGLE THEIR KEYS LIKE THAT UNLESS THEY'RE GOING TO THE STORE.
YEAH.
KIRKMAN & SCOTT

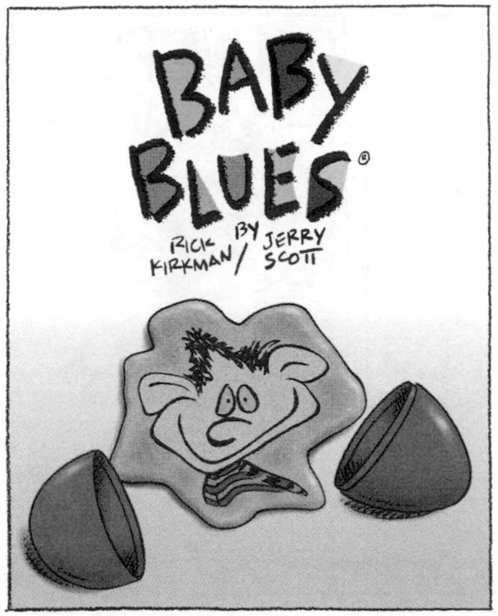
BABY BLUES®
RICK KIRKMAN / BY JERRY SCOTT

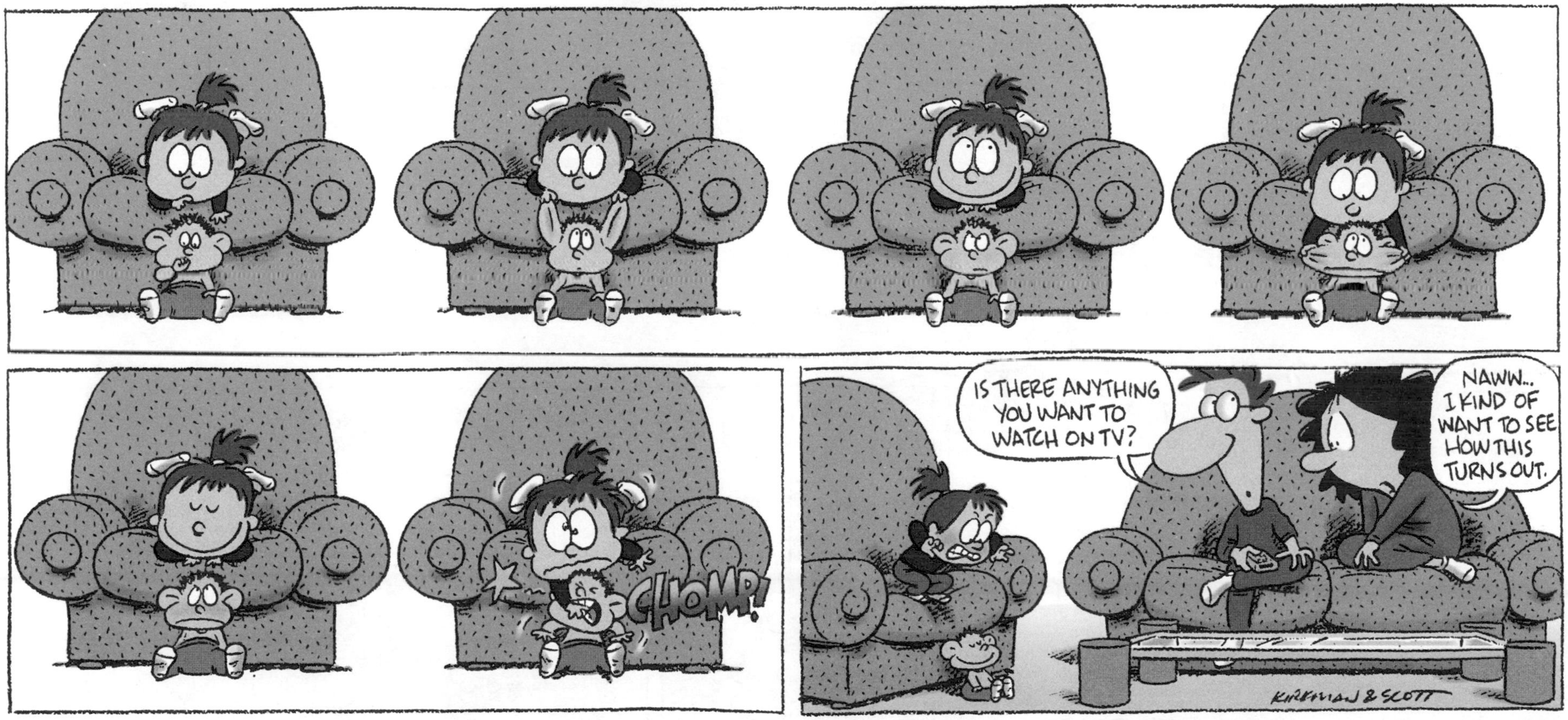
CHOMP!
IS THERE ANYTHING YOU WANT TO WATCH ON TV?
NAWW... I KIND OF WANT TO SEE HOW THIS TURNS OUT.
KIRKMAN & SCOTT

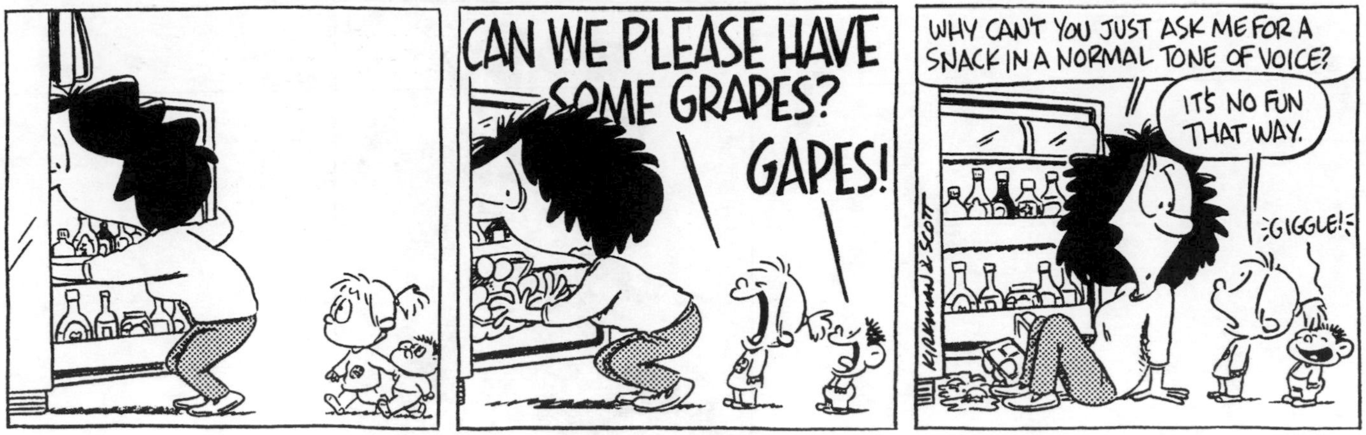
CAN WE PLEASE HAVE SOME GRAPES?
GAPES!
WHY CAN'T YOU JUST ASK ME FOR A SNACK IN A NORMAL TONE OF VOICE?
IT'S NO FUN THAT WAY.
GIGGLE!
KIRKMAN & SCOTT

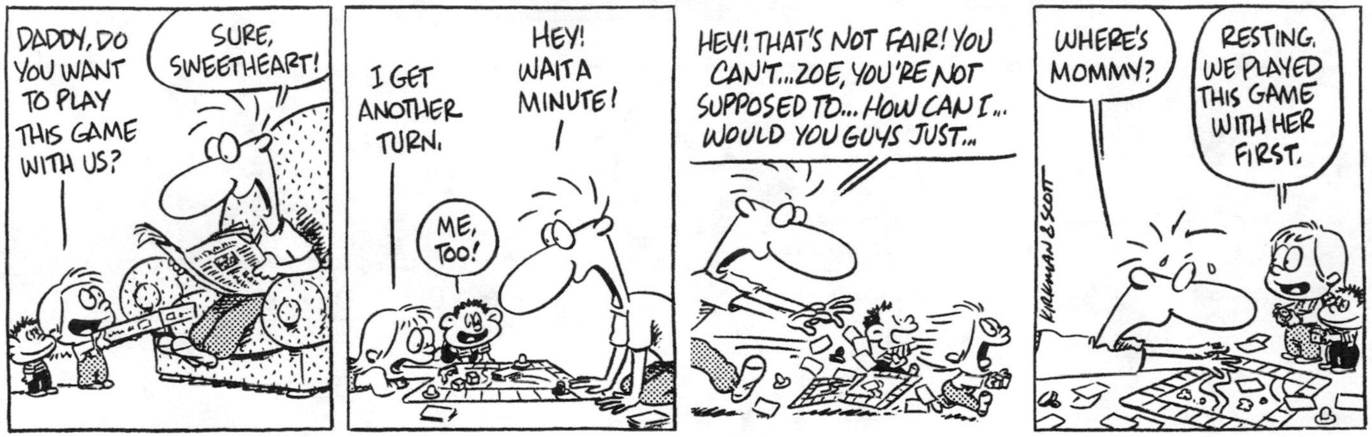
DADDY, DO YOU WANT TO PLAY THIS GAME WITH US?
SURE, SWEETHEART!
I GET ANOTHER TURN.
HEY! WAIT A MINUTE!
ME, TOO!
HEY! THAT'S NOT FAIR! YOU CAN'T...ZOE, YOU'RE NOT SUPPOSED TO... HOW CAN I... WOULD YOU GUYS JUST...
WHERE'S MOMMY?
RESTING. WE PLAYED THIS GAME WITH HER FIRST.
KIRKMAN & SCOTT

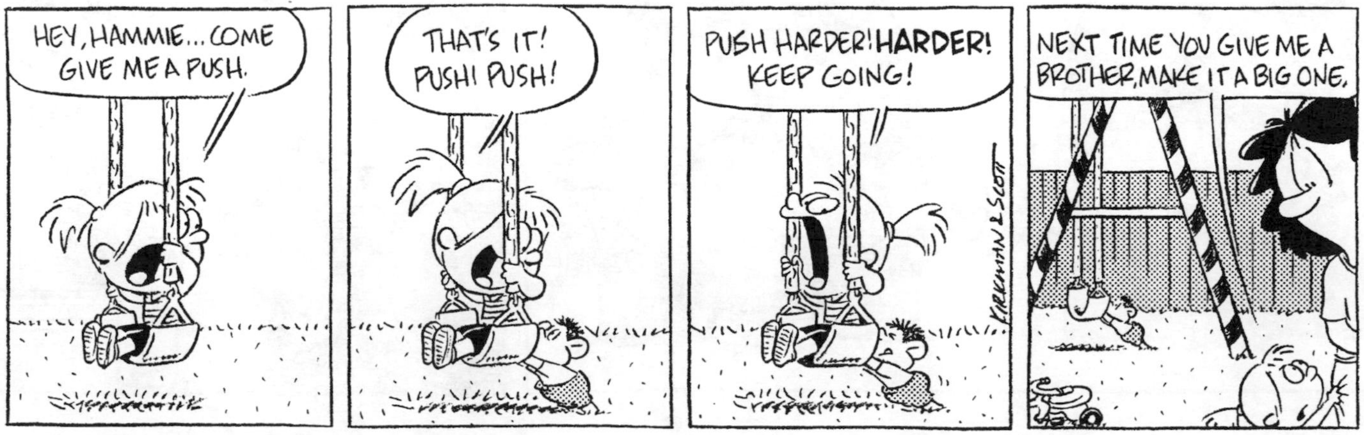
HEY, HAMMIE... COME GIVE ME A PUSH.
THAT'S IT! PUSH! PUSH!
PUSH HARDER! **HARDER!** KEEP GOING!
KIRKMAN & SCOTT
NEXT TIME YOU GIVE ME A BROTHER, MAKE IT A BIG ONE.

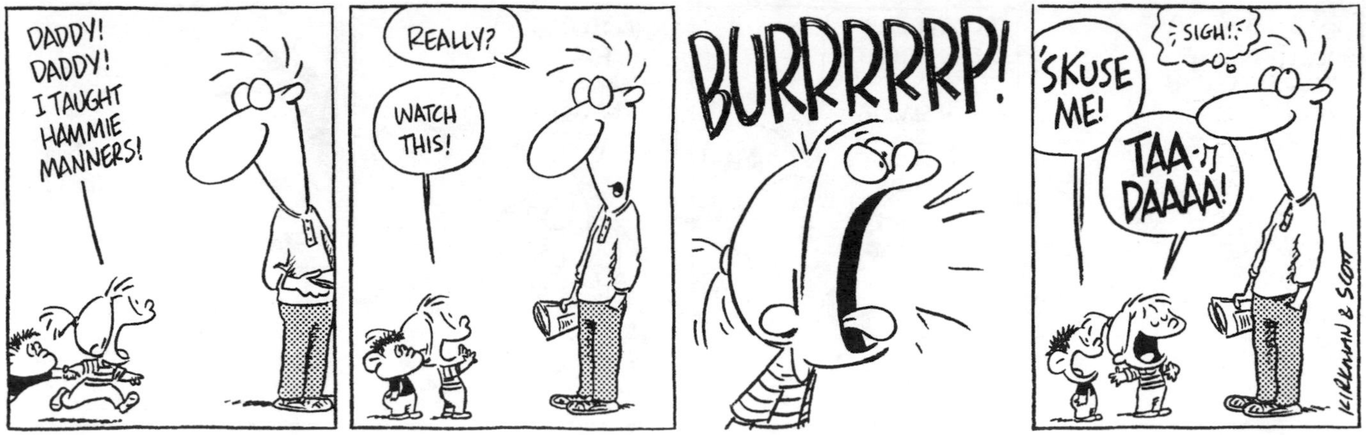
DADDY! DADDY! I TAUGHT HAMMIE MANNERS!
REALLY?
WATCH THIS!
BURRRRRP!
'SKUSE ME!
TAA-♫ DAAAA!
SIGH!
KIRKMAN & SCOTT

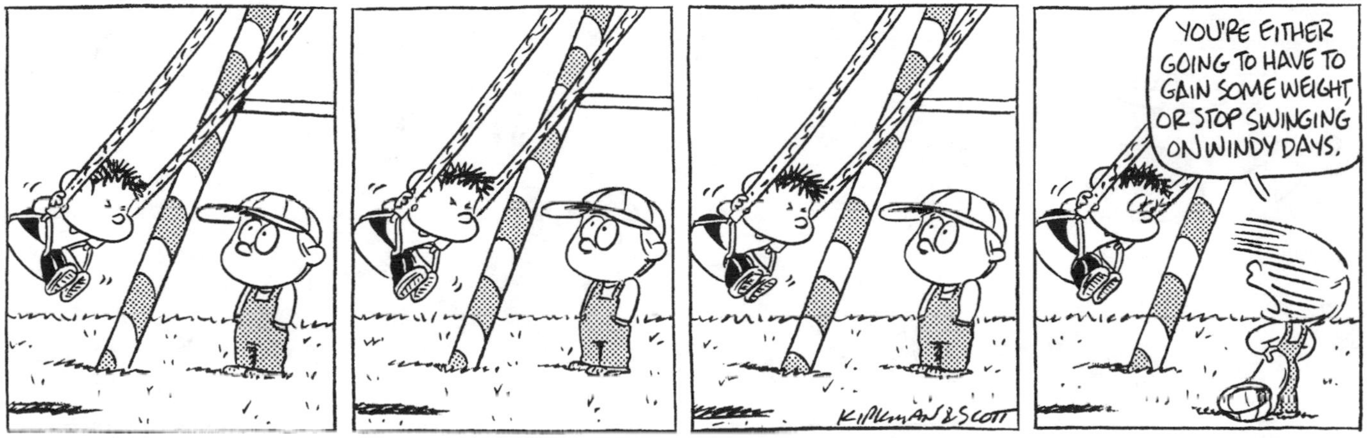
KIRKMAN & SCOTT
YOU'RE EITHER GOING TO HAVE TO GAIN SOME WEIGHT, OR STOP SWINGING ON WINDY DAYS.

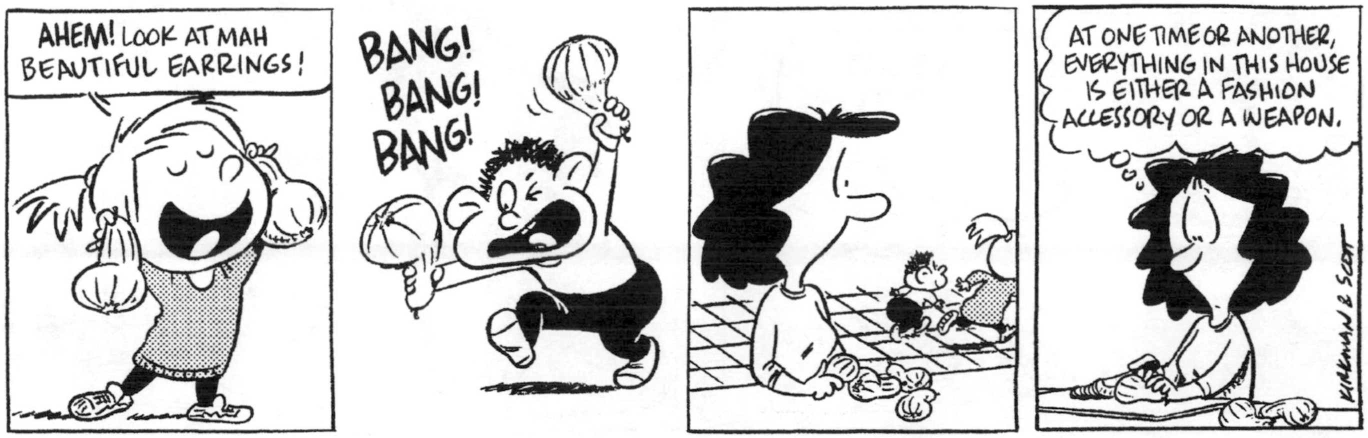
AHEM! LOOK AT MAH BEAUTIFUL EARRINGS!
BANG! BANG! BANG!
AT ONE TIME OR ANOTHER, EVERYTHING IN THIS HOUSE IS EITHER A FASHION ACCESSORY OR A WEAPON.
KIRKMAN & SCOTT

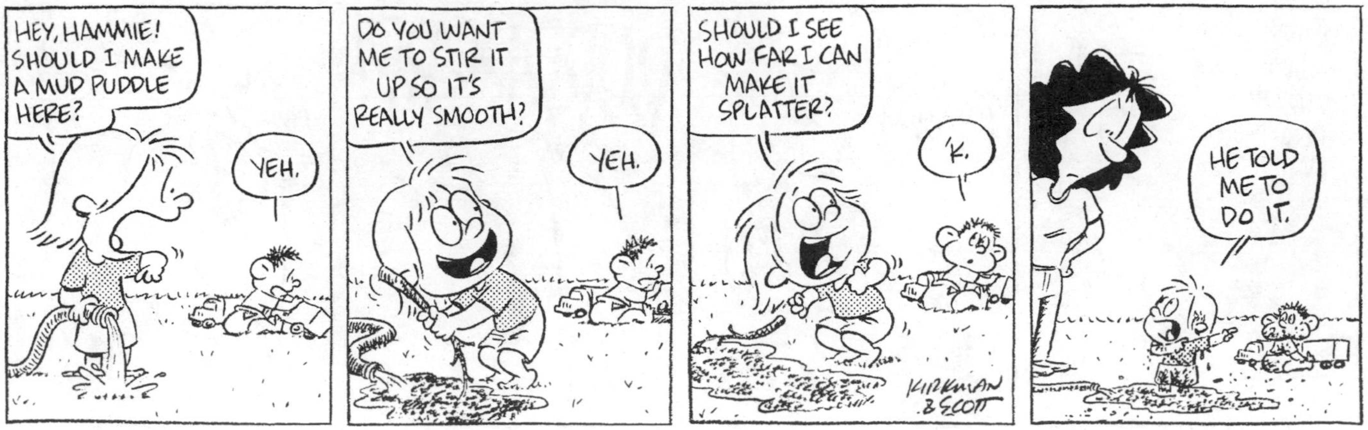
HEY, HAMMIE! SHOULD I MAKE A MUD PUDDLE HERE?
YEH.
DO YOU WANT ME TO STIR IT UP SO IT'S REALLY SMOOTH?
YEH.
SHOULD I SEE HOW FAR I CAN MAKE IT SPLATTER?
'K.
KIRKMAN & SCOTT
HE TOLD ME TO DO IT.

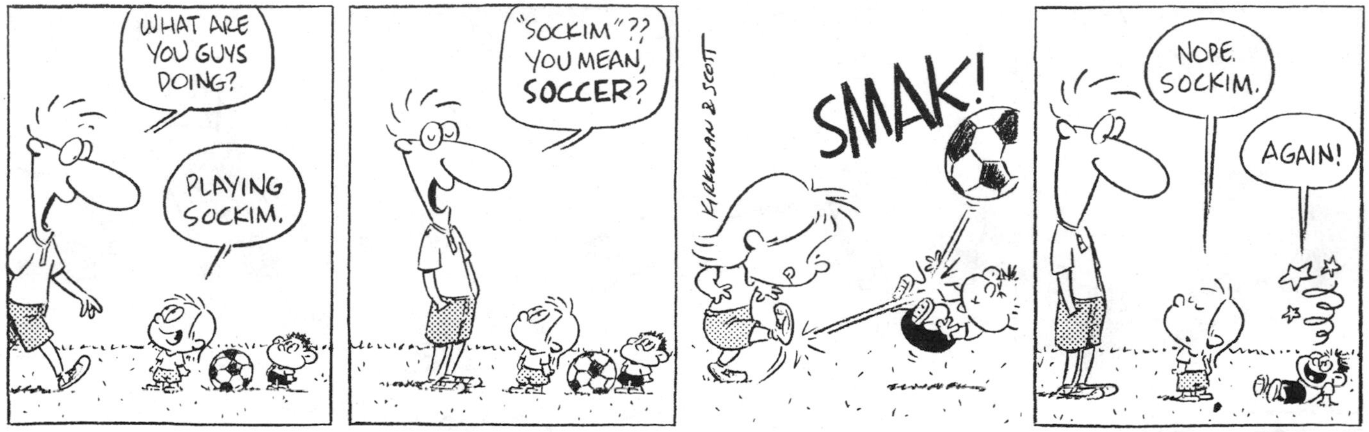
WHAT ARE YOU GUYS DOING?
PLAYING SOCKIM.
"SOCKIM"?? YOU MEAN, SOCCER?
KIRKMAN & SCOTT
SMAK!
NOPE. SOCKIM.
AGAIN!

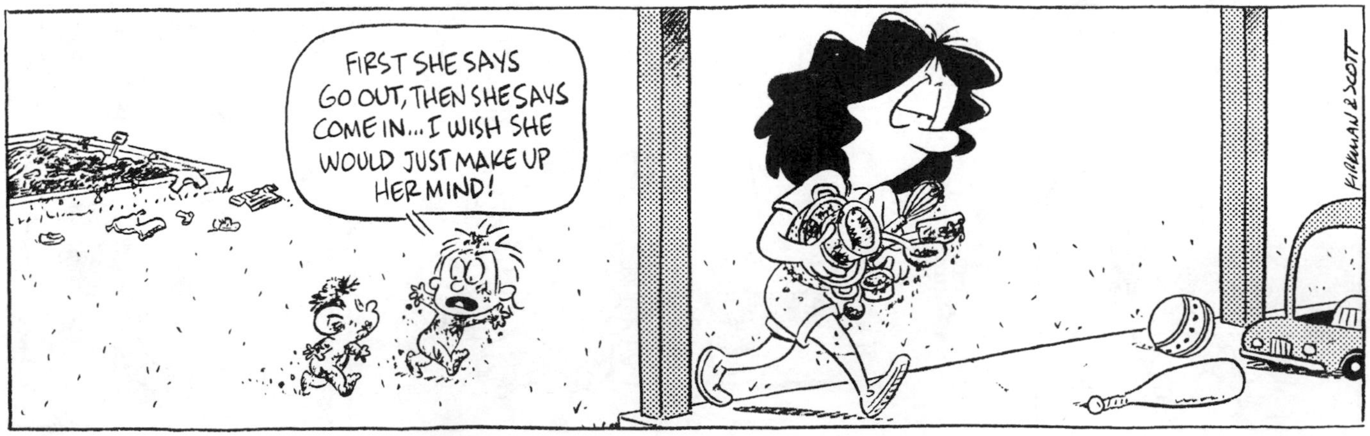
FIRST SHE SAYS GO OUT, THEN SHE SAYS COME IN... I WISH SHE WOULD JUST MAKE UP HER MIND!
KIRKMAN & SCOTT

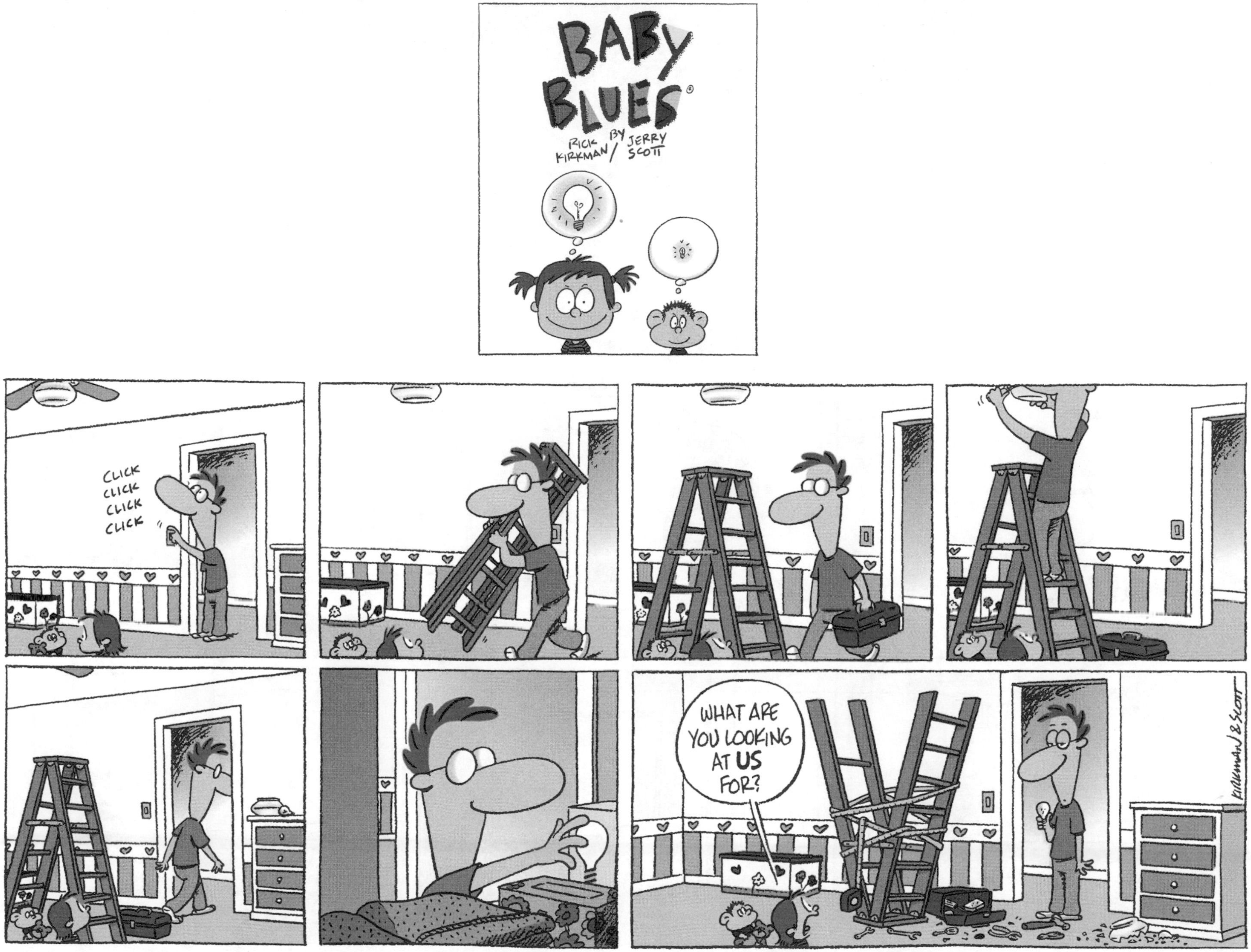
BABY BLUES®
BY RICK KIRKMAN / JERRY SCOTT
CLICK
CLICK
CLICK
CLICK
WHAT ARE YOU LOOKING AT US FOR?
KIRKMAN / & SCOTT

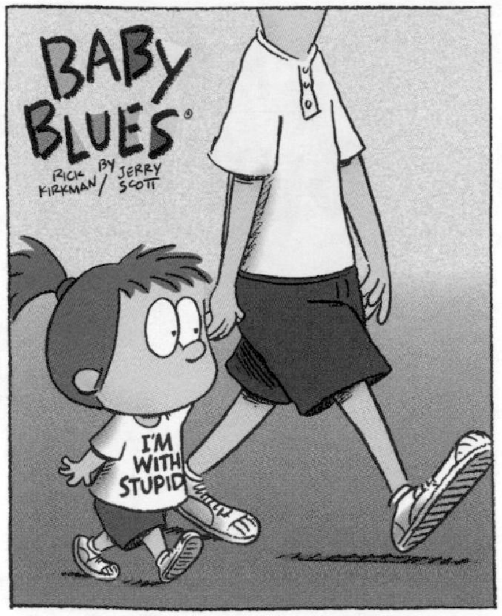
BABY BLUES®
BY RICK KIRKMAN / JERRY SCOTT
I'M WITH STUPID

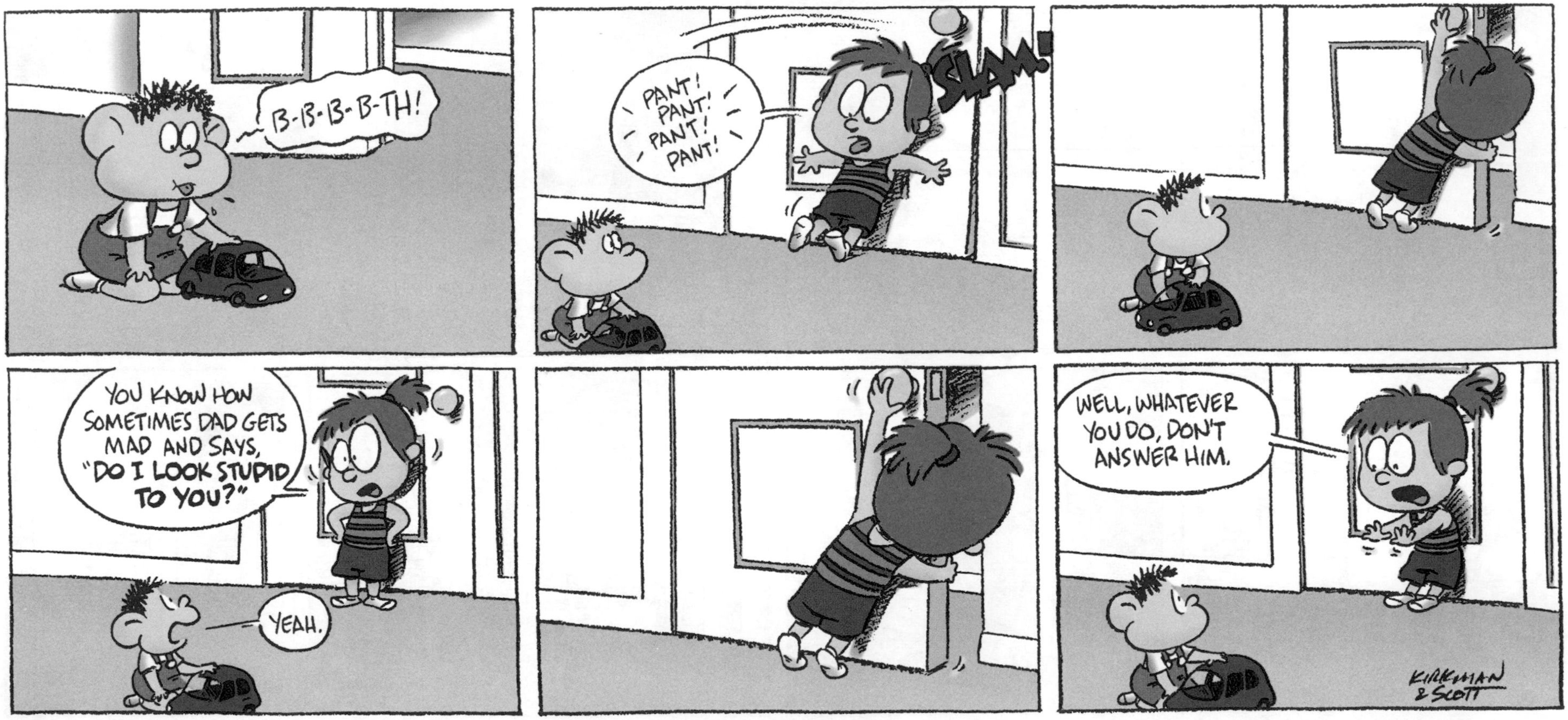
B-B-B-B-TH!
PANT! PANT! PANT! PANT!
SLAM!
YOU KNOW HOW SOMETIMES DAD GETS MAD AND SAYS, "DO I LOOK STUPID TO YOU?"
YEAH.
WELL, WHATEVER YOU DO, DON'T ANSWER HIM.
KIRKMAN & SCOTT

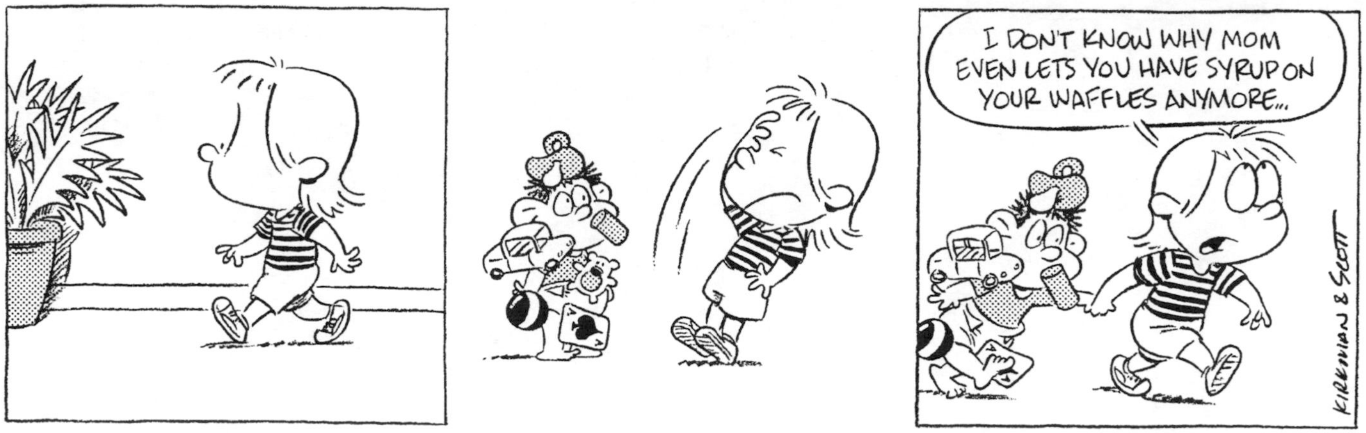
I DON'T KNOW WHY MOM EVEN LETS YOU HAVE SYRUP ON YOUR WAFFLES ANYMORE...
KIRKMAN & SCOTT

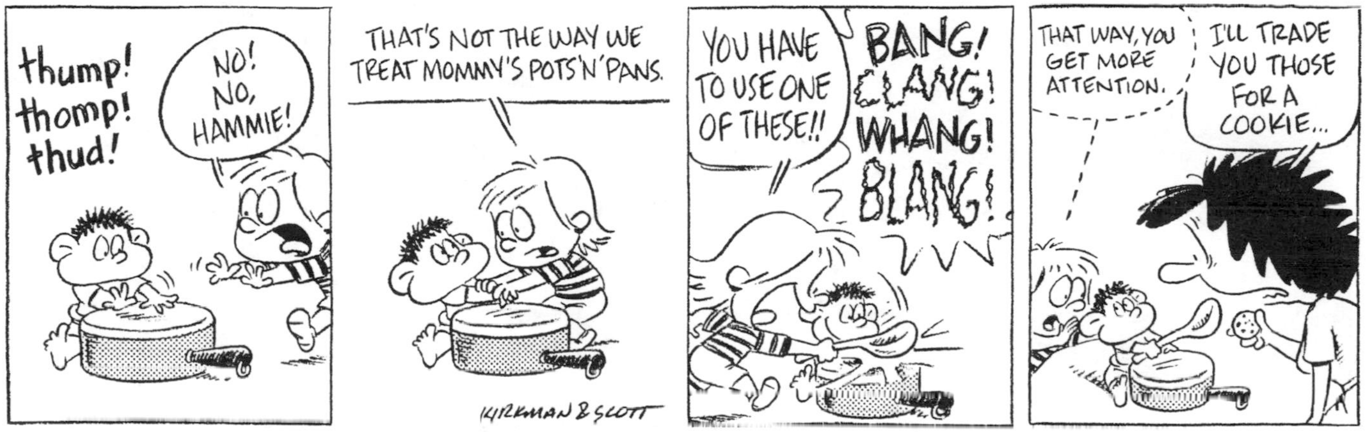
thump! thomp! thud!
NO! NO, HAMMIE!
THAT'S NOT THE WAY WE TREAT MOMMY'S POTS'N'PANS.
KIRKMAN & SCOTT
YOU HAVE TO USE ONE OF THESE!!
BANG! CLANG! WHANG! BLANG!
THAT WAY, YOU GET MORE ATTENTION.
I'LL TRADE YOU THOSE FOR A COOKIE...

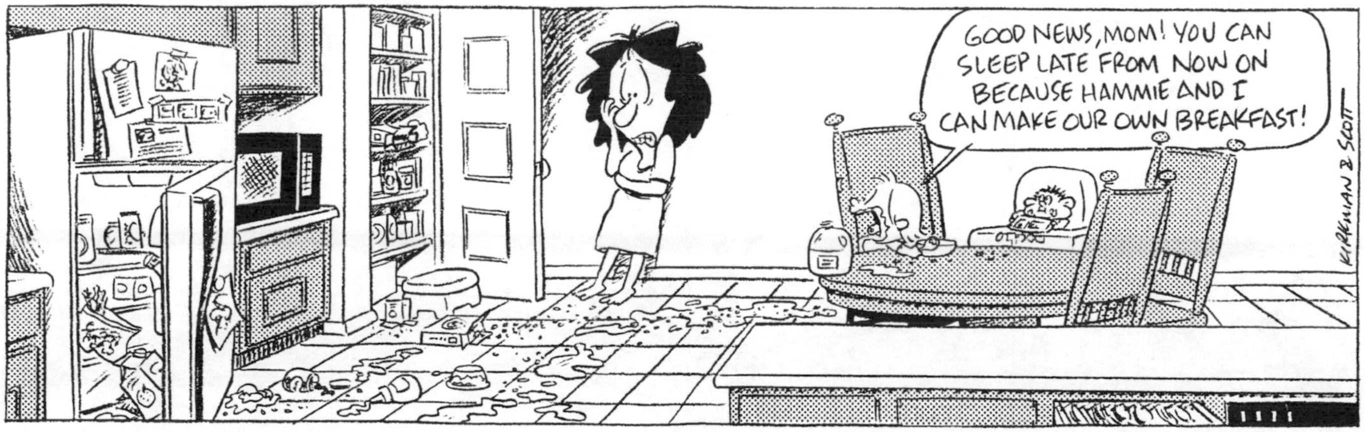
GOOD NEWS, MOM! YOU CAN SLEEP LATE FROM NOW ON BECAUSE HAMMIE AND I CAN MAKE OUR OWN BREAKFAST!
KIRKMAN & SCOTT

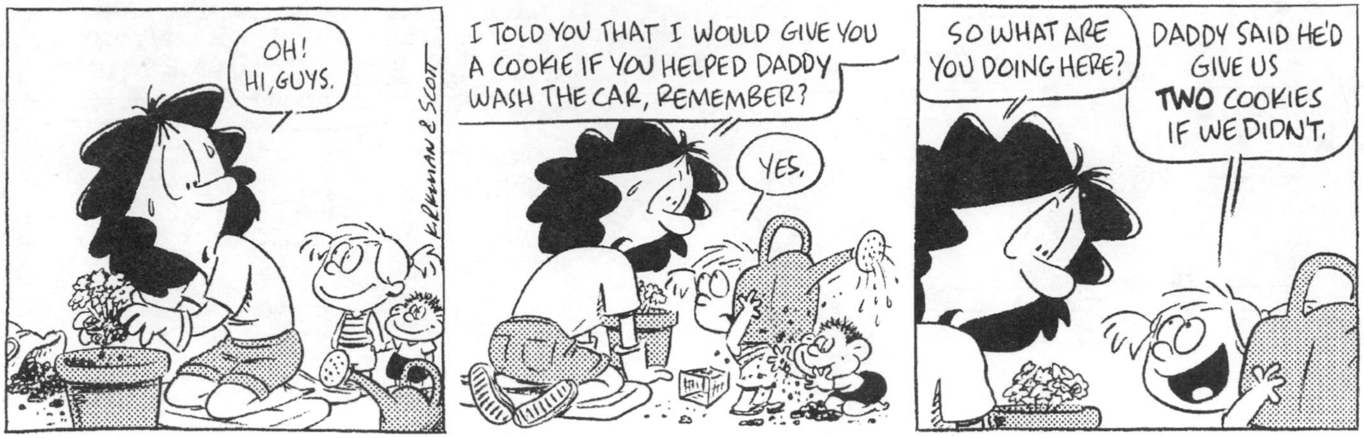
OH! HI, GUYS.
I TOLD YOU THAT I WOULD GIVE YOU A COOKIE IF YOU HELPED DADDY WASH THE CAR, REMEMBER?
YES.
SO WHAT ARE YOU DOING HERE?
DADDY SAID HE'D GIVE US **TWO** COOKIES IF WE DIDN'T.

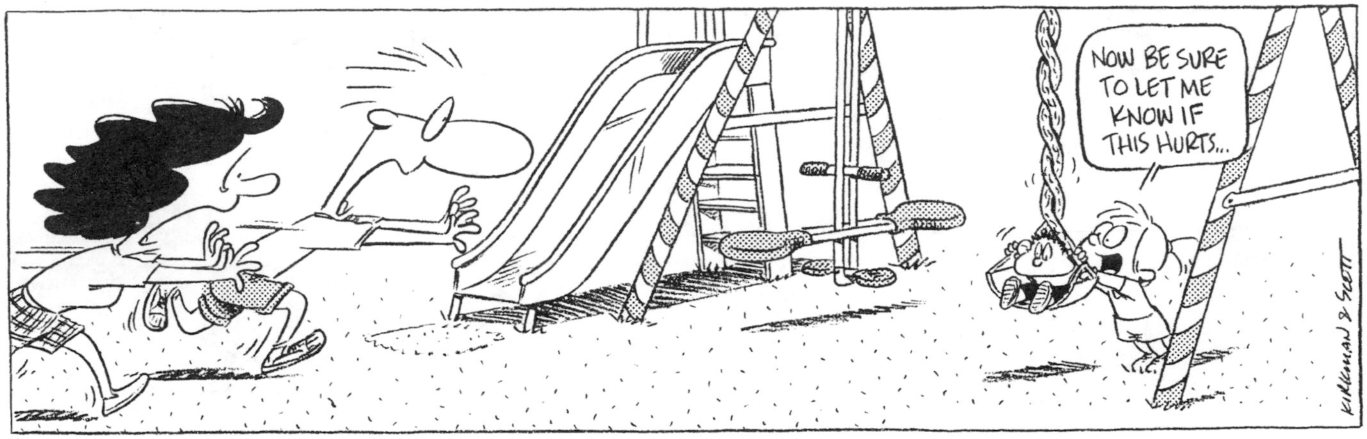
NOW BE SURE TO LET ME KNOW IF THIS HURTS...

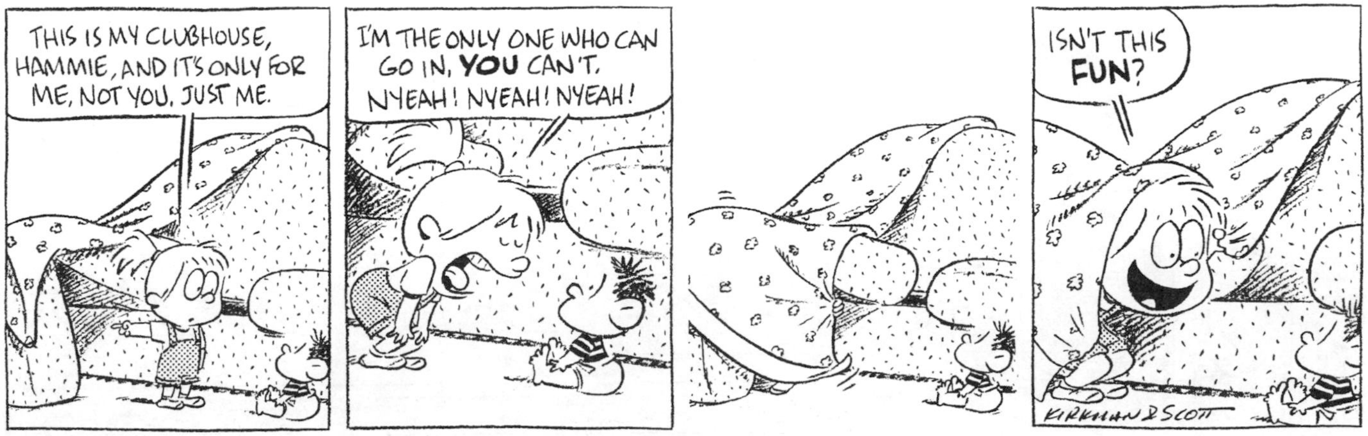
THIS IS MY CLUBHOUSE, HAMMIE, AND IT'S ONLY FOR ME, NOT YOU, JUST ME.
I'M THE ONLY ONE WHO CAN GO IN, **YOU** CAN'T. NYEAH! NYEAH! NYEAH!
ISN'T THIS **FUN**?

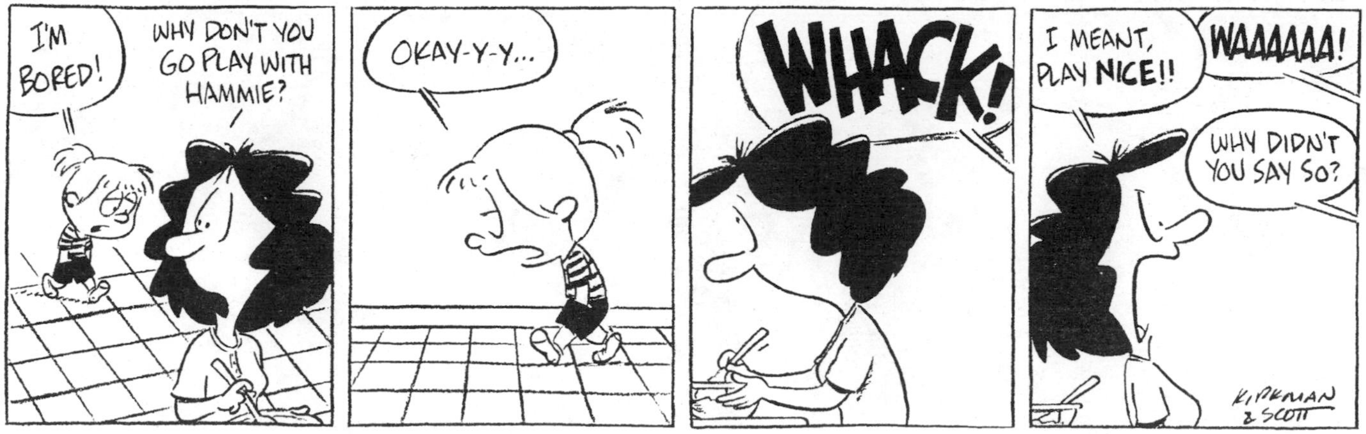
I'M BORED!
WHY DON'T YOU GO PLAY WITH HAMMIE?
OKAY-Y-Y...
WHACK!
I MEANT, PLAY **NICE**!!
WAAAAAAA!
WHY DIDN'T YOU SAY SO?
KIRKMAN & SCOTT

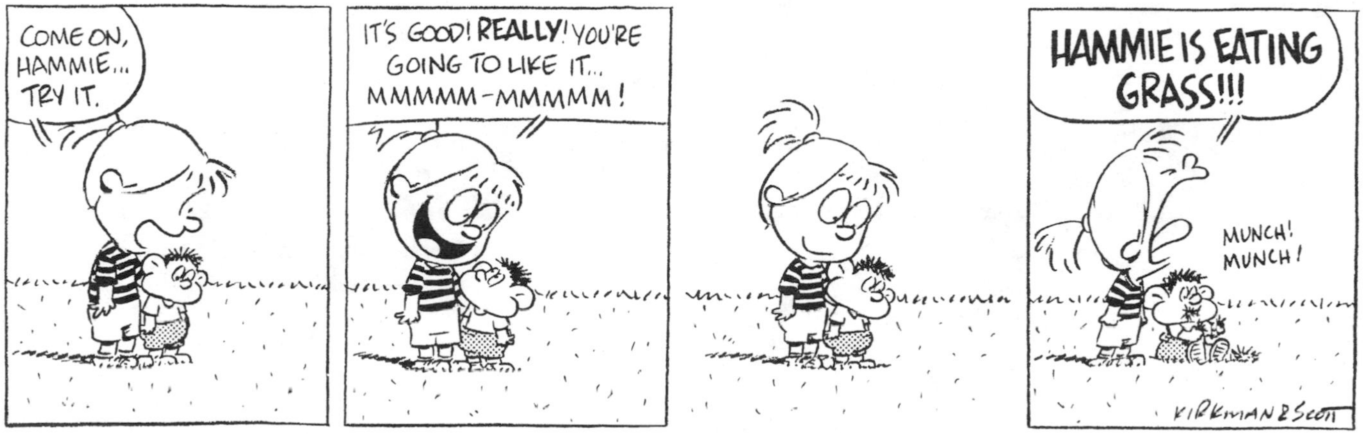
COME ON, HAMMIE... TRY IT.
IT'S GOOD! **REALLY**! YOU'RE GOING TO LIKE IT... MMMMM-MMMMM!
HAMMIE IS EATING GRASS!!!
MUNCH! MUNCH!
KIRKMAN & SCOTT

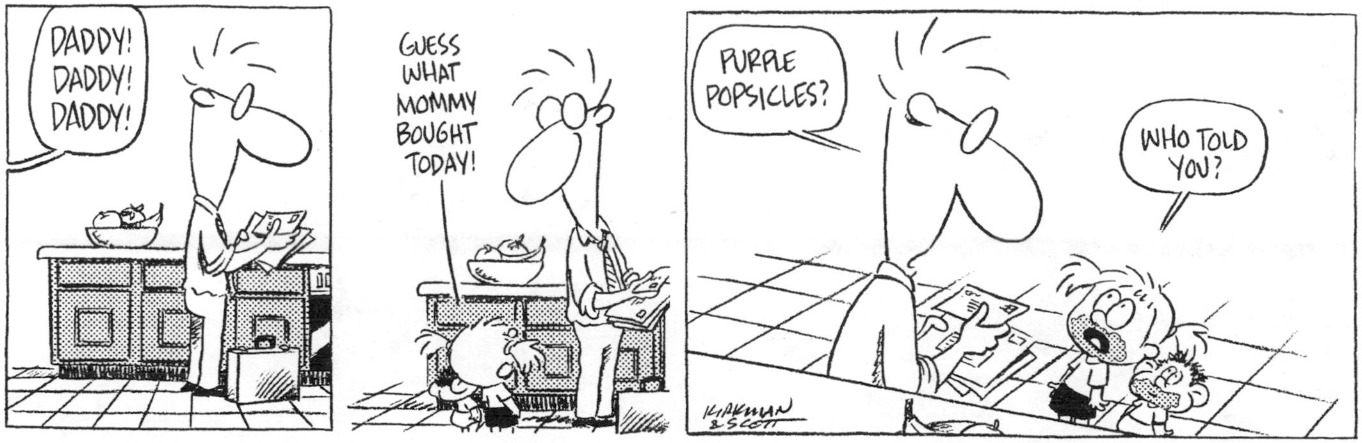
DADDY! DADDY! DADDY!
GUESS WHAT MOMMY BOUGHT TODAY!
PURPLE POPSICLES?
WHO TOLD YOU?
KIRKMAN & SCOTT

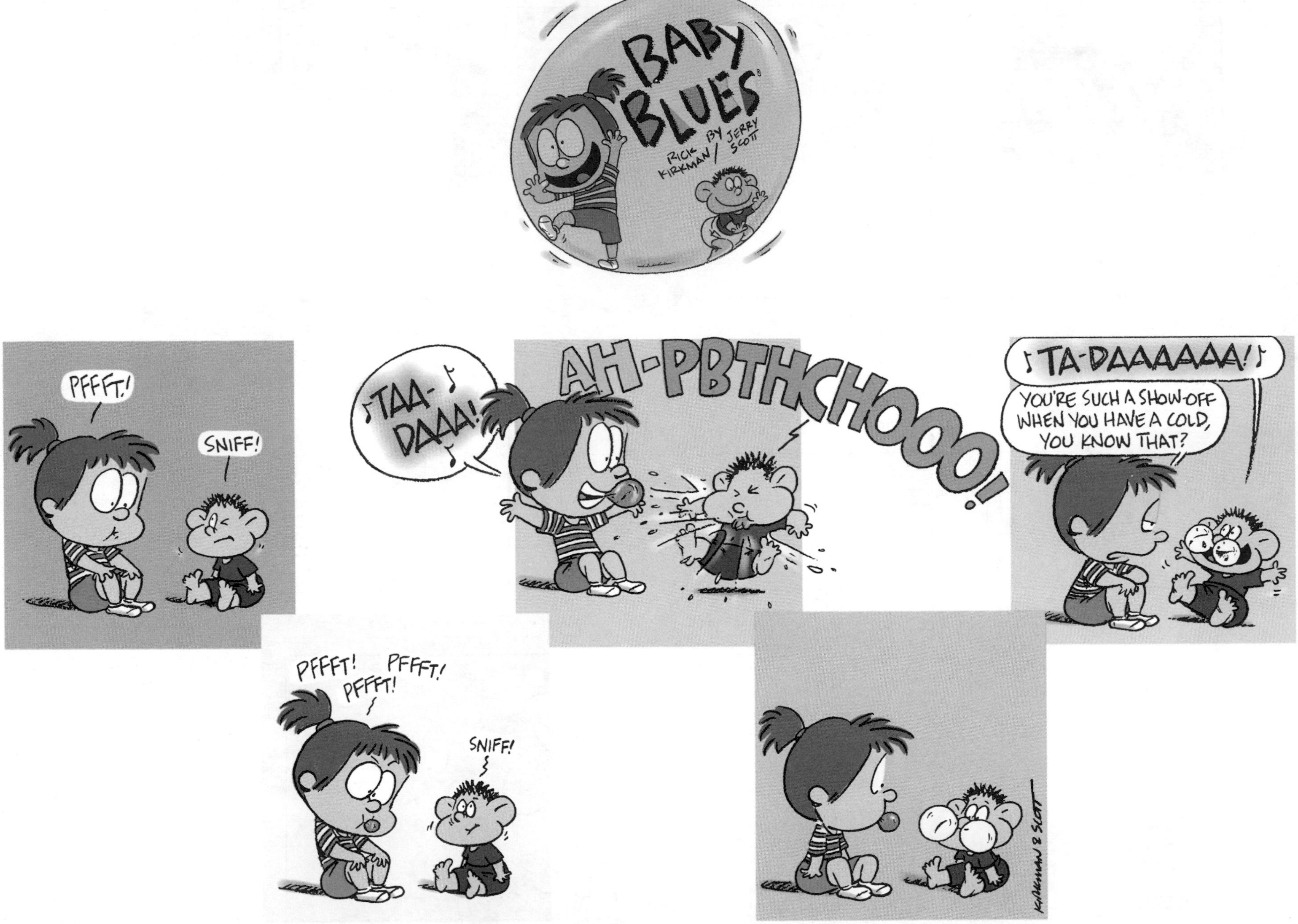
BABY BLUES®
BY RICK KIRKMAN / JERRY SCOTT
PFFFT!
SNIFF!
PFFFT! PFFFT! PFFFT!
SNIFF!
♪TAA-DAAA!♪
AH-PBTHCHOOOO!
♪TA-DAAAAAA!♪
YOU'RE SUCH A SHOW-OFF WHEN YOU HAVE A COLD, YOU KNOW THAT?
KIRKMAN & SCOTT

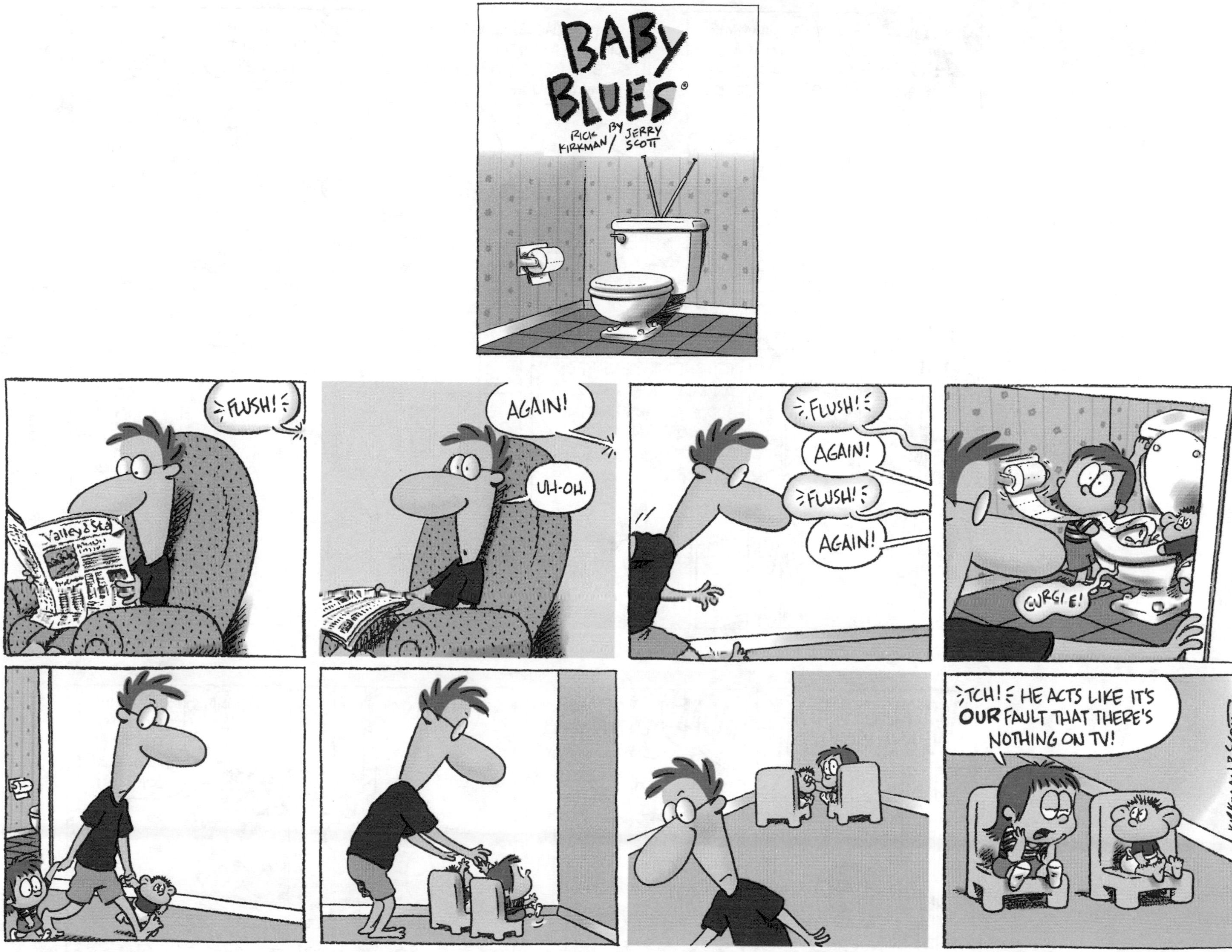
BABY BLUES®
BY RICK KIRKMAN / JERRY SCOTT
FLUSH!
AGAIN!
UH-OH.
FLUSH!
AGAIN!
FLUSH!
AGAIN!
GURGLE!
TCH! HE ACTS LIKE IT'S OUR FAULT THAT THERE'S NOTHING ON TV!
KIRKMAN & SCOTT

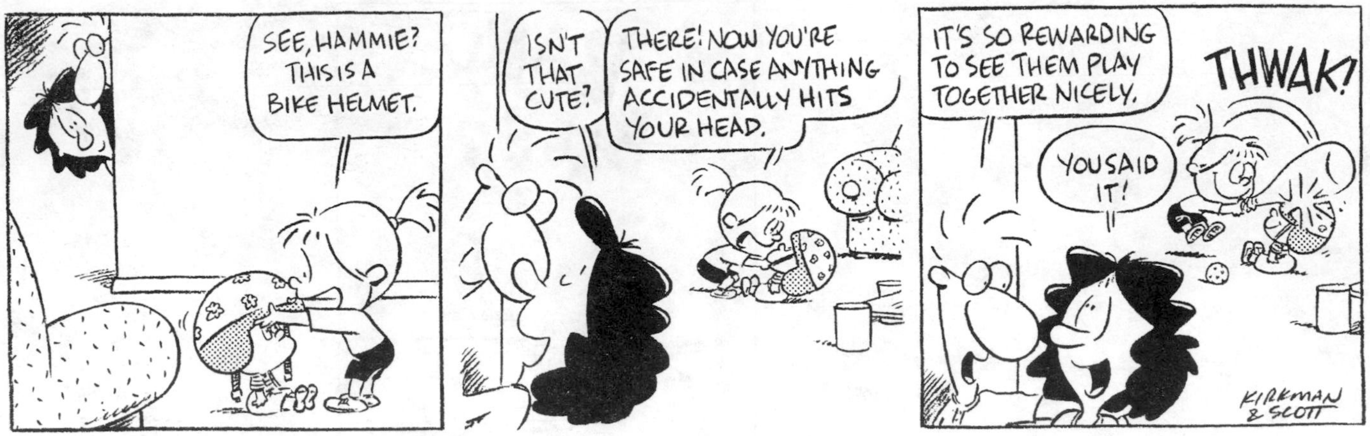
SEE, HAMMIE? THIS IS A BIKE HELMET.
ISN'T THAT CUTE?
THERE! NOW YOU'RE SAFE IN CASE ANYTHING ACCIDENTALLY HITS YOUR HEAD.
IT'S SO REWARDING TO SEE THEM PLAY TOGETHER NICELY.
YOU SAID IT!
THWAK!
KIRKMAN & SCOTT

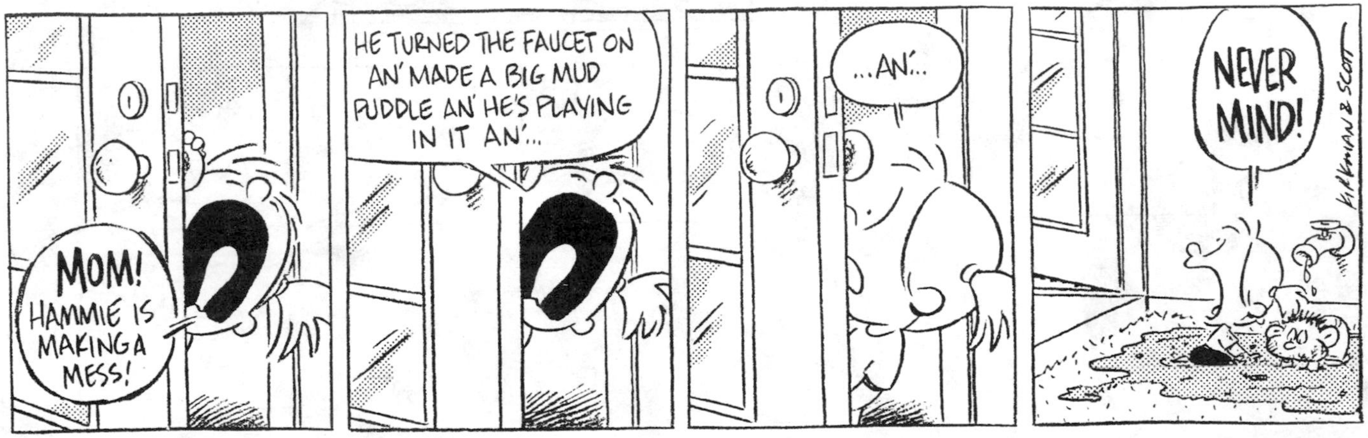
MOM! HAMMIE IS MAKING A MESS!
HE TURNED THE FAUCET ON AN' MADE A BIG MUD PUDDLE AN' HE'S PLAYING IN IT AN'...
...AN'...
NEVER MIND!
KIRKMAN & SCOTT

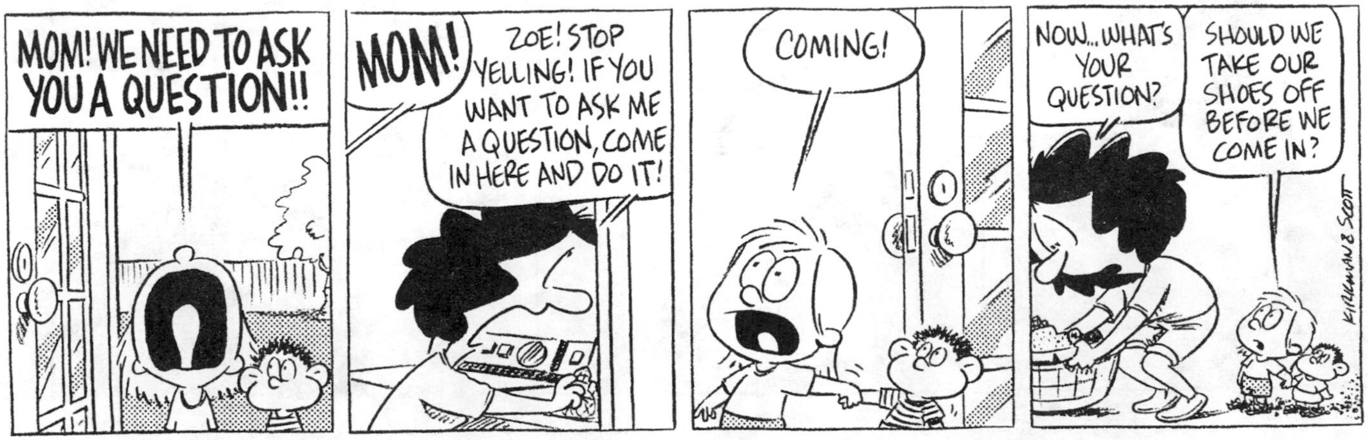
MOM! WE NEED TO ASK YOU A QUESTION!!
MOM!
ZOE! STOP YELLING! IF YOU WANT TO ASK ME A QUESTION, COME IN HERE AND DO IT!
COMING!
NOW... WHAT'S YOUR QUESTION?
SHOULD WE TAKE OUR SHOES OFF BEFORE WE COME IN?
KIRKMAN & SCOTT

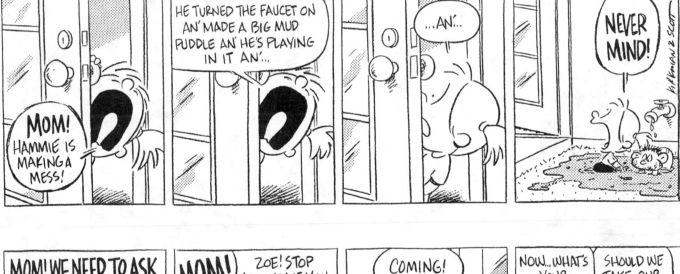

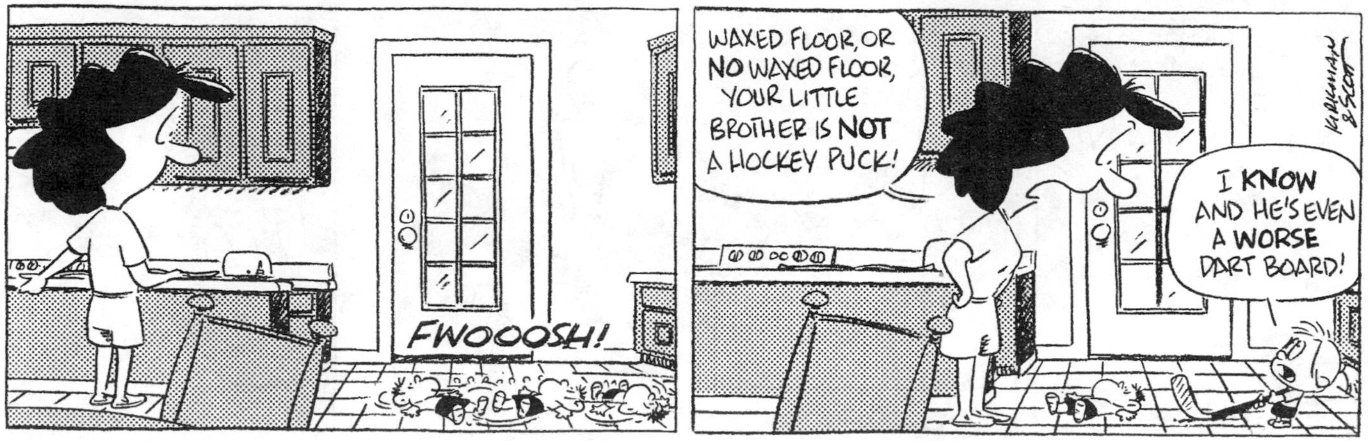
FWOOOSH!
WAXED FLOOR, OR **NO** WAXED FLOOR, YOUR LITTLE BROTHER IS **NOT** A HOCKEY PUCK!
I **KNOW** AND HE'S EVEN A **WORSE** DART BOARD!
KIRKMAN & SCOTT

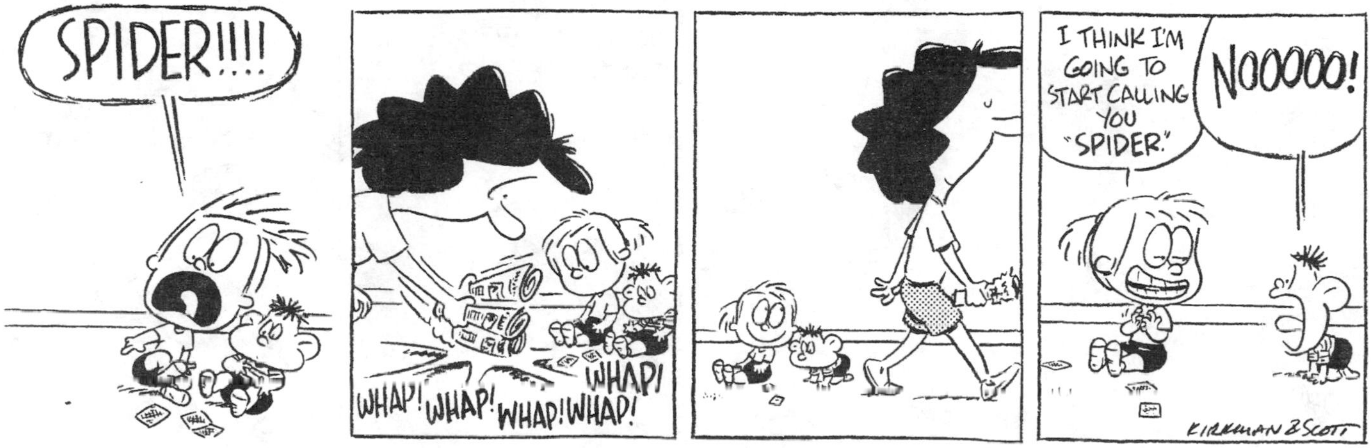
SPIDER!!!!!
WHAP! WHAP! WHAP! WHAP! WHAP!
I THINK I'M GOING TO START CALLING YOU "SPIDER."
NOOOOO!
KIRKMAN & SCOTT

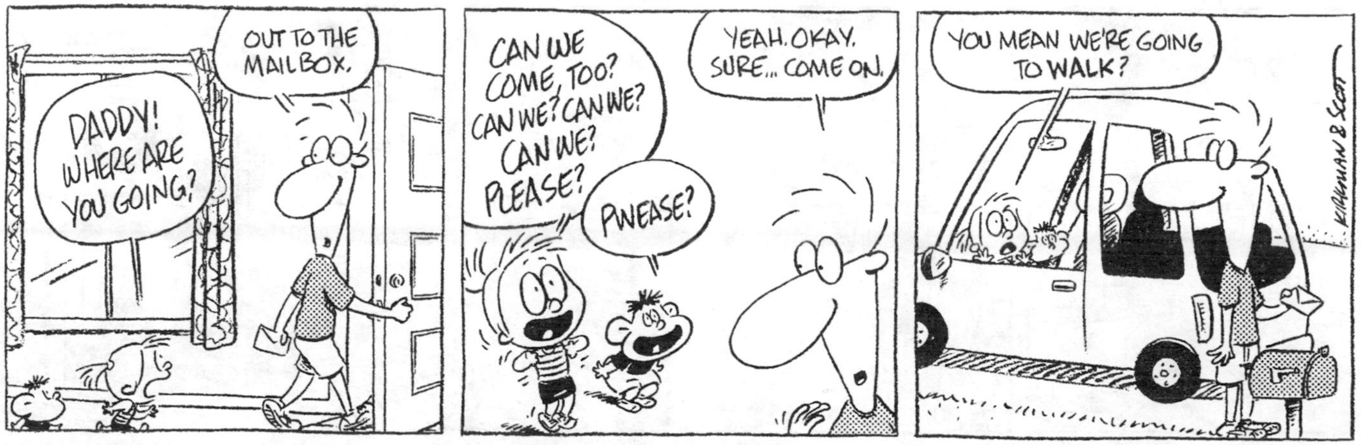
DADDY! WHERE ARE YOU GOING?
OUT TO THE MAILBOX.
CAN WE COME, TOO? CAN WE? CAN WE? CAN WE? PLEASE?
PWEASE?
YEAH. OKAY. SURE... COME ON.
YOU MEAN WE'RE GOING TO **WALK**?
KIRKMAN & SCOTT

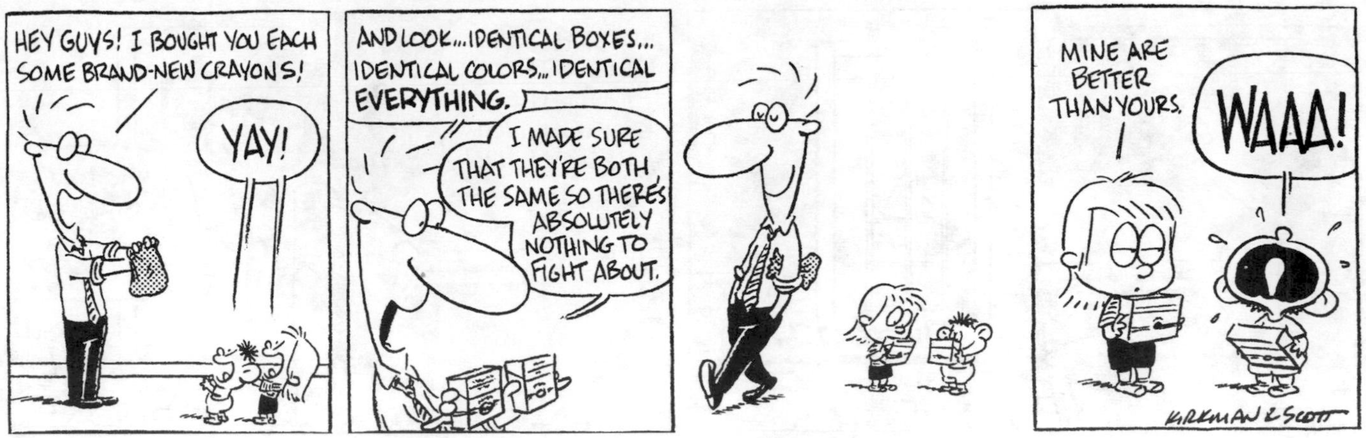
HEY GUYS! I BOUGHT YOU EACH SOME BRAND-NEW CRAYONS!
YAY!
AND LOOK... IDENTICAL BOXES... IDENTICAL COLORS... IDENTICAL **EVERYTHING.**
I MADE SURE THAT THEY'RE BOTH THE SAME SO THERE'S ABSOLUTELY NOTHING TO FIGHT ABOUT.
MINE ARE BETTER THAN YOURS.
WAAA!
KIRKMAN & SCOTT

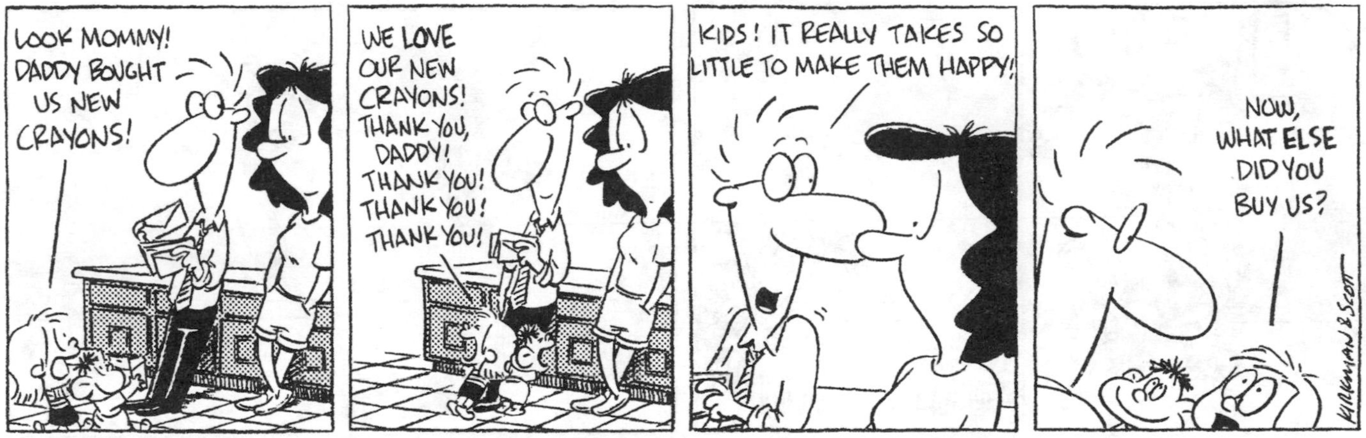
LOOK MOMMY! DADDY BOUGHT US NEW CRAYONS!
WE **LOVE** OUR NEW CRAYONS! THANK YOU, DADDY! THANK YOU! THANK YOU! THANK YOU!
KIDS! IT REALLY TAKES SO LITTLE TO MAKE THEM HAPPY!
NOW, WHAT **ELSE** DID YOU BUY US?
KIRKMAN & SCOTT

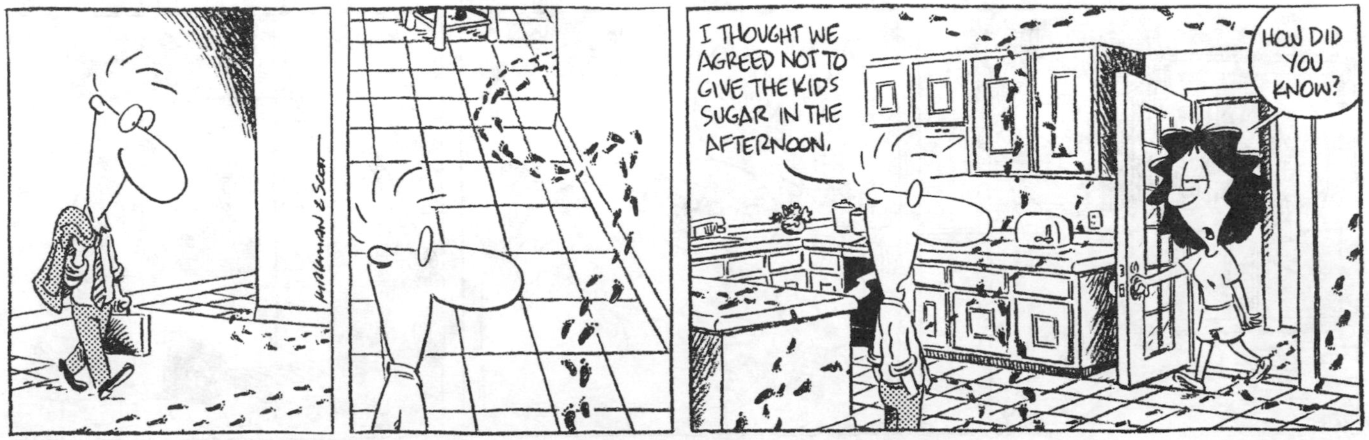
KIRKMAN & SCOTT
I THOUGHT WE AGREED NOT TO GIVE THE KIDS SUGAR IN THE AFTERNOON.
HOW DID YOU KNOW?

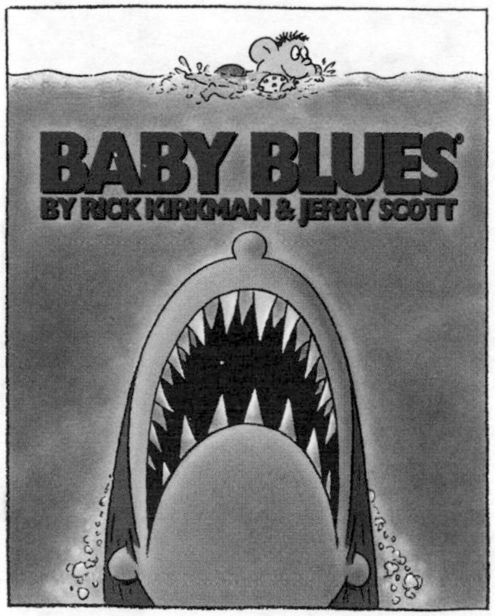
BABY BLUES®
BY RICK KIRKMAN & JERRY SCOTT

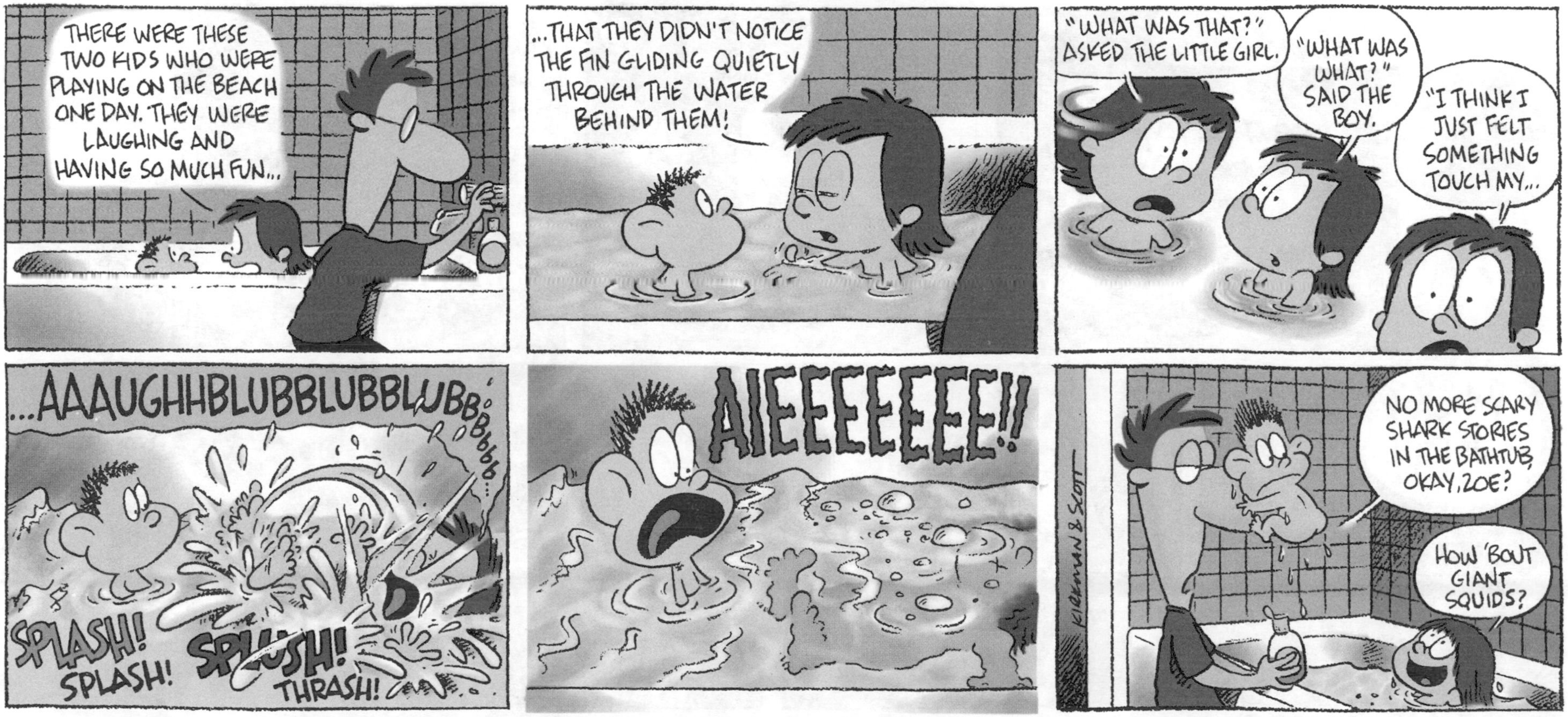
THERE WERE THESE TWO KIDS WHO WERE PLAYING ON THE BEACH ONE DAY. THEY WERE LAUGHING AND HAVING SO MUCH FUN...
...THAT THEY DIDN'T NOTICE THE FIN GLIDING QUIETLY THROUGH THE WATER BEHIND THEM!
"WHAT WAS THAT?" ASKED THE LITTLE GIRL.
"WHAT WAS WHAT?" SAID THE BOY.
"I THINK I JUST FELT SOMETHING TOUCH MY...
...AAAUGHHBLUBBLUBBLUBBBbbb...
SPLASH! SPLASH! SPLUSH! THRASH!
AIEEEEEEEE!!
KIRKMAN & SCOTT
NO MORE SCARY SHARK STORIES IN THE BATHTUB, OKAY, ZOE?
HOW 'BOUT GIANT SQUIDS?

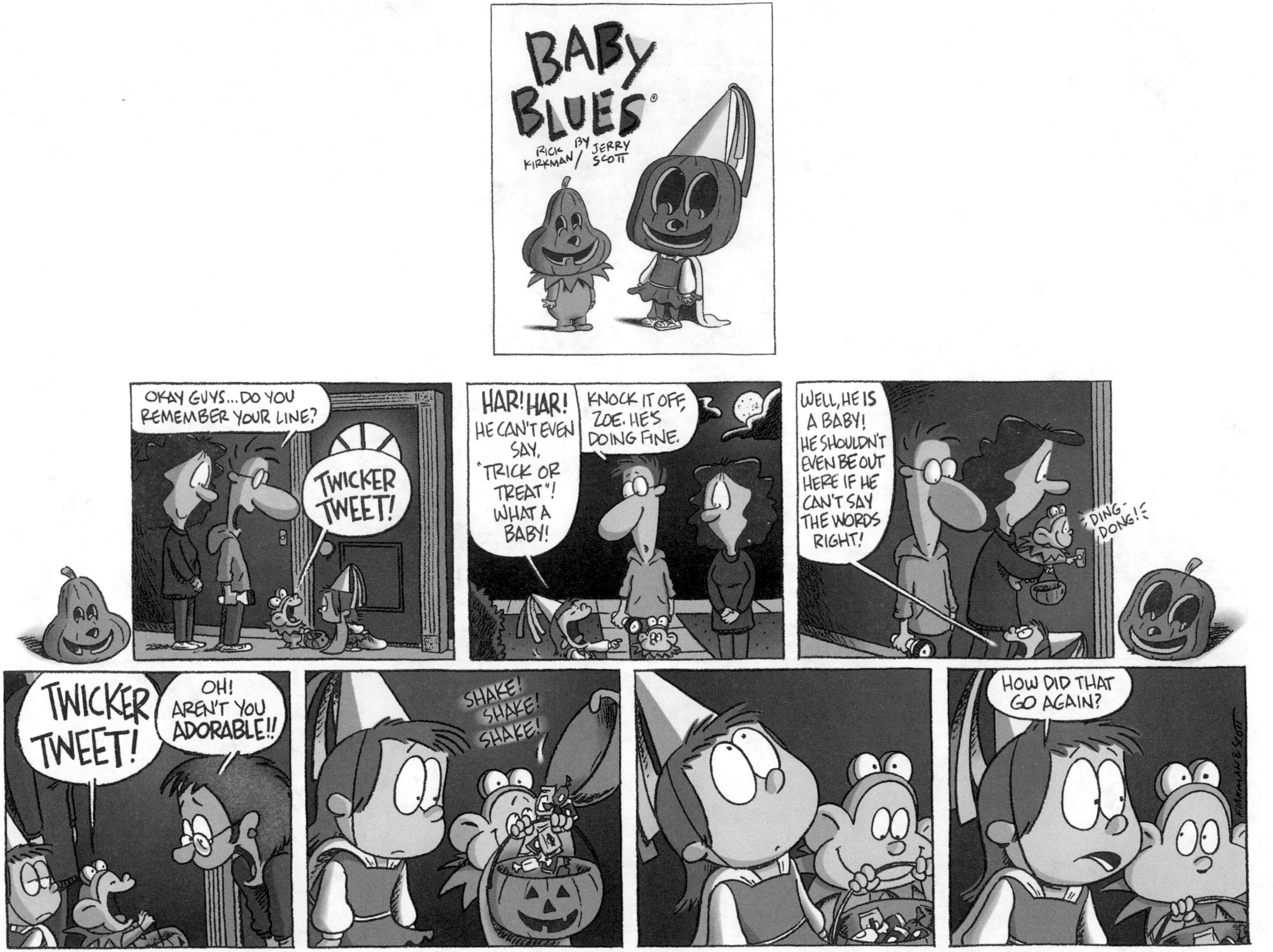
BABY BLUES®
RICK KIRKMAN / BY JERRY SCOTT
OKAY GUYS... DO YOU REMEMBER YOUR LINE?
TWICKER TWEET!
HAR! HAR! HE CAN'T EVEN SAY, "TRICK OR TREAT"! WHAT A BABY!
KNOCK IT OFF, ZOE. HE'S DOING FINE.
WELL, HE IS A BABY! HE SHOULDN'T EVEN BE OUT HERE IF HE CAN'T SAY THE WORDS RIGHT!
DING-DONG!
TWICKER TWEET!
OH! AREN'T YOU ADORABLE!!
SHAKE! SHAKE! SHAKE!
HOW DID THAT GO AGAIN?

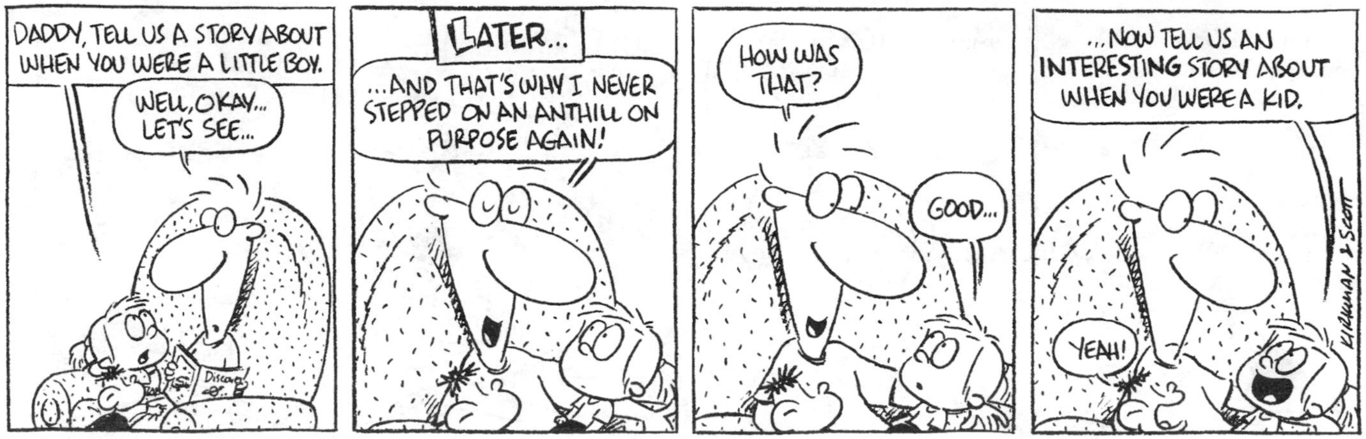
DADDY, TELL US A STORY ABOUT WHEN YOU WERE A LITTLE BOY.
WELL, OKAY... LET'S SEE...
LATER...
...AND THAT'S WHY I NEVER STEPPED ON AN ANTHILL ON PURPOSE AGAIN!
HOW WAS THAT?
GOOD...
...NOW TELL US AN INTERESTING STORY ABOUT WHEN YOU WERE A KID.
YEAH!
KIRKMAN & SCOTT

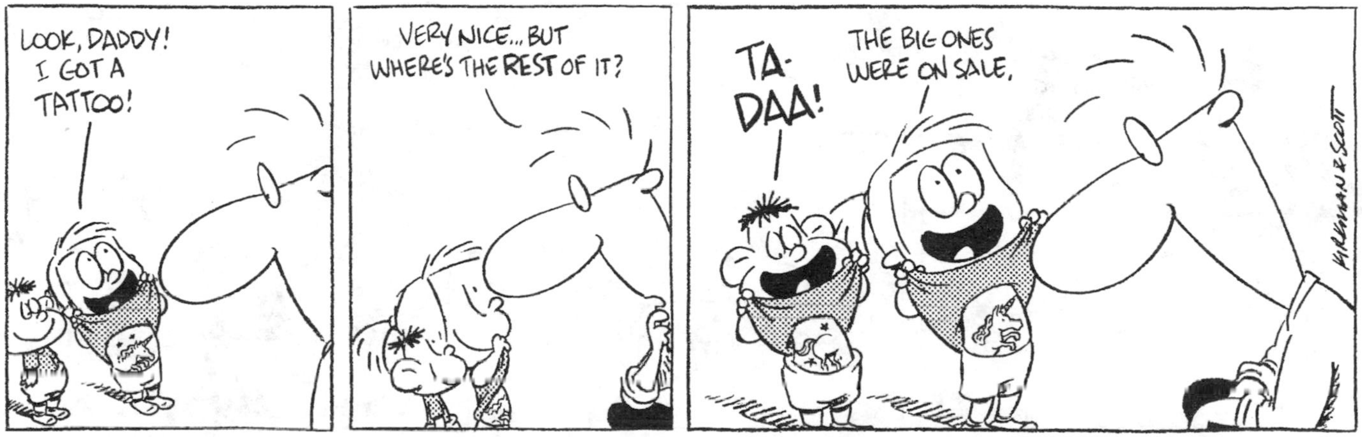
LOOK, DADDY! I GOT A TATTOO!
VERY NICE... BUT WHERE'S THE REST OF IT?
TA-DAA!
THE BIG ONES WERE ON SALE.
KIRKMAN & SCOTT

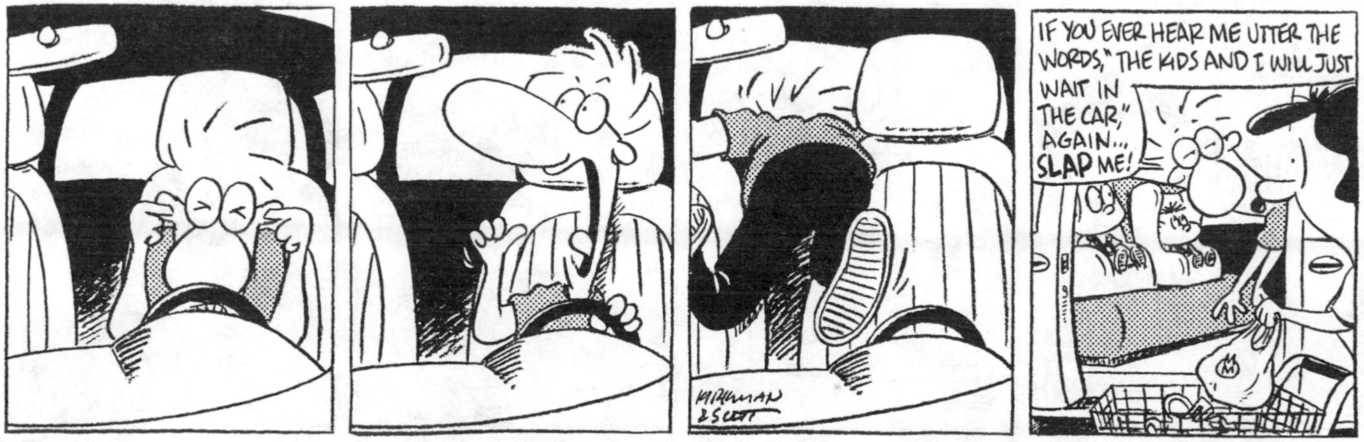
KIRKMAN & SCOTT
IF YOU EVER HEAR ME UTTER THE WORDS, "THE KIDS AND I WILL JUST WAIT IN THE CAR," AGAIN... SLAP ME!

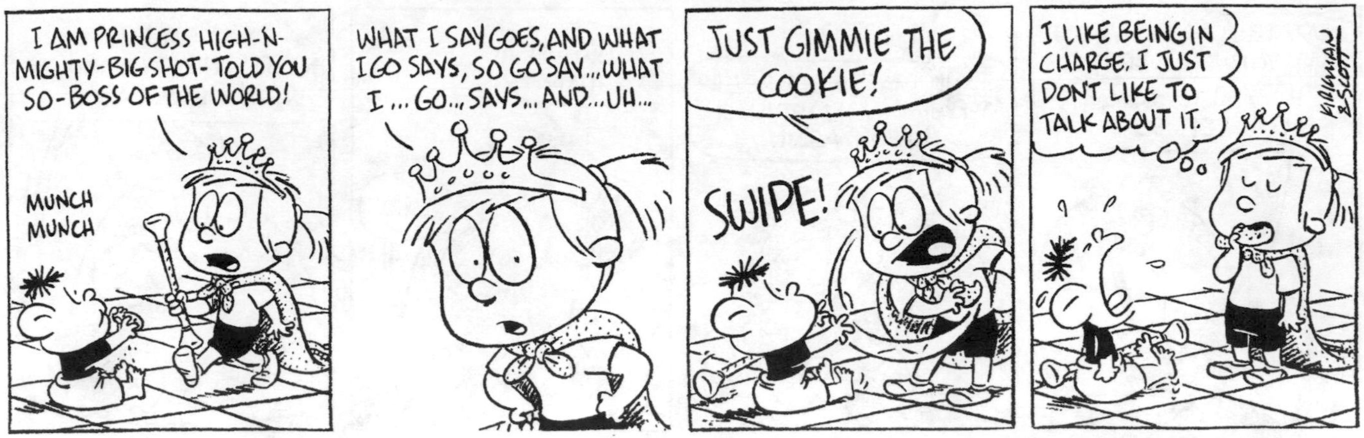
I AM PRINCESS HIGH-N-MIGHTY-BIG SHOT-TOLD YOU SO-BOSS OF THE WORLD!
MUNCH MUNCH
WHAT I SAY GOES, AND WHAT I GO SAYS, SO GO SAY... WHAT I... GO... SAYS... AND... UH...
JUST GIMMIE THE COOKIE!
SWIPE!
I LIKE BEING IN CHARGE. I JUST DON'T LIKE TO TALK ABOUT IT.
KIRKMAN & SCOTT

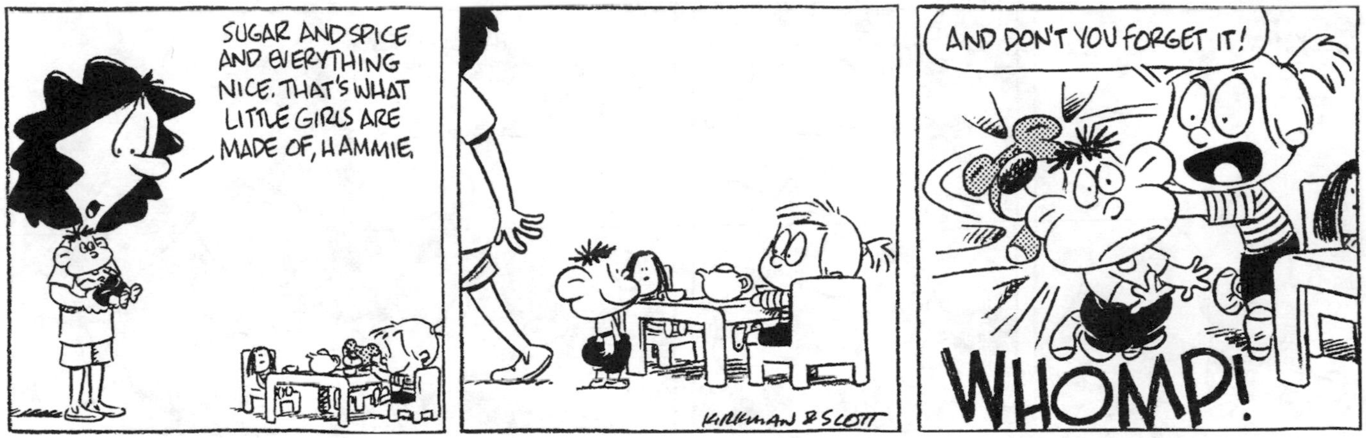
SUGAR AND SPICE AND EVERYTHING NICE. THAT'S WHAT LITTLE GIRLS ARE MADE OF, HAMMIE.
KIRKMAN & SCOTT
AND DON'T YOU FORGET IT!
WHOMP!

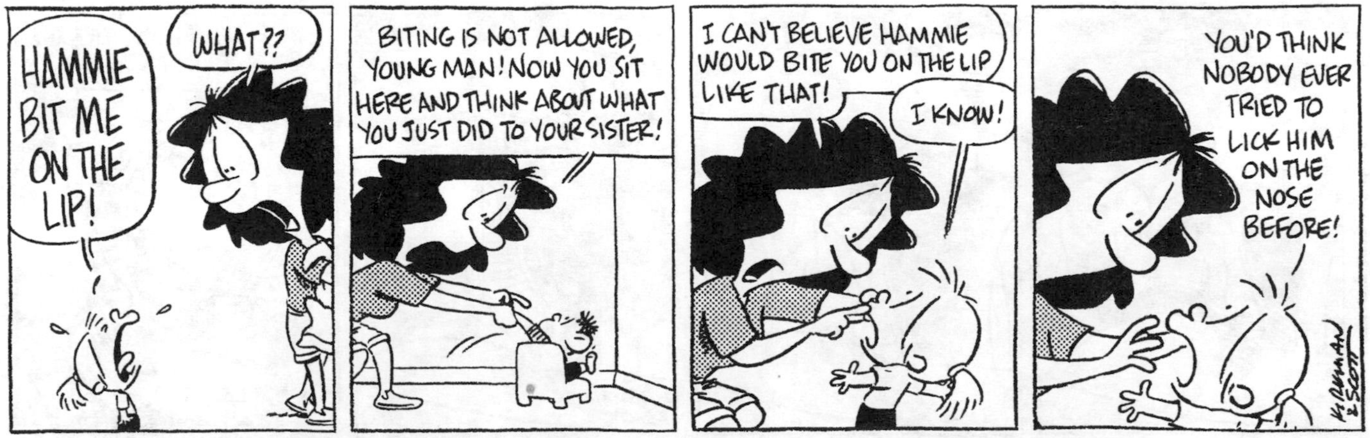
HAMMIE BIT ME ON THE LIP!
WHAT??
BITING IS NOT ALLOWED, YOUNG MAN! NOW YOU SIT HERE AND THINK ABOUT WHAT YOU JUST DID TO YOUR SISTER!
I CAN'T BELIEVE HAMMIE WOULD BITE YOU ON THE LIP LIKE THAT!
I KNOW!
YOU'D THINK NOBODY EVER TRIED TO LICK HIM ON THE NOSE BEFORE!
KIRKMAN & SCOTT

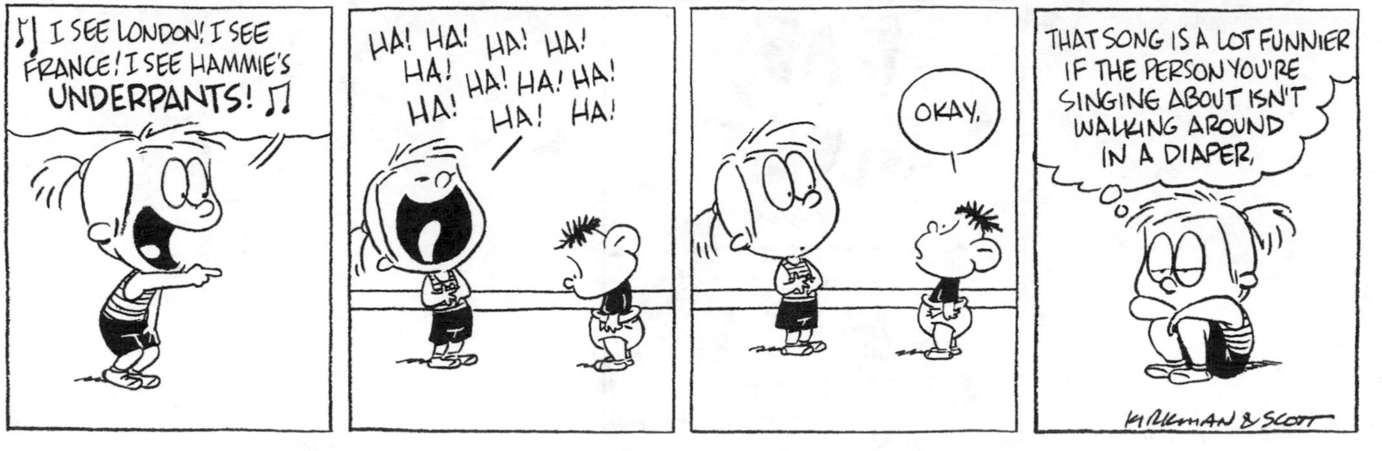
I SEE LONDON! I SEE FRANCE! I SEE HAMMIE'S UNDERPANTS!
HA! HA! HA! HA! HA! HA! HA! HA! HA! HA! HA! HA!
OKAY.
THAT SONG IS A LOT FUNNIER IF THE PERSON YOU'RE SINGING ABOUT ISN'T WALKING AROUND IN A DIAPER.
KIRKMAN & SCOTT

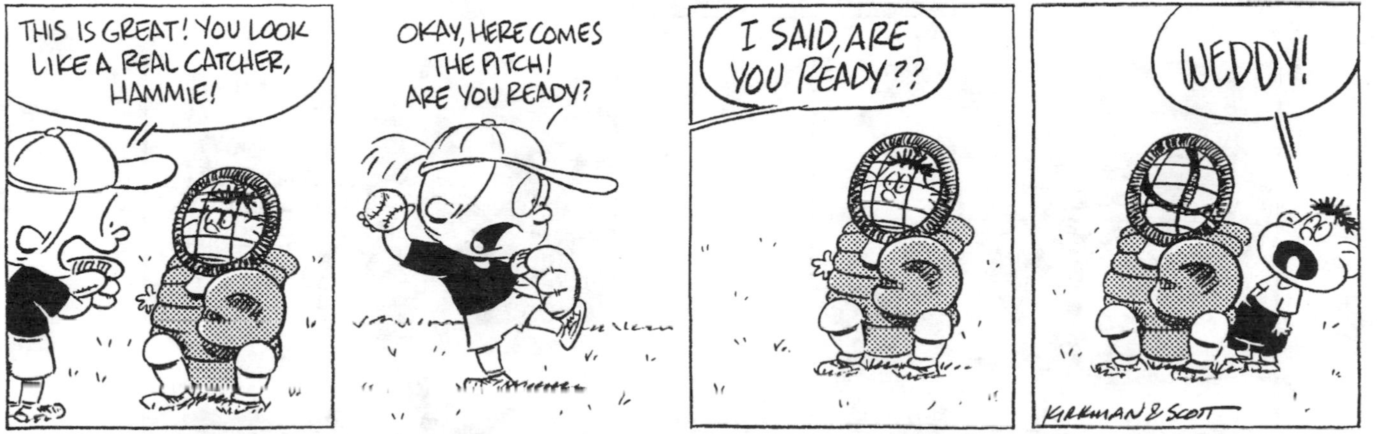
THIS IS GREAT! YOU LOOK LIKE A REAL CATCHER, HAMMIE!
OKAY, HERE COMES THE PITCH! ARE YOU READY?
I SAID, ARE YOU READY??
WEDDY!
KIRKMAN & SCOTT

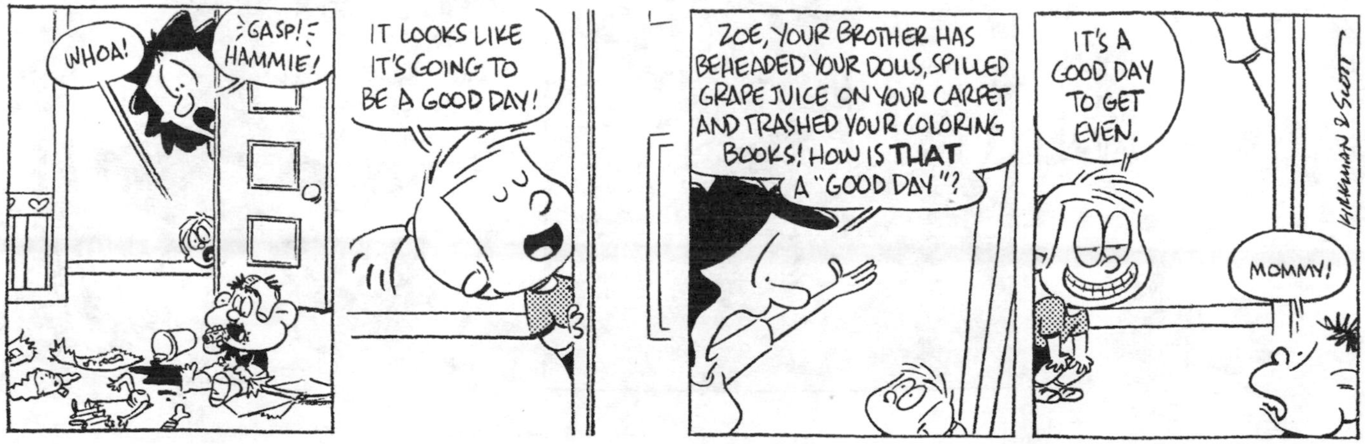
WHOA!
GASP! HAMMIE!
IT LOOKS LIKE IT'S GOING TO BE A GOOD DAY!
ZOE, YOUR BROTHER HAS BEHEADED YOUR DOLLS, SPILLED GRAPE JUICE ON YOUR CARPET AND TRASHED YOUR COLORING BOOKS! HOW IS THAT A "GOOD DAY"?
IT'S A GOOD DAY TO GET EVEN.
MOMMY!
KIRKMAN & SCOTT

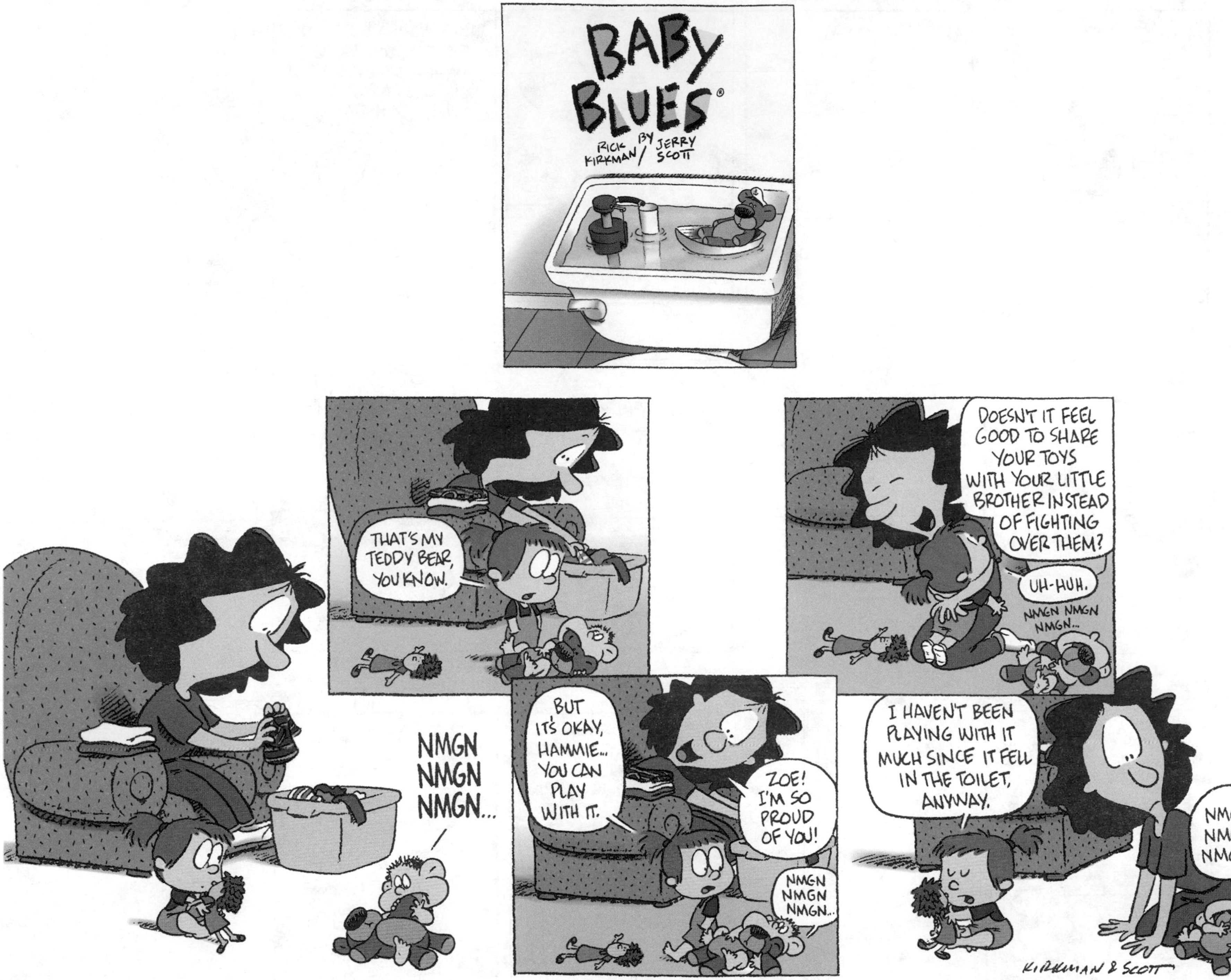
BABY BLUES®
BY RICK KIRKMAN / JERRY SCOTT
THAT'S MY TEDDY BEAR, YOU KNOW.
DOESN'T IT FEEL GOOD TO SHARE YOUR TOYS WITH YOUR LITTLE BROTHER INSTEAD OF FIGHTING OVER THEM?
UH-HUH.
NMGN NMGN NMGN...
NMGN NMGN NMGN...
BUT IT'S OKAY, HAMMIE... YOU CAN PLAY WITH IT.
ZOE! I'M SO PROUD OF YOU!
NMGN NMGN NMGN...
I HAVEN'T BEEN PLAYING WITH IT MUCH SINCE IT FELL IN THE TOILET, ANYWAY.
NMGN NMGN NMGN...
KIRKMAN & SCOTT

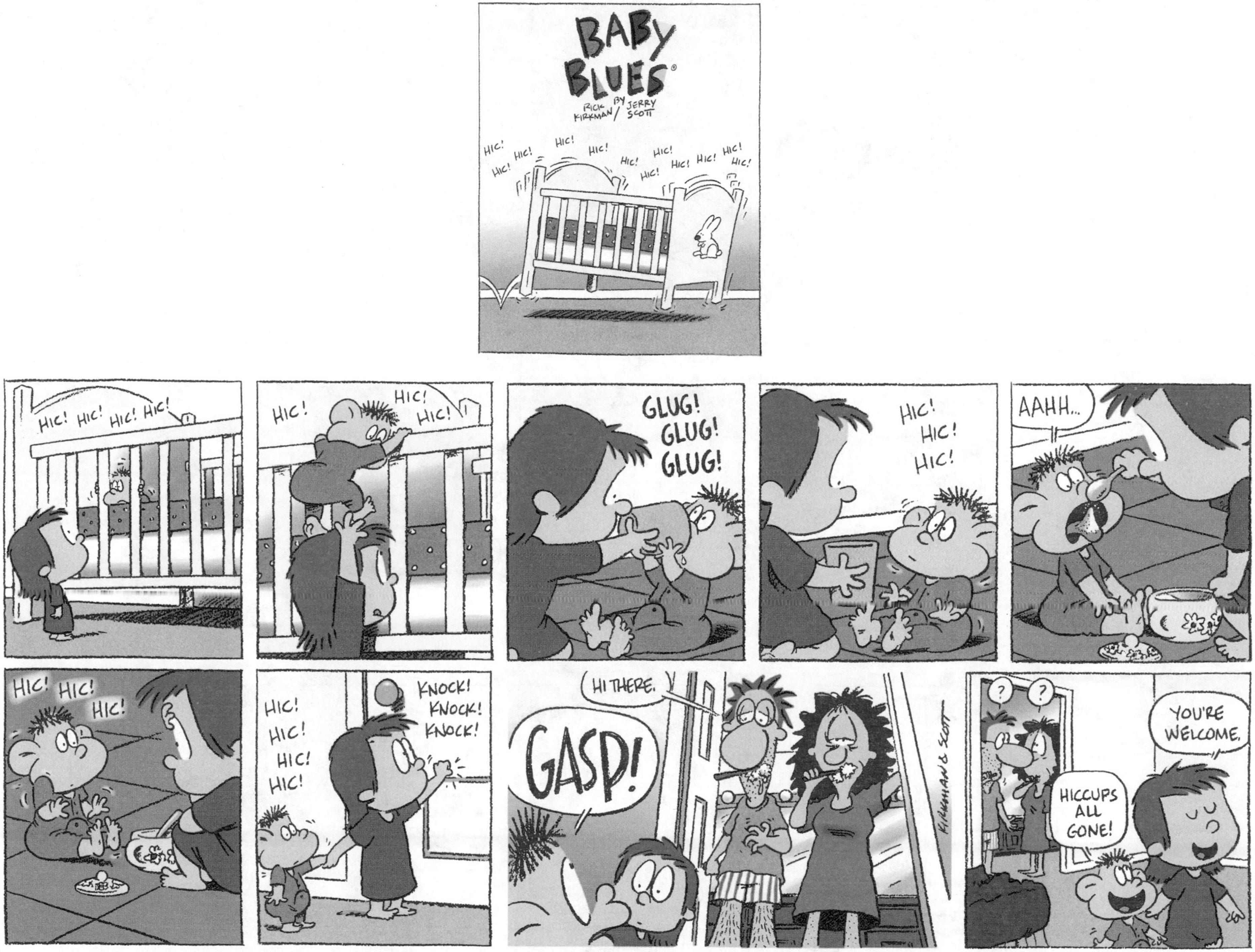

BABY BLUES®
BY RICK KIRKMAN / JERRY SCOTT
HIC! HIC! HIC! HIC! HIC! HIC! HIC! HIC! HIC! HIC! HIC! HIC!
HIC! HIC! HIC! HIC!
HIC! HIC! HIC!
GLUG! GLUG! GLUG!
HIC! HIC! HIC!
AAHH...
HIC! HIC! HIC!
HIC! HIC! HIC! HIC!
KNOCK! KNOCK! KNOCK!
HI THERE.
GASP!
KIRKMAN & SCOTT
?
?
YOU'RE WELCOME.
HICCUPS ALL GONE!

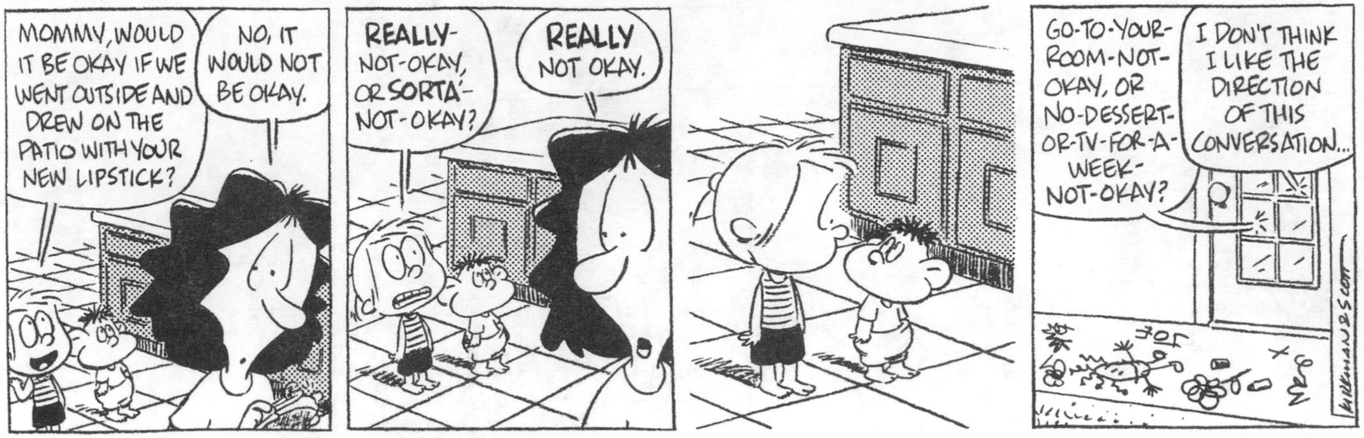
MOMMY, WOULD IT BE OKAY IF WE WENT OUTSIDE AND DREW ON THE PATIO WITH YOUR NEW LIPSTICK?
NO, IT WOULD NOT BE OKAY.
REALLY-NOT-OKAY, OR SORTA'-NOT-OKAY?
REALLY NOT OKAY.
GO-TO-YOUR-ROOM-NOT-OKAY, OR NO-DESSERT-OR-TV-FOR-A-WEEK-NOT-OKAY?
I DON'T THINK I LIKE THE DIRECTION OF THIS CONVERSATION...
KIRKMAN & SCOTT

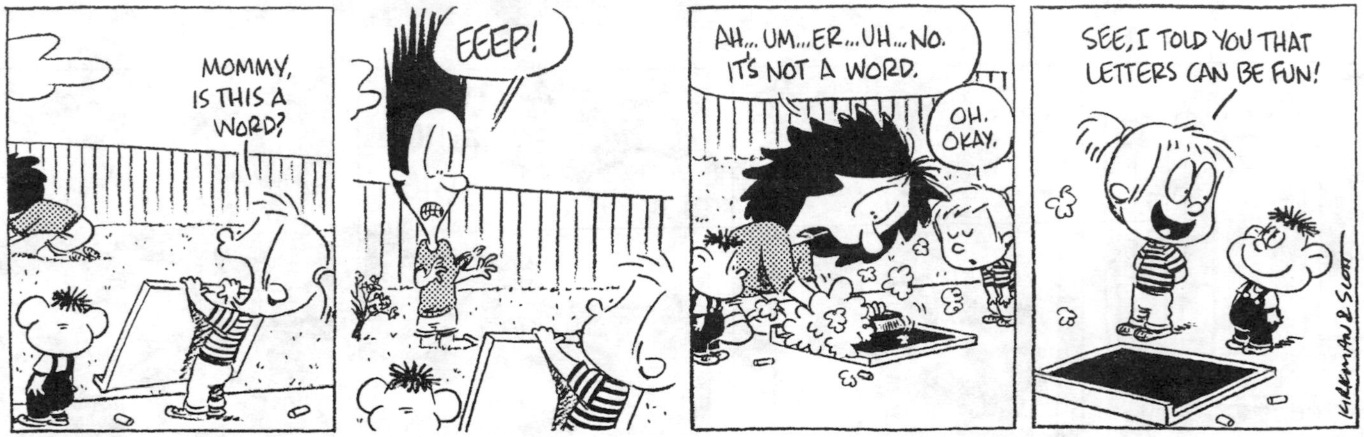
MOMMY, IS THIS A WORD?
EEEP!
AH... UM... ER... UH... NO. IT'S NOT A WORD.
OH. OKAY.
SEE, I TOLD YOU THAT LETTERS CAN BE FUN!
KIRKMAN & SCOTT

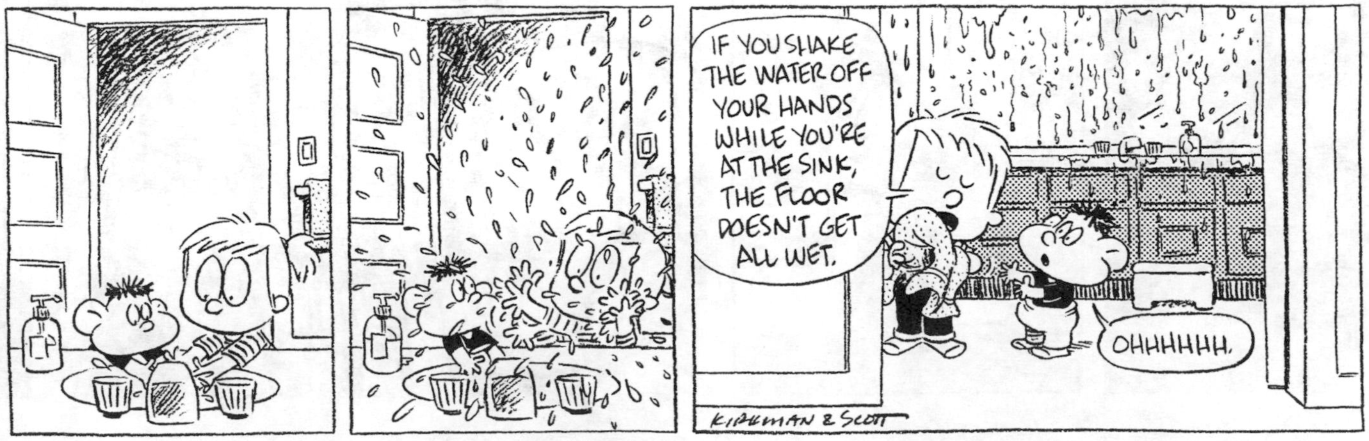
IF YOU SHAKE THE WATER OFF YOUR HANDS WHILE YOU'RE AT THE SINK, THE FLOOR DOESN'T GET ALL WET.
OHHHHHH.
KIRKMAN & SCOTT

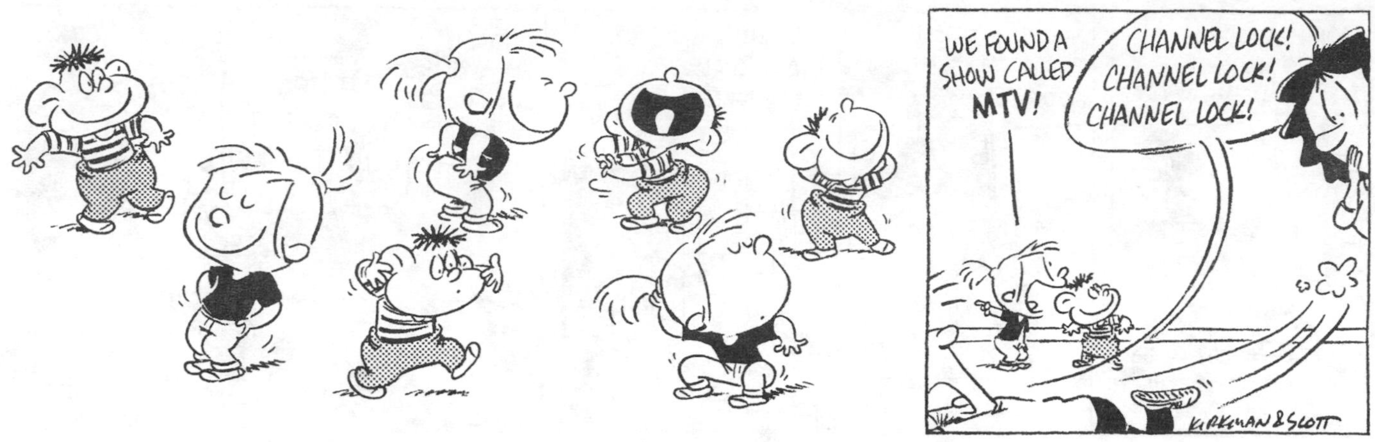
WE FOUND A SHOW CALLED MTV!
CHANNEL LOCK! CHANNEL LOCK! CHANNEL LOCK!
KIRKMAN & SCOTT

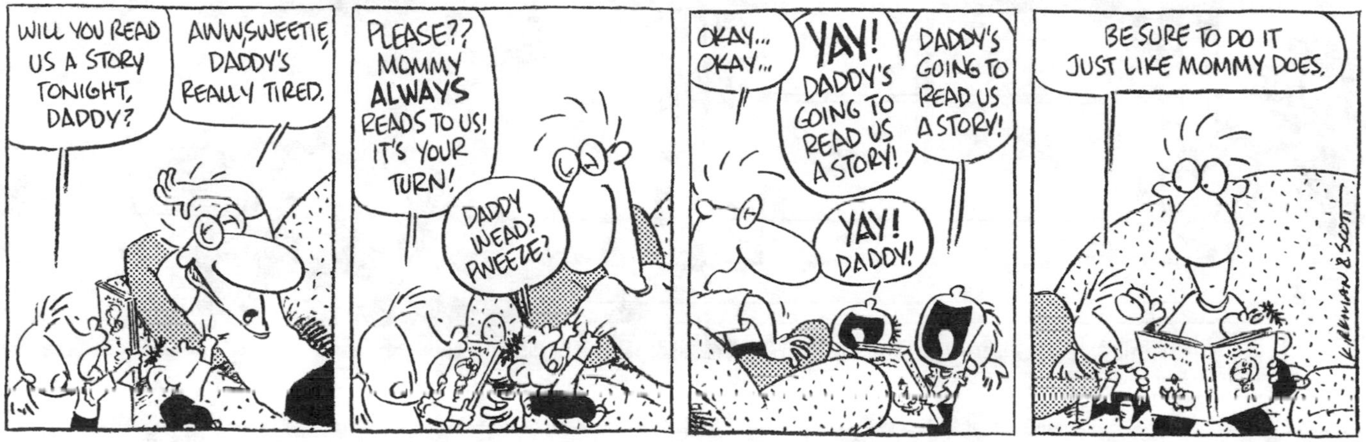
WILL YOU READ US A STORY TONIGHT, DADDY?
AWW, SWEETIE, DADDY'S REALLY TIRED.
PLEASE?? MOMMY ALWAYS READS TO US! IT'S YOUR TURN!
DADDY WEAD? PWEEZE?
OKAY... OKAY...
YAY! DADDY'S GOING TO READ US A STORY!
DADDY'S GOING TO READ US A STORY!
YAY! DADDY!
BE SURE TO DO IT JUST LIKE MOMMY DOES.
KIRKMAN & SCOTT

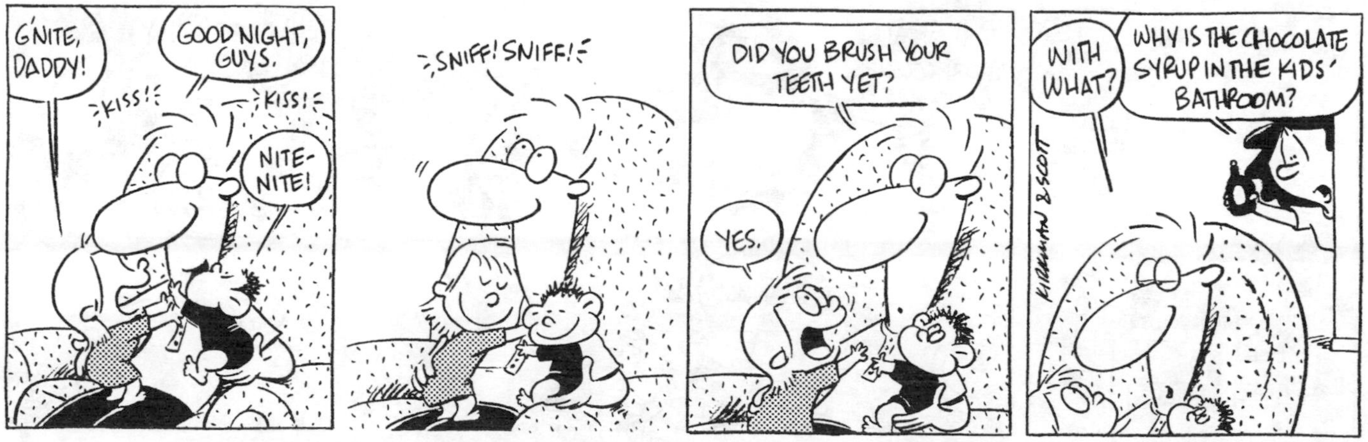
G'NITE, DADDY!
GOOD NIGHT, GUYS.
KISS!
KISS!
NITE-NITE!
SNIFF! SNIFF!
DID YOU BRUSH YOUR TEETH YET?
YES.
KIRKMAN & SCOTT
WITH WHAT?
WHY IS THE CHOCOLATE SYRUP IN THE KIDS' BATHROOM?

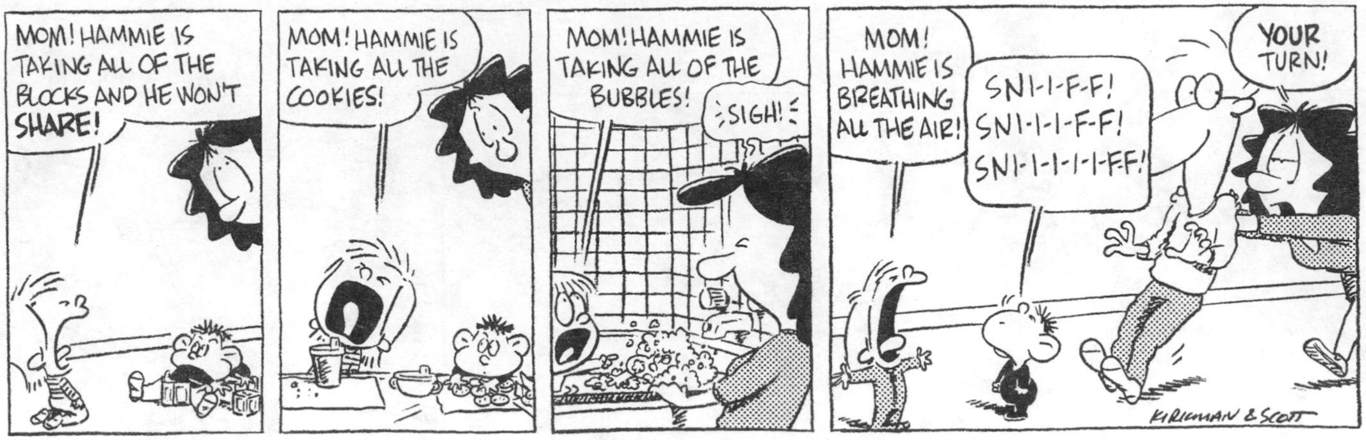
MOM! HAMMIE IS TAKING ALL OF THE BLOCKS AND HE WON'T **SHARE!**
MOM! HAMMIE IS TAKING ALL THE COOKIES!
MOM! HAMMIE IS TAKING ALL OF THE BUBBLES!
SIGH!
MOM! HAMMIE IS BREATHING ALL THE AIR!
SNI-I-F-F! SNI-I-I-F-F! SNI-I-I-I-I-F-F!
YOUR TURN!
KIRKMAN & SCOTT

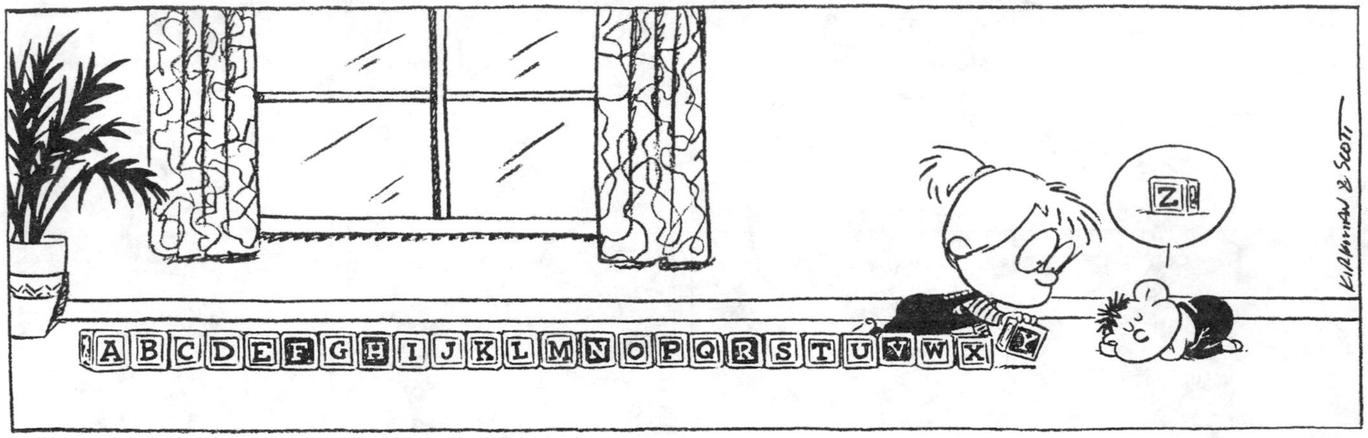
KIRKMAN & SCOTT

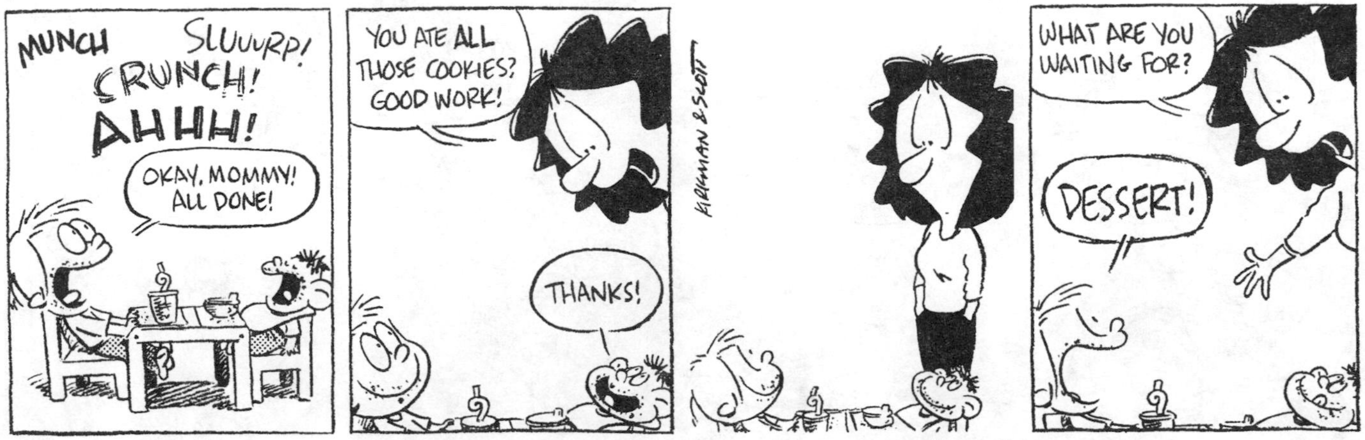
MUNCH
SLUUURP!
CRUNCH!
AHHH!
OKAY, MOMMY! ALL DONE!
YOU ATE **ALL** THOSE COOKIES? GOOD WORK!
THANKS!
KIRKMAN & SCOTT
WHAT ARE YOU WAITING FOR?
DESSERT!

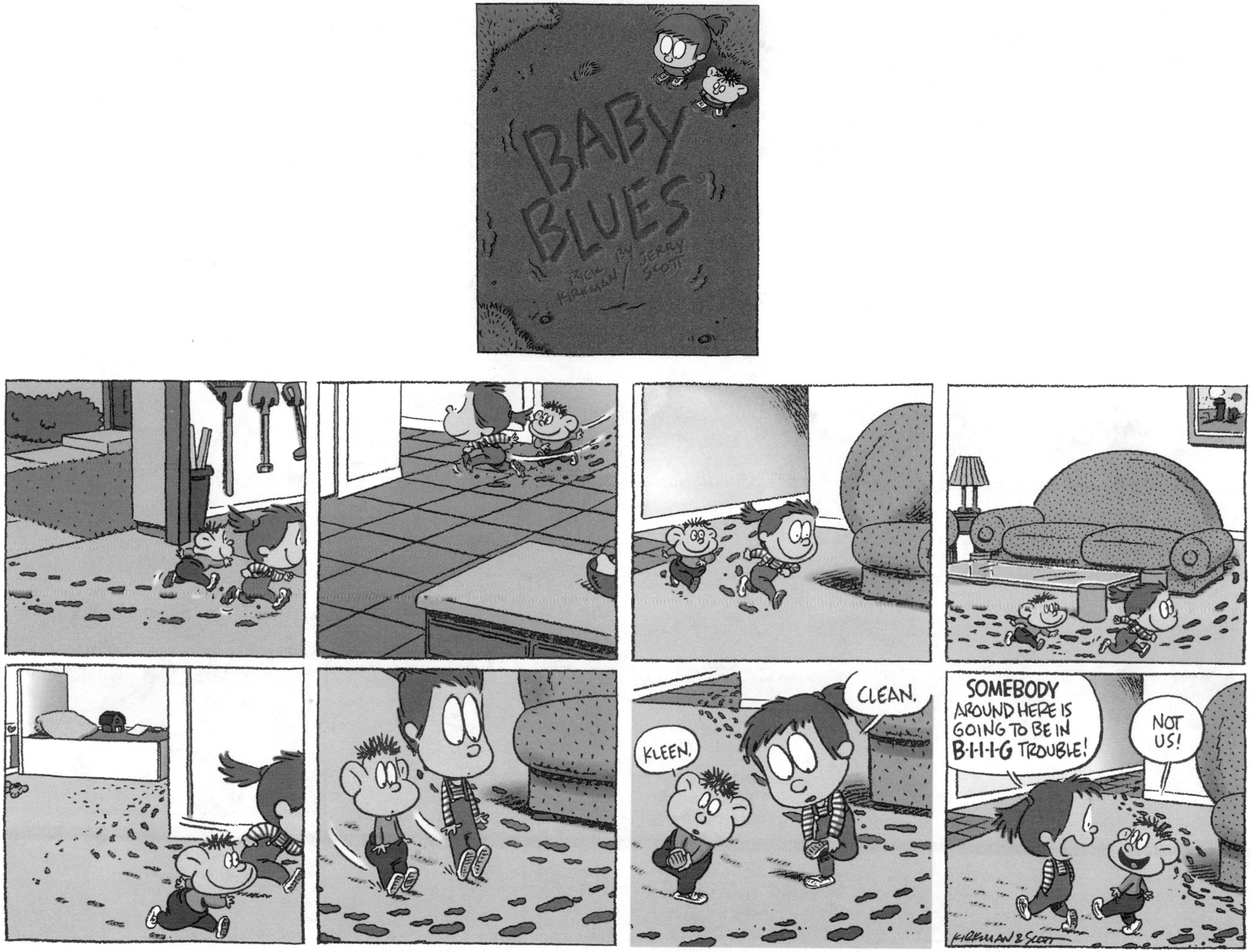
BABY BLUES
BY RICK KIRKMAN / JERRY SCOTT
KLEEN.
CLEAN.
SOMEBODY AROUND HERE IS GOING TO BE IN B-I-I-I-G TROUBLE!
NOT US!
KIRKMAN & SCOTT

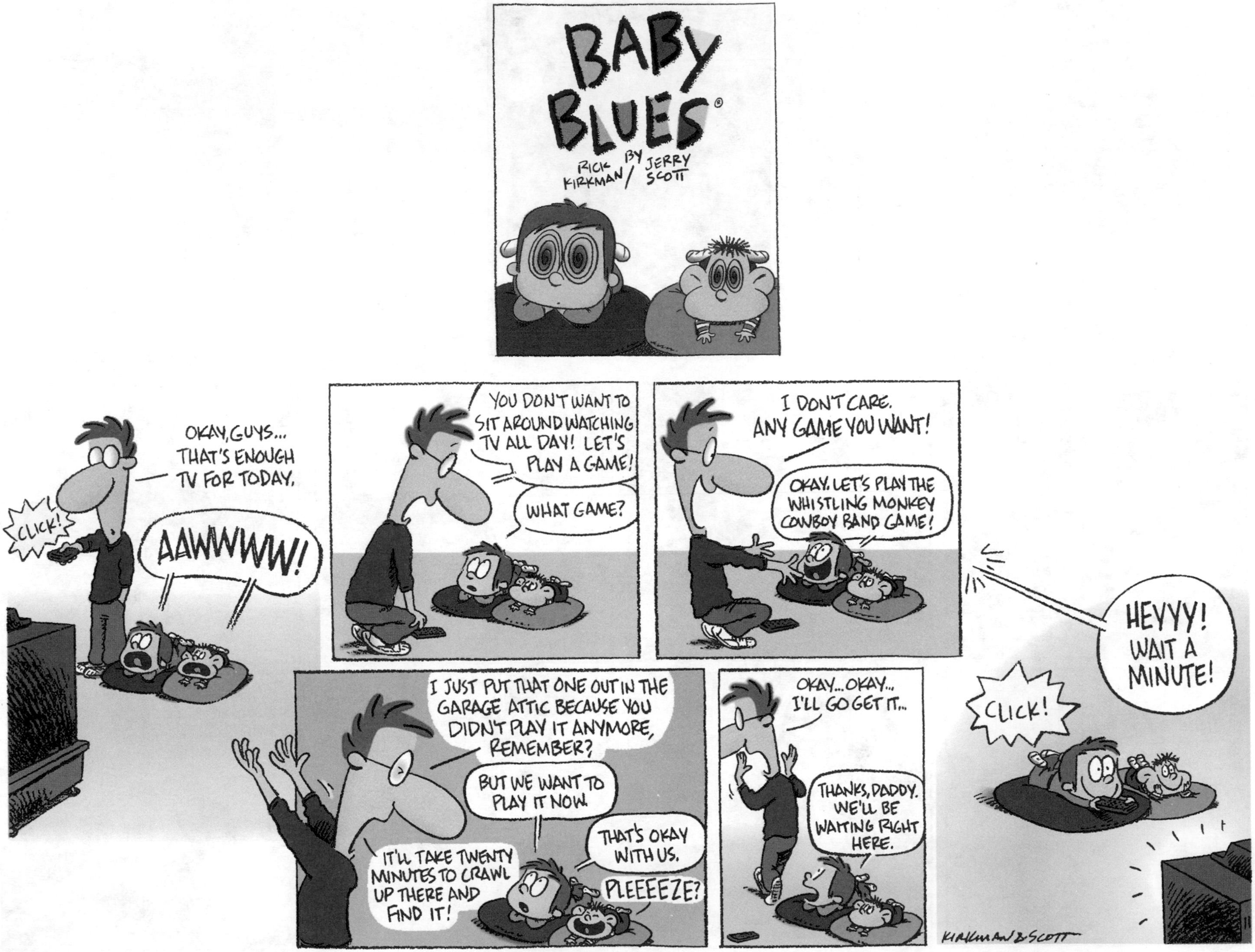
BABY BLUES®
BY RICK KIRKMAN / JERRY SCOTT
OKAY, GUYS... THAT'S ENOUGH TV FOR TODAY.
CLICK!
AAWWWW!
YOU DON'T WANT TO SIT AROUND WATCHING TV ALL DAY! LET'S PLAY A GAME!
WHAT GAME?
I DON'T CARE. ANY GAME YOU WANT!
OKAY. LET'S PLAY THE WHISTLING MONKEY COWBOY BAND GAME!
HEYYY! WAIT A MINUTE!
I JUST PUT THAT ONE OUT IN THE GARAGE ATTIC BECAUSE YOU DIDN'T PLAY IT ANYMORE, REMEMBER?
BUT WE WANT TO PLAY IT NOW.
IT'LL TAKE TWENTY MINUTES TO CRAWL UP THERE AND FIND IT!
THAT'S OKAY WITH US.
PLEEEEZE?
OKAY... OKAY... I'LL GO GET IT...
THANKS, DADDY. WE'LL BE WAITING RIGHT HERE.
CLICK!
KIRKMAN & SCOTT

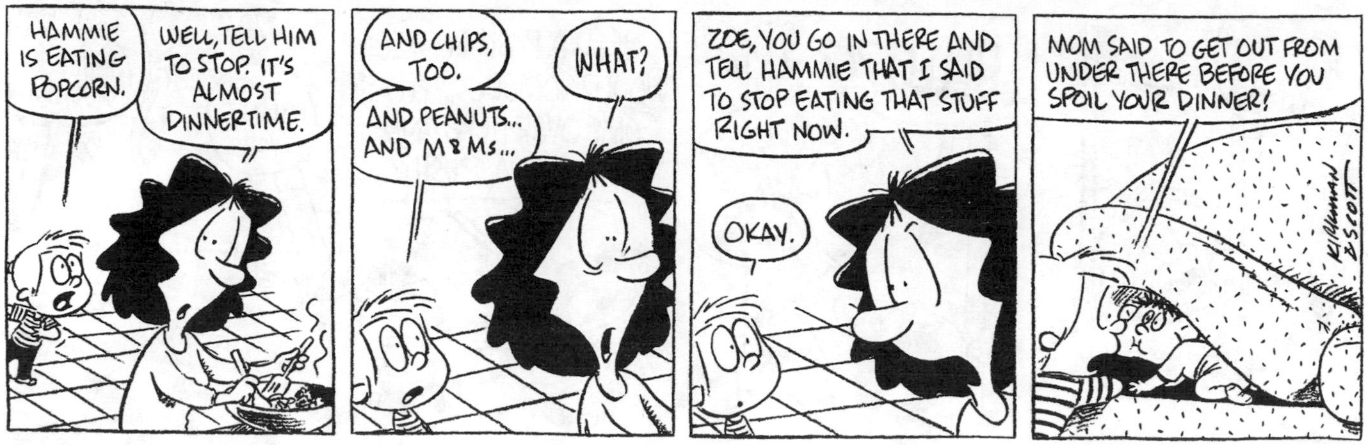
HAMMIE IS EATING POPCORN.
WELL, TELL HIM TO STOP. IT'S ALMOST DINNERTIME.
AND CHIPS, TOO.
WHAT?
AND PEANUTS... AND M&Ms...
ZOE, YOU GO IN THERE AND TELL HAMMIE THAT I SAID TO STOP EATING THAT STUFF RIGHT NOW.
OKAY.
MOM SAID TO GET OUT FROM UNDER THERE BEFORE YOU SPOIL YOUR DINNER!
KIRKMAN & SCOTT

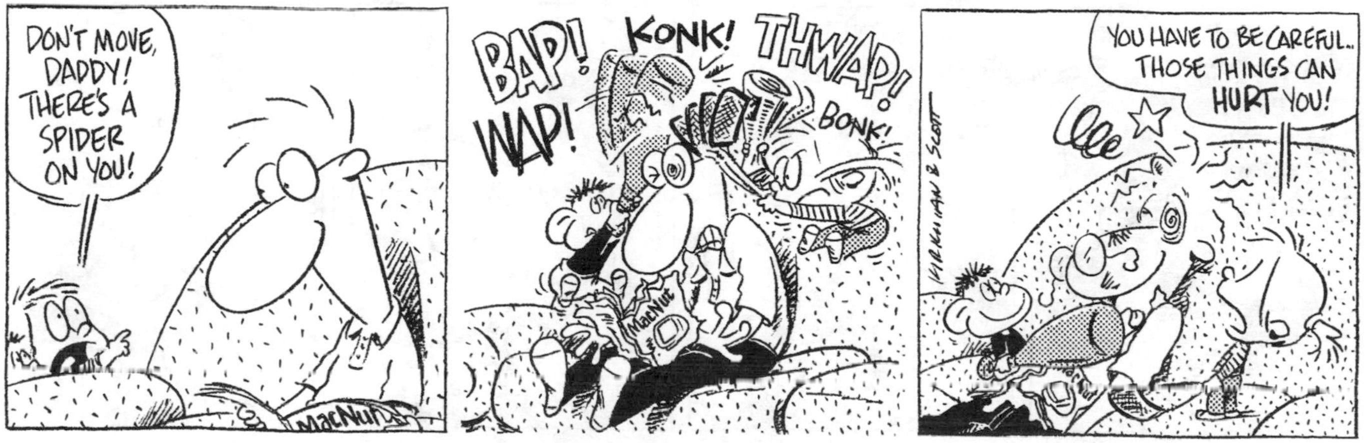
DON'T MOVE, DADDY! THERE'S A SPIDER ON YOU!
MacNut
BAP!
KONK!
THWAP!
WAP!
BONK!
MacNut
KIRKMAN & SCOTT
YOU HAVE TO BE CAREFUL.. THOSE THINGS CAN HURT YOU!

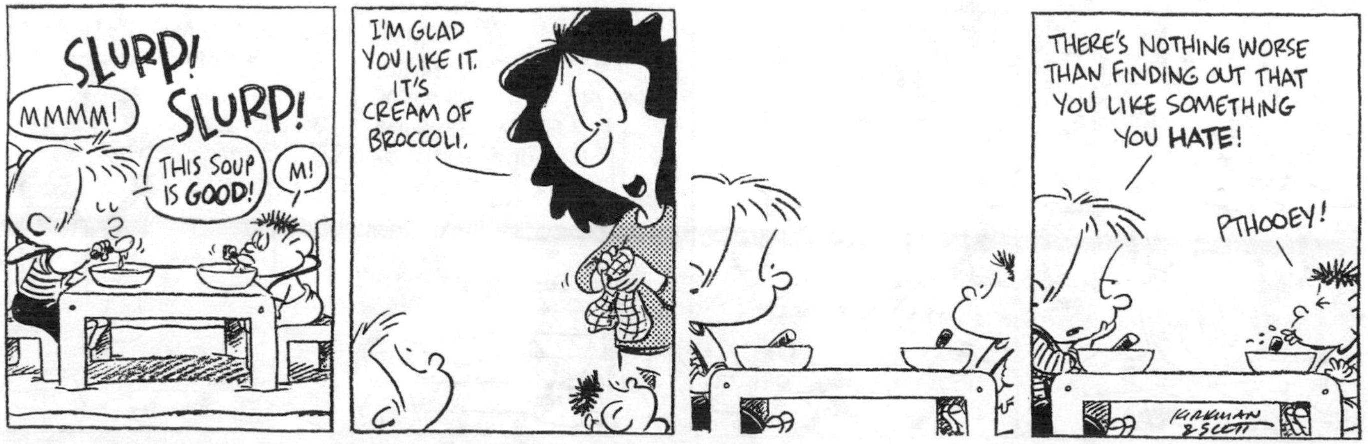
SLURP!
MMMM!
SLURP!
THIS SOUP IS GOOD!
M!
I'M GLAD YOU LIKE IT. IT'S CREAM OF BROCCOLI.
THERE'S NOTHING WORSE THAN FINDING OUT THAT YOU LIKE SOMETHING YOU HATE!
PTHOOEY!
KIRKMAN & SCOTT

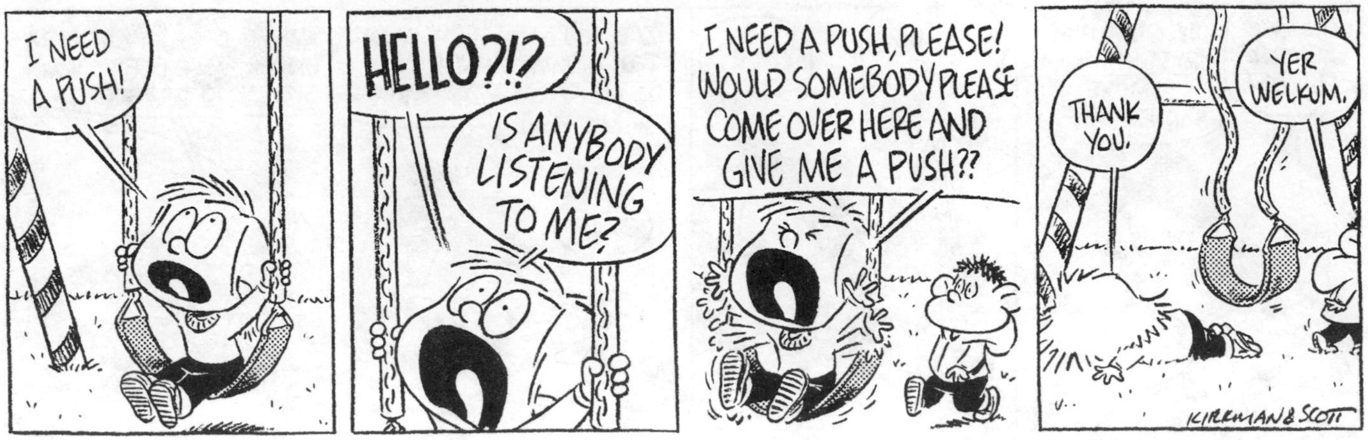
I NEED A PUSH!
HELLO?!?
IS ANYBODY LISTENING TO ME?
I NEED A PUSH, PLEASE! WOULD SOMEBODY PLEASE COME OVER HERE AND GIVE ME A PUSH??
THANK YOU.
YER WELKUM.
KIRKMAN & SCOTT

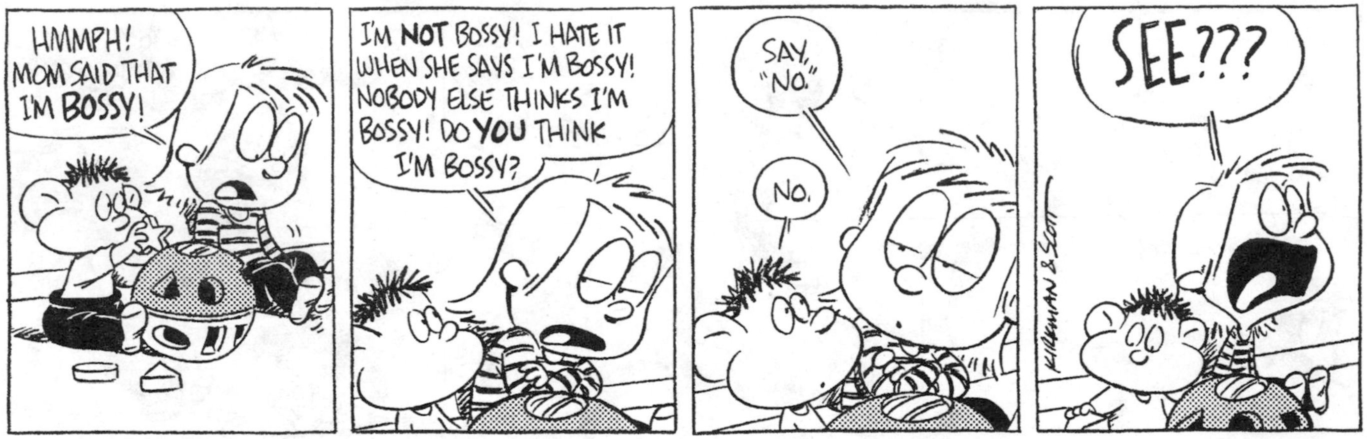
HMMPH! MOM SAID THAT I'M BOSSY!
I'M NOT BOSSY! I HATE IT WHEN SHE SAYS I'M BOSSY! NOBODY ELSE THINKS I'M BOSSY! DO YOU THINK I'M BOSSY?
SAY, "NO."
NO.
KIRKMAN & SCOTT
SEE???

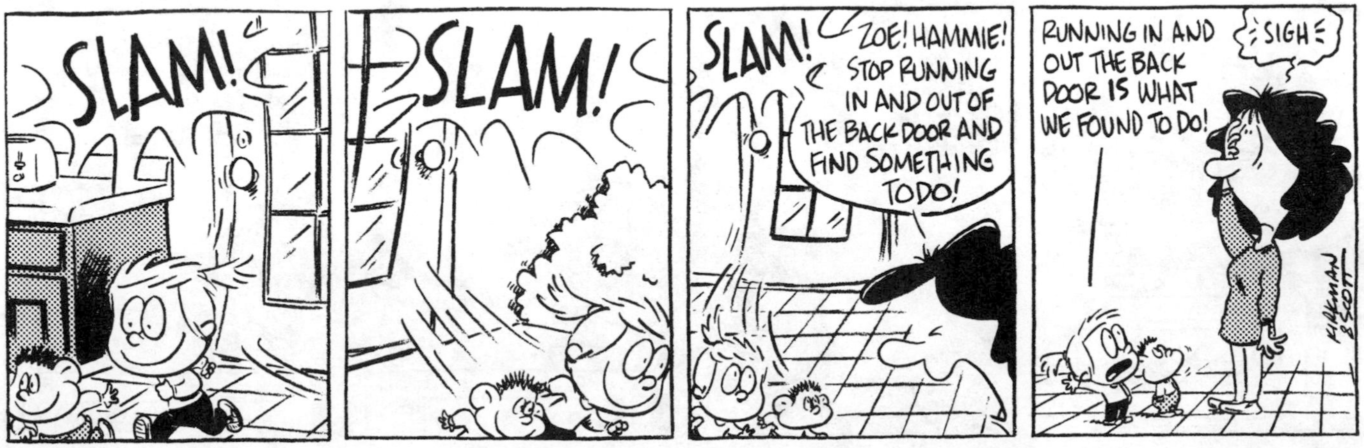
SLAM!
SLAM!
SLAM!
ZOE! HAMMIE! STOP RUNNING IN AND OUT OF THE BACK DOOR AND FIND SOMETHING TO DO!
RUNNING IN AND OUT THE BACK DOOR IS WHAT WE FOUND TO DO!
SIGH
KIRKMAN & SCOTT

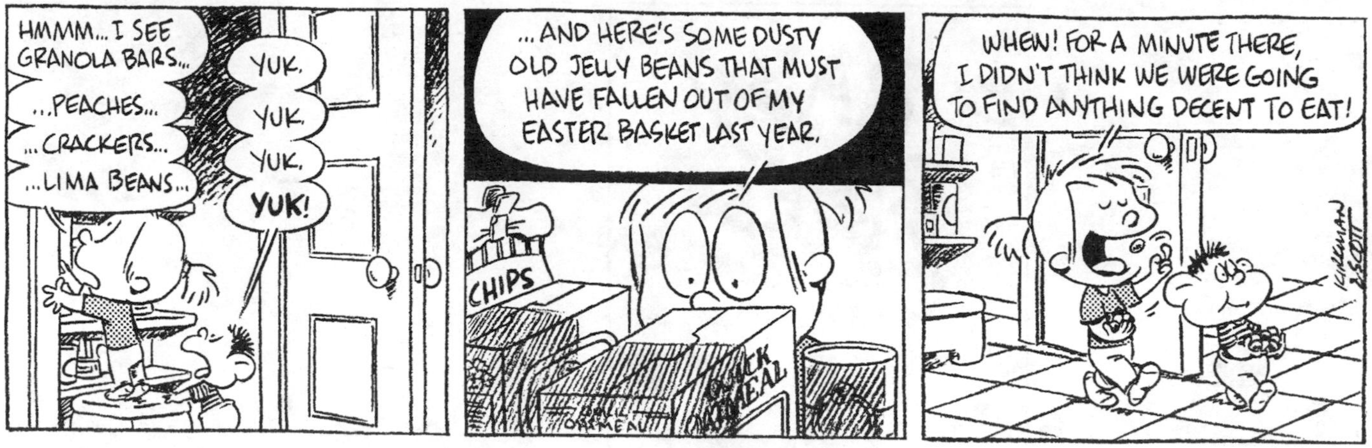
HMMM... I SEE GRANOLA BARS...
YUK.
...PEACHES...
YUK.
...CRACKERS...
YUK.
...LIMA BEANS...
YUK!
...AND HERE'S SOME DUSTY OLD JELLY BEANS THAT MUST HAVE FALLEN OUT OF MY EASTER BASKET LAST YEAR.
CHIPS
WHEW! FOR A MINUTE THERE, I DIDN'T THINK WE WERE GOING TO FIND ANYTHING DECENT TO EAT!
KIRKMAN & SCOTT

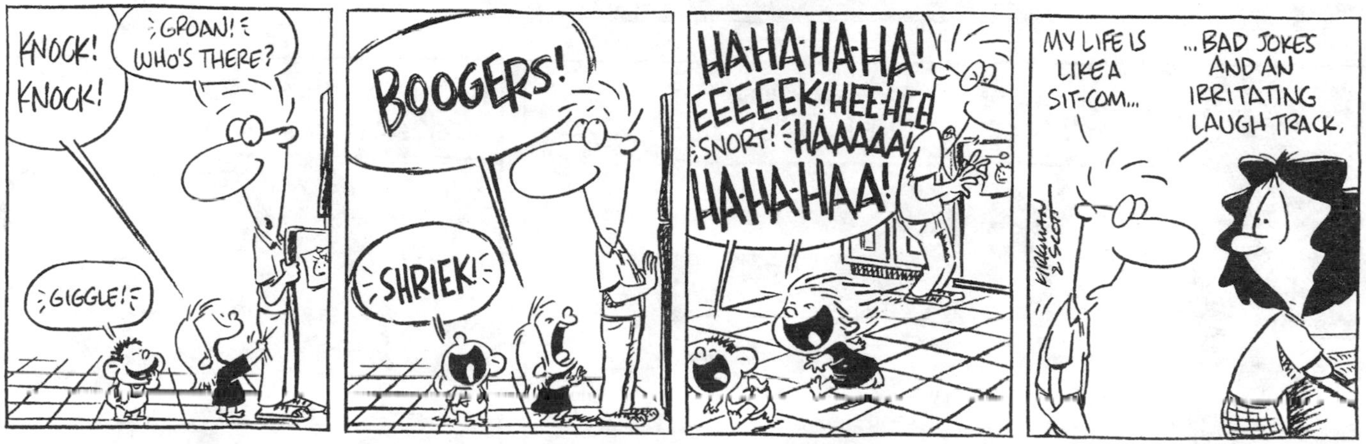
KNOCK! KNOCK!
GROAN! WHO'S THERE?
GIGGLE!
BOOGERS!
SHRIEK!
HA-HA-HA-HA! EEEEEK! HEE-HEE SNORT! HAAAAA! HA-HA-HAA!
KIRKMAN & SCOTT
MY LIFE IS LIKE A SIT-COM...
...BAD JOKES AND AN IRRITATING LAUGH TRACK.

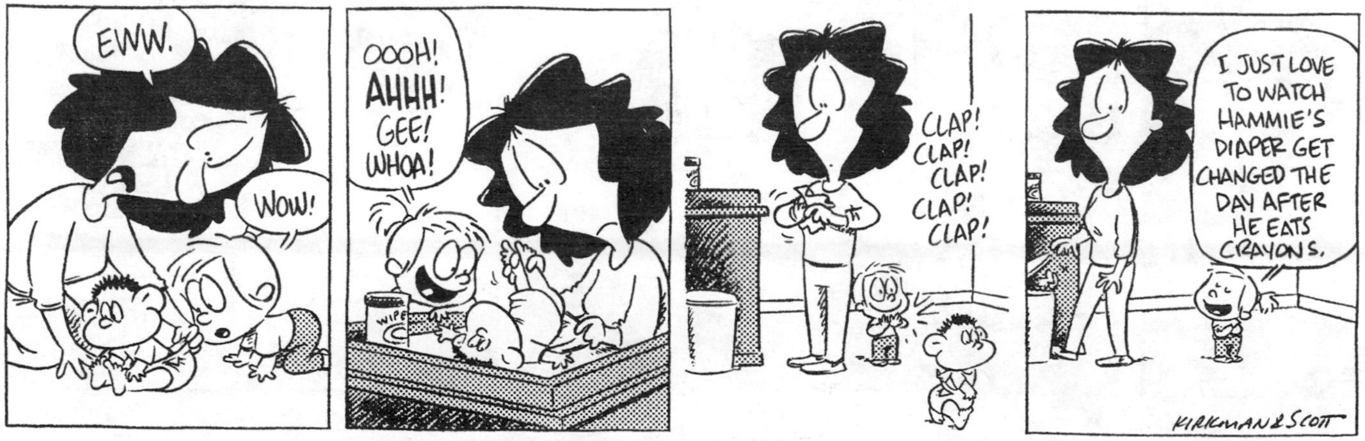
EWW.
WOW!
OOOH! AHHH! GEE! WHOA!
WIPE
CLAP! CLAP! CLAP! CLAP! CLAP!
I JUST LOVE TO WATCH HAMMIE'S DIAPER GET CHANGED THE DAY AFTER HE EATS CRAYONS.
KIRKMAN & SCOTT

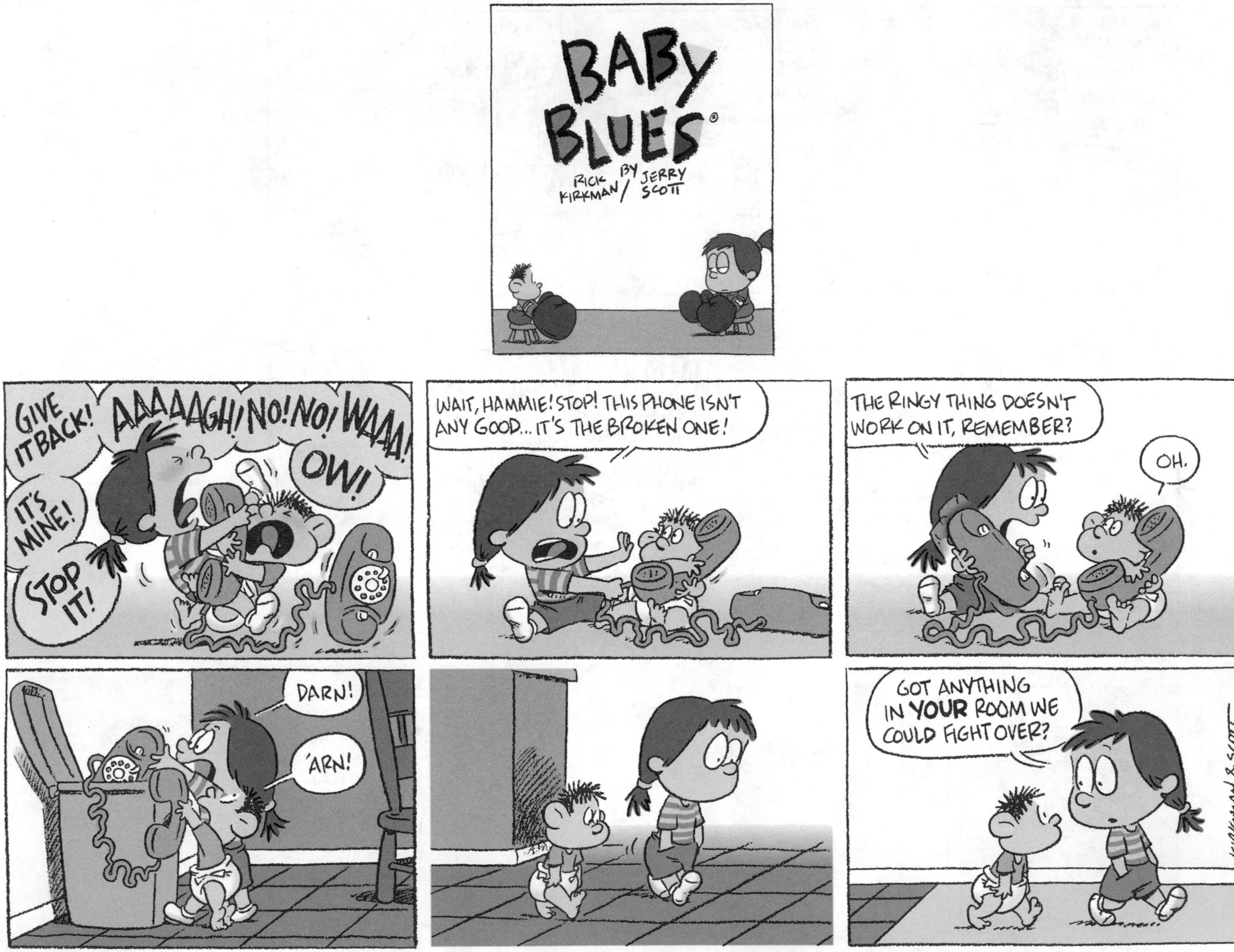
BABY BLUES®
BY RICK KIRKMAN / JERRY SCOTT
GIVE IT BACK!
AAAAAGH!
NO! NO!
WAAA!
OW!
IT'S MINE!
STOP IT!
WAIT, HAMMIE! STOP! THIS PHONE ISN'T ANY GOOD... IT'S THE BROKEN ONE!
THE RINGY THING DOESN'T WORK ON IT, REMEMBER?
OH.
DARN!
'ARN!
GOT ANYTHING IN YOUR ROOM WE COULD FIGHT OVER?
KIRKMAN & SCOTT

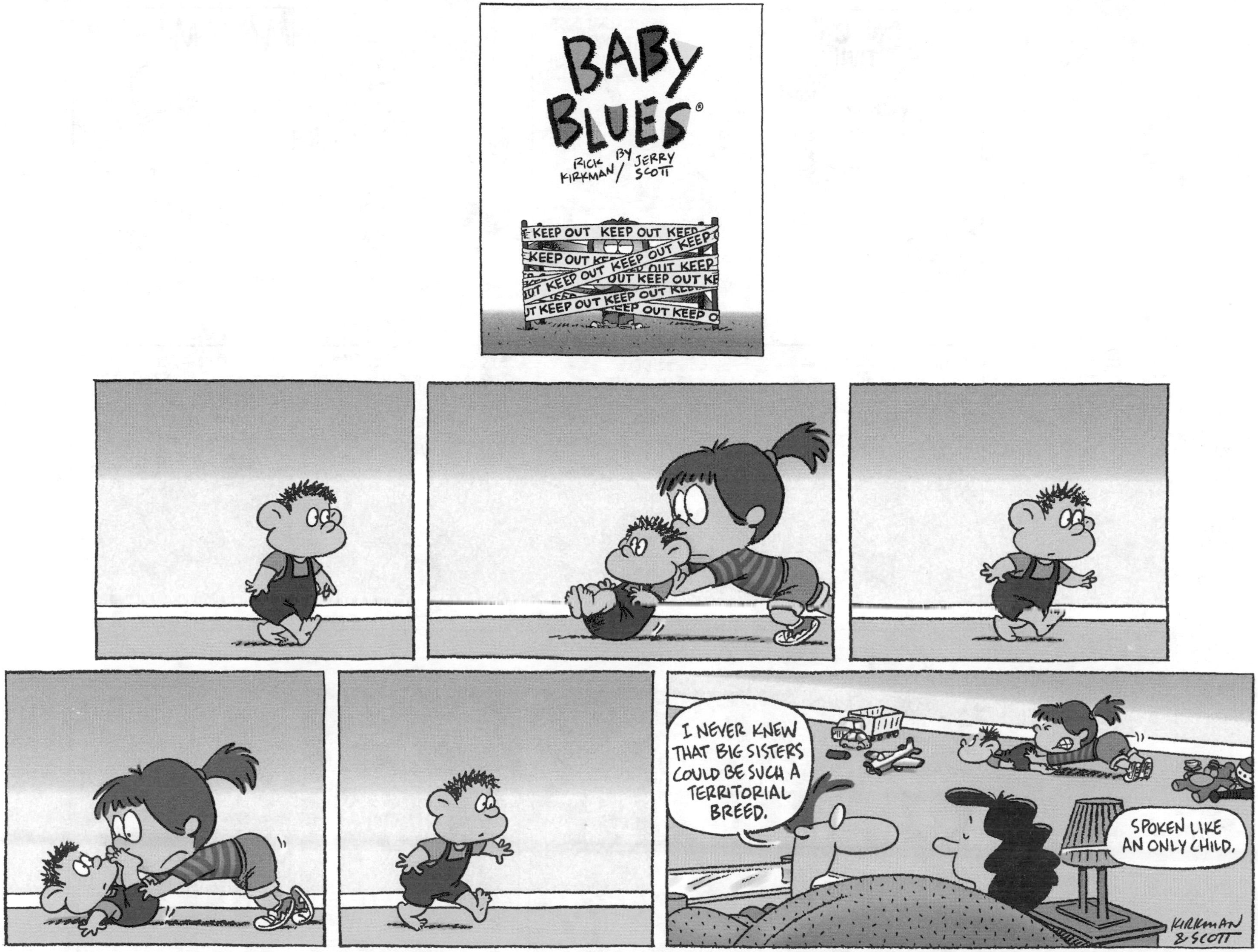
BABY BLUES®
BY RICK KIRKMAN / JERRY SCOTT
KEEP OUT KEEP OUT KEEP
I NEVER KNEW THAT BIG SISTERS COULD BE SUCH A TERRITORIAL BREED.
SPOKEN LIKE AN ONLY CHILD.
KIRKMAN & SCOTT

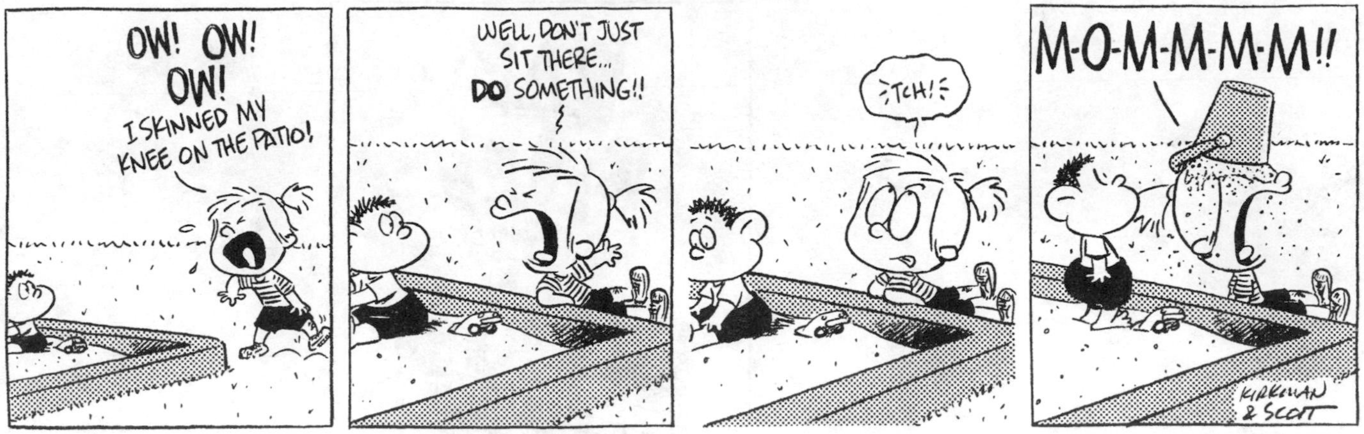
OW! OW! OW!
I SKINNED MY KNEE ON THE PATIO!
WELL, DON'T JUST SIT THERE... DO SOMETHING!!
TCH!
M-O-M-M-M-M!!
KIRKMAN & SCOTT

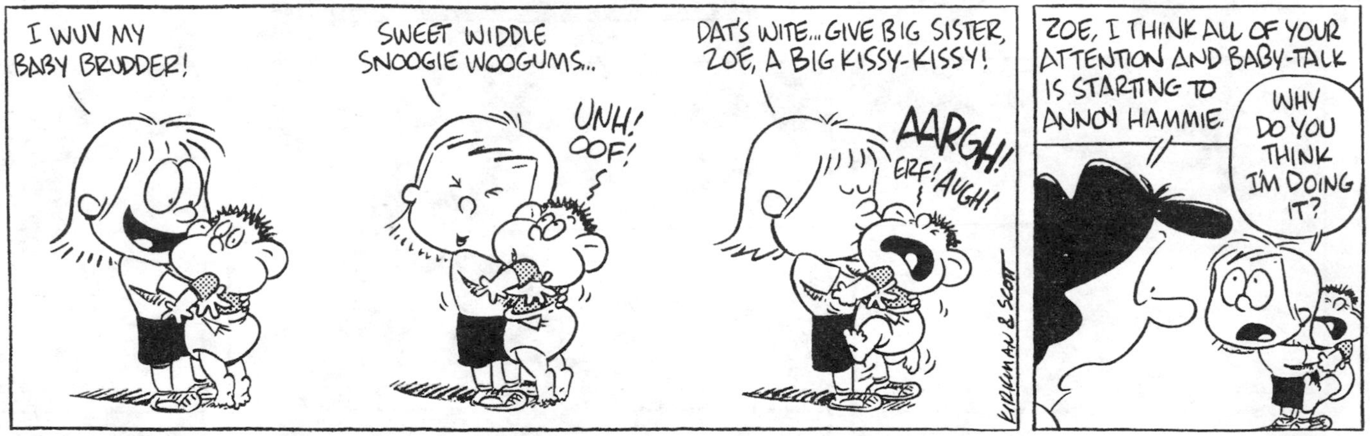
I WUV MY BABY BRUDDER!
SWEET WIDDLE SNOOGIE WOOGUMS...
UNH! OOF!
DAT'S WITE... GIVE BIG SISTER, ZOE, A BIG KISSY-KISSY!
AARGH!
ERF! AUGH!
KIRKMAN & SCOTT
ZOE, I THINK ALL OF YOUR ATTENTION AND BABY-TALK IS STARTING TO ANNOY HAMMIE.
WHY DO YOU THINK I'M DOING IT?

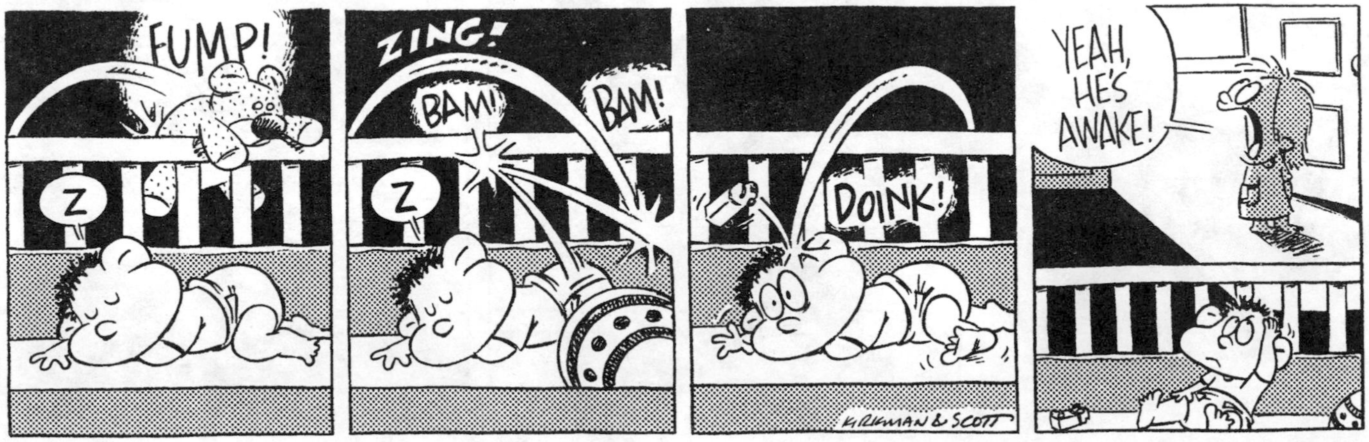
FUMP!
Z
ZING!
BAM!
BAM!
Z
DOINK!
KIRKMAN & SCOTT
YEAH, HE'S AWAKE!

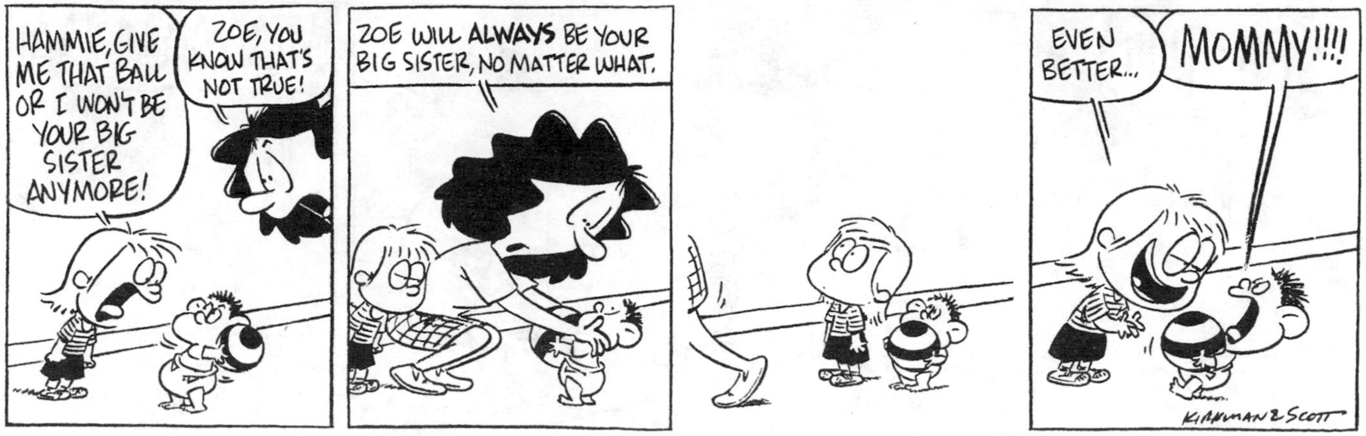
HAMMIE, GIVE ME THAT BALL OR I WON'T BE YOUR BIG SISTER ANYMORE!
ZOE, YOU KNOW THAT'S NOT TRUE!
ZOE WILL **ALWAYS** BE YOUR BIG SISTER, NO MATTER WHAT.
EVEN BETTER...
MOMMY!!!!
KIRKMAN & SCOTT

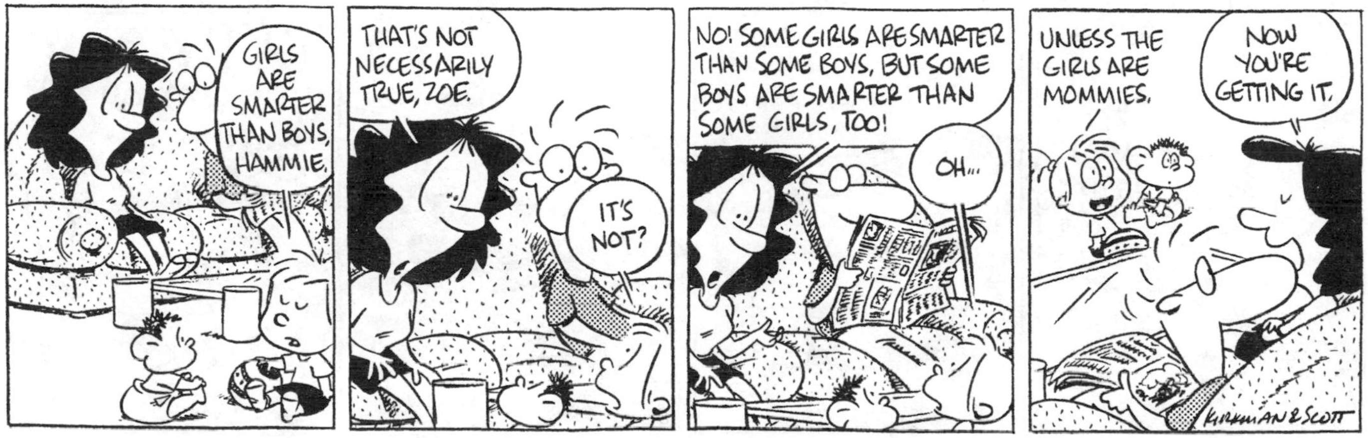
GIRLS ARE SMARTER THAN BOYS, HAMMIE.
THAT'S NOT NECESSARILY TRUE, ZOE.
IT'S NOT?
NO! SOME GIRLS ARE SMARTER THAN SOME BOYS, BUT SOME BOYS ARE SMARTER THAN SOME GIRLS, TOO!
OH...
UNLESS THE GIRLS ARE MOMMIES.
NOW YOU'RE GETTING IT.
KIRKMAN & SCOTT

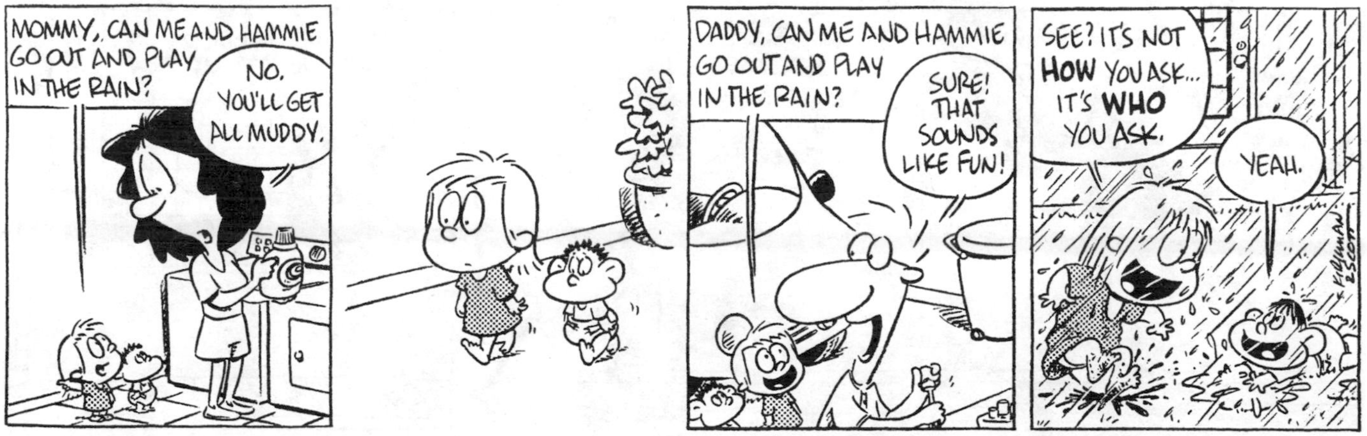
MOMMY, CAN ME AND HAMMIE GO OUT AND PLAY IN THE RAIN?
NO. YOU'LL GET ALL MUDDY.
DADDY, CAN ME AND HAMMIE GO OUT AND PLAY IN THE RAIN?
SURE! THAT SOUNDS LIKE FUN!
SEE? IT'S NOT **HOW** YOU ASK... IT'S **WHO** YOU ASK.
YEAH.
KIRKMAN & SCOTT

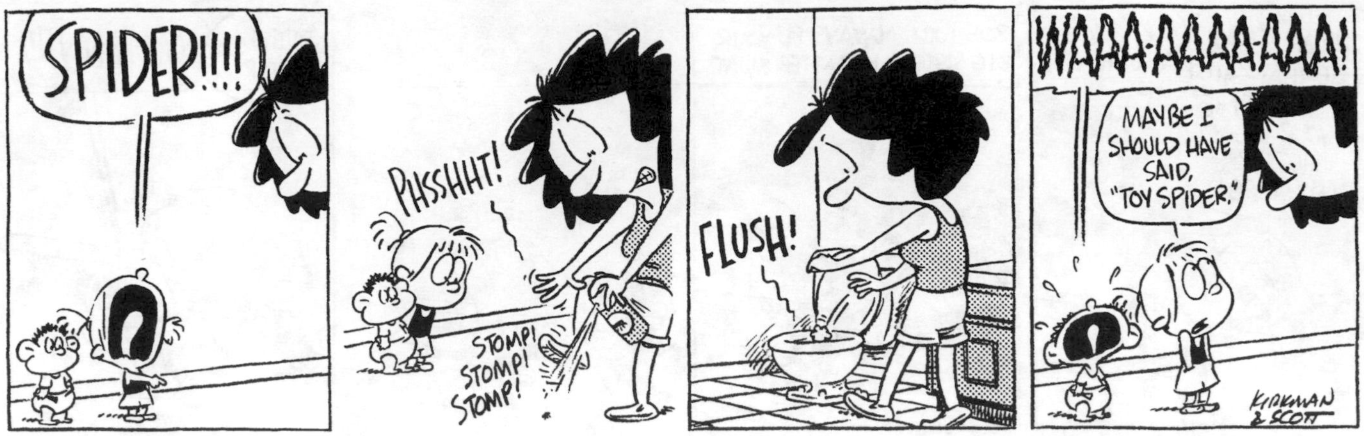
SPIDER!!!!!
PHSSHHT!
STOMP! STOMP! STOMP!
FLUSH!
WAAA-AAAAAAA!
MAYBE I SHOULD HAVE SAID, "TOY SPIDER."
KIRKMAN & SCOTT

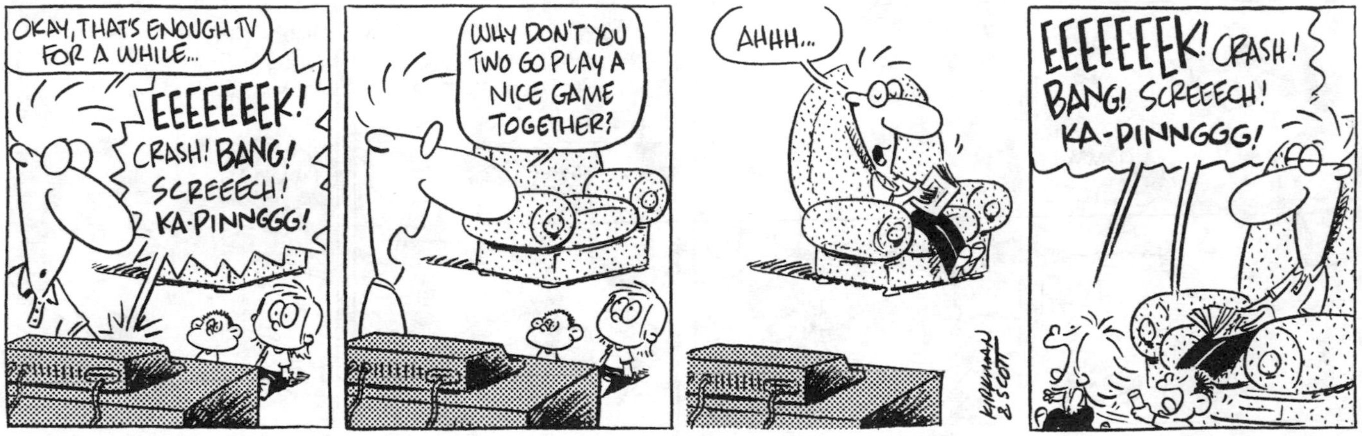
OKAY, THAT'S ENOUGH TV FOR A WHILE...
EEEEEEEK! CRASH! BANG! SCREEECH! KA-PINNGGG!
WHY DON'T YOU TWO GO PLAY A NICE GAME TOGETHER?
AHHH...
KIRKMAN & SCOTT
EEEEEEEK! CRASH! BANG! SCREEECH! KA-PINNGGG!

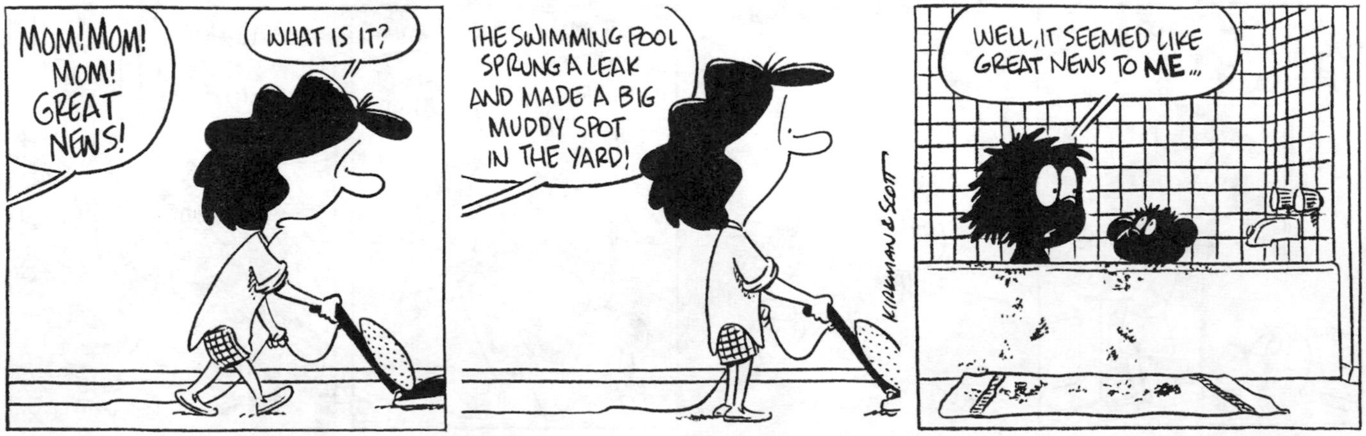
MOM! MOM! MOM! GREAT NEWS!
WHAT IS IT?
THE SWIMMING POOL SPRUNG A LEAK AND MADE A BIG MUDDY SPOT IN THE YARD!
KIRKMAN & SCOTT
WELL, IT SEEMED LIKE GREAT NEWS TO ME...

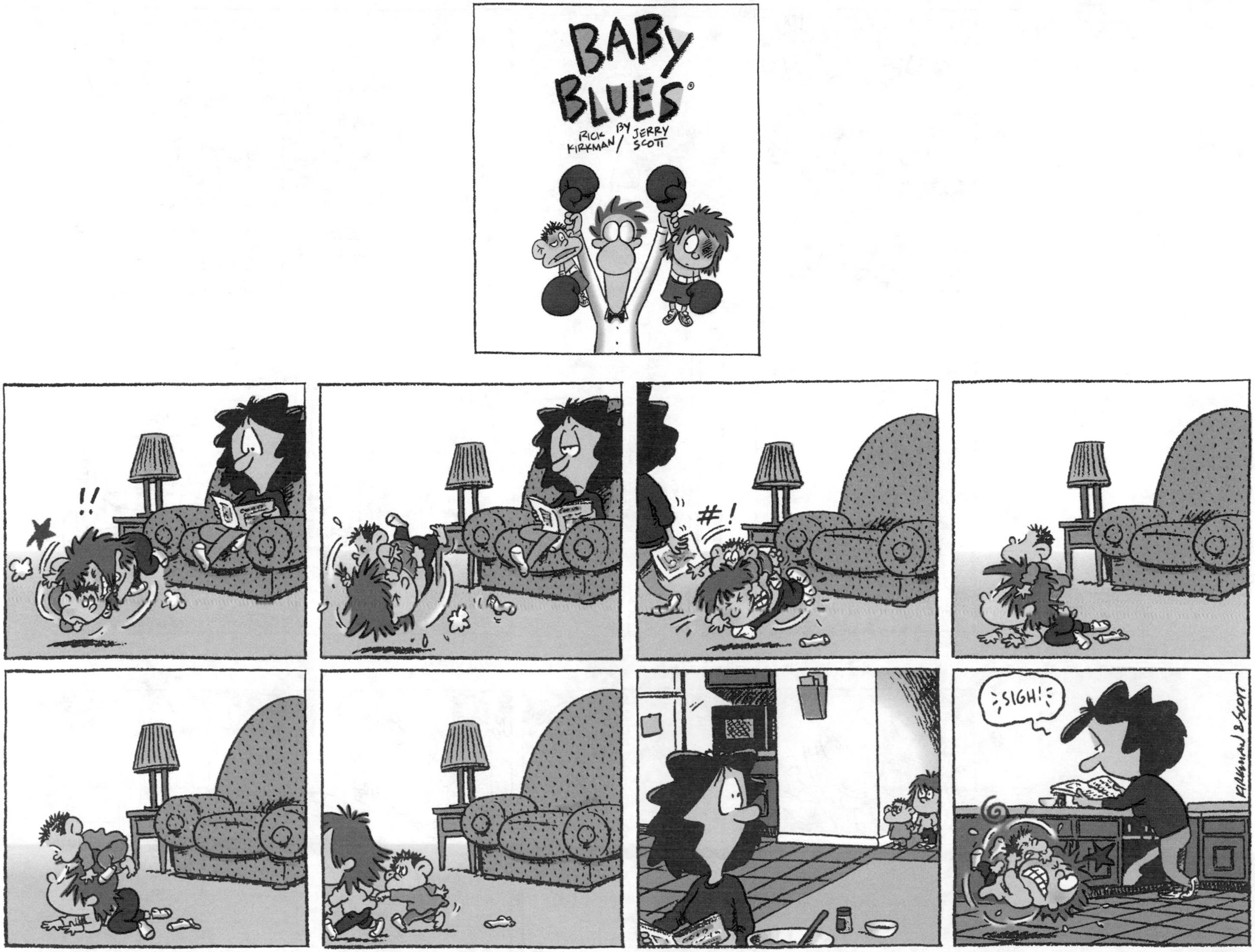
BABY BLUES®
BY RICK KIRKMAN / JERRY SCOTT
!!
#!
SIGH!
KIRKMAN & SCOTT

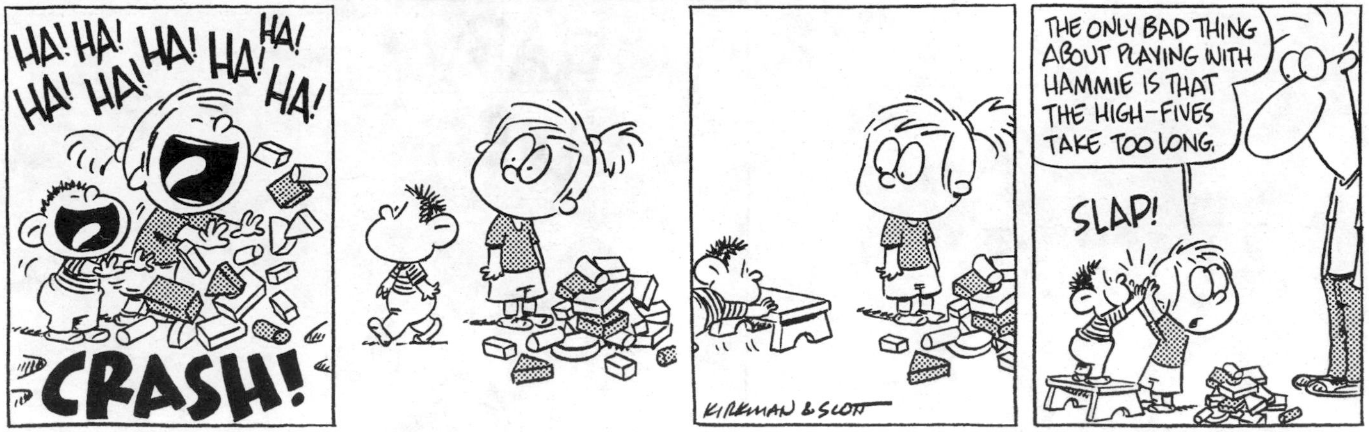
HA! HA! HA! HA! HA! HA! HA! HA!
CRASH!
KIRKMAN & SCOTT
THE ONLY BAD THING ABOUT PLAYING WITH HAMMIE IS THAT THE HIGH-FIVES TAKE TOO LONG.
SLAP!

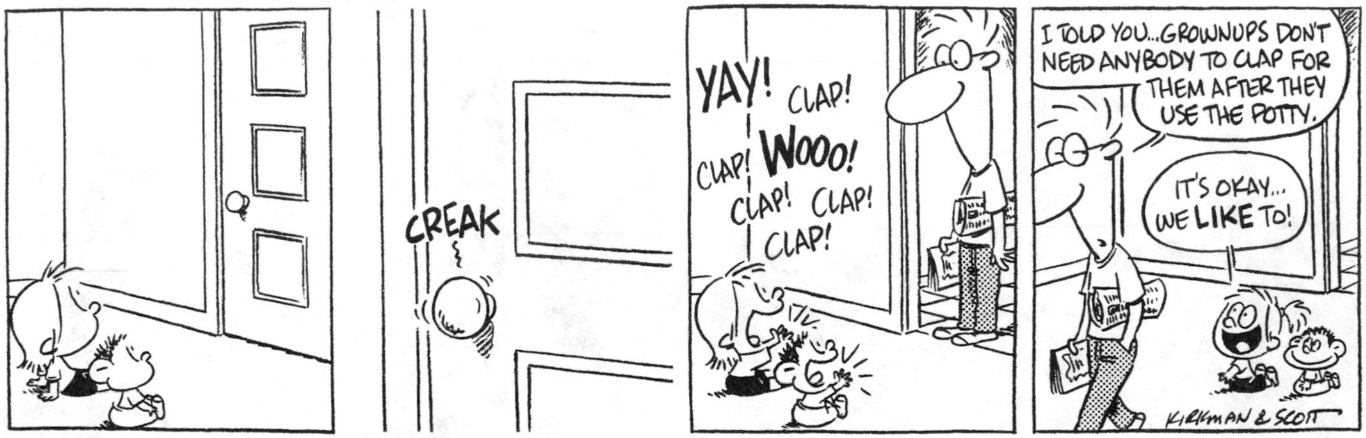
CREAK
YAY! CLAP! CLAP! WOOO! CLAP! CLAP! CLAP!
I TOLD YOU...GROWNUPS DON'T NEED ANYBODY TO CLAP FOR THEM AFTER THEY USE THE POTTY.
IT'S OKAY... WE LIKE TO!
KIRKMAN & SCOTT

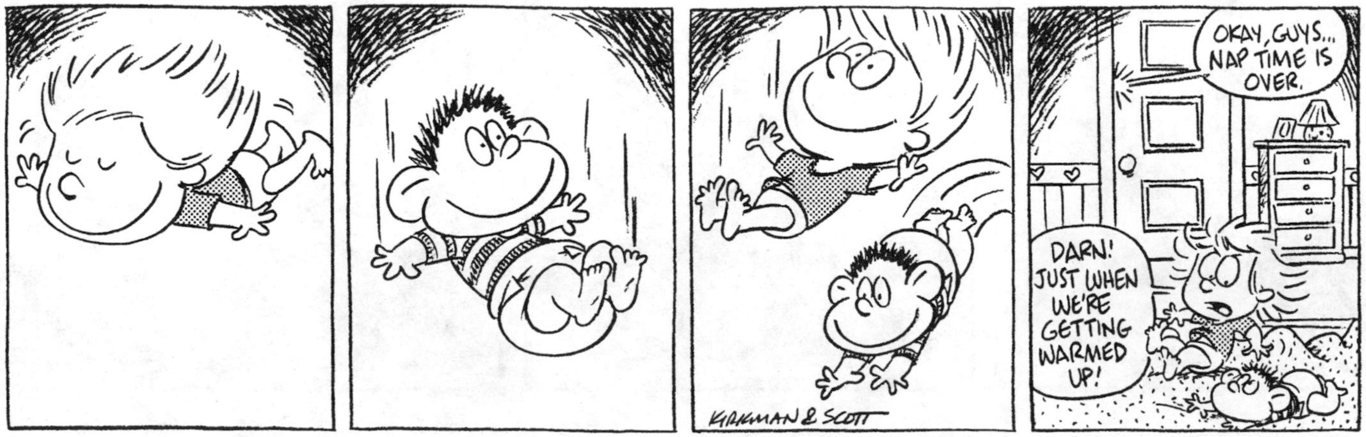
KIRKMAN & SCOTT
OKAY, GUYS... NAP TIME IS OVER.
DARN! JUST WHEN WE'RE GETTING WARMED UP!

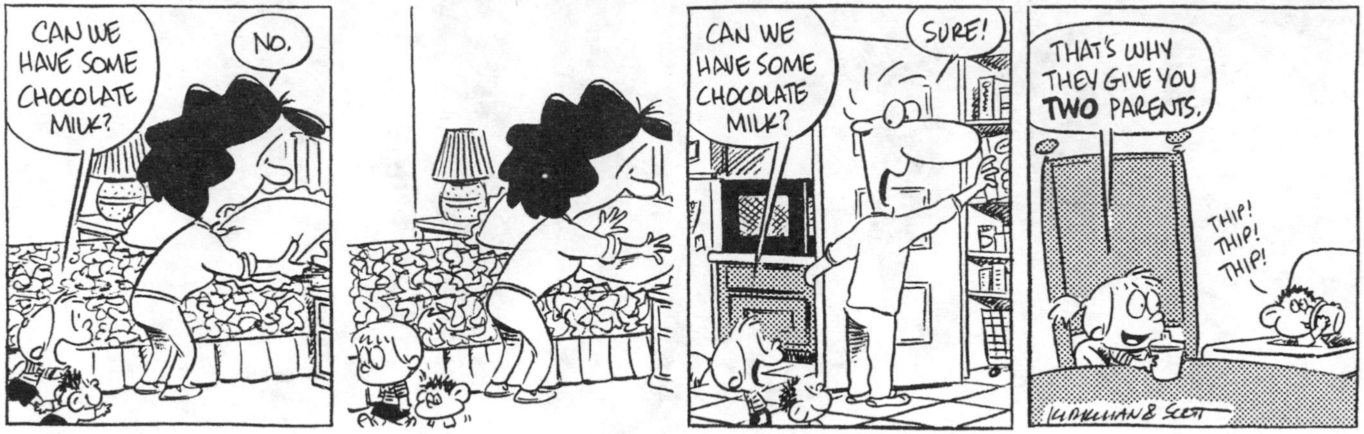
CAN WE HAVE SOME CHOCOLATE MILK?
NO.
CAN WE HAVE SOME CHOCOLATE MILK?
SURE!
THAT'S WHY THEY GIVE YOU **TWO** PARENTS.
THIP! THIP! THIP!
KIRKMAN & SCOTT

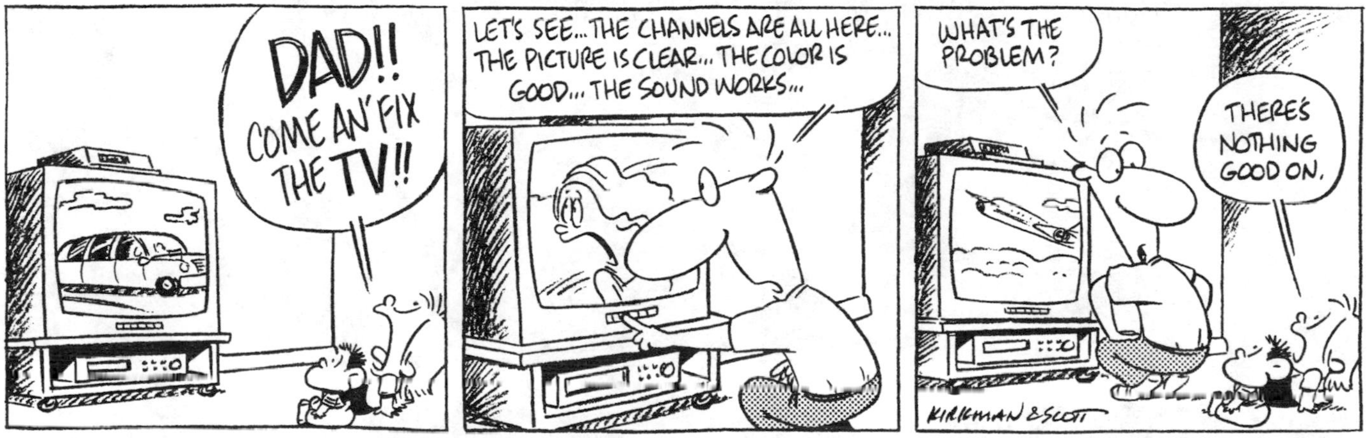
DAD!! COME AN' FIX THE TV!!
LET'S SEE... THE CHANNELS ARE ALL HERE... THE PICTURE IS CLEAR... THE COLOR IS GOOD... THE SOUND WORKS...
WHAT'S THE PROBLEM?
THERE'S NOTHING GOOD ON.
KIRKMAN & SCOTT

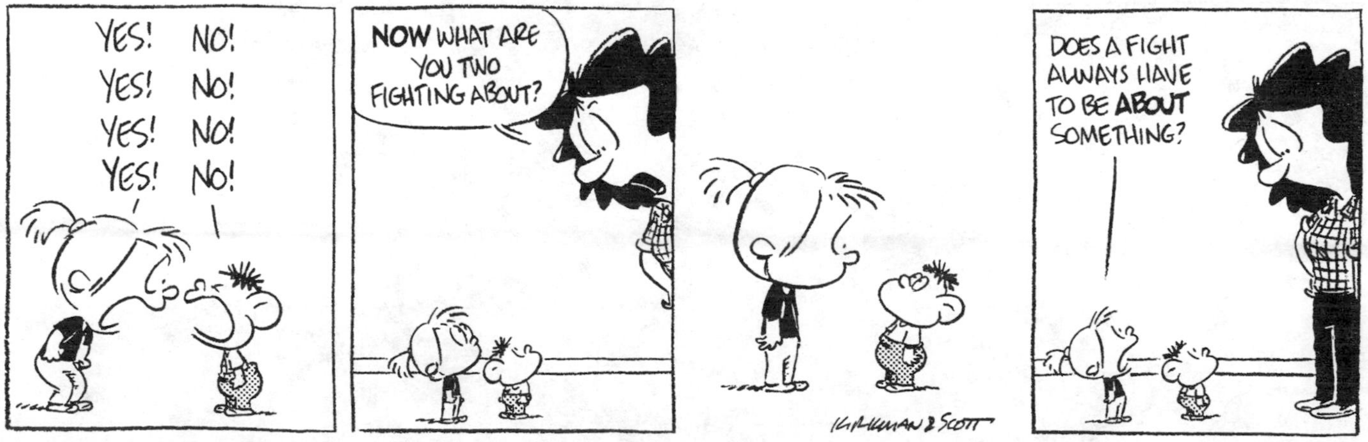
YES! YES! YES! YES!
NO! NO! NO! NO!
NOW WHAT ARE YOU TWO FIGHTING ABOUT?
DOES A FIGHT ALWAYS HAVE TO BE **ABOUT** SOMETHING?
KIRKMAN & SCOTT

STORIES

Stories are the stuff that families are made of: the horrible vacations, the ruined holiday meals, the backyard disasters. Every family has them. The MacPhersons just happen to have them worse.

BACK-TO-SCHOOL SHOPPING

Panel 1:
≥ GASP! ≤ ZOE STARTS PRESCHOOL AGAIN IN TWO WEEKS!

THAT CAN'T BE RIGHT.

Panel 2:
LOOK! I WROTE IT ON THE CALENDAR! IT SAYS RIGHT HERE... SEPTEMBER 8TH, PRESCHOOL STARTS!

SON OF A GUN.

Panel 4:
IS IT JUST ME, OR DID SUMMERS USED TO LAST LONGER?

I THINK WHEN YOU HAVE KIDS, THEY SHORTEN YOUR CALENDARS.

Panel 5:
WE HAVE TO GO SHOPPING FOR BACK-TO-PRESCHOOL CLOTHES FOR ZOE!

WHAT DO YOU MEAN?

Panel 6:
I **MEAN**, WE HAVE TO GO SHOPPING, WE HAVE TO LET HER PICK SOME THINGS OUT AND TRY THEM ON, AND THEN WE HAVE TO BUY THEM!

Panel 7:
DOES THAT HELP?

NO... I MEANT, WHAT DO YOU MEAN "WE"?

KIRKMAN & SCOTT

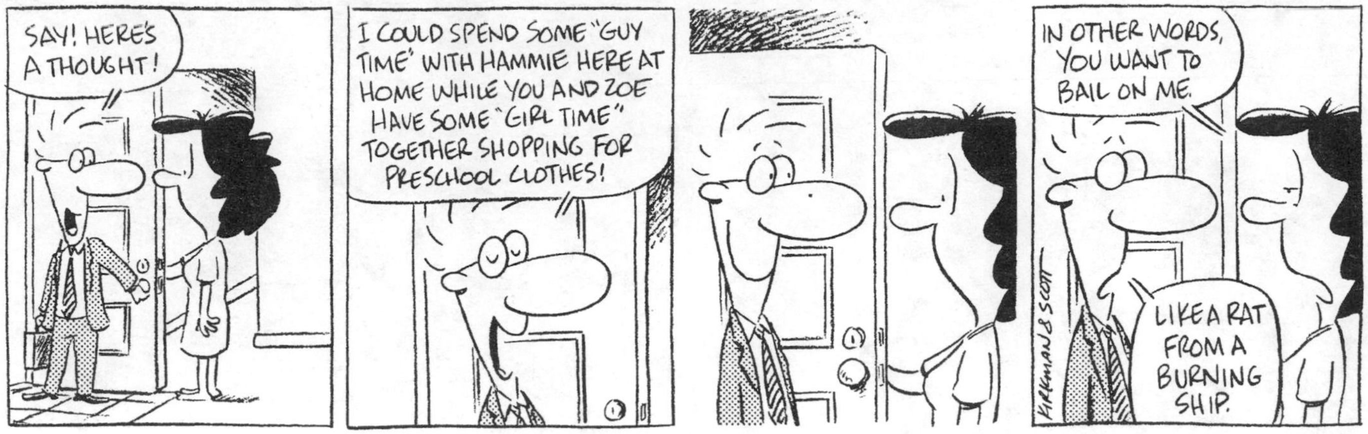
SAY! HERE'S A THOUGHT!
I COULD SPEND SOME "GUY TIME" WITH HAMMIE HERE AT HOME WHILE YOU AND ZOE HAVE SOME "GIRL TIME" TOGETHER SHOPPING FOR PRESCHOOL CLOTHES!
IN OTHER WORDS, YOU WANT TO BAIL ON ME.
LIKE A RAT FROM A BURNING SHIP.
KIRKMAN & SCOTT

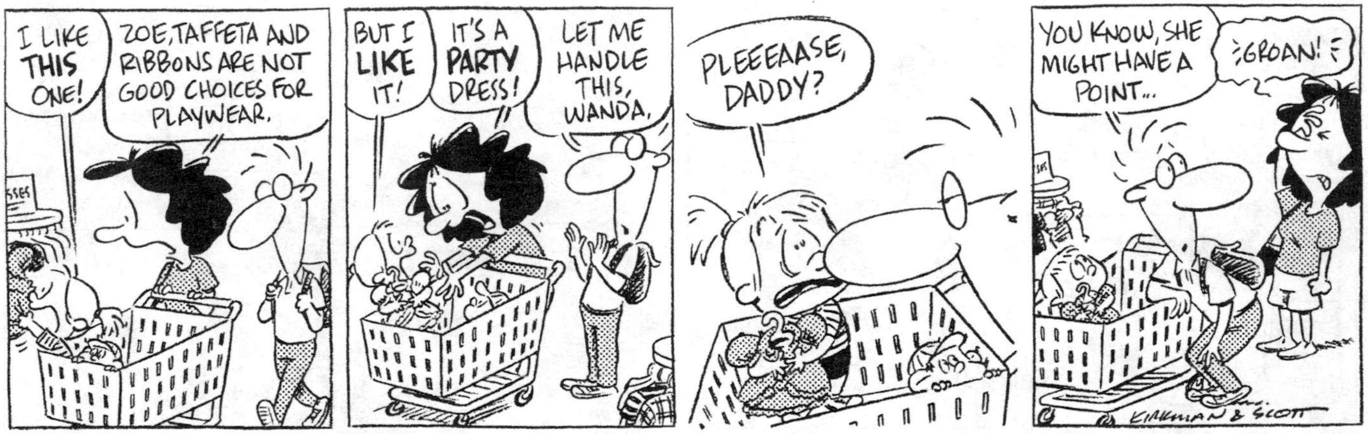
I LIKE **THIS** ONE!
ZOE, TAFFETA AND RIBBONS ARE NOT GOOD CHOICES FOR PLAYWEAR.
BUT I **LIKE** IT!
IT'S A **PARTY** DRESS!
LET ME HANDLE THIS, WANDA.
PLEEEAASE, DADDY?
YOU KNOW, SHE MIGHT HAVE A POINT...
GROAN!
KIRKMAN & SCOTT

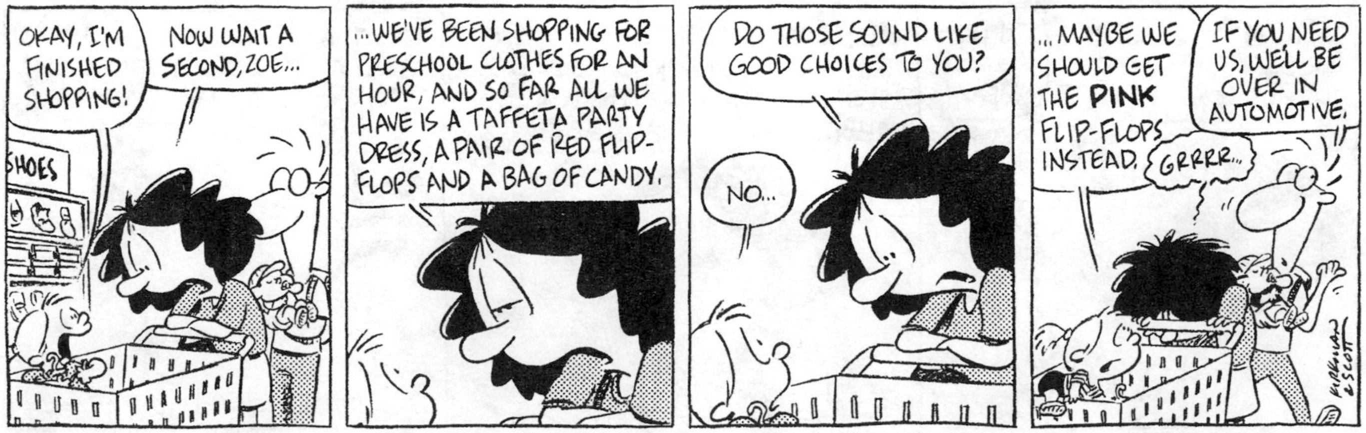
OKAY, I'M FINISHED SHOPPING!
NOW WAIT A SECOND, ZOE...
SHOES
...WE'VE BEEN SHOPPING FOR PRESCHOOL CLOTHES FOR AN HOUR, AND SO FAR ALL WE HAVE IS A TAFFETA PARTY DRESS, A PAIR OF RED FLIP-FLOPS AND A BAG OF CANDY.
DO THOSE SOUND LIKE GOOD CHOICES TO YOU?
NO...
...MAYBE WE SHOULD GET THE **PINK** FLIP-FLOPS INSTEAD.
GRRRR...
IF YOU NEED US, WE'LL BE OVER IN AUTOMOTIVE.
KIRKMAN & SCOTT

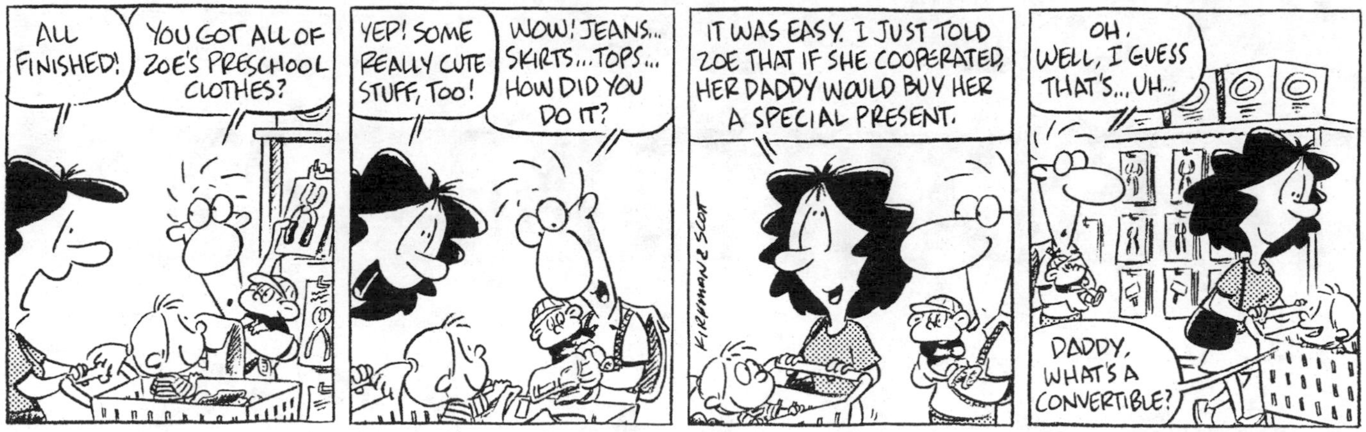
ALL FINISHED!
YOU GOT ALL OF ZOE'S PRESCHOOL CLOTHES?
YEP! SOME REALLY CUTE STUFF, TOO!
WOW! JEANS... SKIRTS... TOPS... HOW DID YOU DO IT?
IT WAS EASY. I JUST TOLD ZOE THAT IF SHE COOPERATED, HER DADDY WOULD BUY HER A SPECIAL PRESENT.
OH. WELL, I GUESS THAT'S... UH...
DADDY, WHAT'S A CONVERTIBLE?
KIRKMAN & SCOTT

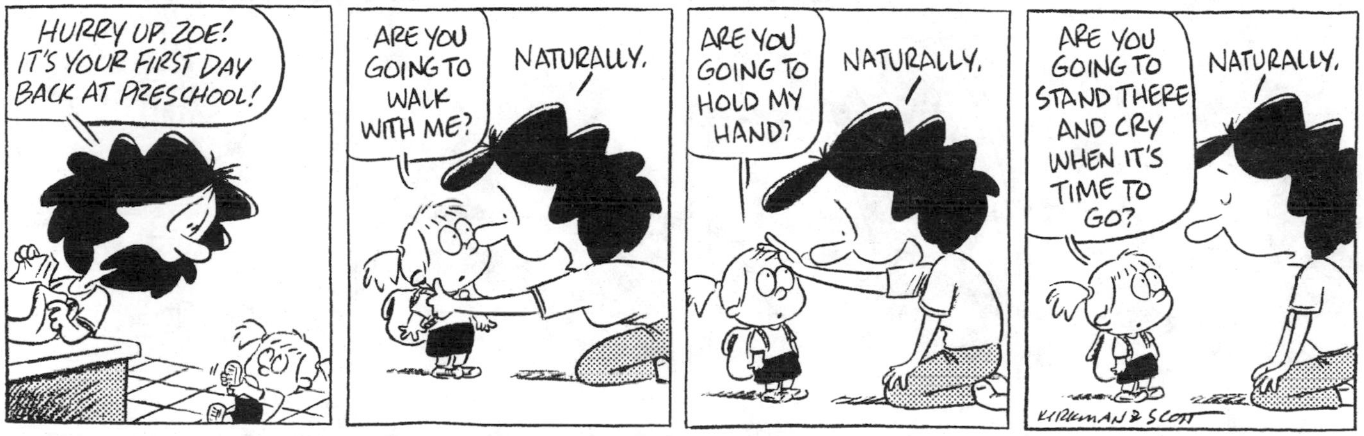
HURRY UP, ZOE! IT'S YOUR FIRST DAY BACK AT PRESCHOOL!
ARE YOU GOING TO WALK WITH ME?
NATURALLY.
ARE YOU GOING TO HOLD MY HAND?
NATURALLY.
ARE YOU GOING TO STAND THERE AND CRY WHEN IT'S TIME TO GO?
NATURALLY.
KIRKMAN & SCOTT

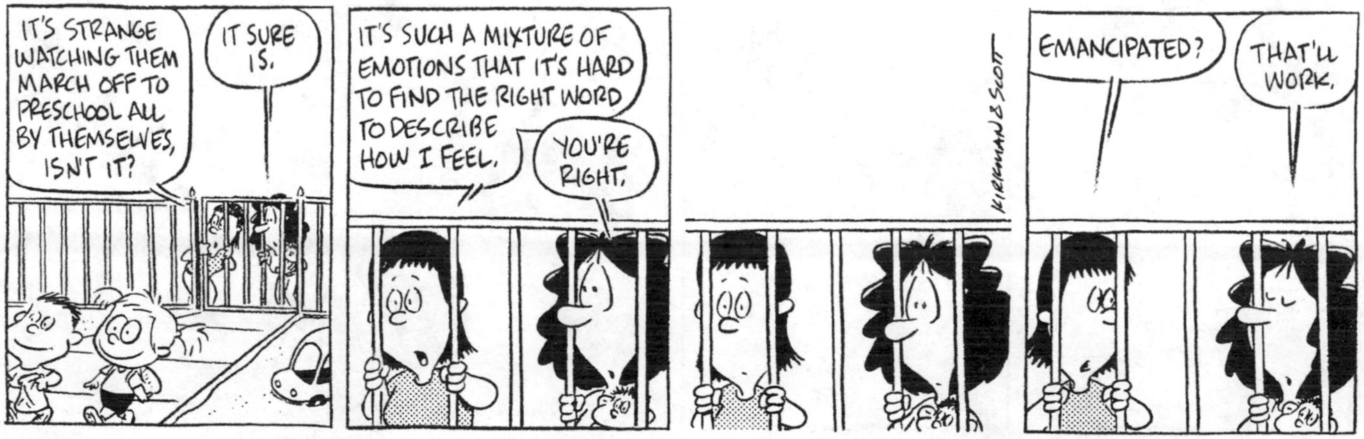
IT'S STRANGE WATCHING THEM MARCH OFF TO PRESCHOOL ALL BY THEMSELVES, ISN'T IT?
IT SURE IS.
IT'S SUCH A MIXTURE OF EMOTIONS THAT IT'S HARD TO FIND THE RIGHT WORD TO DESCRIBE HOW I FEEL.
YOU'RE RIGHT.
KIRKMAN & SCOTT
EMANCIPATED?
THAT'LL WORK.

THE BUG FUNERAL

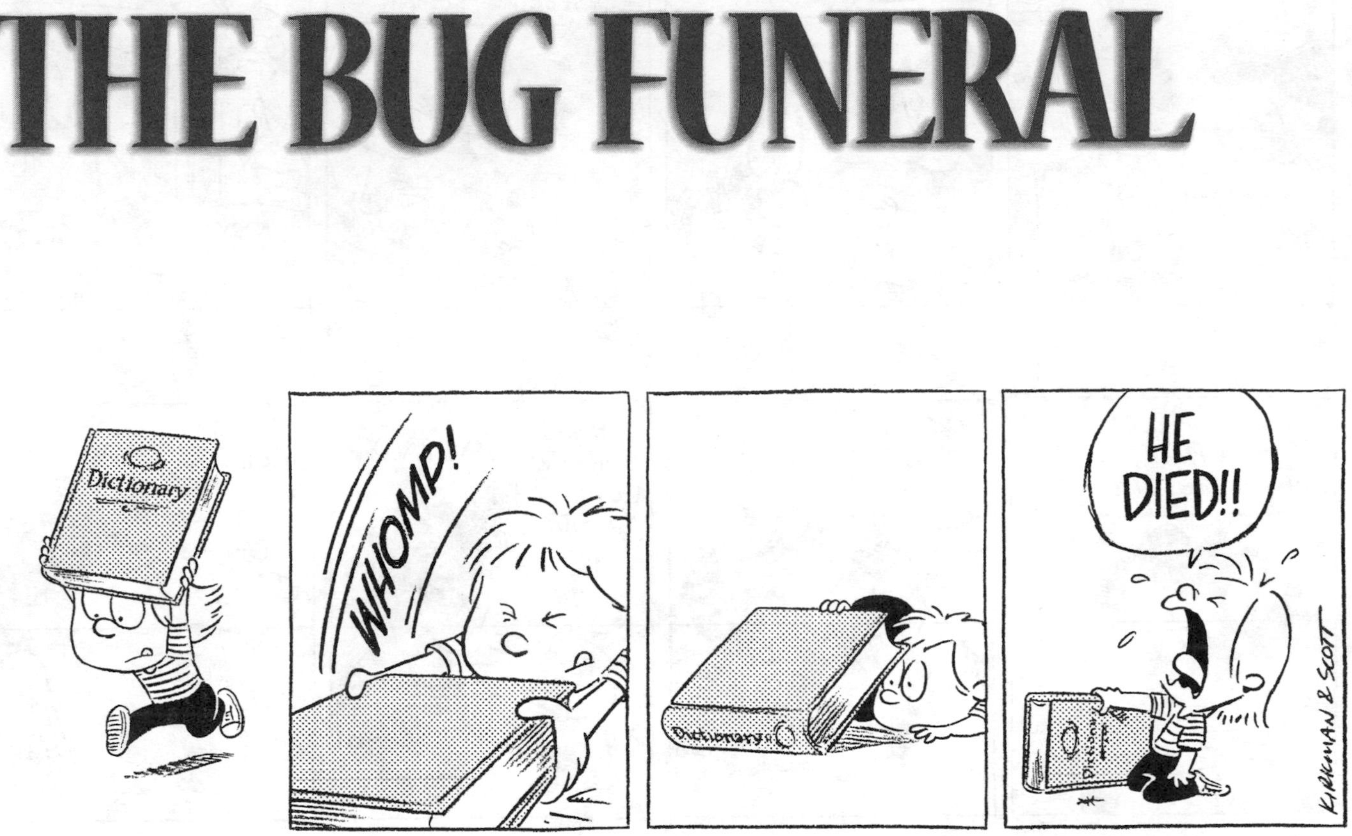
Dictionary
WHOMP!
Dictionary
HE DIED!!
KIRKMAN & SCOTT

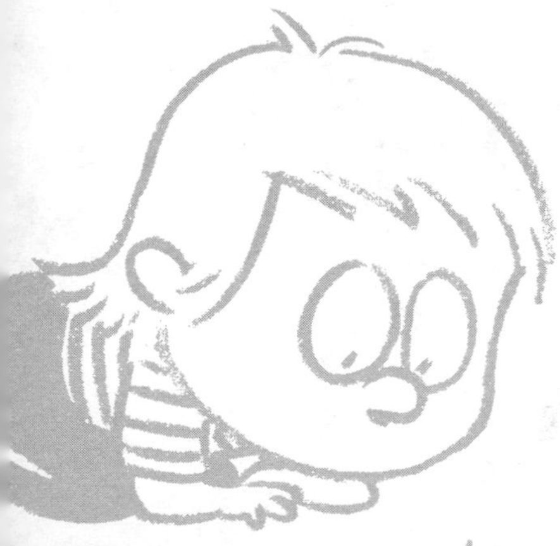

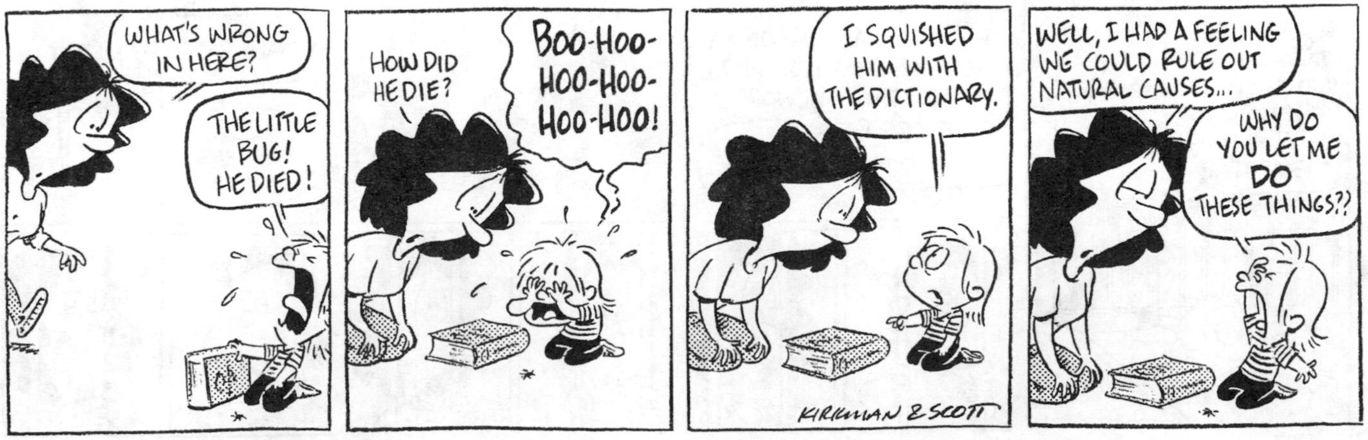
WHAT'S WRONG IN HERE?
THE LITTLE BUG! HE DIED!
HOW DID HE DIE?
BOO-HOO-HOO-HOO-HOO-HOO!
I SQUISHED HIM WITH THE DICTIONARY.
KIRKMAN & SCOTT
WELL, I HAD A FEELING WE COULD RULE OUT NATURAL CAUSES...
WHY DO YOU LET ME DO THESE THINGS??

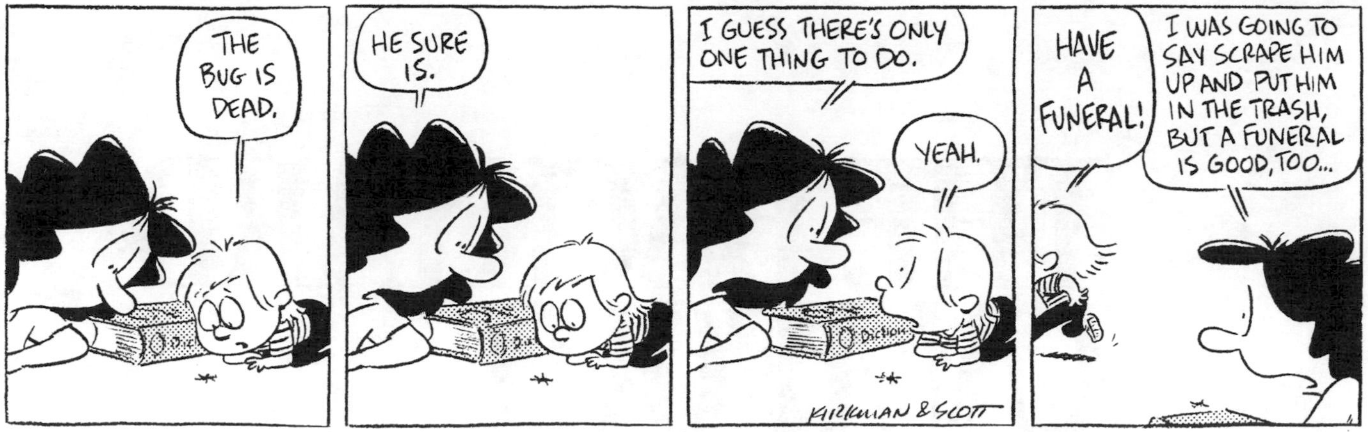
THE BUG IS DEAD.
HE SURE IS.
I GUESS THERE'S ONLY ONE THING TO DO.
YEAH.
KIRKMAN & SCOTT
HAVE A FUNERAL!
I WAS GOING TO SAY SCRAPE HIM UP AND PUT HIM IN THE TRASH, BUT A FUNERAL IS GOOD, TOO...

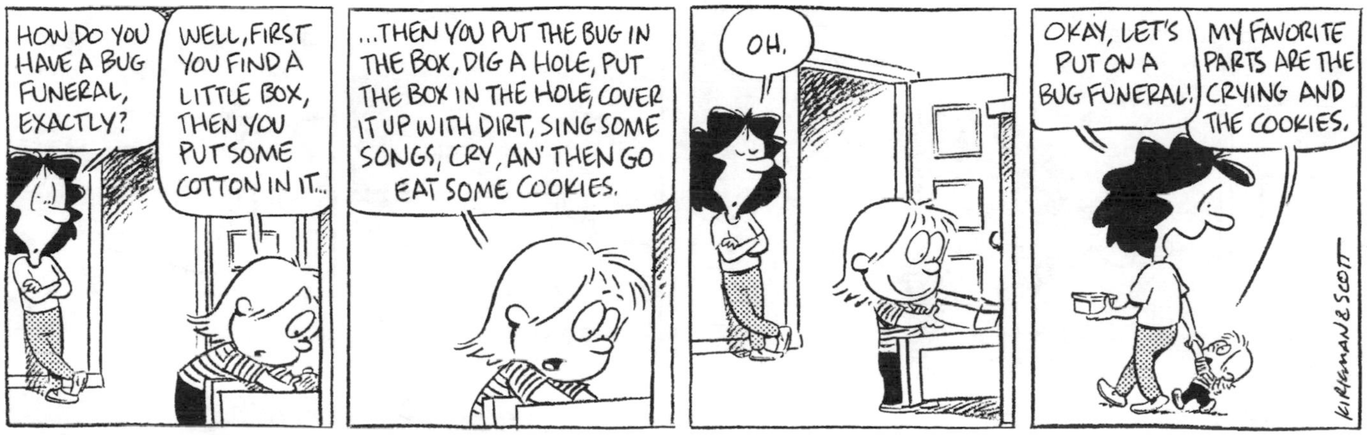
HOW DO YOU HAVE A BUG FUNERAL, EXACTLY?
WELL, FIRST YOU FIND A LITTLE BOX, THEN YOU PUT SOME COTTON IN IT...
...THEN YOU PUT THE BUG IN THE BOX, DIG A HOLE, PUT THE BOX IN THE HOLE, COVER IT UP WITH DIRT, SING SOME SONGS, CRY, AN' THEN GO EAT SOME COOKIES.
OH.
OKAY, LET'S PUT ON A BUG FUNERAL!
MY FAVORITE PARTS ARE THE CRYING AND THE COOKIES.
KIRKMAN & SCOTT

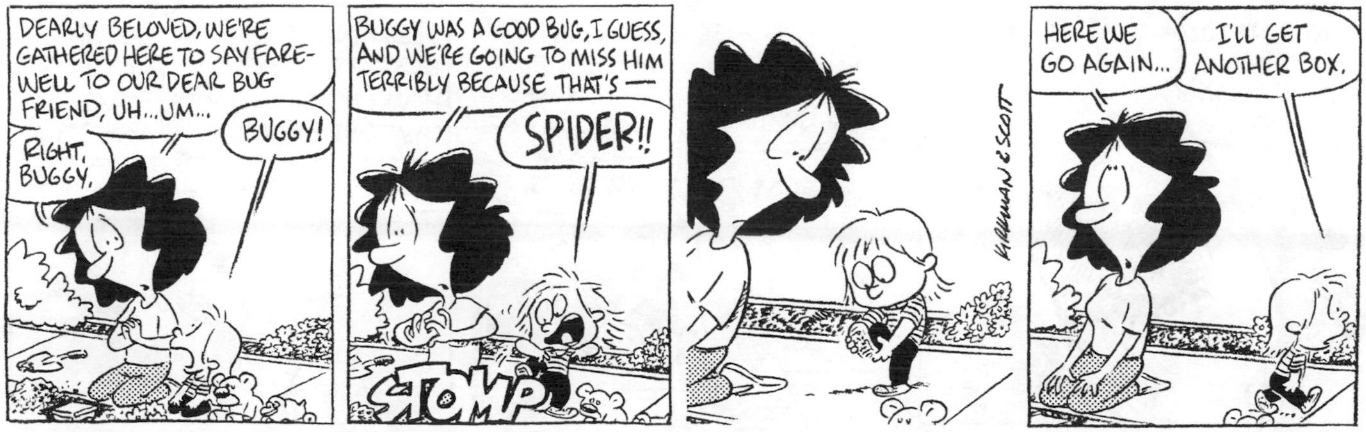
DEARLY BELOVED, WE'RE GATHERED HERE TO SAY FAREWELL TO OUR DEAR BUG FRIEND, UH...UM...
BUGGY!
RIGHT, BUGGY.
BUGGY WAS A GOOD BUG, I GUESS, AND WE'RE GOING TO MISS HIM TERRIBLY BECAUSE THAT'S —
SPIDER!!
STOMP
KIRKMAN & SCOTT
HERE WE GO AGAIN...
I'LL GET ANOTHER BOX.

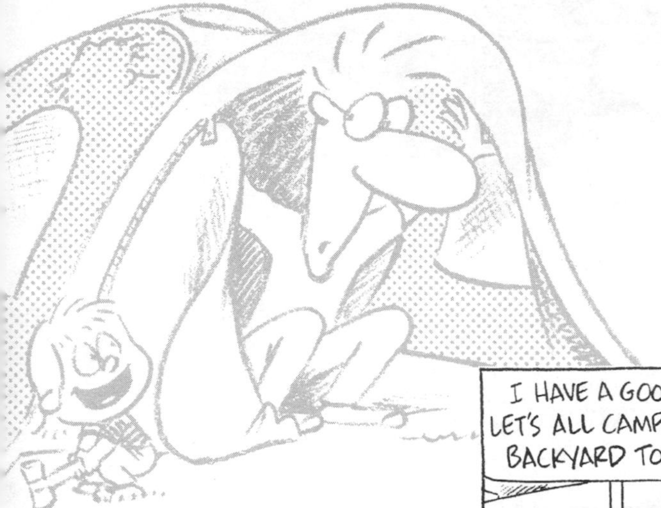

THE BACKYARD CAMPOUT

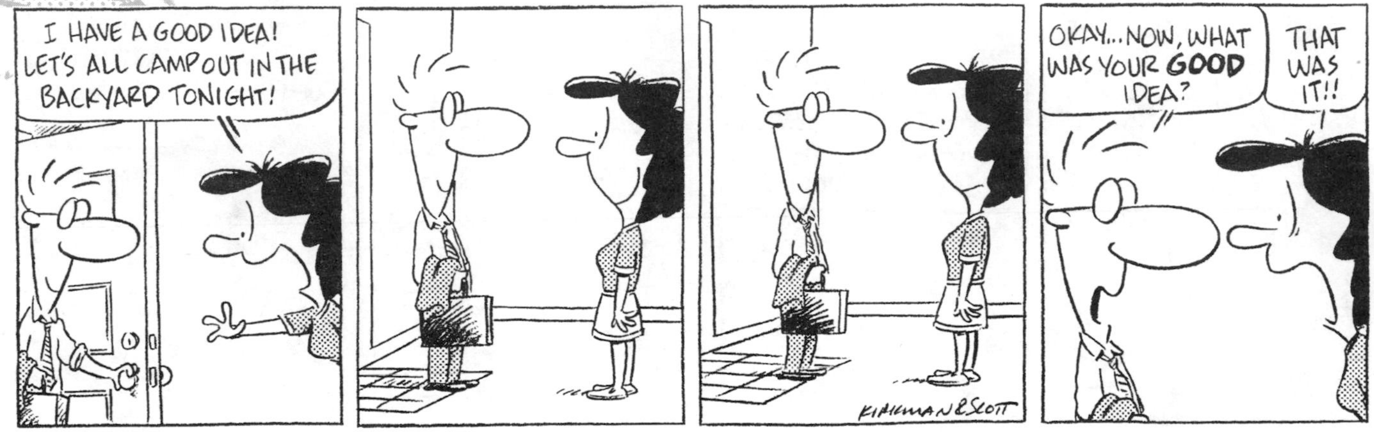

I HAVE A GOOD IDEA! LET'S ALL CAMP OUT IN THE BACKYARD TONIGHT!
OKAY... NOW, WHAT WAS YOUR **GOOD** IDEA?
THAT WAS IT!!
KIRKMAN & SCOTT

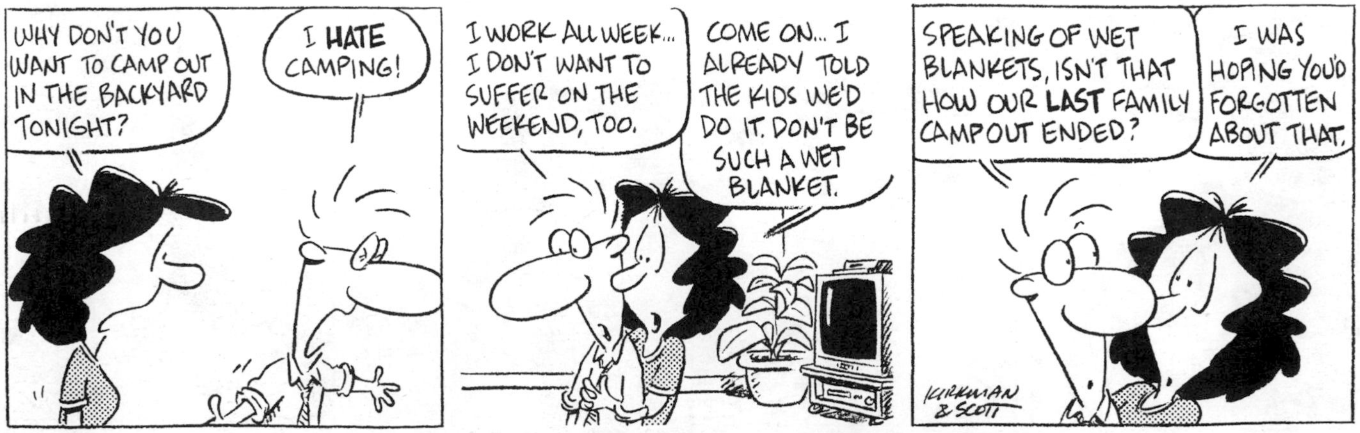

WHY DON'T YOU WANT TO CAMP OUT IN THE BACKYARD TONIGHT?
I **HATE** CAMPING!
I WORK ALL WEEK... I DON'T WANT TO SUFFER ON THE WEEKEND, TOO.
COME ON... I ALREADY TOLD THE KIDS WE'D DO IT. DON'T BE SUCH A WET BLANKET.
SPEAKING OF WET BLANKETS, ISN'T THAT HOW OUR **LAST** FAMILY CAMPOUT ENDED?
I WAS HOPING YOU'D FORGOTTEN ABOUT THAT.
KIRKMAN & SCOTT

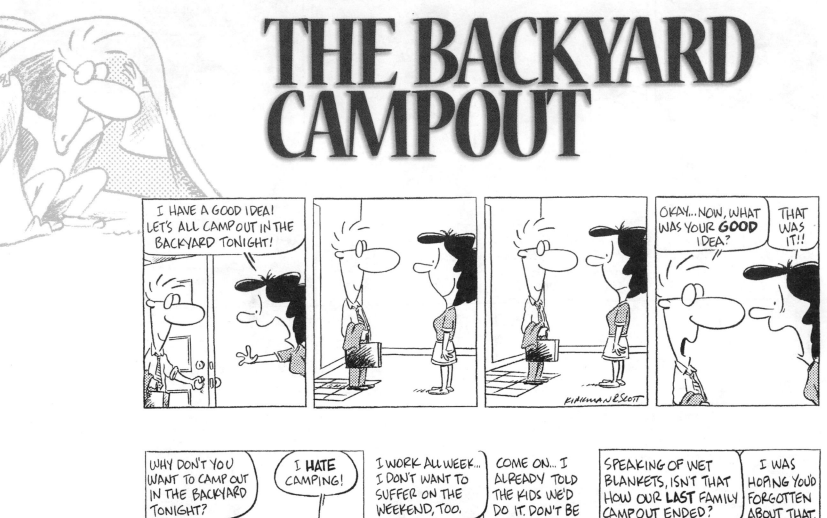

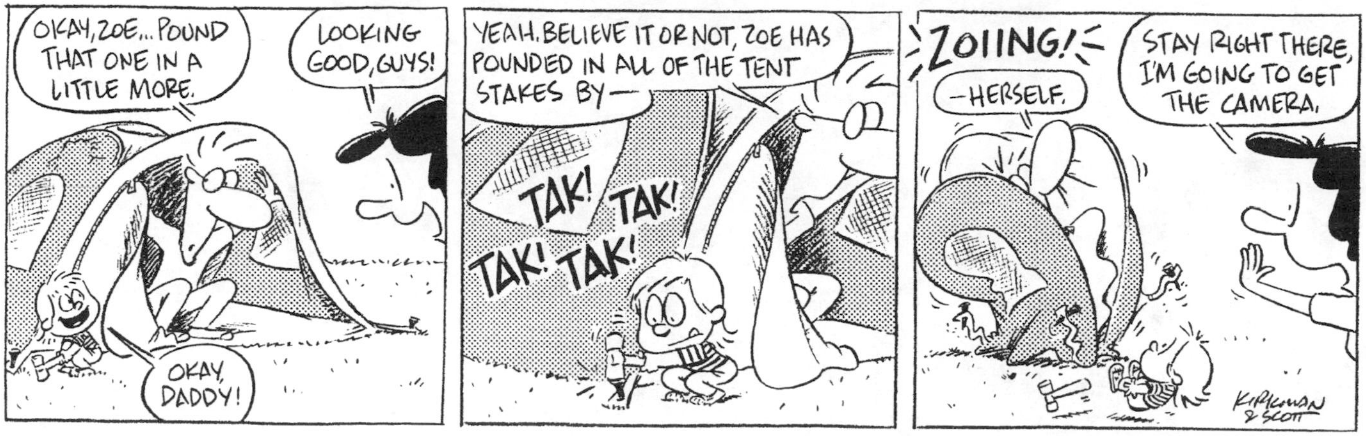
OKAY, ZOE... POUND THAT ONE IN A LITTLE MORE.
LOOKING GOOD, GUYS!
OKAY, DADDY!
YEAH. BELIEVE IT OR NOT, ZOE HAS POUNDED IN ALL OF THE TENT STAKES BY—
TAK! TAK! TAK! TAK!
ZOIING!
—HERSELF.
STAY RIGHT THERE, I'M GOING TO GET THE CAMERA.
KIRKMAN & SCOTT

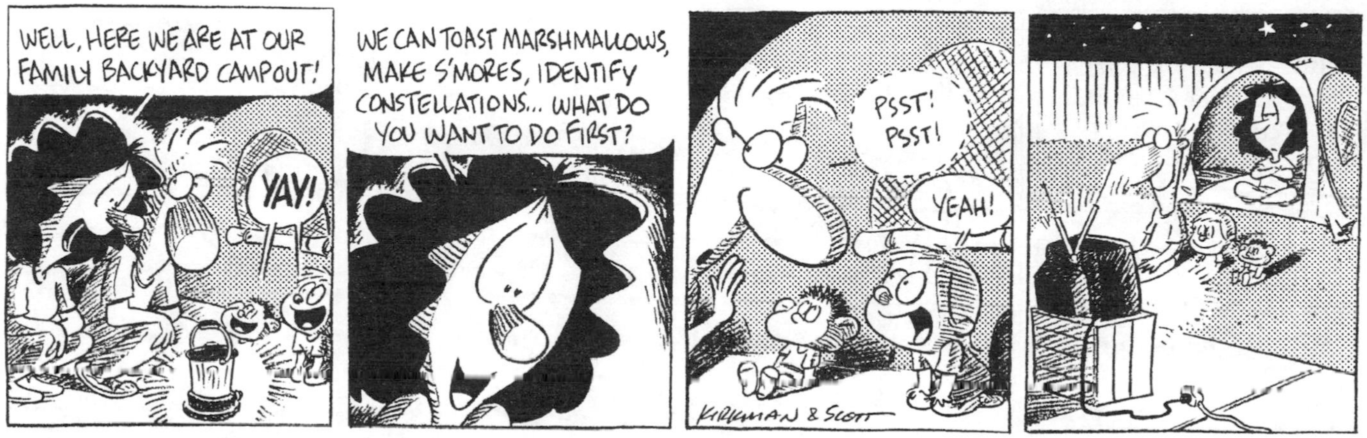
WELL, HERE WE ARE AT OUR FAMILY BACKYARD CAMPOUT!
YAY!
WE CAN TOAST MARSHMALLOWS, MAKE S'MORES, IDENTIFY CONSTELLATIONS... WHAT DO YOU WANT TO DO FIRST?
PSST! PSST!
YEAH!
KIRKMAN & SCOTT

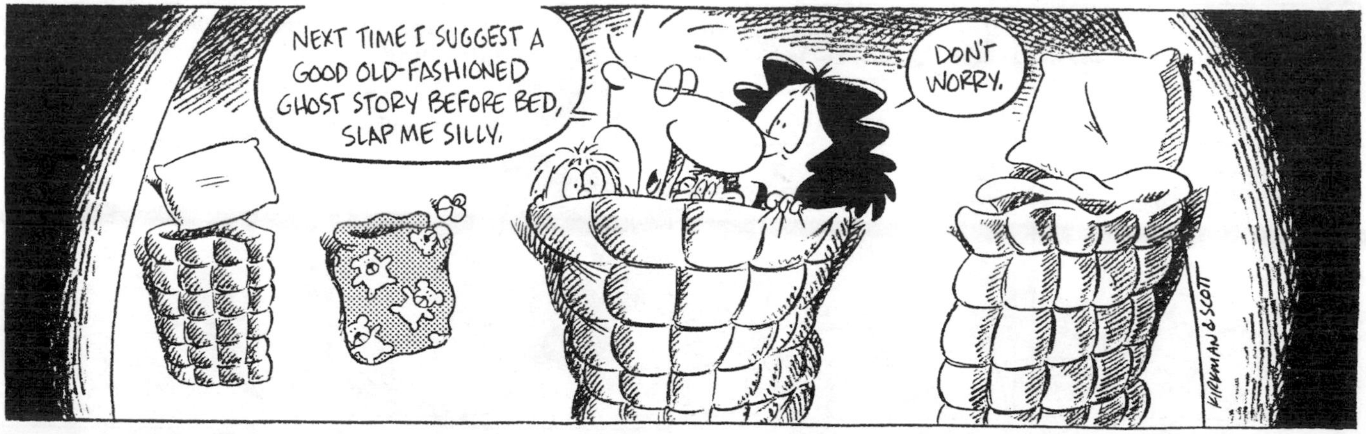
NEXT TIME I SUGGEST A GOOD OLD-FASHIONED GHOST STORY BEFORE BED, SLAP ME SILLY.
DON'T WORRY.
KIRKMAN & SCOTT

THE CLASSROOM VOLUNTEER

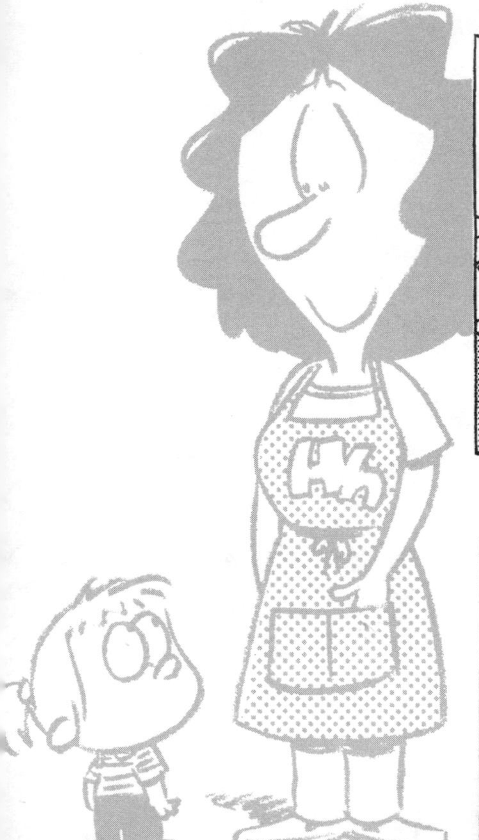

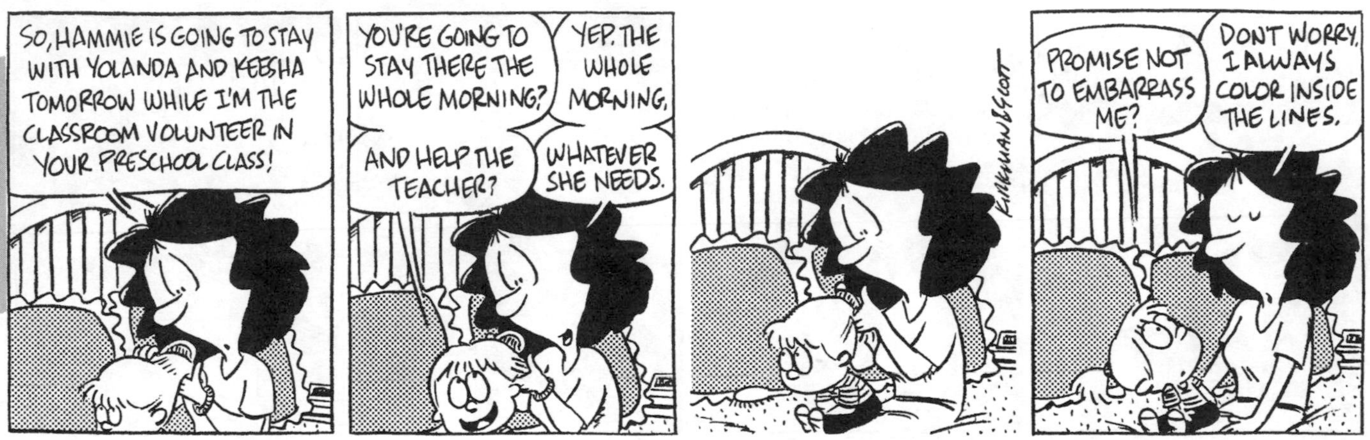

SO, HAMMIE IS GOING TO STAY WITH YOLANDA AND KEESHA TOMORROW WHILE I'M THE CLASSROOM VOLUNTEER IN YOUR PRESCHOOL CLASS!
YOU'RE GOING TO STAY THERE THE WHOLE MORNING?
YEP. THE WHOLE MORNING.
AND HELP THE TEACHER?
WHATEVER SHE NEEDS.
PROMISE NOT TO EMBARRASS ME?
DON'T WORRY. I ALWAYS COLOR INSIDE THE LINES.

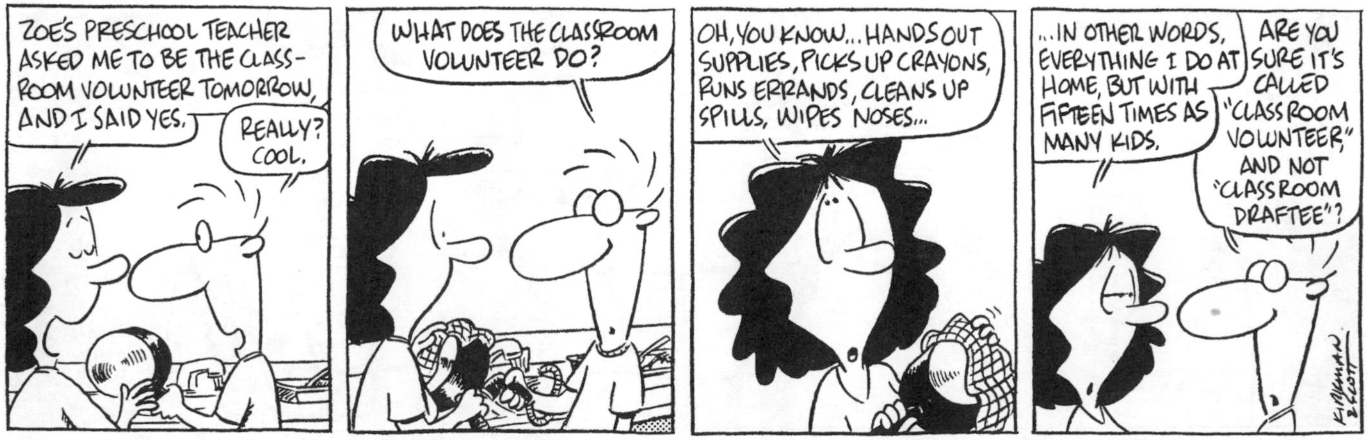

ZOE'S PRESCHOOL TEACHER ASKED ME TO BE THE CLASS-ROOM VOLUNTEER TOMORROW, AND I SAID YES.
REALLY? COOL.
WHAT DOES THE CLASSROOM VOLUNTEER DO?
OH, YOU KNOW... HANDS OUT SUPPLIES, PICKS UP CRAYONS, RUNS ERRANDS, CLEANS UP SPILLS, WIPES NOSES...
...IN OTHER WORDS, EVERYTHING I DO AT HOME, BUT WITH FIFTEEN TIMES AS MANY KIDS.
ARE YOU SURE IT'S CALLED "CLASSROOM VOLUNTEER," AND NOT "CLASSROOM DRAFTEE"?

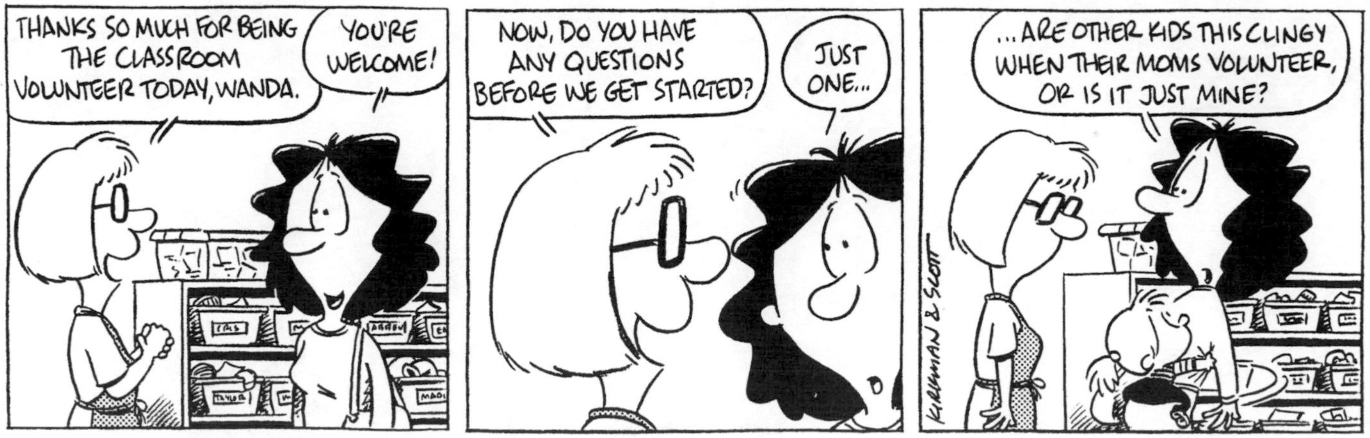
THANKS SO MUCH FOR BEING THE CLASSROOM VOLUNTEER TODAY, WANDA.
YOU'RE WELCOME!
NOW, DO YOU HAVE ANY QUESTIONS BEFORE WE GET STARTED?
JUST ONE...
...ARE OTHER KIDS THIS CLINGY WHEN THEIR MOMS VOLUNTEER, OR IS IT JUST MINE?
KIRKMAN & SCOTT

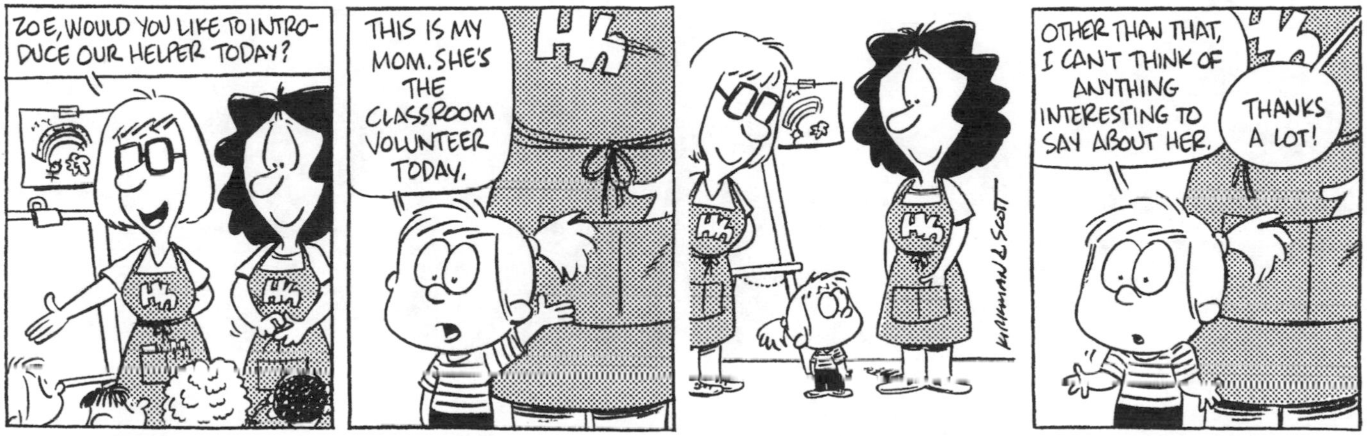
ZOE, WOULD YOU LIKE TO INTRODUCE OUR HELPER TODAY?
THIS IS MY MOM. SHE'S THE CLASSROOM VOLUNTEER TODAY.
KIRKMAN & SCOTT
OTHER THAN THAT, I CAN'T THINK OF ANYTHING INTERESTING TO SAY ABOUT HER.
THANKS A LOT!

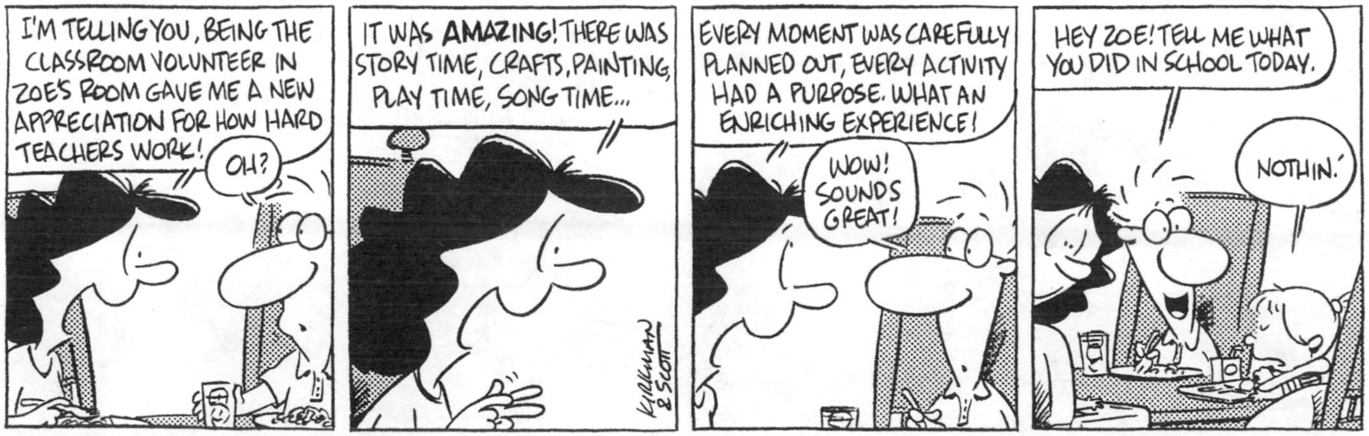
I'M TELLING YOU, BEING THE CLASSROOM VOLUNTEER IN ZOE'S ROOM GAVE ME A NEW APPRECIATION FOR HOW HARD TEACHERS WORK!
OH?
IT WAS AMAZING! THERE WAS STORY TIME, CRAFTS, PAINTING, PLAY TIME, SONG TIME...
KIRKMAN & SCOTT
EVERY MOMENT WAS CAREFULLY PLANNED OUT, EVERY ACTIVITY HAD A PURPOSE. WHAT AN ENRICHING EXPERIENCE!
WOW! SOUNDS GREAT!
HEY ZOE! TELL ME WHAT YOU DID IN SCHOOL TODAY.
NOTHIN'.

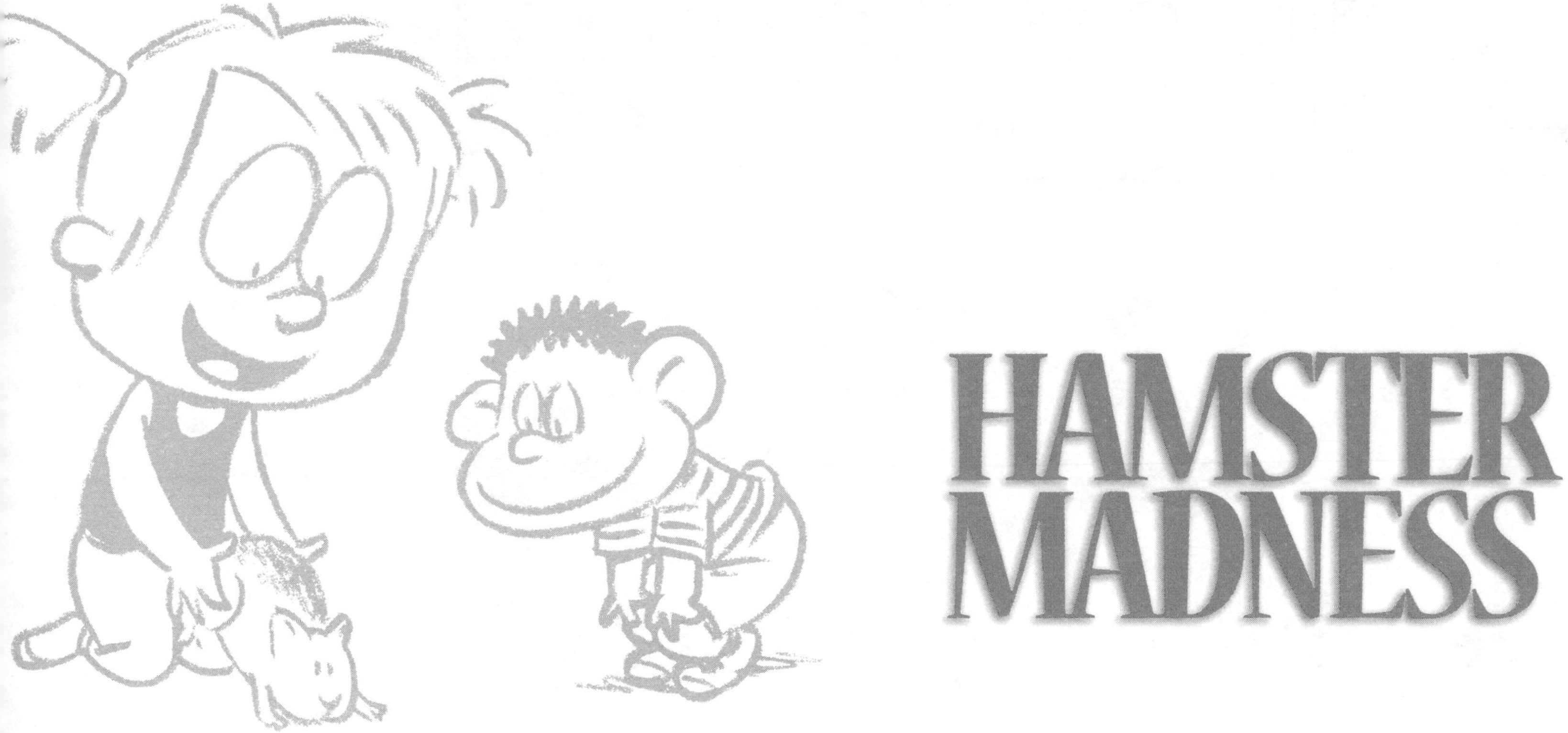

HAMSTER MADNESS

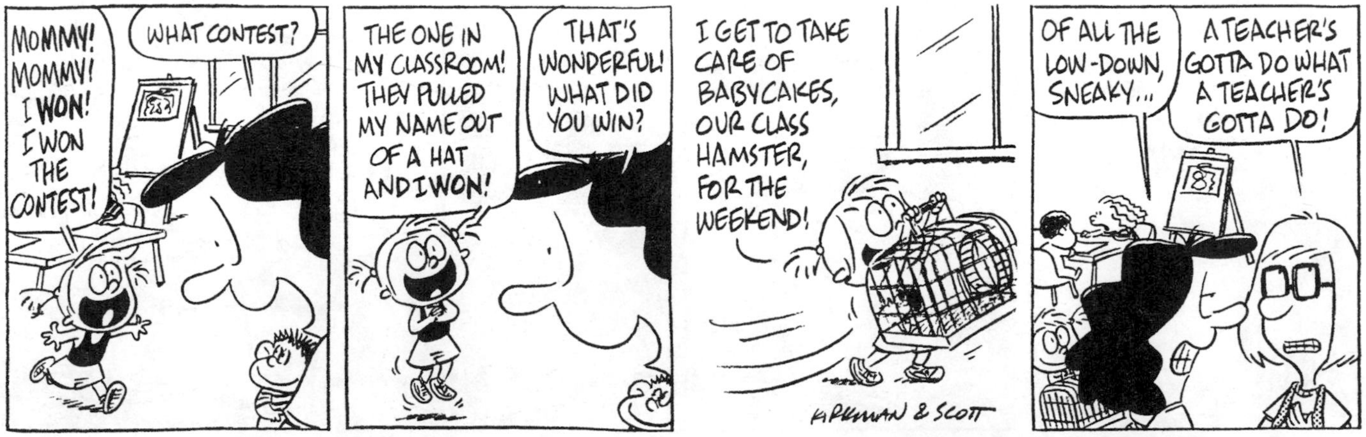
MOMMY! MOMMY! I WON! I WON THE CONTEST!
WHAT CONTEST?
THE ONE IN MY CLASSROOM! THEY PULLED MY NAME OUT OF A HAT AND I WON!
THAT'S WONDERFUL! WHAT DID YOU WIN?
I GET TO TAKE CARE OF BABYCAKES, OUR CLASS HAMSTER, FOR THE WEEKEND!
KIRKMAN & SCOTT
OF ALL THE LOW-DOWN, SNEAKY...
A TEACHER'S GOTTA DO WHAT A TEACHER'S GOTTA DO!

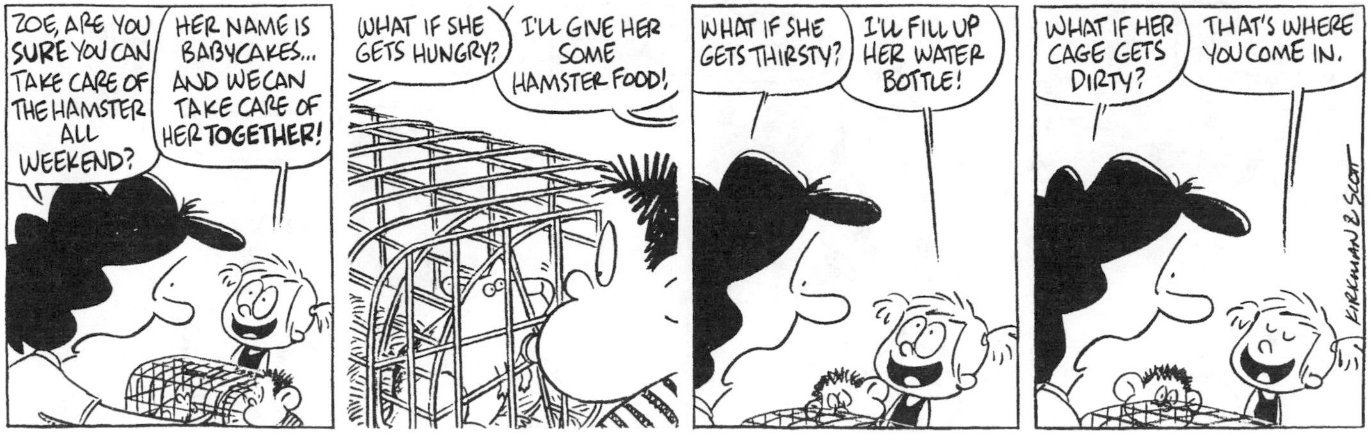
ZOE, ARE YOU SURE YOU CAN TAKE CARE OF THE HAMSTER ALL WEEKEND?
HER NAME IS BABYCAKES... AND WE CAN TAKE CARE OF HER TOGETHER!
WHAT IF SHE GETS HUNGRY?
I'LL GIVE HER SOME HAMSTER FOOD!
WHAT IF SHE GETS THIRSTY?
I'LL FILL UP HER WATER BOTTLE!
WHAT IF HER CAGE GETS DIRTY?
THAT'S WHERE YOU COME IN.
KIRKMAN & SCOTT

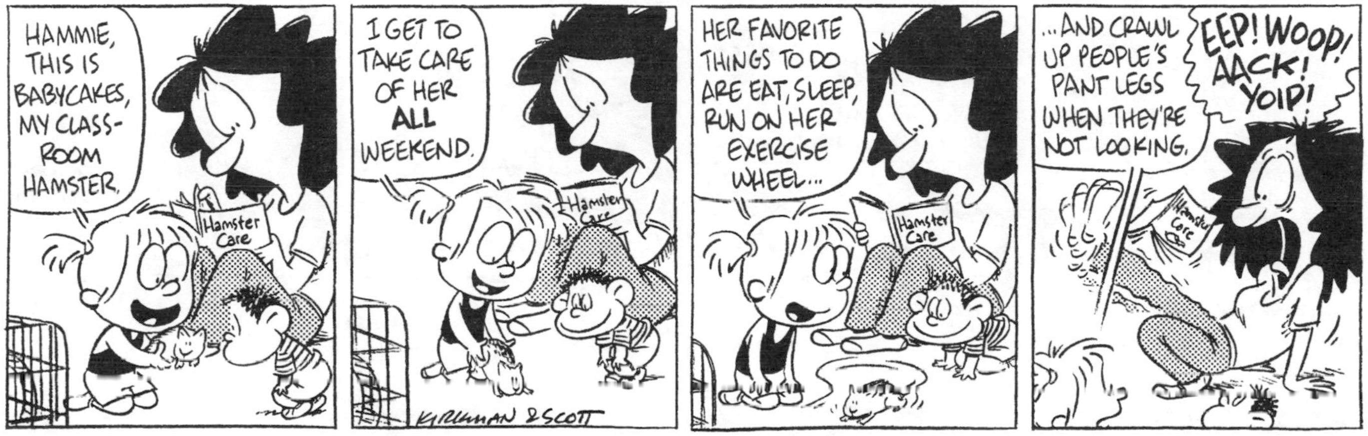
HAMMIE, THIS IS BABYCAKES, MY CLASSROOM HAMSTER.
Hamster Care
I GET TO TAKE CARE OF HER ALL WEEKEND.
Hamster Care
KIRKMAN & SCOTT
HER FAVORITE THINGS TO DO ARE EAT, SLEEP, RUN ON HER EXERCISE WHEEL...
Hamster Care
...AND CRAWL UP PEOPLE'S PANT LEGS WHEN THEY'RE NOT LOOKING.
EEP! WOOP! AACK! YOIP!

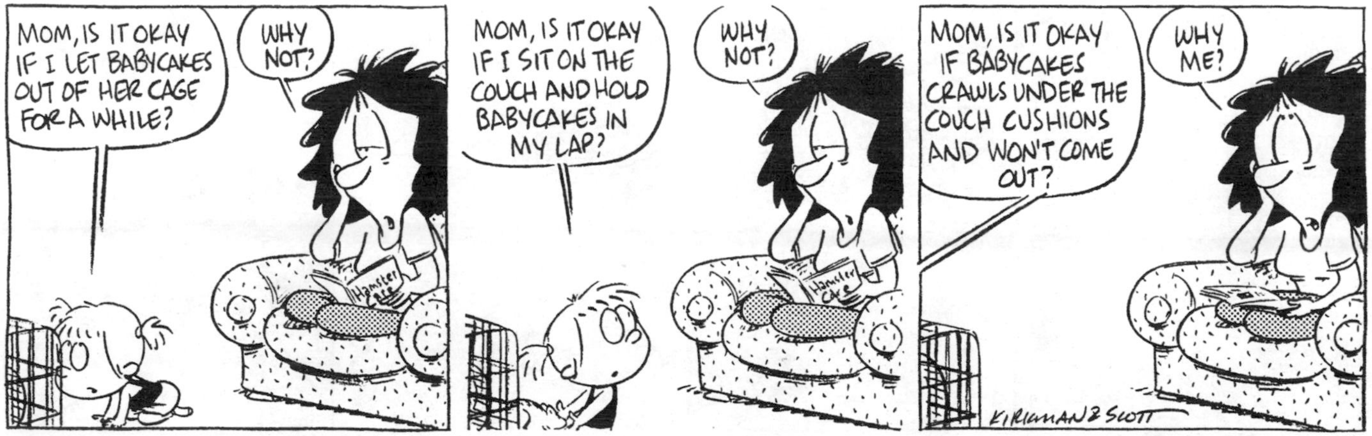
MOM, IS IT OKAY IF I LET BABYCAKES OUT OF HER CAGE FOR A WHILE?
WHY NOT?
MOM, IS IT OKAY IF I SIT ON THE COUCH AND HOLD BABYCAKES IN MY LAP?
WHY NOT?
MOM, IS IT OKAY IF BABYCAKES CRAWLS UNDER THE COUCH CUSHIONS AND WON'T COME OUT?
WHY ME?
KIRKMAN & SCOTT

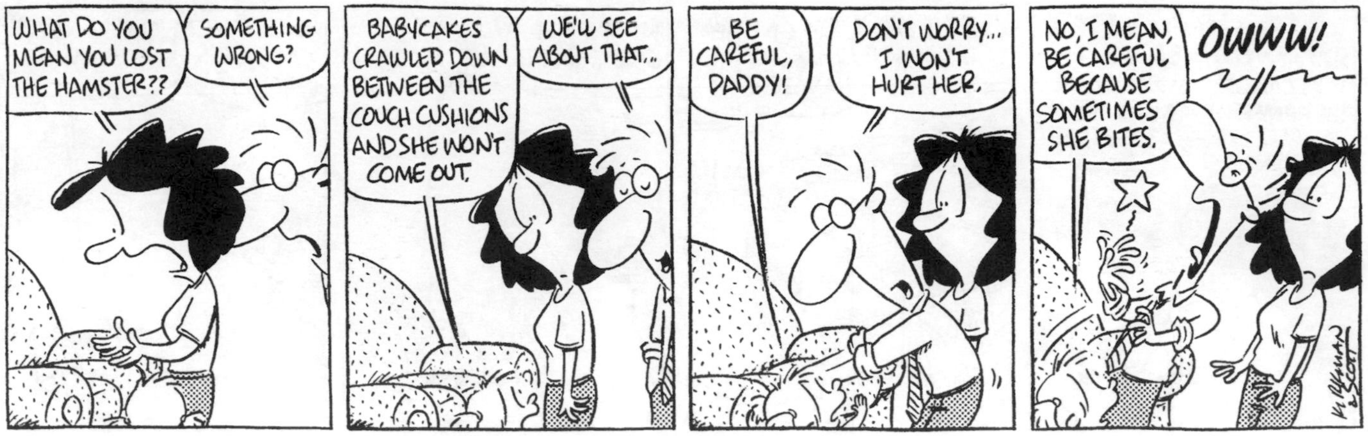
WHAT DO YOU MEAN YOU LOST THE HAMSTER??
SOMETHING WRONG?
BABYCAKES CRAWLED DOWN BETWEEN THE COUCH CUSHIONS AND SHE WON'T COME OUT.
WE'LL SEE ABOUT THAT...
BE CAREFUL, DADDY!
DON'T WORRY... I WON'T HURT HER.
NO, I MEAN, BE CAREFUL BECAUSE SOMETIMES SHE BITES.
OWWW!

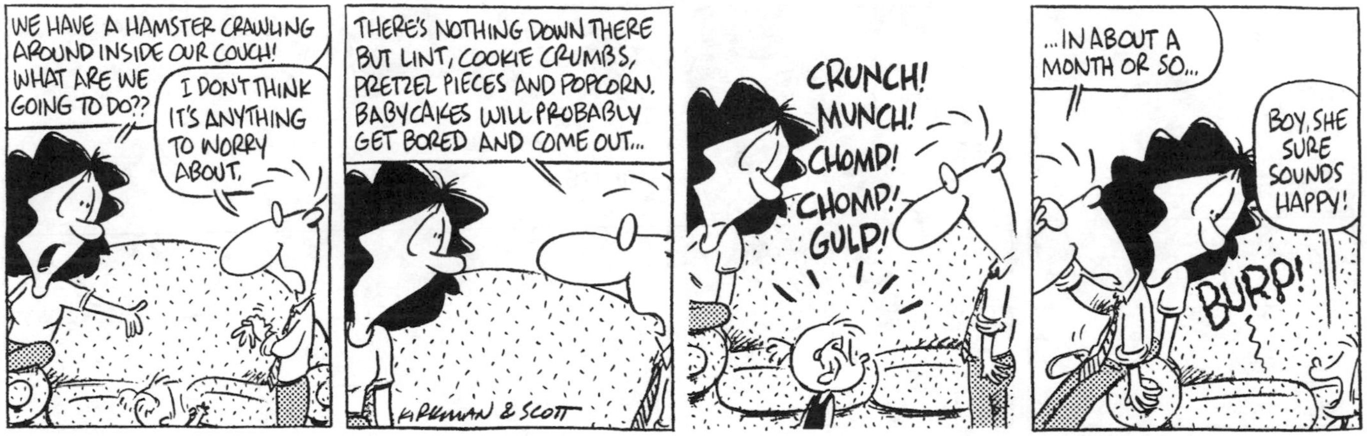
WE HAVE A HAMSTER CRAWLING AROUND INSIDE OUR COUCH! WHAT ARE WE GOING TO DO??
I DON'T THINK IT'S ANYTHING TO WORRY ABOUT.
THERE'S NOTHING DOWN THERE BUT LINT, COOKIE CRUMBS, PRETZEL PIECES AND POPCORN. BABYCAKES WILL PROBABLY GET BORED AND COME OUT...
KIRKMAN & SCOTT
CRUNCH! MUNCH! CHOMP! CHOMP! GULP!
...IN ABOUT A MONTH OR SO...
BOY, SHE SURE SOUNDS HAPPY!
BURP!

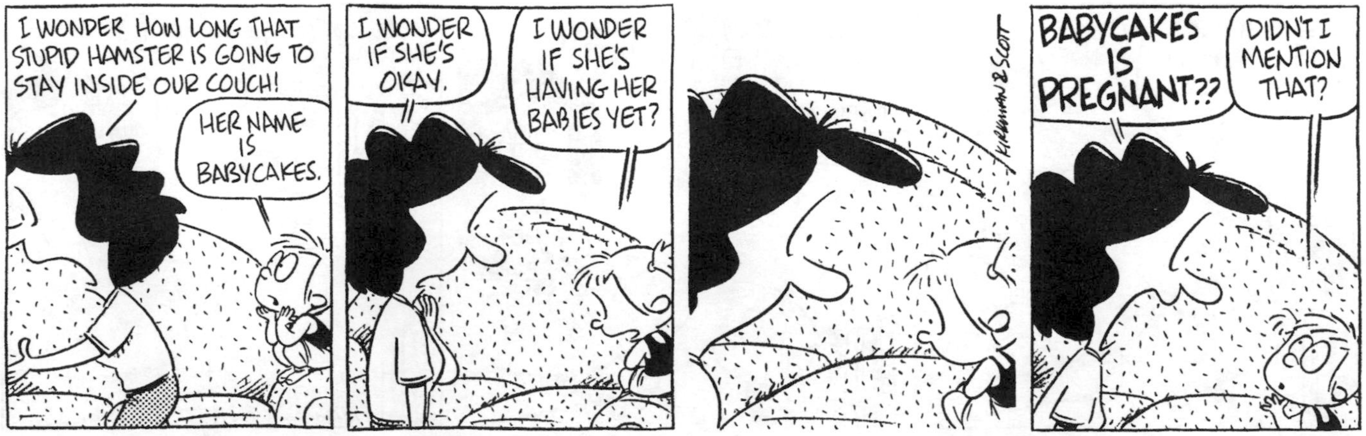
I WONDER HOW LONG THAT STUPID HAMSTER IS GOING TO STAY INSIDE OUR COUCH!
HER NAME IS BABYCAKES.
I WONDER IF SHE'S OKAY.
I WONDER IF SHE'S HAVING HER BABIES YET?
KIRKMAN & SCOTT
BABYCAKES IS PREGNANT??
DIDN'T I MENTION THAT?

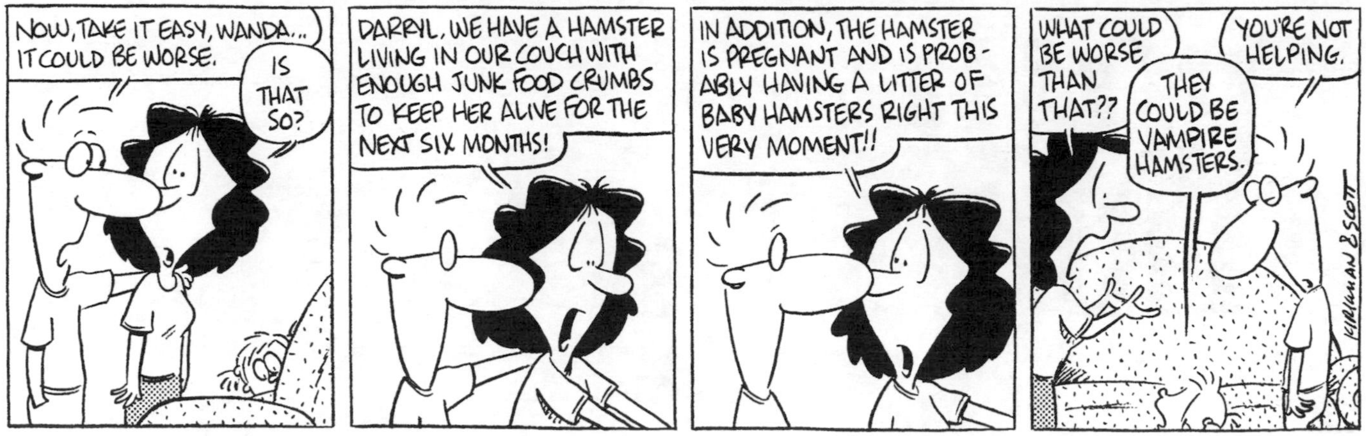
NOW, TAKE IT EASY, WANDA... IT COULD BE WORSE.
IS THAT SO?
DARRYL, WE HAVE A HAMSTER LIVING IN OUR COUCH WITH ENOUGH JUNK FOOD CRUMBS TO KEEP HER ALIVE FOR THE NEXT SIX MONTHS!
IN ADDITION, THE HAMSTER IS PREGNANT AND IS PROB-ABLY HAVING A LITTER OF BABY HAMSTERS RIGHT THIS VERY MOMENT!!
WHAT COULD BE WORSE THAN THAT??
THEY COULD BE VAMPIRE HAMSTERS.
YOU'RE NOT HELPING.
KIRKMAN & SCOTT

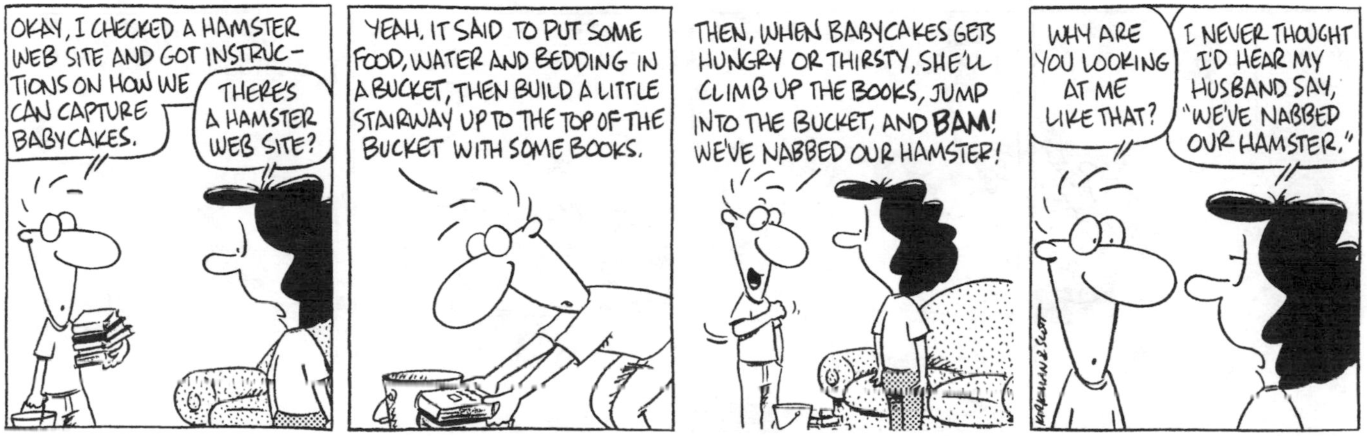
OKAY, I CHECKED A HAMSTER WEB SITE AND GOT INSTRUC-TIONS ON HOW WE CAN CAPTURE BABYCAKES.
THERE'S A HAMSTER WEB SITE?
YEAH, IT SAID TO PUT SOME FOOD, WATER AND BEDDING IN A BUCKET, THEN BUILD A LITTLE STAIRWAY UP TO THE TOP OF THE BUCKET WITH SOME BOOKS.
THEN, WHEN BABYCAKES GETS HUNGRY OR THIRSTY, SHE'LL CLIMB UP THE BOOKS, JUMP INTO THE BUCKET, AND BAM! WE'VE NABBED OUR HAMSTER!
WHY ARE YOU LOOKING AT ME LIKE THAT?
I NEVER THOUGHT I'D HEAR MY HUSBAND SAY, "WE'VE NABBED OUR HAMSTER."

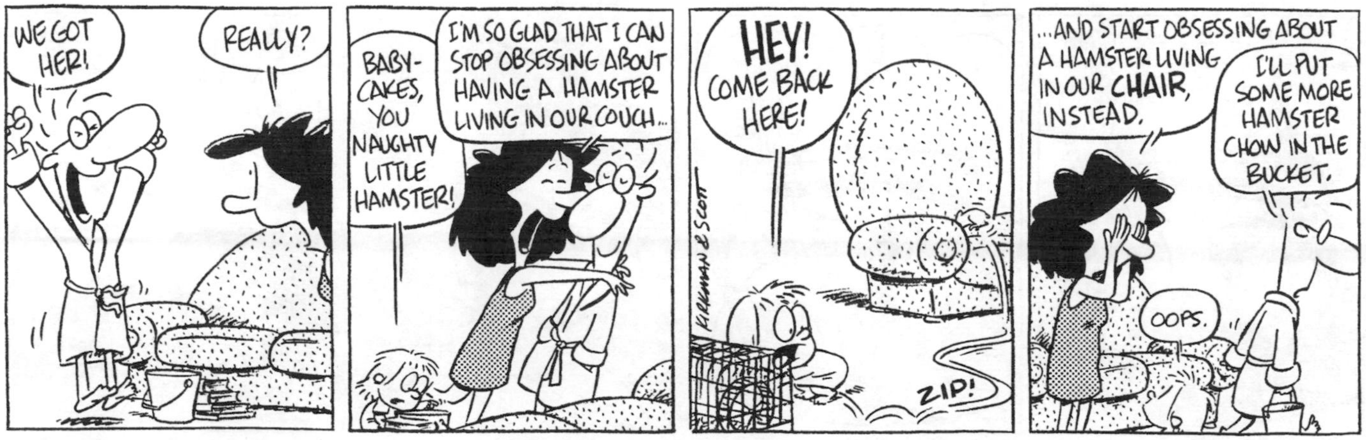
WE GOT HER!
REALLY?
BABY-CAKES, YOU NAUGHTY LITTLE HAMSTER!
I'M SO GLAD THAT I CAN STOP OBSESSING ABOUT HAVING A HAMSTER LIVING IN OUR COUCH...
HEY! COME BACK HERE!
ZIP!
KIRKMAN & SCOTT
...AND START OBSESSING ABOUT A HAMSTER LIVING IN OUR CHAIR, INSTEAD.
I'LL PUT SOME MORE HAMSTER CHOW IN THE BUCKET.
OOPS.

ROAD TRIP

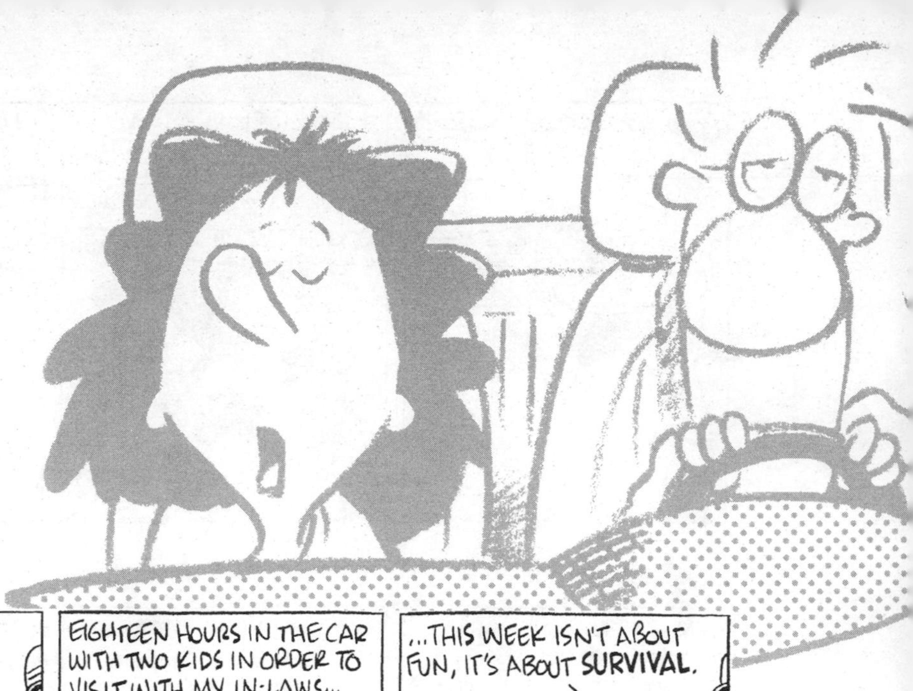

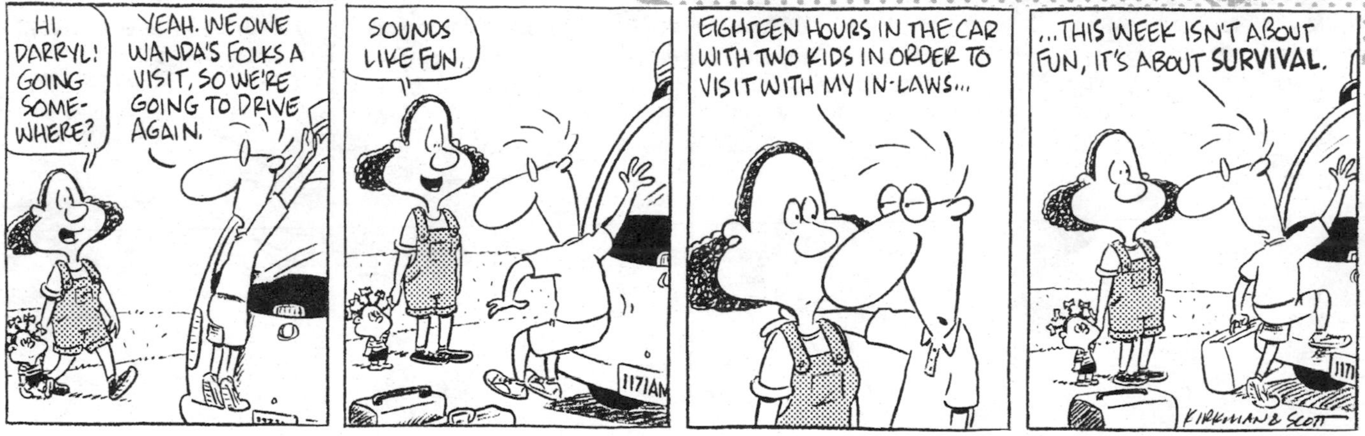

HI, DARRYL! GOING SOME-WHERE?
YEAH. WE OWE WANDA'S FOLKS A VISIT, SO WE'RE GOING TO DRIVE AGAIN.
SOUNDS LIKE FUN.
EIGHTEEN HOURS IN THE CAR WITH TWO KIDS IN ORDER TO VISIT WITH MY IN-LAWS...
...THIS WEEK ISN'T ABOUT FUN, IT'S ABOUT **SURVIVAL**.
KIRKMAN & SCOTT

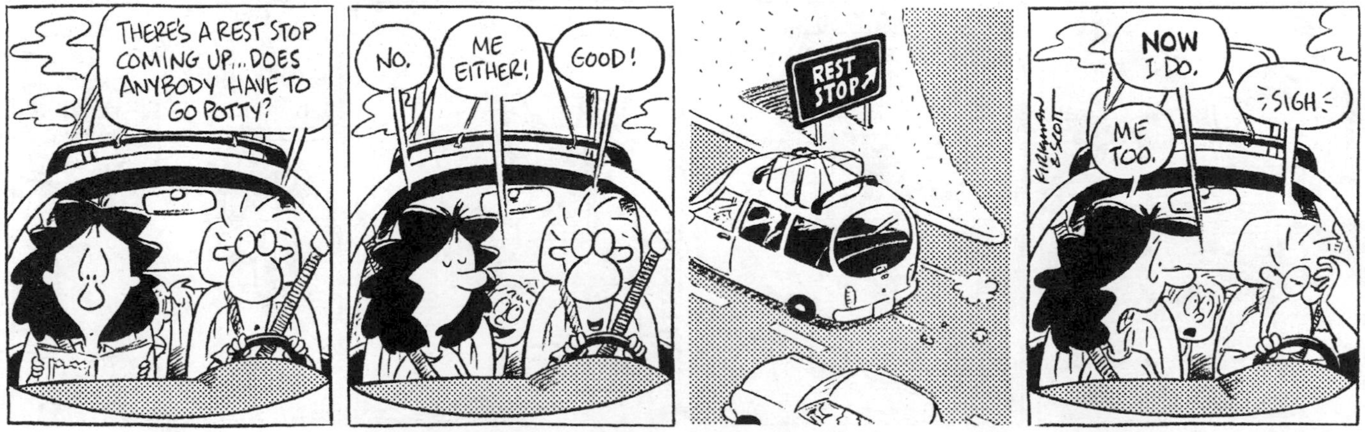

THERE'S A REST STOP COMING UP...DOES ANYBODY HAVE TO GO POTTY?
NO.
ME EITHER!
GOOD!
REST STOP
KIRKMAN & SCOTT
NOW I DO.
ME TOO.
SIGH

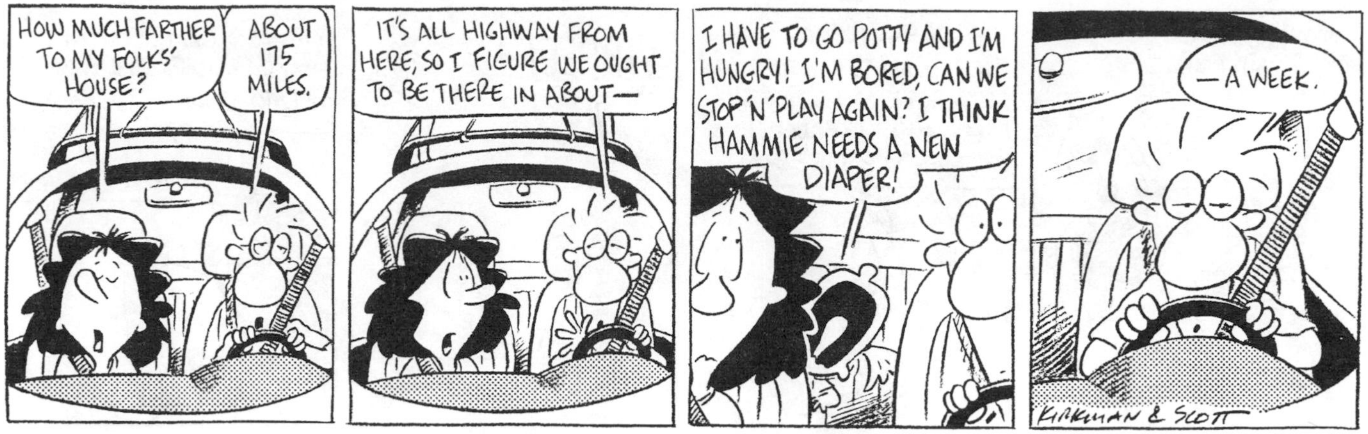
HOW MUCH FARTHER TO MY FOLKS' HOUSE?
ABOUT 175 MILES.
IT'S ALL HIGHWAY FROM HERE, SO I FIGURE WE OUGHT TO BE THERE IN ABOUT—
I HAVE TO GO POTTY AND I'M HUNGRY! I'M BORED, CAN WE STOP 'N' PLAY AGAIN? I THINK HAMMIE NEEDS A NEW DIAPER!
—A WEEK.
KIRKMAN & SCOTT

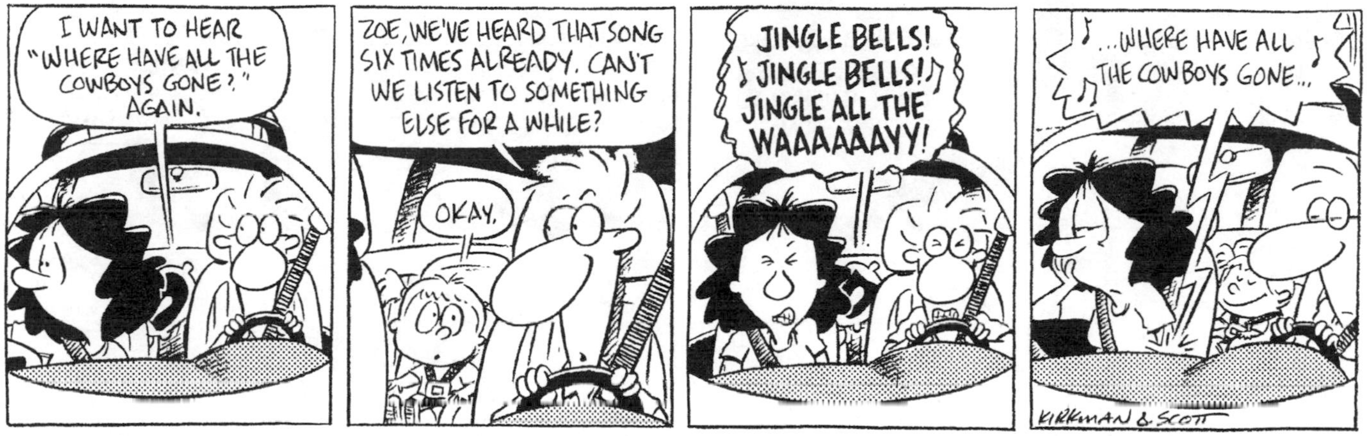
I WANT TO HEAR "WHERE HAVE ALL THE COWBOYS GONE?" AGAIN.
ZOE, WE'VE HEARD THAT SONG SIX TIMES ALREADY. CAN'T WE LISTEN TO SOMETHING ELSE FOR A WHILE?
OKAY.
JINGLE BELLS! JINGLE BELLS! JINGLE ALL THE WAAAAAAYY!
...WHERE HAVE ALL THE COWBOYS GONE...
KIRKMAN & SCOTT

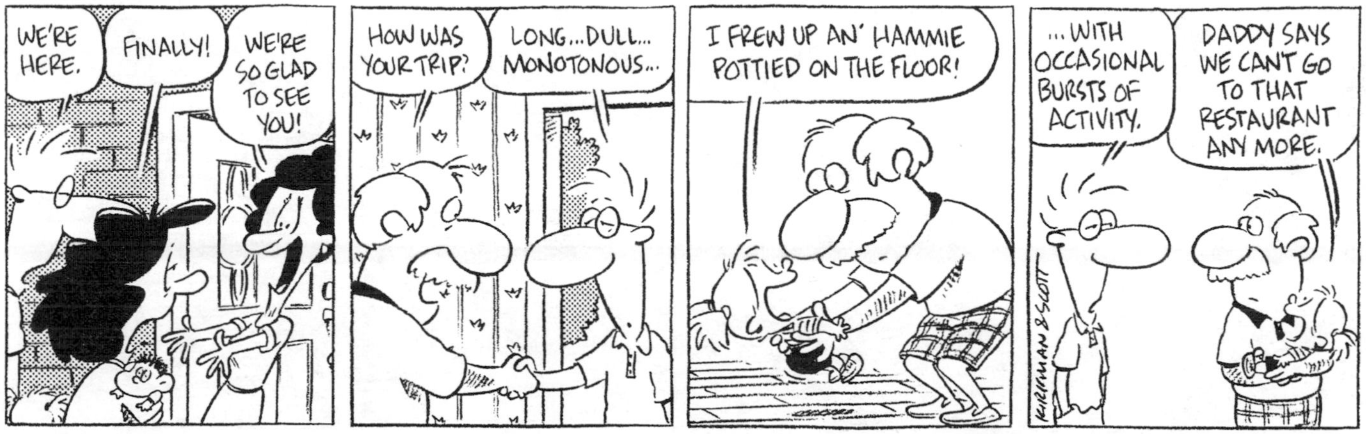
WE'RE HERE.
FINALLY!
WE'RE SO GLAD TO SEE YOU!
HOW WAS YOUR TRIP?
LONG...DULL... MONOTONOUS...
I FREW UP AN' HAMMIE POTTIED ON THE FLOOR!
...WITH OCCASIONAL BURSTS OF ACTIVITY.
DADDY SAYS WE CAN'T GO TO THAT RESTAURANT ANY MORE.
KIRKMAN & SCOTT

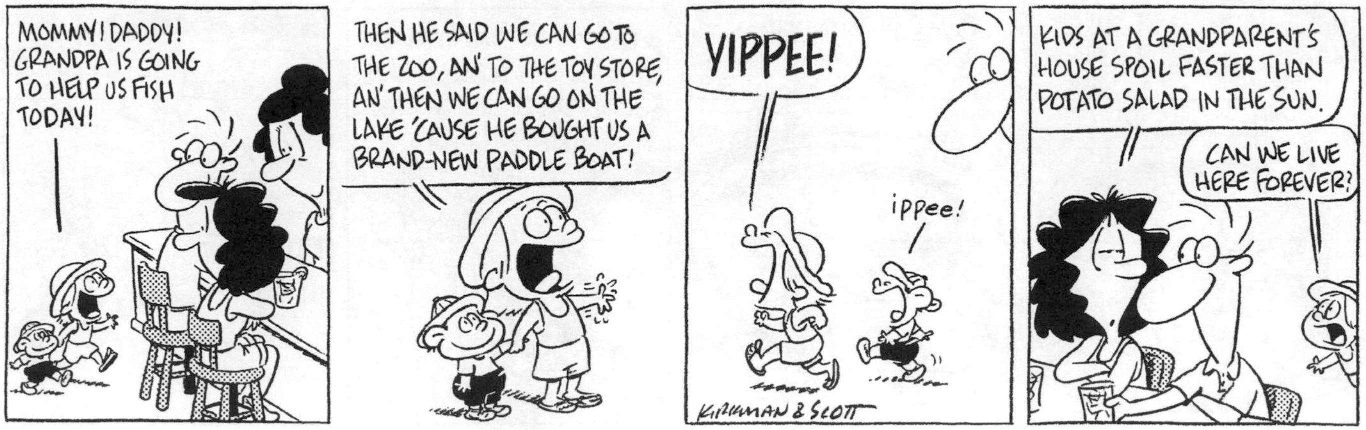
MOMMY! DADDY! GRANDPA IS GOING TO HELP US FISH TODAY!
THEN HE SAID WE CAN GO TO THE ZOO, AN' TO THE TOY STORE, AN' THEN WE CAN GO ON THE LAKE 'CAUSE HE BOUGHT US A BRAND-NEW PADDLE BOAT!
YIPPEE!
ippee!
KIRKMAN & SCOTT
KIDS AT A GRANDPARENT'S HOUSE SPOIL FASTER THAN POTATO SALAD IN THE SUN.
CAN WE LIVE HERE FOREVER?

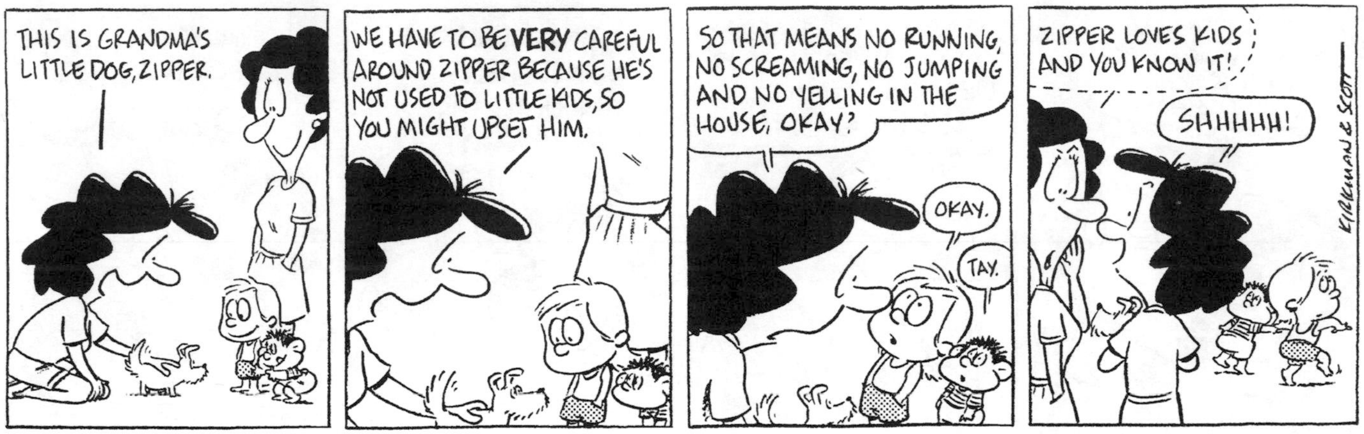
THIS IS GRANDMA'S LITTLE DOG, ZIPPER.
WE HAVE TO BE VERY CAREFUL AROUND ZIPPER BECAUSE HE'S NOT USED TO LITTLE KIDS, SO YOU MIGHT UPSET HIM.
SO THAT MEANS NO RUNNING, NO SCREAMING, NO JUMPING AND NO YELLING IN THE HOUSE, OKAY?
OKAY.
TAY.
ZIPPER LOVES KIDS AND YOU KNOW IT!
SHHHHH!
KIRKMAN & SCOTT

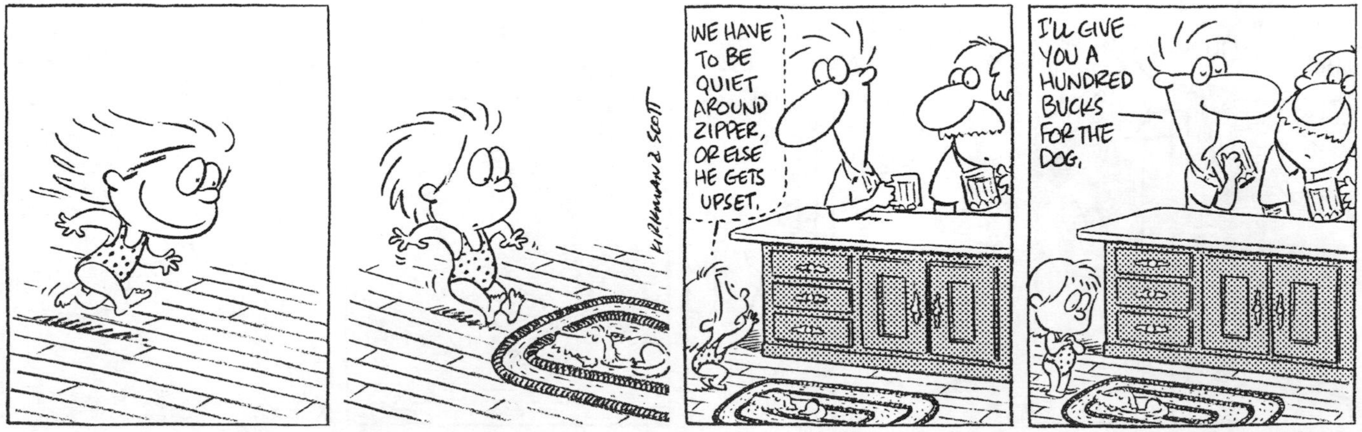
KIRKMAN & SCOTT
WE HAVE TO BE QUIET AROUND ZIPPER, OR ELSE HE GETS UPSET.
I'LL GIVE YOU A HUNDRED BUCKS FOR THE DOG.

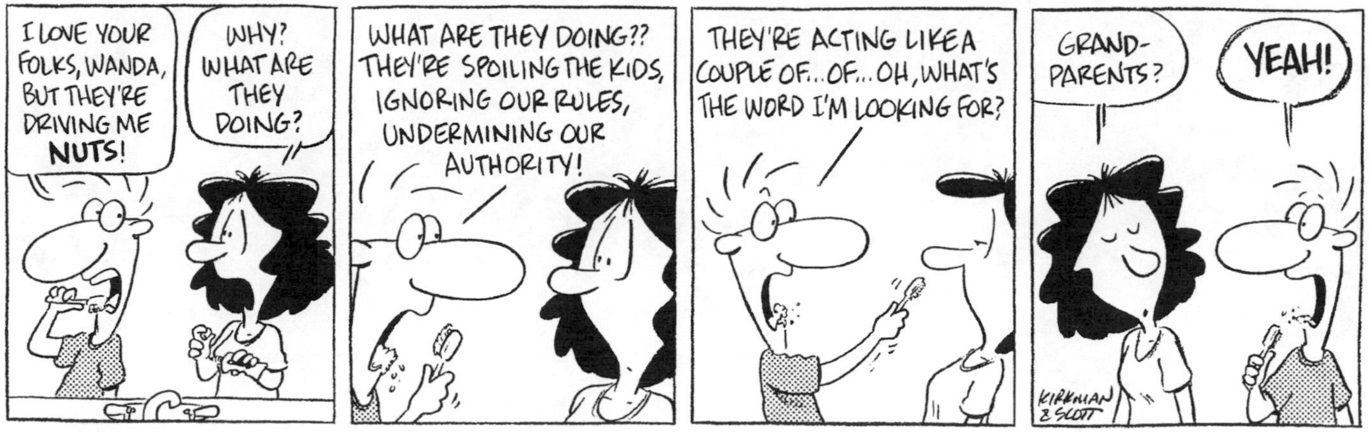
I LOVE YOUR FOLKS, WANDA, BUT THEY'RE DRIVING ME **NUTS**!
WHY? WHAT ARE THEY DOING?
WHAT ARE THEY DOING?? THEY'RE SPOILING THE KIDS, IGNORING OUR RULES, UNDERMINING OUR AUTHORITY!
THEY'RE ACTING LIKE A COUPLE OF...OF...OH, WHAT'S THE WORD I'M LOOKING FOR?
GRAND-PARENTS?
YEAH!
KIRKMAN & SCOTT

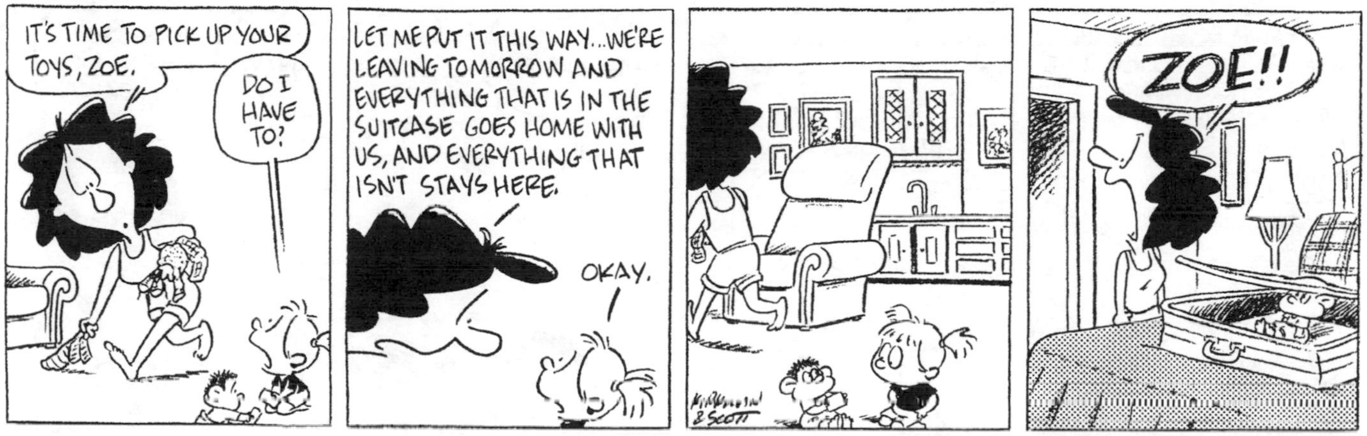
IT'S TIME TO PICK UP YOUR TOYS, ZOE.
DO I HAVE TO?
LET ME PUT IT THIS WAY...WE'RE LEAVING TOMORROW AND EVERYTHING THAT IS IN THE SUITCASE GOES HOME WITH US, AND EVERYTHING THAT ISN'T STAYS HERE.
OKAY.
KIRKMAN & SCOTT
ZOE!!

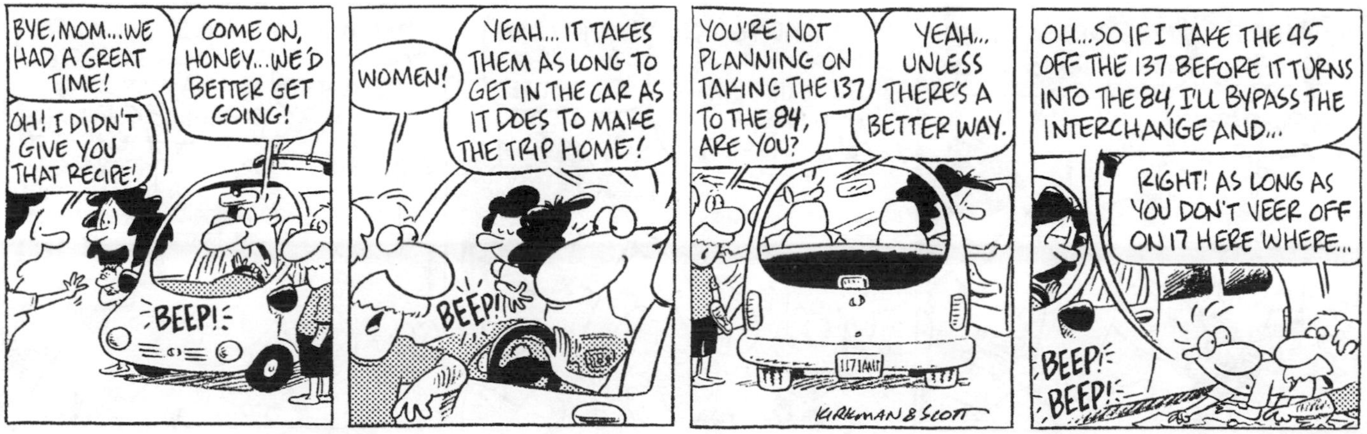
BYE, MOM...WE HAD A GREAT TIME!
COME ON, HONEY...WE'D BETTER GET GOING!
OH! I DIDN'T GIVE YOU THAT RECIPE!
BEEP!
WOMEN!
YEAH... IT TAKES THEM AS LONG TO GET IN THE CAR AS IT DOES TO MAKE THE TRIP HOME!
BEEP!
YOU'RE NOT PLANNING ON TAKING THE 137 TO THE 84, ARE YOU?
YEAH... UNLESS THERE'S A BETTER WAY.
KIRKMAN & SCOTT
OH...SO IF I TAKE THE 45 OFF THE 137 BEFORE IT TURNS INTO THE 84, I'LL BYPASS THE INTERCHANGE AND...
RIGHT! AS LONG AS YOU DON'T VEER OFF ON 17 HERE WHERE...
BEEP! BEEP!

KINDER-GARTEN

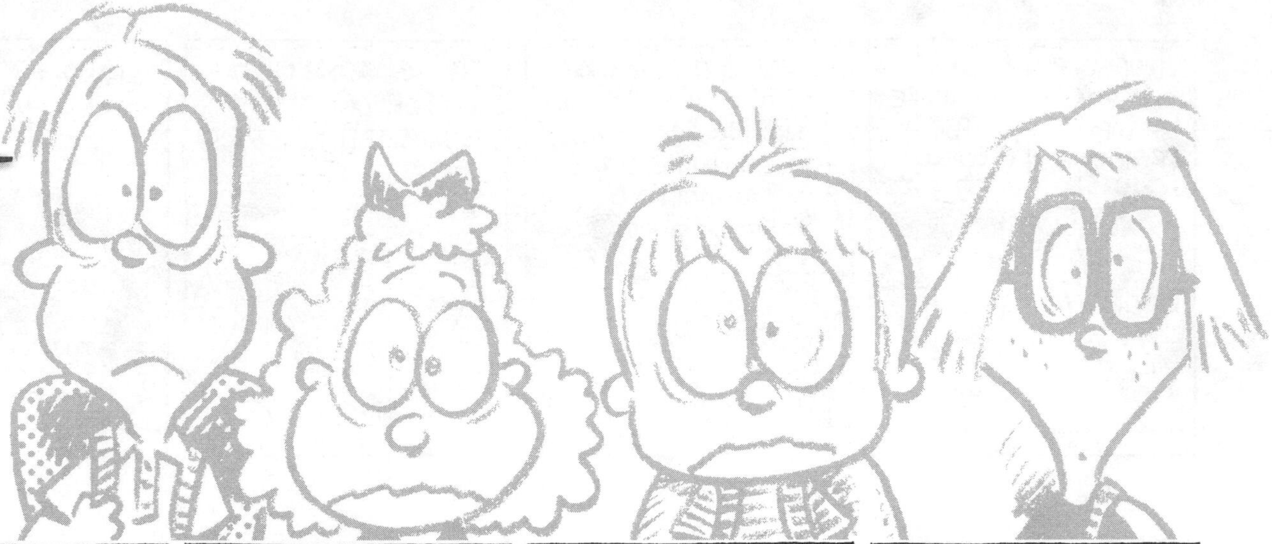

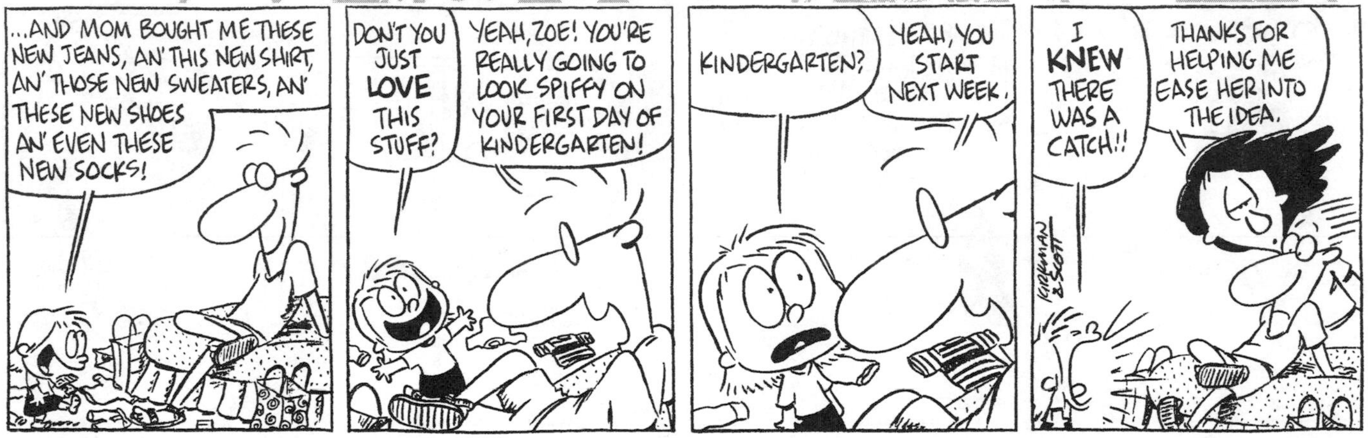
...AND MOM BOUGHT ME THESE NEW JEANS, AN' THIS NEW SHIRT, AN' THOSE NEW SWEATERS, AN' THESE NEW SHOES AN' EVEN THESE NEW SOCKS!
DON'T YOU JUST **LOVE** THIS STUFF?
YEAH, ZOE! YOU'RE REALLY GOING TO LOOK SPIFFY ON YOUR FIRST DAY OF KINDERGARTEN!
KINDERGARTEN?
YEAH, YOU START NEXT WEEK.
I **KNEW** THERE WAS A CATCH!!
THANKS FOR HELPING ME EASE HER INTO THE IDEA.
KIRKMAN & SCOTT

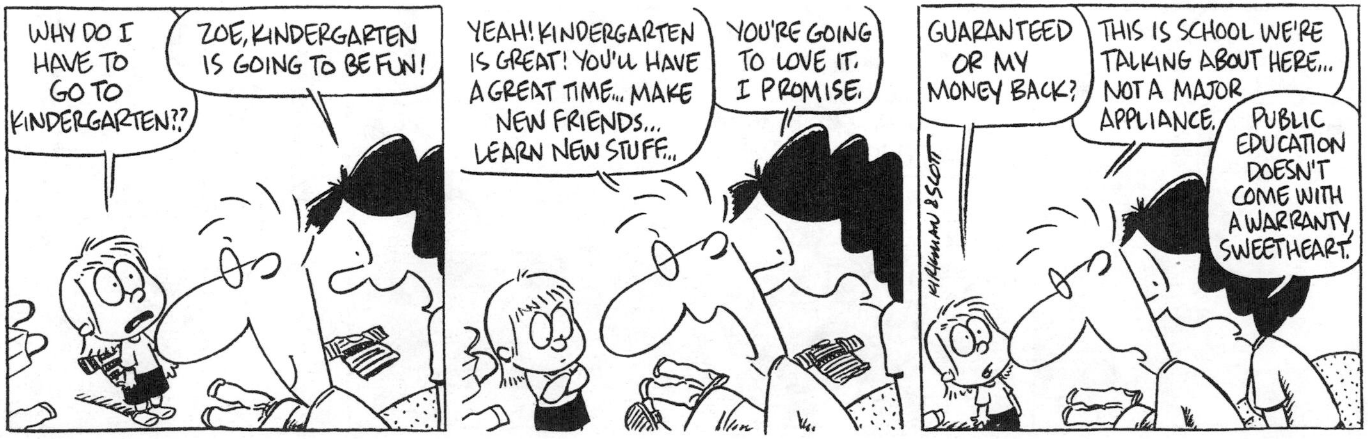
WHY DO I HAVE TO GO TO KINDERGARTEN??
ZOE, KINDERGARTEN IS GOING TO BE FUN!
YEAH! KINDERGARTEN IS GREAT! YOU'LL HAVE A GREAT TIME... MAKE NEW FRIENDS... LEARN NEW STUFF...
YOU'RE GOING TO LOVE IT. I PROMISE.
GUARANTEED OR MY MONEY BACK?
THIS IS SCHOOL WE'RE TALKING ABOUT HERE... NOT A MAJOR APPLIANCE.
PUBLIC EDUCATION DOESN'T COME WITH A WARRANTY, SWEETHEART.
KIRKMAN & SCOTT

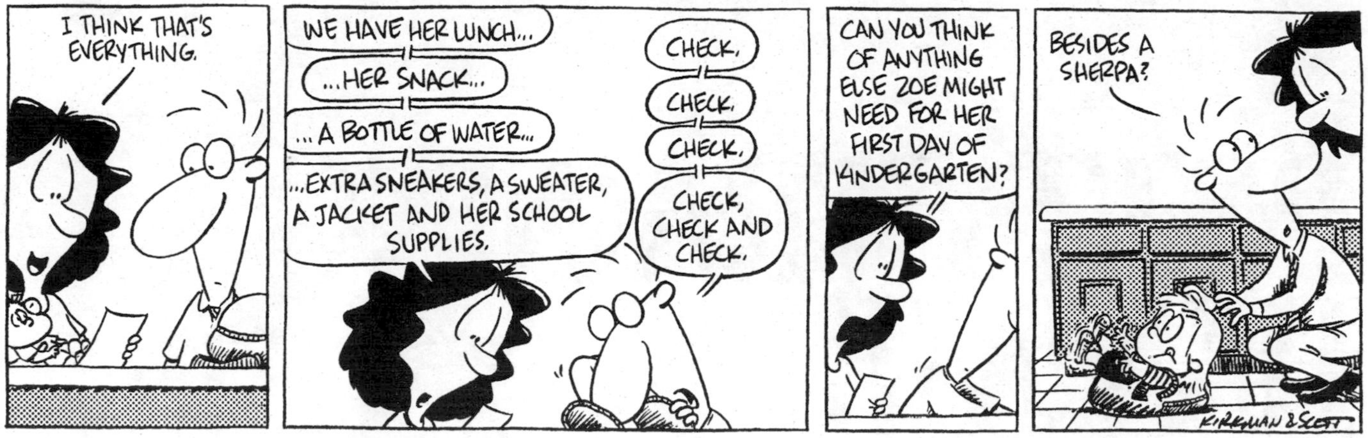
I THINK THAT'S EVERYTHING.
WE HAVE HER LUNCH...
CHECK.
...HER SNACK...
CHECK.
...A BOTTLE OF WATER...
CHECK.
...EXTRA SNEAKERS, A SWEATER, A JACKET AND HER SCHOOL SUPPLIES.
CHECK, CHECK AND CHECK.
CAN YOU THINK OF ANYTHING ELSE ZOE MIGHT NEED FOR HER FIRST DAY OF KINDERGARTEN?
BESIDES A SHERPA?
KIRKMAN & SCOTT

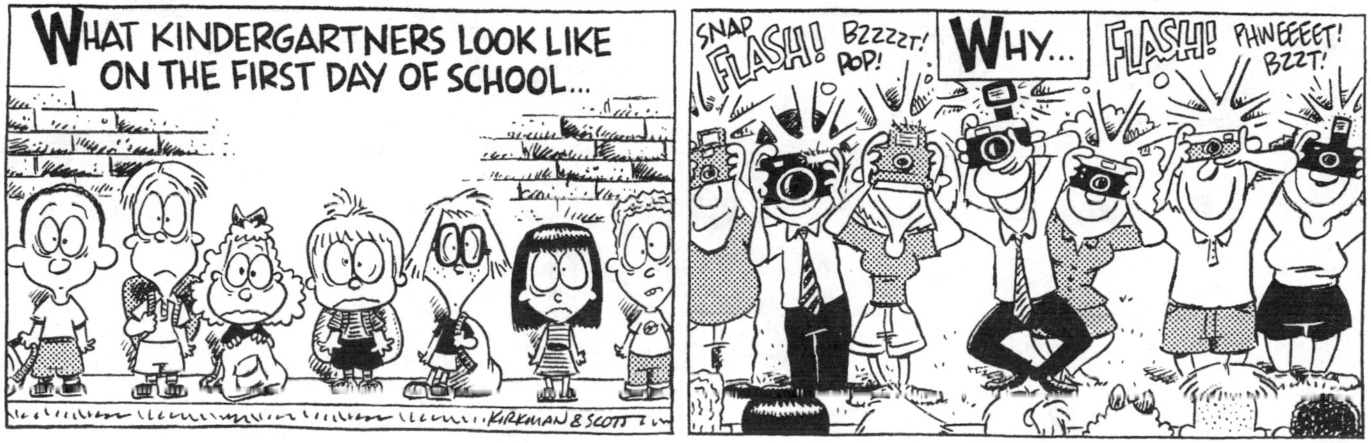
WHAT KINDERGARTNERS LOOK LIKE ON THE FIRST DAY OF SCHOOL...
KIRKMAN & SCOTT
SNAP
FLASH!
BZZZZT!
POP!
WHY...
FLASH!
PHWEEEET!
BZZT!

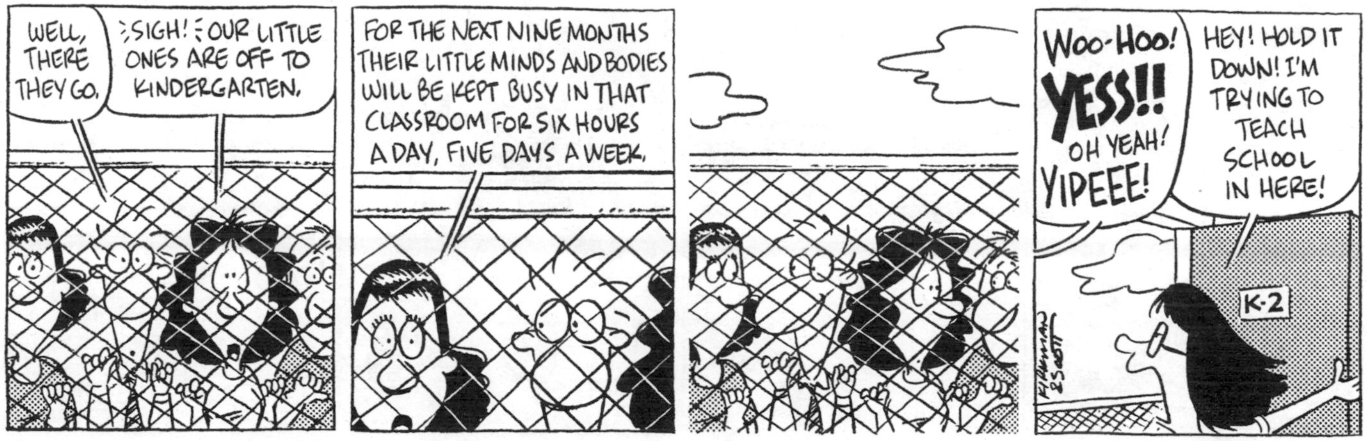
WELL, THERE THEY GO.
SIGH! OUR LITTLE ONES ARE OFF TO KINDERGARTEN.
FOR THE NEXT NINE MONTHS THEIR LITTLE MINDS AND BODIES WILL BE KEPT BUSY IN THAT CLASSROOM FOR SIX HOURS A DAY, FIVE DAYS A WEEK.
WOO-HOO! YESS!! OH YEAH! YIPEEE!
HEY! HOLD IT DOWN! I'M TRYING TO TEACH SCHOOL IN HERE!
K-2

POTTY-TRAINING HAMMIE

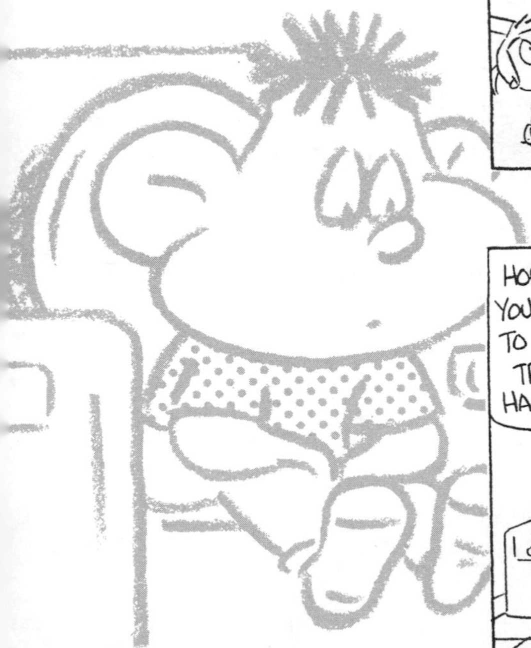

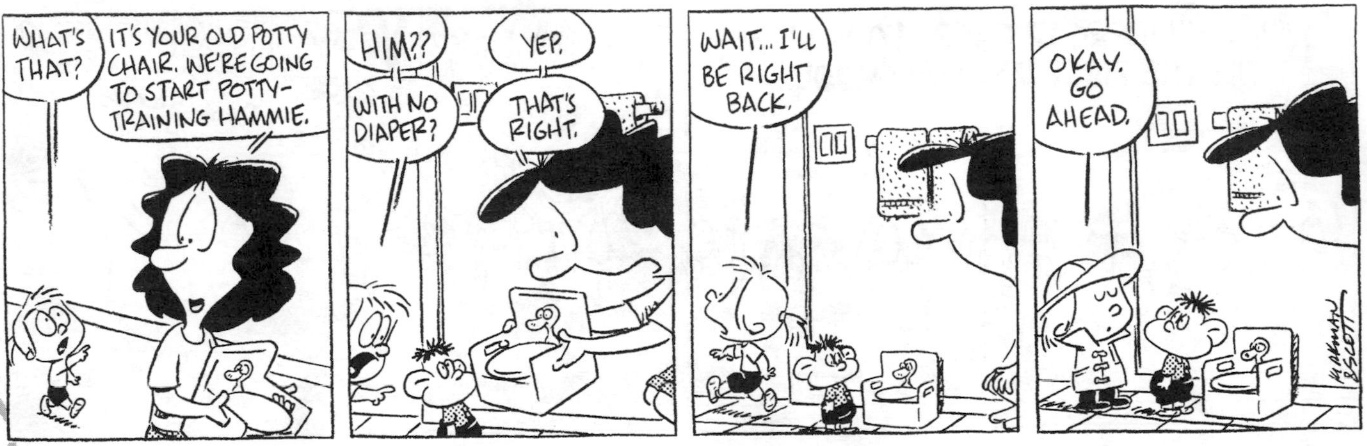

WHAT'S THAT?
IT'S YOUR OLD POTTY CHAIR. WE'RE GOING TO START POTTY-TRAINING HAMMIE.
HIM??
YEP.
WITH NO DIAPER?
THAT'S RIGHT.
WAIT... I'LL BE RIGHT BACK.
OKAY. GO AHEAD.

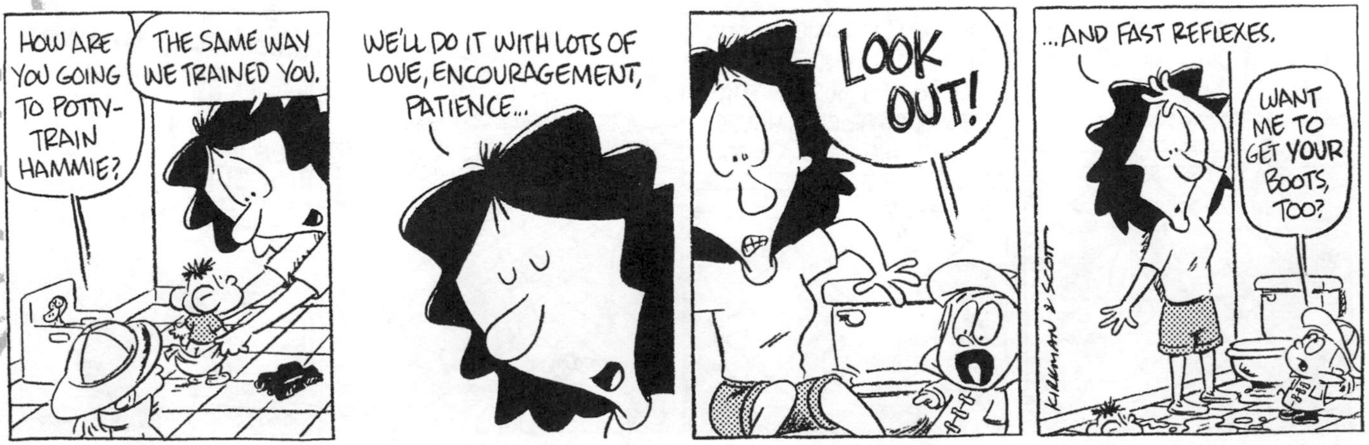

HOW ARE YOU GOING TO POTTY-TRAIN HAMMIE?
THE SAME WAY WE TRAINED YOU.
WE'LL DO IT WITH LOTS OF LOVE, ENCOURAGEMENT, PATIENCE...
LOOK OUT!
...AND FAST REFLEXES.
WANT ME TO GET YOUR BOOTS, TOO?

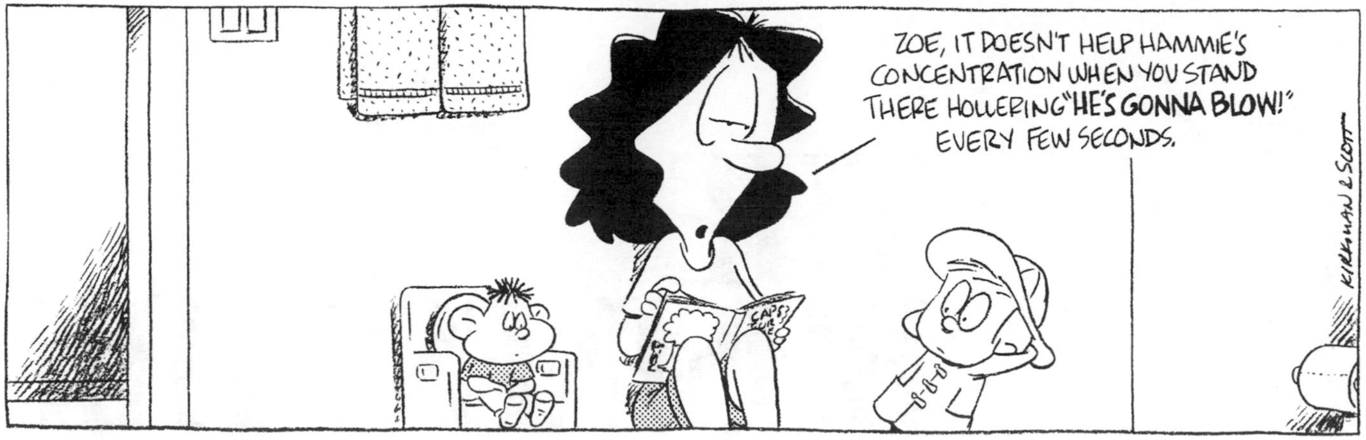
ZOE, IT DOESN'T HELP HAMMIE'S CONCENTRATION WHEN YOU STAND THERE HOLLERING "HE'S GONNA BLOW!" EVERY FEW SECONDS.
KIRKMAN & SCOTT

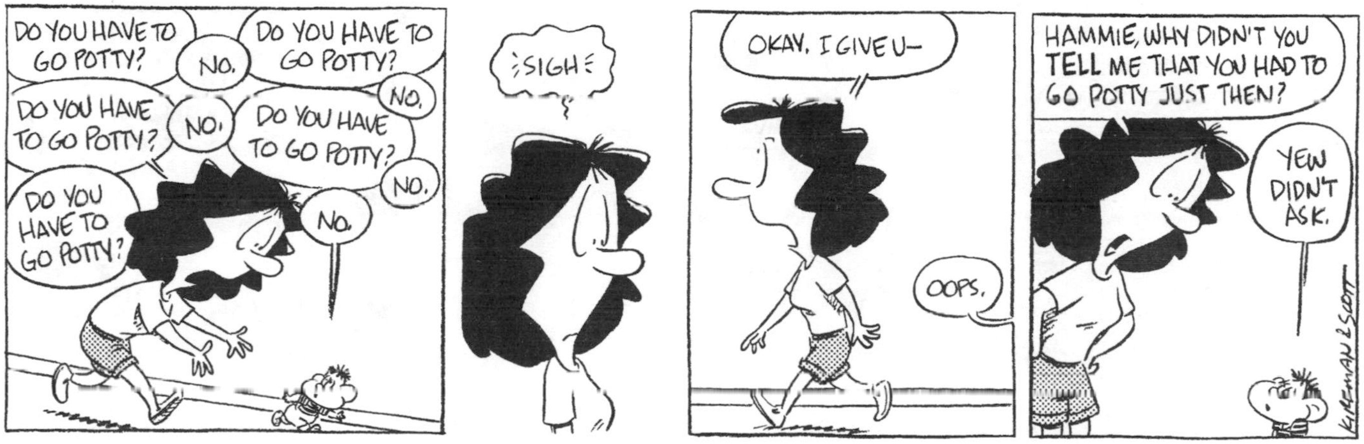
DO YOU HAVE TO GO POTTY?
NO.
DO YOU HAVE TO GO POTTY?
NO.
DO YOU HAVE TO GO POTTY?
NO.
DO YOU HAVE TO GO POTTY?
NO.
DO YOU HAVE TO GO POTTY?
NO.
SIGH
OKAY. I GIVE U–
OOPS.
HAMMIE, WHY DIDN'T YOU TELL ME THAT YOU HAD TO GO POTTY JUST THEN?
YEW DIDN'T ASK.
KIRKMAN & SCOTT

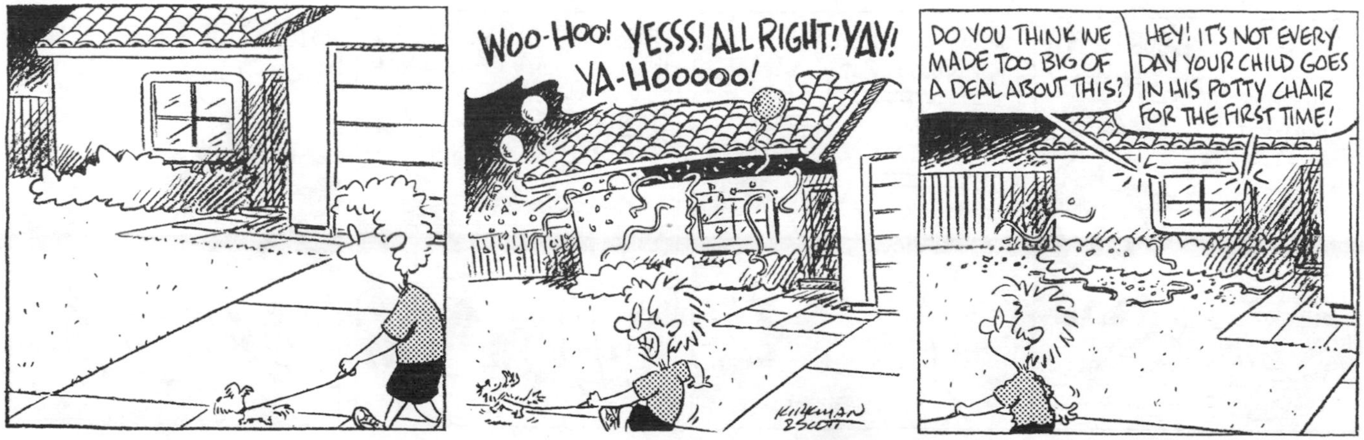
WOO-HOO! YESSS! ALL RIGHT! YAY! YA-HOOOOO!
KIRKMAN & SCOTT
DO YOU THINK WE MADE TOO BIG OF A DEAL ABOUT THIS?
HEY! IT'S NOT EVERY DAY YOUR CHILD GOES IN HIS POTTY CHAIR FOR THE FIRST TIME!

THE BUSINESS TRIP

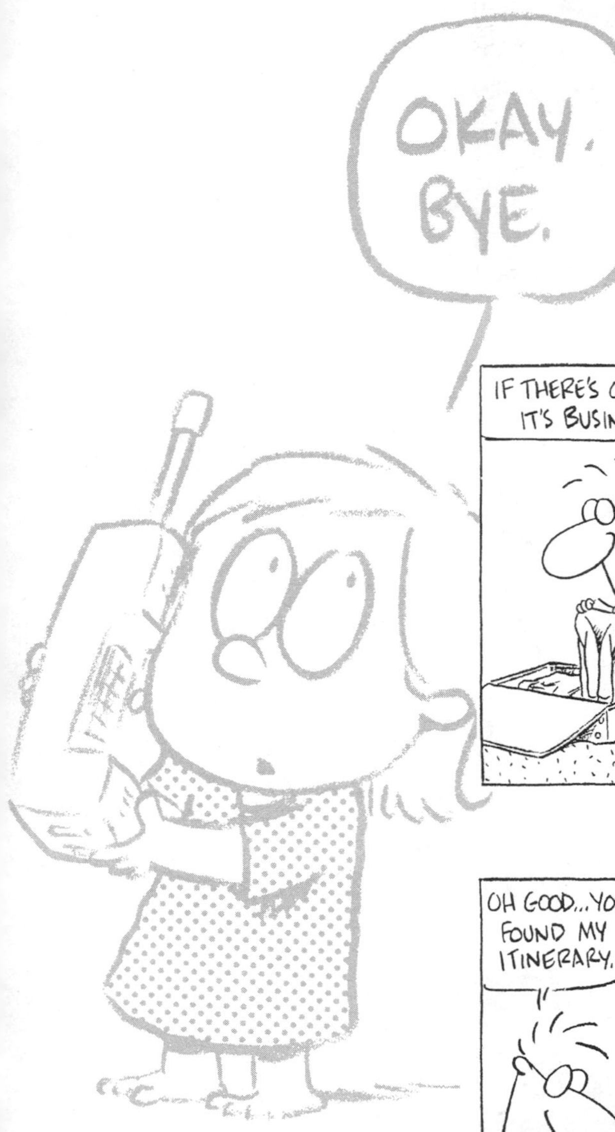

OKAY. BYE.

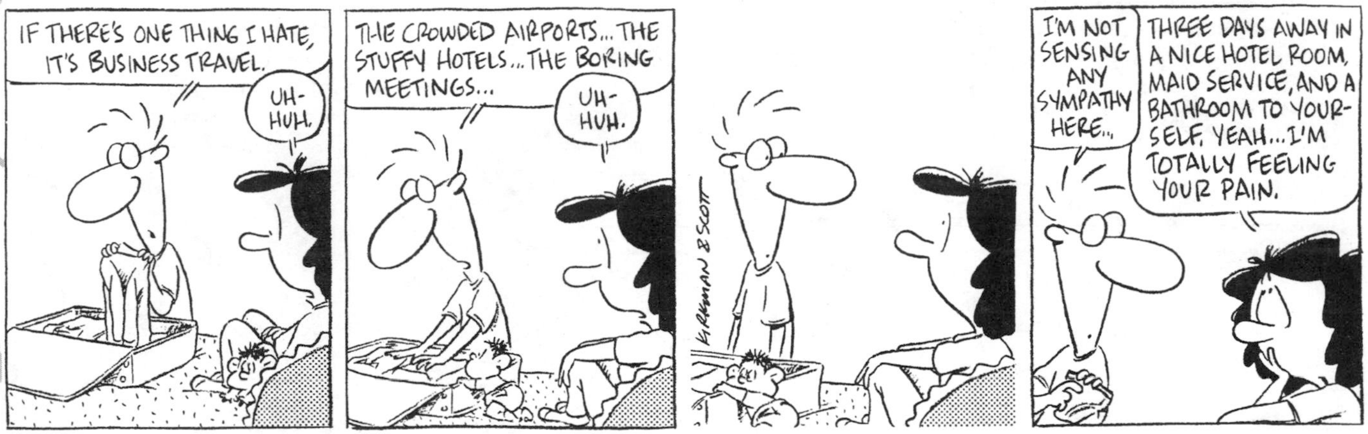

IF THERE'S ONE THING I HATE, IT'S BUSINESS TRAVEL.
UH-HUH.
THE CROWDED AIRPORTS... THE STUFFY HOTELS... THE BORING MEETINGS...
UH-HUH.
KIRKMAN & SCOTT
I'M NOT SENSING ANY SYMPATHY HERE...
THREE DAYS AWAY IN A NICE HOTEL ROOM, MAID SERVICE, AND A BATHROOM TO YOURSELF. YEAH... I'M TOTALLY FEELING YOUR PAIN.

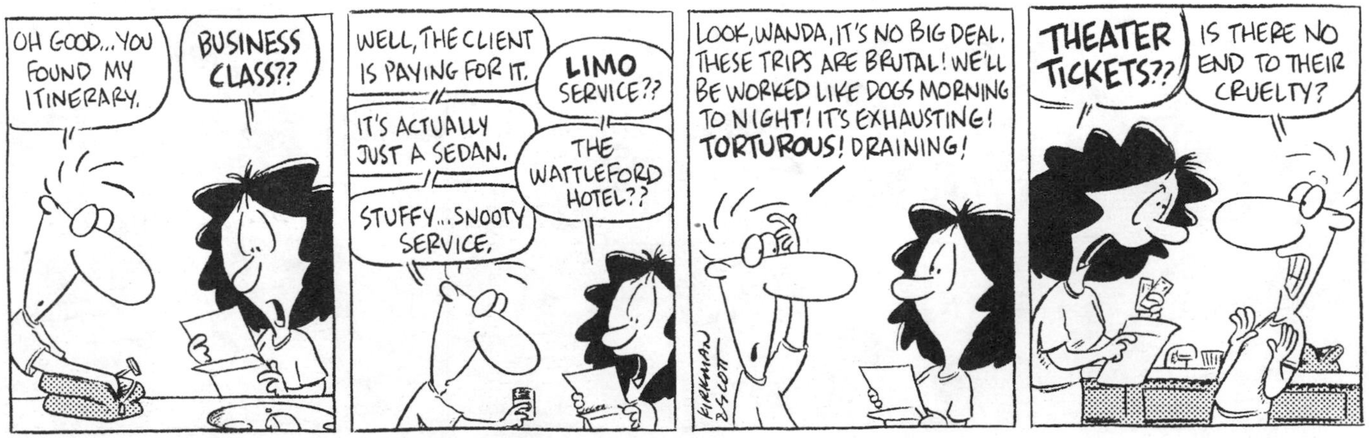

OH GOOD... YOU FOUND MY ITINERARY.
BUSINESS CLASS??
WELL, THE CLIENT IS PAYING FOR IT.
LIMO SERVICE??
IT'S ACTUALLY JUST A SEDAN.
THE WATTLEFORD HOTEL??
STUFFY... SNOOTY SERVICE.
LOOK, WANDA, IT'S NO BIG DEAL. THESE TRIPS ARE BRUTAL! WE'LL BE WORKED LIKE DOGS MORNING TO NIGHT! IT'S EXHAUSTING! TORTUROUS! DRAINING!
KIRKMAN & SCOTT
THEATER TICKETS??
IS THERE NO END TO THEIR CRUELTY?

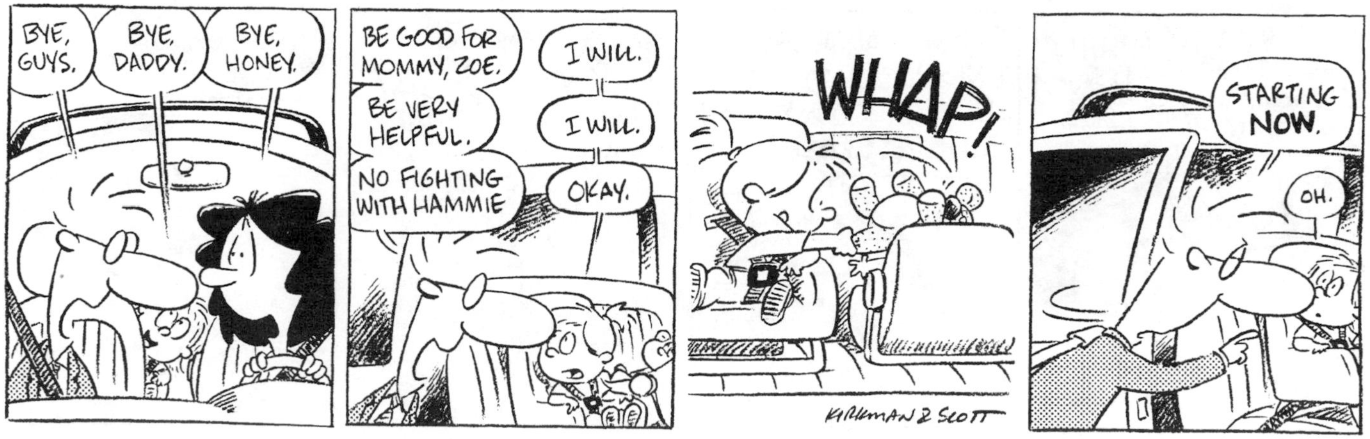
BYE, GUYS.
BYE, DADDY.
BYE, HONEY.
BE GOOD FOR MOMMY, ZOE.
I WILL.
BE VERY HELPFUL.
I WILL.
NO FIGHTING WITH HAMMIE
OKAY.
WHAP!
KIRKMAN & SCOTT
STARTING NOW.
OH.

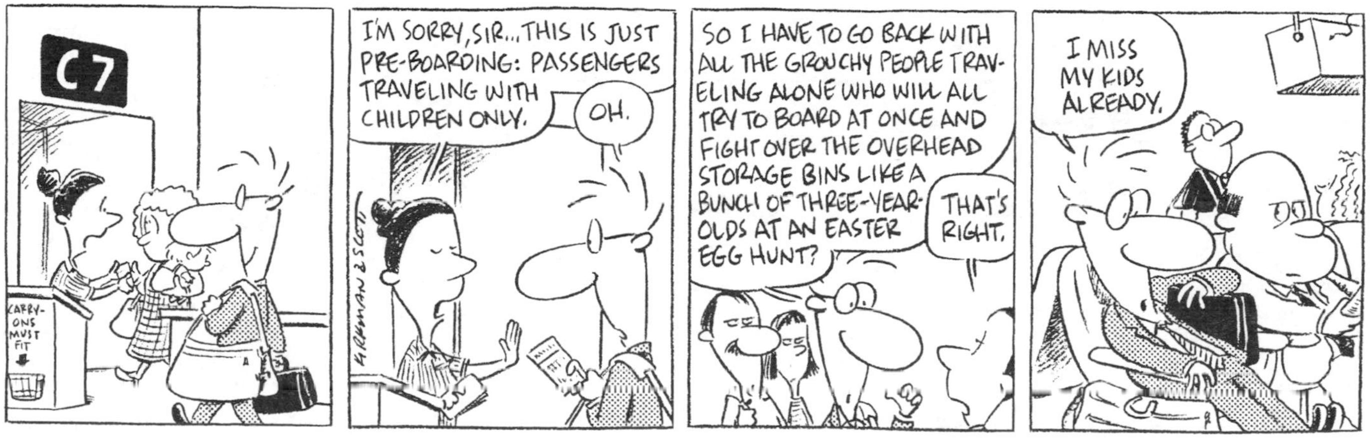
C7
CARRY-ONS MUST FIT
I'M SORRY, SIR... THIS IS JUST PRE-BOARDING: PASSENGERS TRAVELING WITH CHILDREN ONLY.
OH.
KIRKMAN & SCOTT
SO I HAVE TO GO BACK WITH ALL THE GROUCHY PEOPLE TRAVELING ALONE WHO WILL ALL TRY TO BOARD AT ONCE AND FIGHT OVER THE OVERHEAD STORAGE BINS LIKE A BUNCH OF THREE-YEAR-OLDS AT AN EASTER EGG HUNT?
THAT'S RIGHT.
I MISS MY KIDS ALREADY.

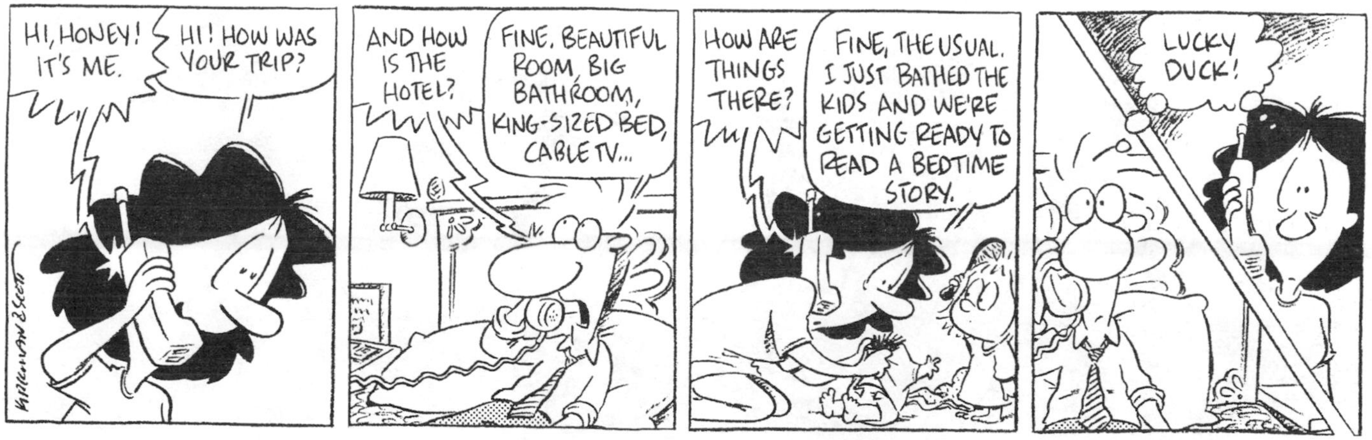
HI, HONEY! IT'S ME.
HI! HOW WAS YOUR TRIP?
KIRKMAN & SCOTT
AND HOW IS THE HOTEL?
FINE. BEAUTIFUL ROOM, BIG BATHROOM, KING-SIZED BED, CABLE TV...
HOW ARE THINGS THERE?
FINE, THE USUAL. I JUST BATHED THE KIDS AND WE'RE GETTING READY TO READ A BEDTIME STORY.
LUCKY DUCK!

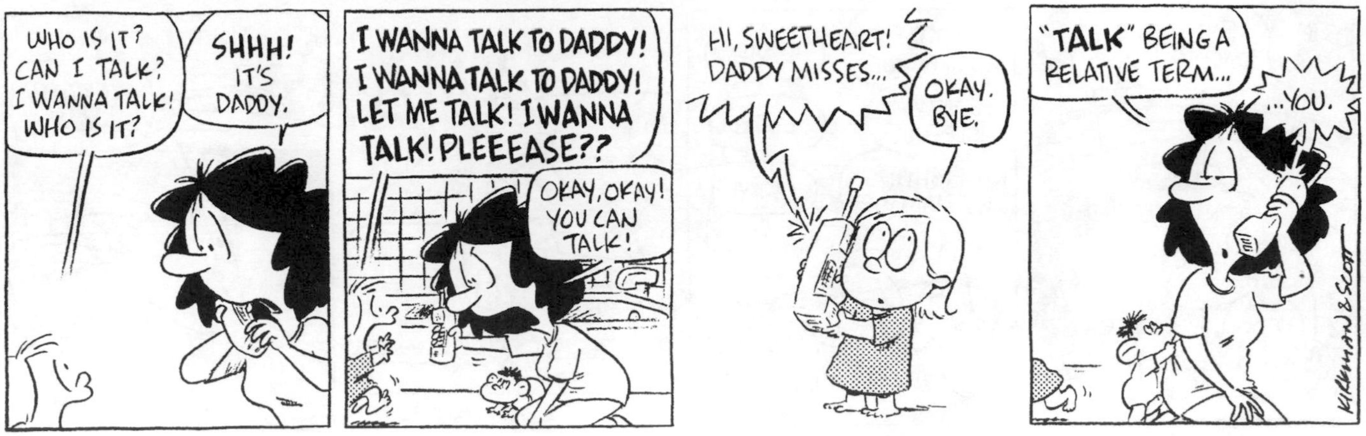
WHO IS IT? CAN I TALK? I WANNA TALK! WHO IS IT?
SHHH! IT'S DADDY.
I WANNA TALK TO DADDY! I WANNA TALK TO DADDY! LET ME TALK! I WANNA TALK! PLEEEASE??
OKAY, OKAY! YOU CAN TALK!
HI, SWEETHEART! DADDY MISSES...
OKAY. BYE.
"TALK" BEING A RELATIVE TERM...
...YOU.
KIRKMAN & SCOTT

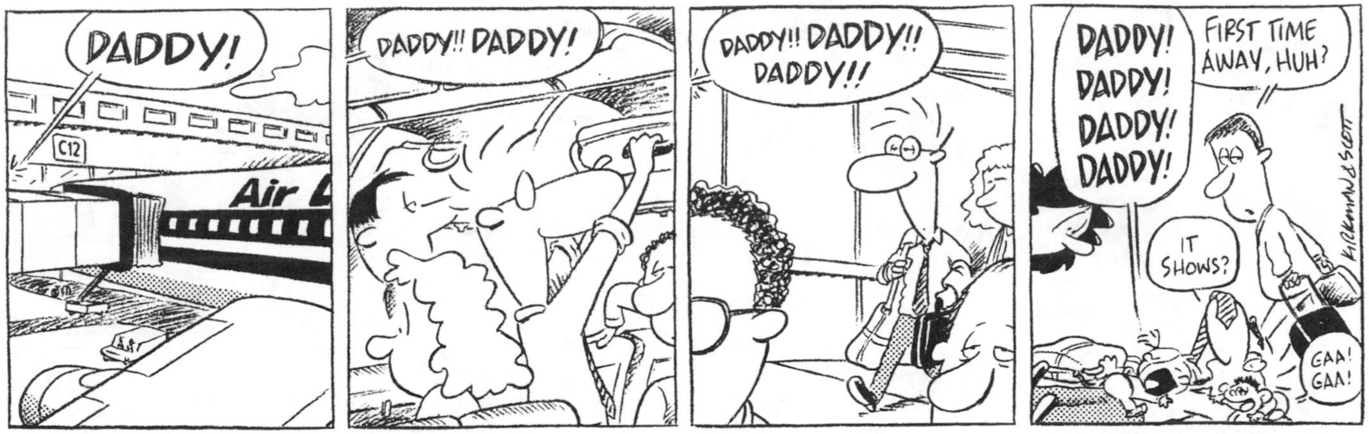
DADDY!
C12
Air
DADDY!! DADDY!
DADDY!! DADDY!! DADDY!!
DADDY! DADDY! DADDY! DADDY!
FIRST TIME AWAY, HUH?
IT SHOWS?
GAA! GAA!
KIRKMAN & SCOTT

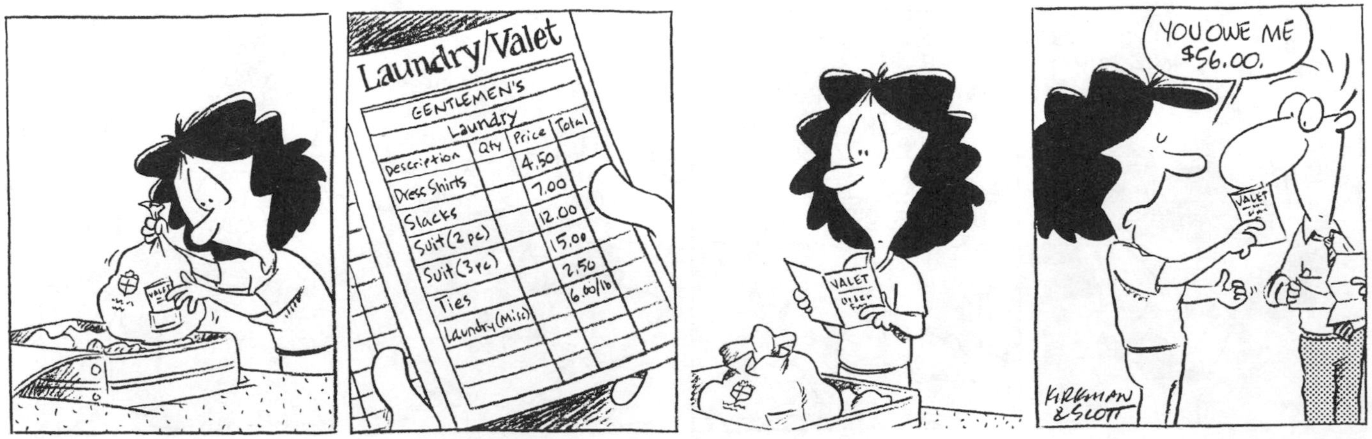
VALET
Laundry/Valet
GENTLEMEN'S
Laundry
Description Qty Price Total
Dress Shirts 4.50
Slacks 7.00
Suit (2 pc) 12.00
Suit (3 pc) 15.00
Ties 2.50
Laundry (Misc) 6.00/lb
VALET
YOU OWE ME $56.00.
KIRKMAN & SCOTT

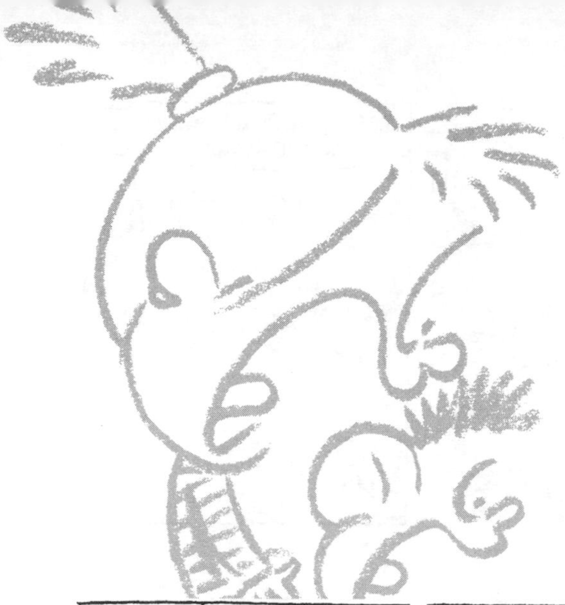

BUTTERFLY FARM

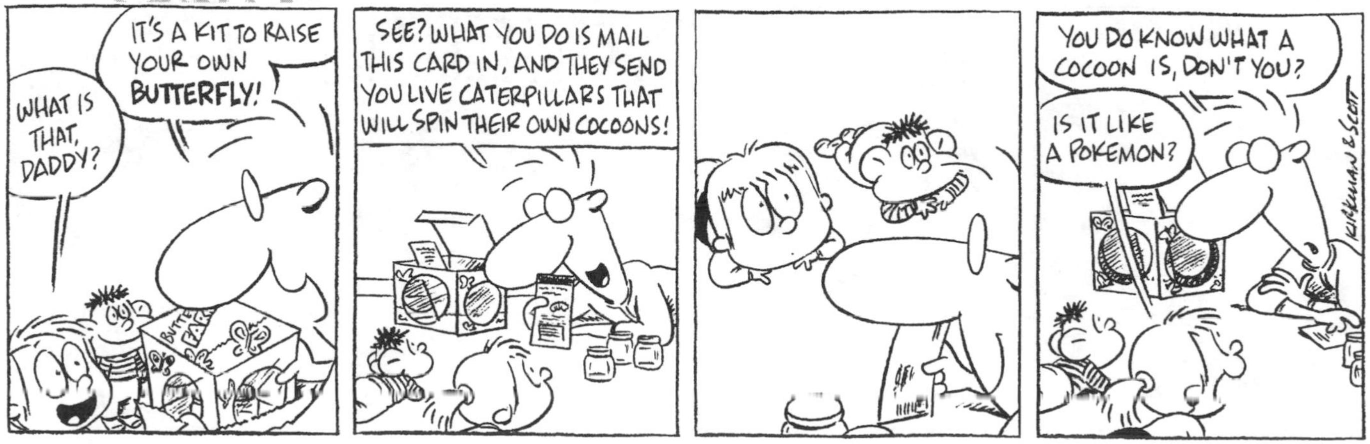
WHAT IS THAT, DADDY?
IT'S A KIT TO RAISE YOUR OWN BUTTERFLY!
SEE? WHAT YOU DO IS MAIL THIS CARD IN, AND THEY SEND YOU LIVE CATERPILLARS THAT WILL SPIN THEIR OWN COCOONS!
YOU DO KNOW WHAT A COCOON IS, DON'T YOU?
IS IT LIKE A POKEMON?
KIRKMAN & SCOTT

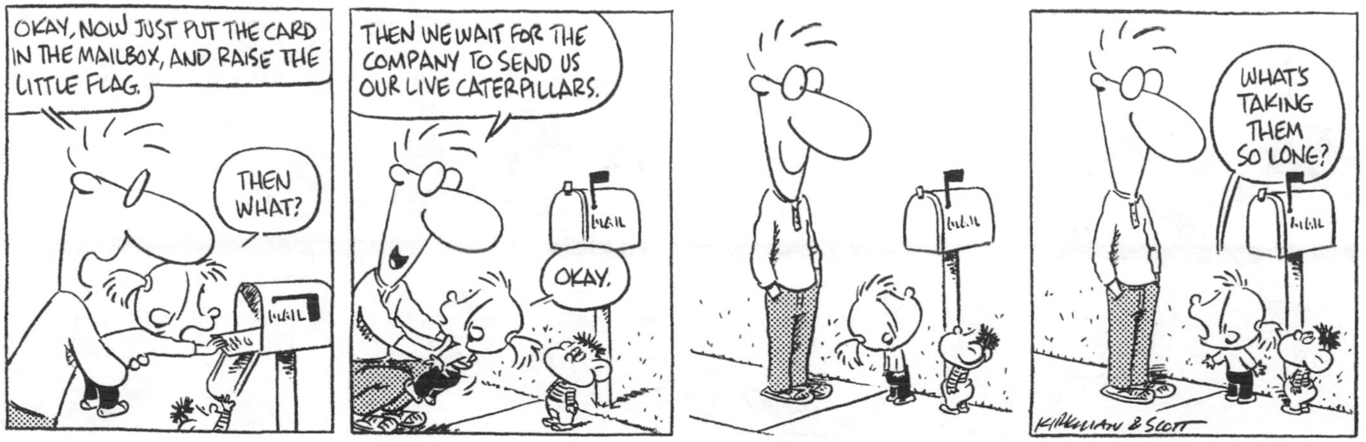
OKAY, NOW JUST PUT THE CARD IN THE MAILBOX, AND RAISE THE LITTLE FLAG.
THEN WHAT?
MAIL
THEN WE WAIT FOR THE COMPANY TO SEND US OUR LIVE CATERPILLARS.
OKAY.
WHAT'S TAKING THEM SO LONG?
KIRKMAN & SCOTT

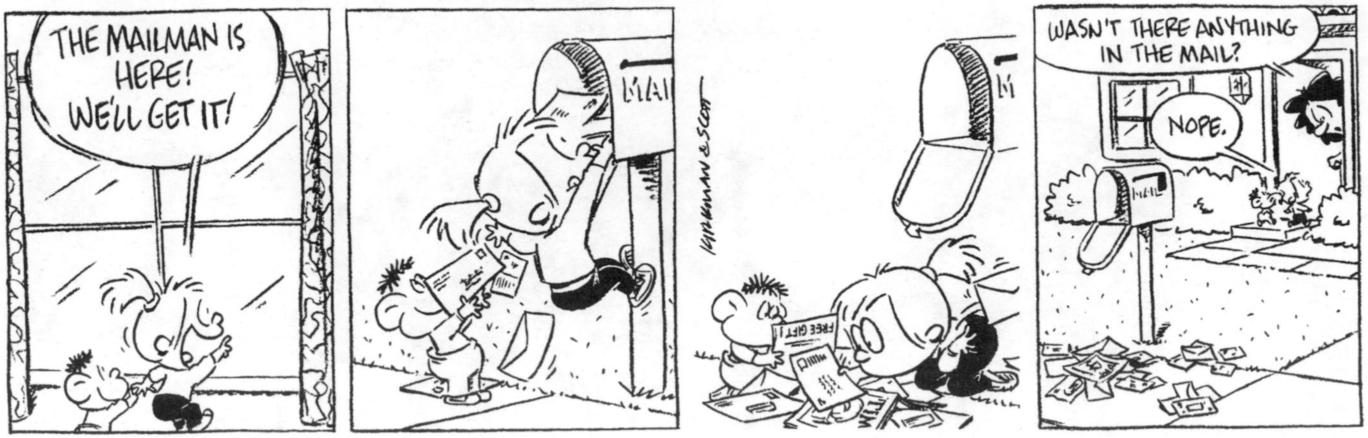
THE MAILMAN IS HERE! WE'LL GET IT!
WASN'T THERE ANYTHING IN THE MAIL?
NOPE.

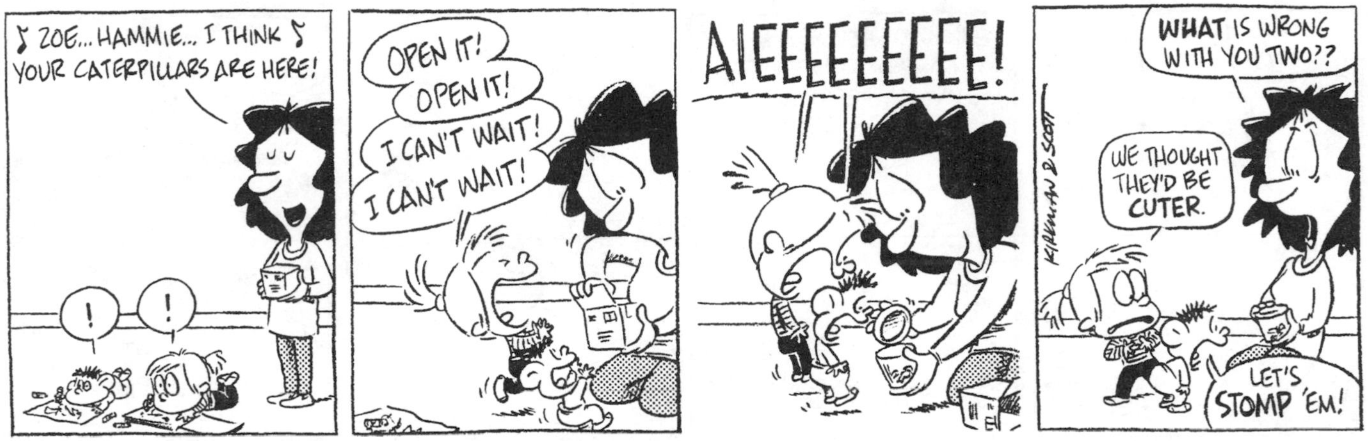
ZOE... HAMMIE... I THINK YOUR CATERPILLARS ARE HERE!
!
!
OPEN IT!
OPEN IT!
I CAN'T WAIT!
I CAN'T WAIT!
AIEEEEEEEEE!
WHAT IS WRONG WITH YOU TWO??
WE THOUGHT THEY'D BE CUTER.
LET'S STOMP 'EM!

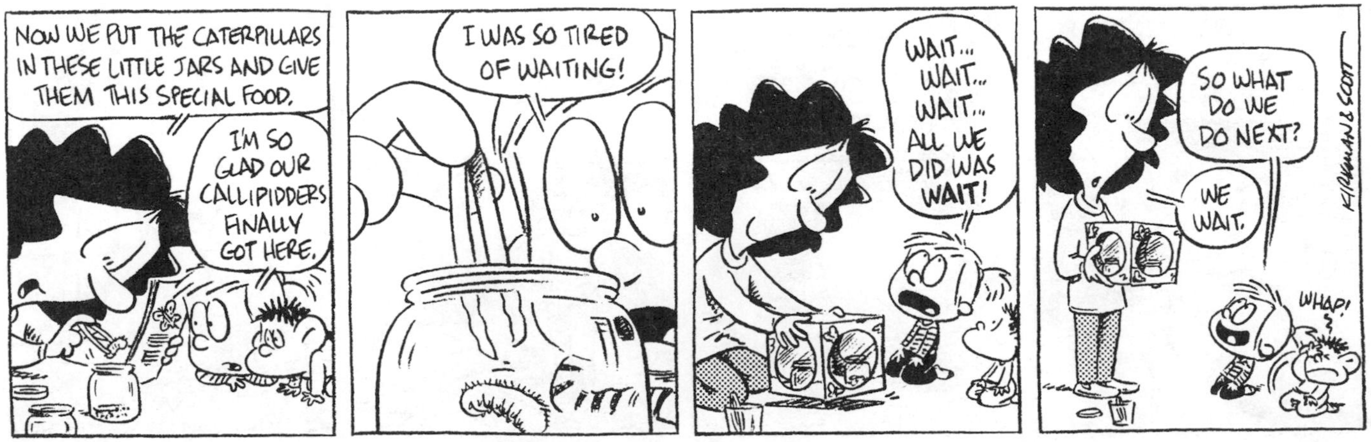
NOW WE PUT THE CATERPILLARS IN THESE LITTLE JARS AND GIVE THEM THIS SPECIAL FOOD.
I'M SO GLAD OUR CALLIPIDDERS FINALLY GOT HERE.
I WAS SO TIRED OF WAITING!
WAIT... WAIT... WAIT... ALL WE DID WAS WAIT!
SO WHAT DO WE DO NEXT?
WE WAIT.
WHAP!

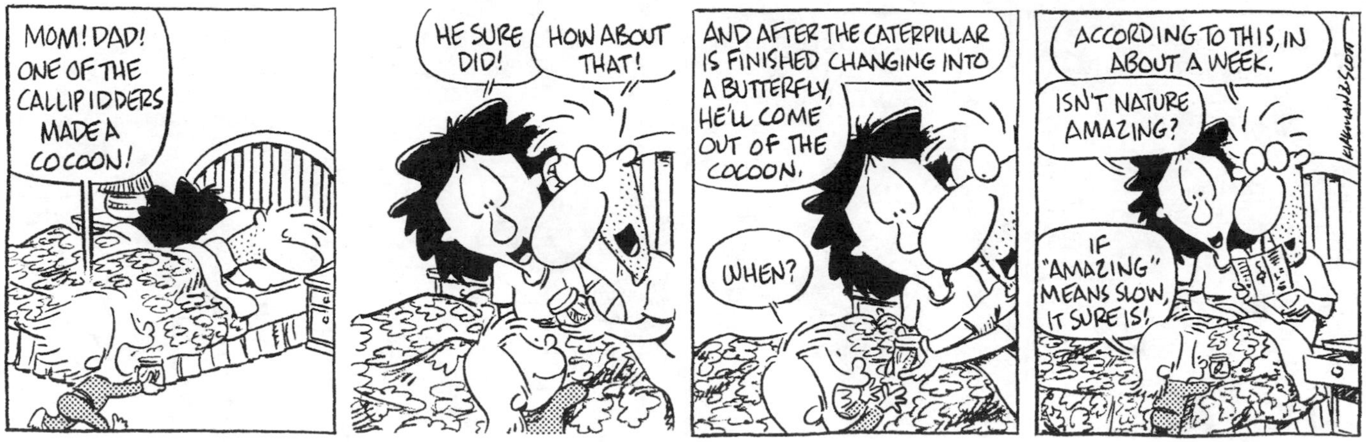
MOM! DAD! ONE OF THE CALLIPIDDERS MADE A COCOON!
HE SURE DID!
HOW ABOUT THAT!
AND AFTER THE CATERPILLAR IS FINISHED CHANGING INTO A BUTTERFLY, HE'LL COME OUT OF THE COCOON.
WHEN?
ACCORDING TO THIS, IN ABOUT A WEEK.
ISN'T NATURE AMAZING?
IF "AMAZING" MEANS SLOW, IT SURE IS!

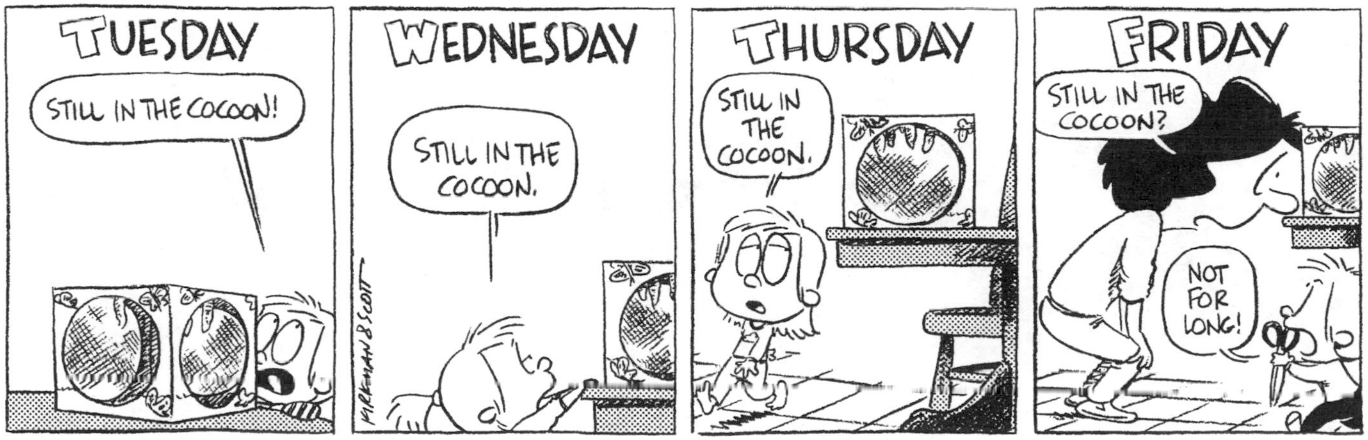
TUESDAY
STILL IN THE COCOON!
WEDNESDAY
STILL IN THE COCOON.
KIRKMAN & SCOTT
THURSDAY
STILL IN THE COCOON.
FRIDAY
STILL IN THE COCOON?
NOT FOR LONG!

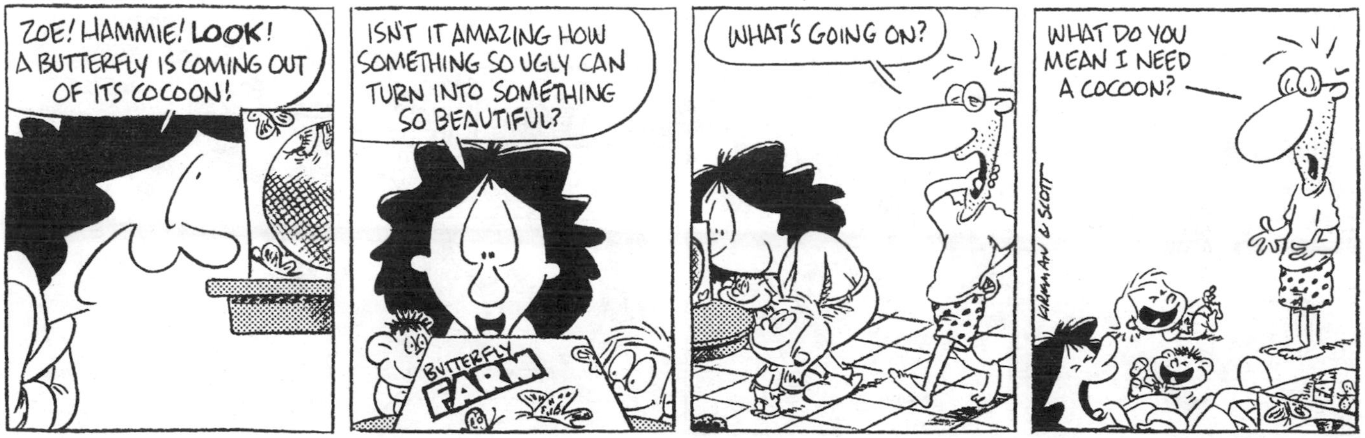
ZOE! HAMMIE! **LOOK**! A BUTTERFLY IS COMING OUT OF ITS COCOON!
ISN'T IT AMAZING HOW SOMETHING SO UGLY CAN TURN INTO SOMETHING SO BEAUTIFUL?
BUTTERFLY FARM
WHAT'S GOING ON?
KIRKMAN & SCOTT
WHAT DO YOU MEAN I NEED A COCOON?

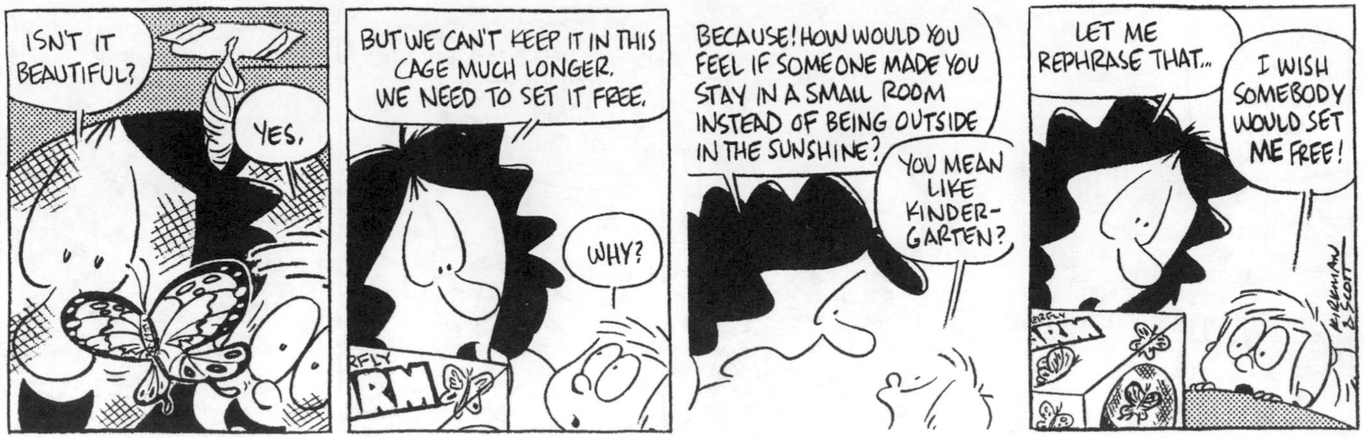
ISN'T IT BEAUTIFUL?
YES.
BUT WE CAN'T KEEP IT IN THIS CAGE MUCH LONGER. WE NEED TO SET IT FREE.
WHY?
BECAUSE! HOW WOULD YOU FEEL IF SOMEONE MADE YOU STAY IN A SMALL ROOM INSTEAD OF BEING OUTSIDE IN THE SUNSHINE?
YOU MEAN LIKE KINDER-GARTEN?
LET ME REPHRASE THAT...
I WISH SOMEBODY WOULD SET ME FREE!
KIRKMAN & SCOTT

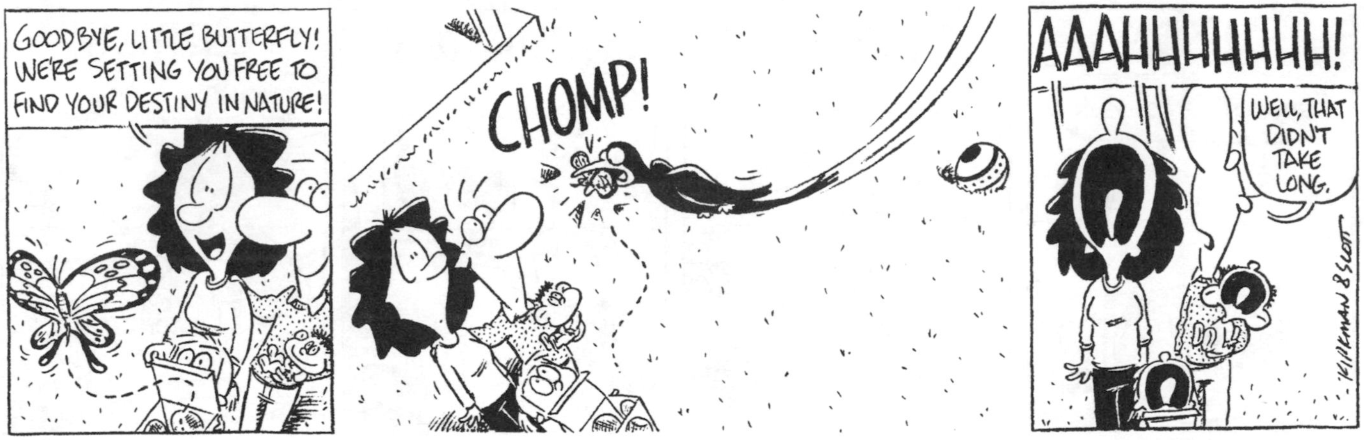
GOODBYE, LITTLE BUTTERFLY! WE'RE SETTING YOU FREE TO FIND YOUR DESTINY IN NATURE!
CHOMP!
AAAHHHHHHH!
WELL, THAT DIDN'T TAKE LONG.
KIRKMAN & SCOTT

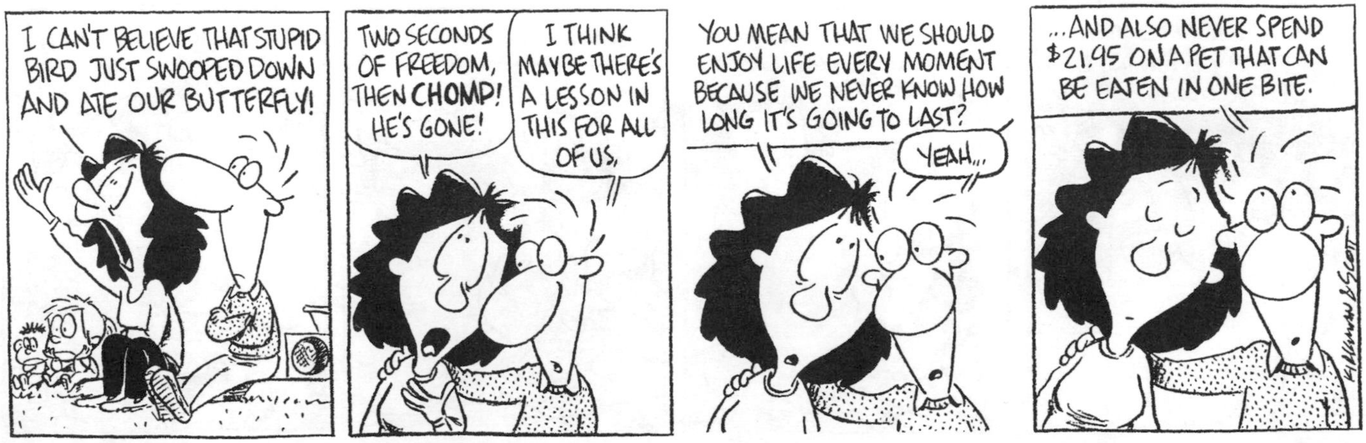
I CAN'T BELIEVE THAT STUPID BIRD JUST SWOOPED DOWN AND ATE OUR BUTTERFLY!
TWO SECONDS OF FREEDOM, THEN CHOMP! HE'S GONE!
I THINK MAYBE THERE'S A LESSON IN THIS FOR ALL OF US.
YOU MEAN THAT WE SHOULD ENJOY LIFE EVERY MOMENT BECAUSE WE NEVER KNOW HOW LONG IT'S GOING TO LAST?
YEAH...
...AND ALSO NEVER SPEND $21.95 ON A PET THAT CAN BE EATEN IN ONE BITE.
KIRKMAN & SCOTT

THE SLEEPOVER

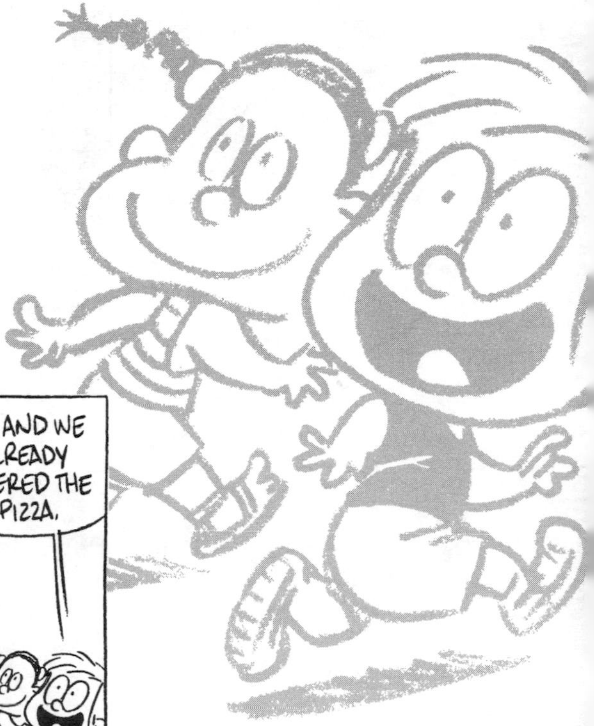

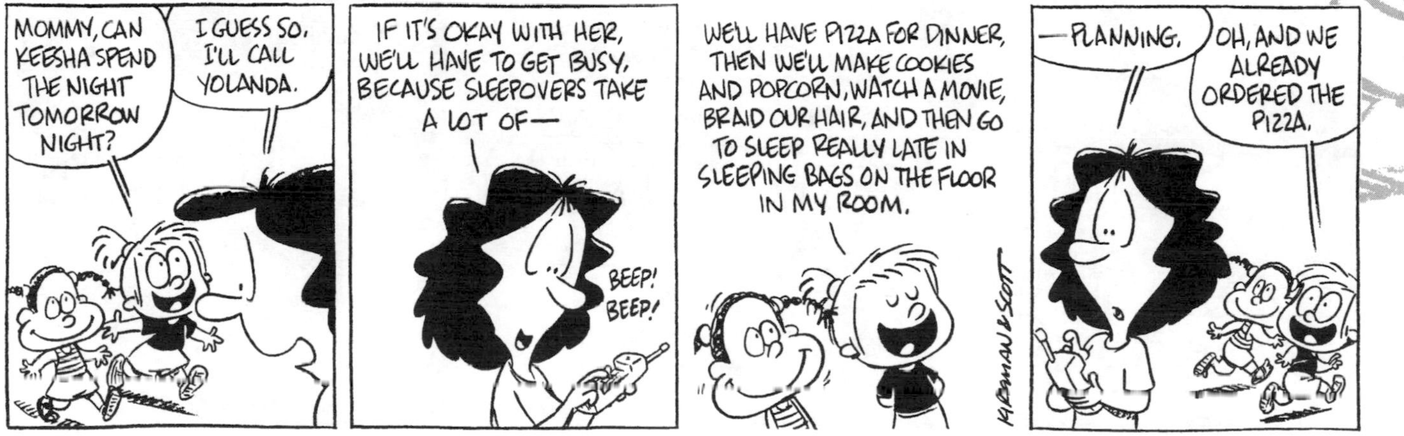

MOMMY, CAN KEESHA SPEND THE NIGHT TOMORROW NIGHT?
I GUESS SO. I'LL CALL YOLANDA.
IF IT'S OKAY WITH HER, WE'LL HAVE TO GET BUSY, BECAUSE SLEEPOVERS TAKE A LOT OF—
BEEP! BEEP!
WE'LL HAVE PIZZA FOR DINNER, THEN WE'LL MAKE COOKIES AND POPCORN, WATCH A MOVIE, BRAID OUR HAIR, AND THEN GO TO SLEEP REALLY LATE IN SLEEPING BAGS ON THE FLOOR IN MY ROOM.
KIRKMAN & SCOTT
—PLANNING.
OH, AND WE ALREADY ORDERED THE PIZZA.

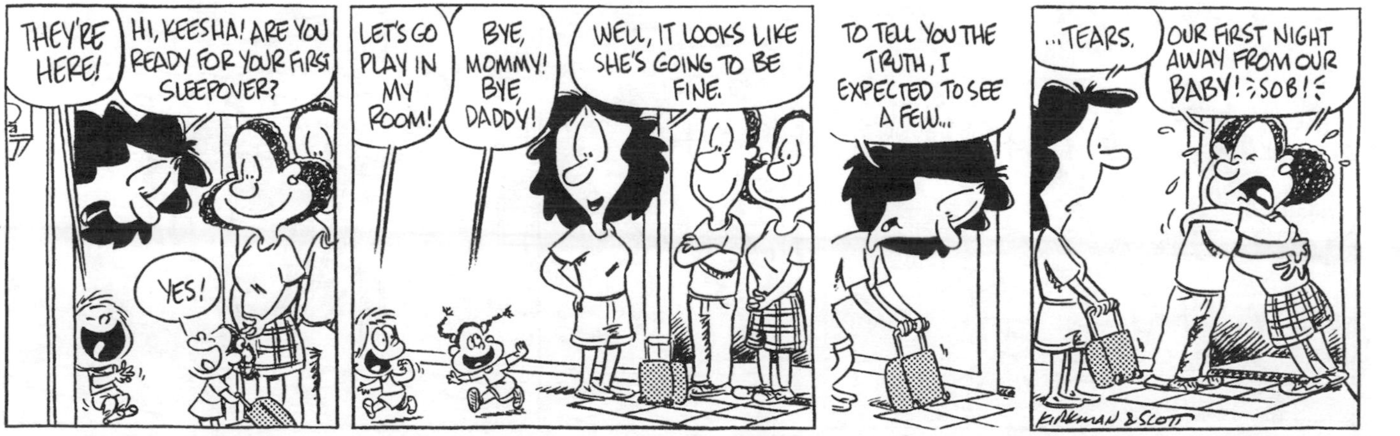

THEY'RE HERE!
HI, KEESHA! ARE YOU READY FOR YOUR FIRST SLEEPOVER?
YES!
LET'S GO PLAY IN MY ROOM!
BYE, MOMMY! BYE, DADDY!
WELL, IT LOOKS LIKE SHE'S GOING TO BE FINE.
TO TELL YOU THE TRUTH, I EXPECTED TO SEE A FEW...
...TEARS.
OUR FIRST NIGHT AWAY FROM OUR BABY! SOB!
KIRKMAN & SCOTT

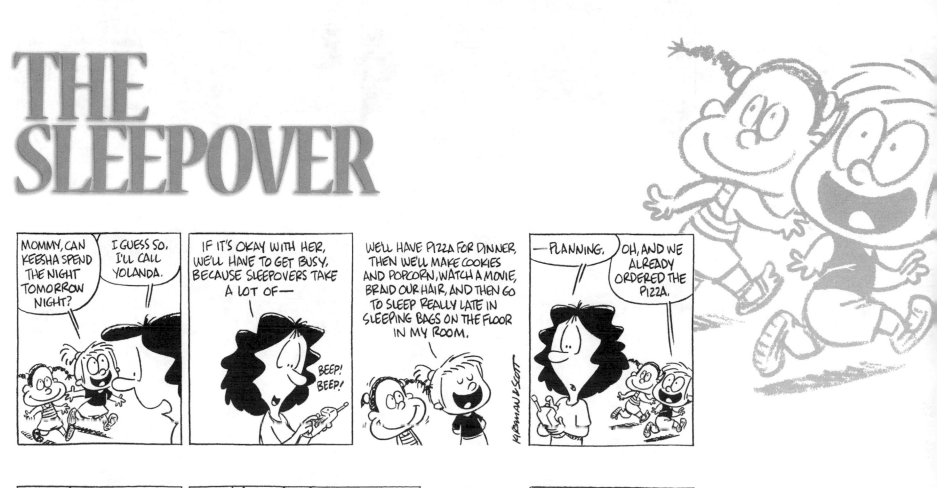

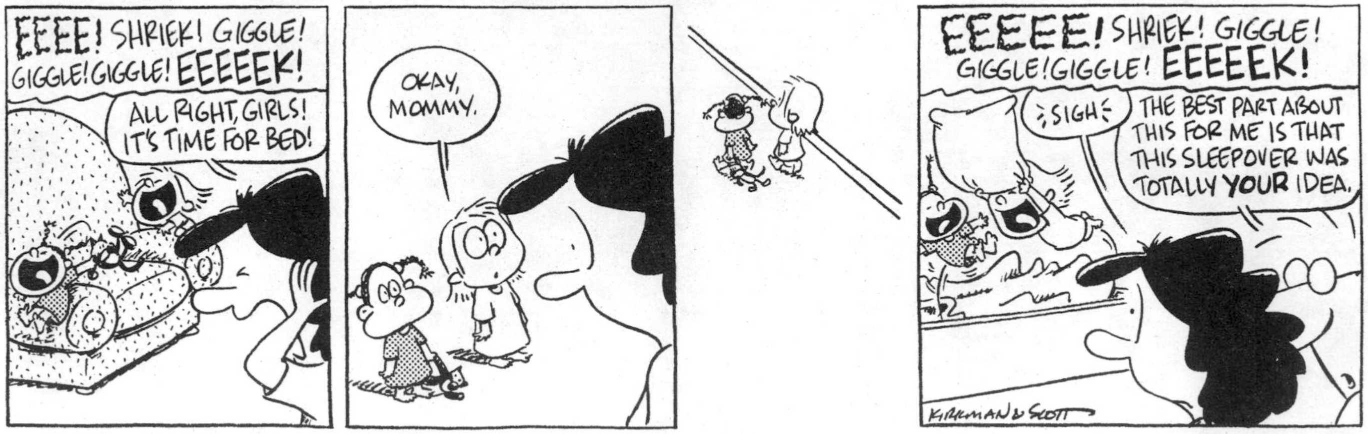
EEEE! SHRIEK! GIGGLE! GIGGLE! GIGGLE! EEEEEK!
ALL RIGHT, GIRLS! IT'S TIME FOR BED!
OKAY, MOMMY.
EEEEE! SHRIEK! GIGGLE! GIGGLE! GIGGLE! EEEEEK!
SIGH
THE BEST PART ABOUT THIS FOR ME IS THAT THIS SLEEPOVER WAS TOTALLY YOUR IDEA.
KIRKMAN & SCOTT

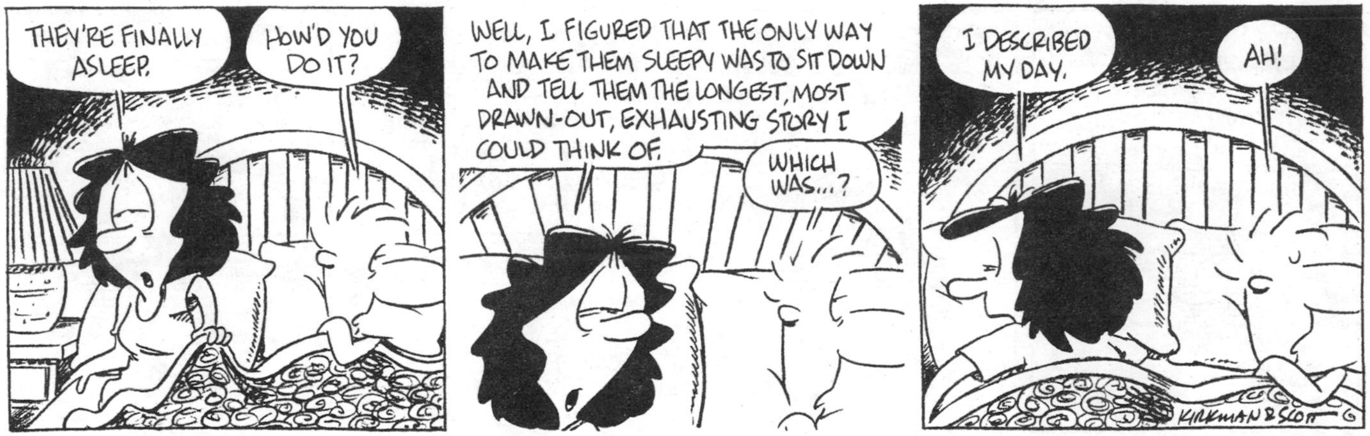
THEY'RE FINALLY ASLEEP.
HOW'D YOU DO IT?
WELL, I FIGURED THAT THE ONLY WAY TO MAKE THEM SLEEPY WAS TO SIT DOWN AND TELL THEM THE LONGEST, MOST DRAWN-OUT, EXHAUSTING STORY I COULD THINK OF.
WHICH WAS...?
I DESCRIBED MY DAY.
AH!
KIRKMAN & SCOTT

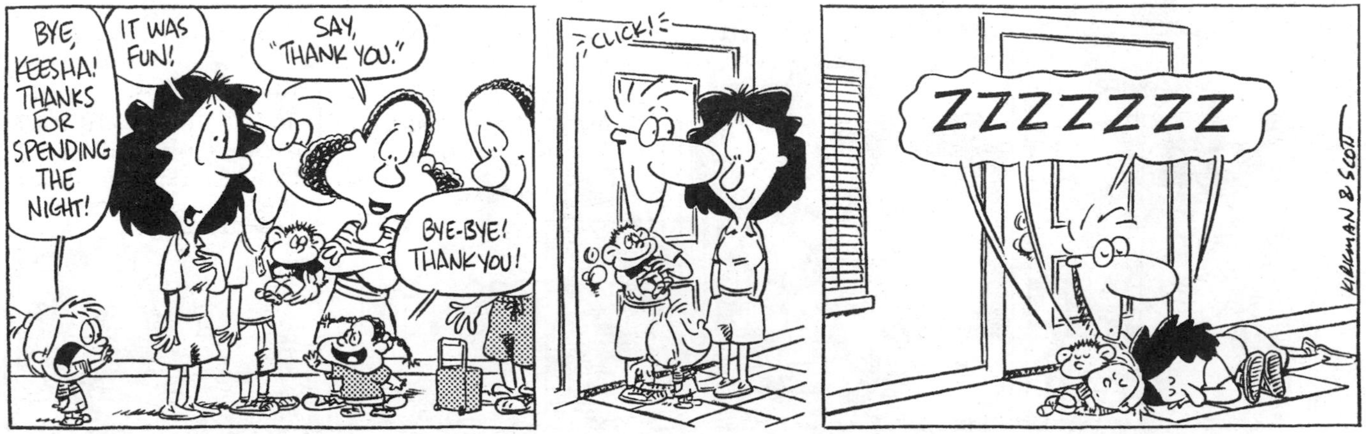
BYE, KEESHA! THANKS FOR SPENDING THE NIGHT!
IT WAS FUN!
SAY, "THANK YOU."
BYE-BYE! THANK YOU!
CLICK!
ZZZZZZZ
KIRKMAN & SCOTT

GRADUATION DAY

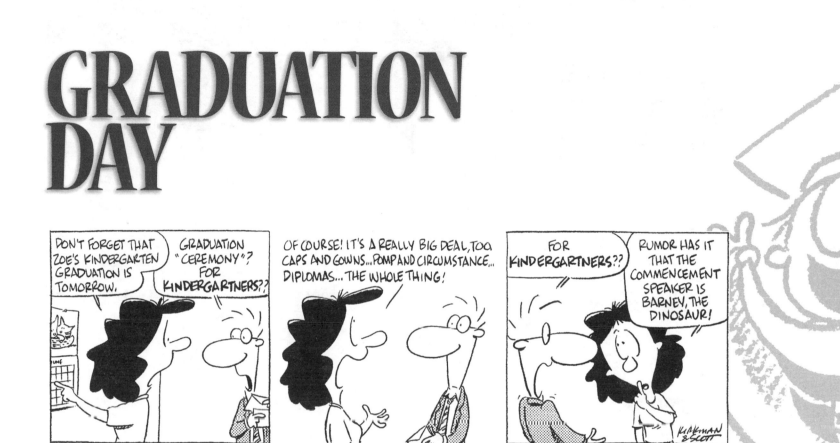

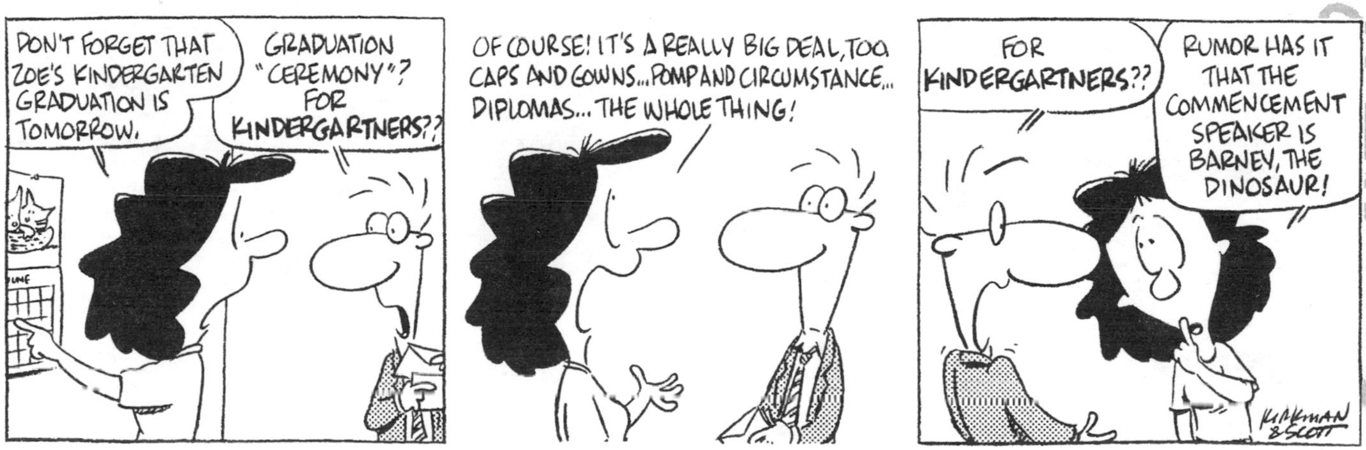
DON'T FORGET THAT ZOE'S KINDERGARTEN GRADUATION IS TOMORROW.
GRADUATION "CEREMONY"? FOR KINDERGARTNERS??
OF COURSE! IT'S A REALLY BIG DEAL, TOO. CAPS AND GOWNS... POMP AND CIRCUMSTANCE... DIPLOMAS... THE WHOLE THING!
FOR KINDERGARTNERS??
RUMOR HAS IT THAT THE COMMENCEMENT SPEAKER IS BARNEY, THE DINOSAUR!
KIRKMAN & SCOTT

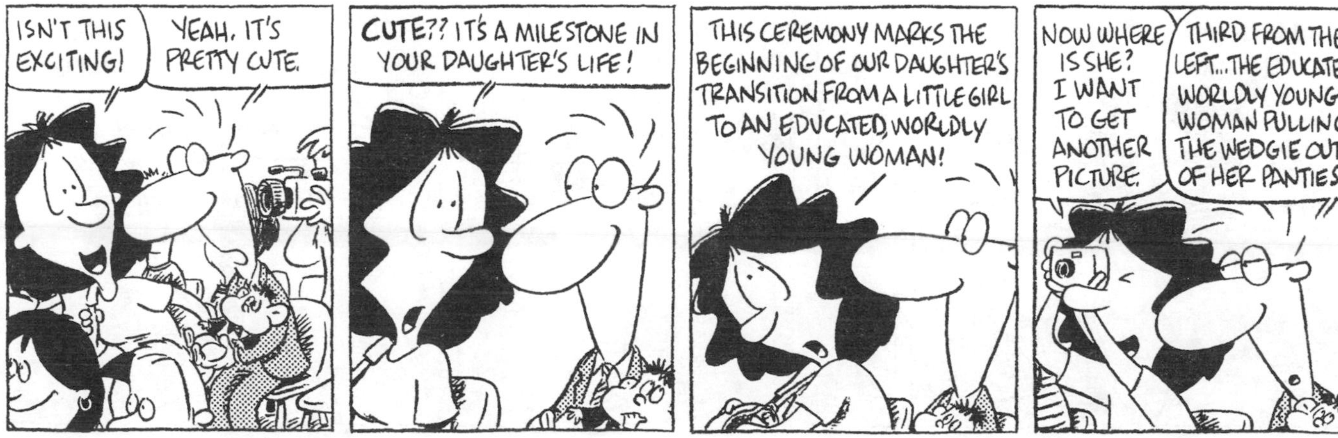
ISN'T THIS EXCITING!
YEAH. IT'S PRETTY CUTE.
CUTE?? IT'S A MILESTONE IN YOUR DAUGHTER'S LIFE!
THIS CEREMONY MARKS THE BEGINNING OF OUR DAUGHTER'S TRANSITION FROM A LITTLE GIRL TO AN EDUCATED, WORLDLY YOUNG WOMAN!
NOW WHERE IS SHE? I WANT TO GET ANOTHER PICTURE.
THIRD FROM THE LEFT... THE EDUCATED, WORLDLY YOUNG WOMAN PULLING THE WEDGIE OUT OF HER PANTIES.
KIRKMAN & SCOTT

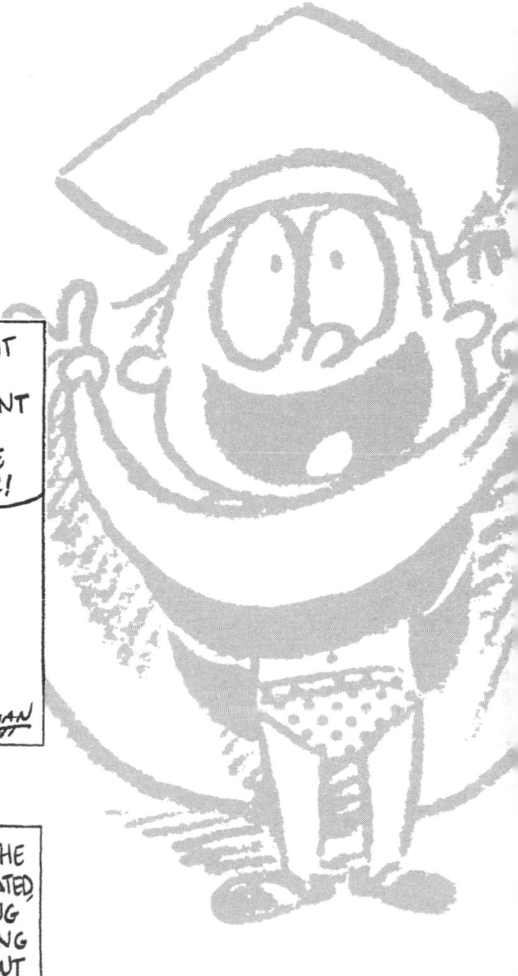

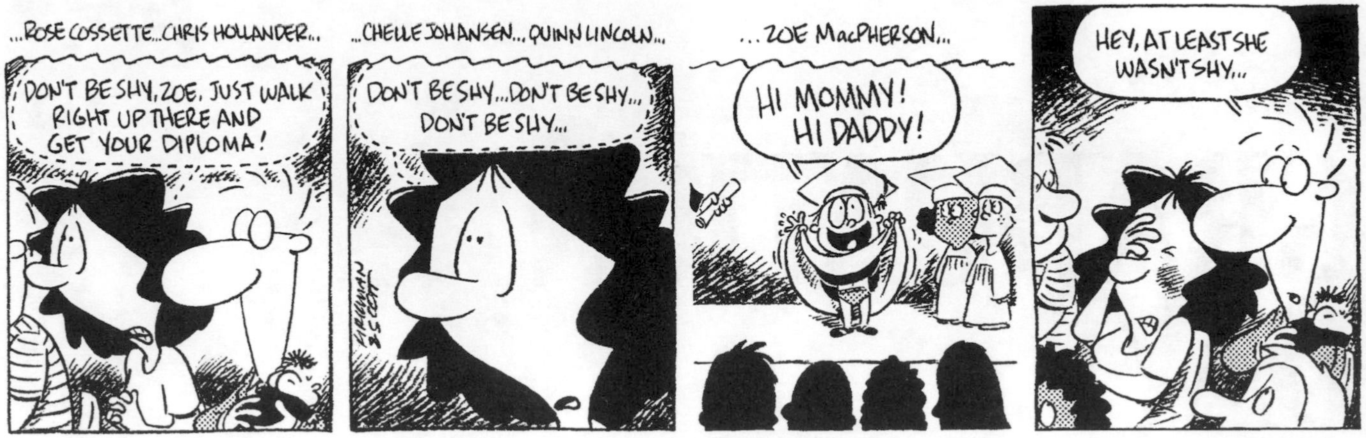
...ROSE COSSETTE...CHRIS HOLLANDER...
DON'T BE SHY, ZOE. JUST WALK RIGHT UP THERE AND GET YOUR DIPLOMA!
...CHELLE JOHANSEN... QUINN LINCOLN...
DON'T BE SHY...DON'T BE SHY... DON'T BE SHY...
... ZOE MacPHERSON...
HI MOMMY! HI DADDY!
HEY, AT LEAST SHE WASN'T SHY...

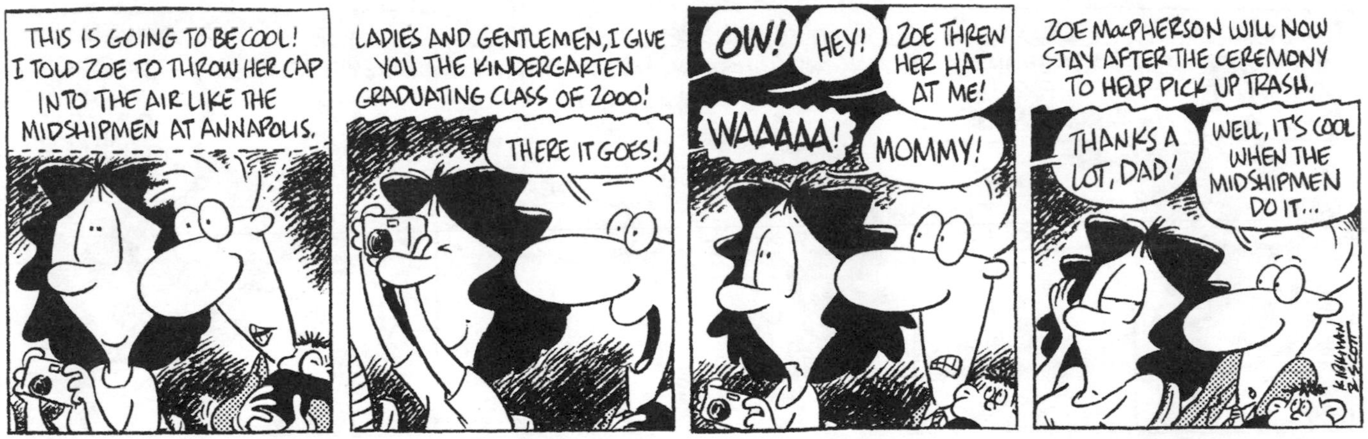
THIS IS GOING TO BE COOL! I TOLD ZOE TO THROW HER CAP INTO THE AIR LIKE THE MIDSHIPMEN AT ANNAPOLIS.
LADIES AND GENTLEMEN, I GIVE YOU THE KINDERGARTEN GRADUATING CLASS OF 2000!
THERE IT GOES!
OW!
HEY!
ZOE THREW HER HAT AT ME!
WAAAAA!
MOMMY!
ZOE MacPHERSON WILL NOW STAY AFTER THE CEREMONY TO HELP PICK UP TRASH.
THANKS A LOT, DAD!
WELL, IT'S COOL WHEN THE MIDSHIPMEN DO IT...

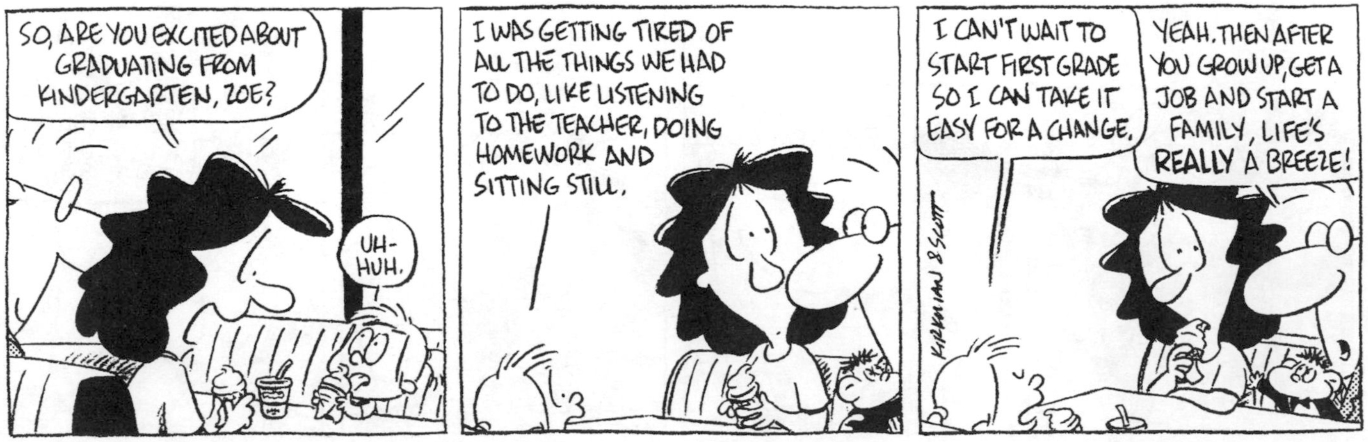
SO, ARE YOU EXCITED ABOUT GRADUATING FROM KINDERGARTEN, ZOE?
UH-HUH.
I WAS GETTING TIRED OF ALL THE THINGS WE HAD TO DO, LIKE LISTENING TO THE TEACHER, DOING HOMEWORK AND SITTING STILL.
I CAN'T WAIT TO START FIRST GRADE SO I CAN TAKE IT EASY FOR A CHANGE.
YEAH. THEN AFTER YOU GROW UP, GET A JOB AND START A FAMILY, LIFE'S REALLY A BREEZE!

PINKEYE

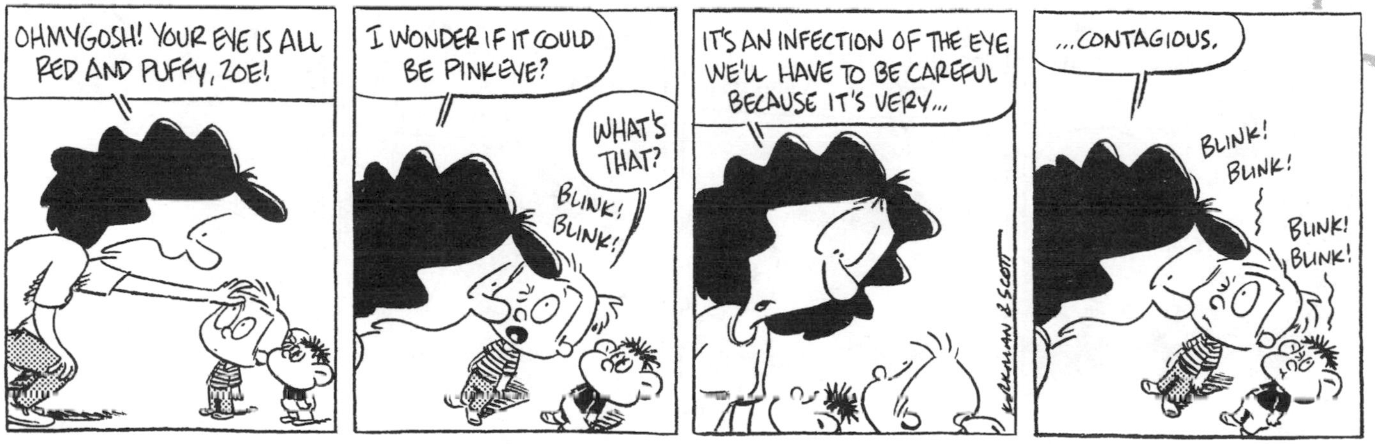
OHMYGOSH! YOUR EYE IS ALL RED AND PUFFY, ZOE!
I WONDER IF IT COULD BE PINKEYE?
WHAT'S THAT?
BLINK! BLINK!
IT'S AN INFECTION OF THE EYE WE'LL HAVE TO BE CAREFUL BECAUSE IT'S VERY...
KIRKMAN & SCOTT
...CONTAGIOUS.
BLINK! BLINK!
BLINK! BLINK!

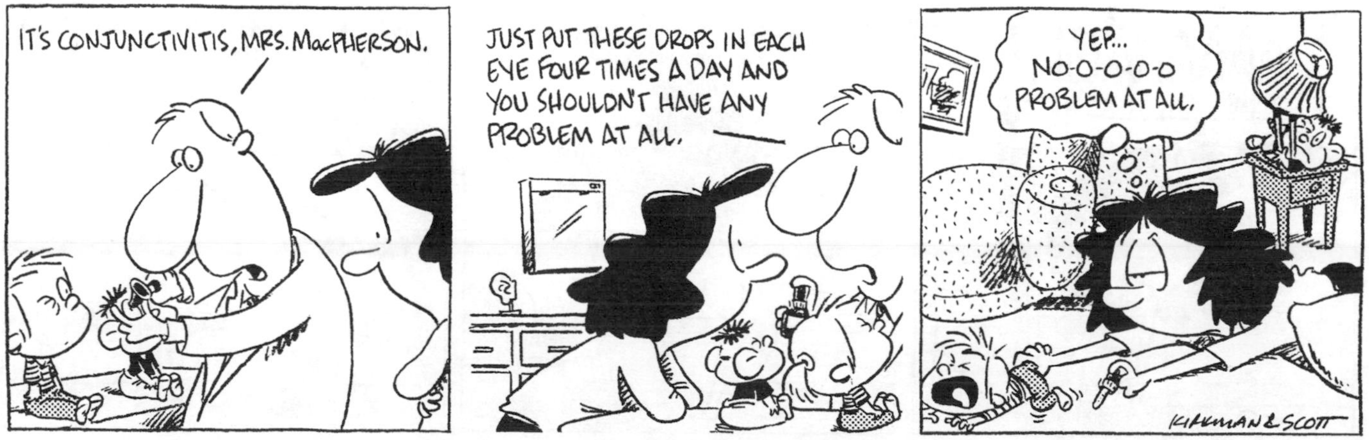
IT'S CONJUNCTIVITIS, MRS. MacPHERSON.
JUST PUT THESE DROPS IN EACH EYE FOUR TIMES A DAY AND YOU SHOULDN'T HAVE ANY PROBLEM AT ALL.
YEP... NO-O-O-O-O PROBLEM AT ALL.
KIRKMAN & SCOTT

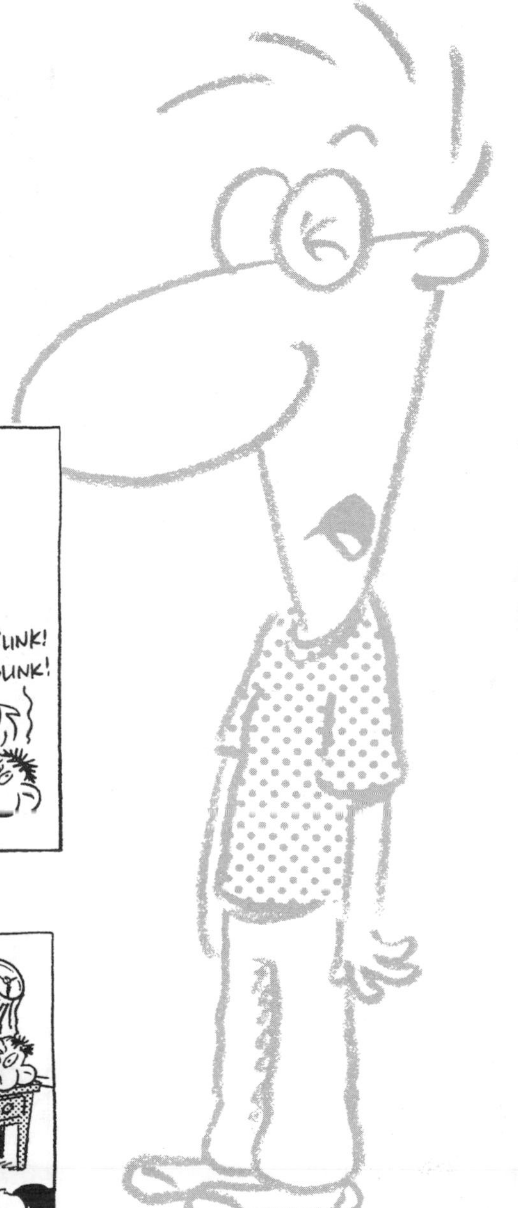

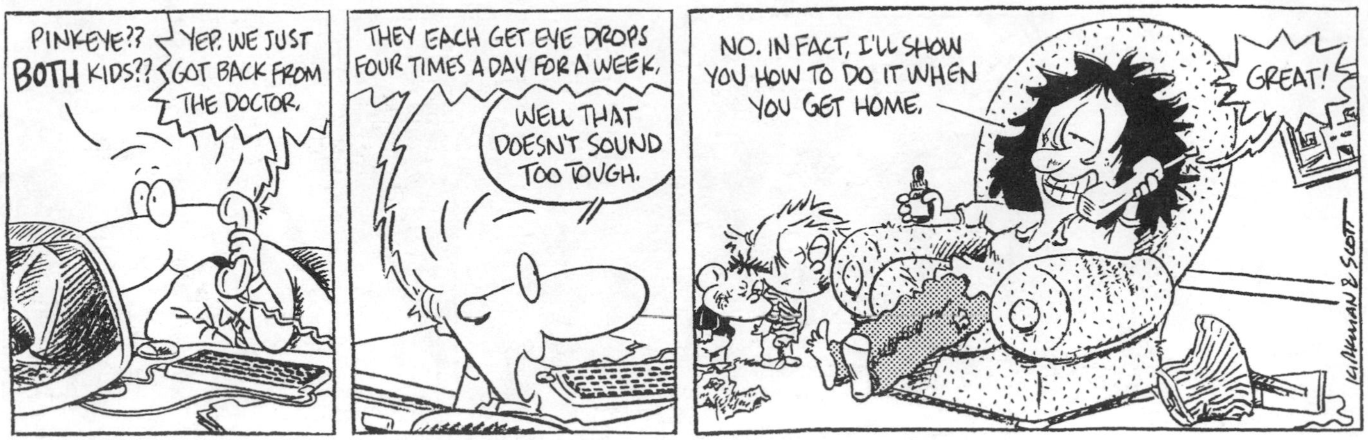
PINKEYE?? BOTH KIDS??
YEP. WE JUST GOT BACK FROM THE DOCTOR.
THEY EACH GET EYE DROPS FOUR TIMES A DAY FOR A WEEK.
WELL THAT DOESN'T SOUND TOO TOUGH.
NO. IN FACT, I'LL SHOW YOU HOW TO DO IT WHEN YOU GET HOME.
GREAT!
KIRKMAN & SCOTT

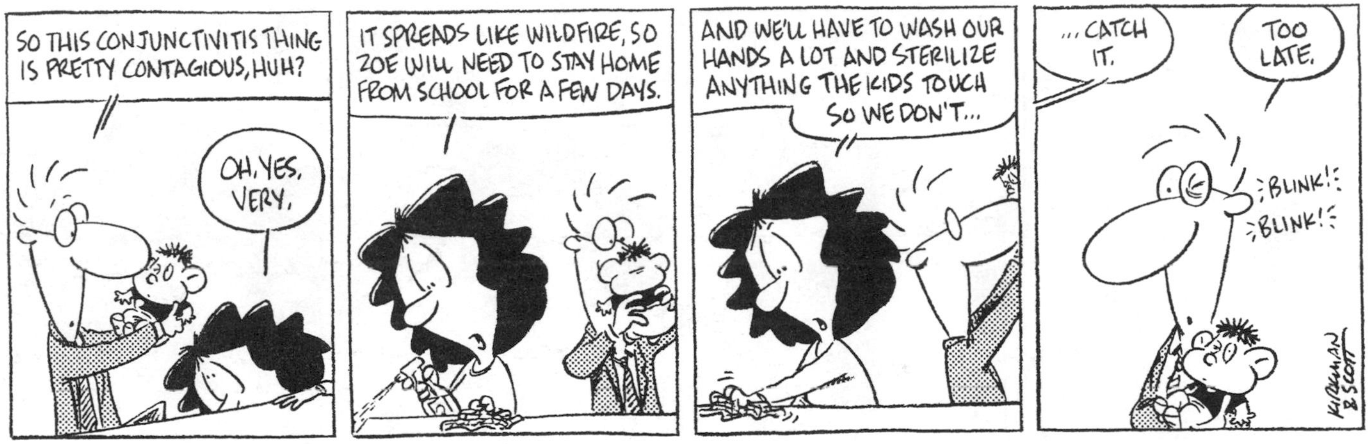
SO THIS CONJUNCTIVITIS THING IS PRETTY CONTAGIOUS, HUH?
OH, YES. VERY.
IT SPREADS LIKE WILDFIRE, SO ZOE WILL NEED TO STAY HOME FROM SCHOOL FOR A FEW DAYS.
AND WE'LL HAVE TO WASH OUR HANDS A LOT AND STERILIZE ANYTHING THE KIDS TOUCH SO WE DON'T...
...CATCH IT.
TOO LATE.
BLINK!
BLINK!
KIRKMAN & SCOTT

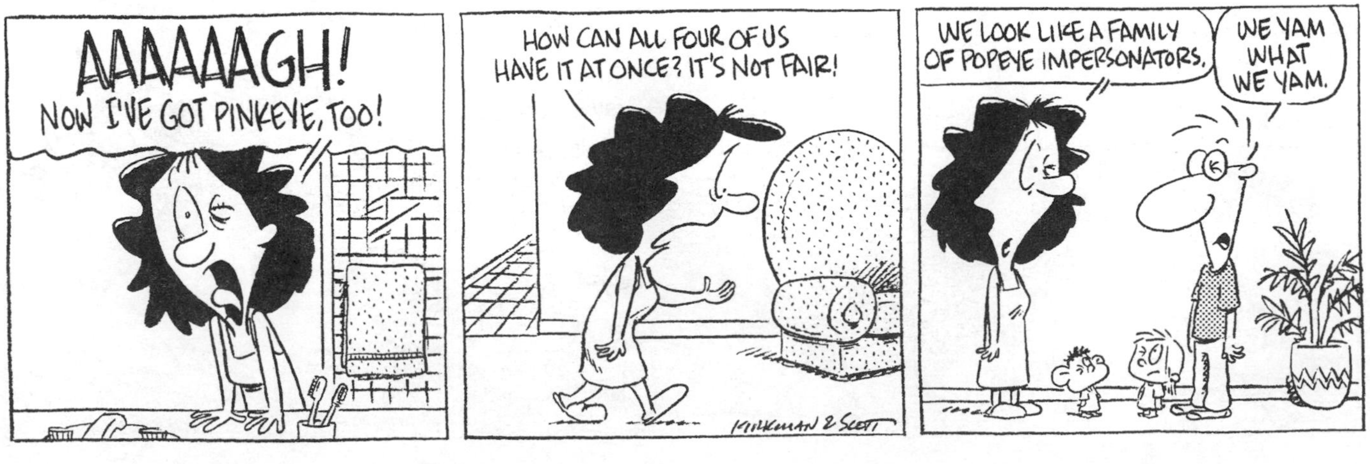
AAAAAAGH! NOW I'VE GOT PINKEYE, TOO!
HOW CAN ALL FOUR OF US HAVE IT AT ONCE? IT'S NOT FAIR!
KIRKMAN & SCOTT
WE LOOK LIKE A FAMILY OF POPEYE IMPERSONATORS.
WE YAM WHAT WE YAM.

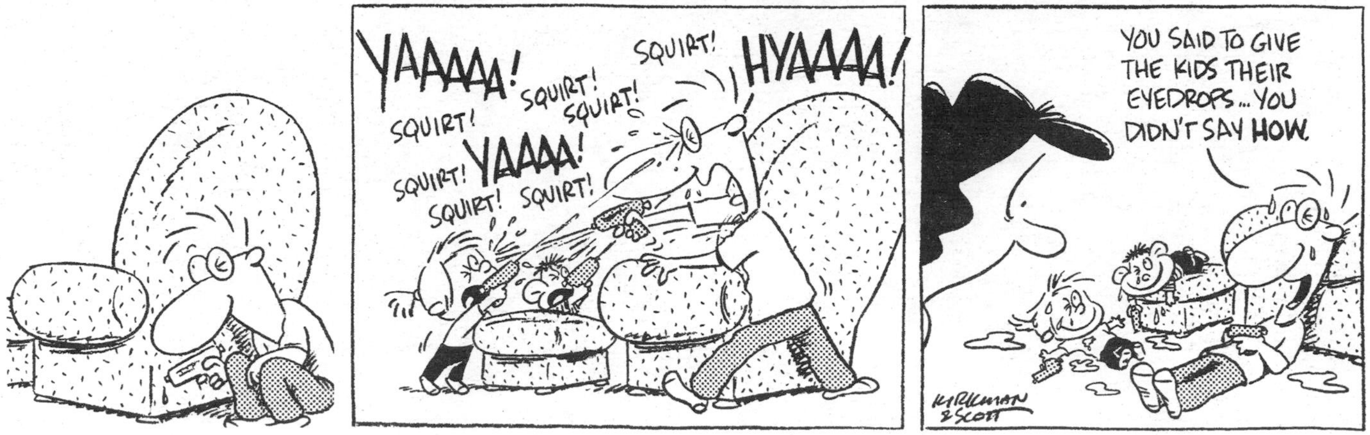
YAAAAA!
SQUIRT!
SQUIRT!
SQUIRT!
SQUIRT!
HYAAAAA!
SQUIRT!
YAAAA!
SQUIRT!
SQUIRT!
SQUIRT!
YOU SAID TO GIVE THE KIDS THEIR EYEDROPS... YOU DIDN'T SAY HOW.
KIRKMAN & SCOTT

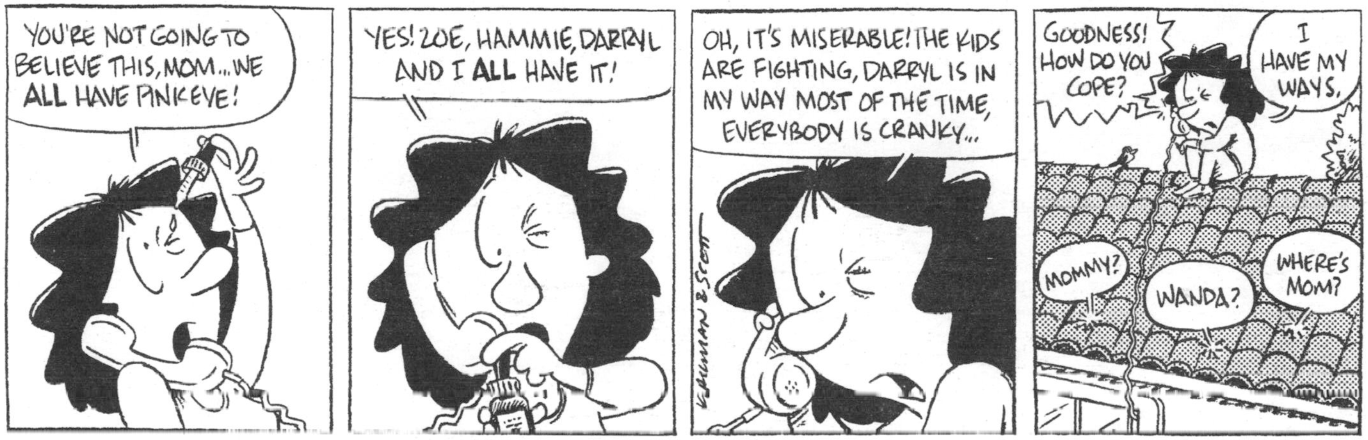
YOU'RE NOT GOING TO BELIEVE THIS, MOM... WE ALL HAVE PINKEYE!
YES! ZOE, HAMMIE, DARRYL AND I ALL HAVE IT!
OH, IT'S MISERABLE! THE KIDS ARE FIGHTING, DARRYL IS IN MY WAY MOST OF THE TIME, EVERYBODY IS CRANKY...
KIRKMAN & SCOTT
GOODNESS! HOW DO YOU COPE?
I HAVE MY WAYS.
MOMMY?
WANDA?
WHERE'S MOM?

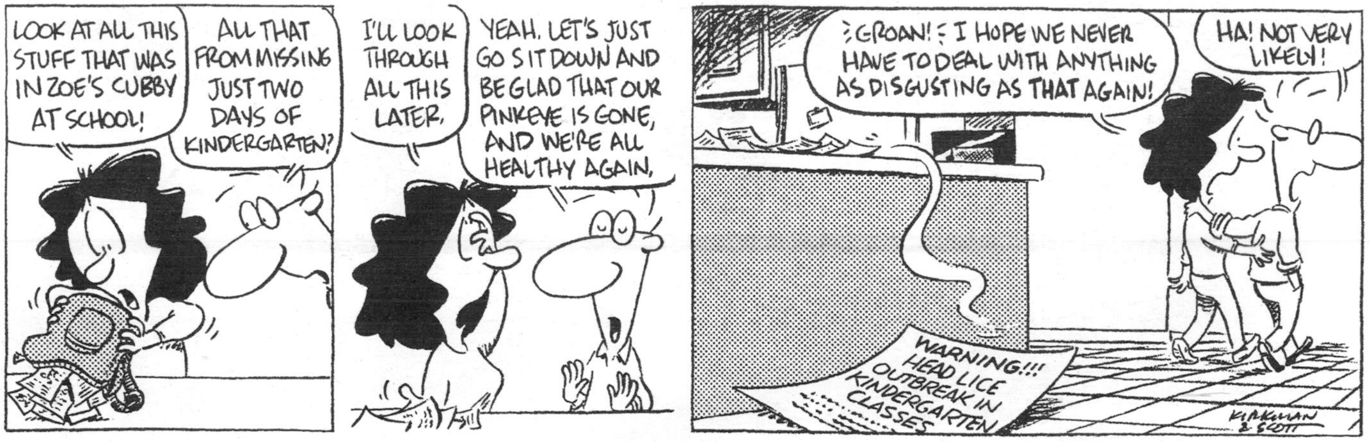
LOOK AT ALL THIS STUFF THAT WAS IN ZOE'S CUBBY AT SCHOOL!
ALL THAT FROM MISSING JUST TWO DAYS OF KINDERGARTEN?
I'LL LOOK THROUGH ALL THIS LATER.
YEAH. LET'S JUST GO SIT DOWN AND BE GLAD THAT OUR PINKEYE IS GONE, AND WE'RE ALL HEALTHY AGAIN.
GROAN! I HOPE WE NEVER HAVE TO DEAL WITH ANYTHING AS DISGUSTING AS THAT AGAIN!
HA! NOT VERY LIKELY!
WARNING!!! HEAD LICE OUTBREAK IN KINDERGARTEN CLASSES
KIRKMAN & SCOTT